Lecture Notes in Artificial Intelligence 12946

Subseries of Lecture Notes in Computer Science

More information about this subseries at http://www.springer.com/series/1244

Frank Dignum · Juan Manuel Corchado ·
Fernando De La Prieta (Eds.)

Advances in Practical Applications of Agents, Multi-Agent Systems, and Social Good

The PAAMS Collection

19th International Conference, PAAMS 2021
Salamanca, Spain, October 6–8, 2021
Proceedings

Springer

Editors
Frank Dignum ⓘD
Umeå University
Umeå, Sweden

Juan Manuel Corchado ⓘD
Universidad de Salamanca
Salamanca, Salamanca, Spain

Fernando De La Prieta ⓘD
University of Salamanca
Salamanca, Spain

ISSN 0302-9743 ISSN 1611-3349 (electronic)
Lecture Notes in Artificial Intelligence
ISBN 978-3-030-85738-7 ISBN 978-3-030-85739-4 (eBook)
https://doi.org/10.1007/978-3-030-85739-4

LNCS Sublibrary: SL7 – Artificial Intelligence

This Springer imprint is published by the registered company Springer Nature Switzerland AG
The registered company address is: Gewerbestrasse 11, 6330 Cham, Switzerland

Preface

Research on agents and multi-agent systems has matured during the last thirty years and many effective applications of this technology are now deployed. An international forum to present and discuss the latest scientific developments and their effective applications, to assess the impact of the approach, and to facilitate technology transfer, became a necessity and was created almost two decades ago.

PAAMS, the International Conference on Practical Applications of Agents and Multi-Agent Systems, is the international yearly conference to present, discuss, and disseminate the latest developments and the most important outcomes related to real-world applications. It provides a unique opportunity to bring multi-disciplinary experts, academics, and practitioners together to exchange their experience in the development and deployment of agents and multi-agent systems.

This volume presents the papers that were accepted for the 2021 edition of PAAMS. These articles report on the application and validation of agent-based models, methods, and technologies in a number of key application areas, including: agents for social good, advanced models for learning, agent-based programming, distributed data analysis, automatic planning, decision-making, social interactions, formal and theoretic models, self-adaptation, mobile edge computing, swarms, and task allocation. Each paper submitted to PAAMS went through a stringent peer-review process by three members of the Program Committee composed of 139 internationally renowned researchers from 34 countries. From the 56 submissions received, 16 were selected for full presentation at the conference; another 11 papers were accepted as short presentations. In addition, a demonstration track featuring innovative and emergent applications of agent and multi-agent systems and technologies in real-world domains was organized. In all, 13 demonstrations were shown, and this volume contains a description of each of them.

We would like to thank all the contributing authors, the members of the Program Committee, the sponsors, IBM, AEPIA, APPIA, the AIR Institute and the University of Salamanca, and the Organizing Committee for their hard and highly valuable work. We acknowledge the funding supporting through the project "Intelligent and sustainable mobility supported by multi-agent systems and edge computing" (ID RTI2018-095390-B-C32). This work contributed to the success of the PAAMS 2021 event.

Thanks for your help – PAAMS 2021 would not exist without your contribution.

July 2021

Frank Dignum
Juan Manuel Corchado
Fernando De la Prieta

Organization

General Co-chairs

Frank Dignum   Umeå University, Sweden
Juan Manuel Corchado   University of Salamanca and the AIR institute, Spain
Fernando De la Prieta   University of Salamanca, Spain

Advisory Board

Bo An   Nanyang Technological University, Singapore
Paul Davidsson   Malmö University, Sweden
Keith Decker   University of Delaware, USA
Yves Demazeau   Centre National de la Recherche Scientifique, France
Tom Holvoet   KU Leuven, Belgium
Toru Ishida   Kyoto University, Japan
Takayuki Ito   Nagoya Institute of Technology, Japan
Eric Matson   Purdue University, USA
Jörg P. Müller   Clausthal Technical University, Germany
Michal Pĕchouček   Technical University in Prague, Czech Republic
Franco Zambonelli   University of Modena and Reggio Emilia, Italy

Program Committee

Emmanuel Adam   University of Valenciennes, France
Analia Amandi   University of Tandil, Argentina
Frederic Amblard   University of Toulouse, France
Francesco Amigoni   Politecnico di Milano, Italy
Bo An   Nanyang Technological University, Singapore
Luis Antunes   University of Lisbon, Portugal
Piotr Artiemjew   University of Warmia and Mazury, Poland
Matteo Baldoni   University of Turin, Italy
Joao Balsa   University of Lisbon, Portugal
Cristina Baroglio   University of Turin, Italy
Michael Berger   DocuWare AG, Germany
Olivier Boissier   École nationale supérieure des mines de Saint-Étienne, France
Vicente Botti   Polytechnic University of Valencia, Spain
Lars Braubach   Universität Hamburg, Germany
Bat-Erdene Byambasuren   Mongolian University of Science and Technology, Mongolia
Javier Carbó   University Carlos III of Madrid, Spain

Luis Castillo   University of Caldas, Colombia
Anders Lynhe Christensen   University of Southern Denmark, Denmark
Helder Coelho   University of Lisbon, Portugal
Rafael Corchuelo   University of Seville, Spain
Luis Correia   University of Lisbon, Portugal
Daniela D'Auria   University of Naples Federico II, Italy
Paul Davidsson   University of Malmö, Sweden
Keith Decker   University of Delaware, USA
Yves Demazeau   CNRS, France
Louise Dennis   University of Liverpool, UK
Andres Diaz Pace   University of Tandil, Argentina
Frank Dignum   University of Utrecht, The Netherlands
Aldo Dragoni   Università Politecnica delle Marche, Italy
Alexis Drogoul   Institut de recherche pour le développement,
                                       Vietnam
Edmund Durfee   University of Michigan, USA
Amal Elfallah   University of Paris 6, France
Ahmad Esmaeili   Purdue University, USA
Rino Falcone   CNR, Italy
Klaus Fischer   DFKI, Germany
Kary Främling   University of Aalto, Finland
Rubén Fuentes   University Complutense de Madrid, Spain
Katsuhide Fujita   Tokyo University of Agriculture and Technology,
                                       Japan
Naoki Fukuta   Shizuoka University, Japan
Stéphane Galland   UBFC - UTBM, France
Amineh Ghorbani   Delft University of Technology, The Netherlands
Daniela Godoy   University of Tandil, Argentina
Jorge J. Gómez-Sanz   University Complutense de Madrid, Spain
Vladimir Gorodetski   University of Saint Petersburg, Russia
Charles Gouin-Vallerand   Télé-Université du Québec, Canada
James Harland   RMIT Melbourne, Australia
Hisashi Hayashi   Advanced Institute of Industrial Technology, Japan
Vincent Hilaire   University of Belfort-Montbeliard, France
Koen Hindriks   University of Delft, The Netherlands
Katsutoshi Hirayama   University of Kobe, Japan
Martin Hofmann   Lockheed Martin, USA
Jomi Hübner   Universidad Federale de Santa Catarina, Brazil
Takayuki Ito   Nagoya Institute of Technology, Japan
Piotr Jędrzejowicz   Gdynia Maritime University, Poland
Yichuan Jiang   Southeast University of Nanjing, China
Vicente Julian   Polytechnic University of Valencia, Spain
Achilles Kameas   University of Patras, Greece
Ryo Kanamori   Nagoya University, Japan
Franziska Kluegl   University of Örebro, Sweden
Matthias Klusch   DFKI, Germany

Ryszard Kowalczyk	Swinburne University of Technology, Australia
Jaroslaw Kozlak	University of Science and Technology in Krakow, Poland
Paulo Leitao	Polytechnic Institute of Bragança, Portugal
Yves Lespérance	University of York, Canada
Henrique Lopes Cardoso	Univerity of Porto, Portugal
Miguel Angel Lopez-Carmona	University of Alcala, Spain
Rene Mandiau	University of Valenciennes, France
Wenji Mao	Chinese Academy of Sciences, China
Ivan Marsa-Maestre	University of Alcala, Spain
Stephen Marsh	University of Ontario, Canada
Viviana Mascardi	University of Genoa, Italy
Philippe Mathieu	University of Lille, France
Shigeo Matsubara	Kyoto University, Japan
Toshihiro Matsui	Nagoya Institute of Technology, Japan
Tsunenori Mine	Kyushu University, Japan
José M. Molina	University Carlos III of Madrid, Spain
Bernard Moulin	Laval University, Canada
Jean-Pierre Muller	CIRAD, France
Aniello Murano	University of Napoli, Italy
Ngoc Thanh Nguyen	Wroclaw University of Technology, Poland
Nariaki Nishino	Tokyo University, Japan
Itsuki Noda	Advanced Industrial Science and Technology, Japan
Paolo Novais	University of Minho, Portugal
Akihiko Ohsuga	University of Electro-Communications, Japan
Andrea Omicini	University of Bologna, Italy
Nir Oren	University of Aberdeen, UK
Mehmet Orgun	Macquarie University, Australia
Ei-Ichi Osawa	Future University Hakodate, Japan
Sascha Ossowski	University of Rey Juan Carlos, Spain
Julian Padget	University of Bath, UK
Juan Pavon	Complutense University de Madrid, Spain
Terry Payne	University of Liverpool, UK
Gauthier Picard	ENS Mines Saint-Etienne, France
Sébastien Picault	University of Lille, France
Faruk Polat	Middle East Technical University, Turkey
David Pynadath	University of Southern California, USA
Luis Paulo Reis	University of Porto, Portugal
Alessandro Ricci	University of Bologna, Italy
Deborah Richards	Macquarie University, Australia
David Robertson	University of Edinburgh, UK
Ana Paula Rocha	University of Porto, Portugal
Sebastian Rodriguez	Universidad Tecnológica Nacional, Argentina
Kristin Yvonne Rozier	Iowa State University, USA
Yuko Sakurai	Advanced Industrial Science and Technology, Japan
Ken Satoh	National Institute of Informatics, Japan

Paul Scerri   Carnegie Mellon University, USA
Silvia Schiaffino   University of Tandil, Argentina
Michael Ignaz   University of Applied Sciences of Western
                                     Switzerland, Switzerland
Franciszek Seredynski   Cardinal Stefan Wyszynski University, Poland
Emilio Serrano   Technical University of Madrid, Spain
Leonid Sheremetov   Instituto Mexicano del Petróleo, Mexico
Jaime Sichman   University of Sao Paulo, Brazil
Viviane Torres da Silva   Universidad Federal Fluminense, Brazil
Petr Skobelev   Smart Solutions, Russia
Sonia Suárez   University of La Coruna, Spain
Toshiharu Sugawara   Waseda University, Japan
Takao Terano   Tokyo Institute of Technology, Japan
Elena Troubitsyna   University of Turku, Finland
Ali Emre Turgut   Middle East Technical University, Turkey
Karl Tuyls   University of Liverpool, UK
Suguru Ueda   Saga University, Japan
Rainer Unland   University of Duisburg, Germany
Domenico Ursino   Università Politecnica delle Marche, Italy
Laszlo Varga   Computer and Automation Research Institute,
                                     Hungary
Wamberto Vasconselos   University of Aberdeen, UK
Javier Vazquez Salceda   Polytechnic University of Catalonia, Spain
Laurent Vercouter   University of Rouen, France
Harko Verhagen   University of Stockholm, Sweden
José R. Villar   University of Oviedo, Spain
Gerhard Weiss   University of Maastricht, The Netherlands
Wayne Wobcke   University of New South Wales, Australia
Gaku Yamamoto   IBM, Japan
Neil Yorke-Smith   University of Delft, The Netherlands
Franco Zambonelli   University of Modena, Italy
Dengji Zhao   ShanghaiTech University, China
Juan Carlos Nieves   Umea University, Sweden
Frédéric Migeon   Université de Toulouse, France
Panagiotis Kouvaros   Imperial College London, UK

Organizing Committee

Juan M. Corchado Rodríguez   University of Salamanca and the AIR Institute, Spain
Fernando De la Prieta   University of Salamanca, Spain
Sara Rodríguez González   University of Salamanca, Spain
Javier Prieto Tejedor   University of Salamanca and the AIR Institute, Spain
Pablo Chamoso Santos   University of Salamanca, Spain
Belén Pérez Lancho   University of Salamanca, Spain
Ana Belén Gil González   University of Salamanca, Spain
Ana De Luis Reboredo   University of Salamanca, Spain

Angélica González Arrieta	University of Salamanca, Spain
Emilio S. Corchado Rodríguez	University of Salamanca, Spain
Angel Luis Sánchez Lázaro	University of Salamanca, Spain
Alfonso González Briones	University of Salamanca, Spain
Yeray Mezquita Martín	University of Salamanca, Spain
Javier J. Martín Limorti	University of Salamanca, Spain
Alberto Rivas Camacho	University of Salamanca, Spain
Elena Hernández Nieves	University of Salamanca, Spain
Beatriz Bellido	University of Salamanca, Spain
María Alonso	University of Salamanca, Spain
Diego Valdeolmillos	AIR Institute, Spain
Sergio Marquez	AIR Institute, Spain
Marta Plaza Hernández	University of Salamanca, Spain
Guillermo Hernández González	University of Salamanca, Spain
Ricardo S. Alonso Rincón	AIR Institute, Spain
Javier Parra	University of Salamanca, Spain

PAAMS 2021 Sponsors and Organizing Institutions

Contents

Multi-agent Techniques to Solve a Real-World Warehouse Problem

Botond Ács, László Dóra, Olivér Jakab, and László Z. Varga$^{(\boxtimes)}$ ⓘ

Faculty of Informatics, ELTE Eötvös Loránd University, 1117 Budapest, Hungary
lzvarga@inf.elte.hu

Abstract. In recent years, many warehouses applied mobile robots to move products from one location to another. We focus on a traditional warehouse where agents are humans and they are engaged with tasks to navigate to the next destination one after the other. The possible destinations are determined at the beginning of the daily shift. Our real-world warehouse client asked us to minimise the total wage cost, and to minimise the irritation of the workers because of conflicts in their tasks. We extend Multi-Agent Path Finding (MAPF) solution techniques. We define a heuristic optimisation for the assignment of the packages. We have implemented our proposal in a simulation software and we have run several experiments. According to the experiments, the make-span and the wage cost cannot be reduced with the heuristic optimisation, however the heuristic optimisation considerably reduces the irritation of the workers. We conclude our work with a guideline for the warehouse.

Keywords: Multi-Agent Path Finding · Task Assignment · Warehouse · Multi-agent optimisation

1 Introduction

In recent years, many warehouses applied mobile robots to move products from one location to another. These applications gave rise to intensive research on problems related to the optimisation of moving a team of agents in discrete time-steps on a graph while avoiding collisions. Big e-commerce companies are interested in this research [16]. This research has become more important nowadays, as the recent pandemic has increased the demand for e-commerce.

In traditional warehouses, the agents go to the shelves, they pick up the products from the shelves and put them into their warehouse cart. Then the agents take the cart to the exit of the warehouse and park the cart for transportation.

The movement of the agents need to be optimised which is the main topic of Multi-Agent Path Finding (MAPF) [13]. The classical MAPF is a "one shot" problem. Each agent has a starting position and a destination position anywhere in the warehouse. In the lifelong MAPF problem [8], the destination positions appear online and the agents are constantly engaged with new tasks to navigate to the next destination. In our traditional warehouse, agents are also engaged

© Springer Nature Switzerland AG 2021
F. Dignum et al. (Eds.): PAAMS 2021, LNAI 12946, pp. 1–13, 2021.
https://doi.org/10.1007/978-3-030-85739-4_1

with tasks to navigate to the next destination one after the other, but the possible destinations are determined at the beginning of the daily shift, because our wholesale warehouse client operates with daily orders. We call this traditional version of the problem "semi-lifelong" MAPF problem.

Our client is a traditional warehouse where the agents are humans. Our real-world warehouse client asked us to tell the number of workers that is needed to be allocated to complete the daily shift in an optimal way. The optimisation goals are to minimise the total wage cost, and to minimise the irritation of the workers when they have to walk around each other or they have to wait in front of a shelf for the other worker to finish. Such real-world scenario is not directly addressed by classic MAPF methods. We advance the state of the art by combining and extending classic MAPF methods to solve a real-world problem.

In Sect. 2, we define the problem to be solved. In Sect. 3, we review the related work. In Sect. 4, we present the proposed solution that we have implemented in a simulation software. In Sect. 5, we describe the simulation experiments that we have done. In Sect. 6, we evaluate the experimental results, and we give a guideline for our real-world warehouse client. Section 7 concludes the paper.

2   Problem Definition

We focus on a traditional warehouse where humans collect the products, but our proposal and results can be applied to robots as well. We use the word agent for human workers. Figure 1 shows the typical layout of the warehouse. The warehouse has a grid layout, and an agent with a warehouse cart occupies one cell in this grid. The shelves are organised in aisles. One shelf occupies one cell. The aisles are wide enough for three agents: one can pass while two other agents stand in front of the shelves.

There is a given set of orders in each daily shift. There are O number of orders per day. The orders consist of several products. The orders have to be split into packages that can be collected into one or more warehouse carts.

The carts are moved by the agents on a route from the entrance door of the warehouse to the exit door. One agent can move maximum one cart. The agent and its cart move together, and they occupy one cell in each time step. When an agent finishes with a route, then it goes back to the entrance outside of the warehouse, and the agent can start its next route after T time.

The products of the orders have to be collected from the shelves. The agent and the cart stays for a short S time in front of a shelf while the products are collected from the shelf. If an agent is in front of a shelf and another agent wants to go to the same shelf, then the later arriving agent has to wait.

The products of an order have to be assigned to carts so that the products fit into the least number of carts. The set of products assigned to a cart is a package. The agent with the cart must visit the shelves containing the products assigned to the package.

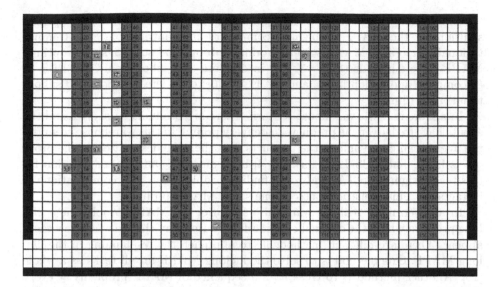

Fig. 1. A typical warehouse layout. The entrance is at the left-hand side and the exit is at the right-hand side. The shelves are indicated with grey cells. The agents pulling the carts are indicated with yellow cells.

There are $\mathcal{N}$ number of agents to move the carts. The daily shift lasts maximum $\mathcal{H}$ hours. The number $\mathcal{H}$ is fixed. The work-time of an agent within a shift starts when the first agent starts with its first cart, and the work-time ends when the last agent exits from the warehouse with its last cart.

Defining the order of the packages is the task assignment (TA). The make-span ($\mathcal{M}$) of the schedule is the time difference between the start of the work-time of the first agent and the end of the work-time of the last agent. The total wage cost is $\mathcal{C} = \mathcal{M} \times \mathcal{N}$. Note that the wage cost is proportional to the make-span, i.e. an agent also incurs cost when it is assigned to the warehouse work, but it is only waiting for the other agents to finish. This is because the agents are assigned to the job for the total make-span.

Our client asked us to solve the following problem: Create a schedule of the packages in accordance with the above description, and assign the packages to the agents. The schedule must fit within the shift. Find the schedule that needs the least amount of wage cost, and in addition, try to minimise the extra movements and waits of the agents.

3   Related Work

A direct approach to solve the "one shot" MAPF problem optimally is to treat the team of agents as a single joint agent and then to apply a version of the A^* algorithm [3]. The Conflict Based Search (CBS) [11] algorithm treats the agents individually and applies a two level search. The optimal and complete

CBS algorithm outperforms the A^* approach in many cases. Finding an optimal solution for the MAPF problem is computationally intractable [17]. Computationally tractable MAPF solvers produce sub-optimal solutions. Sub-optimal MAPF solvers include the CA* [12] (incomplete and suboptimal), the PBS [7] (incomplete and suboptimal), and the ECBS [9] (complete and bounded suboptimal) algorithms.

In a more realistic warehouse scenario, there are products on shelves and the agents have to deliver the products to delivery points. In this warehouse scenario, the agents can chose among the products, but then the destination of the product is fixed. The CBS-TA algorithm [4] is a complete and optimal solution for this task assignment (TA) and route finding problem, but it is computationally intractable. This scenario is also a "one shot" MAPF problem.

In an even more realistic warehouse scenario, the MAPF problem is a lifelong problem where the optimal collision-free routes may change when new tasks appear. There are different methods [5] to approach the re-planning in the lifelong MAPF. One method is to solve the lifelong MAPF for all tasks as a whole [10]. Another method is to treat it as a sequence of MAPF problems at every time-step when a new task is assigned to an agent. At this time-step, the routes for all agents are re-planned [2, 15]. In the third method, the route is re-planned only for those agents which get new tasks [6].

Frequent re-planning makes the computational complexity of the MAPF solvers more difficult to handle. The windowed MAPF approach helps to reduce this computational complexity [5]. In the windowed MAPF solver, the collisions are resolved only for the well chosen next w time-steps ahead. In fact, there is no need to resolve the conflicts for the whole routes, if the routes are re-planned before the agents complete them.

4   Proposed Solution

Two optimisations are already provided to us from our client: the orders are split into packages, and the order of the products within a package is defined. The first optimisation from our client is basically a bin packing problem which can be solved with polynomial algorithm [14]. The second optimisation, finding the best order of the products within a package is similar to the travelling salesman problem [1] which is computationally hard, but there is no need to solve it in the general form. A plain heuristic on the map of the warehouse is good enough, because the agents go from the entrance towards the exit, and they visit the aisles in this order. Once the agents enter an aisle, they collect all the products that are assigned to them and can be found in the given aisle. The order within an aisle follows a U-shape.

In our real-world warehouse, the MAPF problem has lifelong like features on two levels: the agents are engaged with new products one after the other within one package, and the agents are engaged with new packages one after the other within one daily shift. Therefore we have to optimise the route for each package, and we have to optimise the order of the packages within one shift.

The task assignment for the optimisation of the route for a package is given, and we only have to optimise the conflict free routes between the products. We treat this problem as a sequence of MAPF problems at every time-step when an agent starts for a new product. At this time-step, the routes for all agents are re-planned to find the best route for each agent. Although this needs a lot of computing effort, but if only the route for a single agent is re-planned, then completeness is not always guaranteed [5]. We use the CBS algorithm to find the optimal conflict-free routes. The CBS algorithm performs better in the case of bottlenecks, and the warehouse aisles are likely to be bottlenecks. Although the CBS algorithm is computationally hard, we used this algorithm, because the number of agents in the real-world warehouse is expected to be below 20. We used the windowed MAPF approach to reduce computational complexity, although it weakens the optimality of the CBS algorithm.

The classic MAPF solvers do not handle the problem of the waiting time in front of the shelves. Let us consider the situation when an agent arrives at a shelf and wants to stay in front of the shelf for S time-steps to complete its job. If a second agent also arrives at the same shelf during this time, then a classic MAPF solver might produce a solution where the first agent interrupts its job, the second agent stands in front of the shelf, the second agent completes its job, and then the first agent returns. A classic MAPF solver may even consider to interleave the jobs of the two agents. Such solution would not be acceptable in a real-world warehouse, therefore we modified the CBS algorithm to make the S time-steps in front of a shelf indivisible.

In order to optimise the order of the packages within one shift, we would like to avoid that agents have to go to the same shelf at the same time. We know all the packages in advance, but avoiding the conflicts of the packages is a combinatorially hard problem. So we defined a heuristic (Algorithm 1) to solve it. We want to minimise the number of the same product destinations assigned to those agents who are at the same time in the warehouse. This should be true all the time. Because an agent gets a new package when it finishes with the previous package, we want to find an ordering of the packages where there are minimal number of the same product destinations in any $\mathcal{N}$ consecutive packages.

We define the distance $distance(p_1, p_2)$ of two packages p_1 and p_2 with the number of products that are in both packages. Note that if $distance(p_1, p_2) = 0$, then two agents are happy to work on them at the same time. If $distance(p_1, p_2)$ is bigger, then bigger difference in timing is preferable. Given a set of packages P and a package p, then we collect from P the identifiers of packages that are closest to p into the set C with the function $C = closest(P, p)$.

We use the heuristic defined by Algorithm 1. The function $next(R, S)$ returns a package to be assigned to an agent which is free to start to collect a package. The packages that have not yet been assigned to any agent are in set R. The currently assigned packages are in the ordered list $S = \{s_1, s_2, \ldots, s_k\}$. The first agent starts to collect package s_1, the next agent starts to collect package s_2, the next agent starts to collect package s_3, etc. When a package s_i is assigned to an agent, and the agent starts to collect s_i, then s_i is removed from R, and

s_i is appended to the end of S. When an agent finishes with a package s_j, and delivers s_j to the exit, then s_j is removed from S, and the agent asks for another package with $next(R, S)$ if R is not empty.

When the first agent asks for a package with $next(R, S)$, then S is empty, and Algorithm 1 assigns a random package from R to the first agent (lines 2–3). If S is not empty, then we collect the identifiers of those packages from R that are closest to s_1 into a set C (line 7). If there is only one package in this set C, then this package will be assigned to the next agent (lines 8–9). Otherwise we continue with s_2, and we reduce the set C to those packages that are closest to s_2 (line 7). If there is only one package in C, then this package will be assigned to the next agent (lines 8–9). We continue with the packages in S until we reach the number of packages in S. Finally, if C still contains more than one package, then we return a random package from C (line 10).

An additional optimisation is that we do not start the agents at the same time, in order to reduce the collision conflicts in the first aisles. The agents start with a delay bigger than the waiting time $\mathcal{S}$ in front of the shelves.

Algorithm 1: $next(R, S)$: select the next package

Input: A non-empty finite set $R = \{r_1, r_2, \ldots, r_m\}$ of remaining packages, and an ordered list $S = \{s_1, s_2, \ldots, s_k\}$ of currently assigned packages
Output: The package to be assigned to the next agent
1 **begin**
2 | **if** S *is empty* **then**
3 | | **return** r_1
4 | **else**
5 | | $C \leftarrow R$
6 | | **for** $i \leftarrow 1$ *to* k **do**
7 | | | $C \leftarrow closest(C, s_i)$
8 | | | **if** $|C| = 1$ **then**
9 | | | | **return** *the only* $c \in C$
10 | **return** *any* $c \in C$

---

5   Experimental Setup

The above solutions were implemented in a simulation program written in C#. The inputs to the simulation program are the layout of the warehouse, the position of the products in the warehouse, the position of the agents in the warehouse, and the list of packages with the ordered list of products in them. The waiting time $\mathcal{S}$ in front of a shelf and the window w to resolve the conflicts ahead can be set as parameters. The simulation can be run with and without the heuristic optimisation of the order of the packages. When the simulation ran for too long time (one day was the limit), then we stopped it.

The layout of the real-world is similar to the one in Fig. 1. We used this layout in our simulations. Each product type can be found on two neighbouring shelves. The products are evenly distributed among the shelves in the warehouse. The real-world warehouse typically employs about 15 agents to deliver the orders. We created scenarios for agents between 1 and 20. The typical size of a package is around 16 products in the real-world warehouse, and usually only one package has smaller size within an order. In our scenarios, all the packages have 16 products. We have limited the number of packages to 40 in our scenarios to be able to run as many experiments as possible. The package number 40 was selected, because it means two packages per agent in the case of 20 agents, which is the maximum in our scenarios. The scenarios with these settings are similar to the real-world scenarios.

We have created several scenarios for the experiments. Products were randomly generated for two package sets $p1$ and $p2$. We assume that these package sets are the output of the optimal splitting of the orders. The products in the packages are ordered in accordance with the plain heuristic explained in Sect. 4. The scenarios were run with and without the optimisation of Algorithm 1. When Algorithm 1 was not used, the packages were assigned to the agents in the order as they were randomly generated in package sets $p1$ and $p2$.

The window size w has to be greater than the job completion time S, so that the extended CBS algorithm can handle the conflict of two agents aiming to the same shelf at the same time. In order to reduce computation time, we set the job completion time S to 2 time-steps. We chose three different lookahead window sizes: 5, 10 and 100. The window sizes 5 and 10 are about the same as the lookahead range of humans. The lookahead range 100 is about enough to find the optimal solution to the next product anywhere in the warehouse. Because replanning usually occurs more frequently than 10 steps, the plans above 10 steps are almost always dropped.

The simulation scenarios of all the above mentioned parameter combinations were run. Each scenario was a single run, because there is no uncertainty in execution. Most of the simulation runs could be completed in time, however a few of them had to be stopped because they ran for too long time. Table 1 shows which simulation runs were completed. In some cases (e.g. p2/5/2/N or p2/100/2/N for 14 agents) the not optimised simulation could not be completed because of unlucky coincidences causing excessive amount of conflict resolution.

6   Evaluation

The following diagrams show the results of the simulations. The data series legends in the diagrams use the same notations for the parameters as Table 1. If the experiment uses the heuristic optimisation of the order of the packages, then the marker of the data series is a filled circle. If the experiment does not use this heuristic optimisation, then the marker of the data series is a filled triangle. The horizontal axis is the number of agents on all diagrams.

Table 1. The completed simulations (marked with tick signs).

Package set	Window size	Wait steps	Optimisation	1	2	3	4	5	6	7	8	9	10	11	12	13	14	15	16	17	18	19	20
p1	5	2	Y	✓	✓	✓	✓	✓	✓	✓	✓	✓	✓	✓	✓	✓	✓	✓	✓	✓	✓	✓	✓
p1	5	2	N	✓	✓	✓	✓	✓	✓	✓	✓	✓	✓	✓	✓	✓	✓	✓	✓	✓	✓	✓	-
p1	10	2	Y	✓	✓	✓	✓	✓	✓	✓	✓	✓	✓	✓	✓	✓	✓	✓	✓	✓	✓	-	-
p1	10	2	N	✓	✓	✓	✓	✓	✓	✓	✓	✓	✓	✓	✓	✓	✓	-	-	-	-	-	-
p1	100	2	Y	✓	✓	✓	✓	✓	✓	✓	✓	✓	✓	✓	✓	✓	✓	✓	✓	✓	✓	✓	-
p1	100	2	N	✓	✓	✓	✓	✓	✓	✓	✓	✓	✓	✓	-	-	-	-	-	-	-	-	-
p2	5	2	Y	✓	✓	✓	✓	✓	✓	✓	✓	✓	✓	✓	✓	✓	✓	✓	✓	✓	✓	✓	✓
p2	5	2	N	✓	✓	✓	✓	✓	✓	✓	✓	✓	✓	✓	✓	✓	✓	-	✓	✓	✓	-	✓	✓
p2	10	2	Y	✓	✓	✓	✓	✓	✓	✓	✓	✓	✓	✓	✓	✓	✓	✓	✓	✓	✓	✓	✓
p2	10	2	N	✓	✓	✓	✓	✓	✓	✓	✓	✓	✓	✓	✓	✓	✓	-	✓	✓	✓	-	-
p2	100	2	Y	✓	✓	✓	✓	✓	✓	✓	✓	✓	✓	✓	✓	✓	✓	✓	✓	✓	✓	-	✓
p2	100	2	N	✓	✓	✓	✓	✓	✓	✓	✓	✓	✓	✓	✓	✓	✓	-	✓	-	-	-	-

The statistics of the make-span $\mathcal{M}$ (in time-steps) of the experiments are shown in the diagram of Fig. 2. It seems that neither the lookahead window nor the heuristic optimisation has effect on the make-span. We will see on the diagram of Fig. 5 that there are only small differences.

The statistics of the wage cost $\mathcal{C}$ in the experiments are shown in the diagram of Fig. 3. There are significant decreases in the trend of the wage cost when the number of agents is a divisor of the number of packages, because in this case the packages are evenly distributed among the agents, and there is no need for an extra round with only a few agents. The wage cost is about 50% higher when we apply 19 agents instead of 1. It seems that neither the lookahead window nor the heuristic optimisation has effect on the wage cost.

The statistics of the irritation $\mathcal{I}$ in the experiments are shown in the diagram of Fig. 4. The irritation $\mathcal{I}$ is the difference between the sum of the actions of all agents of the given experiment and the number of actions of the single agent experiment. The scenario with one agent is the reference for the total number of steps of an "irritation free" solution. If there is only one agent, then it delivers the packages one after the other, and it can always go on the shortest possible route to the next product. There is a clear difference between the irritation in the heuristically optimised scenarios (circle markers) and the heuristically not optimised scenarios (triangle markers). The heuristic optimisation considerably reduces the irritation of the agents. It seems that the lookahead window does not have effect on the irritation. We will analyse this on the diagram of Fig. 6.

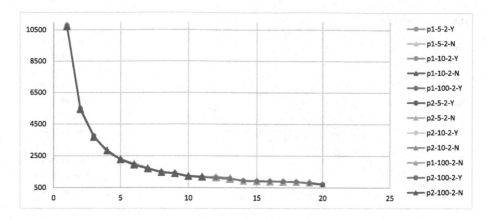

Fig. 2. The make-span $\mathcal{M}$ of the experiments.

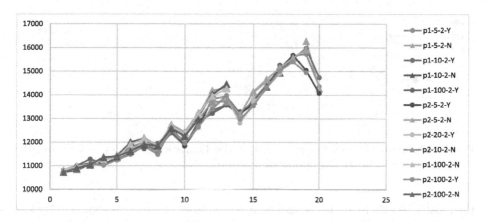

Fig. 3. The total wage cost $\mathcal{C}$ in the experiments.

The effect of the heuristic optimisation and the lookahead window on the wage cost $\mathcal{C}$ is shown in the diagram of Fig. 5. The small sized markers are for the lookahead window 5, the middle sized markers are for the lookahead window 10, and the large sized markers are for the lookahead window 100. The diagram for the make-span ratios would be the same, because $\mathcal{C} = \mathcal{M} \times \mathcal{N}$. There are no big differences between the optimised and the not optimised wage costs. The not optimised wage cost is at most 7% higher than the optimised wage cost, but in few cases the not optimised is at most 2% better. It seems that the lookahead window does not have effect on the wage cost, because there is no clear trend.

The effect of the heuristic optimisation and the lookahead window on the irritation $\mathcal{I}$ is shown in the diagram of Fig. 6. There are significant differences between the optimised and the not optimised irritation. The not optimised irritation is in a few cases 3 times higher than the optimised irritation, and in most of the cases the not optimised irritation is around 2 times higher. The optimisation seems to help

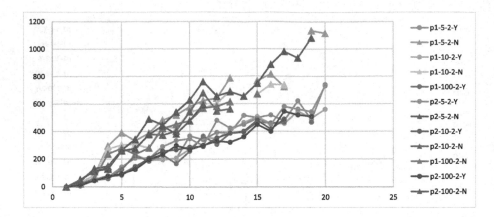

Fig. 4. The irritation $\mathcal{I}$ in the experiments.

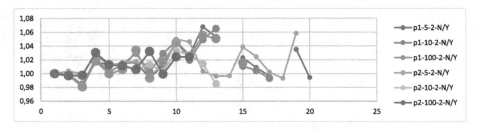

Fig. 5. The ratio between the wage cost of the heuristically not optimised and the wage cost of the heuristically optimised scenarios.

the most when there are fewer agents. If the number of agents is significantly less than the number of packages, then there is more room for optimisation. It seems that the lookahead window does not have effect on the wage cost, because there is no clear trend.

After All, How Many Agents Are Needed? The guideline for our real-world warehouse client is the following: Use Algorithm 1 for the heuristic optimisation of the order of the packages to reduce the irritation of the agents, and apply as few agents as possible, because it reduces both wage cost and irritation. In our experiments, if $\mathcal{H} = 2500$, then (from the diagram of Fig. 2) $\mathcal{N} = 5$. This way the work can be completed within the daily shift (Fig. 2), the wage cost is reduced (Fig. 3), and the irritation of the workers is reduced (Fig. 4).

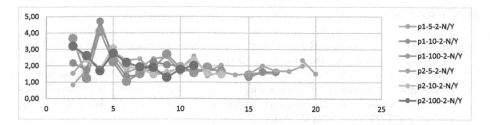

Fig. 6. The ratio between the irritation in the heuristically not optimised and irritation in the heuristically optimised scenarios.

7 Conclusion

In this paper we have investigated the problem of a real-world warehouse. The warehouse want to know the number of workers that is needed to minimise the wage cost, and to minimise the irritation of the workers when they have to walk around each other or they have to wait in front of a shelf for the other worker.

We have proposed a solution which uses MAPF solution techniques with the following additions: 1) We have extended the CBS algorithm to handle the waiting time in front of the shelves as an indivisible action. 2) We have solved a "semi-lifelong" MAPF. We have used the method of re-planning for all agents whenever there is a need for a new destination. 3) We have used the windowed solution to reduce the computing complexity of the "semi-lifelong" MAPF. 4) We have defined a heuristic optimisation for the assignment of the packages.

According to the experiments, the make-span and the wage cost cannot be reduced with the heuristic optimisation, however the heuristic optimisation considerably reduces the irritation of the agents. The lookahead window seems to be indifferent, so the short range of human lookahead may perform as well as a long range computational lookahead. We have concluded our work with a guideline for the real-world warehouse client. We plan to investigate if and how to implement the ideas in the real ERP system of the client.

Acknowledgement. We thank K. Berczi for the optimisations from the real-world client. We thank A. Kiss for facilitating the initial programming work. The work of B. Ács, O. Jakab and L. Dóra was supported by the European Union, co-financed by the European Social Fund (EFOP-3.6.3-VEKOP-16-2017-00002). The work of L.Z. Varga was supported by the "Application Domain Specific Highly Reliable IT Solutions" project which has been implemented with the support provided from the National Research, Development and Innovation Fund of Hungary, financed under the Thematic Excellence Programme TKP2020-NKA-06 (National Challenges Subprogramme) funding scheme.

References

1. Applegate, D.L., Bixby, R.E., Chvátal, V.: The Traveling Salesman Problem. Princeton University Press, Princeton (2007)
2. Grenouilleau, F., van Hoeve, W., Hooker, J.N.: A multi-label A* algorithm for multi-agent pathfinding. In: Proceedings of the Twenty-Ninth International Conference on Automated Planning and Scheduling, ICAPS 2018, Berkeley, CA, USA, 11–15 July 2019, pp. 181–185. AAAI Press (2019)
3. Hart, P., Nilsson, N., Raphael, B.: A formal basis for the heuristic determination of minimum cost paths. IEEE Trans. Syst. Sci. Cybern. **4**(2), 100–107 (1968). https://doi.org/10.1109/tssc.1968.300136
4. Hönig, W., Kiesel, S., Tinka, A., Durham, J.W., Ayanian, N.: Conflict-based search with optimal task assignment. In: Proceedings of the 17th International Conference on Autonomous Agents and MultiAgent Systems, AAMAS 2018, Richland, SC, pp. 757–765 (2018)
5. Li, J., Tinka, A., Kiesel, S., Durham, J.W., Kumar, T.K.S., Koenig, S.: Lifelong Multi-Agent Path Finding in Large-Scale Warehouses, pp. 1898–1900. International Foundation for Autonomous Agents and Multiagent Systems, Richland (2020)
6. Liu, M., Ma, H., Li, J., Koenig, S.: Task and path planning for multi-agent pickup and delivery. In: Proceedings of the 18th International Conference on Autonomous Agents and MultiAgent Systems, AAMAS 2019, International Foundation for Autonomous Agents and Multiagent Systems, Richland, SC, pp. 1152–1160 (2019)
7. Ma, H., Harabor, D., Stuckey, P.J., Li, J., Koenig, S.: Searching with consistent prioritization for multi-agent path finding. Proc. AAAI+ Conf. Artif. Intell. **33**(01), 7643–7650 (2019)
8. Ma, H., Li, J., Kumar, T.K.S., Koenig, S.: Lifelong multi-agent path finding for online pickup and delivery tasks. In: Proceedings of the 16th Conference on Autonomous Agents and MultiAgent Systems, AAMAS 2017, São Paulo, Brazil, 8–12 May 2017, pp. 837–845. ACM (2017)
9. Max, B., Guni, S., Roni, S., Ariel, F.: Suboptimal variants of the conflict-based search algorithm for the multi-agent pathfinding problem. Front. Artif. Intell. Appl. **263**, 961–962 (2014)
10. Nguyen, V., Obermeier, P., Son, T.C., Schaub, T., Yeoh, W.: Generalized target assignment and path finding using answer set programming. In: Proceedings of the Twenty-Sixth International Joint Conference on Artificial Intelligence, pp. 1216–1223, August 2017
11. Sharon, G., Stern, R., Felner, A., Sturtevant, N.R.: Conflict-based search for optimal multi-agent pathfinding. Artif. Intell. **219**, 40–66 (2015)
12. Silver, D.: Cooperative pathfinding. In: Proceedings of the First AAAI Conference on Artificial Intelligence and Interactive Digital Entertainment, AIIDE 2005, pp. 117–122. AAAI Press (2005)
13. Stern, R., et al.: Multi-agent pathfinding: definitions, variants, and benchmarks. In: Proceedings of the Twelfth International Symposium on Combinatorial Search, SOCS 2019, Napa, California, 16–17 July 2019, pp. 151–159. AAAI Press (2019)
14. de la Vega, W.F., Lueker, G.S.: Bin packing can be solved within $1 + \epsilon$ in linear time. Combinatorica **1**(4), 349–355 (1981)

15. Wan, Q., Gu, C., Sun, S., Chen, M., Huang, H., Jia, X.: Lifelong multi-agent path finding in a dynamic environment. In: 2018 15th International Conference on Control, Automation, Robotics and Vision (ICARCV), pp. 875–882. IEEE (2018)
16. Wurman, P.R., D'Andrea, R., Mountz, M.: Coordinating hundreds of cooperative, autonomous vehicles in warehouses. AI Mag. **29**(1), 9 (2008)
17. Yu, J., LaValle, S.: Structure and intractability of optimal multi-robot path planning on graphs. In: Proceedings of the AAAI Conference on Artificial Intelligence, vol. 27, no. 1, June 2013

Towards Quantum-Secure Authentication and Key Agreement via Abstract Multi-Agent Interaction

Ibrahim H. Ahmed[⊠], Josiah P. Hanna, Elliot Fosong,
and Stefano V. Albrecht

School of Informatics, University of Edinburgh, Edinburgh EH8 9AB, UK
{i.ahmed,josiah.hanna,e.fosong,s.albrecht}@ed.ac.uk

Abstract. Current methods for authentication and key agreement based on public-key cryptography are vulnerable to quantum computing. We propose a novel approach based on artificial intelligence research in which communicating parties are viewed as autonomous agents which interact repeatedly using their private decision models. Authentication and key agreement are decided based on the agents' observed behaviors during the interaction. The security of this approach rests upon the difficulty of modeling the decisions of interacting agents from limited observations, a problem which we conjecture is also hard for quantum computing. We release PyAMI, a prototype authentication and key agreement system based on the proposed method. We empirically validate our method for authenticating legitimate users while detecting different types of adversarial attacks. Finally, we show how reinforcement learning techniques can be used to train server models which effectively probe a client's decisions to achieve more sample-efficient authentication.

Keywords: Quantum resistance · Authentication · Key agreement · Multi-agent systems · Opponent modeling · Reinforcement learning

1 Introduction

Authentication and key agreement protocols are the foundation for secure communication over computer networks. Most protocols in use today are based on public-key cryptographic methods such as Diffie-Hellman key exchange, the RSA cryptosystem, and elliptic curve cryptosystems [5]. These methods rely on the difficulty of certain number theoretic problems which can be solved efficiently using quantum computing [19]. Thus, researchers are studying alternative mathematical problems believed to be safe against quantum computing [5]. Standards organizations such as the US National Institute of Standards and Technology [6] are calling for new quantum-safe proposals for standardization.

We propose a novel formulation of authentication and key agreement inspired by research in artificial intelligence (AI) and machine learning. In the proposed

© Springer Nature Switzerland AG 2021
F. Dignum et al. (Eds.): PAAMS 2021, LNAI 12946, pp. 14–26, 2021.
https://doi.org/10.1007/978-3-030-85739-4_2

method, communicating parties are viewed as *autonomous agents* which interact repeatedly using their private decision models. Authentication and key agreement are based solely on the agents recognizing each other from their observed behavior, and no private information is sent at any time during the process. Our approach creates a bridge to AI research in two ways:

Security – The method's security rests upon the difficulty of modeling an agent's decisions from limited observations about its behavior – a long-standing problem in AI research known as *opponent modeling* [1]. We conjecture that the problem is as hard for quantum computing, since the problem is fundamentally one of missing information regarding the causality in an agent's decisions (details in Sect. 3). There are no known quantum algorithms to solve opponent modeling; indeed, if such an algorithm was invented as an attack on our method, it could provide significant novel insights for AI research.

Optimization – By formulating authentication as a multi-agent interaction process, we can employ concepts and algorithms for *optimal decision-making* from reinforcement learning (RL) [21] to optimize the efficiency of the process. The idea is to enable communicating agents to be strategic about probing each other's reactions to maximize authentication accuracy and efficiency. We apply RL methods to our framework to optimize the agent models to reduce the number of interactions required to reach high-confidence authentication decisions.

In summary, our contributions are the following. We introduce a protocol for secure authentication and key agreement based on recognizing an agent from limited observations of its actions. We show empirically that our method obtains high accuracy in rejecting different categories of adversarial agents, while accepting legitimate agents with high confidence. We release a prototype implementation of this protocol, called PyAMI, which allows remote machines to authenticate to one another and generate symmetric session keys. Finally, we introduce an approach for optimizing security based on RL and show empirically that it leads to a significantly more efficient protocol in terms of the required number of client/server interactions than a default random probing server agent.

2 Related Work

Post-quantum Alternatives: Among current post-quantum methods in the literature, those based on the fields of coding theory [20], lattice theory [12], and multivariate quadratic polynomials [15] provide existing entity identification schemes. Such schemes avoid quantum vulnerability by relying on problems for which there is no known quantum algorithm. The use of optimization and decision-theoretic principles, however, makes our approach fundamentally different to other lines of investigation in post-quantum security which rely primarily on the development of new cryptographic operators.

Symmetric AKE: Protocols for symmetric authenticated key-exchange (AKE) such as Kerberos [13] often rely on a third party to provide session keys. Their session key may also be generated independently of the long-term key (LTK).

In our protocol, parties generate session keys without the aid of an extra entity, and derive it based on the LTK. With respect to authentication, protocols like [3] often use a MAC tag based on the LTK, while our protocol uses a test of statistical similarity to determine whether a party possesses the expected LTK.

Information-Theoretic Secrecy: Information-theoretic protocols rely on security which can be achieved without any assumptions on an attacker's computational limits. Shannon's introduction of such protocols required a shared secret key between communicating parties over a noiseless channel [18]. Later protocols replaced this requirement of a shared key by introducing stochasticity [23]. Our key agreement protocol is similar to Shannon's original setting, relying upon a shared secret in the form of the client's decision model, but it is instead used to generate the session key itself for symmetric encryption and decryption.

Multi-agent Modeling/Interactive Processes: Agent-based modeling has been applied quite broadly in the field of security, such as for analyzing dynamics between parties in a computer network [22]. Our protocol is a novel application of multi-agent theory and optimization to cryptographic authentication. Game-theoretic approaches, particularly *security games*, have also been proposed for cyber-defense scenarios between attacker and defenders [10]. Our own work does not rely on equilibrium concepts which are difficult to scale [7] and based on normative rationality assumptions.

3   Authentication via Multi-agent Interaction

This section details our proposed protocol, called **A**uthentication via **M**ulti-agent **I**nteraction (AMI; pronounced "Am I?"). In the following, we use calligraphic letters (e.g., $\mathcal{X}$) to denote sets, lower case letters to denote elements of sets and functions, and upper case letters to denote random variables. We use $\Delta(\mathcal{X})$ to denote the set of all probability distributions over elements of set $\mathcal{X}$.

We consider a setting in which a client seeks to authenticate to a server as a particular user, u. The server must decide whether the client is the intended (*legitimate*) user u or an *adversarial* client attempting to access the server as the intended user.

Protocol: When a client seeks to authenticate, the server initiates an interaction process which proceeds through time steps $t = 0, 1, 2, ..., l$ (cf. Figure 1). At each time step t, the client and server independently choose actions A_c^t and A_s^t, respectively, with values in a finite set of available actions, $\mathcal{A} := \{1, ..., n\}$. The agents then send their chosen actions to each other. The server associates a probabilistic decision model, π_u, with each legitimate user; the decision model is known only to the server agent and the legitimate user. At the end of the interaction process, the server decides whether the interaction history $H_l :=$ $(A_s^0, A_c^0, ..., A_s^l, A_c^l)$ was generated with a client using the model π_u associated with the legitimate user. If the server decides it has been interacting with this model, then it authenticates the client as user u; otherwise, it rejects the client agent.

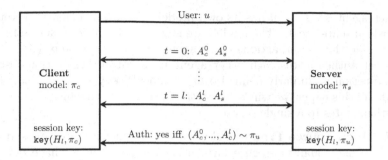

Fig. 1. Multi-agent interaction protocol

We formalize agent decision models as functions mapping the past interaction history to a distribution over the available actions. That is, the client chooses actions with the model $\pi_c : \mathcal{H}_t \to \Delta(\mathcal{A})$ where $\mathcal{H}_t$ is the set of possible interaction histories up to time t. Similarly, the server agent chooses actions with a model π_s. Various model representations could be used, including probabilistic decision trees, probabilistic finite state automata, and neural networks. Jointly, the server and client agent define a distribution on $(l + 1)$-step interaction histories, $p_{s,c}$. If the client in the interaction process is a legitimate client then they use the decision model π_u (i.e., $\pi_c = \pi_u$) that is a shared secret between the server and legitimate client. To perform authentication, the server decides whether a given interaction history has been produced by $p_{s,u}$ or not. To do so, we equip AMI with a test function, test $: \mathcal{H}_l \to \{0, 1\}$ that returns 1 if and only if an interaction $H \sim p_{s,u}$. In Sect. 4 we describe how this function can be implemented with a frequentist hypothesis test.

Key Agreement: If the client is successfully authenticated, a secret session key can be computed as a function $\mathbf{key}(H_l, \pi)$, where the client uses $\mathbf{key}(H_l, \pi_c)$ and the server uses $\mathbf{key}(H_l, \pi_u)$; if $\pi_c = \pi_u$, then the computed keys will be equal. One possible implementation of the key function is by concatenating the probabilities $\pi_u(A_c^t|H_l), t = 0, ...l$ and pushing the resulting bit-string through a suitable hash function to produce a key with a desired length.

Forward Secrecy: AMI supports *forward secrecy* [9] to ensure that a compromised (e.g. stolen) legitimate user model cannot be used to compute past session keys. AMI transforms π_u after each successful authentication process, such that the new model is a function $\pi'_u = \phi(\pi_u, H_l)$ of the old model, and such that ϕ is hard to invert. One possible transformation is to first reset a random seed to the value of the session key. Then, for each $\tau = 0, ..., l$, resample a new probability distribution for $\pi_u(H_\tau)$. Since server and client use the same seed, they produce identical models π'_u and π'_c. The session key cannot be recovered from a transformed model except by exhaustive search in the space of random seeds - with a sufficiently large key size, this is computationally infeasible [16].

Extension to More Than Two Agents: AMI also supports mutual group authentication in which more than two parties authenticate to each other. In this case, each agent $i = 1, ..., m$ has its own model π_i which is a shared secret with all other legitimate agents. The models are now defined over interaction histories which include the chosen actions of all agents at each time step, $(A_1^t, ..., A_m^t)$. Each agent authenticates each other agent using an authentication test, and the key function is similarly defined over all models, $\text{key}(H_l, \pi_1, ..., \pi_m)$. In the remainder of this paper, we will focus on the basic setting in which a single client only authenticates to a single server.

PyAMI Open-Source Framework: Towards further research on and adoption of AMI as a quantum-secure authentication protocol, we have developed an open-source Python application, PyAMI[1]. PyAMI consists of a multi-agent system where agents run on separate (virtual) machines, and communicate to authenticate over network sockets using TCP. During an interaction process, server and client machines transmit actions over a network to build the shared interaction history. After successful authentication, both parties compute identical session keys using the key agreement algorithm.

4   Authentication via Hypothesis Testing

To provide high-confidence authentication decisions, AMI uses the framework of frequentist hypothesis testing to decide whether a given interaction history was generated between the server and a legitimate client or an adversarial client. For a given history, h, we first specify the null hypothesis "h was generated from π_u." To decide on the correctness of this hypothesis, we compute a test statistic from the interaction history and determine whether the test statistic value is too extreme for the distribution of the test statistic under the null hypothesis. More formally, letting $z : \mathcal{H} \rightarrow \mathbb{R}$ denote a test statistic function, a hypothesis test computes the p-value

$$p := \Pr(|z(H)| \geq |z(h)|), \quad H \sim p_{s,u}. \tag{1}$$

Intuitively, p is the probability of observing a z value at least as extreme as $z(h)$ if interacting with the legitimate client model. The p-value is then compared to a pre-determined significance level, α, to determine whether the interaction came from the legitimate client or not:

$$\text{test}(h) = \begin{cases} 1 \text{ (authenticate)} & \text{if } p\text{-value} \geq \alpha \\ 0 \text{ (reject)} & \text{if } p\text{-value} < \alpha \end{cases} \tag{2}$$

We use a hypothesis test which was designed for non-stationary multi-agent interaction [2]. Essentially, this test defines a flexible test statistic for multi-agent interaction, learns the distribution of this test statistic during an interaction (we use the score functions defined in [2]), and computes p from the learned distribution. Our only modification from the original algorithm is to fit the

---

[1] PyAMI code and documentation: https://github.com/uoe-agents/PyAMI

distribution of the test statistic with a normal distribution rather than a skew-normal distribution. This change allows us to compute p-values using the analytic normal CDF instead of the ratio-approximation proposed in [2], which led to more accurate results in our experiments.

An important aspect of the hypothesis testing approach is its interpretability. The p-value has a well-defined semantics and the significance level α allows us to exactly control the false negative rate of the test. Under the null-hypothesis $\pi_c = \pi_u$, p is uniformly distributed in $[0, 1]$ and so a false negative occurs at exactly the rate α. If the legitimate client is incorrectly rejected, the client can retry the interaction process. The probability of k successive false negatives is α^k which rapidly goes to zero.

5   Protocol Security

The problem of modeling the behavior of another agent from limited observations of its actions is widely studied in the AI research literature and known to be hard [1]. The problem is fundamentally one of missing information regarding the causality in an agent's decisions, and this information can be difficult to extract from limited observations. Even with a publicly known agent model structure – which this paper assumes – a complex model will involve large parameter spaces; inferring exact parameter values from a few observed authentications is infeasible. The use of a quantum computer over a classical one will not aid in solving this specific type of problem, as it is more aligned with an *information-theoretic* type of hardness rather than computational hardness [11].

An information-theoretic key agreement protocol is considered (weakly) secure if: (1) the two parties' generated session keys agree with very high probability, (2) the key is nearly uniformly distributed, and (3) is nearly statistically independent of the information leaked to an intruder [11]. AMI is a symmetric key protocol and mandates that client and server generate identical session keys, fulfilling the first condition.

Regarding the second condition; in an experimental setting, AMI uses random instantiation so that the choice of user and server model is uniformly distributed over the space of possible models, which is significant as the session key is a function, $\text{key}(H_l, \pi)$, of these models. Additionally, this key generation procedure includes a hash function as a final step – we note that it is possible to also use a universal hashing mechanism here, similar to [4] where universal hashing is applied so that possible outputs are equiprobable for an intruder.

With respect to the third condition, AMI limits the publicly observable information by which an intruder may attempt to reconstruct π_u and generate the correct session key. It does this in two ways – first, it limits the length of the public interaction required for successful authentication (see optimization in Sect. 8). Second, it implements a forward secrecy transform intended to limit all observations from a specific model π_u to a single interaction session. The only way an intruder may obtain more than a single history from the same client model is in the unlikely event of a false negative, in which a legitimate client is incorrectly rejected (see Sect. 4). We provide an empirical study of such a scenario in Sect. 6 to demonstrate how AMI is robust against a maximum likelihood estimation (MLE) attack[2] even in the absence of the forward secrecy feature.

6   Empirical Study: Authentication

We now present an empirical study of the AMI protocol. Our experiments are primarily designed to answer the following questions: 1) Does AMI correctly accept a legitimate client? 2) Does AMI correctly reject adversarial clients? 3) How does the length of interaction histories affect AMI's accuracy? 4) How robust is AMI to Maximum Likelihood Estimation attacks? 5) How much time does PyAMI need to complete an interaction process?

6.1   Authentication Empirical Set-Up

In our basic empirical setting, agents choose actions from $\mathcal{A} = \{1, ..., 10\}$. The server model and legitimate client model are probabilistic decision trees (PDTs) – decision trees in which each node has a probability distribution over actions. The tree is traversed using the $k = 5$ most recent actions of the other agent (i.e., the client tree is traversed with the server's actions). We choose PDTs as they are computationally cheap to sample actions from and easy to randomly generate.

For each experimental trial run, we randomly generate the server and true user decision model by setting each node in the PDT to be a softmax distribution with logit values sampled uniformly in $[0, 1]$ and temperature parameter τ. The server decision model uses the value $\tau = 1.0$ for near-uniform random action selection; the client uses $\tau = 0.1$. We find lower entropy in the client's action selection leads to better authentication accuracy with shorter interaction lengths. In each experimental trial, we generate interaction histories between the server and legitimate client and measure accuracy of the decisions made by AMI. We also evaluate interactions between the server agent and adversarial agents. We formulate the following adversarial behaviors to create such interactions:

Random: Generate a random adversarial PDT with the same dimensions and temperature τ as the legitimate client PDT.

Replay: Replay client actions from observed interactions between the legitimate client and server to create adversarial "replayed" interaction histories.

Maximum Likelihood Estimation (MLE-k): Compute a maximum likelihood estimate of the legitimate client PDT based on k complete interaction histories with the legitimate client, assuming an identical PDT structure. We set $k = 100$ in these experiments.

---

[2] Assuming a uniform prior distribution over possible models π_u, the best estimate of π_u an attacker can formulate is the MLE; MLE is generally a preferred estimator among frequentist methods due to its statistical and asymptotic properties [8].

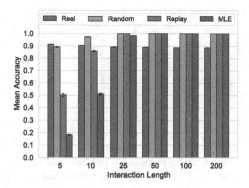

Fig. 2. Authentication accuracy as a function of interaction length. For each considered interaction length we evaluate accuracy on every metric. For Real, Replay, and MLE metrics, results show accuracy on 1000 histories, averaged over 100 different server and legitimate client pairs. For the Random metric, results show accuracy on 1000 histories, averaged over 100 different server models.

To evaluate AMI we generate 1000 interaction histories between the server and legitimate client, and 1000 interaction histories between the server and each type of adversarial behavior for varying interaction history lengths. We report authentication accuracy on each set of interaction histories as the percentage of interaction histories correctly identified as either legitimate or adversarial (Random, Replay, or MLE). For experimental rigor, we repeat this process over 100 different server and legitimate client models, and present the averaged results in Fig. 2. For the hypothesis test we use a significance level of $\alpha = 0.1$.

6.2   Authentication Empirical Results

Figure 2 shows the empirical accuracy of AMI with the legitimate client and against each type of adversary for a varying number of interaction history lengths. As expected, the accuracy for the legitimate client model is unaffected by the interaction history length and always remains around 0.9, due to our chosen significance threshold. For shorter history lengths ($l < 50$), MLE is the strongest attack tested. Once interaction histories are sufficiently long ($l \geq 50$), however, accuracy is perfect against adversarial clients and nothing is gained by further increasing the interaction history length. We emphasize that the MLE adversary cannot successfully authenticate *even after observing 100 interaction histories from the legitimate client* (as used by the MLE agent in Fig. 2). Furthermore, the probability that adversaries observe 100 interaction histories before a forward secrecy transform is applied is $\alpha^{100} = 10^{-100}$.

We conduct an additional experiment to evaluate how many observed interactions are required for an MLE attack to obtain a high probability of authentication (with forward secrecy disabled). Figure 3a plots authentication accuracy on an MLE attack provided with an increasing number of histories. Results are averaged across 100 random client-server pairs, where accuracy is computed on

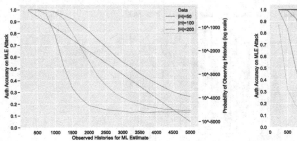
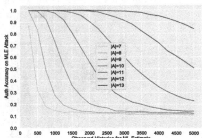

(a) Effect of varying history length for fixed action space size $|\mathcal{A}| = 10$.

(b) Effect of varying size of action space for fixed history length $|H_l| = 100$.

Fig. 3. Average authentication accuracy against MLE attacks versus number of histories used for the MLE attack. Results averaged over 100 different client-server pairs. Standard error not shown due to low variation (<0.01).

100 MLE histories for each pair. It also plots the probability of an intruder observing as many histories. For longer history lengths ($|H_l| = 200$), and with specified model complexity, *at least 500 observed histories are required for an MLE attack to meaningfully lower the authentication accuracy*, and the probability of observing this much data before a forward secrecy transform is 10^{-500} under AMI. These results provide empirical evidence for the difficulty of constructing a successful attack from observed data, even by the best model estimation method, and without bounds on computational power.

We also demonstrate that AMI's parameters can be tuned to further decrease the effectiveness of MLE attacks. In Fig. 3b, we fix the history length at $|H_l| = 100$, then vary the size of the action space $\mathcal{A}$ in the client and server PDT models. The results show that larger action spaces – corresponding to more complex models – are more secure against MLE attacks in terms of number of histories the attacker must observe.

Finally, we include timing experiments for PyAMI's multi-agent interaction process. We measure the time for a full interaction history – the transmission of all actions between separate machines – to complete. For our experiments we use virtual machines on Google Compute Engine situated within the same geographic region (us-west1) and measure the time taken for a server-client interaction in the one-way authentication setup. For interaction lengths of $|H_l| = \{50, 100, 200\}$, we recorded interaction times of $\{(28 \pm 2)$ ms, (54 ± 2) ms, (112 ± 10) ms$\}$ respectively, averaged over 100 trials. These results show that AMI within PyAMI could be feasibly deployed to provide real-time authentication and key agreement.

7   Optimizing Server Actions

Our empirical evaluation demonstrated that AMI robustly rejects various attack types while allowing legitimate clients to authenticate. We now show how the server's decision model can be further optimized for protocol efficiency, as measured by the required interaction length before the p-value is sufficiently small to reject an adversary. When the server interacts with an adversarial client, its actions can probe where the adversary may fail to match the legitimate client's action distributions. Effective probing actions can lead to higher confidence decisions in shorter interaction history lengths. Using shorter histories reduces the amount of observations adversaries can gather, thus improving the security of the protocol against model reconstruction attacks like the MLE attack. We show how an effective server probing model can be learned for a given legitimate client model π_u via reinforcement learning (RL) [21].

We pose the server optimization problem as follows. During training, the server decision model interacts with unknown clients over a series of length l episodes in which each episode runs an AMI authentication process with a fixed client. At the end of the interaction the server receives a reward, $R_l = 1 - p$ where p is the p-value of the hypothesis test. The server is rewarded for producing low p-values when interacting with adversaries. The learning objective is thus:

$$\pi_s \in \arg\max_\pi \mathbf{E}_\pi \left[R_l \mid H_l \sim p_{s,c}, \pi_c \right], \tag{3}$$

in which the client model, π_c, is sampled from an adversarial population (in our experiments we sample random PDTs the same way as Sec. 6). By applying an RL algorithm to optimize (3) w.r.t. the server's decision model, we obtain a model that attempts to quickly reach high-confidence decisions.

We note that the server model is optimized with respect to a particular legitimate client model. After successful authentication, the legitimate client model is transformed via a function ϕ so as to preserve forward secrecy. In principle, this could render the server optimization obsolete since the client model has changed. To address this concern, we can define ϕ to randomly permute the indexing of the client's actions at each leaf node of its PDT. The random permutation generator is seeded by the session key, which depends on exact knowledge of the user model. From an outside observer's perspective the distribution over elements of $\mathcal{A}$ will have changed, and is uniform on expectation assuming the permutation is sampled uniformly-randomly; thus an attacker could never learn anything but the uniform distribution over actions. However, since the permutation is known to both the legitimate client and the server, the server model can un-permute the actions received from the client and apply the trained server model.

8   Empirical Study: Optimized Probing

We conduct an empirical study to addresses the question: does effective probing lead to more efficient authentication relative to random probing?

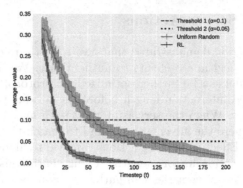

Fig. 4. Average p-value per timestep over 10 different optimized servers interacting with Random adversaries. Shaded areas show standard error.

In these experiments, the server model is a feedforward neural network which outputs the logits of a softmax distribution over the action space. We use $|\mathcal{A}| = 5$ and train with maximum interaction lengths of 50 steps. To more clearly show the benefit of server model optimization, we use legitimate client PDT models with higher entropy action selection ($\tau = 0.5$) than in Sect. 6. Such client models would be harder for an attacker to learn but also necessitate longer interaction histories for high confidence rejection decisions. Thus, server policy optimization is more crucial to shorten the required interaction histories.

Using the PPO RL algorithm [17], we train the server model for 5 million steps with 5,000 environment steps across three parallel processes for each model update. We train the server for a fixed legitimate client model against an adversarial population of 100 randomly generated PDTs. After training, we evaluate the rate of p-value convergence for the trained server. We compute the average p-value per timestep, averaged over a different population of 100 held-out adversarial PDTs. As a baseline, we evaluate a uniform-random probing server model. We repeat the server optimization process 10 times for different randomly generated legitimate clients (and unique populations of adversarial clients), to ensure our optimization method is effective not just for a specific server-client pair.

Figure 4 shows that the RL-trained server model leads to substantially faster convergence of p-values than uniform probing, reducing the required number of timesteps by 70% and 79% on average for thresholds of $\alpha = 0.1$ and $\alpha = 0.05$, respectively. The trained model is able to identify sequences of actions which lead to more informative observations for authenticating client agents.

9   Conclusion and Future Work

We contributed a novel protocol for secure authentication and key agreement based on abstract multi-agent interaction and agent modeling. We have shown empirically that our protocol is highly accurate in authenticating legitimate users and rejecting different types of adversarial attacks. The protocol allows for control over authentication accuracy by choice of hypothesis test parameters, and by the chosen complexity of agent models. We released an open-source framework which employs our protocol in a distributed setting, and demonstrated the feasibility of this framework through timing experiments between remote server-client pairs. Finally, we showed how reinforcement learning can be used to train server models to achieve highly sample-efficient authentication.

Importantly, this work lays the ground work for multi-party authentication through multi-agent systems. Such a system raises new questions for how agents can jointly optimize security and efficiency; we believe that multi-agent reinforcement learning may offer a promising solution [14]. Future work could consider variable-length interaction histories, as such an authentication test could be more active in collecting additional information when facing decision uncertainty.

References

1. Albrecht, S.V., Stone, P.: Autonomous agents modelling other agents: a comprehensive survey and open problems. Artif. Intell. **258**, 66–95 (2018)
2. Albrecht, S.V., Ramamoorthy, S.: Are you doing what I think you are doing? Criticising uncertain agent models. In: Proceedings of UAI 2015 (2015)
3. Avoine, G., Canard, S., Ferreira, L.: Symmetric-key authenticated key exchange (sake) with perfect forward secrecy. In: IACR Cryptology ePrint Archive (2019)
4. Bennett, C.H., Brassard, G., Robert, J.M.: Privacy amplification by public discussion. SIAM J. Comput. **17**(2), 210–229 (1988)
5. Fauzi, P., Hovd, M.N., Raddum, H.: A Practical adaptive key recovery attack on the LGM (GSW-like) cryptosystem. In: Cheon, J.H., Tillich, J.-P. (eds.) PQCrypto 2021 2021. LNCS, vol. 12841, pp. 483–498. Springer, Cham (2021). https://doi.org/10.1007/978-3-030-81293-5_25
6. Chen, L., et al.: Report on post-quantum cryptography. Technical report, National Institute of Standards and Technology (2016)
7. Daskalakis, C., Goldberg, P.W., Papadimitriou, C.H.: The complexity of computing a Nash equilibrium. SIAM J. Comput. **39**(1), 195–259 (2009)
8. Eliason, S.R.: Maximum Likelihood Estimation Logic and Practice. Quantitative Applications in the Social Sciences. 96. SAGE, Newbury Park (1993)
9. Günther, C.G.: An identity-based key-exchange protocol. In: Quisquater, J.-J., Vandewalle, J. (eds.) EUROCRYPT 1989. LNCS, vol. 434, pp. 29–37. Springer, Heidelberg (1990). https://doi.org/10.1007/3-540-46885-4_5
10. Manshaei, M.H., Zhu, Q., Alpcan, T., Başar, T., Hubaux, J.P.: Game theory meets network security and privacy. ACM Comput. Surv. **45**, 1–39 (2013)
11. Maurer, U.M.: The role of information theory in cryptography. In: Proceedings of 4th IMA Conference on Cryptography and Coding (1993)
12. Micciancio, D., Vadhan, S.P.: Statistical zero-knowledge proofs with efficient provers: lattice problems and more. In: Boneh, D. (ed.) CRYPTO 2003. LNCS, vol. 2729, pp. 282–298. Springer, Heidelberg (2003). https://doi.org/10.1007/978-3-540-45146-4_17
13. Neuman, D.C., Hartman, S., Raeburn, K., Yu, T.: The Kerberos Network Authentication Service (V5). RFC 4120, July 2005. https://doi.org/10.17487/RFC4120
14. Papoudakis, G., Christianos, F., Rahman, A., Albrecht, S.V.: Dealing with non-stationarity in multi-agent deep reinforcement learning. arXiv preprint arXiv:1906.04737 (2019)

15. Sakumoto, K.: Public-key identification schemes based on multivariate cubic polynomials. In: Fischlin, M., Buchmann, J., Manulis, M. (eds.) PKC 2012. LNCS, vol. 7293, pp. 172–189. Springer, Heidelberg (2012). https://doi.org/10.1007/978-3-642-30057-8_11
16. Schneier, B.: Applied Cryptography. Wiley, Hoboken (1993)
17. Schulman, J., Wolski, F., Dhariwal, P., Radford, A., Klimov, O.: Proximal policy optimization algorithms. arXiv preprint arXiv:1707.06347 (2017)
18. Shannon, C.E.: A mathematical theory of communication. Bell Syst. Tech. J. **27**(3), 379–423 (1948)
19. Shor, P.: Polynomial-time algorithms for prime factorization and discrete logarithms on a quantum computer. SIAM Rev. **41**(2), 303–332 (1999)
20. Stern, J.: A new identification scheme based on syndrome decoding. In: Stinson, D.R. (ed.) CRYPTO 1993. LNCS, vol. 773, pp. 13–21. Springer, Heidelberg (1994). https://doi.org/10.1007/3-540-48329-2_2
21. Sutton, R., Barto, A.: Reinforcement Learning: An Introduction. MIT Press, Cambridge (1998)
22. Wagner, N., Lippmann, R., Winterrose, M., Riordan, J., Yu, T., Streilein, W.: Agent-based simulation for assessing network security risk due to unauthorized hardware. In: SpringSim (2015)
23. Wyner, A.D.: The wire-tap channel. Bell Syst. Tech. J. **54**(8), 1355–1387 (1975)

HAIL: Modular Agent-Based Pedestrian Imitation Learning

André Antakli[✉], Igor Vozniak, Nils Lipp, Matthias Klusch,
and Christian Müller

German Research Center for Artificial Intelligence (DFKI), Stuhlsatzenhausweg 3,
66123 Saarbruecken, Germany
andre.antakli@dfki.de

Abstract. In the area of autonomous driving there is a need to flexibly configure and simulate more complex individual pedestrian behavior in critical traffic scenes which goes beyond predefined behavior simulation. This paper presents a novel human-oriented, agent-based pedestrian simulation framework, named HAIL, that addresses this challenge. HAIL allows to simulate human pedestrian behavior through means of imitation learning by virtual agents. For this purpose, HAIL combines the 3D traffic simulation environment OpenDS with an integrated imitation learning environment and hybrid agents with AJAN. For predictive behavior planning on the tactical and strategical level, AJAN is extended with Answer Set Programming. For pedestrian behavior imitation learning on the operational level, HAIL utilizes the module InfoSalGAIL for generation of pedestrian paths learned from demonstration by its human counterpart as expert. Among others, an application example has been demonstrated that HAIL can be applied to solve a common challenge in the Neural Network domain, namely the out-of-distribution (OOD), e.g. never shown scenarios would raise an uncertainty prediction level, by unison work of the two different behavior generation frameworks.

Keywords: Pedestrian simulation framework · Multi-agent system · Imitation learning

1 Introduction

Pedestrian simulations are mostly considered in crowd scenarios. In such simulations the individual pedestrians are mathematical functions called particles, that can implement only a limited variety of emerging behavior. In state-of-the-art traffic simulation frameworks like Carla[1] or LGSVL[2] pedestrians follow only predefined trajectories. However, if higher-order behavior is to be simulated because the focus is set on the individual pedestrian, these models are no longer suitable, since

---

[1] Carla: https://carla.org/.
[2] LGSVL: https://www.lgsvlsimulator.com/.

. © Springer Nature Switzerland AG 2021
F. Dignum et al. (Eds.): PAAMS 2021, LNAI 12946, pp. 27–39, 2021.
https://doi.org/10.1007/978-3-030-85739-4_3

various aspects of a pedestrian, such as activity planning through to actual movement, are no longer covered. In general (cf. [10]), a distinction is made between three layers of pedestrian behavior: the strategic level includes high-level decision-making, e.g. activity or trip planning based on interests; the tactical level, which divides the high-level activity plan into intermediate targets and tries to achieve them using atomic actions; and the operational level, which implements the actual action like a walking task and adjusts pedestrian speed, gait, and alignment. The agent paradigm is suitable for encapsulating these layers into a single autonomous entity. Especially the fields of video games or robotics have successfully used this model. In these areas, the simulation environment is represented abstractly in the Strategic and Tactical layer of the agent and is often processed via Behavior Trees. Instead, the Operational layer works directly with environmental properties, like its geometry or physics. Nevertheless, all simulation systems either use pre-modelled approximations of real human behavior (cf. [12,18]), or only certain aspects of the behavior model are considered but hardly transferable to other simulation scenarios due to their lack of modularity (cf. [11,19]).

To this end, we developed a novel approach called HAIL (human-oriented agent-based imitation learning) for the simulation of pedestrians in virtual traffic scenes. The resulting framework follows the above mentioned pedestrian behavior model, and combines modular predictive agents with imitated real pedestrian behavior in order to simulate more realistic traffic situations. With HAIL, it is possible to imitate demonstrated expert behavior of on-street walking on the operational level. For this purpose, HAIL leverages the imitation learning approach InfoSalGAIL [20] and the 3D driving simulation software OpenDS[3] (version 6.0) to set up traffic environment and visualize imitated pedestrian behavior in it. Finally, the agent system AJAN [2] is used in HAIL to represent more complex pedestrian behaviors on the strategic and tactical level based on both intrinsic and extrinsic pedestrian needs. The behavior model in AJAN relies on so called SPARQL-BTs, which was extended by means of Answer Set Programming (ASP) to realize utility-based foresighted activity planning.

The paper is structured as follows. Section 2 gives a brief introduction into the background required and discusses relevant state of the art on pedestrian agent engineering and pedestrian imitation learning. In Sect. 3, we present our contribution HAIL, the interplay of its components and describe how ASP is integrated for foresighted action planning. In Sect. 4, an application example in the context of simulated pedestrians is presented. Finally, we conclude the paper in Sect. 5.

2   Related Work

2.1   Pedestrian Agent Engineering

In the field of pedestrian simulation we mainly find solutions to simulate crowds, see PTV Viswalk[4], VADERE[5] or PEDSIM[6]. According to [18], these solutions

---

[3] OpenDS - open source driving simulation: https://opends.dfki.de/.

[4] PTV Viswalk: https://www.ptvgroup.com/de/loesungen/produkte/ptv-viswalk/.

[5] VADERE Crowd simulation: http://www.vadere.org/.

[6] PDESIM - pedestrian crowd simulation: http://pedsim.silmaril.org/.

are often based on social force, cellular or magnetic force models and are inspired as well by the work of [16]. The individuals of a crowd are purely reactive agents who do not pursue their own goals. The direct interaction between individuals is usually not considered in these approaches and the individual modeling of a autonomous higher order behavior is not given. However, if, for example, critical situations in road traffic are to be simulated in which the vehicle gains a "close" view of individual pedestrian behavior, these solutions are no longer useful. Due to the immense efforts that have recently been made in the field of autonomous driving, the need for individual pedestrian behavior simulation has increased. Prominent traffic simulation environments available in this context are Carla and LGSVL. These solutions only have primitive pedestrian models that usually follow a predefined path. Since Carla is based on the Unreal Engine it is possible to model the individual pedestrian behavior with Behavior Trees[7] (BT). BTs are widely used in the gaming industry and in robotics (see [15]) to realize deliberative agents. However, a predictive utility-based behavior covering intrinsic and extrinsic needs is hard to be implemented with BTs.

Modular Agent Engineering with AJAN. AJAN (Accessible Java Agent Nucleus) is an agent engineering framework, in which SPARQL-enhanced BTs, so called SPARQL-BTs (SBT) are used as an agent behavior model and agent models are defined in RDF (Resource Description Framework). Beside of dictionaries with key value pairs, which are often used in other BT solutions, the RDF data model is domain-independent and thus a more flexible and in combination with SPARQL a powerful alternative [5]. For an intuitive modeling of AJAN agents, a web editor is provided. AJAN has already been used to control virtual humans, see [2]. AJAN is available as open-source software[8] and is used in our approach to control single virtual pedestrians. An AJAN agent has one or more behaviors, each consisting of a SBT and a corresponding RDF-based execution knowledge (EKB), which stores internal behavior knowledge (e.g. procedural variables); one agent specific RDF-based knowledge base (AKB), storing internal agent knowledge, which can be accessed by all agent behaviors[9]; one or more events and goals, each holding RDF data; and one or more agent endpoints, which are the agent's interfaces to its domain and forward incoming RDF messages as events. Behaviors are linked to such events or goals but can also create these. If an event occurs, the behaviors linked to it are executed. SBTs are used to perform contextual SPARQL queries for state checking (e.g. realized with a SPARQL-ASK query), updating, constructing RDF data used for action executions, or to control the internal execution of an AJAN agent behavior. Furthermore, SBTs are defined in RDF, whereby a semantic description of

---

[7] Unreal-BTs: https://docs.unrealengine.com/InteractiveExperiences/BehaviorTrees.

[8] AJAN-service: https://github.com/aantakli/AJAN-service AJAN-editor: https://github.com/aantakli/AJAN-editor.

[9] Not like EKs, where only the corresponding agent behavior has access to.

the behaviors they implement is available. SBTs use standard BT primitives (see [7]) and are processed like typical BTs[10].

2.2 Imitation of Pedestrians in Simulated Environment

Behavior Cloning (BC) and Apprenticeship Learning (AL) are common approaches to address imitation learning challenges. Considering BC it suffers from moderate generalization due to compounding errors and covariant shift [17]. In contrary, AL tends to reconstruct the reward function [1] at high computational costs because of solving a reinforcement learning problem in the training loop. Generative Adversarial Imitation Learning (GAIL) [8], is a prominent approach in solving AL problems. The objective of which is to learn the optimal strategy for a given task without estimating an explicit reward function. An extension of GAIL was introduced in InfoGAIL [13], where the policy of a simulated car agent is estimated based on the mixture of expert trajectories, adding a direct relationship to the latent variables as in [6].

Pedestrian Imitation Learning with InfoSalGAIL. For the imitation learning module of HAIL, we selected the InfoSalGAIL [20] system. In particular, this system uses saliency maps of experts (recorded during a comprehensive study) for a more human-like imitation of virtual pedestrian walking behavior. It was shown that visual attention, represented in the form of saliency maps, indeed plays an important role in trajectory generation. However, the service-oriented architecture of HAIL also allows to integrate other imitation learning modules than InfoSalGAIL.

In InfoSalGAIL, the imitated behavior of a simulated pedestrian is considered safe or risky. This classification is based on the learned expert trajectories and the traffic areas entered with them, such as streets (risky) or crosswalks (safe) (cf. Fig. 3). In the context of a visual attention model, the task is to identify the most probable area of interest at any given point in time, which can be seen as a set of highlighted pixels as shown in Fig. 1. The training objective or loss function (cf. Eq. 1) is defined as follows and has been experimentally shown to be efficiently working for the generation of different types of pedestrian walking behaviors:

$$\min_{\theta,\psi,\Delta} \max_{\omega} \mathbb{E}_{\pi_\theta}[D_\omega(s_{vis,sal}, a)] + \mathbb{E}_{\pi_E}[D_\omega(s_{vis,sal}, a)] - \lambda_0\eta(\pi_\theta)$$
$$-\lambda_1 L_1(\pi, Q) - \Delta_E(s) - \lambda H(\pi)$$

where π stands for the agent's policy, π_E the policy of the subject, D is the discriminative classifier with the overall goal to distinguish state-action pairs (synthetic vs. real). $H(\pi) \triangleq \mathbb{E}[-\log \pi(a|s)]$ denotes the γ - discount casual entropy of the policy π_θ as defined by [4]. λ_1 is the hyper-parameter for the information maximization regularization term L_1 as in [13]. The term $\eta(\pi_\theta) = \mathbb{E}_{s\sim\pi_\theta}[s_r]$ reflects the tendency towards learning of the desired behavior, thus,

---

[10] AJAN uses LibGDX-BTs: https://github.com/libgdx/gdx-ai/wiki/Behavior-Trees.

stands for the main reinforcement learning component which is obtained directly from the simulator. Δ_E is the pixel-wise loss based on the binary cross-entropy function, which helps to optimize the saliency map generation objective.

3 HAIL Framework

3.1 Overview

The HAIL framework is designed to imitate fore-sighted human-like behavior of pedestrians in previously unseen virtual traffic scenarios based on prior knowledge of prerecorded expert demonstrations, e.g. walking in virtual environment. HAIL can also be used to simulate pedestrians in traffic scenarios for which no prior training data exist. Figure 1 shows the high-level architecture of HAIL, which consists of three main components, namely OpenDS as the simulation software, AJAN for controlling pedestrian agents, and InfoSalGAIL as Imitation Learning framework to account for the human-like trajectories learned during the training given the ground truth data of recorded subjects.

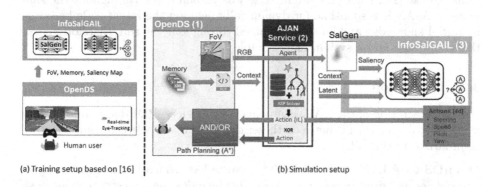

Fig. 1. HAIL framework overview. (a) Setup (cf. [20]) to learn from expert demonstrations. (b): Field of View (FoV) is the input image from OpenDS, where the memory contains current and previous simulation information. Path planning (A*) is supported within OpenDS to deliver a path if no imitation model in a OOD situation. SalGen generates saliency maps for the FoV images, where the context and latent variable are used as input information for the policy generator. The $4d$ action vector comes from InfoSalGAIL to control the pedestrian.

The starting component of HAIL is the open-source driving simulation software OpenDS (cf. Fig. 1b(1)), which is used to simulate and visualize virtual traffic scenarios. OpenDS manages a scenario with a three-dimensional scene with semantic information about objects like traffic lights but also points-of-interest (POI), simulated vehicles, integrated path planning (A*) and atomic actions on the operational level. Such actions include performing animations like waving or operating a traffic light, navigating a pedestrian agent to a given destination via path planning and directly setting the steering vector of a pedestrian agent. In addition, it provides a training environment (cf. Fig. 1(a)) for the imitation learning used in HAIL [20]. Moreover, it manages AJAN agents controlling simulated pedestrians and provides them with dynamic scenario information.

AJAN (cf. Sect. 2.1), the "man-in-the-middle" component of HAIL (cf. Fig. 1b(2)), is used for decision-making of the pedestrian agent, to execute OpenDS atomic actions, and to obtain new avatar transformations for it via the imitation learning service InfoSalGAIL. In this context, two strategies can be applied: Either (i) AJAN controls the virtual pedestrian using input from InfoSalGAIL, if an imitation model is available for a given agent state; or (ii) AJAN controls the pedestrian directly via OpenDS actions, if no such model exists. Which strategy is chosen actually depends on the SBTs and goals of the particular agent and its beliefs. When the beliefs are updated by OpenDS, the decision-making with SBTs is triggered. This involves evaluating which capabilities are available in the current state to achieve an existing goal.

InfoSalGAIL (cf. Sect. 2.2), the imitation learning component of HAIL (cf. Fig. 1b(3)), allows to bring human-like behavior into the simulation through means of learning an optimal navigation policy by means of expert demonstrations. Unlike [20], where the latent code was manually set throughout the simulation, AJAN is responsible for dynamically defining the latent code based on its initial knowledge and knowledge gained throughout the run, therefore makes the overall simulation system more flexible.

3.2 Integration

For the integration of the HAIL components or services, RDF-based information is exchanged over HTTP between these; the interaction between components is summarized in the following.

OpenDS to AJAN: OpenDS initializes an AJAN-controlled pedestrian agent and defines its initial beliefs and goals. This includes the pedestrian agent position and information about the given traffic scene at $time = 0$. After initialization, updates on scene changes are sent to the agent, after which OpenDS listens for calls to perform atomic actions. An update includes "seen" POIs, positions of dynamic objects such as simulated vehicles and other pedestrians, but also states of virtual objects such as traffic lights. In order to simulate a human-like perception module, OpenDS has been extended with an additional visual module to cover the POIs only and the distances to the same, if they fall within the field of view (FoV) of the pedestrian agent. For the use of InfoSalGAIL, additional information about the current body orientation of the pedestrian agent, its speed and "view" (RGB image in combination with yaw and pitch angles for the head) as well as historical information about previously executed actions is also broadcast. The agent receives these updates and sends them to an SBT which updates the agent knowledge base and decides which navigation strategy to use. When it is recognized that an InfoSalGAIL model exists[11] in the current situation to perform a navigation task, the input data required by InfoSalGAIL is forwarded by the agent, otherwise OpenDS-based navigation is used.

AJAN to InfoSalGAIL: An important aspect of AJAN, besides to which destination to navigate for a given goal, is to determine the latent variable used in InfoSalGAIL. The latent variable specifies how risky a pedestrian should navigate. For example (cf. Fig. 3, Scenario A), a simulated pedestrian may initially try to cross the street because of an approaching car. However, if the pedestrian agent realizes that the potential danger has passed, it decides to riskily cross the street. To execute InfoSalGAIL, the data received from OpenDS is merged with the adapted latent variable and forwarded by AJAN. After receiving the information, InfoSalGAIL responds immediately with a new action input for the pedestrian agent, which is forwarded by AJAN to OpenDS. The $4d$-input vector consists of *turning angle*, *speed*, and head orientation (*pitch* and *yaw* angles).

Execution in OpenDS: OpenDS provides multiple HTTP/RDF endpoints to perform pedestrian agent actions, such as *"set transformation"* in case we use InfoSalGAIL, or *"walk to target"* in case we use the path planner. During simulation, these endpoints listen for incoming action commands from AJAN. For example, if a target (a 3D-vector) is received to which the pedestrian agent should walk to, a path to the target is generated using A* and applied to the avatar. However, if the avatar transformation based on the output of InfoSalGAIL is to be adjusted directly, this action input is applied to the avatar and its history and the RGB image of the FoV are updated accordingly.

3.3   AJAN Extensions

AJAN is used in HAIL to realize the strategic and tactical layers of a simulated pedestrian and therefore to control its navigation. For this purpose, a destination is selected and, depending on the strategy, performed directly via OpenDS navigation or with InfoSalGAIL. A set of destinations to be reached sequentially can be manually defined using SBTs. In order to implement more complex scenarios in which the agent dynamically creates navigation sequences based on intrinsic or extrinsic needs, we implemented an ASP-SBT node[12] for reasoning, problem solving or to plan intention sequences. For this purpose, we adapted the RDF-to-ASP translation approach in [9] to translate RDF-based AJAN agent beliefs into ASP rules. Table 1 shows the five most important transformation rules with an example in Fig. 2 left.

---

[11] Upon initialization, an AJAN agent receives RDF descriptions of available InfoSalGAIL models defining trained street configurations.

[12] ASP-SBT-node: https://github.com/aantakli/AJAN-service/tree/master/pluginsystem/plugins/ASPPlugin.

Table 1. Basic RDF-to-ASP transformation rules.

	RDF version:	⇔	ASP version:
Triple:	\<S\> \<P\> \<O\>	⇔	_t("S", "P", "O")
Graph:	\<IRI\> { \<S\> \<P\> \<O\> }	⇔	_g(_t("S", "P", "O"), "IRI")
IRI:	IRI	⇔	"IRI"
Literal:	"l" ∧∧ \<XSD\>	⇔	_l("l", "XSD")
Blank:	_:blank123	⇔	_b("blank123")
Prefix:	@prefix react: \<IRI\>	⇔	_p("react", "IRI")

If beliefs are available for solving navigation problems, then additional ASP rules (e.g., planning rules, see Fig. 4 and [3] Sect. 2) need to be added. Pedestrian behavior could also integrate the social context of the environment (e.g., traffic norms modeled ins ASP [14]) such that the trajectories that are generated by the ASP planner can be evaluated from a normative point of view. The specified problem can then be solved using an ASP solver[13]. If no stable model is found then the ASP-SBT node returns FAILED as status otherwise SUCCEEDED; each model is stored by the agent as a RDF named graph (cf. Fig. 2 right).

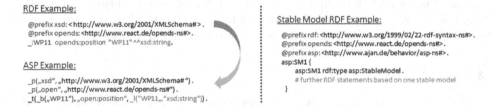

Fig. 2. Left: RDF-to-ASP example. Right: RDF representation of a stable model.

4   Application Example

This section outlines two applications of HAIL for using learned pedestrian street crossing behavior with a foresighted agent. AJAN is used to detect these situations during simulation and to send appropriate requests based on the configured agent model to InfoSalGAIL. The situations that the imitation learning model cannot mimic due to an unevenly balanced training dataset, e.g., navigating in an "unseen" street configurations, are handled by built-in actions in AJAN and OpenDS and meant to solve the OOD challenge of imitation learning.

---

[13] In AJAN we use the Potassco clingo solver: https://potassco.org/clingo/.

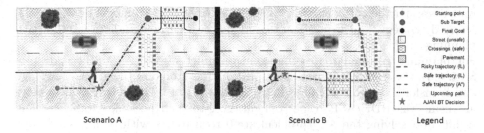

Fig. 3. Chosen use-case scenarios. Left: Scenario A - stands for the use-case shown to IL framework in the form of experts demonstrations. Right: Scenario B - out-of-distribution (OOD) scenario that only partially is known ("seen") to the IL framework. In scenario B, only part of the path (red trajectory) can be guided by the trained model, with the remaining path (blue trajectory) being realized by A* path planner.

4.1 Scenarios Description

Fig. 3 shows the traffic scenarios in which a pedestrian agent shall navigate from a given starting point to a destination like its human counterpart. In the considered scenarios A and B multiple strategies are possible, e.g., risky crossing of the road directly to the destination. Which strategy is finally chosen depends on different parameters like configured maximum time to reach the target, degree of risk aversion and interests. Strategies can also be dynamically switched in response to events, such as an approaching vehicle. In scenario A, e.g., the pedestrian agent initially walks safely because it has seen an approaching vehicle; if there is no longer any potential danger, the agent changes its strategy and crosses the road directly and riskily to the intermediate destination and then walks on to its final location. In scenario B, however, the pedestrian first behaves riskily and then also safely. During the simulation, the pedestrian agent must dynamically decide whether to reach the respective destinations with InfoSalGAIL or A*.

4.2 Agent Model

HAIL enables to configure different pedestrian agents by setting their behavioral parameters like the available definitions of InfoSalGAIL imitation models, the degree of risk taking, and individual interests. These parameters are taken into account during execution of the pedestrian agent SBTs, hence affect its behavior in the scene and are set while agent initialization and updated in runtime.

The application SBT defines the processing of strategy or rout choices depending on the given pedestrian agent state. In each simulation step the agent receives input from OpenDS with which this SBT is executed. While in one sub-tree of the SBT incoming information is saved and the will to take risks is adapted, the simulated behavior is implemented in parallel in another sub-tree as follows. If a critical event occurs, then the SBT is aborted, otherwise, the first step of the iteration is to use an ASP SBT-node to create multiple weighted routes to the agent goal. Then, a strategy is selected based on the agent risk-taking and the rout costs. Further, it is checked whether an InfoSalGAIL model exists for the selected strategy, and if positive, this model is used next; otherwise, the path planning in OpenDS is used.

For planning weighted routes the agent parameters, the ASP SBT-node (see Sect. 3.3), the scene configuration graph, which is stored in the agent knowledge and transformed into ASP, and the rules shown in Fig. 4 are used. These rules are using the RDF/ASP scene configuration to plan possible strategies. The result after solving the ASP problem are 0 to n routes with their costs, which are available to the SBT as named graphs.

```
1    cost(0,0).
2    time(1..steps).
3    edge(I,O,C) :-  _t(E,"rdf:type","opends:Edge"), _t(E,"opends:out",O), _t(E,"cost",C), _t(I,"opends:risky",O), not risky.
4    number(C) :- C = #count{N : node(N)}.
5    1 { walktTo(G,T) : node(G) } 1 :- time(T).
6    at(G,T) :- walktTo(G,T), at(A,T-1), edge(A,G,_).
7    cost(T,C1+C2) :- walktTo(X,T), at(Y,T-1), edge(Y,X,C1), cost(T-1,C2), Y!=X.
8    cost(Max) :- Max = #max{C : cost(T,C)}.
9    :- walktTo(G,T), not edge(A,G,_), at(A,T-1).
10   :- not at(X,T), T = steps, goal(X).
```

Fig. 4. ASP navigation planning rules, generating 0 to n stable models each containing one weighted *walkTo*-action sequence. In line 3 RDF based edges are defined and possible edges are removed, if risk-taking is not considered. In 5 a search space is built and filtered by constraints in lines 9 and 10. In lines 7 and 8 costs are calculated.

Figure 5 depicts several views of scenario A: (A) shows the scene configuration as a graph available to the agent in RDF. Red edges are marked as risky and green edges as safe. Based on this graph, a route is calculated via ASP in which interests (green node) are taken into account by decreasing the route costs. (B) is a partially risky route to an intermediate destination at time 0 of scenario A. Instead, (C) is a safe route of the same scenario and time. (D) displays the graphical representation of the semantic description of an available InfoSalGAIL model. Both routs or strategies (B) and (C) are matching this model. InfoSal-GAIL is used then, by the presented SBT for navigation. The same model can be used in scenario B, if the pedestrian wants to riskily reach the intermediate destination. If it is to be reached safely, the navigation planning in OpenDS must be used instead, if no matching imitation model is available. The choice of a strategy depends mainly on the agent's willingness to take risks. This depends on the current agent state and is based on its initial configuration and incoming events. If, as in scenarios A and B, such an event is received, the originally safely (scenario A) or risky (scenario B) strategy is discarded (star in Fig. 3) by AJAN and a new route is computed and executed by HAIL or A*.

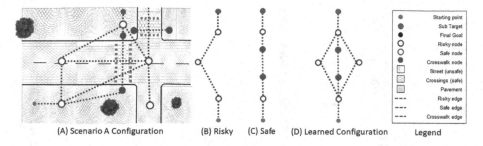

Fig. 5. (A) street configuration in OpenDS. (B) and (C) generated ASP plans for risky and safe behavior. (D) street definition for available imitation models.

4.3 Imitation Model

For the application scenarios, we train imitation models given the training data (see [20]), e.g., pairs consisting of the FoV images and saliency maps, including memory information of six human subjects on nine different scenarios (~140K pairs) in accordance to German-in-Depth-Accident-Study (GIDAS), excluding the safe part of the use-case scenario B (special OOD scenario). Each model represents a single street configuration (for which there is an RDF representation). Here, the risk-free and high-risk navigation was considered in a scene with a zebra crossing. As input signals, InfoSalGAIL accepts an RGB image of size $224 \times 224 \times 3$ and prior information from frames $t-1$ and $t-2$, respectively. This information comes from OpenDS and is passed to InfoSalGAIL via AJAN with a scenario-dependent latent code (safe or risky) for a given trained model. The resulting $4d$ action (turn, speed, yaw, pitch) is then passed back to OpenDS.

4.4 Experimental Evaluation

For training, validation and testing purposes with OpenDS and InfoSalGAIL, we utilized a Tesla V100 (32 GB vRAM) GPU under ~14 GB of vRAM due to usage of a pre-trained model for the saliency generator provided in [20], and a 2018 MacBook with Windows 10 to control the pedestrian agent with AJAN. For the processing of incoming data from OpenDS, the forwarding of information required by InfoSalGAIL, and the passing of resulting 4d-actions, AJAN needs no more than ~17 ms. If a navigation plan needs to be created with the ASP-SBT node, no more than ~94 ms are additionally required for the application scenarios. A detailed evaluation of ASP based action planning is presented in [3]. The generated pedestrian agent trajectories for the application scenarios A[14] and B are shown in Fig. 6.

---

[14] Videos of the FoV of the pedestrian agent in scenario A can be found at: https://cloud.dfki.de/owncloud/index.php/s/HAf5wQtMAx3F9K5.

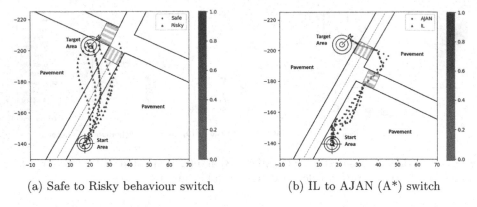

(a) Safe to Risky behaviour switch   (b) IL to AJAN (A*) switch

Fig. 6. (a): Plots of generated pedestrian agent trajectories of Scenario A, where the change from safe to risky behavior is triggered by AJAN depending on the road situation, e.g. potential dangerous collisions by an arriving car. (b): Plots of the trajectories of scenario B, where the agent is faced with the OOD problem (new street layout). Accordingly, navigation path is taken from A*-planning, where less variation is seen.

5   Conclusion

We presented a novel approach, named HAIL, for modular agent-based pedestrian imitation learning in traffic scenarios to generate human-like trajectories under the constraints of previously unseen traffic scenarios. HAIL combines the AJAN, OpenDS and InfoSalGAIL subsystems to realize the tactical and strategic as well as the operational level of pedestrian behavior, making HAIL suitable for the generation of critical traffic scenarios and tests. We presented an application example to show how HAIL virtually imitates real pedestrian trajectories on the one hand and how OOD scenarios are solved on the other hand. For this, ASP is used to decide whether an imitation model is available for partial execution of navigation plans and to dynamically create these plans.

Acknowledgements. The work described in this paper has been funded by the German Federal Ministry of Education and Research (BMBF) through the project REACT (grant no. 01/W17003) and in part by Huawei Munich Research Center.

References

1. Abbeel, P., Ng, A.Y.: Apprenticeship learning via inverse reinforcement learning. In: Proceedings 21st International Conference Machine Learning (ICML) (2004)
2. Antakli, A., et al.: Agent-based web supported simulation of human-robot collaboration. In: Proceedings International Conference Web Information Systems and Technologies (WebIST) (2019)
3. Antakli, A., Zinnikus, I., Klusch, M.: ASP-driven BDI-planning agents in virtual 3D environments. In: Klusch, M., Unland, R., Shehory, O., Pokahr, A., Ahrndt, S. (eds.) MATES 2016. LNCS (LNAI), vol. 9872, pp. 198–214. Springer, Cham (2016). https://doi.org/10.1007/978-3-319-45889-2_15

4. Bloem, M., Bambos, N.: Infinite time horizon maximum causal entropy inverse reinforcement learning. In: International Conference Decision and Control. IEEE (2014)
5. Brambilla, M., Facca, F.M.: Building semantic web portals with a model-driven design approach. In: Web Technologies: Concepts, Methodologies, Tools, and Applications, pp. 541–570. IGI Global (2010)
6. Chen, X., Duan, Y., Houthooft, R., Schulman, J., Sutskever, I., Abbeel, P.: Info-GAN: interpretable representation learning by information maximizing generative adversarial nets. In: Proceedings 29th International Conference Neural Information Processing Systems (NeurIPS), pp. 2172–2180 (2016)
7. Colledanchise, M., Ögren, P.: Behavior Trees in Robotics and AI: An Introduction. CRC Press, Boca Raton (2018)
8. Ho, J., Ermon, S.: Generative adversarial imitation learning. In: Proceedings 29th International Conference Neural Information Processing Systems (NeurIPS) (2016)
9. Ianni, G., Martello, A., Panetta, C., Terracina, G.: Efficiently querying RDF (S) ontologies with answer set programming. Logic Comput. **19**(4), 671–695 (2009)
10. Ishaque, M.M., Noland, R.B.: Behavioural issues in pedestrian speed choice and street crossing behaviour: a review. Transp. Rev. **28**(1), 61–85 (2008)
11. Karamouzas, I., Heil, P., van Beek, P., Overmars, M.H.: A predictive collision avoidance model for pedestrian simulation. In: Egges, A., Geraerts, R., Overmars, M. (eds.) MIG 2009. LNCS, vol. 5884, pp. 41–52. Springer, Heidelberg (2009). https://doi.org/10.1007/978-3-642-10347-6_4
12. Lee, J., Li, T., De Vos, M., Padget, J.: Using social institutions to guide virtual agent behaviour. In: The AAMAS Workshop on Cognitive Agents for Virtual Environments (CAVE-2013). Citeseer (2013)
13. Li, Y., Song, J., Ermon, S.: InfoGAIL: interpretable imitation learning from visual demonstrations. In: Proceedings 30th International Conference Neural Information Processing Systems (NeurIPS) (2017)
14. Panagiotidi, S., Nieves, J.C., Vazquez-Salceda, J.: A framework to model norm dynamics in answer set programming. In: Proceedings International Workshop Multi-agent Logics, Languages, and Organisations (MALLOW), vol. CEUR 494 (2009)
15. Paxton, C., Hundt, A., Jonathan, F., Guerin, K., Hager, G.D.: CoSTAR: instructing collaborative robots with behavior trees and vision. In: Proceedings IEEE International Conference Robotics and Automation (ICRA). IEEE (2017)
16. Reynolds, C.W.: Steering behaviors for autonomous characters. In: Game Developers Conference, vol. 1999, pp. 763–782. Citeseer (1999)
17. Ross, S., Bagnell, D.: Efficient reductions for imitation learning. In: Proceedings 13th International Conference Artificial Intelligence and Statistics (2010)
18. Teknomo, K., Takeyama, Y., Inamura, H.: Review on microscopic pedestrian simulation model. arXiv preprint arXiv:1609.01808 (2016)
19. Vizzari, G., Crociani, L., Bandini, S.: An agent-based model for plausible wayfinding in pedestrian simulation. Eng. Appl. Artif. Intell. **87**, 103241 (2020)
20. Vozniak, I., Klusch, M., Antakli, A., Müller, C.: InfoSalGAIL: visual attention-empowered imitation learning of pedestrians in critical TRAFC scenarios. In: International Conference Neural Computation Theory and Application (NCTA). IEEE (2020)

Towards Collaborative Creativity in Persuasive Multi-agent Systems

Jean-Paul Calbimonte$^{(\boxtimes)}$, Davide Calvaresi, and Michael Schumacher

University of Applied Sciences and Arts Western Switzerland HES-SO,
3960 Sierre, Switzerland
jean-paul.calbimonte@hevs.ch

Abstract. Persuasive systems play a crucial role in supporting and counseling people to achieve individual behavior change goals. Intelligent systems have been used for inducing a positive adjustment of attitudes and routines in scenarios such as physiotherapy exercises, medication adherence, smoking cessation, nutrition & diet changes, physical activity, etc. Beyond the specialization and effectiveness provided by these systems on individual scenarios, we provide a vision for collaborative creativity based on the multi-agent systems paradigm. Considering novelty and usefulness as fundamental dimensions of a creative persuasive strategy, we identify the challenges and opportunities of modeling and orchestrating intelligent agents to collaboratively engage in exploratory and transformational creativity interactions. Moreover, we identify the foundations, outline a road-map for this novel research line, and elaborate on the potential impact and real-life applications.

Keywords: Collective intelligence · Collaborative agents · Social agents

1 Introduction

Innovation and development of novel solutions to address complex problems derives from both incremental contributions and chiefly from creative processes. Although creativity has been traditionally been associated solely to individual inspiration, nowadays we cannot disregard its social components. Indeed, collaborative ideation is one of the driving forces of cutting edge developments in diverse areas such as medicine, computer science, space engineering, physics, or bio-engineering [1,20,32]. In particular, in the field of computational persuasion, the challenge of providing dynamic, personalized and engaging strategies for positive behavior change, calls for novel unconventional and creative approaches.

Although the importance and impact of human collaborative creativity have been analyzed in psychology and cognitive studies [24,25], it has gathered relatively little attention in the context of artificial intelligence (AI) for persuasion purposes. In the last decade, computational methods for reasoning, reinforcement learning, and machine learning have remarkably advanced, focusing on specialized and optimized problem-solving methods [8,19,29]. While these results

F. Dignum et al. (Eds.): PAAMS 2021, LNAI 12946, pp. 40–51, 2021.
https://doi.org/10.1007/978-3-030-85739-4_4

have had a tremendous impact in several application domains, there is a limited understanding of how individual knowledge-based systems and data-driven methods can find ways to cooperate, even beyond the boundaries of their own assumptions, and engage in collaborative creative interactions.

Nevertheless, ideation often requires considering behaviors and criteria, which are not typical of common AI approaches. Beyond the strive for precision/accuracy of given tasks, focusing on creative processes would emphasize the novelty of ideas, even if they might seemingly contradict previous assumptions or knowledge. Moreover, such processes are intended to explore and test new hypotheses, knowing that they may mostly lead to dead-ends or contradictory results. Similar to human creativity, collaboration is pivotal, and it can significantly improve the entire process, leading to more innovative and impactful results.

In this paper, we provide a vision of collaborative creative intelligent entities, embodied as autonomous agents. We argue for the use of multi-agent models as the building blocks to design decentralized computational entities capable of proposing and exploring novel ways of addressing a particular problem, based not only on their own knowledge but also on the shared experience with other entities. As depicted in Fig. 1, our collaborative creativity model considers knowledge extracted from one or multiple domains, which is used by individual agents to explore and propose novel approaches and ideas, which are in turn submitted to a particular field (or multiple fields) where other agents may verify, examine or test them. From this social process creative outcomes are produced and reinserted into the domains of application. This envisioned collective creative process entails the necessity of considering different aspects such as specialization, knowledge sharing, hypotheses modeling, simulation, and novelty metrics. In the following, we identify the challenges (Sect. 2) emerging from this vision, as well as the opportunities of using multi-agent technologies and other building blocks (Sect. 3). Then we indicate the potential impact in different application domains (Sect. 4), before providing a research road-map in Sect. 5.

2   Challenges

Stemming from the agents' internal knowledge and vision, the key challenges revolve around the mechanisms generating new or rearranging existing knowledge. Following and expanding on theories in creative human communication [33] we illustrate in Fig. 2 how a creative process may include several stages, from the common agreement of the problem to solve, to the different preparation, incubation, idea generation and verification of collectively created solutions. The cyclic nature of this model entails the possibility of jumping from different stages and iterating depending on the quality, originality and usefulness of the outcomes. In the following we expand on the identified challenges.

CH1: Shared Language. A creative process can only happen in a collaborative environment if the diverse entities involved can rely on a shared understanding of the subject in question [7]. This common ground may span from domain-specific

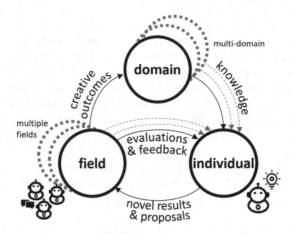

Fig. 1. Our agent collaborative creativity model, based-on, and extending the model in [10,30]

representations of a specific problem, to complex interaction languages describing creative conceptual discussions about a particular topic [37]. The language must imply more than vocabularies or abstract models. Including interaction protocols and patterns may help to govern the different activities among the participants. Thus, a key challenge is to identify the appropriate expressiveness of such languages, so that an appropriate computational complexity balance is found. Moreover, given that different agents with entirely different backgrounds may interact with each other, the reconciling language must also allow representing high-level orthogonal concepts as well as more specific ones. The former can be used to exchange ideas and hypotheses, while the latter may allow deeper exploration and evaluation interactions to pursue a specific objective.

CH2: Shared Knowledge. Once a common language is established, representing the problems/topics under discussion with machine-understandable models is the upcoming challenge. In particular, such mechanisms should be able to specify different types of knowledge, such as background and results stemming from previous studies or interactions, representations of simulations, probabilistic scenarios, validation criteria, novel ideas represented as thought processes, mental models, etc. [2]. Unlike traditional knowledge management approaches that mainly operate on facts, the new sharing scheme needs to handle possibilities, even risking to pursue possible invalid/unfeasible paths. Furthermore, shared knowledge may also need to deal with inconsistencies and conflicts coming from different participants.

CH3: Interdisciplinarity. Creativity, in the form of novel ideas, often arise from cross-fertilization and exchanges of ideas coming from entirely different backgrounds. Reconcile expertise heterogeneity is a fundamental challenge to be addressed, exacerbated by the degree of specialization of current AI systems. Nevertheless, the richness of this collective diversity also entails the difficulty of

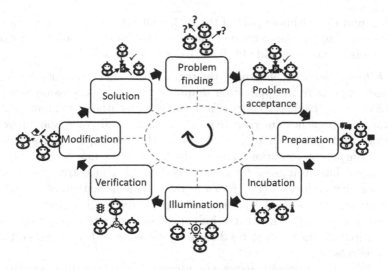

Fig. 2. Collaborative agent creativity cycle.

overcoming barriers across disciplines and completely different perspectives over the same subject [2]. For example, in the case of physical rehabilitation support, while a deep-learning-based system may accurately predict different outcomes regarding progression in physical exercises, a stress knowledge-based system may detect mental health risks due to anxiety or pain-coping mechanisms.

CH4: Collaboration and Exploration. Contributions from heterogeneous AI systems need to be circumscribed in a collaboration scheme that allows sufficient freedom to innovate, while maintaining longer term objectives. Beyond the individual goals and intentions of agents possibly wrapping ad-hoc AI systems (i.e., specific ML predictors), these may agree on different targets upon which they may explore different approaches and variations, taking into account other participants' proposals. Moreover, this collaboration should encourage considering risky options or challenging current assumptions. For instance, two coaching systems may have contradicting results concerning a patient's adherence to knee rehabilitation therapy. Through a contrasting exchange of assumptions and outcomes, a third system (i.e., agent) might propose an alternative treatment based on experimental hypotheses coming from physiotherapy research in areas such as hip strength reinforcement.

CH5: Competition. Although pursuing similar interests, collaborative entities might share the same goals only partially. Therefore, the established cooperation strategies might entail competing for solving specific problems or even claim their share after a common solution was found. Drawing a line is necessary to protect individual interests while sharing ideas and potential elements that will constitute a collaborative effort. This may entail sharing data resources (or aggregated understanding upon them), which are vital for many AI systems. For example, let us consider the case of a smoking cessation persuasion system.

It may temporarily withhold part of the technical details of its approach due to patenting constraints, while exposing the general strategy in order to encourage other systems to either provide feedback or competing solutions.

CH6: Ethics. Several concerns arise regarding the implementation of new approaches, especially in application domains in which persuasion techniques are applied. First, to enforce the user's trust, it is essential to explain how these collaborative approaches emerged (e.g., providing a full trace and provenance descriptions and explicable results). Second, the participating systems must establish transparent conditions under which any data has been used, and if proper consent has been given for these tasks. Third, transparency characterizing collaborative endeavors (i.e., how the result is achieved) must be extended to the contributions brought by the several participants (i.e., how they collectively contributed to it). Finally, the influence that one party may play over the other participating entities may need to be regulated or at least assessed to avoid undesired effects [6].

The challenges proposed above are remarkably interconnected with each other. In particular, *sharing knowledge* (CH2) requires a *shared language* (CH1) among the collaborating entities/agents. *Collaborating & exploring* unexpected or irrational paths (CH4) can entail *competition mechanisms* (CH5) and *bridging interdisciplinary viewpoints, rules, and representations* (CH3). Finally, it is worth mentioning that each of these challenges already raises ethical concerns on its own. Nevertheless, their intersection can entangle the ethical boundaries to a point in which harmonization mechanisms might need to deal with cross-domain-related inconsistencies.

3   Opportunities and Building Blocks

Following the challenges above, this section discusses on the opportunities defining the building blocks, singularly and altogether.

Persuasive Multi-agent Systems: The agent paradigm represents a convenient approach to embody persuasive systems. Several ideas relied on multi-agent systems (MAS) to tackle behavioral change exploiting contextual knowledge and persuasion goals [3,28,34]. Nevertheless, the agents' strategies employed in most of these approaches tend to adopt rigid persuasion strategies. In particular, being highly specialized, such strategies are difficult to be generalized, henceforth, unable to cope with new user-scenarios. Within the collective creativity paradigm, persuasive agents may need first to identify shortcomings in their own strategies and then brainstorm on potential ideas that may contribute to each other's persuasion assumptions and knowledge. For example, a cancer survivor support agent may find that some of their unsuccessful persuasion interactions may be linked to technology-related biases, which were not initially considered in its model. Nevertheless, it could be detected by another agent specialized in diet recommendations. Then, agents will be challenged to question their own facts to revise or enforce them within the collective creativity dynamics, for instance through argumentation [16]

Collective Computational Creativity: Creativity is a human-centered concept. Yet, scientific studies passed from defining machines only able to perform to designed for [21] to defining with several models of computational creativity [11–13]. Creative machines have been envisioned collaborating with, mimic, and inspire humans. The need for a framework to model and reach collective, collaborative, and improvisational computational creativity as intended to be for the human society is well-known [11]. The enaction theory relies on the assumption that cognition is based on improvised (possibly real-time) environmental stimuli [36]. Moreover, further studies tried to understand how to introduce intentional creativity in virtual agencies and foster their emergence [14]. According to Froese & Ziemke, the purpose of an intentional agent determining its intrinsic goals is the maintenance of its existence [13]. Thus, pursuing creativity, computational and interaction models could be merged to actualize conversational creativity models for interdisciplinary debating agents.

Agent Simulation: As mentioned above, we envision agents undertaking or verifying both reasonable and possibly untenable plans and theories. Conversations are at the base of the agents' interaction. Nevertheless, the only way to verify a *point* might verify it (reasonably via simulations). Agent-based simulations have been extensively employed to implement inter-agent behaviors and decision-making processes in a controlled (and most of the times shared among all the agents) environment to verify the feasibility, cost, and sustainability of given solutions [26,38]. By doing so, discussing agents willing to prove their point might generate pools of simulations to validate or confute each other standing. Besides the inherent advantages of employing simulations, persuasive agents might further benefit from them extracting unexpected outcomes, which can strengthen the motivations of their recommendation.

Domain Models and Knowledge Graphs: Knowledge graphs are broadly used to structure data and linking them according to models that accurately reflect a particular domain [23]. Furthermore, knowledge graphs enable logical reasoning to infer implicit information and answer queries through structured sub-graph matching [31]. Although ontologies and semantic vocabularies have already been proposed to represent persuasive agent knowledge, expectations, and goals [5,15], they could further be used as the foundations for a cross-domain transformational creativity language. By doing so, agents with entirely different backgrounds would be able to exchange different hypotheses and engage in brainstorming sessions, extending each domain model beyond its current limits and assumptions. For example, an agent specialized in post-cancer support adherence may expand its domain model by importing knowledge graph concepts from other agents specialized in physical exercise. These agents may propose strength and balance exercises suitable for cancer survivors, which were not included in the original support strategy. Nevertheless, this process is not straightforward, as the *merging* knowledge graphs are not necessarily compatible, nor may have the same level of expressiveness. Moreover, a well-defined protocol should be defined to pass from the stages of incubation, illumination, and verification of the proposed integration of heterogeneous models.

4 Application Scenarios

Collaborative creativity in persuasive intelligent agents can have a substantial impact in different scenarios. In particular, in applications related to support users in managing health behavior, lifestyle changes, education, adherence to treatments, and concept exploration. Although potentially different, the use-cases mentioned above share the complexities of handling strategies that may span over extended periods and may need to adapt dynamically to changes in context and scope.

A first type of application regards the combination of previous knowledge from different multi-agent systems, using existing evidence across multiple domains. Examples include interplays between closely related topics (i.e., smoking cessation and dietary eHealth applications [4,9]), as well as distant areas (i.e., music recommendation and mental health [17]). More specifically, in these applications users could build their behavior change plan with the assistance of a multi-agent system. Beyond traditional coaching agents, this would enable establishing co-creation schemes, where persuasion strategy goals are not imposed but mutually agreed upon. Collective interactions with other agents would allow these strategies to be revised and potentially enriched with others' experiences. For example, a coaching agent for stress and mental health may discover musical therapy and its positive effect from another agent specialized in leisure distracting activities. Based on the novelty, potential impact, and analysis of other validating criteria, the agent may need to revise evidence of this approach's adequateness or launch a pilot test to observe potential consequences.

A second type of scenario is the exploration of entirely new ideas among collaborative agents. In this case, the creative process undergoes a more elaborated path, in which agents require questioning certain limits of current strategies. Examples of such applications may include persuasive agents in physiotherapy. Targeting rehabilitation [27] (e.g., post-acute phase in knee intervention), an agent may initially plan a progressive introduction of exercises focusing solely on strength to enable a smooth transition towards recovery. Nevertheless, other agents may contribute with new evidence indicating that patients with similar characteristics may benefit from new approaches based on simultaneous and more intensive balance-strength routines, which could circumvent future complications. In this exchange, a specialized literature-review agent may initiate providing evidence for exploring a specific idea, while a decision-support agent may counsel the physiotherapist, and monitoring agents may verify compliance with the suggested treatment. In this way, collaborative exploration is not limited to foster creativity among agents, but it can include human intervention (if necessary).

A third kind of application refers to paradigm shifts in the way a problem is addressed. In this case, the agents interactions may lead to questioning assumptions and fundamental decisions, paving the way for a different type of solution that can be further explored and validated. For example, consider a treatment and medication adherence agent-based system based on ML for patient data analysis [35]. An agent in the system may infer that persuasion strategies based on ML predicted outcomes might not be enough to achieve the desired adherence goals. Another agent may then propose using adherence persuasive messages typical of logic reasoning applied to existing knowledge graphs that describe contextual medication advice [18]. Other agents involved in the incubation process of these ideas may then propose a third approach that integrates both the ML predictions and knowledge graph entailments in order to provide explainable persuasion elements to the adherence strategy [28]. This new approach actually disregards the original paradigm, even if it borrows certain aspects of the original ones it has diverged from.

5 Road-Map

This paper has introduced the main challenges stemming from the problem of adaptability and evolution of persuasion strategies implemented through multi-agent systems that incorporate different collective creativity types. Such challenges have been translated into opportunities and backed by solid foundations. From such a ground, we derive our vision of decentralized agents that are able to formulate common problems, debate on different ideas, and propose novel solutions that are both unique and useful. As discussed above, this novel type of agent system has great potential in persuasion-related scenarios, where strategies: need to cope with dynamic impulses, require to adapt to fast-changing assumptions and multi-disciplinary knowledge, and benefit from interdisciplinary influences producing unforeseen solutions. To foster the development of this research line, we foresee the following directions:

Collective Creativity Language: In all the different types of creative interactions discussed in the paper, we anticipate the need for establishing a common language that enables agents to exchange ideas and hypotheses at both high (aggregated concepts) and in-depth (granular and specialized details) levels. This flexibility can only be achieved using semantically rich models that allow interconnecting knowledge expressed at different levels of complexity and across multiple disciplines. Moreover, this language should also explore the different protocols that will allow these different types of exchange. Agent combination of existing ideas, exploration protocols, brainstorming sessions, exchange of hypotheses, and verification procedures are examples of this type of collaboration schemes that should be formalized in such a language.

Combination: Collaborative combinations of existing specialized approaches will require further studies of how agents may share and evaluate each other's strategies. Agreement technologies can be used at the different stages of the creative process, with a special emphasis on the comparison and homogenization of all proposals exposed by the participating agents. In particular, we see the need for alignment of knowledge and goals from highly heterogeneous agents so that the problem finding and incubation phases can lead to meaningful co-created ideas that can be later implemented and verified by the agents. This verification will also require the establishment of meaningful criteria that focus not only on the effectiveness aspects, but also on the novelty. Different types of creativity assessment methods exist, although there should be a focus on the collaborative nature of the outcomes.

Exploration: Regarding the exploratory analysis of novel proposals emerging from collaborative creation, we expect further research regarding data-driven simulation and dynamic evaluation of divergent alternative paths of action. Collaborative exploration implies that simulations may need to include predictions from multiple agents with entirely different contributed datasets and algorithms. The simulation process may also need to consider when to stop scrutinizing and probing in a given direction before switching to a different path. During the incubation phase, agents may experiment several options independently. In turn, the singularly identified outcomes are shared and processed iteratively. The study of techniques exploiting this type of mechanism will also need to consider the limitations of relying only on simulations and may examine human-agent exploration scenarios, in which experts may use the agents' collective outcome as a guiding starting point for future persuasion strategies.

Transformation: Persuasion strategies need to change over time as the individuals' conditions and their context change as well. Moreover, the knowledge in the application domain is in constant evolution (e.g., due to increased availability of relevant data, new discoveries in adherence/effectiveness, the introduction of novel technologies, or the testing of new theories). We argue that collaborative agents should be part of these innovations, incurring in transformational creativity tasks that emerge from contrasting and contributing ideas that defy the current assumptions. To make this possible, a collective knowledge model should be studied—thus, building a social representation per topic or application area. This knowledge should include the specification of risks and a computational representation of hypotheses and assumptions, possibly challenged by the participating agents. This type of information is currently manually curated by scientists in systematic reviews, discussed in conferences and papers, but we expect agents to take leading roles in these activities, contributing to a transformational generation of novel persuasion paradigms and concepts.

Ethical Creativity: To consider the risks of inducing or exerting a certain influence in a given person's decisions is essential in computational persuasion. If misused, inappropriate manipulations or undesired effects might occur. This could generate even worse consequences affecting users possibly unaware of the usage of his/her data. In this context, transparency and accountability mechanisms need to be studied and proposed [6,22]. Thus, the entire collective creative process and its outcomes can be presented and exposed to all the concerned parties. To this end, multi-agent explainability is a fundamental aspect to be investigated [28]. The generation of explicable representations of the entire creative process would surely boost the trust in the system and facilitate to spot potential errors or agents' misbehavior. Furthermore, these explanations must deal with the degree of complexity, which may need to be translated from a domain to another, or even to comprehensible outcomes for end-users. Finally, the ethical aspects of data (re)use during the experimentation phases of the creative process need to consider privacy aspects and the justification of its inclusion.

Acknowledgements. This research has been partially supported by the HES-SO RCSO ISNet project PERSA: Computational Persuasion in eHealth Support Applications.

References

1. Adler, P.S., Chen, C.X.: Combining creativity and control: understanding individual motivation in large-scale collaborative creativity. Account. Organ. Soc. **36**(2), 63–85 (2011)
2. Besold, T.R., Schorlemmer, M., Smaill, A. (eds.): Computational Creativity Research: Towards Creative Machines. ATM, vol. 7. Atlantis Press, Paris (2015). https://doi.org/10.2991/978-94-6239-085-0
3. Black, E., Coles, A.J., Hampson, C.: Planning for persuasion. In: Proceedings of the 16th Conference on Autonomous Agents and MultiAgent Systems, pp. 933–942 (2017)
4. Calvaresi, D., Schumacher, M., Marinoni, M., Hilfiker, R., Dragoni, A.F., Buttazzo, G.: Agent-based systems for telerehabilitation: strengths, limitations and future challenges. In: Montagna, S., Abreu, P.H., Giroux, S., Schumacher, M.I. (eds.) A2HC/AHEALTH -2017. LNCS (LNAI), vol. 10685, pp. 3–24. Springer, Cham (2017). https://doi.org/10.1007/978-3-319-70887-4_1
5. Chen, H., Finin, T., Joshi, A.: The SOUPA ontology for pervasive computing. In: Tamma, V., Cranefield, S., Finin, T.W., Willmott, S. (eds.) Ontologies for Agents: Theory and Experiences, pp. 233–258. Springer, Basel (2005). https://doi.org/10.1007/3-7643-7361-X_10
6. Cointe, N., Bonnet, G., Boissier, O.: Ethical judgment of agents' behaviors in multi-agent systems. In: Proceedings of the 2016 International Conference on Autonomous Agents & Multiagent Systems, pp. 1106–1114 (2016)
7. Colton, S., Charnley, J., Pease, A.: Computational creativity theory: the face and idea descriptive models. In: 2nd International Conference on Computational Creativity, ICCC 2011, pp. 90–95 (2011)
8. Colton, S., Wiggins, G.A.: Computational creativity: the final frontier? In: Proceedings of the 20th European Conference on Artificial Intelligence, pp. 21–26 (2012)
9. Costa, A., Heras, S., Palanca, J., Jordán, J., Novais, P., Julián, V.: Argumentation schemes for events suggestion in an e-health platform. In: de Vries, P.W., Oinas-Kukkonen, H., Siemons, L., Beerlage-de Jong, N., van Gemert-Pijnen, L. (eds.) PERSUASIVE 2017. LNCS, vol. 10171, pp. 17–30. Springer, Cham (2017). https://doi.org/10.1007/978-3-319-55134-0_2
10. Csikszentmihalyi, M.: 16 implications of a systems perspective for the study of creativity. In: Handbook of Creativity, p. 313 (1999)
11. Davis, N., Hsiao, C.-P., Popova, Y., Magerko, B.: An enactive model of creativity for computational collaboration and co-creation. In: Zagalo, N., Branco, P. (eds.) Creativity in the Digital Age. SSCC, pp. 109–133. Springer, London (2015). https://doi.org/10.1007/978-1-4471-6681-8_7

12. De Loor, P., Manac'h, K., Tisseau, J.: Enaction-based artificial intelligence: Toward co-evolution with humans in the loop. Minds Mach. **19**(3), 319–343 (2009)
13. Froese, T., Ziemke, T.: Enactive artificial intelligence: investigating the systemic organization of life and mind. Artif. Intell. **173**(3–4), 466–500 (2009)
14. Guckelsberger, C., Salge, C., Colton, S.: Addressing the "why?" in computational creativity: a non-anthropocentric, minimal model of intentional creative agency (2017)
15. Hendler, J.: Agents and the semantic web. IEEE Intell. Syst. **16**(2), 30–37 (2001)
16. Heras, S., Atkinson, K., Botti, V., Grasso, F., Julián, V., McBurney, P.: How argumentation can enhance dialogues in social networks. In: Computational Models of Argument, pp. 267–274. IOS Press (2010)
17. Ivascu, T., Manate, B., Negru, V.: A multi-agent architecture for ontology-based diagnosis of mental disorders. In: 2015 17th International Symposium on Symbolic and Numeric Algorithms for Scientific Computing (SYNASC), pp. 423–430. IEEE (2015)
18. Larsen, K.R., et al.: Behavior change interventions: the potential of ontologies for advancing science and practice. J. Behav. Med. **40**(1), 6–22 (2017)
19. Loughran, R., O'Neill, M.: Application domains considered in computational creativity. In: ICCC, pp. 197–204 (2017)
20. Mamykina, L., Candy, L., Edmonds, E.: Collaborative creativity. Commun. ACM **45**(10), 96–99 (2002)
21. Menabrea, L.F., Lovelace, A.: Sketch of the analytical engine invented by charles babbage (1842)
22. Murukannaiah, P.K., Ajmeri, N., Jonker, C.M., Singh, M.P.: New foundations of ethical multiagent systems. In: Proceedings of the 19th International Conference on Autonomous Agents and MultiAgent Systems, pp. 1706–1710 (2020)
23. Paulheim, H.: Knowledge graph refinement: a survey of approaches and evaluation methods. Semant. Web **8**(3), 489–508 (2017)
24. Paulus, P.B., Brown, V.R.: Toward more creative and innovative group idea generation: a cognitive-social-motivational perspective of brainstorming. Soc. Pers. Psychol. Compass **1**(1), 248–265 (2007)
25. Paulus, P.B., Dzindolet, M., Kohn, N.W.: Collaborative creativity–group creativity and team innovation. In: Handbook of Organizational Creativity, pp. 327–357. Elsevier (2012)
26. Railsback, S.F., Lytinen, S.L., Jackson, S.K.: Agent-based simulation platforms: review and development recommendations. Simulation **82**(9), 609–623 (2006)
27. Roda, C., Rodríguez, A., López-Jaquero, V., González, P., Navarro, E.: A multi-agent system in ambient intelligence for the physical rehabilitation of older people. In: Bajo, J., et al. (eds.) Trends in Practical Applications of Agents, Multi-Agent Systems and Sustainability. AISC, vol. 372, pp. 113–123. Springer, Cham (2015). https://doi.org/10.1007/978-3-319-19629-9_13
28. Rosenfeld, A., Kraus, S.: Strategical argumentative agent for human persuasion. In: Proceedings of the Twenty-Second European Conference on Artificial Intelligence, pp. 320–328 (2016)
29. Rowe, J., Partridge, D.: Creativity: a survey of AI approaches. Artif. Intell. Rev. **7**(1), 43–70 (1993)
30. Saunders, R., Grace, K.: Towards a computational model of creative cultures. In: AAAI Spring Symposium: Creative Intelligent Systems, pp. 67–74 (2008)
31. Sheth, A., Padhee, S., Gyrard, A.: Knowledge graphs and knowledge networks: the story in brief. IEEE Internet Comput. **23**(4), 67–75 (2019)

32. Siangliulue, P., Arnold, K.C., Gajos, K.Z., Dow, S.P.: Toward collaborative ideation at scale: leveraging ideas from others to generate more creative and diverse ideas. In: Proceedings of the 18th ACM Conference on Computer Supported Cooperative Work & Social Computing, pp. 937–945 (2015)
33. Sonnenburg, S.: Creativity in communication: a theoretical framework for collaborative product creation. Creativity Innov. Manage. **13**(4), 254–262 (2004)
34. Subagdja, B., Tan, A.H., Kang, Y.: A coordination framework for multi-agent persuasion and adviser systems. Expert Syst. Appl. **116**, 31–51 (2019)
35. Tucker, C.S., Behoora, I., Nembhard, H.B., Lewis, M., Sterling, N.W., Huang, X.: Machine learning classification of medication adherence in patients with movement disorders using non-wearable sensors. Comput. Biol. Med. **66**, 120–134 (2015)
36. Varela, F.J., Thompson, E., Rosch, E.: The Embodied Mind: Cognitive Science and Human Experience. MIT Press, Cambridge (2016)
37. Wiggins, G.A.: A preliminary framework for description, analysis and comparison of creative systems. Knowl. Based Syst. **19**(7), 449–458 (2006)
38. Wooldridge, M.J., Jennings, N.R.: Intelligent agents: theory and practice. Knowl. Eng. Rev. **10**(2), 115–152 (1995)

Automated Planning and BDI Agents: A Case Study

Rafael C. Cardoso[1]([⊠])[iD], Angelo Ferrando[2][iD], and Fabio Papacchini[3][iD]

[1] The University of Manchester, Manchester M13 9PL, UK
rafael.cardoso@manchester.ac.uk
[2] University of Genova, 16145 Genova, Italy
angelo.ferrando@dibris.unige.it
[3] University of Liverpool, Liverpool L69 3BX, UK
fabio.papacchini@liverpool.ac.uk

Abstract. There have been many attempts to integrate automated planning and rational agents. Most of the research focuses on adding support directly within agent programming languages, such as those based on the Belief-Desire-Intention model, rather than using off-the-shelf planners. This approach is often believed to improve the computation time, which is a common requirement in real world applications. This paper shows that even in complex scenarios, such as in the Multi-Agent Programming Contest with 50 agents and a 4 s deadline for the agents to send actions to the server, it is possible to efficiently integrate agent languages with off-the-shelf automated planners. Based on the experience with this case study, the paper discusses advantages and disadvantages of decoupling the agents from the planners.

Keywords: Automated planning · BDI agents · Multi-agent programming contest

1 Introduction

Automated (or also referred to as Artificial Intelligence) planning consists of using a search algorithm to find a solution to a problem [18]. The planner receives as input information about the domain (predicates and actions that can be applied) and the problem (initial state of the environment and goals) and will apply a search algorithm to transition between states until the goals have been achieved. The output of a planner is a plan containing a sequence of actions that achieves the goals of the problem. The action theory in STRIPS (STanford Research Institute Problem Solver) [12] is the backbone of later formalisms such as the widely used PDDL (Planning Domain Definition Language) [16]. PDDL

Work supported by UK Research and Innovation, and EPSRC Hubs for "Robotics and AI in Hazardous Environments": EP/R026092 (FAIR-SPACE) and EP/R026084 (RAIN). Cardoso's work is also supported by the Royal Academy of Engineering under the Chairs in Emerging Technologies scheme.

© Springer Nature Switzerland AG 2021
F. Dignum et al. (Eds.): PAAMS 2021, LNAI 12946, pp. 52–63, 2021.
https://doi.org/10.1007/978-3-030-85739-4_5

has been the de-facto standard formalism for representing classical planning problems, but it has also been extended to support temporal, probabilistic, and other types of planning. In this paper, we focus on classical PDDL/STRIPS task planning.

Autonomous agents and Multi-Agent Systems (MAS) have vast and diverse subareas of research. In particular, we focus on Agent-based programming [9], which uses agent-oriented languages to implement some of the concepts found in MAS. The Belief-Desire-Intention (BDI) model [7,20] is used in most agent-based programming languages [4], as well as in research in the area of agent programming [15]. The BDI model consists of a reasoning cycle based on three main concepts: *beliefs* – represent knowledge about the world, *desires* – goals to achieve, and *intentions* – steps that can be made towards achieving something. A simple reasoning trace starts with changes in the belief base which can trigger plans to achieve a goal. Once a plan is triggered, its stack of intentions are executed one by one.

Most agent-based programming languages have some form of inherent task planning. Agents have access to a plan library and, based on certain triggering events, a search is made to find applicable plans from their library. The difference to more traditional task planning is that in the former case interpreting actions (i.e., their pre-conditions and effects) is delegated to the environment and is not a concern of the agent. This kind of planning is more similar to the non-primitive tasks that can be found in Hierarchical Task Planning (HTN) [19]. Even though action descriptions are still needed for HTN planning, the non-primitive tasks (also called methods) are very similar to what plans represent in BDI programming in terms of search. That is, they allow the search space to be effectively pruned. Note that this is different from adding explicit support for automated planning in agent-based programming languages. Such an approach is discussed in the Related Work section.

Plans in the agents' libraries are usually pre-designed by a developer. Complex case studies and unpredictable environments may result in a plan library that does not contain the necessary plans to solve some of the problems that may appear. This is where using automated planners to generate those missing plans (either at runtime as we will demonstrate in this paper, or offline at design time) may remove the burden from the developer of trying to encode every possible solution.

In this paper we use an off-the-shelf planner in combination with our agents, which are programmed using a BDI agent-based language, to solve some complex problems in the 14th and 15th Multi-Agent Programming Contest[1] scenarios [1]. We explain how we have made this integration work and what had to change between the 14th and 15th editions to still make this strategy effective. In particular, we have used the Fast Downward[2] [13] planner for the automated planning, and the JaCaMo[3] [2,3] multi-agent oriented programming framework.

---

[1] https://multiagentcontest.org/.
[2] http://www.fast-downward.org/.
[3] http://jacamo.sourceforge.net/.

The paper is organised as follows. In the next section we discuss some approaches that have tried to explicitly incorporate planning in BDI languages, as well as BDI applications that have used off-the-shelf planners in the past. Section 3 briefly explains our case study, with a particular focus on the elements that were advantageous to apply automated planning. In Sect. 4, we describe in detail how we have used an off-the-shelf planner to solve the aforementioned problems. A discussion about our experience with the combination of automated planning and BDI agents is presented in Sect. 5. We conclude the paper and list some future directions in Sect. 6.

2   Related Work

Automated planning and BDI programming have been used individually to solve an assortment of different tasks in the past. An example of the former is [6], where an off-the-shelf planner is used in a manufacturing plant for logical reconfiguration of the control nodes after changes in the environment (production change, fault in physical components, or changes in the production goals). An example of the latter is [10], where agents are implemented in a BDI-based programming language to support ethical reasoning by adding agents that can recommend ethical actions to be executed.

Some approaches have been developed which aim to integrate BDI programming languages with off-the-shelf automated planners. An example of such approach is the work in [8], which uses the SHOP2 HTN planner [19] without requiring any modifications to the planner itself. The agents in the JaCaMo framework call an individual instance of the planner when required to perform multi-agent planning, with planning being coordinated and tasks allocated at runtime using agent communication protocols and techniques. There are several differences between our work and theirs: (a) we do not perform coordinated multi-agent planning, our agents plan independently from each other; (b) we use a PDDL planner while they used HTN; and (c) we focus on a more practical and complex case study.

Conversely, there have been many approaches that tried to integrate automated planning directly into BDI programming languages. In [23] first principles classical planning is introduced to a theoretical (never implemented) BDI language through the derivation of abstract planning operators from BDI programs. A further extension of this work is reported in [22], which adds failure handling and declarative goals on top of the planning. Even though the theoretical contributions were important at the time, the main issue still remains that the language described was never implemented. A more practical approach with a mapping between classical planning formalisms and traditional BDI agent languages is presented in [17], describing a formal translation process from BDI plans to classical planning operators. We believe there are a number of fundamental differences in using off-the-shelf planners and integrating automated planning directly into BDI programming languages. We discuss what these differences are in Sect. 5.

3 Multi-Agent Programming Contest: Agents Assemble

The Multi-Agent Programming Contest (MAPC) is an annual competition with complex multi-agent oriented challenges (such as communication, coordination, and interaction between agents) that aims to promote and strengthen the use of multi-agent programming frameworks, tools, and methodologies. By applying these techniques to difficult scenarios it is possible to identify what features are missing, can be improved, or have to be fixed in agent-based technologies. The scenarios change every few years, with extensions being done to the previous scenarios on off-years. The core structure of the simulations remain mostly the same: it is a synchronous step-based simulation wherein clients (the teams) have to send actions to the server under a certain deadline (usually 4 s per step), and a match is composed of 3 rounds (each with a different map).

MAPC 14th [1] introduced the "Agents Assemble" scenario, where two teams of 10 agents each compete to accumulate the most amount of currency by assembling block structures to match tasks announced by the server in a grid environment. We participated as team LFC (Liverpool Formidable Constructors) [11] and achieved first place. We believe one of the main factors in our performance during that edition of the contest was due to our strategy in using an off-the-shelf planner to generate movement plans at runtime. The scenario has many other details which required an assortment of different strategies, the interested reader can find more information in [1,11]. For the remaining of this paper, we focus only on the elements of the contest that were relevant for the use of the automated planner and its integration with the agents.

The 15th edition of the MAPC[4] used the same scenario but extended it in many interesting ways. Of relevance to our planning strategy was the change from the static 10 agents to 15 agents in round 1, 30 agents in round 2, and 50 agents in round 3. This required us to adapt our strategy, as calling 30 and 50 instances of the planner would slow down the reasoning of our agents and make them unable to send an action before the deadline. Our solution to this was developing a plan cache, which is explained in detail in Sect. 4.2. We achieved second place in the 15th edition of the MAPC, however we believe our planning strategy performed very well and we only lost due to the lack of optimisation in some of our other strategies (such as task assembly).

In this paper, we focus on performing efficient movement in the contest. Map grids during the 14th and 15th MAPC ranged from 50 × 50 (2500 cells) to 100 × 100 (10000 cells). Each agent has a local view of 61 cells around them. Initially, we tried to encode the agents' movements directly into the agent program, however, we soon realised that there were too many edge cases to consider and that our solution resulted in longer routes and even a few deadlocks. Using an automated off-the-shelf planner allowed us to focus on the other strategies while knowing that the movement of our agents were very efficient.

The main challenge for planning the agents' movement (either directly in the agents' program or in an automated planner) is the dynamic nature of the

---

[4] https://multiagentcontest.org/2020/.

environment and the lack of knowledge of the agent about cells outside its local vision. For example, the following dynamic events can happen during a step: (a) an agent from the other team (or from our own team, if we do not disclose movement information to other agents) may move into one of the cells that are a part of our agent's route, generating a conflict; (b) a special event called a *clear* event has a random chance of occurring at each step, which may remove obstacle cells, create obstacle cells, disable agents, and remove blocks; and (c) agents also have access to a *clear* action, however, compared to the environment event, this action has a reduced radius and can not create obstacles.

4   Automated Planning and BDI Agents

Our team[5] is programmed in the JaCaMo multi-agent oriented development framework using its Eclipse plugin. JaCaMo has three main programming dimensions (agent, environment, and organisation), each handled by a different tool that has been developed over many years and then integrated to work well with each other. Jason [5] is a popular BDI-based agent programming language that we used to define our agent programs. CArtAgO [21] is based on the notion of artifacts that are used to represent and interact with the environment. In our case this means interfacing with the server of the MAPC as well as interfacing with the off-the-shelf planner. Finally, Moise [14] provides organisation constructs to determine roles and norms in groups of agents, which our team uses to aid in the coordination of certain tasks.

Fast Downward (FD) is a well-established planner which has been used several times in the International Planning Competition (IPC). Clear actions take three steps to be successfully used by an agent, and they need to be encoded as a planning operator because clearing obstacles can make much more optimal routes. FD, however, does not support numeric planning. To workaround this problem, we made use of action costs where all movement actions have a cost of 1 and the clear action has a cost of 3, and then the planner is asked to find plans that can minimise the cost.

Next, we describe our planning strategies for the 14th MAPC (Local Vision Planning) as well as the necessary extensions for it to work well in the 15th MAPC (Plan Cache).

4.1   Local Vision Planning

We limited the use of the planner only for performing the movement of the agents in the grid (which includes the clear action for more efficient routes). If the grid cells were static and the map was completely observable, then it would have made more sense to try to plan the entire route of the agent at once. However, apart

---

[5] Our team code for the 14th MAPC:
  https://github.com/autonomy-and-verification-uol/mapc2019-liv
  Our team code for the 15th MAPC:
  https://github.com/autonomy-and-verification-uol/mapc2020-lfc.

from the fact that this solution would likely result in performance problems, the cells in the grid are dynamic and could change because of clear actions or agents' actions. The local vision and the lack of knowledge of the remaining cells in the map also made it pointless to plan too far in advance. Therefore, we call the planner with a target cell that is inside the local vision of the agent. An example of how this works is given later on.

Planning is performed at runtime and an instance of the FD planner is invoked by the agent. The workflow is defined as follows:

1. The agent wants to move to a target position in the grid
2. Is the target position inside the agent's vision? If yes jump to step 4
3. Select the closest cell to the target position that is inside the agent's vision
4. Determine what type of domain will be used, planning operators change depending on specific circumstances:
   - if the agent has enough energy to perform clear actions enable clear as a planning operator
   - if the agent has a block attached (maximum one block attached for planning movement) enable operators to move with one block
5. Call a CArtAgO artifact which will generate the problem file based on the local vision of the agent (obtained through the perceptions observed in that step from the server), with the target cell as a goal, and the appropriate domain (based on the flags determined in previous steps)
6. Call an instance of the FD planner with the generated problem file and the appropriate pre-generated domain file
7. The solution plan is saved onto a file which the CArtAgO artifact reads and then translates it back to the agent
8. If a plan was found, the agent simply executes each action of the plan at each step (jump to step 10)
9. If a plan is not found, then the agent tries to move (without the planner) in a direction that would bring it closer to the final target, and then calls the planner again (back to step 2)
10. If the agent is not in the final target cell after executing all actions in the plan, the process goes back to step 2, otherwise planning has finished

The 14th edition of the MAPC had 10 agents per team. Initially, we thought that if all of our 10 agents started an instance of the planner at the same step, then we may have encountered some performance problems. To circumvent this, we introduced a planning counter which would limit the number of agents allowed to start an instance of the planner at any given step when the counter hits the maximum number allowed. Setting this number varied depending on the processing power of the computer that was being used. During the contest, we disabled this feature, as the used computer was powerful enough to handle comfortably the maximum number of agents.

Example
To better explain the difference between local and final target selection we exemplify some scenarios in Fig. 1 and Fig. 2.

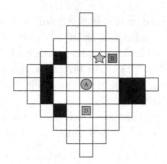

Fig. 1. Example of a final target position (star) inside the vision of the agent (A). Black squares are obstacles, green squares with a (D) are dispensers that can spawn blocks when requested by an agent, and red squares are blocks (B). (Color figure online)

Figure 1 shows an example of when the final target position is inside the vision of the agent. Since we are dealing with local vision, the coordinates are all local with respect to the agent[6], which is located at the centre cell $(0, 0)$. Therefore, the target position in this example is set to cell $(1, -2)$, one cell to the right and two cells above. This is the simplest scenario, and when the agent arrives at the destination planning is concluded.

Figure 2a has a target cell that is outside the local vision of the agent. It would be inefficient to plan the whole route since things could change and then it would require replanning the route multiple times. Therefore, first we must find a target cell inside the agent's vision that would bring it closer to the final target, which in this case is shown in Fig. 2b to be cell $(-5, 0)$. Upon arriving at the local target the agent recalculates the difference to its final target, which in this example would result in cell $(-2, 0)$, and then calls the planner once again.

4.2   Plan Cache

Using automated planning at runtime is far from being an easy task. The entire process, from encoding the state of the agent as a problem file, to solving it with a planner, is computationally demanding. This can be reasonable for small and simple applications, but it becomes an issue when applied to large and complex systems, such as a MAS. Even though the planning problem for a single agent is feasible, it might not be for a coalition of agents as well. Let us assume we have N agents, we would need to call the planner N times (one per agent). Considering the MAPC scenario, this could happen in each step of the simulation.

Since physical resources (CPU, memory) and time (how long an agent can wait) are finite, it is always possible to pick a number N of agents for which it is not possible to solve the planning problem in less than a certain amount of time (4 s for each simulation step in the MAPC). As mentioned previously, the

---

[6] Please note that cells to the north and to the west of cell $(0, 0)$ have negative values, while cells to the south and to the east have positive values.

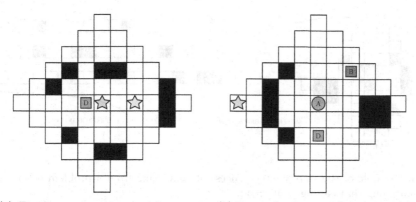

(a) Final target position with respect to Figure 2b. The faded star represents the expected position of the agent after Figure 2b.

(b) Example of a partial target position (star) with a final target outside the vision of the agent.

Fig. 2. Examples of planning targets (destination cells) for when the target is outside the vision of the agent.

15th edition of the contest extended the scenario to have 15 agents in round 1, 30 agents in round 2, and 50 agents in round 3. Through testing, we noticed that our previous strategy managed to hold up for 15 agents, but it did not work for 30 and 50 agents. Because of this, alternatives to speed the planning process up must be considered.

We investigated alternatives to speed up the process, and found that one possible way to make the planning process faster is by *caching* the plans. By caching, we refer to the act of storing previously generated plans, instead of forgetting about them after execution. When an agent asks the planner to solve a problem, if such a problem has been already solved in the past, then there is no reason for the planner to waste time and resources in solving it again. This can be achieved by keeping a mapping between *Problem → Plan*, which, given a problem file, returns its corresponding plan (if present in the cache). When a problem file does find a match in the cache, it means that it has never been solved before (cache miss), in which case the execution continues by calling the planner and then updating the cache. Note that the problem representation does not depend on the size of the grid, number of agents, or any other parameter. This means that the cache can be used in any configuration to speed up the planning process.

The first aspect we have to consider about caching is how to encode a problem file, so it can be straightforwardly retrieved from the cache. Such an encoding must uniquely identify a problem file. Thus, all information which describe the agent's local view needs to be considered. In Fig. 3, we report an example of how we generate such encoding.

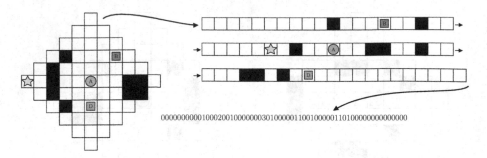

00000000001000200100000000301000001100100000110100000000000000

Fig. 3. Example of the step by step process of converting from a problem description to an encoding that can be easily read.

Starting from the agent's local view (left side of Fig. 3), a possible encoding can be obtained by unrolling the grid as a one-dimensional array (top right of Fig. 3). The unrolling of the agent's local view, starts from the upper most cell, and then all rows are appended one by one from left to right. Finally, in the bottom right of Fig. 3, we can see a possible encoding of the unrolling; where empty spaces are mapped to 0 (dispensers and the agent current position are considered empty), obstacles to 1, blocks to 2, and the goal to 3.

Once the encoding is created, it can be used to query the cache. Since we want to use the cached plans amongst different executions, the cache is stored in the secondary memory. Specifically, a file is created for each cached plan. The encoding of the agent's local view is used to name such a file. Consequently, to check if a certain planning problem has already been solved, it is enough to look if there exists a file named as the encoding of the problem. If such a file exists, there is no need to call the planner since the corresponding plan is already available inside the file, otherwise, the planner is called and a new file is stored (named after the encoding of the problem).

In the example of Fig. 3, the plan returned and stored as a file (named using the encoding) contains the sequence of actions reported in Listing 1.1.

```
1  clear(-3,0)
2  move(w)
3  move(w)
4  move(w)
5  move(w)
6  move(w)
```

Listing 1.1. Plan returned by the planner for Fig. 3, and stored in the cache.

As we have seen previously, it is possible to call the planner in two different settings. The first one is calling for a plan to the agent by itself, which we have already covered how to encode it. The second is that we may call for a plan to the agent with a block currently attached. The encoding for this is almost identical, except that in this case we append the local view coordinates of the block that is attached (note that our planning domain only supports movement with up to one attached block). For example, if there is a block attached to the agent and the block is located one cell below the agent, then we would append 01 to the beginning of the encoding. Finally, for both settings there is an additional encoding to determine if it can perform clear actions. If the agent has enough energy, then it can use clear actions to remove obstacles on its way. Otherwise, it has to go around them, if possible. This is obtained by simply adding a 1 (clear enabled) or a 0 (clear disabled) at the beginning of the encoding. Thus, for the same problem description, four different encodings can be generated depending on the presence of an attached block, and the availability of clear actions.

5   Discussion

The most glaring benefit of using an off-the-shelf planner is that we are able to take advantage of the many sophisticated and efficient tools that have been developed over the years in the community of automated planning. Re-implementing the features provided by these tools in an agent programming language can take a lot of effort. A more subtle advantage is that if the application domain requires distinct planning techniques for different types of problems in the system then we can use multiple off-the-shelf planners that are most appropriate for each problem. For example, different type of planning, such as probabilistic and temporal, might be needed at different stages of the task under consideration.

A limiting factor in using off-the-shelf planners with autonomous agents at runtime in time critical applications is that the solution may not be produced inside acceptable time bounds. Initially, we did not consider using automated planners to be feasible because we thought we would run into this issue. However, after testing we noticed that for 10 agents we could comfortably perform planning under a four seconds restriction. When the number of agents increased to 30 and 50, then we had to modify our solution by performing plan caching which provided excellent results. Our initial analysis indicates that using off-the-shelf planners in domains with loosely coupled agents (low or no interactions between agents) and/or low number of agents should generate results very quickly. Note that determining if the result can be produced inside the time constraint depends specifically on the application domain. Alternative solutions such as plan caching can also make previously unfeasible planning scenarios work well, but the size of the cache must be controlled since it can eventually increase up to a point where it is no longer worth using.

The seamless integration of automated planning in an agent programming language has the advantage that the computing performance can be vastly superior. This is not only because the agents themselves can perform planning directly without having to call a separate process, but also because *lookahead* online planning can be used, wherein only a subset of the problem is planned for and then executed before proceeding to plan for the rest.

The direct integration of planning in agents can restrict the type of planning supported, which can limit its applicability to certain domains. Furthermore, it can make the code difficult to port to other agent languages. For example, the MAPC requires all teams to make their source code available after the contest. This can help new teams (or underperforming teams) to look for inspiration in strategies that have worked well in the past. Because we used an off-the-shelf planner, other teams can easily make similar use of it without being tied to the agent development framework we used (JaCaMo).

6   Conclusion

In this paper, we have described our experience in applying an off-the-shelf automated planner at runtime for a very complex problem requiring a solution under a strict deadline. We have integrated this solution with agents that were developed in a BDI agent programming language. Our case study was based on the scenario first introduced in the 14th edition of the MAPC (and then later extended on the 15th edition). There are advantages and disadvantages to either using off-the-shelf planners or integrating automated planning directly in an agent programming language. Ultimately, the best choice is going to depend on the complexity and limitations imposed by the application/case study as well as the tools and languages that are available to solve the problem.

Future work involves trying to categorise different classes of applications and case studies to understand at a more general level when an off-the-shelf planner can be used alongside an agent programming language with minimal effort, as well as listing possible combinations of planners and agent-based languages that could work well together.

References

1. Ahlbrecht, T., Dix, J., Fiekas, N., Krausburg, T.: The multi-agent programming contest: a résumé. In: Ahlbrecht, T., Dix, J., Fiekas, N., Krausburg, T. (eds.) MAPC 2019. LNCS (LNAI), vol. 12381, pp. 3–27. Springer, Cham (2020). https://doi.org/10.1007/978-3-030-59299-8_1
2. Boissier, O., Bordini, R., Hubner, J., Ricci, A.: Multi-agent Oriented Programming: Programming Multi-agent Systems Using JaCaMo. Intelligent Robotics and Autonomous Agents Series. MIT Press, Cambridge (2020). https://books.google.com.br/books?id=GM_tDwAAQBAJ
3. Boissier, O., Bordini, R.H., Hübner, J.F., Ricci, A., Santi, A.: Multi-agent oriented programming with JaCaMo. Sci. Comput. Program. **78**(6), 747–761 (2013). https://doi.org/10.1016/j.scico.2011.10.004
4. Bordini, R.H., Seghrouchni, A.E.F., Hindriks, K.V., Logan, B., Ricci, A.: Agent programming in the cognitive era. Auton. Agents Multi Agent Syst. **34**(2), 37 (2020). https://doi.org/10.1007/s10458-020-09453-y
5. Bordini, R.H., Wooldridge, M., Hübner, J.F.: Programming Multi-agent Systems in AgentSpeak using Jason. John Wiley & Sons, Hoboken (2007)
6. Borgo, S., Cesta, A., Orlandini, A., Umbrico, A.: A planning-based architecture for a reconfigurable manufacturing system. In: Proceedings of the 26th ICAPS. ICAPS 2016, pp. 358–366, London, UK (2016)

7. Bratman, M.E.: Intentions, Plans, and Practical Reason. Harvard University Press, Cambridge (1987)
8. Cardoso, R.C., Bordini, R.H.: Decentralised planning for multi-agent programming platforms. In: Proceedings of the 18th AAMAS. AAMAS 2019, pp. 799–807. International Foundation for Autonomous Agents and Multiagent Systems, Richland, SC (2019). http://dl.acm.org/citation.cfm?id=3306127.3331771
9. Cardoso, R.C., Ferrando, A.: A review of agent-based programming for multi-agent systems. Computers 10(2), 16 (2021). https://doi.org/10.3390/computers10020016
10. Cardoso, R.C., Ferrando, A., Dennis, L.A., Fisher, M.: Implementing ethical governors in BDI. In: 9th International Workshop on Engineering Multi-agent Systems (2021)
11. Cardoso, R.C., Ferrando, A., Papacchini, F.: LFC: combining autonomous agents and automated planning in the multi-agent programming contest. In: Ahlbrecht, T., Dix, J., Fiekas, N., Krausburg, T. (eds.) MAPC 2019. LNCS (LNAI), vol. 12381, pp. 31–58. Springer, Cham (2020). https://doi.org/10.1007/978-3-030-59299-8_2
12. Fikes, R.E., Nilsson, N.J.: Strips: a new approach to the application of theorem proving to problem solving. Artif. Intell. 2(3), 189–208 (1971). https://doi.org/10.1016/0004-3702(71)90010-5, http://www.sciencedirect.com/science/article/pii/0004370271900105
13. Helmert, M.: The fast downward planning system. J. Artif. Intell. Res. 26, 191–246 (2006). https://doi.org/10.1613/jair.1705
14. Hübner, J.F., Sichman, J.S., Boissier, O.: Developing organised multiagent systems using the MOISE+ model: programming issues at the system and agent levels. Int. J. Agent Orient. Softw. Eng. 1(3/4), 370–395 (2007)
15. Logan, B.: An agent programming manifesto. Int. J. Agent Orient. Softw. Eng. 6(2), 187–210 (2018)
16. Mcdermott, D., et al.: PDDL - The Planning Domain Definition Language. Technical Report TR-98-003, Yale Center for Computational Vision and Control (1998)
17. Meneguzzi, F., Luck, M.: Declarative planning in procedural agent architectures. Expert Syst. Appl. 40(16), 6508–6520 (2013)
18. Nau, D., Ghallab, M., Traverso, P.: Automated Planning: Theory and Practice. Morgan Kaufmann Publishers Inc., San Francisco, CA (2004). https://doi.org/10.1016/B978-1-55860-856-6.X5000-5
19. Nau, D.S., Ilghami, O., Kuter, U., Murdock, J.W., Wu, D., Yaman, F.: SHOP2: an HTN planning system. J. Artif. Intell. Res. 20(1), 379–404 (2003). https://doi.org/10.1613/jair.1141
20. Rao, A.S., Georgeff, M.: BDI Agents: From Theory to Practice. In: Proceedings 1st International Conference Multi-agent Systems (ICMAS), pp. 312–319. San Francisco, USA, June 1995
21. Ricci, A., Piunti, M., Viroli, M., Omicini, A.: Environment programming in CArtAgO. In: El Fallah Seghrouchni, A., Dix, J., Dastani, M., Bordini, R.H. (eds.) Multi-Agent Programming, pp. 259–288. Springer, Boston (2009). https://doi.org/10.1007/978-0-387-89299-3_8
22. Sardina, S., Padgham, L.: A BDI agent programming language with failure handling, declarative goals, and planning. Auton. Agents Multi Agent Syst. 23(1), 18–70 (2011)
23. de Silva, L., Sardina, S., Padgham, L.: First principles planning in BDI systems. In: Proceedings of The 8th International Conference on Autonomous Agents and Multiagent Systems - Volume 2. AAMAS 2009, pp. 1105–1112. International Foundation for Autonomous Agents and Multiagent Systems, Richland, SC (2009)

Auction Mechanisms for Management of Steam Generated by High Temperature Reactors

Błażej Chmielarz[1,2(✉)], Cédric Herpson[2], Alexandre Bredimas[1], and Zahia Guessoum[2,3]

[1] USNC Europe, 91190 Gif-sur-Yvette, France
blazej.chmielarz@lip6.fr
[2] Sorbonne Université, CNRS, LIP6, 75005 Paris, France
[3] CReSTIC, EA, 3804, URCA, 5100 Reims, France

Abstract. Steam networks in existing chemical facilities are typically highly centralized and operate on long-term contracts. It results in energy systems with overcapacity of production, exceeding the demand several times. Facilities which remain idle or utilize fuel sub-optimally create unnecessary costs and possess high carbon footprint. To optimize fuel consumption, increase profits and lower emissions, we propose to decentralize and trade steam distribution with energy producers, chemical facilities and energy storage constituting autonomous agents. In this paper we describe a model of short-term trading of steam through multi-stage auction mechanisms. The goal of this model is to sell all produced steam every timestep while meeting the demand and including both smaller and larger parties in the negotiations fairly.

Keywords: Energy · Nuclear · CHP · VPP · Steam · Multi-agent · Auction

1 Introduction

Steam is a common energy carrier which industry complexes require an uninterrupted flow of to operate correctly. In some cases, live steam is used in chemical processes [1]. The demand of each consumer of steam in real systems is typically not a constant. Failing to meet the demand results in pressure changes in the main steam loop, which, in real systems, could cause lower efficiency, or even outright cease, of processes in a facility of the end user. This level of importance often leads owners of the chemical complexes to overbuild their energy installations where energy production capacities exceed 200% of demand. The large installed redundancies are dictated by the probability of spikes in demand coinciding with maintenance or malfunctioning of multiple boilers. Various kinds of energy generating technologies can be found in the complexes. Different physical principles of operation among the technologies require trading mechanisms which can accommodate them fairly.

Steam users have highly specific contracts with steam producers which ensure steam delivery on demand. The contracts often span a year or more but they cannot accurately put a price for minute-to-minute costs of operation a year ahead due to highly varied demand throughout the year [2]. It leads to complicated annual renegotiations between

© Springer Nature Switzerland AG 2021
F. Dignum et al. (Eds.): PAAMS 2021, LNAI 12946, pp. 64–76, 2021.
https://doi.org/10.1007/978-3-030-85739-4_6

producers and consumers based on past energy consumption and deviations from quotas. The potential impact of day-to-day decisions regarding current energy demand on future contracts cannot be fully understood at the moment of making said decisions. It can lead to economically and environmentally disadvantageous decisions of both consumers and producers of steam [3].

Considering how crucial steam is to the business of everyone in the system, the customers need to have more than one mean of establishing future supply and demand to better plan their operations. The current approach to meet the steam demand of chemical complexes works but is sub-optimal. Having multiple boilers on standby is costly, due to committed capital and recurring fixed costs, which need to be recuperated by the system. Addressing swift changes in demand could happen in a more cooperative fashion through market-driven approach - dynamic pricing is used to keep as many power plants as close to optimal operating conditions as possible.

The energy system proposed in this paper presents an alternate approach in which control of energy production is decentralised. The model trades steam in multi-stage auctions. The goal of the model is to sell all available steam every time-step while meeting the demand, including both smaller and larger parties in the negotiations fairly and lowering emissions without losing profits. Decentralisation of energy sales is achieved through agent-based modelling, where the agents, who represent energy producers, consumers or prosumers of the system, trade steam and electricity through auctions in two different time-frames: short- and long-term. High Temperature Reactors (HTRs) are added to the energy mix to assess their impact on emissions and economics.

The paper is organized as follows. Section 2 presents the entire system and the different types of agents and mechanisms. Section 3 describes the methodology of the short-term auctioning. Section 4 describes the setup of the test system and its implementation as well as the data that will be used for simulations. Section 5 presents a brief overview of the literature and highlights open issues before concluding.

2 System Overview and Agentification

The proposed approach agentifies the entities that make up the Hybrid Cogeneration Plant[1] into two main agent categories - concrete and special.

Physical components are represented by a set of discrete, concrete agents - boilers, nuclear reactors, energy storage, steam turbines, chemical plants or hydrogen production plants. The special agents are responsible for trade between concrete-agents, broadcasting external system variables or managing steam delivery (Fig. 1).

Each of the concrete agents contains a logical and a physical model. The system separates concrete agents at the common denominator of the physical system - steam. This separation facilitates arranging the concrete agents into *Virtual Power Plants* (VPPs). A VPP is any aggregate of concrete agents who will be represented as a singular trade participant (Fig. 2). Additionally, the high-level separation between agents permits the sale

---

[1] A hybrid energy system is one where there is typically more than one product out of one or more energy sources, like co-generation of steam and electricity from both gas and coal boilers. It can also refer to more than one energy source producing the same ware.

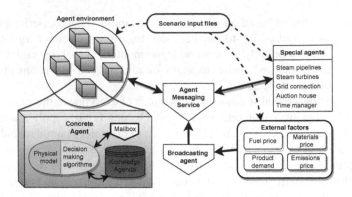

Fig. 1. Overview of the system

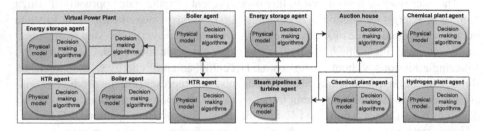

Fig. 2. Visualisation of aggregated agents and connections between them

of energy in the system while allowing agents whose inner workings are black boxes, which is necessary in real-life energy systems where operational details are typically classified.

Steam is a fungible good which should be sold in its entirety once it is produced in order to avoid upsetting the stability of the entire system. Separate auction mechanisms exist for long- and short-term trades. The short-term trade covers no more than a few minutes, trading steam produced inevitably in that short timeframe due to operational constraints of steam producers. The long-term sales offer steam *futures* - executable options to buy a certain amount of steam sometime in the future at a set price, and long-term contracts for steam at a constant volume and price. Contrary to short-term trades which are frequently suboptimal, long-term trades are well established processes not considered as an issue for the sector's players. We thus focus on the former in this work.

Two auction systems will be presented in the paper - *classic* and *reverse dutch auctions* [4]. *Classic* auctions are ones issued by sellers. *Reverse* auctions are issued by buyers. Dutch auctions are more suited to sales of bulk goods, such as electricity, fuel or grains, whereas english auctions are better suited for single item sales [5]. The need to sell the entirety of produced steam in the short-term trade has led us to dutch-style auctions.

In summary, the system is designed to sell the entirety of its wares through auctions, with short-term auctions being either classic or reverse dutch auctions. Agents of the system can have logical and physical layers. Special agents lack either the physical or logical layer. Concrete agents contain both layers. They are capable of independent decision-making and can aggregate into VPPs and be represented as one trade participant.

3   Short-Term Auction Mechanisms

The short-term trade of steam is separated into three protocols that are described in the following sections: 1) Prediction of aggregated supply and demand of steam, 2) Two-phase auctioning of steam and 3) Execution of accepted trades.

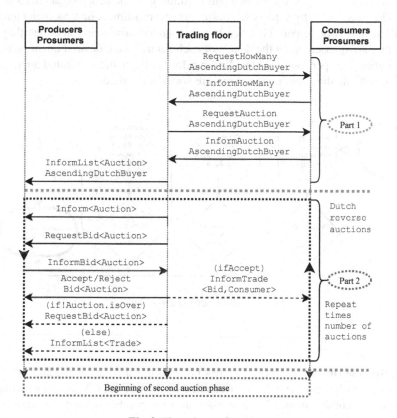

Fig. 3. First phase of auctions

3.1   Prediction of Aggregated Supply and Demand

The goal of prediction protocol is to inform producers and consumers of what is feasible in the present timestep to let them place realistic bids and auctions.

The first step of the protocol is auction participants and the auction house agent identifying each other in their respective roles. Then, the auction house verifies who will participate in the upcoming auctions and asks them about their expected supply and demand in the next short-term trade. The agent will wait until everyone responds or enough time passes. Next, aggregated results are sent to all participants. Protocol ends with a message to each participant informing of that end.

3.2   Algorithm for the First Auction Phase

All the auctions in the first phase are reverse closed dutch auctions. This phase contains two parts - establishing the number of auctions taking place and running the auctions. The phase starts by a query to consumers and prosumers on how many auctions they will submit (Fig. 3, part 1). The second part is running all the accepted auctions (Fig. 3, part 2). The phase starts by a query to consumers and prosumers on how many auctions they will submit (Fig. 3, part 1). Once buyers respond how many auctions they will submit, they are queried about the details of each auction - the desired quantity, budget and the initial price per ton of steam. Trading floor collects the submitted auctions. At the end of part one the submitted auctions are sorted and broadcasted.

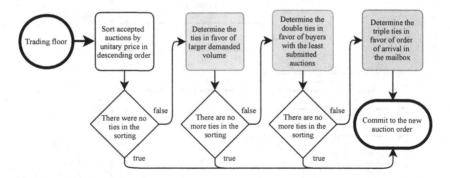

Fig. 4. Auction sorting algorithm

Sorting Reverse Dutch Auctions. Figure 4 presents the auction sorting algorithm. The first auctions are the ones with the highest unitary price of steam. Secondary sorting criterion is the purchase volume. Tertiary criterion is the number of auctions an agent has submitted - the lower the number, the higher the priority. If the previous criteria were insufficient to sort the auctions, the time of auction submission is considered. The chosen sorting order is dictated by several factors - the system consists of several players who may vary greatly in terms of size of their demand, which would give a natural advantage to larger buyers. Large share of control over demand would normally mean that steam producers focus on addressing their demand. Smaller buyers can compete with large vendors in terms of auction priority by raising base prices in auctions. The

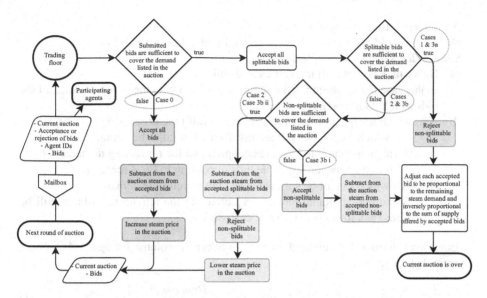

Fig. 5. Flowchart of one round of bid acceptance algorithm - starts at Trading Floor. Case 0: all incoming bids are accepted as the sum of offered volume does not cover the demand. Case 1: all bids are accepted but steam sold by each producer may be adjusted to meet its weighted average. Case 2: no steam is sold and the next round starts with a higher price. Case 3: some bids may be rejected. Red and orange paths lead to the next round. Green and blue steps conclude the auction. (Color figure online)

large vendors still have the advantage in the secondary order priority. The tertiary sorting criterion is aimed at limiting the possibility of scheming by the large vendors who submit a large amount of small auctions at various price points with the goal of gaining priority over small vendors while keeping the weighted average price across the auctions lower.

Accepting Bids for Every Reverse Dutch Auction. Once all the auctions are in and sorted, the list of auctions is announced to the participants and producers as well as prosumers are invited to bid in the first auction. The auction proceeds in the following fashion (Fig. 5): the trading floor sends the current unitary price to the bidders. They can respond how much volume they are willing to provide at the listed price and whether their bids are subject to partial acceptance. The bids are either accepted or rejected.

The rules of bet acceptance were created specifically for this trading system (see Fig. 5. Several cases are considered for each bid. When all submitted bids do not cover the demand of an auction, all bids are accepted, steam price is increased in the next round and the following cases do not apply (see Fig. 5, case 0).

1. All bidders accept incomplete orders
   The simplest situation is when all the bidders accept that their bid may be only partially accepted. In that case, the purchase volume accepted for each bidder is calculated as a weighted average (see Eq. 1 and Fig. 5, case 1)

2. All bidders refuse incomplete orders:
   No steam is sold and the auction is reiterated with a lower price (Fig. 5, case 2)
3. Some bidders accept incomplete orders
   (a) Bids which accept split are sufficient to fulfil the orders:
       In this case the resolution is the same as in case a with the exception that all the bids which do not permit splitting are rejected
   (b) Bids which accept split are not sufficient to fulfil the orders (Fig. 5, case 3a)
       i. Bids which cannot be split are insufficient to fulfil the demand:
          All the non-splittable bids are accepted and the remaining demand volume will be split between splittable bids according to Eq. 1 (case 3b i)
       ii. Bids which cannot be split are sufficient to fulfil the demand:
          All the non-splittable bids are rejected and the remaining volume will be offered at a lower price (Fig. 5, case 3b ii)

Equation 1 defines the weighted average of accepted volume for agent A_x in case of partial bid acceptance.

$$Accepted(A_x) = Demand \times \frac{Proposed(A_x)}{\sum_{i=1}^{n} Proposed(A_i)} \tag{1}$$

The following examples illustrate how bid sorting would proceed when auction lists demand for volume v_1 at price p_1.

Example 1. All participants submit bids equal to v_1 and p_1 and make them splittable. In this case, all bids are accepted at p_1 but volume accepted from each bidder is equal to v divided by number of bidders (Case 1, green).

Example 2. One participant submits a bid equal to $v_2 = \frac{v_1}{2}$ and makes it non-splittable, other participants submit bids equal to $v(p_i)$, where the sum of $v(p_i)$ is lower than v_1 but higher than v_2, and p_1 and make them splittable. All bids are accepted and the auction concludes. Bid of v_2 was accepted entirely whereas bids $v(p_i)$ were divided according to (Eq. 1), where demand is equal to $v_1 - v_2$. (Case 3 b I, blue)

Example 3. All participants submit bids equal to $v(p_i)$ and p_1 and make them non-splittable. The sum of $v(p_i)$ is lower than v_1. All bids are accepted and the auction proceeds to next phase, with volume v_1 minus the sum of $v(p_i)$ and price $p_2 > p_1$ (Case 0, red).

The first phase of auctions is the main mechanism of steam trading in the system and aims at establishing fair market prices for both buyers an sellers while taking into account their limitations, such as flexibility and total size of their demand or supply.

3.3   Algorithm for the Second Auction Phase and Delivery Protocol

The second auction phase is a descending dutch auction, starting at the lowest steam price in the first auction phase. This step is necessary to force sale of already produced steam at any price. Steam sellers are discouraged to sell steam through this auction as the price is now equal to the lowest established price in the previous auction phase.

First, sellers are asked for steam remaining after the first auction phase. The data is collected and, if there is any remaining steam, announced as a classic Dutch auction to

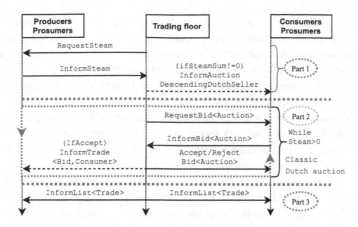

Fig. 6. Second phase of auctions

buyers (Fig. 6, part 1). The auction starts at the lowest price steam was sold for in the first auction phase and the rules for bid acceptance are similar to those in Fig. 5 except only partial bets are allowed and price for remaining steam in the next round strictly goes down in increments until it reaches zero (Fig. 6, part 2). Once the steam is sold, lists of accepted trades are sent to respective buyers and sellers (Fig. 6, part 3). This concludes the protocol for short-term auctions and begins the delivery protocol.

The purpose of delivery protocol is twofold - bookkeeping and calculating the physical state of the steam network each timestep. The bookkeeping includes accounting for all established trades relevant to the timestep - both long-term and short-term.

4 Implementation and Illustrative Scenario

The system is written in Java using JADE framework. Physical models of boilers and steam transport are simulated in MATLAB and integrated in Java. A special class, AugmentedAgent, was created to encompass basic functionalities needed by all agents in the system - address books, internal time tracking, role assignment. Its children are specific implementations for different technologies - boilers, energy storage, chemical plants, turbines, trading floors and broadcasters. Ontologies, protocols and other basic utility functions are used as decorators for instances of AugmentedAgent (see Fig. 7).

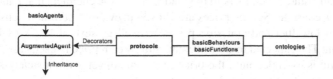

Fig. 7. Overview of code structure

Our platform allows us to model physical systems (boilers, heat storage,..) using MATLAB components and market participants through decision-making algorithms. The agents can generate demand curves, assess technical feasibility of meeting demand, production cost, CO2 emissions, long-term impact of possible decisions, implement strategy for efficient or optimal operation. For the end-users, the two major advantages of using a multi-agent approach are its flexibility and its privacy capabilities.

Data for simulations comes from real sources - historical data on fuel and electricity pricing from the European Energy Agency, prognoses of carbon emission certificates, performance tables of real boilers and High Temperature Gas-cooled Reactor (HTGR) designs. Real demand curves of chemical plants provided by our industrial partners will be used as a basis for simulating testing scenarios. We implemented several ontologies that are referred in our protocols. *TradingOntology* is common to all auction types, prediction and delivery protocols. *SubscriptionOntology* is used exclusively to update agents with current resource pricing and make questions regarding past pricing. The agents do not know future pricing in advance, with the exception of ExternalAgent.

The initial scenario consists of a HTGR, a gas boiler, a chemical plant and a turbine (Fig. 8). It is a very basic setup capable of both baseload and load following.

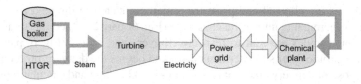

Fig. 8. Visualization of a physical layer of the illustrative scenario

HTGR is simulated with table values of max ramp-up and down speeds as well as a simple Xenon decay model which will reduce the max speeds. Gas boiler is a simpler model, based around fuel efficiency curve and max ramp-up and down speeds. Both units is of equal thermal power - 100 MW. They are connected to a back-pressure turbine, presumed to handle the load. Its isentropic efficiency is considered constant for every load factor. In the basic scenario, only high-pressure steam is sold, with lower pressures being converted to electricity. Electricity sales are handled by the grid agent at market prices at the time of trade as direct sales. The purpose of the scenario is to test the functionality of the system, agent responses in steadily changing conditions and efficiency of multi-stage short-term auction mechanisms.

In the Steady-state scenario, both the load factor of the chemical plant and pricing of all resources is constant. Several prices are chosen to evaluate common-sense decisions with high and low fuel and emission prices as well as several levels of load of the chemical plant. The expected result is a converging steam price in each case. Timeframe of this scenario is extended until the price of steam converges to a steady state or one year. Timestep for short-term auctions is set to one minute.

Different load and pricing scenarios implement three variations: a) variable load factor with constant pricing, b) constant load factor with variable pricing and c) variable load factor and pricing. They investigate the extent to which a decision-making based on production cost as a sole criterion for profitability can ensure continued supply.

5 Related Work

Decarbonisation of industrial heat production is among most challenging tasks in the field. The main reason is the dependence of the industry on reliable and flexible supply of high-temperature heat, mostly in the form of steam. While combustion of fossil fuels yields high temperatures easily, potential emission-free sources have great difficulty providing it. HGTRs are a solution to the problem but are burdened with high capital cost, lower flexibility and both legal and political hurdles [6,7]. To maintain economic viability, industrial complexes should consider new approaches to energy management.

The challenge of decarbonizing industrial complexes with alternative management methods and introduction of HGTRs relates to a more general problem of managing distributed energy production. Several algorithms and methods have been proposed to achieve it [8]. There are three main approaches to simulating systems operations – Discrete Event, System Dynamics and Agent-Based Simulation [9, 10]. Discrete Event Simulations are highly procedural. System Dynamic methods focus on modelling state dynamics with equations defining rates of change, it is analogous to physics simulations. Agent modelling is based on autonomous actors interacting with each other within a set of rules. They can have complex decision-making algorithms and can exhibit self-coordination [11] while ensuring the privacy of the various actors they represent. The two properties are among the key factors for selecting the agent modelling approach.

Multi-agent approach has been successfully applied to energy systems. MAS is used in many smart grids applications [12, 13], where the challenge of load balancing with intermittent energy production is common. Microgrids and District heating are two examples where MAS have been successfully deployed [11, 14, 15]. The examples share common traits with energy systems of industrial complexes. The differences are the covariance between process heat and electricity, the constrained number of actors in the system combined with the paramount importance of QoS and co-dependence between consumers and producers.

On a spectrum of classification of MAS, our system is a case of decentralized control system with overall objectives. The agents are heterogeneous and their hierarchy is holonic – outside of special agents responsible for coordination of actions, the only commitments between agents are ongoing energy contracts [14, 16]. One of the related multi-agent tools is GRENAD [17]. It uses a similar division of roles into distribution, production and consumption as our system. It is not open-source, though, and is designed for smart grids rather than production facilities.

Market-based approach to meeting supply and demand with MAS is a well-known and promising approach [18]. Typical approach in energy markets is based around establishing market clearing prices, where all energy is sold at a set price and every producer margins are different, or sealed-bid auctions, where either buyers or sellers make "take it or leave it" offers. Other approaches use indicators of importance to allocate optimal energy production and distribution [16, 18]. However, chemical plants cannot properly schedule their production in face of large price and supply volatility, leading to overbuilt energy supply systems in real life. The nature of our system has led us to develop our own method of allocating resources through adapting market mechanisms. Our long and short-term auctioning approach combines traits of both approaches and minimizes the risk of excess energy production and should enable fair profit margins to every actor, if one's decision making is sound.

Unlike energy grid or stock market, industrial complexes have few actors. Combined with volatile demand, it leads to low resilience compared to a grid or an entire market. Additionally, the allocated goods – heat and electricity – have more complex cost structures compared to electricity on the grid, as the chemical plants are fully dependent on heat supplied from boilers. The setup creates a coopetition - energy producers need to remain profitable themselves while ensuring long-term profitability of chemical plants. Power plants in the complexes were not designed for efficient electricity production and will not sustain themselves without heat consumers. Both parties need to make fair trades to ensure mutual success. One of the promising approaches to solve the coopetition problem using MAS are cooperative VPPs, which would lead to fewer but more reliable auction participants and could take better advantages of potential synergies among technologies [19].

One of the difficulties with validating the systems is the environment – for both economic and safety reasons, the tests cannot be easily carried out on real energy systems. It was faced in multiple cases for smart grids. Obtaining both realistic data and parameters to model agents is challenging [20]. Special tools were created as testbeds for MAS and for monitoring their performance. A potential step to test its real-life performance is a test loop available for research at INL [21]. MAS studies of energy systems have based their validation on parameters and historical data of real-life systems and we will follow this approach [22].

6   Conclusion and Perspectives

This paper proposes a decentralized control system of energy in chemical complexes with multi-stage auction mechanisms for short-term steam trading to optimize fuel consumption, increase profits and lower CO_2 emissions. The proposed auction mechanism sells all produced steam every timestep while meeting the demand and including all parties in the negotiations fairly. It combines classic and reverse dutch auctions with custom rules. This proposal is a first step towards an industrially deployable steam distribution system with multiple producers and consumers in the context of a HTR used as steam producer in chemical complexes and Hybrid Energy Systems (HES).

To evaluate our work, we developed a simulator standing on real physical models and datasets. It will be tested with simple scenario parameters - steady-state or variable load and demand, based on historical data. The next step involves adding long term trade and increased the complexity of the system, with new and more advanced physical agents and long-term scenarios. Once all elements are introduced, scenarios with malfunctions, outages and system changes will be assessed.

References

1. Botros, B.B., Brisson, J.G.: Targeting the optimum steam system for power generation with increased flexibility in the steam power island design. Energy **36**(8), 4625–4632 (2011)
2. Haverhill North Coke Company and Sunoco Inc. (R&M): Steam supply and purchase agreement (2010)
3. Kumana Associates: How to calculate the true cost of steam, U.S. Dept. of Energy (2003)
4. Shoham, Y., Leyton-Brown, K.: Multiagent Systems: Algorithmic, Game-Theoretic, and Logical Foundations, vol. 9780521899, pp. 1–483. Cambridge University Press, New York (2008)
5. Buchanan, J., Gjerstad, S., Porter, D.: Information effects in uniform price multi-unit Dutch auctions. Southern Econ. J. **83**(1), 126–145 (2016)
6. Bredimas, A., Kugeler, K., Fütterer, M.A.: Strengths, weaknesses, opportunities and threats for HTR deployment in Europe. Nucl. Eng. Des. **271**, 193–200 (2014)
7. Ruth, M.F., Zinaman, O.R., Antkowiak, M., Boardman, R.D., Cherry, R.S., Bazilian, M.D.: Nuclear-renewable hybrid energy systems: opportunities, interconnections, and needs. Energy Conv. Manage. **78**, 684–694 (2014)
8. Kulasekera, A.L., Gopura, R.A., Hemapala, K.T., Perera, N.: A review on multi-agent systems in microgrid applications. In: 2011 IEEE PES International Conference on Innovative Smart Grid Technologies-India, ISGT India 2011, no. December, pp. 173–177 (2011)
9. Maidstone, R.: Discrete event simulation, system dynamics and agent based simulation: discussion and comparison. System, **1**, 1–6 (2012)
10. Baldwin, W.C., Sauser, B., Cloutier, R.: Simulation approaches for system of systems: events-based versus agent based modeling. Proc. Comput. Sci. **44**(C), 363–372 (2015)
11. Gonzalez-Briones, A., De La Prieta, F., Mohamad, M.S., Omatu, S., Corchado, J.M.: Multi-agent systems applications in energy optimization problems: a state-of-the-art review. Energies **11**(8), 1–28 (2018)
12. Gil-Quijano, J.: Post-doctorate: Distributed optimal scheduling of energy resources. Application to district heating (2013)
13. Dötsch, F., Denzinger, J., Kasinger, H., Bauer, B.: Decentralized real-time control of water distribution networks using self-organizing multi-agent systems. In: Proceedings - 2010 4th IEEE International Conference on Self-Adaptive and Self-Organizing Systems, SASO 2010, no. September, pp. 223–232 (2010)
14. Ghribi, K., Sevestre, S., Guessoum, Z., Gil-Quijano, J., Malouche, D., Youssef, A.: A survey on multi-agent management approaches in the context of intelligent energy systems. In: 2014 International Conference on Electrical Sciences and Technologies in Maghreb, CISTEM 2014, no. January 2015 (2014)
15. Souissi, M.A., Bensaid, K., Ellaia, R.: Multi-agent modeling and simulation of a stock market. Invest. Manage. Fin. Innov. **15**, 123–134 (2018)
16. Kamphuis, J., Kok, C.J., Warmer, I.G.: PowerMatcher: multiagent control in the electricity infrastructure. Energy Res. Center Netherlands (ECN) **32**(18), 151–155 (2010)
17. Ductor, S., Gil-Quijano, J.J., Stefanovitch, N., Mele, P.R.: GRENAD, a modular and generic smart-grid framework. In: Proceedings of the 2015 Federated Conference on Computer Science and Information Systems, FedCSIS 2015, vol. 5, pp. 1781–1792 (2015)
18. Ygge, F., Akkermans, H.: Power load management as a computational market. In: Proceedings of the Second International Conference on Multi-Agent Systems (ICMAS), no. March, pp. 1–14 (1996)
19. Chalkiadakis, G., Robu, V., Kota, R., Rogers, A., Jennings, N.R.: Cooperatives of distributed energy resources for efficient virtual power plants. In: 10th International Conference on Autonomous Agents and Multiagent Systems 2011, AAMAS 2011, vol. 2, no. May 2014, pp. 737–744 (2011)

20. Atif, Y., et al.: Multi-agent Systems for Power Grid Monitoring, pp. 1–16 (2018)
21. O'Brien, J.E., Sabharwall, P., Yoon, S.: A multi-purpose thermal hydraulic test facility for support of advanced reactor technologies. Trans. Am. Nucl. Soc. **111**, 1639–1642 (2014)
22. Ren, H., Zhou, W., Nakagami, K., Gao, W., Wu, Q.: Multi-objective optimization for the operation of distributed energy systems considering economic and environmental aspects. Appl. Energy **87**(12), 3642–3651 (2010)

Dial4JaCa – A Communication Interface Between Multi-agent Systems and Chatbots

Débora Engelmann[1,3]($\boxtimes$)(iD), Juliana Damasio[1](iD), Tabajara Krausburg[1,4](iD),
Olimar Borges[1](iD), Mateus Colissi[1](iD), Alison R. Panisson[2](iD),
and Rafael H. Bordini[1](iD)

[1] School of Technology, Pontifical Catholic University of Rio Grande do Sul,
Porto Alegre, Brazil
{debora.engelmann,juliana.damasio,tabajara.rodrigues,olimar.borges,
mateus.colissi}@edu.pucrs.br, rafael.bordini@pucrs.br
[2] Department of Computing, Federal University of Santa Catarina, Araranguá, Brazil
alison.panisson@ufsc.br
[3] DIBRIS, University of Genoa, Genoa, Italy
[4] Department of Informatics, Clausthal University of Technology,
Clausthal-Zellerfeld, Germany

Abstract. Multi-agent techniques have become mature technologies with many tools, programming languages, and methodologies currently available. As a result, it is a practical approach for the development of complex AI systems. However, there are still challenges in developing an interface that enables a more natural communication interface between software agents and human agents, for example, using natural language. We believe chatbot technologies can provide the support needed to face this challenge. In this paper, we propose an approach to the integration of multi-agent systems and chatbot technologies named Dial4JaCa. The resulting integration makes it possible to apply both those technologies together to a variety of domains. In this particular work, we use JaCaMo as a multi-agent programming platform and Dialogflow as a chatbot platform. We evaluate the Dial4JaCa integration using two different multi-agent applications.

Keywords: Multi-agent systems · Natural language · Chatbots

1 Introduction

A conversational agent, also known as chatterbot or chatbot, is a computer program that interact with users through natural language. It has been around since the 1960s, and its first application was to check whether it could deceive users, who are real humans, or not [23]. Over time, it has been noticed that these systems could not only imitate human dialogues, but also be useful in areas such as education, commerce, health, business, among others [16]. It appears that

© Springer Nature Switzerland AG 2021
F. Dignum et al. (Eds.): PAAMS 2021, LNAI 12946, pp. 77–88, 2021.
https://doi.org/10.1007/978-3-030-85739-4_7

virtual assistants are an evolution of chatbots. Besides being an interface for conversation, virtual assistants can also take action to support human activities. In addition, they use inputs such as the user's voice, text, and contextual information to provide assistance by answering questions in natural language [12].

In the light of the advances in Natural Language Processing (NLP), conversational agents have started to play an essential role in various domains, such as: healthcare, to help physicians identify symptoms and improve assessment skills, diagnosis, interview techniques, and interpersonal communication [21]; helping elderly people with cognitive disabilities by providing proactive functions by sending messages to help them in situations where they are distracted [25]; in education to facilitate the teaching and learning process [24]; in tourism to provide information to guests about hotel services and to accompany them through the hotel spaces [26].

In recent years, many companies have invested resources to create platforms for the development of chatbots. To name a few, Google maintains Dialogflow[1], IBM provides Watson[2], and Luis[3] is developed by Microsoft. These platforms provide mechanisms for NLP and dialog management. In those platforms, *intents* are one of the main components. The user's input (i.e., what the user says/types), is mapped to an intent to provide an appropriate response (or action) to the user, which is based on the current input and the context of the conversation [20]. Then, the developer is responsible for registering each intent, which may call *external services*. External services allow the implementation of task-oriented systems. An intent can have a large set of inputs provided by the user; this is because a human can speak the same thing in various ways.

Multi-Agent Systems (MAS) are built upon core concepts such as distributed systems, reactivity, and individual rationality. Agents have been widely studied and a large range of tools have been developed, such as agent-oriented programming languages and methodologies [7]. Thus, practical applications of multi-agent technologies have become a reality to solve complex and distributed problems, e.g., [22]. In addition, it also allows the execution of different tasks and makes it possible the integration with different technologies. Given this, MAS are a promising area for integrating chatbot platforms. To the best of our knowledge, there is still a lack of research on this topic. Much of the research in the area does not use chatbots, it only simulates the user input using datasets [11,27] and, consequently, there is no interaction between agents and humans.

In this paper, we propose an approach that implements a communication interface between MAS and a platform for developing chatbots, which we named Dial4JaCa. Dial4JaCa is an integration between JaCaMo and Dialogflow. While the JaCaMo framework provides a multi-agent oriented programming [6] perspective (Jason for programming agents, CArtAgO for the environment, and Moise for the organisation of agents), Dialogflow supports natural language processing. Thus, our communication interface makes it possible to implement

---

[1] https://dialogflow.com/.

[2] https://www.ibm.com/watson/br-pt/.

[3] https://www.luis.ai/home.

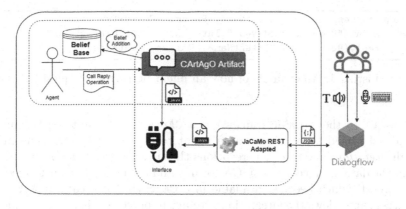

Fig. 1. The Dial4JaCa architecture

multi-agent systems in which agents and humans are able to have dialogues in natural language. Dial4JaCa is general and it can be integrated into different applications for different domains. In this particular piece of work, we demonstrate our approach using two different real-world scenarios: (1) in the Education domain, we developed a MAS to support the coordination of group tasks; (2) in the Health domain, we implemented an approach to support hospital bed allocation.

2   Dial4JaCa – A Communication Interface Between Multi-agent Systems and Chatbots

Dial4JaCa[4] integrates the JaCaMo framework [6] with Dialogflow and, therefore, allows us to implement intelligent agents that are able to communicate with humans through natural-language interaction. We aim at making our approach sufficiently adaptive so that it can be applied to different applications and domains. To do so, we use modular components which can be imported into any multi-agent system developed in JaCaMo. Figure 1 depicts an overview of the Dial4JaCa architecture.

To develop the bridge that links a MAS application, developed using JaCaMo, to a natural language processing platform, e.g., Dialogflow, we use part of the open-source project `JaCaMo REST`[5] [3]. `JaCaMo REST` allows a MAS to interact with services or applications on the web, and to be managed and updated by other applications [3]. In our approach, Dial4JaCa receives requests from `Dialogflow` through `JaCaMo REST`, then it conveys that information to a `CArtAgO Artefact` responsible for making the requests available to the agents. A `CArtAgO Artefact` is a first-class abstraction to develop the environment where the agents inhabit. They can represent resources and tools that the agents dynamically instantiate, share, and use to support their individual and collective

---

[4] https://github.com/smart-pucrs/Dial4JaCa.
[5] https://github.com/jacamo-lang/jacamo-rest.

```
1  +request(ResponseId, IntentName, Params, Contexts) :true
2  <-  .print("Request received ",IntentName," of Dialog");
3       !reply(ResponseId, IntentName, Params, Contexts).
```

Listing 1: An example of how an agent perceives a request.

activities [6]. In the JaCaMo framework, a `CArtAgO Artefact` is programmed in Java and provides the means to an agent to interact with the environment through *operations* and receive perceptions through *observable properties*. In our system, the data are received in JSON format and immediately transformed into a Java object, which becomes available in a `CArtAgO Integration Artefact`. This `Interface` allows the integration artefact to perceive whenever a request is received. Upon realising the arrival of a requisition, the artefact performs a *belief addition* in the *belief base* of all agents who are observing it (i.e., the observable properties). That belief contains all relevant information about the request. Doing so, the agents that *focus* on that artefact are able to decide whether they are going to react such requests or not.

Regarding `Dialogflow`, it uses the `fulfillment`[6] service to communicate to external APIs. We use this service to integrate Dialogflow with the MAS, passing requests through the resource-oriented abstraction layer from `JaCaMo REST`. With the resulting communication interface, intelligent agents developed in JaCaMo perceive not only information about an intent triggered by the user's speech, but also parameters and contexts that have been collected by Dialogflow in each interaction.

Contexts[7] are another important concept in Dialogflow. They are similar to contexts in natural language conversations, that is, it is a relationship between the text and the situation in which it occurs. To process a user's expression in natural language, Dialogflow can use the context to correctly match it with an intent. Doing so, it is possible to control the flow of a conversation. In addition, intents can also have parameters[8] that are values extracted from the user's expression.

Listing 1 shows an example of a plan in Jason (an agent-oriented programming language) that agents can use to react to a belief addition (`+request`). It informs to the agent that a new request from the user has arrived. In this simple example, the agent creates a new goal to `!reply()`, which will result in a sequence of instructions to be carried out.

In addition to the intention's name, Dial4JaCa also allows the agent to have access to `contexts` and `parameters`, which are captured by Dialogflow. This information is recorded in its belief base and might be used during its reasoning cycle. `Contexts` is a list, as shown in the Listing 2, where for each element of this list: `Name` corresponds to the context name; `LifeSpanCount` corresponds to the context lifespan; and `[param(Key, Value), param(Key1, Value1)]` matches the context parameter list. Even if there is no context, it is possible to receive a

---

[6] https://cloud.google.com/dialogflow/es/docs/fulfillment-overview.

[7] https://cloud.google.com/dialogflow/es/docs/contexts-overview?hl=en.

[8] https://cloud.google.com/dialogflow/es/docs/intents-overview?hl=en.

```
1  context(Name, LifeSpanCount, [param(Key, Value), param(Key1, Value1)])
```

Listing 2: An example of context.

```
1  +!reply(ResponseId, IntentName, Params, Contexts)
2    : (IntentName == "Reply With Context")
3  <- .print("The context will be created next.");
4     contextBuilder(ResponseId, "test context", "1", Context);
5     .print("Context created: ", Context);
6     replyWithContext("Hello, I am your Jason agent, and I am
7                       responding with context", Context).
```

Listing 3: An example of a plan to reply to a request with a context.

list of parameters. That list has the same structure as the parameter list in the context, where Key corresponds to the parameter's key, and Value corresponds to the value recorded by Dialogflow.

Dial4JaCa also allows an agent to send new contexts to Dialogflow along with the response to a request. An operation named contextBuilder is available for this purpose. This operation receives as a parameter the response *id* (responseId), the name of the context to be created (contextName), and the lifespan of the context (lifespanCount), and returns a context formatted according to the Dial4JaCa specification. To reply with a context, the agent calls the operation replyWithContext, which takes as parameter a string with the text that the chatbot must tell the user and the context created by the contextBuilder. We exemplify this process in Listing 3.

Dial4JaCa also provides the reply operation in case an agent does not need to send out a context and the replyWithEvent operation that allows an agent to send events to Dialogflow.

One should be particularly careful when dealing with timeouts in Dialogflow. They indicate that the conversation flow should continue and a reply from the MAS is no longer expected. This behaviour can be triggered, for instance, when an agent calls upon external services in order to reason about an appropriate response. Upon realising that an agent is taking too long to respond, Dial4JaCa automatically fires an event in Dialogflow, containing the same name as the current remote intent (getting rid of the blank spaces). Doing so, it gets more time for the agent to finish its reasoning. This process is perceived by neither the user nor the agent. Dialogflow allows these sorts of events to be fired up to three times in a row. In our tests, this mechanism has provided sufficient time for an agent to deliver a response with no endless waiting time on the user side.

In this first implementation, we have approached only the Dialogflow platform. However, preliminary investigations have shown that with small changes in our code, we can also use other natural language processing platforms such as the open-source Rasa[9], Watson, or Luis.

---

[9] https://rasa.com/docs/.

3   Proof of Concept

We show the applicability of Dial4JaCa, demonstrating its versatility in two different scenarios. The first addresses the coordination of group tasks in an classroom environment, and the second provides support to hospital staff during bed allocation process.

3.1   Collaborative Environment

We have developed a group coordinating system[10] that explores the use of a chatbot and a MAS in a collaborative environment [8]. Our multi-agent system assists in the coordination of group tasks, in particular educational environments. The agents in the MAS represent and assist the users participating in a project group. They are also responsible for assisting the group organisation and communication. The communication within the group is performed through a chatbot, and the information about the organisation is available to any group member at any time. Figure 2 depicts an overview of the multi-agent system architecture for this particular application.

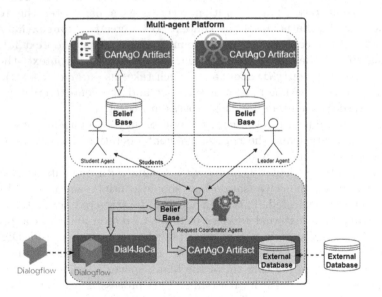

Fig. 2. Coordinating system for groups tasks.

In this particular MAS application, each group of study registered in the system contains a leader and 18 students. Three types of agents are used: (1) **request coordinator**, an agent responsible for requests the system receives

---

[10] https://github.com/Colissi/jacamo-groupwork-coordination.

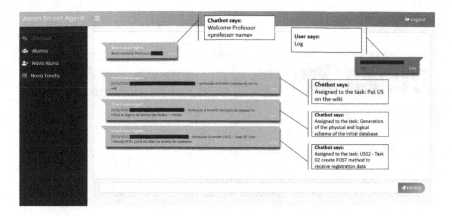

Fig. 3. Screenshot of the coordination system using a chatbot.

from Dialogflow and for handling information of Firebase Realtime Database[11]; (2) `leader`, an agent responsible for coordinating the group, that is, it is the agent that sets up the group (creation of the group artefacts and workspace) in addition to initialising the organisation of agents and handling group requests; and (3) `student`, an agent responsible for achieving tasks and asking for information to the leader of the group (this type of agent represents a student).

The chatbot uses Dial4JaCa to communicate with the MAS responsible for coordinating the group of students. It contains information about the tasks and members of the groups. Also, it returns requested information through the chatbot in natural language form. Figure 3 depicts the interface of our chatbot.

The system was evaluated with two groups of students, with no human supervision during the interaction with the system, in which each group consisted of 18 students and a lecturer responsible for the groups. A total of 577 messages were exchanged (i.e., requests to the chatbot), of which only 53 the chatbot could not identify the user's intention. There were reported no problems regarding the integration of the MAS and the Dialogflow. All messages properly received and recognised by Dialogflow were sent to the multi-agent system through Dial4JaCa. Similarly, Dialogflow successfully received all responses sent by the agents. The cases in which the chatbot was not able to recognise the user's intention were due to failures in the Dialogflow component.

3.2 Bed Allocation

The second application aims at providing decision support for hospital staff during bed allocation process[12]. This application extends our previous work [9] in order to use the Dial4JaCa integration. In [9], we developed an specific integration between the MAS and the Dialogflow, in which a hospital staff could

---

[11] https://firebase.google.com/docs/database.
[12] https://github.com/smart-pucrs/bed-allocation-system.

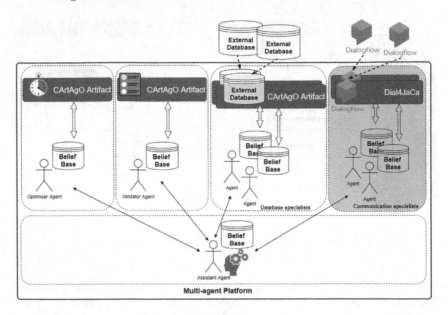

Fig. 4. Bed allocation system

interact with the system using natural language. In this work, we adapt that multi-agent application to use Dial4JaCa, given that it provides more flexibility.

An overview of the proposed architecture for this application is depicted in Fig. 4. The `assistant agent` establishes communication between the user and the other agents to look up for information. The system also may have one or more agents specialised in database queries, named `Database specialists`. Those agents use a CArtAgO artefact to connect to the hospital databases or other databases necessary for our approach's correct operation. Doing so, the MAS is able to look up for important information related to the current state of the application universe (e.g., free beds) so that the `Assistant Agent` can use it for reasoning and decision-making.

The `communication specialists` handle the communication between the `assistant agent` and the end users. They are important, for example, to customise responses to each user based on a previously defined (or learned) profile. This way an application can avoid giving too many explanatory answers to a user who has a specialist background, as well as avoid giving very superficial answers to users with little background. The ability to instantiate multiple communication expert agents, one for each user of the system, also allows the `assistant agent` to engage in multiparty conversations, helping a team or a group of users to make joint decisions.

Moreover, there are two other agents populating the MAS application: the `optimiser agent` and the `validator agent`. The `optimiser agent` is responsible for communicating with a GLPK[13] (Gnu Linear Programming Solver)

---

[13] http://winglpk.sourceforge.net/.

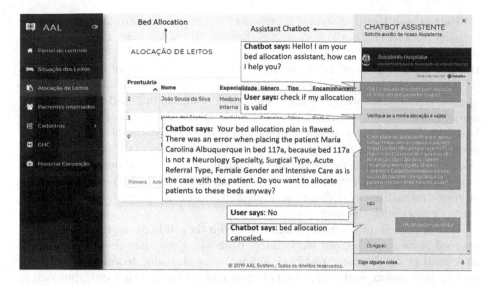

Fig. 5. Web simulator—bed allocation screen with chatbot.

solver to generate optimal bed allocations, and the `validator agent` communicates with a PDDL (Planning Domain Definition Language) validator[14] to validate the bed allocation plans made by the user. Figure 5 depicts the graphical interface that our users use to chat with the chatbot.

The current version of this MAS application has not yet been evaluated by professionals responsible for allocating beds in hospitals, but we intend to do it in the near future. Dial4JaCa has fulfilled its role in our preliminary tests by supporting communication and other functionalities as expected, and providing a complete integration between the MAS application and Dialogflow. In the next version of this multi-agent system application, we intend to use argumentation-based techniques [18,19] and ontology techniques [10], allowing agents to explain their suggestions for bed allocation. Explainability becomes an essential part of decision support systems, and Dial4JaCa can support this type of sophisticated interactions.

4   Related Work

One of the first advances in this direction was made by Alencar and Netto [2]. They developed an approach combining AIML and MAS for Virtual Learning Environment. The work was implemented using the JADE framework [5]. They applied the approach on Moodle, in which intelligent agents exchange information and access a MySQL database to observe what is happening in the forum, providing the status of activities undertaken by students to the Assistant Tutor. They apply an experiment with 10 students from a technical course.

---

[14] https://github.com/smart-pucrs/PDDL-plan-validator.

Hettige and Karunananda [13] presents Octopus, an improved version of the existing Sinhala chatbot [15], designed through the MAS using the agent development framework MaSMT [14]. Octopus has a module for NLP that handles all the user inputs and provides the output as required. They did not cite evaluation.

The work by Bayser et al. [4] is the most related to our approach. They developed Ravel, a MAS with Natural Language Understanding and Dialog components. Ravel enables communication between agents and users. They used MAS based on Microservices-driven architecture [17] and Watson. Using Ravel, it is possible to specify deontic logic for conversation norms (social), especially useful in contexts where multiple agents and human users are communicating in natural language. They demonstrated the approach applicability in a chat-based finance adviser system (finch) designed as a chat group of five participants, where 37 users interact with the finch.

Our approach differs from [2] and [13], given they did not use a chatbot development platform. Also, our work differs from [4], given that they used Watson as a chatbot development platform, but focusing on using deontic logic to obligation, permission, and prohibition of messages. We argue that our approach is more general, in which any multi-agent system application can be implemented using Dial4JaCa integration, which provides support to natural language communication between humans and agents.

5   Conclusion and Future Work

In this paper, we proposed Dial4JaCa, an approach to integrate MAS and Chatbots. Our approach was built using JaCaMo [6] and Dialogflow, and it provides significant progress toward natural language communication interfaces between humans and multi-agent systems. The scenarios presented in this paper demonstrate the use of Dial4JaCa in practice, also showing promising preliminary results. This also confirms that our approach can be applied to different scenarios from different application domains.

In the first scenario presented in this paper, Dial4JaCa was used to create a group coordination system that promotes a collaborative and educational environment. Throughout its development, the system was evaluated by two groups of 18 students each and a lecturer responsible for the groups. No problems were reported on the use of the integration, although there were failures related to Dialogflow recognising the users' intents. In the second scenario presented in this paper, Dial4JaCa was used to develop a decision support system for hospital bed allocation. The evaluation was performed using simulated hospital bed allocation scenarios. This limitation was due to the pandemic caused by COVID-19, which made evaluation in hospitals not possible at this particular time. During the simulations, Dial4JaCa worked as expected and no problems were reported.

Providing a communication interface between JaCaMo and Dialogflow is an important step to increase the use of MAS in conjunction with chatbot systems. We believe that several other applications can be developed using Dial4JaCa, for example, in the domains of ambient intelligence, law, e-commerce, hotel booking, and software engineering. Moreover, we believe our approach provides support to the development of hybrid intelligence [1], in which human-agent collaboration is fundamental. In our future work, we intend to expand the integration to other chatbot development platforms. We also intend to apply Dial4JaCa in other application domains.

Acknowledgements. This study was financed in part by CAPES—Finance Code 001.

References

1. Akata, Z., et al.: A research agenda for hybrid intelligence: augmenting human intellect with collaborative, adaptive, responsible, and explainable artificial intelligence. Computer **53**(8), 18–28 (2020)
2. Alencar, M., Netto, J.M.: Improving cooperation in virtual learning environments using multi-agent systems and AIML. In: 2011 Frontiers in Education Conference (FIE), pp. F4C–1. IEEE (2011)
3. Amaral, C.J., Hübner, J.F., Kampik, T.: Towards JaCaMo-rest: a resource-oriented abstraction for managing multi-agent systems. arXiv preprint (2020)
4. Bayser, M.G., et al.: Ravel: a MAS orchestration platform for human-chatbots conversations. In: The 6th International Workshop on Engineering Multi-Agent Systems (EMAS@ AAMAS 2018), Stockholm, Sweden (2018)
5. Bellifemine, F.L., Caire, G., Greenwood, D.: Developing Multi-agent Systems with JADE, vol. 7. Wiley, Hoboken (2007)
6. Boissier, O., Bordini, R.H., Hübner, J.F., Ricci, A., Santi, A.: Multi-agent oriented programming with JaCaMo. Sci. Comput. Program. **78**(6), 747–761 (2013)
7. Bordini, R.H., Dastani, M., Dix, J., Seghrouchni, A.E.F.: Multi-Agent Programming: Languages, Tools and Applications, 1st edn. Springer, New York (2009)
8. Colissi, M., Renata, V., Mascardi, V., Bordini, R.: A chatbot that uses a multi-agent organization to support collaborative learning. In: Proceedings of the Human Computer Interaction International (2021, Forthcoming)
9. Engelmann, D.C.: An interactive agent to support hospital bed allocation based on plan validation. Dissertation, Pontifícia Universidade Católica do Rio Grande do Sul (2019)
10. Freitas, A., Panisson, A.R., Hilgert, L., Meneguzzi, F., Vieira, R., Bordini, R.H.: Integrating ontologies with multi-agent systems through Cartago artifacts. Int. Conf. Web Intell. Intell. Agent Technol. **2**, 143–150 (2015)
11. Griol, D., Molina, J.M.: A multiagent-based technique for dialog management in conversational interfaces. In: Demazeau, Y., Ito, T., Bajo, J., Escalona, M.J. (eds.) PAAMS 2016, vol. 9662, pp. 121–132. Springer, Cham (2016). https://doi.org/10.1007/978-3-319-39324-7
12. Hauswald, J., et al.: Sirius: an open end-to-end voice and vision personal assistant and its implications for future warehouse scale computers. In: Proceedings of International Conference on Architectural Support for Programming Languages and Operating Systems, pp. 223–238 (2015)
13. Hettige, B., Karunananda, A.: Octopus: a multi agent chatbot. In: Proceedings of 8th International Research Conference, pp. 41–47. KDU Library (2015)
14. Hettige, B., Karunananda, A., Rzevski, G.: MaSMT: a multi-agent system development framework for English-Sinhala machine translation. Int. J. Comput. Ling. Nat. Lang. Process. **2**(7), 411–416 (2013)

15. Hettige, B., Karunananda, A.S.: First Sinhala chatbot in action. In: Proceedings of the 3rd Annual Sessions of Sri Lanka Association for Artificial Intelligence (SLAAI). University of Moratuwa (2006)
16. Júnior, C.P., Francisco, R., Silva, L., Veiga, E., Fernandes, M., Dorça, F.: Uso de ontologias para agentes conversacionais no contexto de ensino-aprendizagem: Uma revisão sistemática da literatura. In: Proceedings of Brazilian Symposium on Computers in Education, pp. 183–192 (2017)
17. Newman, S.: Building Microservices: Designing Fine-grained Systems. O'Reilly Media Inc., Sebastopol (2015)
18. Panisson, A.R., Bordini, R.H.: Towards a computational model of argumentation schemes in agent-oriented programming languages. In: International Joint Conference on Web Intelligence and Intelligent Agent Technology, pp. 9–16. (2020)
19. Panisson, A.R., Engelmann, D.C., Bordini, R.H.: Engineering explainable agents: an argumentation-based approach. In: International Workshop on Engineering Multi-Agent Systems (2021)
20. Rahman, A., Al Mamun, A., Islam, A.: Programming challenges of chatbot: current and future prospective. In: Humanitarian Technology Conference (R10-HTC), 2017 IEEE Region 10, pp. 75–78. IEEE (2017)
21. Rizzo, A., Kenny, P., Parsons, T.D.: Intelligent virtual patients for training clinical skills. J. Virtual Real. Broadcast. **8**(3), 1–16 (2011)
22. Schmidt, D., Panisson, A.R., Freitas, A., Bordini, R.H., Meneguzzi, F.R., Vieira, R.: An ontology-based mobile application for task managing in collaborative groups. In: Proceedings of the 29th Florida Artificial Intelligence Research Society (FLAIRS), 2016, Estados Unidos (2016)
23. Shawar, B.A., Atwell, E.: Chatbots: are they really useful? In: Proceedings of LDV Forum, pp. 29–49 (2007)
24. Silva, M., de Melo, S., Silva, M., Lima, L.: Integração de um agente conversacional no processo de ensino e aprendizagem utilizando as teorias mce e mmeeb para a retenção do conhecimento. In: Proceedings of Brazilian Symposium on Computers in Education, pp. 99–107 (2018)
25. Wargnier, P., et al.: Towards attention monitoring of older adults with cognitive impairment during interaction with an embodied conversational agent. In: Proceedings of IEEE International Workshop on Virtual and Augmented Assistive Technology, pp. 23–28 (2015)
26. Zalama, E., et al.: Sacarino, a service robot in a hotel environment. In: Proceedings of Iberian Robotics Conference, pp. 3–14 (2014)
27. Zolitschka, Jan Felix: A novel multi-agent-based chatbot approach to orchestrate conversational assistants. In: Abramowicz, Witold, Klein, Gary (eds.) BIS 2020. LNBIP, vol. 389, pp. 103–117. Springer, Cham (2020). https://doi.org/10.1007/978-3-030-53337-3_8

Are Exploration-Based Strategies of Interest for Repeated Stochastic Coalitional Games?

Josselin Guéneron[✉] and Grégory Bonnet

Normandie Univ, UNICAEN, ENSICAEN, CNRS, GREYC, Caen Cedex 5, France
{josselin.gueneron,gregory.bonnet}@unicaen.fr
https://www.greyc.fr/

Abstract. Coalitional games are models of cooperation where selfish agents must form groups (coalitions) to maximize their utility. In these models, it is generally assumed that the utility of a coalition is fixed and known. As these assumptions are not realistic in many applications, some works addressed this problem by considering repeated stochastic coalitional games. In such games, agents repeatedly form coalitions and observe their utility a posteriori in order to update their knowledge. However, it is generally assumed that agents have a greedy behavior: they always form the best coalitions they estimate at a given time step. In this article, we study if other strategies (behaviors) that allow agents to explore under-evaluated coalitions may be of interest. To this end, we propose a model of repeated stochastic coalitional game where agents use a neural network to estimate the utility of the coalitions. We compare different exploration strategies, and we show that, due to the structure of the coalitional games, the greedy strategy is the best despite the fact exploration-based strategies better estimate the utilities.

Keywords: Sequential decision · Coalition formation · Cooperative game theory · Multi-agent systems

1 Introduction

In multi-agent systems, individual agents are not always able to realize some tasks on their own. In such case, they can decide to cooperate with each other in forming coalitions, i.e. forming groups of agents able to realize a given task, and sharing the gains generated afterwards. As agents are selfish and rational, they will try to earn as much as possible, and can refuse to form certain coalitions deemed uninteresting for themselves. In the literature, the majority of works about coalition formation makes two strong hypotheses. The first one is that agents have perfect *a priori* knowledge of their payoff when forming a given coalition. The second hypothesis is that this payoff is deterministic. These two hypotheses do not seem to fit with real situations where the exact payoff brought by a coalition is known only a posteriori. Moreover, if this coalition is formed

© Springer Nature Switzerland AG 2021
F. Dignum et al. (Eds.): PAAMS 2021, LNAI 12946, pp. 89–100, 2021.
https://doi.org/10.1007/978-3-030-85739-4_8

again, this payoff may not always be the same, if the agents are more or less efficient in their tasks. For example, we can consider scientists having to repeatedly form consortia in order to temporarily work on projects. These consortium formations are repeated with the same pool of scientists but the quality of the results produced by each consortium may vary due to internal factors. For example, a internal factor can be the individual skills of the scientists and their ability to interact better with some rather than others. Moreover, externalities independent of the consortia formed may also stochastically impact the quality of the result. In the literature, some works proposed to relax these hypotheses by considering repeated stochastic coalitional games. The agents play the same game – and thus form coalitions – repeatedly. They observe the payoff they obtain and use this information to estimate the value of each coalition at the next time step. However, in those works agents use greedy strategies: they form the coalitions they estimate the best. We can thus wonder if exploration-based strategies, which are successful in other contexts, may be of interest in the coalition formation domain. We then propose in this article a high-level repeated stochastic coalition formation model, and we experimentally assess the performance of several strategies compared to a greedy strategy. We finally highlight that, due to the structure of the coalitional games, the greedy strategy remains the best. This article is structured as follows. In Sect. 2, we present the basic notions related to coalitional games, then we review some works both on stochastic characteristic functions and repeated coalitional games. In Sect. 3, we describe our repeated stochastic coalitional game model, and detail how agents learn the characteristic function, and the different strategies they can use. Finally, Sect. 4 is devoted to evaluate these strategies.

2   State of the Art

We present here the basic notions about coalitional games [13], repeated coalitional games [1–3] as well as stochasticity in coalitional games [3,5,9].

2.1   Coalition Formation

In a coalition game, a set of agents is partitioned into separate *coalitions* which produce an amount of *utility*. Such partition is called a *coalition structure*.

Definition 1 (Coalitional game). *A game is a tuple* $\mathcal{G} = \langle N, v \rangle$ *where:*

- $N = \{a_1, \ldots, a_n\}$ *is a set of agents,*
- $v : 2^N \to \mathbb{R}$ *is a characteristic function that assigns a real value to each coalition, called the coalition utility and denoted* $v(C_k)$ *where* $C_k \subseteq N$.

We consider in this article coalitional games with *transferable utility*, i.e. where agents must decide how to distribute the coalition utility among its members [7]. A *solution* to such a game is defined as follows.

Definition 2 (Solution). *A solution to* $\mathcal{G}$ *is a tuple* $S_{\mathcal{G}} = \langle \mathcal{C}, \boldsymbol{x} \rangle$ *where:*

- $\mathcal{C}$ is a coalition structure of N,
- $\boldsymbol{x} = \{x_1, \ldots, x_n\}$ is a payoff vector where $x_i \geq 0$ is the payoff of agent a_i.

As agents are selfish, when a solution is proposed, all of them must accept it, i.e. that they must not wish to form or join another coalition where they could earn more. This is why we are interested in solutions which belong to a *solution concept*. A solution concept is the set of solutions that respect a certain notion of stability. While many concepts have been proposed in the literature such as the nucleolus or the kernel [4], we focus in this article on the concept of core and its generalization, the ϵ-*core* [12,16]. The core is the set of solutions $\langle \mathcal{C}, \boldsymbol{x} \rangle$ for which no other coalition that could be formed produces a sum of gains greater than that which agents obtain with $\boldsymbol{x}$. The ϵ-core allows agents to make a concession, i.e. agree to reduce their gain by ϵ, in order to form a stable coalition structure.

Definition 3 (ϵ-core). *A solution $(\mathcal{C}, \boldsymbol{x})$ belongs to the ϵ-core if and only if:*

$$\forall C \subseteq N, x(C) \geq v(C) - \epsilon \ with \ x(C) = \sum_{i \in C} x_i$$

The ϵ-core allows to define the *least core*, which contains all ϵ-core solutions for the smallest value of ϵ that make the solution concept non-empty.

2.2 Stochastic Characteristic Functions

In the literature, some works have proposed stochastic coalitional games [3,5, 6,9]. The nature of uncertainty in these models differs. For instance, Ieong and Shoham proposed a probability distribution on worlds representing coalitional games, each of them having a deterministic characteristic function [9]. Chalkiadakis and Boutilier considered a deterministic characteristic function modeled in a stochastic environment with partially observable Markovian decision processes [3]. Agents have beliefs about capabilities of other agents and the same coalition structure can lead to different world states. Charnes and Granot simply considered that the value of a coalition is a random variable [5,6]. The characteristic function is then rewritten as $v : 2^N \to \mathcal{X}_{2^N}$. Thus, when a coalition is formed, the utility produced is determined by the random variable, that follows a normal distribution. In this model, they compute their payoff vectors by associating to each agent in a coalition an equal part of the expectation of the random variable associated to the coalition. In this article, we position ourselves in the continuity of the Charnes and Granot's work. Indeed, their model allows us to deal with the heterogeneity of stochasticity (both internal and external factors as cited in Sect. 1) through the use of a single random variable.

2.3 Repeated Coalitional Games

If we also relax the hypothesis of perfect knowledge of the characteristic function, whether it is stochastic or not, it becomes interesting to move on to a repeated game [1–3,10]. For instance, Konishi and Debraj [10] have shown that repeated coalition formation processes converge towards equilibria if agents sequentially form Pareto-efficient coalition structures. Moreover, repeated coalitional games allow to observe the utilities when coalitions are formed in order to learn an estimation of the characteristic function. Agents can then use this estimation, and can be able to find an optimal stable solution over time. Models in the literature essentially differ on the nature of what the agents learn and how they estimate the coalitions. For instance, Blankenburg *et al.* [2] learn a reliability value for each agent, which impact the utility of coalitions. In Chalkiadakis and Boutilier [3], agents learn both the others' skills and a stochastic transition between a given coalition structure and the states it may reach (and therefore a payoff). In all those works, agents use a greedy strategy: they form the coalition structure which is estimated the best at each time step. As in other sequential decision-making problems it has been demonstrated that there is an interest to explore, i.e. making *a priori* sub-optimal decision in order to acquire knowledge [8,11], we study in this article if exploration-based strategies are efficient in the context of coalition formation.

3   A General Model of Repeated Stochastic Coalitional Game

First of all, let us define a model of repeated stochastic coalitional game.

3.1   Game and Solution

Definition 4 (Repeated stochastic coalitional game). *Let* $\mathcal{G} = \langle N, \mathbb{T}, v \rangle$ *be a repeated stochastic coalitional game (RSCG) where:*

- $N = \{a_1 \ldots a_n\}$ *is a set of agents,*
- $\mathbb{T} \subset \mathbb{N}^+$ *is a set of distinct time steps,*
- $v : 2^N \rightarrow \mathcal{X}^{2^N}$ *is a characteristic function that associates a random variable to each coalition. For a given coalition* $C \subseteq 2^N$*, we note* $v(C) = \mathcal{X}^C$*. This characteristic function is unknown to the agents.*

At each time step, agents in N have to decide on a solution to the game, despite the fact that they do not know the characteristic function v *a priori*. A solution is, like in a deterministic context, a tuple made of a coalition structure and a payoff vector. Here, the payoff is an *ex ante* payoff, i.e. the estimated payoff based on what the agents know about v.

Definition 5 (Solution to a RSCG). *A solution* S^t *at the time step* $t \in \mathbb{T}$ *to a RSCG* $\mathcal{G}$ *is a tuple* $S^t = (\mathcal{C}^t, \boldsymbol{x}^t)$ *such as:*

- $\mathcal{C}^t$ *is a coalition structure (disjointed partition) of* N*,*
- $\boldsymbol{x}^t = \{x_1^t, \ldots, x_n^t\}$ *is a payoff vector such as* $x_i^t \geq 0$ *is the gain of the agent* a_i *calculated according to the estimated value of the coalition of which he is a part in the structure* $\mathcal{C}^t$*.*

3.2   Coalition Formation Process

We consider the following process:

1. Agents are initialized with an *a priori* knowledge about the game, i.e. an estimation of the characteristic function, which may reflect either ignorance, or an expert-knowledge (e.g. larger coalitions produce a higher value);
2. Agents form a coalition structure according to a given strategy based on their current knowledge of the characteristic function (see Sect. 3.4);
3. Agents observe the payoff they obtain by forming the structure, and they update their knowledge of the characteristic function (see Sect. 3.3). We assumed that all agents observe the payoff produced by each coalition: hence they have the same knowledge, and consequently the same estimation;
4. The process is repeated from step 2.

3.3   Estimating the Characteristic Function

As we assume the *ex-post* payoffs are observed by all the agents, we denote by X_t^C the observation of the payoff of coalition C at the time step t.

Definition 6 (Observations). *Let $\mathcal{O}_t = \{(C, t', X_{t'}^C)) : C \subseteq 2^N, t' \in \mathbb{T}, t' < t\}$ be a set of observations at time step t corresponding to the set of the coalitions formed at each time step before t and their ex-post payoffs. Knowing a solution S^t of a RSCG at time step t, $\mathcal{O}_{t+1} = \mathcal{O}_t \cup \{(C, t, X_t^C)) : \forall C \in \mathcal{C}^t\}$.*

Thereafter, let us note $\mathcal{O}_t(C)$ the set of observations at time step t associated with the coalition $C \subseteq 2^N$. Then the agents can use different methods to estimate the future payoff, e.g. tabular representation, bayesian network, or neural network. In order to remain general, we simply consider that the agents know a function that produces an estimation according to the observations. Such function has to be instanciated (see experiments in Sect. 4).

Definition 7 (Payoff estimation). *Let $\mathbb{E}(C, t)$ be the payoff estimation of a coalition $C \subseteq 2^N$ at time step $t \in \mathbb{T}$.*

3.4   Decision Strategies

Once the agents have estimated the characteristic function, they need to decide which coalitions to form, according to a given strategy that take exploration into account. We consider two kinds of strategies: ϵ-greedy strategies (also known as semi-uniform strategies) and contextual strategies. Adapted in the context of coalition formation, ϵ-greedy strategies are strategies where agents choose the best coalition structure according to the least core solution concept with a given probability, or choose a random coalition structure otherwise.

Definition 8 (ϵ-greedy strategy). *The ϵ-greedy strategy selects a solution from the least core solution concept with a probability of ϵ, or a solution drawn uniformly at random among all solutions otherwise.*

Obviously, when ϵ is set to 1, the ϵ-greedy strategy becomes a simple greedy strategy as considered in the literature [1–3,10]. When ϵ is set to 0, the agents choose their coalition structure uniformly at random among all coalition structures. Contextual strategies are strategies where agents value the information they can gain as they value a payoff. We consider firstly a strategy, we called UCB-core strategy, inspired from UCB strategies in multi-armed bandits problem [8,11]. Information value is a bias defined as follows.

Definition 9 (Exploration bias). *Let* $\gamma(C,t) : 2^N \mapsto \mathbb{R}$ *a bias such as:*

$$\gamma(C,t) = \sqrt{\frac{2.\log(|\mathcal{O}_t|+1)}{|\mathcal{O}_t(C)|+1}}$$

We now adapt the UCB-strategy in the context of coalition formation. To this end, we consider a variant of the ϵ-core solution concept, called the UCB-core.

Definition 10 (UCB-core). *A solution* $S^t = (\mathcal{C}^t, \boldsymbol{x}^t)$ *belongs to the UCB-core solution concept if, and only if:*

$$\forall C \in N, x^t(C) + \Gamma(C,t) \geq \mathbb{E}(C,t) - \epsilon + \gamma(C,t),$$

with:

$$x^t(C) = \sum_{a_i \in C} x_i^t \quad and \quad \Gamma(C,t) = \sum_{a_i \in C} \frac{\gamma(C_{a_i},t)}{|C_{a_i}|},$$

where C_{a_i} *is the coalition of* a_i *in* $\mathcal{C}^t$

The previous definition means a coalition structure is stable if, and only if, there is no coalition such that its payoff plus its exploration bias is higher than what its members earn currently in the coalition structure, knowing the value given by the exploration bias is equally shared between agents. Hence,

Definition 11 (UCB-core strategy). *The* UCB-core strategy *selects a solution uniformly at random from the non-empty UCB-core solution concept with the smallest* ϵ.

The UCB-core strategy may allow solutions that are irrational for some agents, i.e. solutions where the payoff of at least one agent is lesser than the payoff he would have received alone. As rationality is an important concept in coalition formation, we propose another contextual strategy that preserves the rationality, called the δ-core strategy. The idea is to allow agents to sacrifice a part of their surplus, i.e. the part of the payoff they received in excess of their singleton coalition, proportional to the exploration biais.

Definition 12 (Surplus). *Let* $\Omega^t(a_i, S^t)$ *be the surplus of the agent* a_i *for a given solution* S^t *at time step* $t \in \mathbb{T}$. *This surplus is computed as*

$$\Omega^t(a_i, S^t) = x_i^t - \mathbb{E}(C,t)$$

where $C = \{a_i\}$, *i.e. the singleton coalition of the agent* a_i. *If the surplus is negative, it means that the given solution is* irrational *for agent* i, *so it will never be stable.*

Secondly, let us consider a normalized exploration bias.

Definition 13 (Normalized exploration bias)

$$\zeta(C,t) = \frac{\gamma(C,t)}{\max_{\forall C' \subseteq 2^N} (\gamma(C',t))}$$

Once the normalization of exploration factors done, agents can compute how much of their surplus they accept to not gain. Thus, the payoff an agent can sacrifice is given by:

Definition 14 (Sacrificable payoff). *The* sacrificable payoff *for a agent a_i and a given solution S^t at time step t is given by $\delta^t(a_i, S^t) = \Omega^t(a_i, S^t) \times \zeta(C,t)$ where C is the coalition of a_i in S^t.*

We can now define the δ-core solution concept. In this solution concept, a coalition structure is stable if there are no coalitions – that are not part of the structure – whose estimated payoff, minus the payoff that agents accept not to earn to form the structure, is greater than the estimated payoff the agents obtain with the structure.

Definition 15 (δ-core). *The solution $S^t = (C^t, \boldsymbol{x}^t)$ belongs to the δ-core solution concept if, and only if:*

$$\forall C \in N, x^t(C) \geq \mathbb{E}(C,t) - \mathfrak{c} - \Delta^t(C),$$

where:

$$x^t(C) = \sum_{a_i \in C} x_i^t \quad and \quad \Delta^t(C) = \sum_{a_i \in C} \delta^t(a_i, S^t)$$

Hence obviously,

Definition 16 (δ-core strategy). *The δ-core strategy selects a solution uniformly at random from the δ-core solution concept.*

4 Experimentations

To compare the different strategies given above, we generate random games where agents play repeatedly and observe the evolution of the chosen solutions.

4.1 Experimental Protocol

We generate games with 5, 6 and 7 agents, thus for 52, 203, 877 possible coalition structures respectively. The stochastic characteristic functions of those games are generated with normal distributions whose their μ parameter is drawn from the normal, uniform and NDCS model proposed in [14,15]. Hence for each coalition $C \subseteq N$, the μ parameter is $|C| \times \mathcal{N}(1, 0.1)$ for normal models, $|C| \times \mathcal{U}(0, 1)$ for uniform models and $\mathcal{N}(|C|, \sqrt{|C|})$ for NDCS models. The variance σ associated to each coalition is given by $\sigma = \mathcal{U}(0, \frac{\mu}{2})$. As the maximal variance is related to μ and as μ is higher with large coalitions, the larger a coalition, the higher its variance may be.

We now need to instantiate the payoff estimation function (Definition 7). In order to be general and abstract, we use in the experiments a neural network with two hidden layers. Each layer is a dense layer with a ELU activation function. The input layer represents coalitions with one neuron dedicated to each agents: input of 1 for his presence in the coalition, 0 otherwise. The output layer consists in a single neuron that produces a real value. Such neural network is able to learn non-linear functions. Here, we use stochastic gradient descent with adaptive moment estimation to train the network. The loss function is the mean square error. It is important to notice that this network is not trained offline before playing the repeated game, but trained at the runtime. Each time the agents observe a payoff (see the process described in Sect. 3.2), the network is trained with a set of examples (coalition, payoff).

For each kind of model (normal, uniform or NDCS) we perform 1000 runs with different characteristic functions each time (but their type does not change) where the agents play over 100 time steps. We made two experiments: the first one compares the performances of the ϵ-greedy strategy when ϵ varies; the second one highlights the performances of the UCB-core and δ-core strategies compared to the greedy and the random strategy.

4.2   Performance Measure

In order to evaluate our model, we measure both the efficiency of the decisions taken (seen as the optimality of the stable solutions found) over time, and the accuracy of the estimated characteristic function. The efficiency is measured from the *instant regret* at step t, which is the sum of the differences between the maximum social welfare (the maximum sum of the real expected utilities of the coalition structures) and the sum of the actual expected utilities of the coalitions of the structure formed at time step t. Formally, instant regret is defined as:

Definition 17 (Instant regret). *At one time step t, let $S^* = (\mathcal{C}^*, \boldsymbol{x}^*)$ be the optimal solution, the instant regret at this time step, noted R^t, is defined by:*

$$R^t = \sum_{C^* \in \mathcal{C}^*} \mu_{C^*} - \sum_{C \in \mathcal{C}^t} \mu_C$$

As instant regret can oscillate due to stochasticity, we consider in the sequel the *cumulative regret*, i.e. the sum of instant regrets from the beginning of an experiment to a given time step. The accuracy of the estimated characteristic functions is given by the *mean absolute error* (MAE) measure over the coalitions.

Definition 18 (Mean absolute error). *The distance D^t_{MAE} between two characteristic functions at time step t is defined by:*

$$D^t_{MAE} = \frac{\sum_{C \in 2^N} |\hat{v}(C) - v(C)|}{|2^N|}$$

4.3   Results

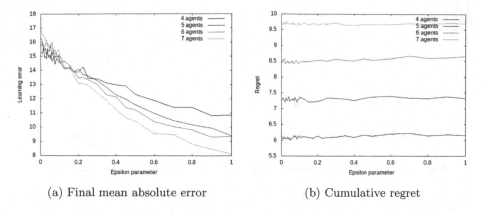

(a) Final mean absolute error   (b) Cumulative regret

Fig. 1. Results for the ϵ-greedy strategy on normal characteristic functions

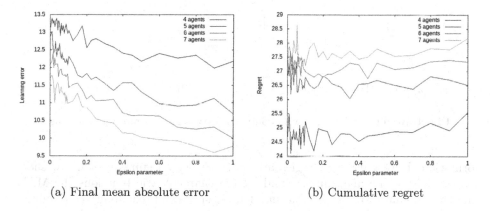

(a) Final mean absolute error   (b) Cumulative regret

Fig. 2. Results for the ϵ-greedy strategy on uniform characteristic functions

Figures 1, 2 and 3 show respectively for normal, uniform and NDCS characteristic functions the MAE and regret at the end of the experiment for the ϵ-greedy strategy, when ϵ vary between 0 and 1, and when the number of agents increase. The oscillations when ϵ is low are due to the higher number of data points. Independently of the number of agents, the learning error decreases when ϵ increases, i.e. when going from a greedy strategy to a random exploration. However, the regret remains the same or increases when ϵ increases. Thus, while semi-uniform exploration is interesting to better estimate the characteristic function as expected, it is helpless to decrease the regret in the context of coalition

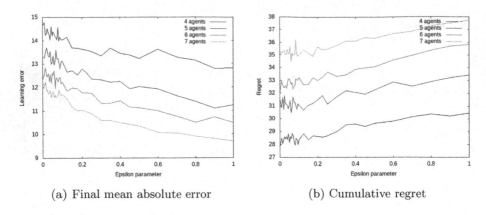

(a) Final mean absolute error   (b) Cumulative regret

Fig. 3. Results for the ϵ-greedy strategy on NDCS characteristic functions

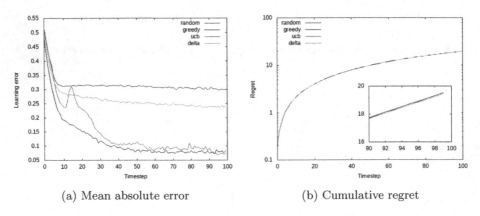

(a) Mean absolute error   (b) Cumulative regret

Fig. 4. Results for 7 agents with contextual strategies on normal functions

formation. Pure greedy strategies are still the best. Figures 4, 5 and 6 show respectively for normal, uniform and NDCS characteristic functions the MAE and the cumulative regret for 7 agents. Due to space and readability constraints, we do not give the figures for 5 and 6 agents, but in all experiments, they present the same shapes. Concerning the MAE, as expected, the random strategy learns the best, while the greedy strategy learns the worse. UCB-core strategy is very efficient and close to the random strategy. δ-core strategy is worse but better than the greedy strategy. Concerning the cumulative regret, we can see its convergence. As the curve as close to each other, we provide a zoom on the final steps. For the NDCS model, the greedy strategy remains the best, followed by UCB-core strategy, δ-core strategy (and finally random strategy). Greedy strategy remains the best for uniform models. In the particular case of normal models, all strategies tend to be confounded.

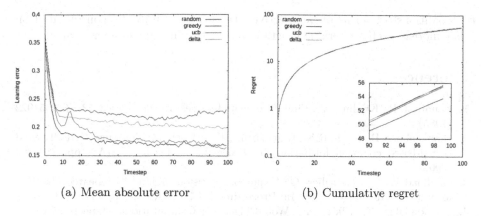

(a) Mean absolute error   (b) Cumulative regret

Fig. 5. Results for 7 agents with contextual strategies on uniform functions

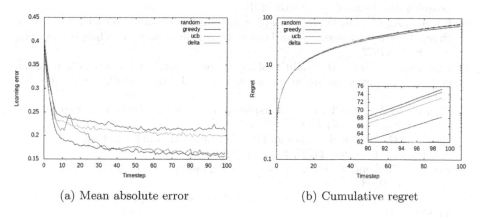

(a) Mean absolute error   (b) Cumulative regret

Fig. 6. Results for 7 agents with contextual strategies on NDCS functions

5 Conclusion

We studied in this article repeated stochastic coalitional games, which relax hypothesis which may be too strong for real work application. In such models, agents use greedy strategies, i.e. they form at each time step the best coalition structure they estimate, form the coalitions, and update their knowledge accordingly. However, are exploration-based strategies, known to be efficient in other contexts, interesting for such games? To answer this question, we proposed a high-level model of repeated coalitional games, and experiment several strategies: ϵ-greedy strategy, UCB-core strategy and δ-core strategy. The results show that, as expected exploration-based strategies allows to better estimate the characteristic function. However, the greedy strategy remains the best for repeated coalition formation. Indeed, learning the precise value of each coalition independently is not useful in coalition formation as long as the agents correctly rank the coalitions. In terms of perspectives, these results must be consolidated on other models of characteristic function, and with a higher number of agents.

References

1. Benoit, J.-P., Krishna, V.: Finitely repeated games. Econometrica **53**(4), 905–922 (1985)
2. Blankenburg, B., Dash, R.K., Ramchurn, S.D., Klusch, M., Jennings, N.R.: Trusted kernel-based coalition formation. In: Proceedings of 4th AAMAS, pp. 989–996 (2005)
3. Chalkiadakis, G., Boutilier, C.: Sequential decision making in repeated coalition formation under uncertainty. In: Proceedings of 7th AAMAS, pp. 347–354 (2008)
4. Chalkiadakis, G., Elkind, E., Wooldridge, M.: Computational Aspects of Cooperative Game Theory. Synthesis Lectures on Artificial Intelligence and Machine Learning, vol. 5, no. 6, pp. 1–168 (2011)
5. Charnes, A., Granot, D.: Prior solutions: extensions of convex nucleus solutions to chance-constrained games. Texas University, Austin Center for Cybernetic Studies, no. CS-118 (1973)
6. Charnes, A., Granot, D.: Coalitional and chance-constrained solutions to n-person games. I: the prior satisficing nucleolus. SIAM J. Appl. Math. **31**(2), 358–367 (1976)
7. Debraj, R.: A Game-Theoretic Perspective on Coalition Formation. Oxford University Press, Oxford (2007)
8. Gittins, J.C.: Bandit processes and dynamic allocation indices. J. Roy. Stat. Soc. Ser. B Stat. Methodol. **41**(2), 148–164 (1979)
9. Ieong, S., Shoham, Y.: Bayesian coalitional games. In: Proceedings of 23rd AAAI, pp. 95–100 (2008)
10. Konishi, H., Debraj, R.: Coalition formation as a dynamic process. J. Econ. Theory **110**(1), 1–41 (2003)
11. Mahajan, A., Teneketzis, D.: Multi-armed bandit problems. In: Hero, A.O., Castañón, D.A., Cochran, D., Kastella, K. (eds.) Foundations and Applications of Sensor Management, pp. 121–151. Springer, Boston (2008). https://doi.org/10.1007/978-0-387-49819-5_6
12. Mochaourab, R., Jorswieck, E.: Coalitional games in MISO interference channels: epsilon-core and coalition structure stable set. IEEE Trans. Sig. Process. **62**(24), 6507–6520 (2014)
13. Morgenstern, O., von Neumann, J.: Theory of Games and Economic Behavior. Princeton University Press, Princeton (1953)
14. Rahwan, T., Michalak, T., Wooldridge, M., Jennings, N.R.: Anytime coalition structure generation in multi-agent systems with positive or negative externalities. AI **186**, 95–122 (2012)
15. Rahwan, T., Ramchurn, S.D., Giovannucci, A., Jennings, N.R.: An anytime algorithm for optimal coalition structure generation. JAIR **34**, 521–556 (2009)
16. Shapley, L.S., Shubik, M.: Quasi-cores in a monetary economy with non-convex preferences. Econometrica **34**(4), 805–827 (1966)

Typologies of Persuasive Strategies and Content: A Formalization Using Argumentation

Esteban Guerrero$^{(\boxtimes)}$ (iD) and Helena Lindgren (iD)

Department of Computing Science, Umeå University, Umeå, Sweden
{esteban,helena}@cs.umu.se

Abstract. *Persuasion* is an active research topic in artificial intelligence (AI), human-computer interaction (HCI), and social sciences. When persuasive technology has been designed, some HCI guidelines have commonly used disregarding the current AI state of the art, for example, ignoring *autonomy* and *proactive* AI behavior. In this paper, a systematic review of HCI persuasive strategies and their corresponding content is *mapped* to a formal AI approach using argumentation theory. We also present experimental results using as context a mobile application for behavior change in the Swedish context.

Keywords: Persuasive technology · Argumentation theory · Persuasive dialogue · Persuasive strategies

1 Introduction

The study of *persuasion* remains vital for contemporary social psychology and philosophy, impacting other research areas such as artificial intelligence (AI). In social psychology, different models of a persuasion process have been proposed (*e.g.* [4,18]), in which a *receiver* is able and properly motivated, s/he will elaborate, or systematically analyze, a *persuasive message*. If the message is well reasoned, data-based, and logical (*i.e.*, strong), it will persuade; if it is not, it will fail [5]. In general, this persuasion process has been adapted and used in AI literature to model *dialogues* [12], *interfaces* [15], and for serious games, the so-called *gamification* approaches [13]. General guidelines for designing these persuasive systems have been proposed from the human-computer interaction (HCI) perspective (*e.g.* PSD framework [17], and Nemery's work [15]). However, those guidelines although suitable for defining *what* a persuasive system should provide (*e.g.* suggestions, reminders, etc.), disregard progress in the area of *software agents* of AI, when defining the *how* such content (*e.g.* persuasive messages) should be generated and provided by the software to an individual.

Conversely, *computational persuasion* [12] as it is defined in formal approaches of *argumentation* in AI, diverges from those HCI guidelines for persuasive systems, due to technical capabilities or ethical barriers that prevent

F. Dignum et al. (Eds.): PAAMS 2021, LNAI 12946, pp. 101–113, 2021.
https://doi.org/10.1007/978-3-030-85739-4_9

fully encompassing social science perspectives regarding persuasive mechanisms. The impact of disregarding AI-based persuasion capabilities has led to a perception that some AI-methods for engagement are limited [20], and that human-AI interaction may trigger negative emotional reactions [6], consequences of computational mechanisms incapable of select a suitable persuasive strategy and content.

In this paper, we proposed a mapping between well-established human-AI interaction design guidelines and formal methods of computational persuasion with the aim of design general mechanisms for tailoring persuasive strategies and content. We focus on a gamification perspective of persuasion given its current technological raising and applicability. This mapping serves as a general ground for AI practitioners when persuasive technology is designed, and it represents a revision of those aforementioned HCI guidelines by integrating a formal AI perspective. Concretely, three contributions are presented: 1) a typology of persuasive strategies and content; 2) a mapping between those typologies and formal persuasive dialogue games; and 3) a novel algorithm for strategy and content selection that can be used in persuasive technology. We exemplify our framework using the design of an *intelligent coaching system* (as a persuasive technology) for sustainable behavior change in northern Sweden [16].

2   Methodology

This paper followed a three-arm methodological approach (see Fig. 1). In the following, we present methods used in the three phases.

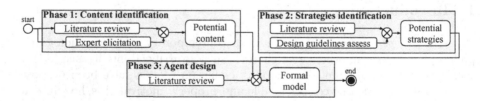

Fig. 1. Methodological process: Phase 1) content identification, Phase 2) strategies identification, and Phase 3) agent design.

2.1   Persuasive Content and Strategies (Phases 1 and 2)

Identification of general features of persuasive or coaching systems was performed using two data collection mechanisms: 1) a *systematic literature review* (SLR), aiming at identify features (or content) used in persuasive/coaching systems within the health-care literature; and 2) *expert elicitation process* in which a multidisciplinary group of researchers identified features of those systems focused on specific scientific areas. We describe the data collection procedure in the following.

Literature Review on Features Identification

The questions that the SLR was aiming to solve were: Q1: *What features w.r.t. content a persuasive or coaching system has?* and Q2: *What strategies w.r.t. behavior of the software presenting content a persuasive or coaching system has?*

Details of the SLR protocol and procedure can be found in an external document due to limited space http://s.cs.umu.se/lare8b. As a result, 36 from 329 potential papers were selected using a set of assessment criteria to evaluate the quality of every paper.

Expert Elicitation

The expert elicitation process was conducted as follows: 1) eight researchers from seven different areas (physical activity and sedentary behaviour, ageing and disability, social work, social welfare, nutrition, psychology and governance, and health economics) volunteered to participate in the study; 2) five questions directed a one-hour interview: a) *What should be the main goal for the digital coach?* b) *What are the main functionalities of the system?* c) *How the visual aspect of the main functionality would be?* d) *What direct benefits a user should receive from the digital coach use?* e) *What direct risks could the user have when using the digital coach?* 3) *Grounded theory* [3] was used. We use RQDA: Qualitative Data Analysis[1] package with RStudio version 3.6.3 to make the codes, code categories, and the analysis of cases of every interview. Details of the expert elicitation process can be found in an external document http://s.cs.umu.se/c6yw7v.

2.2   Agent Design Background (Phase 3)

In this paper, we make the following design assumptions of our agents (Ag): 1) an Ag has an independent knowledge base Σ, potentially inconsistent and containing formulas of a propositional language $\mathcal{L}$. 2) Formal argumentation is used in the Ag's decision-making process, and in the communication process (argument-based dialogue) that has a persuasive nature, between a persuadee (Ag_c) and a persuader (Ag_p). We use a propositional logic with connectives: $\wedge, \leftarrow, \neg, \top$; the consequence operator: $\leftarrow$ is non monotonic.

Formal Argumentation Reasoning

An *argument* is a tuple $Arg = \langle support, conclusion \rangle$, fulfilling next conditions: 1) $supp \subseteq \Sigma$; 2) $supp$ is consistent; 3) $supp \vdash conc$ and 4) $\nexists supp' \subset supp$ such that $supp' \vdash conc$. $supp$ and $conc$ are usually called the *support* and *conclusion* of an argument. All the arguments built from Σ are noted as $\mathcal{A}$. Two arguments may have logically *conflicting* information (henceforth Conflicts $\mathcal{C}$), *e.g.* $Arg_1, Arg_2 \in \mathcal{A}$, Arg_1 has a conflict type *undercut* with Arg_2 iff. $\exists conc \in$ Supp(Arg_2) | $conc \equiv \neg$Conc(Arg_1). A graph structure containing all the arguments and conflicts is called an *argumentation system* $AS = (\mathcal{A}, \mathcal{C})$. *Argumentation semantics* are patterns of selection for obtaining *winner* arguments [8], we

---

[1] http://rqda.r-forge.r-project.org.

this concept using a handy function $\mathsf{SEM}(AS) = \{\{Arg_1, \ldots, Arg_i\}\}$ that has as output sets of non-conflicting arguments called *extensions*.

Argumentation-Based Dialogue. A *dialogue* ($\mathcal{D}$) has two agents, both have an argument-based decision-making process and they communicate through a *moves*-based *protocol*. Agents have a shared knowledge base called *commitment store* (CS) that is updated at every agent's move. A move in $\mathcal{D}$ contains: 1) a *speech act* ($sa \in SA$) that is a function defining the move intention; 2) a move *content* (ct); and 3) the targeted or opponent agent towards is directed the speech act and the content. Formally, a move is a tuple $m = \langle sa, ct, Ag_i \rangle$, that will be defined in the following sections. We use the following speech acts *assert, accept, challenge, question, ignore* and *reject*. Then, agents may have different *attitudes* towards propositional speech-acts from other agents: 1) assertion attitude: an agent is confident if it can assert any proposition p for which it can build an argument $\langle S, p \rangle$, or it is thoughtful if asserts any proposition p for which it can build an *acceptable* argument $\langle S, p \rangle$. 2) Acceptance attitudes: an agent is credulous if it accepts any proposition p that is backed by an argument, or it is skeptical if accepts any proposition p if there is an *acceptable* argument $\langle S, p \rangle$. 3) Challenging attitudes: an agent is curious if it challenges or questions any proposition p that has an argument, or it is inquisitive if it challenges or questions proposition p backed by an acceptable argument $\langle S, p \rangle$. *ignore* and *reject* speech acts do not change CS, ending the dialogue as outcome.

3   Results

This section presents two main results of the systematic process to find *what* content and *how* such content should be presented (strategies) to an individual by an agent-based coaching or persuasive system, that we call *intelligent coaching system*.

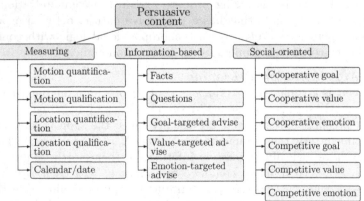

Taxonomy 1: Taxonomy of gamification content

3.1 Persuasive Content Typology and Strategies

Content Typology. The elicitation process with multidisciplinary experts and our systematic literature review reveled three types of content that is preferred and expected by experts, and well-known used in the state of the art: 1) *measuring and monitoring* content; 2) *information-based* content; and 3) *social-oriented* content. In this taxonomy of content (Taxonomy 1), different general types were found for example: *motion* type relates to complex activities or simple motion logs or data tracking, *location* relates to context or specific spatial information, *facts* regard to information-based content presented in different modalities (text, audio, visual, haptic, etc.), and *goal-targeted advises* or *value-targeted advises* or *emotion-targeted advises* relate to information-based content integrating a goal or a value or an emotion to stimulate another individual (or agent in general)). For lack of space, we do not provide the full list of papers linked to every branch of the taxonomy.

Persuasive Strategies Typology. Our systematic review on persuasive strategies in gamification, revealed the existence of nine main types of strategies commonly used in persuasive and coaching systems, as is presented in Taxonomy 2. We mapped these gamification strategies with three key software *agency* characteristics: *proactiveness*, *reactiveness* and *social awareness* [23]. From a software agent perspective, a *reactive* strategy are those that generate an *output after* the execution of an action by another agent (*e.g.* an individual). A proactive strategy refers to action-based outputs that are not-preceded by other agent's action; and a social behavior is any output where collective relations information regarding cooperation and competition is shared. For a lack of space we do not add further examples neither references, we hope to provide these additional material in the future.

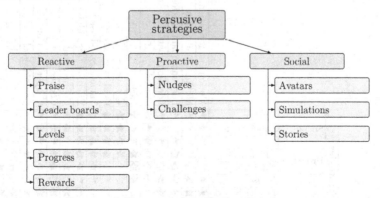

Taxonomy 2: Taxonomy of gamification strategies

Content and Strategies Compatibility

Not all the content can be used in different gamification strategies [13], therefore we propose a set of dynamic constraints that the persuader agent should use during the strategy-protocol-content selection as follows.

3.2   Formal Framework for Content and Strategy Selection

This section introduces two computational mechanisms for selecting content and strategies (*w.r.t.* Taxonomy 1 and Taxonomy 2) using formal argumentation. We simplify our characterization in order to introduce related results.

Decision-Making Algorithm for Content Selection. We present a decision-making algorithm allowing an agent select the most *aligned* type of content depending on the persuadee agent status.

An *opponent agent, i.e.* the agent towards persuasive content is directed (a persuadee) is modeled as a tuple $Ag_c = \langle S, Act, G, V, E, \preceq^* \rangle$, where $S, Act, G, V, E \subseteq \Sigma$, G, V, E are mental states representing *beliefs*, *values* and *emotions* respectively, extending the Belief-Desire-Intention (BDI) model [2] by following recent work on the *attitudinal theory of emotions* [7] and the value orientations theory [21]. This extension allows us to model a *human agent* with capabilities closer to a real individual, endowing a software agent with possibilities to perceive and take decisions given potential emotions and values of a person. The rationale for such a design is that the identification of belief, desires, and intentions (included emotions and values) is useful when the system must communicate with humans [19]. The decision-making process that we propose (see Algorithm 1) takes as *input* observations of the world in terms of rule-based facts, and the agents model, and it returns as *output* an ordered set of hypotheses about the current state of the persuadee agent, from which the persuader may take a preferred explanation. For example generating sets of goal hypotheses such as:

Table 1. Content-strategies compatibility

		Motion quantification	Motion qualification	Location quantification	Location quantification	Calendar/date	Facts	Questions	Goal-targ. advise	Value-targ. advise	Emotion-targ. advise	Cooper. goal	Cooper. value	Cooper. emotion	Compet. goal	Compet. value	Compet. emotion
		Measuring					Information					Social					
Social	Avatar	⚑	⚑	⚑	⚑	★	★	★	★	★	★	⚑	⚑	⚑	⚑	⚑	⚑
Social	Simulations	⚑	⚑	⚑	⚑	⚑	★	★	★	★	★	★	★	★	★	★	★
Social	Stories	⚑	⚑	⚑	⚑	★	★	★	★	★	★	⚑	⚑	⚑	⚑	⚑	⚑
Proactive	Challenges	☆	☆	☆	☆	☆	★	★	★	★	★	★	★	★	★	★	★
Proactive	Nudges	☆	☆	☆	☆	☆	☆	☆	★	★	★	★	★	★	★	★	★
Reactive	Praise	★	★	★	★	★	★	☆	⚑	⚑	⚑	☆	☆	☆	☆	☆	☆
Reactive	Leader boards	★	★	★	★	★	☆	☆	⚑	⚑	⚑	★	★	★	★	★	★
Reactive	Levels	★	★	★	★	★	☆	☆	☆	☆	☆	☆	☆	☆	☆	☆	☆
Reactive	Progress	★	★	★	★	★	☆	☆	☆	☆	☆	⚑	⚑	⚑	⚑	⚑	⚑
Reactive	Rewards	★	★	★	★	☆	☆	☆	☆	☆	☆	☆	☆	☆	☆	☆	☆

★: complete compatibility.
⚑: partial compatibility.
☆: incompatibility.

$$h_{g1} = \langle\{\ \overbrace{S}^{\text{background}} \wedge \overbrace{\text{show}(goal\_oriented\_content) \wedge \text{"be healthy"} \wedge \overbrace{\text{amazement}}^{\text{emotion}}}^{\text{action}} \},$$

$$\underbrace{\overbrace{\text{"improve physical activity"}}^{\text{goal}}}_{\text{conclusion}}\rangle$$

Hypothesis h_{g1} intuitively says: *"in order to improve physical activity as goal, given that persuadee values to be healthy and is currently amazed, then it is necessary to show goal-oriented content"*. This algorithm is an extension of an argument-based practical reasoning mechanism [10], generating goal, emotion and value-oriented hypotheses.

Algorithm 1: Generation and selection of goal, value, emotion-oriented hypotheses

---

    Input : Agent framework $Ag' = \langle S, Act, G, V, E, \preceq^* \rangle$
    Output: Lattice of preferred non conflicting Hypotheses
1 Set GHypoth,VHypoth,EHypoth,Support, RelatedRules $= \emptyset$;
    // **Persuadee model update**
2 $G = $ UpdateAttitude $(G', \preceq^G, p(G))$;
3 $V = $ UpdateAttitude $(V', \preceq^V, p(V))$;
4 $E = $ UpdateAttitude $(E', \preceq^E, p(E))$

    // **Hypotheses generation**
5 **for** $\forall$ *conclusion* $\in$ G, V, E **do**
6      $S = $ ConnectedRules(*conclusion*);
7   RelatedRules $= 2^S$;
8   **for** *set* $\in$ RelatedRules **do**
9   **if** Support $\neq \perp$ **then**
10   Support $= $ min(Support) $\cup$ ASP(*set*);
11   GHypoth $= \cup$ GHypoth $= \langle$Support, *conclusion*$\rangle$;
           // *w.r.t.* **V,E, VHypoth or EHypoth respectively**
12   **end**
13   **end**
14 **end**
    // **Hypotheses selection**
15 Graph $= $ buildGraph(GHypoth, Conflicts)// **or VHypoth or EHypoth**
16 $P = \sum_{i \in \text{Graph}} p(i)$;
17 NonConflicting $= $ SEM(Graph)// **Argumentation semantics process**
18 Output $= \langle$Graph,$\preceq^*$,P$\rangle$ // $* \in \{G, V, E\}$

Algorithm 1 has three phases, a model update (lines 1–3), a hypotheses generation (lines 4–16), and a hypotheses selection (lines 17–18). The UpdateAttitude function, updates the G, V, E attitudes with their respective preferences. In the hypotheses generation (line 8), ASP() is an *answer set* solvers—function that generates *stable models* (see [11]). In line 15, *Conflicts* is a logical relation set that emerge from different hypotheses. buildGraph (in line 15) is a function creating a graph with the entire set of hypotheses $\mathcal{H}$ as nodes, and Conflicts as edges, and in line 16 SEM() is an argument-based pattern of selection where conflicting hypotheses are discarded [8]. Finally, the output of the algorithm is a ordered set of hypotheses that are selected to be used by the persuader agent during a dialogue exchange.

Our proposed strategies' classification $w.r.t$ the type of agency is based on the underlying assumption that the protocol selection depends on an *uncertainty level* of the persuadee's G, V, E. In other words, gamification strategies (and their respective protocols) for proactive or social behavior cannot be used when there are limited information (high uncertainty) about goals, values or emotions modeling the agent persuadee. Moreover, such uncertainty can be modeled as a *probabilistic distribution* representing an uncertainty degree to which parts of the hypotheses premises (*e.g.* G, V, E) are true, or *believed* to be true, more formally, a belief function on $U \subseteq \Sigma$ is a probabilistic function $p : \Sigma \rightarrow [0, 1]$ on Σ *iff* for each U: $p(U) = \sum_{i \in U} p(i)$ (see lines 2–4 in Algorithm 1). If we consider only *consistent* probabilistic distributions $\sum_{i \in U} p(i) = 1$, and

Example 1 (Generating value-oriented hypothetical actions). A persuader uses Algorithm 1 to establish the status of a persuadee, knowing that it has a preference to follow emotional cues (*i.e.* $\preceq^e$). Let P be a *program* capturing the persuadee behavior with following rules: $\{g1 \leftarrow S_1 \wedge v_1 \wedge e_1 \wedge act_1; g2 \leftarrow S_2 \wedge v_2 \wedge e_2 \wedge act_2; g3 \leftarrow S_3 \wedge v_3 \wedge e_3 \wedge act_3; act_1, act_2, act_3 \leftarrow \top; v_1, v_2, v_3 \leftarrow \top; e_1, e_2, e_3 \leftarrow \top; S_1, S_2, S_3 \leftarrow \top\}$. Where g_1 = "improve physical activity", g_2 = "stay at bed", g_3 = "keep social network", v_1 = "be healthy", v_2 = "seek pleasure", v_3 = "be social", e_1 = "amazement", e_2 = "grief", e_3 = "vigilance", act_1 = show(*goal_oriented_content*), act_2 = show(*value_oriented_content*), act_3 = show(*emotion_oriented_content*), S_1, S_2, S_3 are observations, considering that $g_1 \equiv \neg g_2$, and show is a propositional action to present content, *e.g.* "show goal-targeted advise" (see Taxonomy 1).

Using Algorithm 1, two non-contradictory sets of hypotheses are generated in line 16:

$$\left\{ \begin{cases} h_{g1} = \langle\{S_1 \wedge v_1 \wedge e_1 \wedge act_1\}, g_1\rangle, \\ h_{g2} = \langle\{S_2 \wedge v_2 \wedge e_2 \wedge act_2\}, g_2\rangle \end{cases} \right\}, \{h_{g3} = \langle\{S_3 \wedge v_3 \wedge e_3 \wedge act_3\}, g_3\rangle\}\right\} \quad (1)$$

Then, in line 17, persuader agent selects from the output lattices (1) one of them considering $\preceq^e$, for example prioritizing emotion e_1 = "amazement" than e_2 = "grief". Therefore, the agent will decide that h_{g1} explains the current state of the persuadee agent.

Gamification Strategies as Agent Dialogues

We map gamification persuasive strategies (Taxonomy 2) to dialogue protocols using formal argumentation. Argument-based dialogues are *strategic games* between two agents [22] (*e.g.* persuader and persuadee), then gamification strategies for persuasion are "translated" to moves' specifications. In this paper, dialogues have the following characteristics: 1) agents' communications is based on tactical *moves* within a *protocol*; 2) the persuader agent has a well-defined decision-making mechanism (see Sect. 3) and follows strict protocols; and 3) the persuadee agent (*e.g.* a person) may not follow some postulates of well-defined dialogues [1] and can brake protocols. In the following, we introduce our mapping starting with an analysis of protocols and moves, then we present how agents compute a dialogue *outcome*.

Protocol and Moves. We present three general move alternatives with the respective *atomic protocols* mapping gamification strategies and types of software agency. This mapping, as a key contribution of this paper, is presented in Table 2, in which we use $\bullet$ and $\odot$ to represent the starting and ending points of a protocols, $p, q \in S$ are propositions (*e.g.* $q =$ show($value\_oriented\_content$)), and every move is called by one or the other agent using an additional parameter to identify it (Ag_c or Ag_p), for example $assert$(show($value\_oriented\_content$), Ag_c)).

Protocols 1 to 7 in Table 2, are initiated by the persuader agent (Ag_p) directed to the persuadee (Ag_c). Conversely, $Protocol_8$ to $Protocol_{10}$ can be seen as a "reactive" moves that a persuader can take considering that the persuadee initiates the dialogue. This mapping requires formal requirements/constraints of the persuader's internal decision-making (Algorithm 1), such as the imposition that a persuader cannot ignore or reject an assert or quest move from the persuadee (see $Protocol_8$ to $Protocol_{10}$). We summarize these constraints as follows:

Proposition 1 (Constraints for gamification persuasive moves). *Let out be the output set from Algorithm 1 or any argument-based decision-making process that considers the next move of a persuader agent in a dialogue. Then, the following formal requirements need to hold: R1) For $Protocol_1$ to $Protocol_3$, Ag_c can reject or ignore quest moves; R2) For $Protocol_8$ to $Protocol_{10}$, out $\in$ SEM(AF) and out $\neq \emptyset$; and R3) For every assert, challenge or quest move, compatible content w.r.t the strategy should be selected (see Table 1).*

Table 2. Typology of gamification strategies used in intelligent persuasive/coaching systems

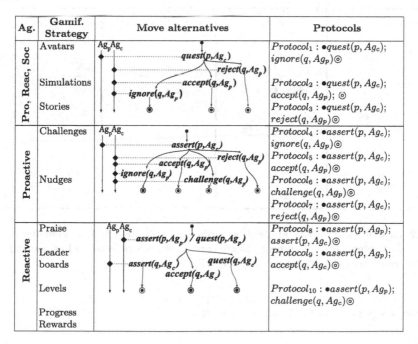

Ag.	Gamif. Strategy	Move alternatives	Protocols
Pro, Reac, Soc	Avatars		$Protocol_1 : \bullet quest(p, Ag_c)$; $ignore(q, Ag_p)\odot$
	Simulations		$Protocol_2 : \bullet quest(p, Ag_c)$; $accept(q, Ag_p); \odot$
	Stories		$Protocol_3 : \bullet quest(p, Ag_c)$; $reject(q, Ag_p)\odot$
Proactive	Challenges		$Protocol_4 : \bullet assert(p, Ag_c)$; $ignore(q, Ag_p)\odot$
	Nudges		$Protocol_5 : \bullet assert(p, Ag_c)$; $accept(q, Ag_p)\odot$
			$Protocol_6 : \bullet assert(p, Ag_c)$; $challenge(q, Ag_p)\odot$
			$Protocol_7 : \bullet assert(p, Ag_c)$; $reject(q, Ag_p)\odot$
Reactive	Praise		$Protocol_8 : \bullet assert(p, Ag_p)$; $assert(p, Ag_c)\odot$
	Leader boards		$Protocol_9 : \bullet assert(p, Ag_p)$; $accept(q, Ag_c)\odot$
	Levels		$Protocol_{10} : \bullet assert(p, Ag_p)$; $challenge(q, Ag_c)\odot$
	Progress Rewards		

Move Selection and Outcome. The persuader agent requires a fine-grained mechanism for protocol and move selection, then we use a utility function $\mathcal{Q}$: $2^{\mathcal{D}} \rightarrow \mathbb{R}$, which evaluates the attitude uncertainty P (line 16 in 1) in a dialogues $\mathcal{D}$. We compute such utility as an attitude achievement $w.r.t.$ goals, values and emotions. For example, a persuadee has as reference $goal_1$ and $goal_2$, then every hypothesis that a persuader obtains from Algorithm 1 will provide evidence of $goal_1$ and/or $goal_2$ achievement if those goals belong to out, formally: if $m = \langle sa, ct, Ag_c \rangle$ is a move generated by agent Ag_p targeting agent Ag_c, with $ct \in H \subseteq$ out $= SEM(AF)$, and $G^R, V^R, E^R \subseteq \mathcal{R}$ be the reference attitudes of Ag_c, then a dialogue outcome quantifier is given by: $\mathcal{Q} = \mathsf{Sim}(\arg \max_{G,V,E}(ct), \mathcal{R})$, considering a *similarity function* $\mathsf{Sim} : 2^{G,V,E} \times 2^{G,V,E} \rightarrow \mathbb{R}$.

3.3   Experimentation

We used our framework for selecting and re-ordering mobile application *cards* that have a persuasive nature (see Fig. 2). We focus our experimentation in how a persuasive agent (the application) may update the user interface suggesting to a persuadee (a mobile application user) different persuasive content, *i.e.* information cards. In this context, hypotheses contain cards as content; the persuadee moves (*accept, ignore, quest*) were coded as response buttons. For our experiment, we manipulated a probability distribution causing different uncertainty levels of the persuadee model. We implemented Algorithm 1 and the move selection mechanism using Java with the *Tweety Project library*[2]. We used Ionic framework[3] to build the cards. We consider the following information: $g_1 =$

Fig. 2. Experiment 1: Mobile application cards used as content within persuader moves. Left and left-center (card 1 and card 2) are cards using information and measuring type content respectively: card 2, type progress with a calendar date

---

[2] TweetyProject acceded on April 2021 https://tweetyproject.org/.
[3] Ionic acceded on April 2021 https://ionicframework.com.

"improve physical activity", g_2 = "improve diet", g_3 = "reduce alcohol consumption", v_1 = "achievement", v_2 = "tradition", v_3 = "hedonism", e_1 = "amazement", e_2 = "grief", e_3 = "vigilance", act_1 = show($goal\_oriented\_content$), act_2 = show($emotion\_oriented\_content$), act_3 = show($location\_quant\_content$), act_4 = show($calendar\_date\_content$), act_5 = show($question\_content$).

With this information, several hypotheses were built using Algorithm 1, for lack of space we refrain to show them. In Algorithm 1, we modify P = $\{0.01, 0.5, 0.99\}$ in the set of created hypotheses, we limited set $\mathcal{H}$ to a size of 10 hypotheses. We found that in general, the persuader agent (Agp in Fig. 3) "wins" the dialogue when it has more knowledge than the persuadee, $i.e.$ that it will provide more cards connected with proactive strategies. Conversely, as it is expected, the more uncertainty in the persuadee, the more chances that the persuder selects reactive content. For example, when uncertainty was highest (0,99 in Fig. 3), where the persuader has no previous information about G, V, E then, only reactive cards were placed on the top of the application, $i.e.$ changing the order from card 1 to card 2 in Fig. 2, where every card is associated with an action, $e.g.$ act_2 = show($emotion\_oriented\_content$).

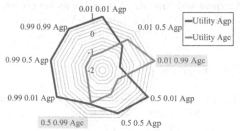

Fig. 3. Uncertainty P of the agent's model vs protocol winner.

4   Conclusions

There is a discrepancy between formal approaches of AI literature and commonly used guidelines for designing persuasive technology in HCI, which is reflected in the design of computational mechanisms that do not cover all the dimensions of what persuasion entails in other research areas. Using a compound systematic methodology, we investigated persuasion through the lenses of *gamification* that is currently a vital fundamental in practical applications. We presented two typologies that summarize an extensive body of knowledge that we systematically interpreted with the support of a multidisciplinary team of researchers focused on behavior change. We addressed a recurrent problem in software agents and AI literature, that is the design of decision-making algorithms selecting persuasive strategies and content, to be used in practical applications. This issue has been mainly addressed using three main types of computational mechanisms for decision-making of persuasive agents: 1) using practical reasoning [2] for example in [9], 2) with ontology-based reasoning see [14], and 3) with formal and natural argumentation. We extend previous work on non-monotonic reasoning using argumentation [11] to build an algorithm that: 1) selects a persuasive strategy and the corresponding content from a knowledge base (strategies and content taxonomies); 2) generates a persuasive dialogue as output; and 3) adapts its *agency* (*w.r.t* reactive, proactive, social). As future work, we would like to extend our systematic review with further conclusions that we found, also presenting formal details about our framework as well as technical details in our implementation.

Acknowledgment. Research was supported by Forte, the Swedish Research Council for Health, Working Life and Welfare, which supports the STAR-C project during 2019–2024 (Dnr. 2018-01461).

References

1. Amgoud, L., de Saint-Cyr, F.D.: An axiomatic approach for persuasion dialogs. In: 2013 IEEE 25th International Conference on Tools with Artificial Intelligence, pp. 618–625. IEEE (2013)
2. Bratman, M.: Intention, Plans, and Practical Reason. Harvard University Press, Cambridge (1987)
3. Charmaz, K.: Grounded theory: methodology and theory construction. In: International Encyclopedia of the Social & Behavioral Sciences, pp. 6396–6399. Pergamon, Oxford, January 2001
4. Chen, S., Chaiken, S.: The heuristic-systematic model in its broader context. In: Dual-Process Theories in Social Psychology, pp. 93–96. Guilford Publications (1999)
5. Crano, W.D., Prislin, R.: Attitudes and persuasion. Ann. Rev. Psychol. **57**, 345–374 (2006)
6. Dennison, L., Morrison, L., Conway, G., Yardley, L.: Opportunities and challenges for smartphone applications in supporting health behavior change: qualitative study. J. Med. Internet Res. **15**(4), e2583 (2013)
7. Deonna, J.A., Teroni, F.: Emotions as attitudes. Dialectica **69**(3), 293–311 (2015)
8. Dung, P.M.: On the acceptability of arguments and its fundamental role in non-monotonic reasoning, logic programming and n-person games. Artif. Intell. **77**(2), 321–357 (1995)
9. Guerini, M., Stock, O., Zancanaro, M.: A taxonomy of strategies for multimodal persuasive message generation. Appl. Artif. Intell. **21**(2), 99–136 (2007)
10. Guerrero, E., Lindgren, H.: Practical reasoning about complex activities. In: Demazeau, Y., Davidsson, P., Bajo, J., Vale, Z. (eds.) PAAMS 2017. LNCS (LNAI), vol. 10349, pp. 82–94. Springer, Cham (2017). https://doi.org/10.1007/978-3-319-59930-4_7
11. Guerrero, E., Nieves, J.C., Lindgren, H.: Semantic-based construction of arguments: an answer set programming approach. Int. J. Approx. Reason. **64**, 54–74 (2015)
12. Hunter, A.: Modelling the persuadee in asymmetric argumentation dialogues for persuasion. In: Proceedings of the Twenty-Fourth International Joint Conference on Artificial Intelligence, IJCAI 2015, Buenos Aires, Argentina, 25–31 July 2015, pp. 3055–3061 (2015)
13. Johnson, D., Deterding, S., Kuhn, K.A., Staneva, A., Stoyanov, S., Hides, L.: Gamification for health and wellbeing: a systematic review of the literature. Internet Interv. **6**, 89–106 (2016)
14. Maimone, R., Guerini, M., Dragoni, M., Bailoni, T., Eccher, C.: PerKApp: a general purpose persuasion architecture for healthy lifestyles. J. Biomed. Inf. **82**, 70–87 (2018)

15. Némery, A., Brangier, E.: Set of guidelines for persuasive interfaces: organization and validation of the criteria. J. Usability Stud. **9**(3), 105–128 (2014)
16. Ng, N., et al.: Sustainable behavior change for health supported by person-tailored, adaptive, risk-aware digital coaching in a social context: study protocol for the STAR-C research programme. Front. Public Health **9**, 593453 (2021)
17. Oinas-Kukkonen, H., Harjumaa, M.: Persuasive systems design: key issues, process model, and system features. Commun. Assoc. Inf. Syst. **24**(1), 28 (2009)
18. Petty, R.E., Briñol, P.: The elaboration likelihood model. In: Handbook of Theories of Social Psychology, vol. 1, pp. 224–245 (2011)
19. Rao, A.S., Georgeff, M.P., et al.: BDI agents: from theory to practice. In: ICMAS, vol. 95, pp. 312–319 (1995)
20. Sama, P.R., Eapen, Z.J., Weinfurt, K.P., Shah, B.R., Schulman, K.A.: An evaluation of mobile health application tools. JMIR Mhealth Uhealth **2**(2), e3088 (2014)
21. Schwartz, S.H.: Universals in the content and structure of values: theoretical advances and empirical tests in 20 countries. In: Advances in Experimental Social Psychology, vol. 25, pp. 1–65. Elsevier (1992)
22. Walton, D., Krabbe, E.C.W.: Commitment in Dialogue: Basic Concepts of Interpersonal Reasoning. SUNY Series in Logic and Language, State University of New York Press, Albany (1995)
23. Wooldridge, M., Jennings, N.R.: Agent theories, architectures, and languages: a survey. In: Wooldridge, M.J., Jennings, N.R. (eds.) ATAL 1994. LNCS, vol. 890, pp. 1–39. Springer, Heidelberg (1995). https://doi.org/10.1007/3-540-58855-8_1

A Practical Application of Market-Based Mechanisms for Allocating Harvesting Tasks

Helen Harman[✉][iD] and Elizabeth I. Sklar[iD]

Lincoln Institute for Agri-Food Technology, University of Lincoln, Lincoln, UK
{hharman,esklar}@lincoln.ac.uk

Abstract. Market-based task allocation mechanisms are designed to distribute a set of tasks fairly amongst a set of agents. Such mechanisms have been shown to be highly effective in simulation and when applied to multi-robot teams. Application of such mechanisms in real-world settings can present a range of practical challenges, such as knowing what is the best point in a complex process to allocate tasks and what information to consider in determining the allocation. The work presented here explores the application of market-based task allocation mechanisms to the problem of managing a heterogeneous human workforce to undertake activities associated with harvesting soft fruit. Soft fruit farms aim to maximise yield (the volume of fruit picked) while minimising labour time (and thus the cost of picking). Our work evaluates experimentally several different strategies for practical application of market-based mechanisms for allocating tasks to workers on soft fruit farms, identifying methods that appear best when simulated using a multi-agent model of farm activity.

Keywords: Task allocation mechanism · Multi-agent system · Agent-based simulation

1 Introduction

Due to the increasing demand for soft fruits and shortages in seasonal workers [6,17,27], farms are requiring innovative solutions for managing their fruit harvesting processes. Typically, on such farms, each day a harvest manager determines which fields are ready for picking and how many workers should be assigned to each field. In the field, supervisors assign tasks to individual workers, who place harvested fruit into containers ("punnets", in the case of strawberries) that must be carried (i.e. transported) to a centralised location, such as a permanent pack house or mobile trailer adjacent to the fields, where they are weighed, scanned for quality and tallied so that the picker responsible is compensated correctly. The task of transporting punnets to the central location is often performed by a worker called a "runner". This task allocation problem thus involves decisions about which tasks to assign to which workers and how many workers to assign to each role (picker and runner). In the not too

© Springer Nature Switzerland AG 2021
F. Dignum et al. (Eds.): PAAMS 2021, LNAI 12946, pp. 114–126, 2021.
https://doi.org/10.1007/978-3-030-85739-4_10

distant future, robots may soon be filling gaps in the shortages of seasonal workers [4,17,20,30,32]; and therefore, robotic co-workers will need to be managed alongside the human workforce.

Multi-robot task allocation (MRTA) problems address situations in which a group of robots must work together to complete a *mission*—a set of *tasks* to be executed. A key challenge is to decide which tasks should be assigned to which robots so that the overall execution of the mission is efficient: resources are used effectively, so that time and energy are not wasted and, often, some reward is maximised. A range of methods for allocating tasks in multi-robot teams are described in the literature, for example handling heterogeneous teams of robots [26] and multi-robot swarms [24], assigning tasks dynamically [34] and limiting robots to local input from immediate neighbours [2]. Recent real-world applications include disinfecting public areas in order to reduce spread of contagious diseases [28] and delivering food [14].

In the work presented here, we posit that approaches designed to address task allocation in a multi-robot team can be adapted to manage the human workforce on a soft fruit farm. Fruit picking and transporting harvested fruit are two types of tasks that need to be allocated to workers, who are often assigned one of two roles (*picker* or *runner*, respectively). Here, we apply market-based MRTA strategies and investigate two questions: (1) What is the most efficient ratio of runners to pickers? (2) What is the most efficient strategy for allocating tasks to runners? We investigate these questions empirically, using a multi-agent based simulation that emulates the activity of human workers on a soft fruit farm.

The paper is organised as follows. Section 2 provides brief background on multi-robot task allocation problems, focussing on market-inspired approaches, and also highlights related work in *agricultural robotics*. Section 3 describes the methodology we employed for our simulation. Section 4 explains our experiment design, and Sect. 5 presents the results of our simulation experiments. Section 6 closes with a summary of results.

2   Background

The *multi-robot task allocation (MRTA)* problem has been classified in the literature according to several taxonomies that distinguish specific features of tasks and task environments [9,18,21]. From that literature, the parameters that are particularly relevant for the work presented here are: static (SA) vs dynamic (DA) assignment—whether all the tasks are known at the start of a mission (static) or new ones may appear during the mission (dynamic); independent (IT) vs constrained (CT) task—whether or not the assignment of one task is dependent on the completion of another; and the further distinction between in-schedule (ID), cross-schedule (XD) and complex (CD) dependencies for CT tasks. Our soft fruit farm task allocation scenario is unusual because it combines SA and DA tasks within an XD environment (runner tasks are dependent on picker tasks and vice-versa).

Market-based mechanisms, especially *auctions*, are a popular approach to the MRTA problem [5,13]. Auctions are typically executed in *rounds*, comprised of three phases: (1) a centralised auction manager advertises one or more tasks to a set of robots (or agents); (2) each agent determines its individual (private) valuation (cost or utility) for one or more of the announced tasks and presents that valuation in the form of a *bid* to the auction manager; and (3) then the auction manager compiles the bids and decides which tasks to assign to which agents. Multiple rounds can occur, until all the tasks advertised are assigned. One prominent auction-based method is the *sequential single-item (SSI)* method [16] (described in Sect. 3). SSI has been a popular choice for multi-robot task allocation, and many variants have been studied, for example *TeSSI* [25], to efficiently allocate a set of tasks with temporal constraints to a team of robots, and *sequential single-cluster (SSC)* auctions [12] for solving pick-up and delivery tasks in a dynamic environment.

One area of application for multi-robot teams that has been gaining attention recently is *agricultural robotics* [6]. State-of-the-art work includes use of autonomous robots and machine learning methods, for example to identify ripe fruit [15], map regions in need of irrigation [3]. or locate weeds [22]. A wide range of robotic solutions for picking and transporting crops are currently being developed, including harvesting sweet peppers [7,20], and other fruiting vegetables [32], When harvesting crops, if a container has been filled, it must be transported to a storage and/or packing location. Some have evaluated hybrid human-robot solutions, where robots perform the transporting tasks while humans do the picking [4,30,31].

3   Methodology

In order to investigate our two research questions, we have constructed a multi-agent based simulation of operations on a soft fruit farm, where each human worker is represented by an agent. We assume that there are two different roles for workers (picker and runner), that each task can be completed by one worker on their own and that each worker performs one type of task (picking or transporting, respectively). Pickers harvest fruit in the field (in this case, a type of greenhouse called a *polytunnel*) and place the produce in punnets; and runners collect trays of full punnets and deliver them to a centralised location called a *packing station*. Our simulator was developed using MASON [23], a discrete-event multi-agent simulation library. We adapted a market-based task allocation mechanism from [29], to advertise a set of fruit picking tasks. Agents bid on these tasks and an auction manager assigns each task to the agent that presents the bid with the lowest cost.

In practice on farms, picking tasks are determined each day by inspecting the rows of crops, to discover the amount of ripe fruit they contain. In our simulation, picking tasks are represented by patches (areas) of *unoccluded* (readily visible) and *occluded* (hidden) fruits that are ripe. Transport tasks are created when a picker's schedule contains a task that will cause its capacity to be reached. According to the taxonomies cited in Sect. 2, we characterise picking task assignment as SA, because this is done *a priori*. Transport task assignment could be characterised either as SA, allocated before the mission when picker tasks are assigned, or DA, allocated during the mission, as pickers fill trays.

3.1 Agents

We define two roles for agents in our simulation:

- A **picker** is defined by the tuple $p = \langle v, l, s_p, c \rangle$, where l is the agent's initial location and v its navigation speed; $s_p = \langle s_o, s_u \rangle$, for which s_o is the speed at which the agent can pick occluded fruit (number of fruits per step); and s_u the agent's unoccluded fruit picking speed. When a picker has reached their capacity (c) they cannot pick any more fruits. Pickers cannot leave trays/punnets on the ground since customers are unwilling to accept fruit covered in mud, and potentially contaminated with pests and disease. They also require empty punnets to be delivered to them. Thus, the agent must wait for a runner to collect the ripe fruits and take them to the pack house.
- A **runner** navigates to a picker, collects the punnet and then returns to the pack house. Runners have a navigation speed and an initial location, i.e., $r = \langle v, l \rangle$. For runners, their initial location is always within the pack house.

3.2 Task Allocation Mechanisms

Similarly to our earlier work [11], we compare the variations in performance resulting from the application of three different auction-based mechanisms to the process of allocating picker and transporter tasks.

- *Round Robin* (RR) assigns the first task to the first agent, the second to the second agent and so forth. After a single task has been assigned to each agent, the agents are re-iterated over to assign each of them a second task. This process continues until all tasks have been assigned to an agent.
- In *Ordered Single Item* (OSI), all agents bid on the first task and the agent with lowest costing bid is assigned the task. The subsequent task is then auctioned. When all tasks are assigned, the process concludes.
- For *Sequential Single Item* (SSI), in each round all unassigned tasks are bid on by all agents. The task of the lowest costing bid is assigned to the agent who placed that bid.

3.3 Allocation of Picking Tasks

Pickers are allocated work by bidding on, winning, and thus being assigned, picking tasks. A picking task is defined as an (x, y) location and a number of ripe fruits. Before bidding begins, the list of picking tasks is sorted, highest first, by the total number of ripe fruits they contain. Pickers are sorted by picking speed, s, which is a combination of speeds for picking unoccluded, s_u, and occluded, s_o, fruits; quickest picker appears first. The cost of a picking bid is the *duration* for the agent to complete all their previously assigned tasks plus the task being auctioned. The duration of a single picking task is the sum of three components:

- The time it takes the agent to navigate to their picking location (d_v). Navigation duration is calculated by dividing the length of the path by the agent's navigation speed (v): $d_v = len(path)/v$.
- The time it takes to pick the ripe fruits (d_p). Picking duration is calculated by combining the time spent picking unoccluded fruits with the time to pick occluded fruits: $d_p = (u/s_u) + (o/s_o)$.
- The time spent waiting for a runner, but only if two conditions are met: (i) the agent's capacity will be reached whilst picking that patch; and (ii) the runner scheduling interweaves the picker scheduling (see Sect. 3.4).

As precise AI path planning (e.g. [10]) causes the bidding process to be computationally expensive, Euclidean distance is calculated as a proxy for the path length. If the agent has not won any tasks (yet), two Euclidean distances are summed: (i) the distance from the picker's initial location to the row in which the new task is located, and (ii) from the end of the new task's row to the location within the row of the new task. For navigating between locations within the same aisle, a single distance is measured. For patches in different aisles, three distances are summed: the distance from the previous location to the end of its row, from the row of the previous location to the end of the row containing the new location, and from that row end to the location itself. When the mission is executed, *Jump Point Search (JPS)* [10] is called to find the precise path.

If executing a task would cause a picker's capacity to be reached, it creates a *provisional transport task* whilst constructing its bid. To facilitate this, the number of fruits the agent will be holding when it completes its schedule and the time step the agent will finish on are updated each time it is assigned a task. To determine the time spent picking before the agent's capacity is reached, we assume that pickers harvest unoccluded fruits before picking the occluded fruits from a patch. Along with the navigation time, this is added to the time the picker will start the task (i.e. the timestep after its previously scheduled task will end). Ideally, a runner will take the picked fruit from the picker on the timestep directly after the picker has reached capacity. In reality, often a picker has to wait for a runner; or vice versa. If the picker's bid wins, then the transport task is no longer provisional; it is appended to a list of transport tasks. When a picker will reach capacity more than once when executing a task, multiple transport tasks are created.

3.4   Allocation of Transport Tasks

Transport tasks contain the location and timestep that a picker will reach maximum capacity. The less time a picker spends waiting for a runner, the sooner it will be able to complete its task. Therefore, the winning transport bid is the bid that causes the picker the shortest delay. If multiple bids have an equally short delay, then the bid with the shortest duration wins. For a transport bid, duration is the sum of the time it takes the runner to navigate to the picker, collect the punnet and return to the packing station. Runners are sorted by navigation speed, quickest appearing first.

Three different modes were implemented and compared for allocating tasks to runners. To differentiate between these and the mechanisms implemented for allocating picking tasks, each adds a prefix to the mechanism name (e.g. W-RR):

- _Whilst scheduling picking_ (W): Runners can be scheduled as soon as a transport task is created. This enables a picker's bid to include the time they would spend waiting for the runner.
- _Post scheduling picking_ (P): The auction manager can wait until all transport tasks have been created (i.e. all picking tasks have all been assigned) before scheduling the runners.
- _Whilst executing picking_ (E): Runners can be scheduled during execution, which facilitates delays (differences between the scheduled duration and execution duration) to be accounted for within the runners' schedules.

The transport bid creation algorithm determines where within the runner's existing schedule the task should be placed. The algorithm iterates over all the runner's already scheduled tasks, selecting those with start time after the ideal end time of the task being auctioned and checking where the new task will fit within this selected list. A record of the location/index is kept, so that if the agent's bid wins, the task can be inserted into the schedule easily.

The delay to the picker, in waiting for the runner to complete its task, is calculated by finding the difference between the time the transport is required and how soon after this time the runner can arrive. If the runner can arrive on time, then the delay is the time it takes to hand over the punnet.

For the three modes (W, P and E), implementations of RR and OSI were developed. In the W and E modes, OSI and SSI are equivalent since only one task at a time is offered to the bidders. The algorithms employed to auction transport tasks are essentially equivalent to the those developed for auctioning picking tasks. In the P mode, before bidding begins, the transport tasks are sorted by the timestep at which the runner is required. Unlike the W and E modes, when a runner is assigned a task, the picker who created the task is required to update its schedule to take into account the delay. The delay amount is added to the start, end and transport-required times of all the tasks proceeding the delayed picking task. The transport-required times of the corresponding (unassigned) transport tasks are updated simultaneously. P-SSI is not performed since a runner's tasks must be in order of when a picker reaches capacity (to prevent deadlocks).

In the E mode, the transport task is only offered to the runners when the picker (actually) reaches capacity. When a runner has no tasks to execute, it will navigate to and wait in front of the polytunnels, so that it has less distance to travel when a picker reaches capacity. These locations are predefined and iterated over (then re-iterated over) to assigned them to the runners. In future work, we will consider selecting different "waiting" locations that take into consideration the current locations of the pickers.

4   Experiments

We designed a series of experiments to evaluate our research questions concerning the ratio of runners to pickers and the strategy for allocating tasks to runners. Two experimental scenarios were defined, below, and results of experiments are presented in Sect. 5. Two key metrics are computed: **execution time**—how long it takes to perform the tasks allocated; and **waiting time**—how long pickers spend waiting for runners. If the system is efficient, then the execution time and wait time is minimised and yield is maximised. To determine the significance of our results, we applied statistical testing and factor analysis, where appropriate. A Shapiro-Wilk test [33] was performed to check if each sample is normally distributed. If there is a greater than 90% chance that the samples are all normally distributed, an ANalysis Of VAriance (ANOVA) test [1,8] was performed (for which the F test statistic is reported). Otherwise, Kruskal-Wallis tests [19] were run (for which the H test statistic is reported). T-test are performed when there are only two samples. The significance of results is indicated by p, the probability of the results occurring randomly.

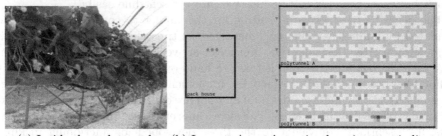

(a) Inside the polytunnel.   (b) Layout. Agents' starting locations are indicated.

Fig. 1. Our strawberry farm. See text for explanation.

We developed two scenarios, one emulating a **small farm** and one a **large farm**. Both are based on existing soft fruit farms and the data used in the scenarios come from each of these farms.

The **Small Farm** (pictured in Fig. 1a) is a small research farm. During Summer 2020, the volume of ripe fruits that were picked per row of crops were recorded. This included information on how many of the fruits were occluded from view. Data was recorded on each picking day (twice per week). In our initial experiments, there was no statistically significant difference between the results for different dates. Therefore, for the experiments presented here, we selected a single date in which a large number of fruits were harvested. The data per row was broken down into patches by adding each fruit to a randomly selected patch from the same row (as depicted in Fig. 1b). The colour of the patches, in Fig. 1b, represents the number of ripe fruits: red patches contain more ripe fruits than orange patches, which contain more than yellow patches and green indicates the patches containing low amounts of ripe fruits. As an element of randomness was included, two random distributions were produced (illustrated as *heatmaps*, like that in Fig. 1b). For this scenario, we employed a 7-agent team of workers.

The **Large Farm** replicates aspects of a commercial fruit farm and we have modeled one of their fields as an example. This single field is about 100 times as large as the small research farm. Based on data provided from this farm, we calculated the average yield per date and the average picking speed. Within our simulation of this field, the yield was uniformly distributed across patches. For all agents, navigation speed was set to ≈1 m per timestep. The capacity of pickers is set to the volume (4000 g) of a standard tray (which contains the punnets of picked fruits). On average, 39 pickers picked each day from this field; therefore our experiment for this scenario contains 39 agents.

5 Results

We analyse our results by looking first at the composition of our workforce (number of pickers and transporters); second at the impact of allocating tasks to transporters at different points in the picking process; and third at the evenness of the distribution of tasks in terms of how much time pickers spend waiting for runners. In all plots presented, error bars indicate ±1 standard deviation.

The whilst scheduling pickers (W) runner mode, is more computationally expensive than the E and P modes, since for every bid that a picker creates (for which transport is required) the transportation task auction is invoked; whereas, for E and P, only the transport tasks of winning picking bids are auctioned. The deliberation time (i.e. the time it takes to allocate the tasks) of RR, OSI and SSI has previously been compared and is nominal in the scheme of the overall run time of our scenarios; thus, deliberation time is not analysed here [29].

5.1 Workforce Composition

As shown in Fig. 2a, the ideal team split, for the small farm is 71% of agents deployed as runners and the remaining agents as pickers; and for the large farm

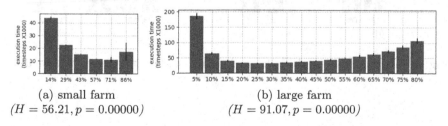

(a) small farm   (b) large farm
$(H = 56.21, p = 0.00000)$ $(H = 91.07, p = 0.00000)$

Fig. 2. Results for **execution time** for different percentages of agents being employed as runners. The H statistic from Kruskal-Wallis tests and associated p values are shown, indicating statistically significant differences for the different ratios for both farms.

is 25% of agents deployed at runners. Although the best percentages differ—due to the large difference in size between the small and large farms and workforces—the trends are the same. The two extremes (highest:lowest and lowest:highest ratios of runners:pickers) represent the worst execution times, but in both cases there is a sweet spot in the middle.

5.2   Transport Task Allocation Mode

We computed factor analysis to compare the three transport task allocation modes: whilst scheduling picking (W), post scheduling picking (P) and whilst executing picking (E), as shown in Fig. 3. For scheduling runners, overall there is no statistically significant difference in execution time between the two task allocation mechanisms (RR and OSI) (plots a and d). Scheduling the runners whilst scheduling the pickers produced a shorter execution time than the alternative modes (plots b and e). The ablated results for the runner scheduling mechanisms and modes show no statistically significant differences (plots c and f). The statistical significance is reported for the small farm; for the large farm, only one heatmap (i.e. distribution of ripe fruit) was evaluated for each run, so it is not possible to compute statistical significance. Future work will involve running over multiple heatmaps (e.g. representing different days in a picking season).

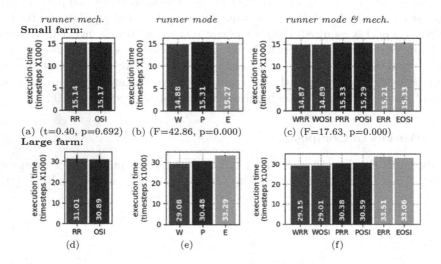

Fig. 3. Factor analysis for the picker and runner mechanisms (mech.) and modes.

5.3   Cost of Waiting

Finally, we compare the cost of waiting. Since pickers are more expensive than runners (i.e. the best pickers are paid higher salaries), we focus on the picker waiting time here. Figure 4 shows the *cumulative* waiting time, summed over all pickers in each run. As expected, when the percentage of runners increases, the pickers' wait time decreases; however, this also results in each picker picking a higher proportion of the fruit.

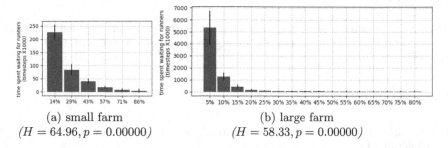

(a) small farm

$(H = 64.96, p = 0.00000)$

(b) large farm

$(H = 58.33, p = 0.00000)$

Fig. 4. Results for **cumulative picker waiting time** for different percentages of agents being employed as runners. The H statistic from Kruskal-Wallis tests and associated p values are shown, indicating statistically significant differences for the different ratios in both farm scenarios.

6 Discussion, Conclusions and Future Work

This paper explored the application of market-based task-allocation mechanisms to the problem of managing workers to harvest fruit. Patches of ripe fruits were auctioned to agents in one of two roles (picker or runner) using three different market-based mechanisms (RR, OSI and SSI) drawn from the MRTA literature and three different modes for assigning dependent tasks to runners (whilst scheduling picking, post scheduling picking and whilst executing picking). The comparative performance of different ratios of pickers and runners was evaluated.

Our experiments were designed to answer two questions. The first question asks what is the most efficient ratio of runners to pickers. Our results show that the ratio of runners to pickers is critical with respect to both execution and picker waiting time, and that the "sweet spot" varies depending on the size of field and workforce. The second question asks what is the most efficient strategy for allocating tasks to runners. Our results show that, for allocating tasks to runners, the *whilst scheduling pickers* (W) mode produces the best results (shortest execution times), with similar results for each of the different auction mechanisms—indicating that the critical factor is identifying the best point in the complex harvesting process to allocate transport tasks.

Current work involves deeper investigation of the large farm scenario, particularly using different distributions of ripe fruit and expanding to consider multiple fields in the allocation (e.g. using market-based mechanisms to allocate the workforce to different fields, as well as allocating tasks within a field).

Ongoing collaboration with both of the farms that served as examples for the scenarios implemented here will allow farm managers to employ our task allocation methods for managing their workforce. These real-world deployments will provide additional verification of our methodology, such that predicted results from our simulation compared to actual results in the field will be presented in future work.

Acknowledgements. This work was supported by Research England [Lincoln Agri-Robotics] as part of the Expanding Excellence in England (E3) Programme.

References

1. Anscombe, F.: The validity of comparative experiments. J. Roy. Stat. Soc. Ser. A (General) **111**(3), 181–211 (1948)
2. Atay, N., Bayazit, B.: Emergent task allocation for mobile robots. In: Proceedings of Robotics: Science and Systems Conference (2007)
3. Chang, C.L., Lin, K.M.: Smart agricultural machine with a computer vision-based weeding and variable-rate irrigation scheme. Robotics **7**, 38 (2018)
4. Das, G., Cielniak, G., From, P., Hanheide, M.: Discrete event simulations for scalability analysis of robotic in-field logistics in agriculture-a case study. In: IEEE International Conference on Robotics and Automation, Workshop on Robotic Vision and Action in Agriculture (2018)
5. Dias, M.B., Zlot, R., Kalra, N., Stentz, A.: Market-based multirobot coordination: a survey and analysis. Proc. IEEE **94**(7), 1257–1270 (2006)
6. Duckett, T., Pearson, S., Blackmore, S., Grieve, B., Smith, M.: Agricultural robotics white paper: the future of robotic agriculture (2018). https://www.ukras. org/wp-content/uploads/2018/10/UK_RAS_wp_Agri_web-res_single.pdf. Accessed 10 Mar 2020
7. Elkoby, Z., van 't Ooster, B., Edan, Y.: Simulation analysis of sweet pepper harvesting operations. In: Grabot, B., Vallespir, B., Gomes, S., Bouras, A., Kiritsis, D. (eds.) APMS 2014. IAICT, vol. 440, pp. 441–448. Springer, Heidelberg (2014). https://doi.org/10.1007/978-3-662-44733-8_55
8. Fisher, R.A.: Statistical methods for research workers (1925)
9. Gerkey, B., Matarić, M.: A formal analysis and taxonomy of task allocation in multi-robot systems. Int. J. Robot. Res. **23**(9), 939–954 (2004)
10. Harabor, D., Grastien, A.: Online graph pruning for pathfinding on grid maps. In: Proceedings of AAAI (2011)
11. Harman, H., Sklar, E.: Auction-based task allocation mechanisms for managing fruit harvesting tasks. In: UK Robotics and Autonomous Systems Network Annual Conference (UK-RAS) (2021)
12. Heap, B., Pagnucco, M.: Repeated sequential single-cluster auctions with dynamic tasks for multi-robot task allocation with pickup and delivery. In: Klusch, M., Thimm, M., Paprzycki, M. (eds.) MATES 2013. LNCS (LNAI), vol. 8076, pp. 87–100. Springer, Heidelberg (2013). https://doi.org/10.1007/978-3-642-40776-5_10
13. Heap, B., Pagnucco, M.: Sequential single-cluster auctions for robot task allocation. In: Wang, D., Reynolds, M. (eds.) AI 2011. LNCS (LNAI), vol. 7106, pp. 412–421. Springer, Heidelberg (2011). https://doi.org/10.1007/978-3-642-25832-9_42

14. Hern, A.: Robots deliver food in Milton Keynes under coronavirus lockdown. The Guardian, 12 April 2020. Accessed 9 Oct 2020
15. Kirk, R., Cielniak, G., Mangan, M.: L*a*b*fruits: a rapid and robust outdoor fruit detection system combining bio-inspired features with one-stage deep learning networks. Sensors **20**(1), 275 (2020)
16. Koenig, S., et al.: The power of sequential single-item auctions for agent coordination. In: Proceedings of AAAI, vol. 2 (2006)
17. Kootstra, G., Wang, X., Blok, P.M., Hemming, J., Van Henten, E.: Selective harvesting robotics: current research, trends, and future directions. Curr. Robot. Rep. (2021)
18. Korsah, G., Stentz, A., Dias, M.: A comprehensive taxonomy for multi-robot task allocation. Int. J. Robot. Res. **32**(12), 1495–1512 (2013)
19. Kruskal, W.H., Wallis, W.W.: Use of ranks in one-criterion variance analysis. J. Am. Stat. Assoc. **47**(260), 583–621 (1952)
20. Kurtser, P., Edan, Y.: Planning the sequence of tasks for harvesting robots. Robot. Auton. Syst. **131**, 103591 (2020)
21. Landén, D., Heintz, F., Doherty, P.: Complex task allocation in mixed-initiative delegation: a UAV case study. In: Desai, N., Liu, A., Winikoff, M. (eds.) PRIMA 2010. LNCS (LNAI), vol. 7057, pp. 288–303. Springer, Heidelberg (2012). https://doi.org/10.1007/978-3-642-25920-3_20
22. Liu, B., Bruch, R.: Weed detection for selective spraying: a review. Curr. Robot. Rep. **1**(1), 19–26 (2020). https://doi.org/10.1007/s43154-020-00001-w
23. Luke, S., Cioffi-Revilla, C., Panait, L., Sullivan, K., Balan, G.: MASON: a multi-agent simulation environment. Simulation **81**(7), 517–527 (2005)
24. McLurkin, J., Yamins, D.: Dynamic task assignment in robot swarms. In: Proceedings of Robotics: Science and Systems Conference (RSS) (2005)
25. Nunes, E., Gini, M.: Multi-robot auctions for allocation of tasks with temporal constraints. In: Proceedings of AAAI (2015)
26. Parker, L.E.: Task-oriented multi-robot learning in behavior-based systems. In: IEEE/RSJ International Conference on Intelligent Robots and Systems (1996)
27. Pelham, J.: The Impact of Brexit on the UK Soft Fruit Industry. British Summer Fruits, London (2017)
28. Reuters: Robots target coronavirus with ultraviolet light at London train station, 23 September 2020. https://uk.reuters.com/article/uk-health-coronavirus-britain-robots/robots-target-coronavirus-with-ultraviolet-light-at-london-train-station-idUKKCN26E2NT. Accessed 9 Oct 2020
29. Schneider, E., Sklar, E.I., Parsons, S., Özgelen, A.T.: Auction-based task allocation for multi-robot teams in dynamic environments. In: Dixon, C., Tuyls, K. (eds.) TAROS 2015. LNCS (LNAI), vol. 9287, pp. 246–257. Springer, Cham (2015). https://doi.org/10.1007/978-3-319-22416-9_29
30. Seyyedhasani, H., Peng, C., Jang, W.J., Vougioukas, S.G.: Collaboration of human pickers and crop-transporting robots during harvesting - Part I: model and simulator development. Comput. Electron. Agric. **172**, 105324 (2020)
31. Seyyedhasani, H., Peng, C., Jang, W.J., Vougioukas, S.G.: Collaboration of human pickers and crop-transporting robots during harvesting - Part II: simulator evaluation and robot-scheduling case-study. Comput. Electron. Agric. **172**, 105323 (2020)
32. Shamshiri, R.R., Hameed, I.A., Karkee, M., Weltzien, C.: Robotic harvesting of fruiting vegetables: a simulation approach in V-REP, ROS and MATLAB. In: Proceedings in Automation in Agriculture-Securing Food Supplies for Future Generations (2018)

33. Shapiro, S.S., Wilk, M.B.: An analysis of variance test for normality (complete samples). Biometrika **52**(3/4), 591–611 (1965)
34. Vail, D., Veloso, M.: Dynamic multi-robot coordination. In: Multi-Robot Systems: From Swarms to Intelligent Automata. Kluwer (2003)

A Multi-agent Approach for Evacuation Support in Mountainous Areas Using UAV

Yasushi Kambayashi[1]([✉]), Itsuki Tago[1], and Munehiro Takimoto[2]

[1] Department of Computer and Information Engineering, Nippon Institute of Technology, Saitama, Japan
yasushi@nit.ac.jp, 2198017@stu.nit.ac.jp
[2] Department of Information Sciences, Tokyo University of Science, Tokyo, Japan
mune@rs.tus.ac.jp

Abstract. We have witnessed natural disasters in several regions. Although people focus on the events of tsunami, landslides in mountainous areas are serious issues to consider. Therefore, we have proposed a system that supports evacuation after the occurrence of a large-scale disaster using multi-agents and multiple unmanned aerial vehicles (UAVs). When the software agent generates an evacuation plan, it considers area characteristics, prioritizes routes, and recommends an optimal guidance flight plan, which is provided to the UAV control agent. We describe the cooperation of two types of UAVs that assist people in evacuation and have conducted a simulation to show the feasibility of the proposed system.

Keywords: Disaster mitigation · Evacuation support · Multi-agent · Cooperative UAVs · Risk reduction · Contingency plan

1 Introduction

Natural disasters such as earthquakes and tsunamis have been occurring not only in Japan but also around the world. In addition, one needs to be careful during evacuation about the occurrence of secondary disasters such as flooding, collapsing houses, and landslides. The evacuees need to focus on these dangerous places during evacuation. Currently, people have to go and check whether a secondary disaster has occurred; as a result, evacuation is delayed, raising the risk that evacuees may be caught in secondary disasters.

Meanwhile, with the development of technologies, people have come to possess smartphones. Smartphones use radio waves transmitted from base stations. Owing to congestion caused by damage to communication base stations and sudden traffic surge owing to an increase in the number of people seeking information, it may be difficult to collect information using the Internet and telephone using smartphones.

We have been studying evacuation guidance support in the event of a disaster using mobile agents. Using the mobile ad hoc network (MANET), we have studied a system that guides evacuees to safe zones, while they collectively confirm the safety of evacuation routes [1]. Moreover, we have proposed a system to notify preferred routes via locations

© Springer Nature Switzerland AG 2021
F. Dignum et al. (Eds.): PAAMS 2021, LNAI 12946, pp. 127–138, 2021.
https://doi.org/10.1007/978-3-030-85739-4_11

that many evacuees have passed through [2] and proposed a configuration with server redundancy to run the system [3, 4].

Katayama et al. have studied evacuation guidance methods based on priorities. The study, however, specifically assumed coastal areas that are prone to tsunamis, and it is not applicable to mountainous areas [5]. For mountainous areas, it is necessary to determine priorities specific to them, and it is desirable to provide evacuation guidance based on such priorities.

This study proposes an approach using priorities specific to mountainous areas. In addition, we perform a simulation with unmanned aerial vehicles (UAVs) necessary in evacuation guidance to determine the number of people that can be evacuated utilizing the UAVs.

The structure of the balance of this paper is as follows: the second section describes the background of the study. The third section describes the formula to determine the priorities of the mountainous area, and how the UAVs operate based on these priorities. The fourth section discusses the results of the simulation. Finally, we conclude our discussion in the fifth section.

2   Background

2.1   Evacuation Route Guidance System

Until now, several studies have investigated evacuation guidance support using mobile agents [1, 6–8, 11, 12]. We have proposed a mobile agent system that collect information related to the areas lying ahead along the direction of the destination of the user [1]. Once a mobile agent is generated for a user, it migrates to the other smartphone of another user situated along the direction of the destination and collects information stored in the smartphone. Thereafter, it repeatedly migrates and collects information, and, at the same time, as part of the migration history, saves the address of the smartphone. After collecting a certain amount of information, the agent traces the migration history to return to the smartphone on which it was originated, and passes the collected information. This enabled the user to collect information about places beforehand along the direction of the destination, thus avoiding danger zones in advance [9].

A few issues, however, were identified in the proposed method when the mobile agent returned to the smartphone of origin. The mobile agent faces difficulty while returning to the user's smartphone, because the user is on the move. Therefore, the smartphones to which the agent had been transferred in the past may not necessarily remain at the same locations later, and it was considered difficult to return to the smartphone of origin based on the previous migrations. We then proposed MANET, a multi-agent system that directly communicates among smartphones, where the collected information is shared among participants to realize the optimal route to the destination [7].

Goto et al. have shown that it can generate evacuation route by applying the ant colony optimization (ACO) algorithm to a multi-agent system where the evacuees are treated as virtual ants. The ACO algorithm performs pheromone update for a minimum distance. This may lead to selecting a dangerous route during a disaster. It has been shown that by making the pheromone volatile and reducing the probability of approaching danger zones with time, a safe route can be formulated [10].

Using the simulation results of Goto et al. and defining what a "safe route" implies, we have estimated the associated realizability and safety [2]. Then, the aforementioned parameters were applied to real smartphones with high penetration rates and Google Maps API for Google Maps, which has many users. The implemented system, however, had a single point of failure. The redundancy issue is required to be configured, and we studied systems that use mobile agents and consider remote procedure calls (RPCs) [3, 4].

2.2 Priority in Coastal Areas

Katayama et al. proposed evacuation guidance plans using agent-based UAVs to reduce the risk of disasters. The software agent creates evacuation guidance plans for UAVs, considering the situation of disasters and regional characteristics, and selects the safest evacuation guidance route. Moreover, the evacuation guidance support was provided through cooperation among multiple UAVs. The system employs seven agents. Their roles are described below [5]:

Device agent: This agent sends the disaster information to the collector agent.
Collector agent: This agent collects the disaster information and shares the information with the navigator agent.
Generator agent: The UAV agent guides individuals to the evacuation route, plans evacuation using Google Maps, and sends the evacuation plans to the navigator agent.
Navigator agent: Using the priority values, the navigator agent selects a safer evacuation route based on the evacuation plans received from the generator agent. This priority was defined by the equation defined after this paragraph. In the equation, α, β, and γ are arbitrary coefficients, d_d denotes the distance between the route and secondary disasters, and t denotes the time necessary to reach the shelter. Moreover, d_{hc} is a combination of h and d_c, which represent the altitude and distance from the coast, respectively, at one point on the horizontal plane. When d_d is less than 30 m, however, the priority value is set to zero because the location is considered dangerous.

$$priority = \alpha d_d + \beta t + \gamma d_{hc}.$$

For this priority, d_c is considered as the distance from the coast. Thus, it implies an evacuation guidance route that avoids secondary disasters, e.g., tsunamis, in coastal areas.
UAV agent: The UAV flight, based on socket-based communications, is controlled with the smartphone of an evacuee. Moreover, the UAV agent shares information, for instance, location, battery charge, work status, areas already searched by UAVs, and segments where secondary disaster has occurred, with other UAV agents. The segment refers to the portion of the route connecting two consecutive waypoints. Moreover, other UAVs can change roles and perform activities in accordance with their roles. The role change is conducted according to the remaining battery charge and evacuation guidance to the shelter, once all the information is shared. Moreover, when the position of a UAV remains unchanged even though the work status is "evacuation guidance," the UAV agent requests another UAV agent for the evacuation guidance work. This way, a UAV, instead of searching for evacuees, can change the role and start guiding evacuees to the shelter.

Moreover, the UAV agent may end up sending the position information to the recognizer agent because of the incorrect detection of an evacuee while searching for evacuees.
Evacuee agent: This agent artificially recognizes evacuees in a simulation environment and sends the position information to the recognizer agent.
Recognizer agent: This agent detects an evacuee when the UAV is closer to the evacuee and sends the detection information to the UAV agent.

As the priority formula implies, this route guidance system focuses the dangers of coastal regions. We, on the contrary, focus the dangers of mountainous regions, and propose a solution using UAVs and multi-agents.

3   Evacuation Support System

This study implements an evacuation guidance system suitable for mountainous regions. Two types of UAVs are used for this purpose: UAVs that create an ad hoc communication network and UAVs that guide evacuees by showing dangerous areas along the route to avoid secondary disasters. It is assumed that the communication network is damaged owing to a disaster.

UAV points are set in advance in the target areas in the event of communication infrastructure damage. UAV1 starts from the source shelter and fly-passes over the points along the route to the target shelter without guiding evacuees. It shares information with UAV2 that operates between two points to guide the evacuees (Fig. 1). The roles of UAV1 and UAV2 are described below.

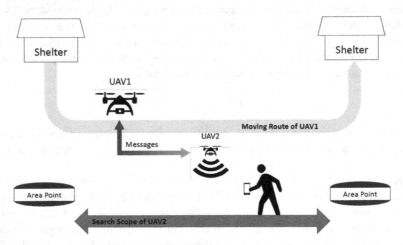

Fig. 1. Relationship between UAV1 and UAV2

UAV1 flies over almost all the area points in between two shelters and collects basic information to share with UAV2. At this time, priority is derived because this is required for each area point along the search movement path of UAV1.

UAV2 is used to search evacuees and generates the evacuation route for the evacuees. UAV2 is positioned to detect evacuees using the signal transmitted from the smartphones of the evacuees and fulfills the role of a router or repeater to relay communication packets.

To achieve the aforementioned purpose, five agents are used in guiding evacuation in mountainous regions using the UAVs. The role of each agent is described below.

Calculate agent: This agent resides on the server at the shelter. At the shelter, it updates the number of persons present in each area point screened by UAV1. The agent estimates the priority information at each area point, which is then dispatched to the find route agent.

Messenger agent: This agent resides in UAV1. It aggregates the number of evacuees obtained from the find evacuee agent in UAV2 and sends the information to the calculate agent. Moreover, it sends the evacuation information, obtained from the shelter, from UAV1 to UAV2.

Find evacuee agent: This agent resides in UAV2. It counts the number of detected evacuees that have smartphones and communicates the total count to the messenger agent in UAV1, along with the status of the UAV itself. Moreover, it transmits essential evacuation information, e.g., accessible roads and possible shelters nearby, to the smartphones of the evacuees.

Find route agent: This agent resides on the server at the shelter. This is not just about proceeding haphazardly along the area points screened by UAV1. The area points are predicted to have more evacuees should be given priority. Moreover, from an evacuation support standpoint, it is meaningless if evacuation at area points prone to secondary disasters is delayed. Accordingly, based on priority analyzed by the calculate agent, this agent decides the route that should be considered. The finalized decision is passed to the UAV control agent.

UAV control agent: This agent resides in UAV1 and controls UAV1 according to the instructions of the find route agent at the shelter, regarding the route to be followed.

The following sections describe the proposed system based on the aforementioned agents (Fig. 2).

3.1 UAV1: UAV for Movement Among Area Points

The priority equation is defined below and calculated as $priority_y$, considering the characteristics of mountainous regions. α, β, γ, and δ are arbitrary coefficients, and d is the distance to the shelter, t is the average time necessary to reach the shelter from the subject location, and U is the proportion of evacuees present around the subject area point. Moreover, D shows how prone the subject location and surrounding areas are to secondary disasters. Here, $priority_y$ can range from 0.0 to 1.0.

$$priority_y = \alpha d + \beta t + \gamma U + \delta D.$$

The number of roads leading to the shelter is few in mountainous regions. Access to roads may be blocked due to landslides. Therefore, it is likely that proceeding toward the shelter may not be feasible owing to such factors. Under such a condition, the value is set as 1.00, and the governor of the prefecture (Fig. 3) issues the request for disaster rescue support of the National Guard.

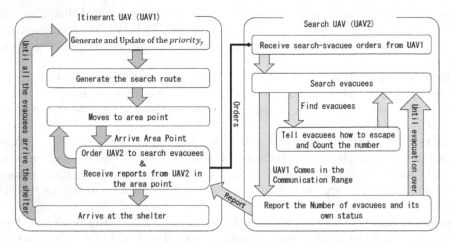

Fig. 2. Evacuation guidance system using UAV

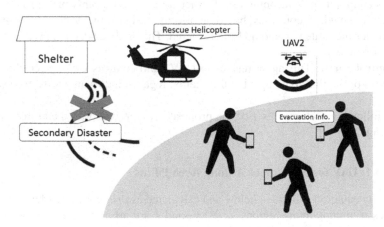

Fig. 3. Blocked evacuation path

priority$_y$, although not equal to 1.00, may be very close to 1.00, i.e., 0.99 or 0.91. In such a case, it indicates that, while there are possibilities of secondary disasters owing to landslides, moving towards the shelter is still feasible and that many evacuees are present around the subject area point. Without knowing when a secondary disaster, however, may occur and considering the worst-case scenario that many disaster victims are unable to evacuate, UAV2 provides information on the evacuation route to the evacuees present in between the two area points. Moreover, it may be likely that as it is a mountainous region, there is no evacuee around the subject area point. In such a case, *priority$_y$* is set to zero, and no evacuee search is conducted around this area point. In addition, the microcomputer installed in UAV1 instructs UAV2 not to generate (or guide) evacuation routes for entry into regions around the area point where *priority$_y$* is zero.

3.2   UAV2: UAV Searching for Evacuees

UAV2 thoroughly searches the area around the nearest area point, dispatches area-wide mail with a request like "follow me" to the smartphones of the evacuees, and guides them to the shelter (Fig. 4). There may be situations where the road leading to the shelter is blocked, which may call for rescue operations conducted by the National Guard using helicopters. In such a case, instead of sending the information on the evacuation route to the evacuees, UAV2 sends rescue information, asking the evacuees to stay where they are.

Fig. 4. Unblocked evacuation path

In addition, UAV2 reports to UAV1 flying nearby about the number of evacuees near the area point, along with the status of the UAV itself. Then it downloads the data in the server at shelters. Therefore, *priority$_y$*, which is necessary to search for a suitable path for UAV1, changes in real time.

4   Experiments

We have implemented a simulator in order to verify the feasibility of the proposed system. The simulated scenario was that a large-scale disaster occurred in a mountainous region, owing to which the communication network was damaged. Twenty-four area points were set in the region, where points 0 and 24 were shelters; and points 3, 4, 8, 9, 13, and 14 were "secondary-disaster-caution areas," where the danger of being stuck in areas prone to secondary disaster was high (Fig. 5). Of these areas, point 4 was designated as "evacuation-impossible area," which was required to raise a rescue request to the National Guard. Moreover, points 15, 16, 20, and 21 were set as "no-one-around areas," indicating no evacuees in the nearby area; and points 7, 12, and 17 were set as "many-evacuee-present areas." When this simulator is launched, the route for UAV1 is generated, and UAV2 is placed above the route screened by UAV1, excluding the points of shelters.

In order to differentiate "secondary-disaster-caution areas," "evacuation-impossible areas," "no-one-around areas," and "many-evacuee-present areas" when this simulator is launched, each area point was assigned a proportion of evacuees and a risk level of secondary disasters. With such settings, assuming the walking speed of evacuees to be 4.00 km/h, the priorities at each area point in the mountainous region were estimated, and the movement route for the initial state of UAV1 was determined.

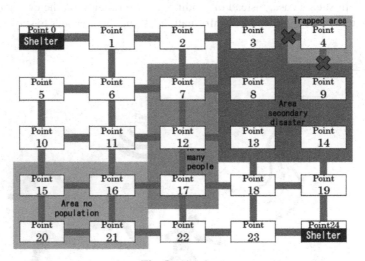

Fig. 5. Simulator

Assuming that a maximum number of 200 evacuees can be present at a certain area point, the proportion of 17.9% at point 1 indicates that 35 evacuees are present around point 1. Moreover, it reports that 135 evacuees have shifted to the shelter, and 18 evacuees present at point 4, where a rescue request was raised to the self-defense force because of secondary disasters.

Assuming that about half of the evacuees present around the area point were guided by UAV2 to proceed to the shelter every time UAV1 passes the area point, the number of evacuees, as listed in Table 1, was able to move to the nearest shelter using the selected route for the initial phase.

When this process was repeated, as listed in Table 2, in the initial phase, the number of people evacuated, including those who had been already evacuated to begin with and who were rescued by the National Guard, was 764, that is 81% of the total, and the remaining 171 evacuees could not proceed to the shelters. Moreover, of the 18 area points, excluding the shelters, evacuation-impossible areas, and no-one-around areas, 11 evacuees could not be evacuated at around point 3 because UAV1 did not fly even once over that area point, which is included among the secondary-disaster-prone areas.

Table 1. Number of persons evacuated in the initial state

Area point no. passed by UAV1	Number of persons evacuated from nearby regions of the area point
1	17
2	22
7	77
12	71
17	61
18	19
19	3

The simulation results revealed that there were low-priority areas where UAV1 did not fly over, even though the areas were not designated as "evacuation-impossible areas," or "no-one-around areas." Accordingly, UAV1 could not provide the necessary evacuation information to UAV2 positioned nearby those area points, resulting in the evacuees near those area points not able to evacuate.

Moreover, in the initial phase, $priority_y$ in "secondary-disaster-caution areas" was nearly the same as that for other undesignated areas. UAV1 should move to such areas with similar priority as "many-evacuee-present areas," because "secondary disaster risk is high," and based on the information of UAV1; UAV2 should issue the evacuation information. Accordingly, the value of $priority_y$ for these two areas should become nearly equivalent. Therefore, adjustments are deemed necessary to make the priorities of "secondary-disaster-caution areas" and "many-evacuee-present areas" same.

Moreover, in the initial phase, more than 80% of the total number of evacuces was able to proceed to the shelters. The remaining less than 20% of the evacuees, however, could not evacuate. Accordingly, it is necessary that more UAV1 should be deployed and that more innovative ways to determine the movement path are devised, so that the remaining evacuees would also be able to evacuate.

Table 2. Simulation results

Point no.	Number of people at the starting point	Evacuation completed	Not yet evacuated
1	35	31	4
2	45	40	5
3	11	0	11
4	18	18	0
5	13	10	3

(*continued*)

Table 2. (*continued*)

Point no.	Number of people at the starting point	Evacuation completed	Not yet evacuated
6	16	12	4
7	155	136	19
8	8	6	2
9	45	34	11
10	0	0	0
11	52	39	13
12	143	126	17
13	34	17	17
14	31	28	3
15	0	–	–
16	0	–	–
17	122	92	30
18	38	19	19
19	7	7	0
20	0	–	–
21	0	–	–
22	26	13	13
23	1	1	0
0, 24 (shelters)	135	135	–
Total	935	764	171

5   Conclusion and Future Work

We have proposed an evacuation guidance system suitable for mountainous regions and implemented a simulator for the system in order to show its feasibility. We have focused evacuation in mountainous regions. The priority of the mountainous areas was defined as *priority*$_y$ based on the regional characteristics, and the number of UAVs necessary was estimated. However, to determine *priority*$_y$ of evacuation, this study did not presume simultaneous occurrence of multiple conditions, i.e., high secondary-disaster risk and a large number of evacuees at one place. Therefore, it is necessary to address flexibly such cases depending on the situation.

In the experiments, areas were separately designated as "secondary-disaster-caution areas" and "many-evacuee-present areas." Therefore, *priority*$_y$ is calculated based on whether the risk of secondary disaster is high or whether there are a large number of evacuees present (the larger the number, the higher the priority). Both of these conditions, however, may hold at the same time and it is possible to evacuate from many subject areas. We have to consider many possible cases and their combinations. We believe that it is possible to address such cases that satisfy more than one condition at the same time by revising the derivation equation of $priority_y$ and the values of α, β, γ, and δ.

Moreover, the simulation was performed with only one UAV (UAV1) that moved between the area points. However, there is no guarantee that by deploying only one UAV, the information on evacuees and disaster situation can be captured in real time. Moreover, unpredictable situations, for instance, low battery power of UAV1, may occur. Accordingly, increasing the number of UAV1s to move between area points is deemed necessary to obtain information in real time.

As mentioned in the previous section, there are many restrictions in our simulation experiments. We are aware of the limitations and unrealistic assumptions in the simulator. As the next step, we are re-designing our simulator where we employ the real map of a mountainous region of North of Japan and multiple UAVs. Based on the results of this simulator, we will build a real multi-agent based evacuation support system using multiple UAVs with large mobile batteries.

Acknowledgements. This work is partially supported by Japan Society for Promotion of Science (JSPS), with the basic research program (C) (No. 20K05010), Grant-in-Aid for Scientific Research (KAKENHI).

References

1. Taga, S., Matsuzawa, T., Takimoto, M., Kambayashi, Y.: Multi-agent base evacuation support system using MANET. Vietnam J. Comput. Sci. **6**(2), 177–191 (2019)
2. Kambayashi, Y., Konishi, K., Sato, R., Azechi, K., Takimoto, M.: A prototype of evacuation support systems based on the ant colony optimization algorithm. In: Borzemski, L., Świątek, J., Wilimowska, Z. (eds.) ISAT 2018. AISC, vol. 852, pp. 324–333. Springer, Cham (2019). https://doi.org/10.1007/978-3-319-99981-4_30
3. Tago, I., Suzuki, N., Matsuzawa, T., Takimoto, M., Kambayashi, Y.: A proposal of evacuation support system with redundancy using multiple mobile agents. In: Jezic, G., Chen-Burger, Y.-H., Kusek, M., Šperka, R., Howlett, R.J., Jain, L.C. (eds.) Agents and Multi-Agent Systems: Technologies and Applications 2019. SIST, vol. 148, pp. 47–56. Springer, Singapore (2020). https://doi.org/10.1007/978-981-13-8679-4_4
4. Tago, I., Konishi, K., Takimoto, M., Kambayashi, Y.: Providing efficient redundancy to an evacuation support system using remote procedure calls. In: Jezic, G., Chen-Burger, J., Kusek, M., Sperka, R., Howlett, R.J., Jain, L.C. (eds.) Agents and Multi-Agent Systems: Technologies and Applications 2020. SIST, vol. 186, pp. 47–56. Springer, Singapore (2020). https://doi.org/10.1007/978-981-15-5764-4_5
5. Katayama, K., Takahashi, H., Yokota, N., Sugiyasu, K., Kitagata, G., Kinoshita, T.: An effective multi-UAVs-based evacuation guidance support for disaster risk reduction. In: 2019 IEEE International Conference on Big Data and Smart Computing, pp. 1–6 (2019)
6. Kambayashi, Y., Nishiyama, T., Matsuzawa, T., Takimoto, M.: An implementation of an ad hoc mobile multi-agent system for a safety information. In: Grzech, A., Borzemski, L., Świątek, J., Wilimowska, Z. (eds.) Information Systems Architecture and Technology: Proceedings of 36th International Conference on Information Systems Architecture and Technology – ISAT 2015 – Part II. AISC, vol. 430, pp. 201–213. Springer, Cham (2016). https://doi.org/10.1007/978-3-319-28561-0_16

7. Taga, S., Matsuzawa, T., Takimoto, M., Kambayashi, Y.: Multi-agent approach for evacuation support system. In: Herik, J., Filipe, J. (eds.) Ninth International Conference on Agents and Artificial Intelligence, vol. 1, pp. 220–227 (2017)
8. Taga, S., Matsuzawa, T., Takimoto, M., Kambayashi, Y.: Multi-agent approach for return route support system simulation. In: Herik, J., Filipe, J. (eds.) Eighth International Conference on Agents and Artificial Intelligence, vol. 1, pp. 269–274 (2016)
9. Goto, H., Ohta, A., Matsuzawa, T., Takimoto, M., Kambayashi, Y., Takeda, M.: A guidance system for wide-area complex disaster evacuation based on ant colony optimization. In: Herik, J., Filipe, J. (eds.) Eighth International Conference on Agents and Artificial Intelligence, vol. 1, pp. 262–268 (2016)
10. Ohta, A., Goto, H., Matsuzawa, T., Takimoto, M., Kambayashi, Y., Takeda, M.: An improved evacuation guidance system based on ant colony optimization. In: Lavangnananda, K., Phon-Amnuaisuk, S., Engchuan, W., Chan, J. (eds.) Intelligent and Evolutionary Systems. PALO, vol. 5, pp. 15–27. Springer, Cham (2016). https://doi.org/10.1007/978-3-319-27000-5_2
11. Taga, S., Matsuzawa, T., Takimoto, M., Kambayashi, Y.: Multi-agent base evacuation support system considering altitude. In: Rocha, A., Steels, L., Herik, J. (eds.) 11th International Conference on Agents and Artificial Intelligence, vol. 1, pp. 299–306 (2019)
12. Taga, S., Matsuzawa, T., Takimoto, M., Kambayashi, Y.: Multi-agent base evacuation support system using MANET. In: Nguyen, N.T., Pimenidis, E., Khan, Z., Trawiński, B. (eds.) ICCCI 2018. LNCS (LNAI), vol. 11055, pp. 445–454. Springer, Cham (2018). https://doi.org/10.1007/978-3-319-98443-8_41

A Simple Agent Based Modeling Tool for Plastic and Debris Tracking in Oceans

Sai Amulya Murukutla📷, S. B. Koushik📷, Sai Pranay Raju Chinthala📷,
Abhishek Bobbillapati📷, and Subu Kandaswamy(✉)📷

Indian Institute of Information Technology, Sri City, Andhra Pradesh, India
{saipranayraju.c17,subu.k}@iiits.in

Abstract. Plastics and the pollution caused by their waste have always been a menace to both nature and humans. With the continual increase in plastic waste, the contamination due to plastic has stretched to the oceans. Many plastics are being drained into the oceans and rose to accumulate in the oceans. These plastics have seemed to form large patches of debris that keep floating in the oceans over the years. Identification of the plastic debris in the ocean is challenging and it is essential to clean plastic debris from the ocean. We propose a simple tool built using the agent-based modeling framework NetLogo. The tool uses ocean currents data and plastic data both being loaded using GIS (Geographic Information System) to simulate and visualize the movement of floatable plastic and debris in the oceans. The tool can be used to identify the plastic debris that has been piled up in the oceans. The tool can also be used as a teaching aid in classrooms to bring awareness about the impact of plastic pollution. This tool could additionally assist people to realize how a small plastic chunk discarded can end up as large debris drifting in the oceans. The same tool might help us narrow down the search area while looking out for missing cargo and wreckage parts of ships or flights. Though the tool does not pinpoint the location, it might help in reducing the search area and might be a rudimentary alternative for more computationally expensive models.

Keywords: Plastic movement · Agent based modelling · Plastics in oceans · Agent based simulation and prediction

1 Introduction

A large number of plastics are being manufactured for numerous purposes. Recycle and reuse seem to be a substitute solution. However, the extensive usage of plastics has never assisted in reducing the pollution level in the environment. With the immense plastic quantity and improper cleaning practices, plastics have ended up in the water bodies like lakes, rivers, sea [3]. The plastics from these water bodies settle up in the oceans amidst the extra plastic pollution.

Over 300 million tons of plastic are manufactured every year. Plastics are utilized in a wide variety of applications. Of all these plastics, at least 8 million

© Springer Nature Switzerland AG 2021
F. Dignum et al. (Eds.): PAAMS 2021, LNAI 12946, pp. 139–150, 2021.
https://doi.org/10.1007/978-3-030-85739-4_12

tons of plastic settle up in the oceans. These deliver 80% of all the oceanic debris from surface waters to deep-sea sediments [22]. The contamination of oceans with plastics is the greatest peril. It jeopardizes the amount of oxygen level present in the oceans, which directly affects marine life. As the surface currents focalize in specific locations, the buoyant debris will tend to assemble in certain regions [24]. These inflation regions are regularly known as great ocean garbage patches [16].

With enormous input of debris into the ocean, most of which are floating on the oceans, there is a considerable chance that the plastics will make their way into endless gyres [1, 23]. For instance, a cargo container of 28,000 plastic bath toys dropped overboard in the middle of the North Pacific Ocean on its route from Hong Kong to the United States in 1992 [18]. The toys kept wafting in the oceans and eventually, these yellow ducks have bobbed halfway, encompassing the world. The question concerning how these ducks settled up in radically distinct locations of the world had helped in understanding the ocean currents [18]. Similarly, debris from the Malaysian airlines crash in 2014 was noticed nearly after 17 months, 4000 km away from the presumed crash site near the shores of South Africa, Mozambique, and Rodrigues Islands [13, 17].

As it is difficult to identify and retrieve the floating debris in the oceans, a tool can help locate and understand the movement of floating debris in the ocean. This tool can also help analyze the formation of large gliding debris clusters at varied locations in the open ocean [7]. Though the harm caused to the environment by humans cannot be reversed, it is important to educate people about plastic pollution. A study [10] stated that environmental education is required to bridge the information gap and enhance possibilities to adopt pro-environmental behaviours. In general, there are four main educational approaches on plastic pollution [5] which are community-based education followed by Japan, government-based education followed by Taiwan, business-based education followed by the U.K, and school-based education followed by Hong Kong. An experiment was conducted on children by the Centre for Education in Environmental Sustainability (CEES) to see which strategy would work better. It was noticed that Simulation Game-Based Teaching Strategy worked better to enrich student's knowledge, behaviour, and attitude towards a safe environment.

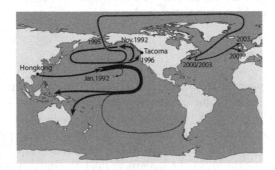

Fig. 1. Picture depicting the travel patterns of the ducks [18]

Simulation-based teaching provides learning with a practice that supports altering and understanding the aspects of reality [4]. Studies have shown that computer-based simulations can be an effective teaching tool in various domains [6]. Hence, a simple computer-based simulation would be swift and easy to understand (Fig. 1).

With this motivation, we have modelled the movement of plastics in the ocean using NetLogo to understand where the plastics can end up when discarded at a specific point. The tool can educate people on the amount of plastic that is being ended up in the oceans and assist in visually tracking the formations of large debris in the oceans. The tool can further give an idea of how ocean currents across the world affect debris tracking. The tool might help minimize the search area and might save time in locating crashed ships or flights by tracking its movement beginning from the crash location. A good start for narrowing down the search.

Since the movement of the floating plastic is constrained by the surface currents, we have acquired the ocean currents and plastics discarded at different shores data and have modelled the movement of the plastic in the oceans with NetLogo. Due to inadequate data, the validation of the model is challenging. Flight wreckage tracking is a handy way to validate the model and we used Malaysian airline's crash data to track the possible locations of wreckage parts [17]. Also, validated the formation of the plastic cluster in the middle of the pacific ocean [1,23] over eight years.

2   Related Work

Historically, researchers practiced propelling devices into oceans to measure wind speed, pressure, temperature, and salinity and then apply complex mathematical models to estimate surface water currents to assume the movements of ocean currents. After the disturbance of toy ducks in 1992 [18], a lot of effort went into understanding ocean surface currents.

OSCURS (Ocean Surface Currents Simulator) [12] is a numerical model with a computation grid of 40 by 140 that stretches laterally across the North Pacific Ocean from the west coast of the U.S. (124°W) to southern Japan (130°E) and stretches longitudinally southward from Bering Strait (67°N) to about latitude 30°N. The key input field used in the model is daily sea-level pressure data acquired from records of the U.S. Navy, FNMOC (Fleet Numerical Meteorology and Oceanography Center) Monterey, California, over the division of the standard FNMOC 380 km (63 by 63) grid between latitude 50°N and 68°N and longitude 100°W and 120°E [12]. Surface pressure signifies the OSCURS model's key attribute, which supports computing ocean currents directions and the surface transport vectors. These vectors are determined by holding frictional influences caused by ocean currents along latitudes and wind speeds. Also, the edge causes like friction at shores are taken into account to simulate the complete OSCURS model.

The Ocean Plastic Generator tool by Cawthron Institute [20] is on similar lines with our model. However, with a limited scope, i.e., it simulates plastic movement only in Cook Strait, Golden Bay, Tasman Bay, Hauraki Gulf, Firth of Thames, and Tauranga Moana areas around New Zealand. Also, it assigns coasts around New Zealand into triangular grids with knowledge on tides, currents, wind, temperature, and salinity in them. So, based on the parameters, it drives plastic in oceans. While these models are reasonably accurate, they tend to be harder to interpret due to complex mathematical equations, which may not suit well as a learning tool. On the contrary, our model is data-driven, simple to follow, rebuild, and educate ordinary people. Additionally, it attempts to cover the entire world without narrowing it to certain locations.

3   Input Data

The data is crucial in delivering a more accurate and effective model. The data required are the surface currents data that stimulate the plastic movement and the quantity of plastic present at diverse shores to understand their movement. Plastic quantity at the east coastline of the US in the Antarctic Ocean and shores around Australia are considered. All the data is converted to shapefiles using QGIS (Quantum Geographic Information System) Software and is loaded into NetLogo with GIS (Geographic Information System) extension. Before deciding on QGIS, we looked into ArcGIS. But comparatively, QGIS is better because it is open-source, free to use, and can be used on any operating system. It loads faster, has better documentation and performs operations more efficiently [14].

World Map Data: The countries data set is loaded into NetLogo with the help of the GIS (Geographic Information Systems) extension. It can load vector features like lines and polygons into the NetLogo model from shapefiles. So, using the World Map shapefile, we have modeled the separation of the landmass from the oceans. This shapefile has an attribute of area, and this attribute holds the area of the region in sq-km. For countries (polygons), this attribute has a numerical value while oceans have a fixed value of 0. So, based on this area attribute, countries and oceans are differentiated.

Ocean Currents Data: The dataset consists of surface currents data obtained by satellite-tracked surface sailing buoys ("drifters") for the NOAA (National Oceanic and Atmospheric Administration) Global Drifter Program [19]. The data contains the following attributes: date, time, surface water temperature, and velocities (eastward, northward) at a specified location (latitude and longitude). Only surface water velocities in east and north direction attributes are considered for this model. The latest available data at each latitude-longitude intersection is retrieved and converted into shape format using QGIS software for easier loading through the GIS extension of NetLogo. With GIS, the global coordinate system latitude-longitude is mapped to the NetLogo world coordinates. The data retrieved is mapped to NetLogo patches. If the patch has no data, interpolation is done by considering the average of neighboring patches data.

Plastic Data: We are using two datasets of the floating debris.

1. Debris in the Atlantic ocean at the east coast of the USA [8]. This dataset has the following attributes: date, plastic pieces/Kilometer-Square collected from 1989 through 2008 at the latitude-longitude location.
2. Debris around the shores of Australia [15]. This dataset consists of date, latitude, and longitude. Also, the plastics are divided into four size categories and have records of weights and particle count. In this dataset, we are utilizing the particle count of thick plastic category attributes at a latitude-longitude location.

As a preprocessing step, the datasets are converted into shape format using QGIS software and loaded into the NetLogo model using GIS extension where plastics, represented as agents, are created at the latitude-longitude location. We are assuming the plastic in data is floating all the time on the ocean's surface and does not sink to the depth.

4   Model Implementation

The model is implemented in NetLogo. NetLogo is a multi-agent programming language and modelling suite that runs simulation based on an agent to agent and agent to environment interactions for each time step called tick. Turtles are represented as agents, and the patches represent a point in the NetLogo world (simulation space). Both, turtles and patches can have multiple properties which the user can define.

In the simulation, patches represent the world as land and ocean. Patches in white colour represent land, and in blue represent the ocean. The plastic/debris are mobile in nature i.e. they move in reaction to the surface currents. Hence, we found it appropriate to simulate them as turtle agents.

With the NetLogo GIS extension, we load shape files. The shape files consist of real-time surface currents, area, and plastics data for distinct coordinate locations, as mentioned in Sect. 3. With the GIS system, a world map bounded with longitudes varying from −180 to 180 and latitudes varying from −60 to 72 is loaded into the model for visualization. In addition to the built-in patch properties, patches have below properties:

- area: area of a region of land, which is zero for oceans.
- p_lat: latitude of the world.
- p_long: longitude of the world.
- speed_north: Speed of ocean current in north direction (km/day).
- speed_east: Speed of ocean current in east direction (km/day).
- magnitude: The measure of the distance that can be travelled (km).
- direction: The direction in which the displacement of plastic happens.

For each individual patch, the values for above properties will be assigned based on the world map data and surface water currents data. The values remain unchanged throughout the simulation. Firstly, each patch is identified using the p_lat and p_long values, and then the speed_north and speed_east values from the dataset mentioned in Sect. 3 are assigned to that patch. To avoid recomputation, the resultant vector is computed as a sum of speed_north and speed_east and stored in the patch variables 'magnitude' and 'direction'.

Turtles have latitude and longitude properties which maintain the location of turtle in the world. At each time step (tick), the latitude and longitude of the turtles are updated. The tool allows the user to control different default values and settings via the user interface, as shown in Fig. 2.

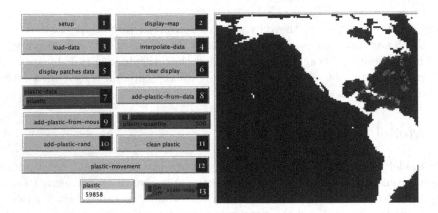

Fig. 2. Interface of the cropped world model with buttons to command simulation

Interface Control

(1) Set Up: Loads the country data required to display the world map mentioned in section 3.1 and fixes the patch size to 3.

(2) Display Map: Designates colours to patches based on the area from the data stated in section 3.1 into blue and white i.e. if the area of land is greater than zero, the [pcolor] property of a patch is set to white, symbolizing the land region else blue indicating the oceans.

(3) Add currents data: Loads the surface currents data and initializes the patch properties: magnitude, direction, latitude, and longitude. The surface currents data which are in the form of shape files are loaded into NetLogo through GIS extension. The data attributes (latitude, longitude, velocity of surface water in north and east direction) are mapped to patch properties. Velocities of ocean currents attributes of data which are in meter per second dimensions are converted to km per day while mapping to patch properties. Patches are assigned with magnitude and direction by calculating from velocities in north and east directions.

$$(V_R)^2 = (V_N)^2 + (V_E)^2 \tag{1}$$

$$Magnitude = (V_R * Time) \tag{2}$$

$$Direction = \tan^{-1}(\frac{V_N}{V_E}) \tag{3}$$

V_N is the velocity of the ocean currents in the north direction in km/day, V_E is the velocity of the ocean currents in the east direction in km/day. Hence Resultant velocity V_R is calculated from Eq. 1. The direction is calculated from Eq. 3, which specifies the angle of the motion of a plastic. NetLogo measures time with the ticks. In this model, each tick signifies one day and the velocity is in the km/day scale, so we calculate the magnitude from Eq. 2 by which a plastic can displace.

(4) Interpolate data: Unfortunately we don't have sufficient data for all the patches spanning across the entire map of the world. So, we used interpolation to make up for missing data. The interpolation is done by averaging eight neighbouring patches' resultant speeds and directions. This step is repeated until there are no more empty patches.

(5) Display patches data: Displays all the patches with surface currents data with red colour, which helps visualize the surface currents data and the blind spots.

(6) Clear display: After displaying the data with patches, this resets the display to enable further functioning.

(7) plastic-data: Here, there are two options to select (1) East of the US east coastline in the Atlantic Ocean, (2) Australia coastline.

(8) add plastic data: For the selected location specified in 7, it loads the plastic into NetLogo from the input data as mentioned in Sect. 3.3. [8,15]. It considers the locations and the plastic quantity. It creates those amount of turtles(representing plastic pollution) at the mentioned locations.

(9) Add plastic from mouse: This allows the user to place plastic pollution anywhere in the ocean using a mouse click. The amount of plastic placed can be controlled using the plastic-quantity slider.

(10) add plastic rand: This initializes the system with random plastic pollution. The amount of plastic can be controlled via the plastic-quantity slider.

(11) clean plastic: removes all the plastic from the simulation.

(12) plastic movement: This simulates the displacement of plastic. A detailed explanation of simulation is mentioned in the below subsection. The basic flow of the model is mentioned in the flow diagram in Fig. 3 below.

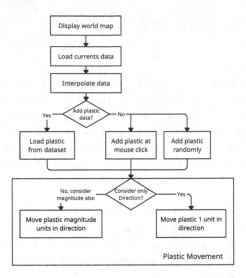

Fig. 3. Flow chart of the model

4.1   Simulation of Plastic Movement

Each patch has properties that specify the magnitude and direction of the current. The plastic modelled as NetLogo agent moves based on the direction and the magnitude of the water current at every tick. Experimented on two conditions to analyse the movement of plastics in the ocean. Started the experiment considering only the direction which was computed from the dataset mentioned in Sect. 3. This parameter specifies in which direction the plastic should move with a constant magnitude of 1. Then along with direction speed is considered for the movement of plastic because adding more input to the model might increase its accuracy. But, the results from the direction-only experiment matched well with the validation data than the direction-speed experiment.

Experimental Condition 1: Here, only the direction in which the plastic should relocate is acknowledged omitting the measure of magnitude it should transfer. Hence the plastic updates only the heading property according to the direction computed in Eq. 3 and displaces 1 unit in that course. We are considering a fixed speed of 1 unit forward per tick since it is the minimum distance a plastic has to move to get into a new patch with different latitude and longitude from the current position. All the plastics proceed forward in their course of the path, i.e. the direction keeps changing for every tick. While modelling, a few assumptions are considered, which are listed below.

Experimental Condition 2: Initially, the plastic fixes its direction, i.e. heading property of the turtle and holds the magnitude from patch properties. This direction and magnitude, along with current latitude and longitude attributes of plastic, are considered to calculate the next latitude and longitude position of plastic using the haversine formula [21]:

$$\phi' = \sin^{-1}(\sin(\phi) * \cos(\frac{d}{R})) + (\cos(\phi) * \sin(\frac{d}{R}) * \cos(b)) \tag{4}$$

$$\lambda' = \lambda + \tan^{-1}(\frac{\sin(b) * \sin(\frac{d}{R}) * \cos(\phi)}{\cos(\frac{d}{R}) - (\sin(\phi) * \sin(\phi'))}) \tag{5}$$

Where ϕ is initial latitude, λ is initial longitude, ϕ' is final latitude, λ' is final longitude, R is earth's radius (mean radius = 6,371 km), b is the direction and d is the magnitude. The calculated latitude and longitude are attributed to the plastics. Thus for every tick i.e. a day, the plastic updates its latitude and longitude properties.

1. The NetLogo world size is set in such a way that each patch accounts for one coordinate (longitude, latitude).
2. As only one data record can be assigned to a single patch, the speed and direction of surface water currents are identical between two coordinates (longitude, latitude) i.e. in a patch.
3. The model delivers the latest ocean current information for a particular latitude, longitude (i.e. patch) from the dataset.
4. The data that the model is built on assumes to have no influence by the cyclone, turbulence, or any other causes.
5. Though surface currents are influenced by additional factors like temperature and abrupt calamities. These are not reflected in the model as the data concerning the same is not consistent.
6. While all plastics do not float, however, due to inadequate knowledge on how deep a plastic can sink and the types of plastic bodies that affect their sink or float ability. There is no data available to support the above points, and it is troublesome to determine the time after which plastic can sink. Taking these points into account, we have assumed all the plastics here remain to float or maintain a constant depth throughout the simulation.

5   Model Validation

Validating this model was challenging because of the unavailability of data. The only information on which we could rely for validation was the formation of the great pacific patch and the movement of wrecked parts of Malaysian airlines (Figs. 4 and 5).

We ran this model on the plastic data from the US east coastline using condition one and condition two for about 3000 ticks i.e. about 8 years. After this duration of the simulation, we observed that a large debris patch had been created in the middle of the Pacific Ocean, similar to the one mentioned in this paper [23]. The movement of plastics mentioned in the paper [23] is very similar to the ones we simulated. In addition, we considered the recent crash of

Fig. 4. Plastic around the predicted crash site

Fig. 5. Plastic near Africa after running the simulation

Malaysia airline Flight 370 [9] to validate the model. The predicted crash site of this airline is at a remote part of the Indian Ocean 2,500 km (1,500 miles) southwest of Australia at location 35.6°S 92.8°E [2,11]. About 2 years later the parts of the airline are found at the shores of Tanzania, Mozambique, South Africa, Madagascar, and Mauritius.

We simulated this crash with two experimental conditions, with condition one considering the speed and direction of surface water currents and condition two considering only the direction of surface water current—both the simulations starting from the initial plane wreckage point. In experimental condition one, the debris had ended up as clusters near the shores of Australia. This could be happening because the model considers only the latest record in the dataset, and it is having low surface water speeds making the plastic end up in clusters or move towards Australia. In experimental condition two, the plastic ends up near Madagascar and Africa's shores, thus validating our model for the Malaysian airline's crash data. As desired results were not obtained with experimental condition one, we went on with experimental condition two.

6   Discussions and Future Work

This paper proposes an agent-based model for simulating plastic and debris movement in the ocean using the dataset of surface water currents [19,23] collected from drifters. The model works by simulating plastic displacement by calculating the drift based on the direction of surface water currents. It is imperative to educate people that plastic pollution can have a global effect while seemingly local to geography. We posit that our model could be an effective educational tool that enables understanding how 79 thousand tonnes of ocean plastic are floating inside an area of 1.6 million km^2, rapidly accumulating at the Great Pacific Garbage Patch [16]. Additionally, this model is beneficial for those studying and learning the consequence of ocean currents on floating debris movements. While the data for validation is not easily available nevertheless, the model simulation of plastic pollution along the US coast [8] and Australian coast [15] clearly shows how surface water currents can bring plastic debris from different geographical areas to coalesce into garbage patches. While the model shows garbage patch formation, it is too optimistic to claim the accuracy of the garbage patch location, given that in the real world, the debris could be affected by many other factors, including weather, etc. Nevertheless, our model, which is computationally cheap, easy to understand, and accessible to the common public, is a good start to encourage more studies in this area. Thus we claim that our model has high pedagogical value. The easy accessibility enables researchers to modify and test their hypotheses. Though more data is needed to verify, we also posit that this model may help to narrow down ship and flight wreckage in the oceans. While not a high-precision tool, it might still be a rudimentary first step for forming hypotheses about the search area.

In the future, we would like to address some of the limitations of the model and comprehend how natural events like cyclones and turbulence affect plastic movement in the oceans. We would likewise incorporate sinking into the equation to understand how the pollution could reach and affect deep-sea marine organisms and the ocean floors.

References

1. Boxall, S.: From rubber ducks to ocean gyres. Nature **459**(7250), 1058–1059 (2009)
2. Calder, S.: Australia thinks it's finally found the crash site for missing flight MH370 2017. The Independent, August 2017. https://www.independent.co.uk/travel/news-and-advice
3. Chenillat, F., Huck, T., Maes, C., Grima, N., Blanke, B.: Fate of floating plastic debris released along the coasts in a global ocean model. Marine Pollution Bull. **165**, 112116 (2021). https://doi.org/10.1016/j.marpolbul.2021.112116
4. Chernikova, O., Heitzmann, N., Stadler, M., Holzberger, D., Seidel, T., Fischer, F.: Simulation-based learning in higher education: a meta-analysis. Rev. Educ. Res. **90** (2020). https://doi.org/10.3102/0034654320933544
5. Chow, C.-F., So, W.-M.W., Cheung, T.-Y., Yeung, S.-K.D.: Plastic waste problem and education for plastic waste management. In: Kong, S.C., Wong, T.L., Yang, M., Chow, C.F., Tse, K.H. (eds.) Emerging Practices in Scholarship of Learning and Teaching in a Digital Era, pp. 125–140. Springer, Singapore (2017). https://doi.org/10.1007/978-981-10-3344-5_8
6. Curtin, L.B., Finn, L.A., Czosnowski, Q.A., Whitman, C.B., Cawley, M.J.: Computer-based simulation training to improve learning outcomes in mannequin-based simulation exercises. Am. J. Pharm. Educ. **75**(6) (2011)
7. Cózar, A., et al.: Plastic debris in the open ocean. Proc. Natl. Acad. Sci. U.S.A. **111** (2014). https://doi.org/10.1073/pnas.1314705111
8. Eriksen, M.: Plastic Marine Pollution Global Dataset, May 2014. https://figshare.com/articles/dataset/Plastic_Marine_Pollution_Global_Dataset/1015289/1. https://doi.org/10.6084/m9.figshare.1015289.v1
9. Gregersen, E.: Malaysia airlines flight 370 disappearance. Encyclopedia Britannica. https://www.britannica.com/event/Malaysia-Airlines-flight-370-disappearance
10. Hammami, M.B.A., et al.: Survey on awareness and attitudes of secondary school students regarding plastic pollution: implications for environmental education and public health in Sharjah City, UAE. Environ. Sci. Poll. Res. **24**(25), 20626–20633 (2017). https://doi.org/10.1007/s11356-017-9625-x
11. Holmes, O.: MH370: satellite images show "probably man-made" objects floating in sea. The Guardian, August 2017. https://www.theguardian.com/world/2017/aug/16/french-images-bolster-theory-mh370-crashed-north-of-search-area

12. Ingraham, W.J., Miyahara, R.K.: Ocean surface current simulations in the North Pacific Ocean and the Bering Sea (OSCURS-numerical model) (1988). https://repository.library.noaa.gov/view/noaa/5795. Technical Memorandum
13. Jansen, E., Coppini, G., Pinardi, N.: Drift simulation of MH370 debris using superensemble techniques. Nat. Hazards Earth Syst. Sci. **16**(7), 1623–1628 (2016)
14. Khan, S., Mohiuddin, K.: Evaluating the parameters of ArcGIS and QGIS for GIS applications. Int. J. Adv. Res. Sci. Eng. **7**, 582–594 (2018)
15. Lavender Law, K., Proskurowski, G.: Plastics in the North Atlantic subtropical gyre, January 2012. http://doi.iedadata.org/100014. https://doi.org/10.1594/IEDA/100014
16. Lebreton, L., et al.: Evidence that the great pacific garbage patch is rapidly accumulating plastic. Sci. Rep. **8**(1), 4666 (2018). https://doi.org/10.1038/s41598-018-22939-w
17. Lumpur, R.i.K.: Malaysia confirms debris found near Tanzania is from missing MH370 jet. the Guardian, September 2016. http://www.theguardian.com/world/2016/sep/15/malaysia-confirms-debris-near-tanzania-missing-mh370-plane
18. Nelson, B.: What can 28,000 rubber duckies lost at sea teach us about our oceans. Mother Nature Netw. **3**(1), 1–1 (2011). https://www.treehugger.com/what-can-rubber-duckies-lost-at-sea-teach-us-about-4864165
19. NOAA: National oceanic and atmospheric administration's global drifter program home page. https://www.aoml.noaa.gov/phod/gdp/index.php. Accessed 01 July 2021
20. Pūtaiao, P.A.: Tracking plastics in our oceans. Sci. Learn. Hub (2019). https://www.sciencelearn.org.nz/resources/2807-tracking-plastics-in-our-oceans
21. Robusto, C.C.: The cosine-haversine formula. Am. Math. Monthly **64**(1), 38–40 (1957)
22. Thevenon, F., Carroll, C., Sousa, J.: Plastic debris in the ocean: the characterization of marine plastics and their environmental impacts, situation analysis report. Gland, Switzerland: IUCN 52 (2014)
23. Van Sebille, E., England, M.H., Froyland, G.: Origin, dynamics and evolution of ocean garbage patches from observed surface drifters. Environ. Res. Lett. **7**(4), 044040 (2012)
24. Wabnitz, C., Nichols, W.: Editorial: plastic pollution: an ocean emergency. Marine Turtle News Lett. **20** (2010)

Multi-agent CHANS: BDI Farmer Intentions and Decision Making

Tito Julio Muto[1,3] , Elias Buitrago Bolivar[2,3] , Jairo E. Serrano[2,3(✉)] ,
and Enrique González[1,3]

[1] Pontificia Universidad Javeriana, Bogotá, Colombia
{tmuto,egonzal}@javeriana.edu.co
[2] Corporacion Universitaria Republicana, Bogota, Colombia
ebuitrago@urepublicana.edu.co
[3] Universidad Tecnológica de Bolívar, Cartagena, Colombia
jserrano@utb.edu.co

Abstract. This paper extends previous works on multi-agent-based simulation models of Coupled Human and Natural Systems (CHANS), by introducing a farmer agent model capable of interact with environmental, economic, and spatial variables in the context of supply and demand of environmental services. Emphasis is made on how the Farmer Agent implements the BDI framework (Believes, Desires, and Intentions) at its core. Also, insights about its decision-making mechanism based on fuzzy logic are provided. Preliminary results are shown in terms of modulating variables such as knowledge, money, well-being, energy, and productivity.

Keywords: Complex-environmental systems · Multi-agent systems · Emotional BDI · Multi-agent simulation · BDI agent · Fuzzy logic

1 Introduction

The incorporation of models of human decision-making processes in social simulations is a powerfull strategy to understand the effects of human adaptive behavior on global simulation outcomes. In Coupled Human and Natural Systems (CHANS) systems, the focus consist in jointly model humans with communities and their interactions with the territory, following realistic observed patterns, in order to enhance the comprehension of human decisions regarding ecology and how these decisions can be formalized in models created by Schluter et al. [12]. However, this type of modeling is complex due to the multifactorial nature of the human decision-making process concerning ecology, as it involves economic aspects, non-economic benefits, social influence, social impact, emotions, uncertainty, knowledge about the environment, spatial location within the ecosystem, among other factors [5]. There are two predominant approaches to include the individual's decision processes in CHANS simulation models: bio-economic and agent-based models. Bio-economic models focus their attention on investigating questions related to optimal decision making as a function of

© Springer Nature Switzerland AG 2021
F. Dignum et al. (Eds.): PAAMS 2021, LNAI 12946, pp. 151–162, 2021.
https://doi.org/10.1007/978-3-030-85739-4_13

temporal variability in natural resource dynamics. Probabilistic and risk estimation techniques, uncertainty analysis, among others, are used. In addition, these models seek to represent the concepts derived from ecological economics, which, according to Schluter, allows a more realistic modeling of ecological dynamics and the ethical aspects involved in the sustainability of non-renewable resources.

In contrast to the focus on the study of risk in bio-economic models, agent-based models (ABM) allow modeling the social interactions between multiple entities immersed in the simulation, while incorporating decision-making models. In this way, an approximation towards models of human behavior is possible, since agents representing human beings can "actively reevaluate their beliefs, values and functioning to adapt to unexpected environmental changes" [3]. Indeed, systematic literature reviews identify different categories of agent-based decision-making models applied in social simulation: production rule systems, psychologically and neurologically inspired models, BDI models and derivatives [9], normative and cognitive models [2]. An example of psychologically inspired decision-making architectures in CHANS is the one proposed by Malawska and Topping, with a focus on incomplete rationality. Each farmer agent is assigned one of the following objectives: profit-maximizing, yield maximizing, environmentally friendly. Additionally, each agent is assigned one of the following harvesting schemes each year: deliberation, repetition, imitation, or social comparison. The deliberation decision mode is based on a simplified form of micro-economic optimization. The architecture includes a rule to switch to a deliberation strategy if the price of a crop varies by 20% [6].

The objective of this work is to explore in-depth the BDI farmer agent presented in a previous work [8], to explain in more detail the decision-making mechanism as well as preliminary results regarding the modulation of variables such as knowledge, money, emotion, well-being, energy, and productivity. Thus, the structure of the paper is as follows. Section 2 presents the state of the art giving a context on social simulation and the BDI paradigm, whilst details of the interaction of the farmer agent with the Multi-agent-System (MAS) are given in Sect. 3. Meanwhile, the architecture of the model are presented in Sect. 4 and the specific details about the decision-making mechanism are highlighted in Sect. 5. The final two sections were left for results and conclusions.

2   Social Simulation and BDI Architectures

Despite considerable work applying classical dynamical systems models in ecology, agent-based models have demonstrated advantages in CHANS simulations, particularly in land use applications. For instance, Matthews et al. [7], compiled the main advantages described in the literature on the use of ABM for land use modeling, highlighting the following: the ability to couple social and environmental models, incorporate the influence on environmental management of micro-level decision processes, study emerging collective responses to environmental management policies, ability to model decision making at different levels (individuals and organizations), model adaptive behavior at the individual and system level. In this same work, the authors distinguish five categories related to land use, in which ABM models have been performed, namely: policy planning and analysis, participatory modeling, characterization of spatial patterns of land use or settlements, evaluation of concepts derived from social sciences, and explaining land use functions.

Agent-based models exhibit distinguishable characteristics like the search for the fulfillment of predefined objectives and the structured representations of the processes involved in the decision-making mechanism. In fact, rational agents can incorporate a mental state that allows them to make decisions according to contextual situations. This ability of ABMs can be modeled through BDI paradigm (Believes, Desires and Intentions) [9], showing interesting results in the context of social simulation because its capability to represent complex human behavior as Adam's work stated [1].

In addition, other desirable features of social simulation-oriented ABMs are posited as the following: (i) getting the agent to modulate its decision-making process by incorporating a representation of emotions in its mental state (emotions can determine the agent's ability to want to do things and work to achieve them), consistent with recognized psychological theories to bring the agent closer to bounded rationality; (ii) incorporating the representation of uncertainty in decision-making; (iii) maximizing cooperation and coordination between agents; (iv) adding a module that allows the agent to evaluate social norms and cultural values; (v) getting the agent to modulate its decision-making process through individual and collective learning. This last point is emphasized since it is desirable to model the effect that the community has on individual and collective decision-making. In this way, the concept of the social fabric and the effect of collective action on an agent's decision-making could be incorporated.

3   Multi-agent Farmer Interaction Model

This section will describe the multi-agent system and the interactions of the farmer with the other implemented entities. To define the design and behavior of the entities, the AOPOA methodology [10] was applied (this is an approach for agent-based programming with a organizational orientation of recursive decomposition of roles and goals), resulting in the generation of roles or sub-roles of agents, events, objectives, abilities, resources, and tasks of the multi-agent system. Being the entity Farmer as the main agent in the simulation, its role and the interactions it has with the other entities in the simulation will be detailed below.

3.1   General Vision of MAS

In the simulation developed, eight major roles interact (farmer, consumer, market, farm, associations, disturbances, private) as represented in the Fig. 1. These roles are decomposed into sub-roles, some implemented with BESA [4] or BESA-BDI agents and others as cellular automata in the case of land use and cover

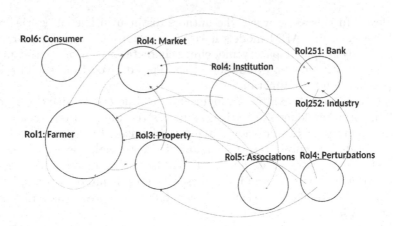

Fig. 1. Multi-agent CHANS SimSAC, Roles and high-level interaction flow.

(plant and/or mineral), water, air, and temperature, these will not be addressed in this article. BESA it's a Java library used to build multi-agent systems, ready for extensions like BDI and others, made by researchers in the Pontificia Universidad Javeriana. Next, the interactions of the Farmer Agent with the other entities in the simulation will be detailed.

3.2 Farmer Interactions

The farmer agent was implemented with a BESA-BDI architecture, whose goals are to maximize its welfare and the optimization of benefits when developing its productive activities. Throughout the simulation, the farmer can play a sub-role as an agricultural, mining, livestock, or ecosystem services producer. To achieve its goals, the agent must interact with the other entities that are part of the simulation, it interacts directly with six of the eight entities in the model and with itself, in the Table 1 the agent with whom it interacts and the description of the possible interaction are listed.

The simulation model takes into account social, economic, and environmental interactions, among others, to achieve the prioritized goals. Social interactions can achieve associativity among peers. It is also possible to observe how institution-type entities can exert influence through training and modify the beliefs of the Farmer agents, achieving incentives and improving their welfare.

4 Farmer's BDI Goal Model

The architecture of the model shows how a BESA-BDI agent (Farmer), based on a fuzzy reasoning system, incorporates its beliefs, desires, and intentions based on the interaction processes among the other agents, starting with those closest to it or having common interests, through its role. These can also change

Table 1. Multi-agent CHANS SimSAC - role descriptions

Agent	Description
Farmer	Demand or supply of products
Property	Soil exploitation or conservation
Market	Demand or supply of products or services and this in turn sells it to consumers
Institution	Receives environmental or regulatory influences, in addition to the supply of public services
Association	Product demand or supply
Bank	Make or collect loans
Industry	Demand for or supply of products or services
Perturbation	Receives negative or positive influences from the environment

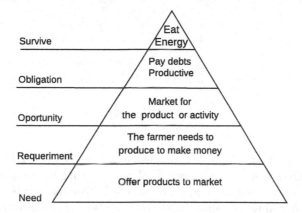

Fig. 2. Hierarchical pyramid of BDI goals

with the interaction with other external agents such as the market, institution, associations, industry, or banks. These can modify the BDIs of the financier agent based on the interaction and the financier's objectives, which change as he interacts, incorporating data and information to act, either with other agents in the same role or in a different one, or to perform actions on the automatons.

There is a disturbing agent that randomly generates events in the system, and that generates a positive or negative influence in the BDI reasoning, affecting directly in the decision-making process. The farmer agent is guided by a pyramid of priorities as shown in Fig. 2, this process is described in more detail in the Table 2. For example, in the case where the farmer agent has no energy to work and fulfill a goal related to making money by planting, it is necessary to execute the action of eating, the survival of the agent takes precedence over the productivity needs, this decision-making process will be explained in the next section in more detail.

The general process for the execution of the BDI model in the Farmer Agent is presented below, followed by a description of the beliefs and goals established in the model for reasoning and decision making.

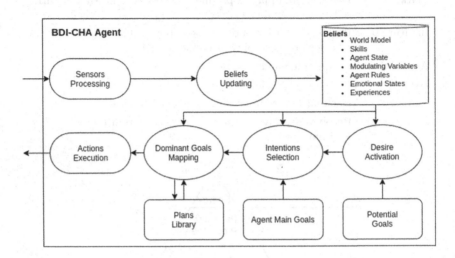

Fig. 3. BDI process

The overall goal execution flow process is based on the BDI-CHANS architecture and differs from a traditional BDI architecture in the proactivity with which beliefs, desires, and intentions are handled. To achieve this, agents include multiple threads running concurrently; there is also a series of internal events to update beliefs, evaluate goals, launch plans, or perform goal modification.

The Farmer Agent, represented in the Fig. 3, detects the conditions of its environment using different types of sensors, processes and shares the information with the process **Beliefs Update**, this process has the database of the Beliefs, composed by the model of the world, skills, the state of the agent, the modulating variables, the experiences and the rules of the agent itself. Once the Beliefs are updated, the **Desire Activation** process starts, in this process, the **Potential Goals** are analyzed and according to their activation function (consulting the Beliefs) the goal with the best valuation is activated, becoming a desire. Once the goals are activated, they go to the process of **Intention Selection**, in which the contribution is measured by evaluating the current state of the world (Beliefs) and the pyramid of priorities (explained in the decision-making model), concerning to **Agent Main Goals**. When the intent is selected, **Dominant Goals Mapping** selects an action or a set of these from the **Plans Library** to be executed or updated with an improvement for its next use.

Table 2. Farmer goals by BDI priority pyramid

Goal type	Goal	Activation	Action triggered
Survival	Farmer agent must eat	No energy	The ability to feed is activated
	Farmer agent must work to earn money	Improve their conditions	Working in productive activity
Obligation	Farmer agent must pay bank obligations	Time to pay the debt	Check if you have money to pay, and pay
	Farmer agent must take care of his productive activities	Definition of productive activities	Technical knowledge and change to the desired activity
	Farmer agent must cultivate the soil	Crop demand	Learn about agriculture
	Farmer agent must work his livestock	Demand for livestock	Learn about livestock
	Farmer agent must work his mine	Mining demand	Lear about mining
	Farmer agent must take care of his Ecological service	Demand for ecosystem services	Learn about ecosystem services
	Farmer agent must consult the market price system, demand and supply of products	Pre-requisite of an economic activity to be performed	Negotiation of product purchase
Opportunity	Farmer agent must attend the trainings offered by the training entity	Being encouraged to be socially responsible Need to be trained to carry out an economic activity	Technical knowledge of ecosystem services
	Farmer agent must review the opportunity for assistance in the development of sustainable projects	Being encouraged to be socially responsible	High environmental and ecological awareness and technical expertise
	Farmer agent must partner with others to sell their products	There is a market for the product or activity	Sales and business persuasion skills are activated
Requirements	Farmer agent must apply for a loan in order to have money and develop his activity	The farmer needs to produce and has no money to invest	He asks for a loan from the bank
Needs	Farmer agent must sell his products	Offer the market	Negotiation and sale

5   Decision-Making Model

The decision-making model in this simulation is an integration of the BDI architecture, presented before, with a Mamdani fuzzy logic inference system. The fuzzy rules are used to evaluate the agent state using the information registered in the believes. This evaluation process is achieved by using modulating variables and making decisions by applying fuzzy logic techniques as described below. The agent state is used to active and measure the contribution of the agent's goals. Then, the final action decisions are taking into account the goals according to the pyramid of priorities in which the base (or lowest priority) is the needs, moving up to the requirements, opportunities, obligations, with the highest priority being the survival of the agent itself.

5.1   Modulating Variables

A variable is considered to be a modulating variable when it is used to modify the value it contributes to an independent variable over a dependent one used to take decisions. In this case, they are used to quantify the status of the Farmer Agent in the decision-making process. The farmer's modulating variables are:

Activity type - the agent has the option to change his productive activity according to the influence of the received training, trying to maximize his investment and improving the quality of life of his family.

Personal variables - the agent can select the best way to use his property taking into account the environment and the implication of his decisions.

Terrain-dependent variables - the agent is influenced by its neighbors and by the basic needs satisfied by them.

Opportunity - the agent's opportunity goals are related to the development of productive activities that minimize environmental impact. This is achieved by improving the agent's knowledge, raising environmental awareness, or receiving an economic incentive for carrying out these actions.

Need - the need for training, sale of products, money for the development of their activity, and access to loans.

Survival - the agent must be attentive to his daily feeding and direct survival.

Obligation - the agent must pay bank obligations, carry out productive activities, take care of his family, check prices, available offers, and demand for market products.

Requirements - the agent must apply for loans from the bank to develop its activity if required.

These modulating variables define the values stored in the beliefs of the BDI Farmer agent and are necessary to determine the predominant goal at any instant of time. These variables are knowledge of the productive activity, level of proactivity, energy, emotional situation, well-being, and the amount of money available for basic needs or to develop productive activities.

The modulated variables change value as the simulation progresses and alter the beliefs of each agent as it interacts with other agents or its environment.

As beliefs change, intentions are also updated and prioritized differently, executing different actions according to the agent's internal decision-making process. This process was designed by applying fuzzy logic techniques as it is possible to apply reasoning in levels of uncertainty like humans, explained in the next section.

5.2   Decision Making with Fuzzy Logic

The decision-making process, used to evaluate the farmer goals, was implemented based on fuzzy logic inference. A set of simple fuzzy rules was generated, based on expert knowledge. The rules are if-then sentences, which approximate a fuzzy reasoning process that simulates the dynamics of each of the key decision variables of the farmer.

Figure 4 shows an example of two of the fuzzy variables, related to the six modulated variables of the Farmer Agent, that are used in the reasoning process. By applying four simple rules (see an example in Proposition 1), once the defuzzification process is done, the agent can calculate the level of productivity achieved in some commercial activity such as planting, selling or buying products.

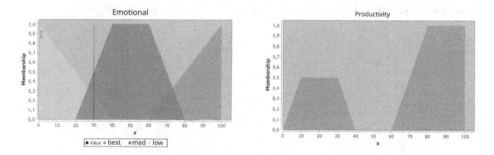

Fig. 4. SimSAC decision making: fuzzy

Proposition 1. *IF emotional IS best OR knowledge IS best OR money IS med OR energy IS best THEN production IS high.*

For example, a Farmer Agent might have 50% of his knowledge in agriculture, which may vary according to the occupation of activity, he has 50% of the money, money increases or decreases according to the sale, purchase, and welfare expenditure, 80% of energy, which may decrease in proportion to the day and the activities he performs, and 40% of welfare. Well-being is conditioned to the fulfillment or satisfaction of basic needs and increases depending on whether the farmer has more income. Emotional level 30%, calculated according to their level of work, well-being, and energy. If these are the values of the farmer's modulating variables at time t of the simulation process, the productivity level is calculated using the fuzzy inference system; in this case, a result of 62.92% is obtained for the variable associated to the agent's productivity level.

This fuzzy oriented approach is very useful, as it allows to express in a very intuitive and understandable way, closer to the real world situation, the relations between the key variables associated to the farmer's decision process. A more detailed explanation of the fuzzy decision system is out of the scope of this paper.

6   Results

An experiment was designed in which 156 plots were created in the upper basin of the Rancheria River (using data from [11]) and one was assigned to each farmer. Then, the modulating variables of the farmer, such as knowledge, money, emotion, well-being, energy, and productivity, were configured. These variables change as the farmer interacts with other agents or with his context.

In the experiment was used as independent variable the number of agents, the dependent variable was the welfare of the Farmer Agent and the intervening variable, fixed for each experiment, was defined as the level of initial knowledge of the Farmer agent, using qualitative values low, medium, high. The simulation was run with the same number of agents for five periods (five years), with a factorial design, starting with 20 agents and increasing up to 156.

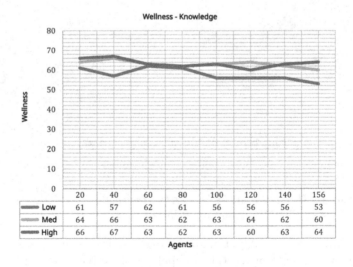

Wellness - Knowledge

	20	40	60	80	100	120	140	156
Low	61	57	62	61	56	56	56	53
Med	64	66	63	62	63	64	62	60
High	66	67	63	62	63	60	63	64

Fig. 5. SimSAC results: wellness-knowledge

The results can be seen in Fig. 5. The simulation response shows characteristics of emergence and self-organization, with a very slight tendency towards welfare. Although it is clear, as expected, that agents who start with higher knowledge tend to retain a higher degree of welfare, and the more agents with low knowledge, the lower their welfare.

7   Conclusions

A recently addressed aspect in the CHANS literature consists of simulating the potential effect of the decision-making processes of agents that represent human individuals in order to model causality between humans beings actions and ecology systems sustainability. Therefore, for a given scenario of ecosystem services, biodiversity, and productivity, this approach can be very useful to predict both economic and environmental impacts.

Based on a project that was implemented in the Rancheria river basin, real data is used to verify in an experimental and controlled way how the BDI Farmer Agents exhibiting opportunity behavior to attend training can increase their level of knowledge, which therefore leads to an increase in their well-being. However, the evidence from the experiment pointed out that in the case of the BDI Farmer Agent, it is not necessarily enough to have excellent knowledge, but on the contrary, behavioral modulating variables such as emotions, money, productivity, and their energy, are fundamental in the generation of levels of well-being or others that can be combined in the CHANS simulator model, to obtain environmental prediction scenarios.

In this work, lines of action were shown that would allow us to understand from a more holistic point of view, the relationship between agent's decision-making processes and the nature of changes in terms of land use, consumption of ecosystem services, or productivity. Despite, it is not clear yet the effect that the community has on decision-making to an individual and collective level, BDI Farmer Agents can incorporate the social fabric concept and the effect of collective action on the decision-making of a unique agent. In this way, one of the most significant contributions of this work consists in highlighting the importance of CHANS research, incorporating the representation of decision-making process based on BDI architecture involving modulating variables of the internal state of the agent as knowledge of the productive activity, level of proactivity, energy, emotional level, well-being, and the amount of money available for basic needs or to develop productive activities. Future work will include a more complex model of the influence of the community in the agent's decisions by incorporating new interactions between farmers, modulating variables and rules that will modify the evaluation of the agent's goals.

Acknowledgements. The author Jairo Enrique Serrano Castañeda thanks MIN-CIENCIAS, the Pontificia Universidad Javeriana and the Universidad Tenológica de Bolívar for the support received to pursue a doctoral degree within the programme "Becas de la Excelencia Doctoral del Bicentenario (corte 1)".

References

1. Adam, C., Gaudou, B.: BDI agents in social simulations: a survey. Knowl. Eng. Rev. **31**(3), 207–238 (2016). https://doi.org/10.1017/S0269888916000096
2. Balke, T., Gilbert, N.: How do agents make decisions? A survey. JASSS 17(4), 1 (2014). https://doi.org/10.18564/jasss.2687

3. Filatova, T., Verburg, P.H., Parker, D.C., Stannard, C.A.: Spatial agent-based models for socio-ecological systems: challenges and prospects. Environ. Model. Softw. **45**, 1–7 (2013). https://doi.org/10.1016/j.envsoft.2013.03.017
4. González, E., Avila, J., Bustacara, C.: BESA: Behavior-Oriented, Event-Driven, Social-Based Agent Framework. Undefined (2003)
5. Groeneveld, J., et al.: Theoretical foundations of human decision-making in agent-based land use models - a review. Environ. Model. Softw. **87**, 39–48 (2017). https://doi.org/10.1016/j.envsoft.2016.10.008
6. Malawska, A., Topping, C.J.: Applying a biocomplexity approach to modelling farmer decision-making and land use impacts on wildlife. J. Appl. Ecol. **55**(3), 1445–1455 (2018). https://doi.org/10.1111/1365-2664.13024
7. Matthews, R.B., Gilbert, N.G., Roach, A., Polhill, J.G., Gotts, N.M.: Agent-based land-use models: a review of applications (2007). https://doi.org/10.1007/s10980-007-9135-1. https://link.springer.com/article/10.1007/s10980-007-9135-1
8. Muto, T.J., Bolivar, E.B., González, E.: BDI multi-agent based simulation model for social ecological systems. In: De La Prieta, F., et al. (eds.) PAAMS 2020. CCIS, vol. 1233, pp. 279–288. Springer, Cham (2020). https://doi.org/10.1007/978-3-030-51999-5_23
9. Rao, A., Georgeff, M.P.: Modeling rational agents within a BDI-architecture. In: Proceedings of the 2nd International Conference on Principles of Knowledge Representation and Reasoning (1991). https://doi.org/10.5555/3087158.3087205. https://dl-acm-org.ezproxy.javeriana.edu.co/doi/10.5555/3087158.3087205
10. Rodríguez, J., Torres, M., González, E.: La Metodología Aopoa. Avances en Sistemas e Informática **4**(2) (2007)
11. Ruiz Agudelo, C.A., et al.: Hacia una economía verde en Colombia: diseño e implementación de un esquema de Pago por Servicios Ecosistémicos (PSE) en el marco del ordenamiento territorial. Fases de diseño e implementación temprana. Caso cuenca del rio Ranchería. Departamento de la Guajira-Colombia. Reflexiones sobre el Capital Natural de Colombia (3) (2013)
12. Schulze, J., Müller, B., Groeneveld, J., Grimm, V.: Agent-based modelling of social-ecological systems: achievements, challenges, and a way forward. J. Artif. Soc. Soc. Simul. **20**(2) (2017). https://doi.org/10.18564/jasss.3423

Modelling Individual Preferences to Study and Predict Effects of Traffic Policies

Johannes Nguyen[1,2]([✉]), Simon T. Powers[2], Neil Urquhart[2],
Thomas Farrenkopf[1], and Michael Guckert[1]

[1] KITE, Technische Hochschule Mittelhessen, Friedberg 61169, Germany
{Johannes.Nguyen,Thomas.Farrenkopf,michael.guckert}@mnd.thm.de
[2] School of Computing, Edinburgh Napier University, Edinburgh EH10 5DT, UK
{S.Powers,n.urquhart}@napier.ac.uk

Abstract. Traffic can be viewed as a complex adaptive system in which systemic patterns arise as emergent phenomena. Global behaviour is a result of behavioural patterns of a large set of individual travellers. However, available traffic simulation models lack of concepts to comprehensibly capture preferences and personal objectives as determining factors of individual decisions. This limits predictive power of such simulation models when used to estimate the consequences of new traffic policies. Effects on individuals must not be ignored as these are the basic cause of how the system changes under interventions. In this paper, we present a simulation framework in which the self-interested individual and its decision-making is placed at the center of attention. We use semantic reasoning techniques to model individual decision-making on the basis of personal preferences that determine traffic relevant behaviour. As this initially makes the simulations more complex and opaque the simulation framework also comprises tools to inspect rule evaluation providing a necessary element of explainability. As proof of concept we discuss an example scenario and demonstrate how this type of modelling could help in evaluating the effects of new traffic policies on individual as well as global system behaviour.

Keywords: Traffic simulation · Agent modelling · Policy assessment

1 Introduction and Motivation

Infrastructure and mobility have a strong influence on societal progress and economic growth and can become obstacles in the process of developing an economy [5]. However, change and extension of infrastructure are extremely costly and may take long time periods before showing the desired effects. Moreover, infrastructure extension often requires massive interventions with strong ecological effects and environmental impact that is counterproductive to the good intentions. This may lead to open resistance and public opposition (e.g. [20]) slowing

© Springer Nature Switzerland AG 2021
F. Dignum et al. (Eds.): PAAMS 2021, LNAI 12946, pp. 163–175, 2021.
https://doi.org/10.1007/978-3-030-85739-4_14

down infrastructure projects thus further prolonging the time before measures get effective. Beyond that, actual outcomes of measures are difficult to predict, e.g. it is well known that an extension of streets with excessive traffic often does not lead to an improved flow of vehicles but may attract more individuals than before, deteriorating the situation even more (see [15]). Therefore, innovative ideas for new mobility services (e.g. car/ride-sharing) that achieve more efficient and sustainable use of available resources can have a high leverage effect on mobility and the environment. Problems, such as frequent traffic jams and perpetual lack of parking space, are obvious indicators of a system in overload mode that requires a fundamental change in the concepts of everyday mobility. Private companies and public institutions are already working intensely on alternative strategies that exploit contemporary technological innovation [12], but need more elaborate tools for working out new mobility strategies. Before designing new mobility services cause and effect of the current traffic situation must be scrutinised in order to develop services that are accepted by the public and can eventually provide relief. Measures in complex public systems are threatened by rebound effects [4], e.g. car sharing services at first sight encourage people to abandon their private vehicles thus freeing up space in urban areas. However, if they apply to the wrong audiences effects end up worsening the inner-city traffic. It has been observed that car sharing services were accepted as an alternative to *public transport*, which in consequence has increased the number of people travelling in individual vehicles [13].

Computer-based simulations can be applied to analyse measures in complex traffic systems and to foresee such effects in advance. State of the art research has been investigating traffic as an emergent phenomenon, rather than a problem that can be modelled from a global perspective where system behaviour is modelled based on aggregated and abstract parameters (see [18] for a discussion). Emergent traffic models assume that global system behaviour results from the interactions between the personal behaviours and preferences of a large set of individuals [7]. Therefore, the application of agent models is particularly suitable for the simulation of traffic. However, available models have focused on simulating traffic as the primary subject, thus not prioritising individuals pursuing personal objectives, such as travelling to work or going to shop for grocery. In order to achieve these objectives, movement of individuals to a different location should merely be regarded as a necessary means. Consequently, road traffic itself should not be considered the sole focus when modelling traffic scenarios as individual traveller objectives are just as relevant. These objectives strongly depend on individual preferences. Hence, it is important to include these individual preferences in the process of modelling. At the same time, analysis of individual-based simulation models is difficult, because the results are based on many reciprocally influencing variables. A detailed modelling of individuals adds complexity, and therefore requires a methodical approach that achieves a higher degree of transparency through explainability.

In this paper, we create a simulation model that focuses on the individual in order to examine how new policies on mobility affect both individual and global system behaviour. For this purpose, we make use of semantic reasoning mechanisms which helps to improve analysis of individual-based simulation results. The following section provides an overview of related work and presents capabilities and scope of available modelling options. Following this, in Sect. 3 we reflect on modelling aspects that are relevant to modelling individuals and their self-interested decision behaviour. In Sect. 4, we describe modelling procedures and implement an example simulation using AGADE Traffic simulator. We then perform experimentation for a demonstration scenario and discuss results using the analysis instruments of our simulator. Finally, in Sect. 6 conclusions are drawn and possible options for future work are indicated.

2   Related Work

Multi-agent systems have become established tools for traffic simulation and there is a variety of simulators that range from general purpose platforms to systems specifically designed for specific traffic scenarios. In [18], we have studied and discussed a broad range of available simulation tools. However for this work, we will focus on three applications with functionality appropriate for modelling individual traffic participants.

1. *ITSUMO* is an open-source agent-based microscopic simulator that has been applied for the simulation of route choice scenarios. However, primary focus of the application is on traffic control [2,21]. In ITSUMO, travel demand is modelled using global origin-destination matrices. Traffic actors such as drivers and traffic lights are modelled as autonomous software agents. Regarding the aspects of agent modelling, the ITSUMO approach is fairly detailed. ITSUMO distinguishes between prejourney planning and the en route (re)planning. En route replanning refers to route changes that occur during the journey. Route selection is based on established routing algorithms. The application supports both centralised and decentralised routing.
2. *MATISSE* is a large-scale agent-based simulation platform for Intelligent Transportation Systems (ITS) [17,25]. The application focuses on the simulation of scenarios related to traffic safety. Agents are used for the representation of both vehicles as well as intersection controllers. MATISSE provides options for modelling inter-vehicle communication as well as communication with intersection controllers. Similar to the ITSUMO approach, MATISSE also supports centralised and decentralised routing for both, prejourney and en route (re)planning. However, MATISSE goes one step further in modelling the individual by including a parameter that imitates a virtual level of distraction for driver agents which causes unpredicted driving behaviour.
3. *SimMobility* is an agent-based multi-scale simulation platform that has been used to simulate the effects of different fleet sizes for on-demand autonomous mobility [1,16]. It uses an activity-based approach to generate travel demand. Agents are used to represent all sorts of entities and communication in the system such as travellers, vehicles, phones, traffic lights, etc. SimMobility

also supports prejourney and en route (re)planning. This not only refers to route choices but also to scheduling of activities that ultimately causes travel demand. Going one step further, SimMobility includes a mechanism that enables day-to-day agent learning. Key figures of the previous day are calculated to update agent knowledge for new decisions.

The applications covered demonstrate current features implemented in available traffic simulators. In the following section, we discuss the gaps and limitations as well as unused potential in the modelling of individuals.

3   Gaps and Limitations in the Modelling of Individuals

Modelling of individual traveller behaviour must consider several aspects (see Fig. 1) and usually starts with the choice of travel destination which is closely related to modelling of travel demand. For this purpose, different options of *demand modelling* have been addressed in related work. Models that make use of activity based demand generation allow a more detailed modelling of the individuals in comparison to global origin-destination matrices (see [24, 26]). Agents make a series of decisions depending on the modelled scenario. *Cost-based decision-making* is an evident criterion for decisions. However, available models have mostly been limited to obvious metrics such as travel time or distance. In order to assess the effects of traffic policies on the individual, further aspects such as *individual preferences* related to traffic as well as the simulated domain are required to be included in the modelling. Simulation models also differ in the timing of decision-making. Models that consider both prejourney and en route decisions let travellers spontaneously deviate from their initial travel plans based on situational conditions. Continuous access to real-time information via smartphones has led to *dynamic decision behaviour*. However, only a few approaches even include simple en route replanning of the travel route. SimMobility is the only approach that has gone one step further and includes replanning of the personal activity schedule. Other types of decisions such as spontaneously changing modes in the event of a sudden weather change have not been considered. This is why more work on modelling this type of spontaneous decision behaviour is required. The final modelling

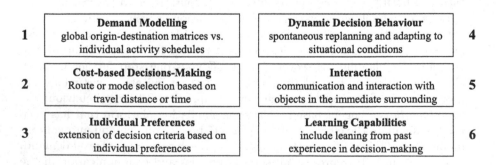

Fig. 1. Aspects of modelling individuals in traffic simulations.

aspect refers to agent capabilities to individually *learn* from past experiences. To date, there has been almost no implementation of this in available traffic models. SimMobility is the only exception that has shown any concepts towards individual agent learning in traffic simulation.

In this work we focus on modelling individual preferences using semantic reasoning techniques to improve explainability of the effects of traffic policies on both the individual and global system behaviour.

4   Modelling Individuals with AGADE Traffic

AGADE Traffic is an agent-based traffic simulator that integrates a rule-based component for modelling knowledge and individual preferences. In particular, ontologies are used to express agent knowledge in a formalised machine readable form [10]. Using rules enables the application of reasoning algorithms to infer additional agent knowledge from explicitly formulated facts. In our own previous work, we have demonstrated effectiveness and efficiency of this approach for application in agent simulation [8]. Agents can be equipped with personal ontologies that contain knowledge on domains relevant for the simulated scenario. The following scenario simulates mobility of individuals that is associated with their grocery shopping. Agents are assigned a randomly generated list of food items selected from a set of products available in the supermarkets of the simulation. This set is categorised (e.g. fruit, vegetable, grains) and probability distributions over the categories can be defined and assigned to different agent types. Agents aim at purchasing items in their lists in the course of which they have to make decisions, e.g. choosing a supermarket together with a mode of travel. Available modes of travel are using private vehicles, cycling or walking. As of now we have simplified the scenario by excluding public transport due to current state of implementation. Moreover, modelled supermarkets not only differ in product supply, but also in which products they stock, price tendency, product quality, and sustainability. In consequence, individuals may purchase the items on their assigned shopping list from more than one supermarket, which causes additional travelling to other target locations.

An agent a has a set of attributes A. A is the disjoint union of descriptive attributes Δ and preference attributes $P = T \cup \Phi$ with traffic related preferences T and food related preferences Φ. While ranges of attributes in Δ all are nominally scaled, attributes in P take values from a *Likert scale* of 1 to 5 (1="not important" and 5="very important"). Selection of attributes relevant for modelling is based on behavioural surveys on mobility [6] and grocery shopping [3] (see Table 1). Agents are given values for attributes of Δ, whereas attributes of P are derived using provided survey data. For this purpose, we modelled rules in the ontology with which for each preference a probability distribution over the Likert scale is derived. For this, descriptive attributes $\delta \in \Delta$ are used as input for the rules which output probabilities for each value on the Likert scale. For each agent a and each of its preferences τ let $p(\tau, \delta, l)$ be the probability that l will

Table 1. Attributes and preferences assigned at initialisation of an agent.

Δ	T	Φ
Age	Flexibility	Price tendency
Education	Time	Product quality
Gender	Reliability	Eco-friendliness
Occupation	Privacy	Fair trade
Marital status	Safety	
	Monetary costs	
	Environmental impact	
	Convenience	

be assigned to τ for agent a depending on the values of attributes δ. As agent preference is influenced by all its attributes $\delta \in \Delta$ the values are aggregated over Δ into the weighted sum $p(\tau, l) = \sum_{\delta \in \Delta} \lambda_\delta \cdot p(\tau, \delta, l)$ with $\sum_{\delta \in \Delta} \lambda_\delta = 1$. In this sum we weigh all attributes as of equal importance: $\lambda_\delta = \frac{1}{|\Delta|}$.

An example will illustrate this: Assume that Δ contains the two attributes *age* and *occupation* and P consists of a single preference $\tau = Environmental\ Impact$. Let a_1 with $\Delta_{a_1} = \{18\text{-}25,\ student\}$ and a_2 with $\Delta_{a_2} = \{46\text{-}55,\ factory\ worker\}$ be agents. Given their difference in descriptive attributes Δ, a_1 and a_2 probably differ in their personal preference on τ. Survey data for *age* $=18\text{-}25$ indicates that higher values for agent a_1 have higher probabilities (see Table 2). For the second descriptive attribute *occupation* again probabilities for Likert scale values are concluded from the empirical distribution of data in the survey. The weighted sum of the values for *age* and *occupation* yields $p(Environmental\ Impact, l)$ for each Likert scale value. Roulette wheel selection is used, based on the aggregated probabilities $p(\tau, l)$, to determine the value l which is then assigned to preference τ. Computation of the $p(\tau, \delta, l)$ uses rules in the ontology. By logging rule evaluation a detailed protocol of firing and non firing rules can be obtained. This log transparently explains how preferences of an individual were determined. This concludes initialisation of agent a.

Table 2. Example inference of preference probabilities for agent a_1.

Probabilites/Likert values l	1	2	3	4	5
$p(Environmental\ Impact, age, l)$	0.05	0.1	0.15	0.3	0.4
$p(Environmental\ Impact, occupation, l)$	0.1	0.1	0.2	0.3	0.3
$p(Environmental\ Impact, l)$	**0.075**	**0.1**	**0.175**	**0.3**	**0.35**

During the simulation, agents undergo two phases. The first phase is referred to as *prejourney* planning. Preference values serve as input to utility functions which are used in the planning process for the *selection of supermarkets* as well as the *choice of travel mode*. A characteristic of this scenario is that decisions are mutually interdependent and have to happen simultaneously e.g. distant supermarkets can only be reached by car while choosing to walk will likely determine a nearby market. Thus, decision making is multi-criteria and not only based on traffic related aspects but also on individual preferences relevant for the selection and purchasing of food items. In order to purchase all items on its shopping list an agent has to visit supermarkets following its personal preferences. Therefore, preferences as well as the degree to which these are satisfied is quantified in compound utility functions. The agent successively constructs a shopping journey consisting of legs from supermarket to supermarket (and from home to the first supermarket and back home from the last) with appropriate traffic modes. Supermarkets and traffic mode are chosen to maximise the utility of the agent. We first define a utility that reflects all traffic related preferences of an agent a. For a given attribute $\tau \in T$ (T the set of traffic related attributes) and a traffic mode $m \in M$ (M the set of available traffic modes), let $u(\tau, m)$ be the given utility of mode m with regard to a specific mode attribute τ and a_τ the preference value of τ for agent a. Spontaneous modal change en route accounts for extra effort and therefore involves costs which we model with a function $c : M \times M \to \mathbb{R}$ with $c(m, m')$ the associated cost for changing from mode m to mode m' with $c(m, m') = 0$ for $m = m'$. Note that we add an artificial mode m_{null} to represent the start of the food shopping journey and that $c(m_{null}, m) = 0$ for all $m \in M$. Based on this, the total traffic utility U_{TT} of traffic mode m for agent a is defined. Note that the value of this function also depends on the traffic mode m_c of the last leg.

$$U_{TT}(a, m, m_c) = \sum_{\tau \in T} u(\tau, m) \cdot a_\tau - c(m_c, m) \qquad (1)$$

Supermarkets $s \in S$ (S the set of supermarkets) are assigned utilities $u(\phi, s)$ that rate their products with regard to $\phi \in \Phi$ (Φ the set of food related attributes) (see Table 1). Furthermore, a_ϕ is the value for preference ϕ of agent a. Based on this a shopping utility $U_\Phi(a, s)$ is determined:

$$U_\Phi(a, s) = \sum_{\phi \in \Phi} u(\phi, s) \cdot a_\phi \qquad (2)$$

Besides personal utility we assess supermarkets by the degree to which the products they stock cover the items on the shopping list of an agent and by its vicinity to the current whereabouts of an agent. If the agent a has r_a open items on its list q_s of which are available in supermarket s the quotient $\frac{r_a}{q_s}$ quantifies the product coverage of s for a. Furthermore, for each agent a a randomly generated value e_a models aversion of a towards additional trips to other supermarkets based on probabilities provided by [22]. The *euclidean distance* $d(a, s)$ from the current position of a to the supermarket s is used as an estimate for the travel distance to s. For each agent values for U_{TT}, U_Φ and $d(a, s)$ are normalised with *min-max normalisation* so that they lie in [0,1]. As decisions on mode of travel and selection of supermarket are interdependent, we aggregate the traffic and food related utilities into a single utility function with which an agent determines which supermarket to go to next and how. Therefore, the leg $r = (m, s)$ to the next supermarket s is an element in $M \times S$ (with M travel modes and supermarkets S) that has a utility:

$$U(a, r, m_c) = (1 - d(a, s)) + U_{TT}(a, m, m_c) + U_{\Phi}(a, s) + \frac{r_a}{q_s} * e_a. \tag{3}$$

Algorithm 1 shows how an agent successively selects supermarkets and determines rides that are concatenated into a journey. We assume that the overall supply of all supermarkets covers all items on shopping lists and that items are abundantly available. Furthermore, no additional optimisation with respect to order is performed as we try to simulate natural behaviour of individuals. This concludes planning phase for agent a.

Algorithm 1: Algorithm to determine agent journey.

Input: agent a, location origin, set of supermarkets S, list of shopping items I_a
journey=emptylist;
while I_a *is not empty* **do**
    $r = (m, s) = \underset{r \in M \times S}{\mathrm{argmax}}\, U(a, r)$;
    journey=journey+r;
    $I_a = I_a \backslash$supply(s);
end
Result: journey

The following phase refers to agents travelling *en route*. As decisions about travel mode and target supermarkets primarily depend on preferences, which currently do not change en route, agent decisions from prejourney planning remain the same. However, agents are able to spontaneously change routes depending on present traffic load. Routing was implemented using the A* algorithm based on shortest time. Let W be a route with $w \in W$ being a continuous section of route W with same speed limit $v(w)$. Travel speed of an agent is defined $v(w, m) = min\{v(w), v(m)\}$ for $v(m)$ the maximum speed of travel mode m. Furthermore, $d(w)$ defines distance to be covered on w and $n(w)$ an indicator for present traffic load. Thus, overall travel time T is computed:

$$T(W, m) = \sum_{w \in W} \frac{d(w)}{v(w, m)} + n(w) \tag{4}$$

5   Proof-of-Concept

As an example, we look at a scenario situated in the German city of Wetzlar. According to data from the German census of 2011 [23], Wetzlar has circa 50,000 inhabitants distributed over 20 residential areas. For performance reasons, we assume that one person shops for one household and 20% of the household shop during the simulated time interval. We therefore created a population of 2130 agents which is distributed over the 20 residential areas, replicating the empirical distribution of residents. Google maps search produced 29 supermarkets. Furthermore, a consumer study [9] defines the most significant social groups in the German demographic from which we derived 12 agent types (see [19]). Agents in our population are assigned to one of these agent types respecting the distribution of these social groups in the areas under investigation. Agent types define values for the descriptive properties required for rule evaluations on preferences. Details of simulation data as well as source code of the simulation are available at GitHub.[1] Note that our current implementation uses stochastic elements only while computing preference values, thus keeping the subsequent decision processes deterministic. This simplifies analysis and proof of concept making comparison of simulations easier.

We performed two simulation runs with identical agent populations. In the second run the value for the traffic preference *Environmental Impact* changed, ceteris paribus, for 35% of the agents, meaning that 756 agents were affected, 42 of which changed their preference value from 1 to 5, 200 from 2 to 5, and 514 from 3 to 5. This models a change of attitude of 35% of the inhabitants to traffic and its environmental consequences. In the real-world, this experiment could be used to answer the research question *"How does awareness on environmentally friendly transportation affect traffic behaviour?"*.

We now analyse effects that result from this change of attitude on the decisions *selection of supermarkets* and *mode choice*. Using the analysis instruments of our simulator on data that is logged during the simulations, calculated metrics and visualisations show that in total 300 agents, i.e. circa 40% of agents affected by change of attitude, have changed from their original mode of travel. Table 3 compares modal choices of both simulation runs. The number of agents travelling by car has decreased while the percentage of pedestrians and cyclist has increased as 33 agents have changed from travelling by car to cycling, 266 from car to walking, and a single agent from cycling to walking. We assume that policy makers prefer agents to choose green transportation modes such as *walking* or *cycling* to avoid emission of exhaust fumes. In the simulation, this is mirrored through key performance indicators on aggregated travelled distances.

Table 3. Comparison of modal choices.

Modal Choice	Simulation 1	Simulation 2	Difference
Car	77.18%	63.15%	−14.03%
Bike	1.69%	3.19%	+1.5%
Walking	21.13%	33.66%	+12.53%

---

[1] see https://github.com/kite-cloud/agade-traffic.

Table 4. Evaluation indicators.

KPI	Simulation 1	Simulation 2	Difference
Global travel distance [km]	9752.14	8771.92	−10.1%
Combustion distance [km]	9009.25	7520.85	−16.5%
Avg. traveller satisfaction (normalised)	0.882525	0.881825	−0.079%

Environmental impact is measured by the indicators *global travel distance* which is the sum of the overall distances travelled by the set of all agents, and *combustion distance* that only considers modes of travel that produce exhaust gases (see Table 4). Hence, results indicate a favourable shift in modal choices. At this stage, policy makers need to evaluate whether implementation of this type of policy is worth the effort, considering that changes in modal choice in total affected circa 14% of the entire population.

In addition to this, 36 agents (4.8% of agents affected by change of attitude and 1.6% of the entire population) have changed their journey because of their selection of supermarkets. We assume policy makers to prefer agents to visit markets in their immediate neighborhood as this reduces overall traffic load. However, individual preferences may lead to selection of markets that are farther away. For example, some agents prefer to travel if products are more affordable at the target store than in their direct vicinity. Results show that 20 of these agents have in fact travelled a shorter distance but also that for the remainder travel distance has actually increased. Even though the number of agents reducing their travel distance is relatively equal to the number of agents that travelled longer distances, *global travel distance* as well as *global combustion distance* show a significant drop in the second simulation. This implies that agents reducing their travel distance have caused more impact and thus larger changes in comparison to changes caused by agents with increasing travel distance. Consequently, this is an improvement of global system behaviour with respect to the amount of traffic and pollution. In most simulation models assessment of policies ends with findings on global system behaviour due to the limited information about the individual. However, the detailed modelling of individuals enables further interpretation of results. For assessing interventions in a system by (individual) utility, we necessarily have to take a utilitarian perspective on utility [11]. Experienced utility has been associated with happiness measures [14]. We are aware that this relation between utility and happiness is debatable, but so far there is no consensus on this matter (see [11] for a discussion). Hence, we use experienced utility as an indicator for satisfaction of individuals. *Average traveller satisfaction* (see Table 4) has changed only to a minimal extent as a result of changes in surrounding social conditions. Negative effects on individuals are thus barely noticeable. Based on this, results have shown how change of attitude affects travel behaviour in this example scenario.

6   Conclusion and Future Work

As urban mobility is in constant transformation, there is a need for computer-based simulation tools to study and predict effects of new policies. However, available simulation models lack of concepts for capturing preferences and personal objectives of individuals. This makes evaluation of traffic policies difficult, as lack of information about individual behaviour limits analysis of its effects on global system behaviour. Especially, as it is well known that opposing impact of individuals can lead to counterproductive global effects. In this paper, we created a simulation model that focuses on modelling individual preferences. We demonstrated that modelling individual preferences using semantic technology can help achieve more transparent and meaningful agent decisions that are accessible to the user and increase explainability of simulation results. For future work, we will extend our models of personal preferences and utility to apply instruments of game theory and mechanism design. This will allow creation of richer simulation models for investigating effects of interventions into traffic systems as well as new mobility services on individual traffic.

Acknowledgement. This research has been supported by a grant from the Karl-Vossloh-Stiftung (Project Number S0047/10053/2019).

References

1. Adnan, M.,et al.: Simmobility: a multi-scale integrated agent-based simulation platform. In: 95th Annual Meeting of the Transportation Research Board Forthcoming in Transportation Research Record (2016)
2. Bazzan, A., do Amarante, M., Sommer, T., Benavides, A.: Itsumo: an agent-based simulator for its applications. In: Proceedings of the 4th Workshop on Artificial Transportation Systems and Simulation, p. 8. IEEE (2010)
3. Berger, M., Müller, C., Nüske, N.: Digital nudging in online grocery stores : towards ecologically sustainable nutrition. In: Proceedings of the 41st International Conference on Information Systems (ICIS 2020). AIS Electronic Library, Hyderabad, India (Dezember 2020). https://eref.uni-bayreuth.de/57729/
4. Dimitropoulos, A., Oueslati, W., Sintek, C.: The rebound effect in road transport: a meta-analysis of empirical studies. Energy Econ. **75**, 163–179 (2018). https://doi.org/10.1016/j.eneco.2018.07.021, https://www.sciencedirect.com/science/article/pii/S0140988318302718
5. Égert, B., Koźluk, T., Sutherland, D.: Infrastructure and growth (mar 2009). https://doi.org/10.1787/225682848268, https://www.oecd-ilibrary.org/content/paper/225682848268
6. Engel, U., Pötschke, M.: Mobilität und verkehrsmittelwahl 1999/2000. GESIS Datenarchiv, Köln. ZA4203 Datenfile Version 1.0.0 (2013). https://doi.org/10.4232/1.11591
7. Erol, K., Levy, R., Wentworth, J.: Application of agent technology to traffic simulation. In: Proceedings of Complex Systems, Intelligent Systems and Interfaces (1998)

8. Farrenkopf, T.: Applying semantic technologies to multi-agent models in the context of business simulations. Ph.D. thesis, Edinburgh Napier University (2017)

9. GfK Consumer Panels: consumers' choice '17 - neue Muster in der Ernährung: die Verbindung von Genuss, Gesundheit und Gemeinschaft in einer beschleunigten Welt : eine Publikation anlässlich der Anuga 2017. GfK Consumer Panels and Bundesvereinigung der Deutschen Ernährungsindustrie e.V. (2017), https://www.bve-online.de/presse/infothek/publikationen-jahresbericht/consumers-choice-2017

10. Guarino, N., Oberle, D., Staab, S.: What Is an ontology? In: Staab, S., Studer, R. (eds.) Handbook on Ontologies. IHIS, pp. 1–17. Springer, Heidelberg (2009). https://doi.org/10.1007/978-3-540-92673-3_0

11. Hirschauer, N., Lehberger, M., Musshoff, O.: Happiness and utility in economic thought–or: what can we learn from happiness research for public policy analysis and public policy making? Soc. Indicat. Res. **121**(3), 647–674 (2015)

12. Hotten, R.: Bmw and daimler invest 1bn in new car venture (2019). https://www.bbc.com/news/business-47332805, Accessed 30 Nov 2019

13. Jung, J., Koo, Y.: Analyzing the effects of car sharing services on the reduction of greenhouse gas (GHG) emissions. Sustainability **10**(2), 539 (2018). https://doi.org/10.3390/su10020539

14. Kahneman, D., Wakker, P., Sarin, R.: Back to Bentham? Explorations of experienced utility. Q. J. Eono. **112**(2), 375–406 (1997)

15. Kolata, G.: What if they closed 42d street and nobody noticed. New York Times **25**, 38 (1990)

16. Marczuk, K., et al.: Autonomous mobility on demand in SimMobility: case study of the central business district in Singapore. In: 2015 IEEE 7th International Conference on Cybernetics and Intelligent Systems (CIS) and IEEE Conference on Robotics, Automation and Mechatronics (RAM). pp. 167–172. IEEE, July 2015. https://doi.org/10.1109/iccis.2015.7274567

17. MAVS: Agent-based intelligent traffic simulation system (2015). https://www.utdmavs.org/matisse/. Accessed 25 May 2020

18. Nguyen, J., Powers, S., Urquhart, N., Farrenkopf, T., Guckert, M.: An overview of agent-based traffic simulators (2021)

19. Nguyen, J., Powers, S., Urquhart, N., Farrenkopf, T., Guckert, M.: Using semantic technology to model persona for adaptable agents. In: ECMS (in press, 2021)

20. Oltermann, P.: Activists try to stop autobahn being built through German forest (2020). https://www.theguardian.com/world/2020/oct/04/activists-try-to-stop-autobahn-being-built-through-german-forest. Accessed 3 Jan 2021

21. Rossetti, R., Liu, R.: Advances in Artificial Transportation Systems and Simulation. Academic Press, San Diego (2014)

22. Statista: Lebensmittelkauf in deutschland (2020). https://de.statista.com/statistik/studie/id/12521/dokument/einkauf-und-konsum-von-lebensmitteln-statista-dossier/

23. Statistische Ämter des Bundes und der Länder: Zensus 2011: Methoden und Verfahren. Statistisches Bundesamt. Wiesbaden (2015)

24. Thulasidasan, S., Kasiviswanathan, S., Eidenbenz, S., Galli, E., Mniszewski, S., Romero, P.: Designing systems for large-scale, discrete-event simulations: experiences with the fasttrans parallel microsimulator. In: 2009 International Conference on High Performance Computing (HiPC), pp. 428–437. IEEE, December 2009. https://doi.org/10.1109/hipc.2009.5433183

25. Torabi, B., Al-Zinati, M., Wenkstern, R.Z.: MATISSE 3.0: a large-scale multi-agent simulation system for intelligent transportation systems. In: Demazeau, Y., An, B., Bajo, J., Fernández-Caballero, A. (eds.) PAAMS 2018. LNCS (LNAI), vol. 10978, pp. 357–360. Springer, Cham (2018). https://doi.org/10.1007/978-3-319-94580-4_38
26. Ziemke, D., Nagel, K., Bhat, C.: Integrating CEMDAP and MATSIM to increase the transferability of transport demand models. Transportation Research Record: J. Transp. Res. Board **2493**(1), 117–125 (2015). https://doi.org/10.3141/2493-13

Dynamical Perceptual-Motor Primitives for Better Deep Reinforcement Learning Agents

Gaurav Patil[1,2]([✉]), Patrick Nalepka[1,2], Lillian Rigoli[1], Rachel W. Kallen[1,2], and Michael J. Richardson[1,2]

[1] Department of Psychology, Macquarie University, Sydney, NSW 2019, Australia
{gaurav.patil,patrick.nalepka,lillian.rigoli,rachel.kallen,
michael.j.richardson}@mq.edu.au
[2] Centre for Elite Performance, Expertise and Training, Macquarie University, Sydney, NSW 2019, Australia

Abstract. Recent innovations in Deep Reinforcement Learning (DRL) and Artificial Intelligence (AI) techniques have allowed for the development of artificial agents that can outperform human counterparts. But when it comes to multiagent task contexts, the behavioral patterning of AI agents is just as important as their performance. Indeed, successful multi-agent interaction requires that co-actors behave reciprocally, anticipate each other's behaviors, and readily perceive each other's behavioral intentions. Thus, developing AI agents that can produce behaviors compatible with human co-actors is of vital importance. Of particular relevance here, research exploring the dynamics of human behavior has demonstrated that many human behaviors and actions can be modeled using a small set of dynamical perceptual-motor primitives (DPMPs) and, moreover, that these primitives can also capture the complex behavior of humans in multiagent scenarios. Motivated by this understanding, the current paper proposes methodologies which use DPMPs to augment the training and action dynamics of DRL agents to ensure that the agents inherit the essential pattering of human behavior while still allowing for optimal exploration of the task solution space during training. The feasibility of these methodologies is demonstrated by creating hybrid DPMP-DRL agents for a multiagent herding task. Overall, this approach leads to faster training of DRL agents while also exhibiting behavior characteristics of expert human actors.

Keywords: Deep Reinforcement Learning (DRL) · Dynamical Motor Primitives (DMPs) · Multiagent coordination

1 Introduction

Rapid improvements in model-free Artificial Intelligence (AI) and Deep Reinforcement Learning (DRL) techniques [1–4] have resulted in the development of artificial agents capable of performing various tasks at levels equal to or better than human experts. In many cases, however, the success of these DRL agents requires a complex, highly

F. Dignum et al. (Eds.): PAAMS 2021, LNAI 12946, pp. 176–187, 2021.
https://doi.org/10.1007/978-3-030-85739-4_15

tuned, and task-specific structure of DRL methodologies and neural-network architectures along with long and computationally intensive self-play training schemes [1, 2]. Moreover, even after constraining the action space of DRL agents to match human response limitations [1], the behavior of DRL agents is often qualitatively different from humans [5], such that, DRL agents often exhibit action sequences or behavioral strategies that are not readily performed by humans. Although this does not pose a problem if the goal is only to achieve optimal or near optimal performance, it poses a major challenge when the aim is to develop DRL agents capable of effective human-AI agent interaction. Indeed, effective human performance in multiagent contexts requires that co-actors behave reciprocally, are able to anticipate each other's behaviors, and can readily perceive each other's behavioral intentions [6] while maintaining the right interaction flexibility [7]. Thus, developing methods that produce DRL agents that are capable of human-like behavior leading to robust human-centered coordination is often essential.

One way to improve the "human-like" nature of DRL agents is to employ prerecorded human expert data or real-time human gameplay/interventions during the training process; e.g., behavior cloning [8], generative adversarial imitation learning (GAIL) [9], or oracle learning [10]. In addition to increasing the interactive effectiveness of DRL by exposing them to human actions and reciprocal patterns of coordination that are likely to be missed during self-play training [6], the use of human data to pre-train AI agents also helps to scaffold the essential "dynamics of gameplay" (e.g., basic action and coordination patterns that lead to preliminary levels of task success), both ensuring effective task learning and decreasing training time [11]. Unfortunately, these methods rely on the availability of large datasets of human gameplay, which are not readily available for most tasks (both real and computer based), and can suffer sharp performance declines when the expert data is sparse or imperfect [12].

However, despite the variability and complexity of human data within and across task contexts, research exploring the dynamics of human behavior has demonstrated that it typically reflects the context-specific realization of low-dimensional principles. Indeed, a growing body of research [13–17] has revealed that the spatiotemporal patterning of the behavioral actions that define human performance and decision making in both individual and multiagent task contexts can be modelled using a small, fundamental set of dynamical primitives (i.e., nonlinear dynamical functions) [15–18]. Moreover, that the task-specific structure and parameterization of such models can be achieved with small human datasets (i.e., 5 to 10 individuals/teams) and can readily generalize across various task contexts [19–23].

The significant implication of the latter work is that human-inspired, dynamical models could be employed to (a) enhance DRL training across task contexts where large human datasets are not available or augment DRL models to inherit the low-dimensional dynamics of human behavior or decision making and (b) produce DRL agents that enact more human-like behavior, and thus, work more effectively in mixed human-AI multiagent task contexts. Thus, the aim of this paper is to provide a brief background of the application of dynamical primitives to model individual behavior in multiagent task contexts and to provide a methodology for using dynamical primitives to augment DRL agents trained to complete a complex multiagent herding task.

2 Modeling Perceptual-Motor Behaviors

2.1 Dynamical Perceptual-Motor Primitives in Individual Behavior

Research on perceptual-motor behavior [24] has revealed that human actions are composed of two fundamental movement types: (1) *discrete movements*, as when one reaches for an object or target location, taps a key, or throws a dart; and (2) *rhythmic movements*, as when one waves a hand, hammers a nail, or simply walks. Furthermore, previous research has demonstrated how task-defined human perceptual-motor behavior and decision making can be modelled using a relatively small set of nonlinear dynamical primitives: namely, environmentally coupled *fixed-point* (mass-spring) and *limit cycle* (self-sustained oscillator) equations, as well as multi-stable bifurcation functions [13–17]. For instance, research has shown these dynamical primitives can be employed to effectively model human reaching, object passing, rhythmic wiping, cranking tasks [25], goal-directed human navigation within an obstacle-ridden environment, including route selection [21], and drumming and racket ball tasks [20]. The dynamical primitives used to model human perceptual-motor behaviors can be termed as dynamical perceptual-motor primitives (DPMPs).

2.2 DPMPs in Multiagent Tasks

To succeed in human-human multiagent task contexts, individual agents have to plan their action in relation to both the desired goal and their partner's state and action [26]. This results in individuals coordinating their actions physically and temporally to collectively influence the environment [18, 27]. The stable patterns of such coordination, whether between a group of friends clearing a dinner table or teammates playing football, naturally emerge from the changing physical constraints and informational couplings that exist between the environmentally embedded co-acting individuals [28–30]. Thus, the same dynamical primitives used to model human perceptual-motor behavior can also be employed to model the task dynamics of numerous complex multiagent tasks, including cooperative object pick-and-place tasks [31] and goal-directed multiagent navigation and collision avoidance behaviors, as well as multiagent shepherding behavior [14, 19]. The latter research has also demonstrated how these DPMPs can be employed to control the behavior of artificial agents in human-AI agent contexts, with human-AI agent performance equivalent to and indistinguishable from human-human performance. It is also important to note that the DPMPs that underly these models can be readily generalized across a wide range of multiagent task contexts [19, 31–33].

2.3 Use of Deep Reinforcement Learning (DRL) in Conjunction with DPMPs

Importantly, DPMPs have the potential to provide a highly generative set of dynamical functions for developing low-dimensional models of synergistic human perceptual-motor behavior. Several researchers have demonstrated how DPMPs can significantly reduce the dimensionality of motor-skill training and control in artificial systems [34, 35]. For instance, Ijspeert and colleagues [23, 36] have shown how DPMPs can be employed to generatively train a virtual end-effector or multi-joint robotic arm to perform goal-directed reaching, obstacle avoidance movements, and racket swinging. It is important to note here that the use of DPMPs introduces the need for the selection of task-specific models and further optimization of the model parameters. Various machine learning techniques can be used for DPMP model selection and parameter optimization e.g., *imitation-* and *reinforcement*-based techniques [23], supervised learning [37], and search-based optimization techniques [38].

The advantage of reinforcement learning (RL) is that such machine learning approaches do not require the agents have a-priori knowledge of the dynamics of the environment nor the agent's action capabilities or consequences. In RL, agents learn via trial-and-error, modifying their behavior to maximize desired outcomes. Computationally, the goal of machine-based RL is to find the policy (state-action mapping) that results in an agent maximizing its reward within a complex dynamical environment [39]. Combined with deep-neural-network architectures and a "replay-memory", deep reinforcement learning (DRL) methods have gained wide notoriety for their ability to learn various tasks at or above human levels of performance [1–4]. This is in-part due to the powerful function approximation properties of deep neural networks which can learn low-dimensional feature representations from high-dimensional state-action spaces [40]. Most relevant here is the work demonstrating how DRL can be employed to map continuous action or parameter spaces [41, 42]. Interestingly, DRL applied within multiagent contexts can result in more robust behavioral policies than single actor RL [43]. However, although DRL methods have the advantage of generalizing over a wide set of state-action-reward scenarios and mapping high-dimensional states to actions, DRL methods are notoriously slow and computationally intensive resulting in researchers often relying on imitation learning methods to enhance the speed of novel task learning [44, 45].

The advantages and shortcomings of both DPMP and DRL methods necessitate the use of both methodologies in conjunction. Indeed, we propose that the DPMPs can be used in two ways to enhance the training and performance of DRL agents: 1) using DPMPs during DRL training and 2) augmenting DRL model architectures with DPMPs. The former approach is analogous to imitation learning approaches [8–10] while treating the DPMP model as an expert "human" demonstrator. The rest of the paper will however focus on the latter and will specifically present the application of the proposed methods to the multiagent herding problem.

3 The Herding Problem

3.1 Modeling Human Behavior Using DPMPs

The herding problem is a widely studied multiagent paradigm wherein two or more herders (agents) have to corral multiple targets agents (e.g., sheep, autonomous agents) and either contain them or move them from one location to another [19]. The task is ideally suited for the investigation of human group and multiagent coordination and problem-solving behaviors, including task division, behavior-mode switching (corralling to containment), and adaptation to task perturbations (new targets) [46]. In the context of this paper, of particular interest is the recent research demonstrating how DPMPs can be employed to model the emergence of the coordinated perceptual-motor strategies of humans during successful task completion [13, 14, 19]. The task consists of 'herding agents' (HAs) successfully corralling and containing a set of 'target agents' (TAs), typically ranging from 3 to 7 targets, within a red containment region located on a game field. When left unperturbed, TAs exhibit Brownian motion, and thus naturally disperse if left alone. Importantly, however, the TAs are repelled away from the HAs, such that, when an HA is within a critical distance from a TA, the TA flees in the opposite direction. Thus, continuous action by both HAs is required to corral and keep the TAs contained within the containment region. Task trials are typically between 1 to 2 min, with a trial deemed successful if an HA dyad can contain the TAs within the containment area for a specified period or percentage of trial time (e.g., 70% of a 1-min trial or continuously for 10 s). An overview of the task layout is show in in Fig. 1. An effective strategy to complete this task is to select and recover the TA that is farthest from the containment region, such that at each point in time each HA moves towards the farthest-TA closest to their current location (and not currently being corralled by another HA). This strategy, termed as Search and Recover (S&R), can be modelled by a DPMP based task dynamic model taking the form,

$$\ddot{r}_i + \alpha_r \dot{r}_i + \omega_\theta^2 \big(r_i - \big(r_{T,i} + r_{min} \big) \big) = 0 \tag{1}$$

and

$$\ddot{\theta}_i + \alpha_\theta \dot{\theta}_i + \beta \dot{\theta}_i^3 + \gamma \theta_i \dot{\theta}_i + \omega_\theta^2 (\theta_i - \theta_{T,i}) = 0, \tag{2}$$

which model the radial distance and angle of each herder, respectively. More specifically, in Eq. (1), $\dot{r}$, and $\ddot{r}$ represent the velocity and acceleration of HA-i's radial distance, respectively, $r_{T,i}$ is the radial distance of the farthest TA that is being pursued, and r_{min} is a fixed parameter that specifies HA-i's minimum preferred radial distance from a TA during herding to ensure repulsion towards the goal. In Eq. (2), $\dot{\theta}_i$ and $\ddot{\theta}_i$ represent the velocity and acceleration of the radial angle, respectively, α_θ and ω_θ^2 represent the dampness and stiffness parameters, $\theta_{T,i}$ represents the radial angle of the TA pursued by HA-i, and $\beta \dot{\theta}_i^3$ and $\gamma \theta_i \dot{\theta}_i$ are the nonlinear Rayleigh and van der Pol terms. The inclusion of the nonlinear terms captures the amplitude-frequency and peak velocity-frequency relationship exhibited by human actors [25].

The S&R strategy is effective in corralling TAs into a containment region, but when tasked with continuously containing more than four TAs within a containment region for extended periods of time, the S&R strategy becomes unstable (ineffective) and a more robust strategy is adopted by experienced herders. This latter containment strategy involves the HAs performing oscillatory movements that together encircle the entire TA herd and has been termed as coupled oscillatory containment (COC) [19]. A more complex and robust DPMP model can be used to model both S&R and COC behaviors with additional terms for coupling between HAs (see [46] for more details). However, for the scope of this paper, which is concerned with demonstrating the feasibility of using DPMP models to augment DRL agents, the simplified model approximated by Eqs. (1) and (2) is sufficient.

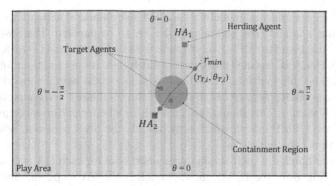

Fig. 1. Top view of the herding environment

3.2 Target Selection (Decision Dynamics)

It is also important to note here that, in general, the DPMP model for the S&R herding approximated by the above equations defines the *action dynamics* of a herder (i.e., the movement dynamics when moving towards and corralling a TA). However, the effectiveness of Eqs. (1) and (2), is dependent on the decision dynamics of *target selection,* which determines the TA to be pursued (i.e., $(r_{T,i}, \theta_{T,i})$). Indeed, research has demonstrated how the specifics of the target selection rule (dynamics) can significantly influence task performance [47]. Auletta et al. [48], for example, showed that the TA selection strategies derived from expert human players can be significantly different and lead to better task performance than those derived from novice human players, while resulting in the same number of task successes.

Of particular importance here, Nalepka et al. [19] demonstrated how human TA selection can be modeled heuristically as: select the TA that was (i) closer to their HA than the other HA and (ii) was furthest from the containment area. Rigoli et al. [49] further demonstrated that this TA selection rule results in robust novice human-AI agent interaction while also providing training equivalent to a human expert.

3.3 Hybrid DRL Agents for Herding

A classical approach to applying DRL techniques to a multiagent problem like herding would be to use a single deep neural network to approximate the target selection and action dynamics policy for each HA where the states of all the TAs and HAs are provided as an input and the network outputs the HA's action. This approach can be further decentralized by using separate networks for target selection and action dynamics which can be trained independently. To draw upon the advantages of DPMP models, the decentralized DRL architectures can be augmented by creating hybrid models such that either the target selection or the action dynamics of the DPMP model described in the previous sub-section is used with a deep neural network which is trained by DRL. Here we will refer to these hybrid models as *DRL-target selection* and *DRL-action dynamic* models, respectively, and their schematic is shown in Fig. 2.

The DRL-target selection model for each HA uses a neural network to observe the states of all the TAs and HAs and outputs the TA to be pursued. The position of this selected TA is used with the DPMP model described by Eqs. (1) and (2) to determine the action of each HA. It is expected that by using this hybrid model and training it by DRL, the HAs would be able to exhibit better task division and the neural network trained for TA selection can compensate for the absence of the oscillatory and coupling behaviors in the action dynamics. This should further result in a better performance as compared to the simplified DPMP model, which only models the S&R behavior, when the goal containment time is higher (>5 s).

On the other hand, the DRL-action dynamics model for each HA uses the heuristic TA selection rule from the DPMP model to select the TA to pursue and the neural network takes the state of that selected TA with the states of all the HAs and outputs the change in position in radial distance and radial angle. In this case, it is expected that the neural network trained to approximate the action dynamics will exhibit the oscillatory and coupling behaviors observed in human experts and thus result in better task performance than the simplified DPMP model.

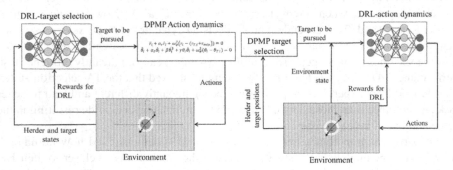

Fig. 2. Schematic of Hybrid DRL agents. (Left) DRL-target selection agent and (right) DRL-action dynamics agent

4   Simulation Experiments

4.1   Task Environment

The herding environment was developed using the Unity game engine (Unity Technologies, San Francisco, USA) and the DRL agents were implemented using the Unity ML-Agents package [50]. The environment size was set to 1 m × 1.8 m with two HAs corralling four TAs which spawned randomly in a ±0.3 m × ±0.6 m rectangle at the center of the field. The task goal was for the HAs to contain the TAs continuously for 10 s while each trial lasted 90 s. The velocity of the HAs was limited to 1 m/s in each direction and the TA behavior and DPMP parameters for Eqs. (1) and (2) were set according to a model tested to approximate human-like behavior (see Nalepka et al. [14] for more details).

4.2 DRL Models and Training

The DRL-target selection model for each HA used a neural network with 2 densely connected hidden layers with 128 neurons each and took the states (position and velocity) of all TAs and HAs as inputs (24 inputs) and outputted a one-hot vector of the TA to pursue. The same neural network was used to approximate the policy of both HAs in any given environment, but the actions and observations were transformed such that each HA observed the playing field from the bottom. The neural network was trained according to the Proximal Policy Optimization (PPO) algorithm for reinforcement learning (RL) for 10 million training steps with observations collected every 15th frame while the environment updated at 50 Hz. A curriculum learning was implemented such that, during the first 3 million training steps, the TA spawn area increased in steps linearly from ± 0.15 m $\times$ ± 0.3 m to ± 0.3 m $\times$ ± 0.6 m.

For the DRL-action dynamics model, the state of the selected TA and the HAs was used as an input (12 inputs) to a neural network with 2 densely connected hidden layers with 128 neurons each and outputted a continuous action vector (2 outputs) of change in radial distance and radial angle for each HA. The neural network was trained according to the Proximal Policy Optimization (PPO) algorithm for reinforcement learning (RL) for 25 million training steps with observations collected every 5th frame while the environment updated at 50 Hz. Between 2 and 10 million training steps, the TA spawn area increased in steps linearly from ± 0.15 m $\times$ ± 0.3 m to ± 0.3 m $\times$ ± 0.45 m while the area of the field increased in steps linearly from 0.8 m $\times$ 1.2 m to 1 m $\times$ 1.8 m. During training, the environment started with 2 TAs and an additional TA was added at 10 and 15 million training steps. Finally, at 5, 7.5, and 10 million training steps the distance within which the HA influenced a TA was stepped from 20 cm to 16 cm to 12 cm and the random motion of TAs when not influenced by HAs proportional to the experimental value (used in [14]) was stepped from 0.25 to 0.5 to 1 times, respectively.

During training, the reward for both hybrid DRL agents was calculated in each environment update such that each HA received a negative (0.01 $\times$ distance of TA from center of environment) reward for every TA outside the containment area and positive 0.01 reward for every TA in the containment area.

4.3 Comparison Between Modeling Methodologies

Twenty hybrid DRL agents were trained by each methodology and the 3 top agents of each type were selected by ranking them by the average episode length in the last 0.25 million training steps. 20 simulation trials were carried out for each selected agent (60 trials per condition) and 60 simulation trials were carried out using the DPMP model (parameters set to values specified in [14]) while they completed the 2-HA, 4-TA herding task where both HAs were controlled by the same model. The trial data (states of HAs and TAs) recorded from all trials was used to discern basic performance outcomes for the three agent types.

The analysis revealed that the DPMP, DRL-action dynamics, and DRL-target selection models were found to be successful in 26.67%, 98.33%, and 100% of the simulation trails, respectively. Further, a similar procedure employed by Nalepka et al. [19, 46] was used to classify oscillatory (COC) behaviour during containment for each agent and proportion of time spent oscillating (%OSC) was then averaged for each agent type. This measure is displayed in Fig. 3 (right).

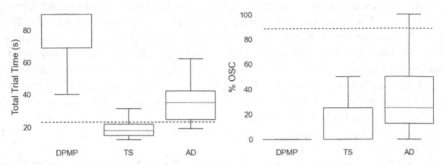

Fig. 3. Boxplots displaying the total time taken to complete a trial (left) and proportion of time spent oscillating during containment (right) for the three agent types, where TS refers to the DRL-target selection model and AD refers to the DRL-action dynamics model. Dotted lines indicate human expert performance for reference.

5 Discussion

The analysis of the performance measures from the simulated trials of the agents modeled by DPMP, DRL-target selection, and DRL-action dynamics methods is in line with the expectation of the hybrid agents performing better than the agent modeled by the simplified DPMP. Indeed, agents trained by both hybrid DRL methods outperform the DPMP agent in terms of task success and total time required for task completion. It is again important to note that the DPMP model used for comparison was a simplified model without the oscillatory and coupling behavior which are characteristic of expert human behavior during successful TA containment [19]. The better performance of the hybrid DRL agents can be attributed to the differences in strategies approximated by the simplified DPMP model and the corresponding deep neural networks. In the case of the DRL-target selection agent, it was observed that the policy diverges from the heuristic policy of the simplified DPMP once the TAs are in the containment region – resulting in higher task success. On the other hand, the policy of the DRL-action dynamics agent when pursuing the TA which is inside the containment region results in oscillatory behavior. This may be due to the fact that the TA selection heuristic encodes information regarding whether all TAs are within the containment region, and thus whether oscillatory behaviors are appropriate. This change in policy is also reflected by the higher proportion of time spent oscillating during containment by the DRL-action dynamics model. Finally, from the box plots in Fig. 3, it can be seen that the total trial time taken by the hybrid DRL agents is comparable to expert human pairs. Further, although the time spent by the hybrid DRL agents oscillating during containment is not even close to the expert human level, it is sufficient for task success and supports the occurrence of a bifurcation in human behavior with the increased skill level [13].

In this paper, we successfully demonstrated the usage of DPMP models for creating better hybrid DRL agents. Although not presented here, an alternative approach of using a single deep neural network, or two separate deep neural networks to approximate both target selection and action dynamics, was unsuccessful in learning the task with similar curriculum learning steps and even longer training times (>100 million steps). If required, the networks from the hybrid DRL agents can be detached and combined to create a completely neural network-based agent for further training using DRL. Finally, as highlighted at the end of Sect. 2, DPMP models can also be used to supplement methods that use expert data (imitation learning) or expert models (oracle learning) for DRL and will need further exploration and testing. Given that the DPMPs capture the essence of human movement behaviors, their use for creating DRL agents can allow for creating DRL agents for a much wider range of tasks without being limited by the complexity of state-action-reward structures and lack of expert datasets. Finally, more research is required to create DRL agents which can exhibit adaptive behavior based on the human teammate's skill level such that DRL agents can be used as a trainer or synthetic teammate for skill-learning.

Acknowledgments. This work was supported by ARC Future Fellowship (Richardson, FT180 100447), Macquarie University Research Fellowship (Nalepka), and Human Performance Research Network (HPRnet, partnership grant ID9024).

References

1. Berner, C., et al.: Dota 2 with large scale deep reinforcement learning. arXiv arXiv:1912. 06680 (2019)
2. Vinyals, O., et al.: Grandmaster level in StarCraft II using multi-agent reinforcement learning. Nature **575**, 350–354 (2019)
3. Pohlen, T., et al.: Observe and look further: achieving consistent performance on Atari. arXiv arXiv:1805.11593 (2018)
4. Mnih, V., et al.: Human-level control through deep reinforcement learning. Nature **518**, 529–533 (2015)
5. Shek, J.: Takeaways from OpenAI Five [AI/ML, Dota Summary] (2019). https://senrigan.io/blog/takeaways-from-openai-5/
6. Carroll, M., et al.: On the utility of learning about humans for human-AI coordination. In: Advances in Neural Information Processing Systems, NeurIPS 2019, vol. 32 (2019)
7. Nalepka, P., et al.: Interaction flexibility in artificial agents teaming with humans. In: CogSci 2021 (2021). https://escholarship.org/uc/item/9ks6n70q
8. Bain, M., Sammut, C.: A framework for behavioural cloning. In: Machine Intelligence 15. Intelligent Agents, pp. 103–129. Oxford University, GBR (1999). St. Catherine's College, Oxford, July 1995
9. Ho, J., Ermon, S.: Generative adversarial imitation learning. arXiv arXiv:1606.03476 (2016)
10. Maclin, R., et al.: Giving advice about preferred actions to reinforcement learners via knowledge-based kernel regression. In: AAAI (2005)
11. Amodei, D., et al.: Concrete problems in AI safety. arXiv arXiv:1606.06565 (2016)
12. Osa, T., et al.: An algorithmic perspective on imitation learning. Found. Trends Robot. **7**, 1–179 (2018)
13. Patil, G., et al.: Hopf bifurcations in complex multiagent activity: the signature of discrete to rhythmic behavioral transitions. Brain Sci. **10**, 536 (2020)

14. Nalepka, P., et al.: Human social motor solutions for human–machine interaction in dynamical task contexts. Proc. Natl. Acad. Sci. U. S. A. **116**, 1437–1446 (2019)
15. Richardson, M.J., et al.: Modeling embedded interpersonal and multiagent coordination. In: Proceedings of the 1st International Conference on Complex Information Systems, pp. 155–164. SCITEPRESS - Science and Technology Publications (2016)
16. Warren, W.H.: The dynamics of perception and action. Psychol. Rev. **113**, 358–389 (2006)
17. Kelso, J.A.S.: Dynamic Patterns: The Self-Organization of Brain and Behavior. MIT Press, Cambridge (1997)
18. Schmidt, R.C., Richardson, M.J.: Dynamics of interpersonal coordination. In: Fuchs, A., Jirsa, V.K. (eds.) Coordination: Neural, Behavioral and Social Dynamics, pp. 281–308. Springer , Heidelberg (2008). https://doi.org/10.1007/978-3-540-74479-5_14
19. Nalepka, P., et al.: Herd those sheep: emergent multiagent coordination and behavioral-mode switching. Psychol. Sci. **28**, 630–650 (2017)
20. Sternad, D., et al.: Bouncing a ball: tuning into dynamic stability. J. Exp. Psychol. Hum. Percept. Perform. **27**, 1163–1184 (2001)
21. Fajen, B.R., et al.: A dynamical model of visually-guided steering, obstacle avoidance, and route selection. Int. J. Comput. Vis. **54**, 13–34 (2003). https://doi.org/10.1023/A:1023701300169
22. Lamb, M., et al.: To pass or not to pass: modeling the movement and affordance dynamics of a pick and place task. Front. Psychol. **8**, 1061 (2017)
23. Ijspeert, A.J., et al.: Dynamical movement primitives: learning attractor models for motor behaviors. Neural Comput. **25**, 328–373 (2013). https://doi.org/10.1162/NECO_a_00393
24. Hogan, N., Sternad, D.: On rhythmic and discrete movements: reflections, definitions and implications for motor control. Exp. Brain Res. **181**(1), 13–30 (2007). https://doi.org/10.1007/s00221-007-0899-y
25. Kay, B.A., et al.: Space-time behavior of single and bimanual rhythmical movements: data and limit cycle model. J. Exp. Psychol. Hum. Percept. Perform. **13**, 178–192 (1987)
26. Vesper, C., et al.: Joint action: mental representations, shared information and general mechanisms for coordinating with others. Front. Psychol. **07**, 2039 (2017)
27. Repp, B.H., Keller, P.E.: Adaptation to tempo changes in sensorimotor synchronization: effects of intention, attention, and awareness. Q. J. Exp. Psychol. Sect. A Hum. Exp. Psychol. **57**, 499–521 (2004)
28. Lagarde, J.: Challenges for the understanding of the dynamics of social coordination. Front. Neurorobot. **7**, 18 (2013)
29. Richardson, M.J., et al.: Challenging the egocentric view of coordinated perceiving, acting, and knowing. In: Mind Context, pp. 307–333 (2010)
30. Schmidt, R.C., O'Brien, B.: Evaluating the dynamics of unintended interpersonal coordination. Ecol. Psychol. **9**, 189–206 (1997)
31. Lamb, M., et al.: A hierarchical behavioral dynamic approach for naturally adaptive human-agent pick-and-place interactions. Complexity, **2019** , 16 (2019). John Wiley & Sons, Inc., USA. https://doi.org/10.1155/2019/5964632
32. Yokoyama, K., Yamamoto, Y.: Three people can synchronize as coupled oscillators during sports activities. PLoS Comput. Biol. **7**, e1002181 (2011)
33. Zhang, M., et al.: Critical diversity: divided or United States of social coordination. PLoS ONE **13**, e0193843 (2018)
34. Schaal, S., Peters, J., Nakanishi, J., Ijspeert, A.: Learning movement primitives. In: Dario, P., Chatila, R. (eds.) Robotics Research. The Eleventh International Symposium. STAR, vol. 15, pp. 561–572. Springer, Heidelberg (2005). https://doi.org/10.1007/11008941_60
35. Schaal, S., et al.: Nonlinear dynamical systems as movement primitives. In: International Conference on Humanoid Robots, Cambridge, MA, vol. 38, pp. 117–124 (2001)

36. Ijspeert, A.J., et al.: Movement imitation with nonlinear dynamical systems in humanoid robots. In: Proceedings 2002 IEEE International Conference on Robotics and Automation (Cat. No. 02CH37292), vol. 2, pp. 1–6 (2002)

37. Mukovskiy, A., et al.: Modeling of coordinated human body motion by learning of structured dynamic representations. In: Laumond, J.-P., Mansard, N., Lasserre, J.-B. (eds.) Geometric and Numerical Foundations of Movements. STAR, vol. 117, pp. 237–267. Springer, Cham (2017). https://doi.org/10.1007/978-3-319-51547-2_11

38. Nalepka, P., et al.: "Human-like" emergent behavior in an evolved agent for a cooperative shepherding task. In: 2017 IEEE/RSJ International Conference on Intelligent Robots and Systems (IROS 2017), Vancouver, Canada (2017)

39. Sutton, R.S., Barto, A.G.: Reinforcement Learning: An Introduction, 2nd edn. MIT Press, Cambridge (2017)

40. Arulkumaran, K., et al.: Deep reinforcement learning: a brief survey. IEEE Sig. Process. Mag. **34**, 26–38 (2017)

41. Mnih, V., et al.: Asynchronous methods for deep reinforcement learning. In: Machine Learning (2016)

42. Lillicrap, T.P., et al.: Continuous control with deep reinforcement learning. In: 4th International Conference on Learning Representations, ICLR 2016 - Conference Track Proceedings. International Conference on Learning Representations, ICLR (2016)

43. Tampuu, A., et al.: Multiagent cooperation and competition with deep reinforcement learning. PLoS ONE **12**, e0172395 (2017)

44. Hester, T., et al.: Learning from demonstrations for real world reinforcement learning. arXiv arXiv:1704.03732 (2017)

45. Hussein, A., et al.: Imitation learning: a survey of learning methods. ACM Comput. Surv. **50**, 1–35 (2017)

46. Nalepka, P., Kallen, R.W., Chemero, A., Saltzman, E., Richardson, M.J.: Practical applications of multiagent shepherding for human-machine interaction. In: Demazeau, Y., Matson, E., Corchado, J.M., De la Prieta, F. (eds.) PAAMS 2019. LNCS (LNAI), vol. 11523, pp. 168–179. Springer, Cham (2019). https://doi.org/10.1007/978-3-030-24209-1_14

47. Auletta, F., et al.: Herding stochastic autonomous agents via local control rules and online global target selection strategies. arXiv arXiv:2010.00386 (2020)

48. Auletta, F., et al.: Human-inspired strategies to solve complex joint tasks in multi agent systems (2021)

49. Rigoli, L.M., et al.: Employing models of human social motor behavior for artificial agent trainers. In: An, B., et al. (eds.) Proceedings of the 19th International Conference on Autonomous Agents and Multiagent Systems (AAMAS 2020), p. 9. International Foundation for Autonomous Agents and Multiagent Systems, Auckland (2020)

50. Juliani, A., et al.: Unity: a general platform for intelligent agents. arXiv (2018)

Inference of the Intentions of Unknown Agents in a Theory of Mind Setting

Michele Persiani$^{(\boxtimes)}$ (iD) and Thomas Hellström$^{(\boxtimes)}$ (iD)

Department of Computing Science, Umeå University, Umeå, Sweden
{michelep,thomash}@cs.umu.se

Abstract. Autonomous agents may be required to form an understanding of other agents for which they don't possess a model. In such cases, they must rely on their previously gathered knowledge of agents, and ground the observed behaviors in the models this knowledge describes by theory of mind reasoning. To give flesh to this process, in this paper we propose an algorithm to ground observations on a combination of priorly possessed Belief-Desire-Intention models, while using rationality to infer unobservable variables. This allows to jointly infer beliefs, goals and intentions of an unknown observed agent by using only available models.

Keywords: Intent recognition · Belief-desire-intention · Unknown agent model · Theory of mind · Planning domain description language

1 Introduction

An important aspect emphasized in recent research on intent recognition is that the actor agent, whose intention should be found, and the observer agent, who attempts to infer the intention, may be using different models to represent each other. In this decoupled setting, the observer must form a model of the actor's decision-making process in order to understand its actions. This creation of another agent's model is commonly referred to as theory of mind reasoning [3], or a first-order theory of mind. However, commonly this model is given a priori to the observer [3,5,11], or is assumed to be equivalent to the one it is already using [8,12,17]. Such assumptions may work well in hand-crafted or simple domains but is unrealistic if the agents are heterogeneous and autonomous. In such cases, they should rather build models of each other through observations and interaction.

The algorithmic creation of a theory of mind that goes beyond simple controlled experiments is still a hard problem [4]. While most research focuses on reconstructing internal beliefs from observations, an additional difficulty seldom addressed is that the observer cannot know the symbols and schemas that the actor is using to create its beliefs or its deliberation model. The only symbols available to the observer are those it itself possesses, and the models it can form through observations must be a function of those symbols alone. In this paper we

© Springer Nature Switzerland AG 2021
F. Dignum et al. (Eds.): PAAMS 2021, LNAI 12946, pp. 188–200, 2021.
https://doi.org/10.1007/978-3-030-85739-4_16

address the following questions: how can the observer realize the actor's model based on schemas that are available to him? And, how can the observer infer the actor's intentions based on those?

To answer these questions, and in agreement with earlier work, we propose that the only key assumption we need is that the actor is intentional, and acts rationally to pursue its goal (commonly, this is referred to as being subject to the *principle of rational action* [1]). Therefore, the models that fulfil these requirements are the candidate hypotheses for the true model of the actor. This resulting space of hypotheses describes what must be true or false if the agent is performing intentionally, both in terms of beliefs and how these beliefs and their representations are combined to form an action schema. Everyone of these models could describe different hypothesis, yet in all of them the actor is explained as being intentional. They are all possible hypothesis for the true world in which the actor is being intentional and therefore we here propose that they are *equivalent* to the true actor's model when trying to understand what are its beliefs and goals. Since these hypothesized models could be symbolically heterogeneous, they may form multiple descriptions of the actor's intention because of their different symbolic forms. Therefore, in order to find the models in which the actor is being intentional, we can project an assumed optimality of observations over the space of possible models, after which the valid models underlying rationality are those that allow to explain the observations as being optimally directed towards a goal. We define this class of models as the equivalent class of rational models.

We propose that the observer can generate an initial guess of this class of models (possibly starting fully unspecified) using its known schemas, then refining it by maximizing the rationality expressed by the observations. This inference is possible from the observer perspective, and doesn't require the true symbols the actor is using to represent its world. Having the set of rational models, we find the probability of a certain goal, or predicate in the agent's belief.

In this paper we propose a novel algorithm for constructing models of an observed agent, based on the maximization of rationality in the observations. The proposed method utilizes the Planning Domain Description Language (PDDL), that allows us to easily perform tests on arbitrary domains. We extend earlier theory of mind and intent recognition formalizations by simultaneously considering multiple candidate models. In Sect. 2 we describe how the proposed methods fit in the current literature. In Sect. 3 we describe our proposed method to find an agent's equivalence class of rational models from observations, followed by a description of how we implemented it using PDDL in Sect. 4. In Sect. 5 we provide a simple illustrative example and experimental results on a joint belief and goal inference task, performed on several standard domains. Finally, Sects. 6 and 7 describe the current limitations, proposed future work, and conclusions.

2   Background and Related Work

Intent recognition is the algorithmic task of finding an agent's intention using some observations as evidence. In planning contexts where agents can move in an artificial world and take decisions, intentions can be understood as an agent's plan of actions and/or desired goal state. As also previously shown, in this setting intent recognition can be realized by goal or plan recognition techniques [15].

Recent research suggests to complement intent recognition with theory of mind reasoning. In its context, intentions form relevant parts of an agent's *state of mind* [10]. An example which motivates the utilization of theory of mind for intent recognition is the following. Let's suppose that an AI autonomously managing a building, in which it is embodied, attempts to infer the goal destination of a person walking an hallway. Clearly, the knowledge in terms of the state of the building is largely different between AI and person. Since the AI can gather a lot of data from its sensors, its instantaneous state is very rich in details e.g. knows who is in the building and where, which doors are open, etc. In this setting, computing the person's intention using the AI's belief is wrongly assuming that the person possesses the same amount of information. Therefore, to correctly make predictions, the AI should first estimate what are the person's beliefs, to then perform intent recognition based on those. i.e. it must form a theory of mind of the person that is focused on his belief about the building. Crucially, this allows to perform tests of *false belief*. For example, supposing that the AI knows that a door is closed, observing a person going towards the door without before taking its key allows to infer that the person has a false belief of the door being open.

An important point often only scratched in the literature is about the prior models that are provided to the agents doing inference. Often, these models are assumed to be completely known such as in [3], where the authors use Bayesian inference on POMDPs to jointly infer an agent's beliefs and goal while navigating a grid environment with multiple possible goals. The authors show that intent recognition using theory of mind reasoning forms predictions that are comparable to humans predictions. However, in their work a model of how the actor perceives, can move, etc. is explicitly required. Rather, in this paper we utilize the class of rational models that are induced by the rationality in the observations, which is the only assumed property of the actor agent. We consider multiple candidate models for the actor rather than a single one. Additionally, these models come from priors internally possessed by the observer, and another relevant divergent point is that we don't require a true model of the actor agent (and in particular its observation function). While in past research on theory of mind reasoning computing an observation function of the actor was considered positively grounded in folk psychology to the mechanism of *spontaneous perspective taking*, recent research is criticizing the position [6] by arguing that there is not enough evidence to claim that humans consistently do perspective-taking in interactions, as well as to describe how humans infer others visual perspectives. Computing an observation function of a robot's human collaborators has been shown to be feasible in highly controlled environments [7], however, in this paper we assume for the observation function of the actor agent to be unknown, with the observations being gathered from the observer's observation model only.

In [16] the authors propose a neural network which learns multiple species of agents moving in a gridworld, each of which described by a POMDP. Their *Machine Theory of Mind* shows that it is possible to memorize multiple models of agents, to then infer posterior distributions about their beliefs and intentions from observations. Despite the diversity of the produced agents, the number of classes of agents is large but still limited by the dataset. An important drawback of this approach is that the dataset must enumerate all of the possible models and observation functions of the POMDP agents, which quickly becomes intractable in complex scenarios.

Other relevant background research is in *Epistemic Plan Recognition* [19], that is a formalization for planning and plan recognition problems in multi-agent settings that explicitly takes into account observers and their beliefs. And the seminal work in plan and goal recognition of [18], over which part of our discussion on rationality is based on.

3   Method

We model the actor agent as a Belief-Desire-Intention (BDI) agent, and the observer agent as an intent recognition agent that infers the best candidates of the actor's BDI components using gathered observations. The BDI architecture [9] is a common framework to model agents. In a BDI agent, the beliefs comprise what is true for the agent. Desires correspond to possible goal states, while intentions are plans of actions, consistent with the beliefs, and obtained through a deliberation model, in which the agent commits to fulfil its desires. In this setting we model intentions as a function of the beliefs and a goal. Intentions are consistent with the beliefs, and could, for example, be generated by deliberation cycles computed at every time step of the agent [2]. Therefore, we assume that whenever the agent model is known, knowing also the agent's goal and beliefs is sufficient to compute its intention, for example by using a plan library or a forward planning procedure. Intent recognition can therefore be seen as a two-step process. First, the observer evaluates belief-goal pairs to find the one best matching the observations. Second, the intentions are found by simulating this selected actor model.

In the space of possible models that the observer uses to explain the actor's actions as intentional we refer to the subset of models that preserve rationality as the actor's equivalence class of rational models. They represent the class of models that are equivalent in preserving the actor's optimality toward a possible goal, by capturing what must be true if the agent is behaving intentionally.

Taking the previously given example of the person walking the hallway, the observations could be explained in a number of ways, each of which ground the person's actions in a different BDI model, such as gridworld model (the person seeks to reach a tile in the world), social model (the person seeks to reach a person), a combination of those or others. Raw observations are grounded in the selected set of models, in which the corresponding intentions are evaluated.

Rather than using a single BDI model, the observer may combine multiple models to understand the actor's actions. This is equivalent to refining an initial distribution of models $P(\Xi; \theta)$ towards the agent's class of rational models $P(\Xi; \theta_R)$, where $\xi = (b, g, a) \sim \Xi$ is a sampled instance which includes a candidate agent model, goal and belief. For simplicity, we assume that all models in Ξ are compatible with the underlying sources of data, or alternatively, the observer considers only the models that are possible given its context.

The inference process of the observer is represented in a graphical form in Fig. 1. The observer has a model of the actor as a joint probability distribution of beliefs, goals and deliberation models $P(\Xi_{act}^{obs}) = P(B, G, A)$. Every instance $\xi \sim P(\Xi)$ contains a fully specified, candidate description of the actor's BDI state. For example, a belief $b \in B$ could be described with a set of truth predicates, a goal $g \in G$ as the desired belief state. A deliberation model $a \in A$ is an action schema as we will later show. We consider an intention $\pi \in \Pi_{act}^{obs}$ as a committed plan recipe consistent with a deliberation model, together with the goal it attempts to achieve. For a particular $\xi = (b, g, a)$ the instantiated intentions are those plans that are consistent with (b, a) and that fulfills g.

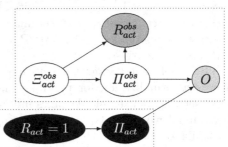

Fig. 1. Graphical model describing the variables involved in intent recognition and their connection in a theory of mind context. Ξ_{obs}^{act}: Inferred agent model, Π_{obs}^{act}: Inferred intention, **O**: Observations, **R**: Rationality. The figure highlights that in order to infer intentions the observer must beforehand internally model the actor agent. The only assumption we make about the actor is that its intentions are rational.

As they unfold, intentions produce observations that can be gathered by the observer. For an agent instance ξ, its candidate intentions are inferred using the set of observations $o = \{o_1, ..., o_n\} \in O$ that, once grounded, describe the effects that the actor's actions had on the world as described by ξ. Therefore, inferred intentions must be consistent both with the considered actor's models and the gathered observations. This is highlighted in the following probability distribution from the Baysian network in Fig. 1:

$$P(\Pi|O)P(O) = P(O|\Pi) \sum_{\Xi} P(\Pi|\Xi)P(\Xi) \propto \sum_{\Xi} P(\Pi|\Xi, O)P(\Xi) \quad (1)$$

where Π is the random variable of possible plans, Ξ of possible BDI instances, and O of possible observations. Equation 1 must provide high likelihoods for intentions that are consistent with both the observations and considered models. This can be achieved by setting $P(O = o|\Pi = \pi) > 0$ only if $o \in \pi$, and $P(\Pi = \pi|\Xi = \xi) > 0$ only if π is a plan consistent with ξ. Additionally, since the actor is assumed to be intentional, $P(\Pi = \pi|\Xi = \xi)$ should reflect the rationality of π in ξ. In Sect. 4 we show how it can be implemented using the Planning Domain Description Language.

3.1 Maximization of Rationality

The key idea driving intentions is that they must be rational. Therefore, in order to find the actor's intentional model the observations should be interpreted in a way that explains them as rational, or, in our case, optimal in some possible ξ. Following this argument we define rationality as a measurable property of observation-instance pairs, $R(o, \xi)$, defined as the expected rationality that the instance's intentions have while being constrained to be consistent with the observations:

$$R(o, \xi) = E_{\pi \sim P(\Pi | \Xi = \xi, O = o)}[R(\xi, \pi)] \tag{2}$$

where $R(\xi, \pi)$ is the rationality of a specific plan computed in ξ. In agreement with the principle of rational action, we set $R(\xi, \pi)$ to be in function of the optimality of π in achieving ξ's goal. This optimality measure for a plan π can be expressed as:

$$R(\xi, \pi) = \exp\{|\pi_{opt, \xi}| - |\pi|\} \tag{3}$$

where $\pi_{opt, \xi}$ is an optimal plan for ξ. Since $|\pi_{opt, \xi}| \leq |\pi|$, $R(\xi, \pi)$ has a value of 1 if the observations are along an optimal plan, a value between 0 and 1 whenever the observations belong to a sub-optimal plan. The observation o is rational in ξ if the intentions produced by $P(\Pi | \Xi = \xi, O = o)$ fulfill the principle of rational action, that is, they likely correspond to the optimal plans obtainable in ξ. When matched against all possible instances from the distribution of models $P(\Xi)$, an expected rationality of the observations is obtained as:

$$R(o) = E_{\xi \sim P(\Xi)}[R(\xi, o)] = E_{\pi \sim P(\Pi | \Xi = \xi, O = o), \xi \sim P(\Xi)}[R(\xi, \pi)] \tag{4}$$

Our proposed method for finding plausible agent models is to maximize the expected rationality of the observations $R(o)$. This is because, as we introduced in Sect. 1, we aim to search the model space to find instances expressing a rational behavior. Therefore, we are interested in finding the planning instances that maximize the degree of rationality $R(\xi, \pi)$ of intentions consistent with the observations, i.e. that also have a high likelihood $p(\pi | \xi, o)$. At the end of the optimization process, sampling from the resulting distribution yields planning instances in which the observations are contained in maximally rational intentions. Therefore, after training, $P(\Xi; \theta_R)$ captures a distribution of BDI models that explain the observed agent behavior as rational. It is the agent's equivalence class of rational models. In order to train $P(\Xi; \theta)$ we start by considering the expected value of rationality of a sequence of observations o and the parameters θ_R that maximize $R(o)$:

$$R(o) = E_{\xi \sim P(\Xi;\theta)}[R(\xi, o)] = \sum_{\Xi} R(\xi, o)p(\xi; \theta), \; \theta_R = \underset{\theta}{\operatorname{argmax}} \sum_{\Xi} R(\xi, o)p(\xi; \theta) \tag{5}$$

This maximization is difficult for two main reasons. The space of planning instances defined by $P(\Xi; \theta)$ can be very large, and in the general case $R(o)$ is non differentiable since it requires to compute plans through e.g. a planner. To overcome this issues we propose the following Expectation-Maximization (E-M) procedure based on sampling, which avoids to compute the derivative of the rationality function.

3.2   E-M Importance Sampling

To speed up the E-M algorithm we introduce an importance sampling buffer $P_R(\Xi)$ with limited capacity that holds past generated planning instance with high rationality. By using the memory buffer, planning instances are sampled using probabilities based on their rationality rather than on the current parameters value of $P(\Xi; \theta)$. Instances sampled during the E-step are sampled from this buffer rather than being freshly generated using $P(\Xi; \theta)$. When sampling instances from the buffer we have:

$$\xi \sim P_R(\Xi), p_R(\xi) = \alpha e^{\beta \cdot R(\xi, o)}, w_\xi = \frac{p(\xi)}{p_R(\xi)} \tag{6}$$

where $p_R(\xi)$ is the probability of ξ inside the buffer, while w_ξ are the importance weights to balance the fact that ξ was sampled using $P_R(\Xi)$ rather than the current distribution $P(\Xi; \theta)$.

Importance sampling has two main advantages: it ensures that all the instances being sampled are possible since the rationality of impossible ones is 0. This prevents wasting computations on irrelevant cases. It also makes the sampling process progress more steadily towards instances with high rationality, since highly rational instances are sampled more often by using $P_R(\Xi)$ rather than $P(\Xi; \theta)$. This speeds up the convergence of the algorithm.

3.3   Training Algorithm

Our proposed optimization procedure based on E-M with importance sampling is implemented by the following algorithm.

Algorithm 1. Rationality-Maximization

1: **procedure** RATIONALITY-MAXIMIZATION(o, k)
2:     $\Delta\theta \leftarrow \infty$
3:     **while** $\Delta\theta > k$ **do**
4:         $\Xi \sim P(\Xi; \theta_t)$ ▷ Sample a set of instances using θ_t
5:         $R_\Xi = $ COMPUTE-RATIONALITY(Ξ, o) ▷ Compute rationality
6:         $P_R(\Xi).update(\Xi, R_\Xi)$ ▷ Update the memory buffer
7:         $\Xi_\mathbf{R} \sim P_R(\Xi)$ ▷ Sample from the memory buffer
8:         $w_{\Xi_R} = \frac{p(\Xi_R; \theta_t)}{p_R(\Xi_R)}$ ▷ Compute the importance weights
9:         $\Delta\theta \leftarrow R_{\Xi_R} \cdot w_{\Xi_R} \cdot \frac{d}{d\theta} p(\Xi; \theta_t)$ ▷ Compute $\Delta\theta$
10:        $\theta_{t+1} \leftarrow \theta_t + lr \cdot \Delta\theta$ ▷ Update the parameters for the next iteration
11:    **end while**
12: **end procedure**

Algorithm 1 performs the following steps: **Line 2–3:** The computation ends when no further progress can be made towards optimizing θ. **Line 4–6:** Randomly sample some planning instances using the current parameters at iteration t and compute their rationality (E-step). Store these in the memory buffer. **Line 7–8:** Sample from the memory buffer using importance sampling. **Line 9–10:** Update the model's parameters for the $t+1$ iteration using the instances sampled from the memory buffer.

4   Implementation in PDDL

We implement BDI models by specifying planning instances using the Planning Domain Description Language (PDDL). PDDL [13] is a standard language to specify planning domains for what is usually referred to as classical planning. A planning instance is obtained by specifying the tuple $\langle \mathcal{P}, \mathcal{A}, I, \mathcal{G}, \mathcal{O} \rangle$. Where I and $\mathcal{G}$ are the initial and goal state respectively, $\mathcal{O}$ is the set of objects available to ground the predicates $\mathcal{P}$, while $\mathcal{A}$ is the set of available actions to transition between states. The observer agent infers equivalent PDDL components $\xi = \langle \mathcal{P}_{obs}^{act}, \mathcal{A}_{obs}^{act}, I_{obs}^{act}, \mathcal{G}_{obs}^{act}, \mathcal{O}_{obs}^{act} \rangle$ that allow to compute intentions Π_{obs}^{act}. $\langle \mathcal{P}_{obs}^{act}, \mathcal{A}_{obs}^{act}, \mathcal{O}_{obs}^{act} \rangle$ is the inferred action schema $a \in A$, $\langle I_{obs}^{act} \rangle$ its inferred belief $b \in B$, while $\langle \mathcal{G}_{obs}^{act} \rangle$ the inferred desire $g \in G$. The probability distribution over the possible instances is defined as a combination of a Bernoulli distribution for the beliefs, and two categorical distributions for action schemas and goals.

$$P(\Xi, \theta) = P(B; \theta_B)P(A; \theta_A)P(G; \theta_G)$$
$$P(B; \theta_B) = \Pi_i P(p_i \in I_{obs}^{act}; \theta_{p_i}), \ p(p_i \in I_{obs}^{act}) = \theta_i$$
$$P(A; \theta_A) = P(A | \{a_0, ..., a_n\}), \ p(A = \langle \mathcal{P}_{obs}^{act}, \mathcal{A}_{obs}^{act}, \mathcal{O}_{obs}^{act} \rangle | \{a_0, ..., a_n\}) = \theta_{ni}$$
$$P(G; \theta_G) = P(G | \{g_0, ..., g_m\}), \ p(G = \langle \mathcal{G}_{obs}^{act} \rangle | \{g_0, ..., g_m\}) = \theta_{mi}$$
$$\sum_i \theta_{ni} = 1, \sum_i \theta_{mi} = 1$$

The rationality of a sequence of observations O in an PDDL instance ξ is measured as proposed in previous research [15]:

$$R(\xi, \pi_O) = \exp\{\tau(|\pi_{opt}| - |\pi_o|)\} \tag{7}$$

where $|\pi_{opt}|$ is the length of an optimal plan of ξ, while $|\pi_o|$ the length of the optimal plan constrained to contain O.

5   Experiments

We tested our model for a series of joint goal and belief recognition tasks, performed on an existing dataset for goal recognition in PDDL [14] on the following domains: *satellite, logistics, ferry, easy-ipc-gridworld, kitchen, intrusion-detection, campus.* For each domain we selected 10 random planning instances. For every planning instance beliefs and goals were randomized, while we kept the action schemas as fixed. Table 1 shows averages of several measures related to the original planning instances: number of operators, number of predicates,

Table 1. Average instance measures over the tested planning domains. $|\mathcal{A}|$: number of operators, $|\mathcal{P}|$: number of predicates, $|I|$: size of the initial state, $|G|$: size of the goals, $|\overline{\pi}|$: length of the optimal plans.

Domain	$|\mathcal{A}|$	$|\mathcal{P}|$	$|I|$	$|G|$	$|\overline{\pi}|$
intrusion	9.0	11.0	1.0	4.75	17.15
kitchen	29.0	23.0	2.0	1.0	10.6
satellite	5.0	12.0	62.8	6.8	16.55
campus	22.0	12.0	1.0	2.75	4.925
blocks-world	4.0	5.0	14.4	4.95	15.25
logistics	6.0	3.0	22.7	2.3	31.25
easy-ipc-grid	3.0	8.0	227.4	1.0	17.2
miconic	4.0	8.0	518.6	6.6	24.85
ferry	3.0	7.0	99.3	8.9	28.27

size of the initial state, size of the goal (number of predicates) and length of the optimal plans.

For each tested sequence of observations we generated a randomized initial estimate of the actor's belief by using the original initial state of the problem, which in our case corresponds to the actor's true belief, further adding randomly generated ground predicates. The number of random ground predicates being added were equal to 10% of the number of possible ground predicates for that instance. The prior likelihood of every belief predicate, was set to 0.5, and the prior likelihoods over the goals were set to $\frac{1}{|G|} = 0.25$ (i.e. the observers started from a maximally entropic estimate of the actor). The memory was initialized with 200 randomly sampled valid planning instances (i.e. instances that reached their respective goal state from the initial state). Table 2 shows the measured hit rate on the correct goal by increasing percentages of observed actions, the columns are %obs: percentage of observations, *hit*: accuracy of recognized goals, $|I^+|$: beliefs size (number of predicates), R_{init}: rationality of the instances in memory priorly to training, R_{mem}: rationality of the instances in memory after training, R_{model}: avg. rationality of the instances from the model after training, D_{avg}: distance of the obtained intentions from the original observations, D_{min}:

minimum distance of the obtained intentions from the original observations. D is a measure of state trajectory distance defined as:

$$D_{avg} = E_{\pi \sim P(\Pi|\xi,O), \xi \sim P(\Xi,\theta_R)}\left[\sum_{i \in 1..n} D(\pi_i, o_i)\right] \tag{8}$$

where $D(\pi_i, o_i)$ is the Jaccard distance between the i-th state obtained by unfolding plans coming from the learned $P(\Xi;\theta_R)$ and the i-th state computed using the ground-truth planning instance.

6   Discussion

Table 2 shows that we were able to jointly find with high accuracies, and for all the tested instances, the correct goal and belief behind the partial plans used as evidence. The rationality measures R_{init} of the original instances, and R_{model} for the final obtained instances, indicates that the algorithm correctly maximizes rationality. The small minimum pairwise state distances of intentions and observations show that some resulting intentions yield state transitions that are close to equal to the state transitions computed on the true instance, however, the larger D_{avg} indicates that the valid rational intentions are sampled from a broader belief space. In general, these measures suggest that the model correctly finds multiple rational interpretations in terms of goals and beliefs for a fixed sequence of observations, that are spread over a probabilistic space of beliefs, in a consistent way for all of the tested domains.

Table 2. Average resulting measures for the tested domains. See text for additional details.

Domain	%obs	hit	$|I^+|$	R_{init}	R_{mem}	R_{model}	D_{avg}	D_{min}
logistics	0.30	1.00	63.69	0.21	0.56	0.05	0.40	0.08
logistics	0.50	1.00	63.69	0.21	0.86	0.23	0.34	0.14
logistics	0.70	1.00	63.69	0.21	0.93	0.36	0.31	0.17
blocks	0.30	0.80	38.30	0.46	0.87	0.21	0.49	0.18
blocks	0.50	0.80	38.30	0.46	0.91	0.24	0.45	0.09
blocks	0.70	0.80	38.30	0.46	0.98	0.34	0.42	0.13
grid	0.30	0.93	664.40	0.17	0.61	0.26	0.27	0.00
grid	0.50	0.93	664.40	0.17	0.74	0.24	0.24	0.02
grid	0.70	0.93	664.40	0.17	0.79	0.23	0.24	0.01
kitchen	0.30	0.80	11.60	0.47	0.87	0.38	0.68	0.21
kitchen	0.50	0.80	11.60	0.47	0.90	0.36	0.66	0.41
kitchen	0.70	0.80	11.60	0.47	0.91	0.41	0.63	0.38
campus	0.30	0.90	10.00	0.12	0.73	0.32	0.69	0.54
campus	0.50	1.00	10.00	0.12	0.82	0.24	0.66	0.41
campus	0.70	1.00	10.00	0.12	0.83	0.14	0.61	0.16
ferry	0.30	1.00	277.50	0.35	0.90	0.20	0.23	0.11
ferry	0.50	1.00	277.50	0.35	0.97	0.42	0.21	0.11
ferry	0.70	1.00	277.50	0.35	1.00	0.55	0.19	0.10
satellite	0.30	0.90	186.10	0.39	0.91	0.26	0.28	0.11
satellite	0.50	0.90	186.10	0.39	0.97	0.46	0.27	0.14
satellite	0.70	0.90	186.10	0.39	1.00	0.57	0.27	0.12
intrusion	0.30	1.00	10.60	0.74	0.89	0.37	0.82	0.64
intrusion	0.50	1.00	10.60	0.74	0.98	0.46	0.75	0.58
intrusion	0.70	1.00	10.60	0.74	1.00	0.56	0.70	0.56
miconic	0.30	1.00	1476.30	0.30	0.95	0.47	0.16	0.06
miconic	0.50	1.00	1476.30	0.30	1.00	0.59	0.15	0.05
miconic	0.70	1.00	1476.30	0.30	1.00	0.60	0.15	0.02
avg	0.30	0.93	304.28	0.36	0.81	0.28	0.45	0.21
	0.50	0.94	304.28	0.36	0.90	0.36	0.41	0.22
	0.70	0.94	304.28	0.36	0.94	0.42	0.39	0.18

However, we had to employ a few tricks to contrast the complexity of computing probabilistic PDDL instances. In particular, populating the memory prior to training, and reusing results from a smaller number of observed plans was necessary to achieve high accuracy for longer sequences. In the absence of these two actions, the algorithm struggled to converge when long sequences of observations were provided. The reason for this is the difficulty in finding, from scratch, planning instances consistent with long plans.

The obtained accuracy is comparable with previous work on joint inference of belief and goal [3].

7 Conclusions

We have presented an algorithm for jointly inferring belief, goals, intentions and action schemas of a BDI agent by maximizing the rationality contained in the observations. The algorithm was implemented and evaluated on several standard PDDL domains. Our results demonstrate that a probability distribution for an actor's model can be constructed using prior assumptions about its action schemas and beliefs, combined with gathered observations as evidence. The intentional state of the agent (its committed plan of action) is a product of those. The proposed method was tested over several standard domains, where the actor's goal, beliefs and intentions were jointly inferred.

This work is related to many contributions in previous research, and attempts to better describe how to model an actor agent without assuming strong prior models. We showed how, building on just the assumption of rationality, it is possible to infer agents models in terms of their action schemas, beliefs, desires and intentions. We referred to the set of models induced by rationality as the equivalence class of rational models. We also proposed an algorithm to obtain such classes of models from observations. We implemented our method using PDDL and showed its applicability in multiple different domains.

Since the model space is usually very large, some starting assumptions on the agent model are necessary to make the proposed iterative procedure converge to a solution. This is expressed by the set of priorly known models of the actor. However, we make no assumption about these prior models used to construct the class of rational models. Intuitively, we expect that the richer they are in descriptive power, and the more similar they are to the observed agent, the better prediction capability they offer.

A relevant point that we would like to highlight is that the presented method based solely on rationality uses models and symbols that are internal to the observer, and therefore accessible for inference in autonomous robots that cannot directly access the state of other agents. This makes the model compatible with a first-order theory of mind setting. Despite its plausability in humans [6], and contrary to most of previous research, we do not use a model of how the actor perceives its environment, but focus only on the observations gathered by the observer. We however achieved accuracies comparable to methods explicitly modeling how the actor perceives. Future research could complement these methods for greater prediction accuracy.

References

1. Tomasello, M., Carpenter, M., Call, J., Behne, T., Moll, H.: Understanding and sharing intentions: the origins of cultural cognition. Behav. Brain Sci. **28**(5), 675–691 (2005)
2. Alzetta, F., Giorgini, P., Marinoni, M., Calvaresi, D.: RT-BDI: a real-time BDI model. In: Demazeau, Y., Holvoet, T., Corchado, J.M., Costantini, S. (eds.) PAAMS 2020. LNCS (LNAI), vol. 12092, pp. 16–29. Springer, Cham (2020). https://doi.org/10.1007/978-3-030-49778-1_2
3. Baker, C.L., Tenenbaum, J.B.: Modeling human plan recognition using Bayesian theory of mind. Plan Activity Intent Recogn. Theory Pract. **7**, 177–204 (2014)
4. Bianco, F., Ognibene, D.: Functional advantages of an adaptive theory of mind for robotics: a review of current architectures. In: 2019 11th Computer Science and Electronic Engineering (CEEC), pp. 139–143. IEEE (2019)
5. Chakraborti, T., Sreedharan, S., Zhang, Y., Kambhampati, S.: Plan explanations as model reconciliation: moving beyond explanation as soliloquy. arXiv preprint arXiv:1701.08317 (2017)
6. Cole, G.G., Millett, A.C.: The closing of the theory of mind: a critique of perspective-taking. Psych. Bull. Rev. **26**(6), 1787–1802 (2019). https://doi.org/10.3758/s13423-019-01657-y
7. Devin, S., Alami, R.: An implemented theory of mind to improve human-robot shared plans execution. In: 2016 11th ACM/IEEE International Conference on Human-Robot Interaction (HRI), pp. 319–326. IEEE (2016)
8. Dragan, A.D., Lee, K.C., Srinivasa, S.S.: Legibility and predictability of robot motion. In: 2013 8th ACM/IEEE International Conference on Human-Robot Interaction (HRI), pp. 301–308. IEEE (2013)
9. Georgeff, M., Pell, B., Pollack, M., Tambe, M., Wooldridge, M.: The belief-desire-intention model of agency. In: Müller, J.P., Rao, A.S., Singh, M.P. (eds.) ATAL 1998. LNCS, vol. 1555, pp. 1–10. Springer, Heidelberg (1999). https://doi.org/10.1007/3-540-49057-4_1
10. Hellström, T., Bensch, S.: Understandable robots: what, why, and how. Paladyn J. Behav. Robot. **9**(1), 110–123 (2018)
11. Kulkarni, A., Srivastava, S., Kambhampati, S.: Signaling friends and head-faking enemies simultaneously: balancing goal obfuscation and goal legibility. In: Proceedings of the 19th International Conference on Autonomous Agents and MultiAgent Systems, pp. 1889–1891 (2020)
12. MacNally, A.M., Lipovetzky, N., Ramirez, M., Pearce, A.R.: Action selection for transparent planning. In: AAMAS, pp. 1327–1335 (2018)
13. McDermott, D.: PDDL-the planning domain definition language (1998)
14. Pereira, R., Oren, N., Meneguzzi, F.: Landmark-based heuristics for goal recognition. In: Proceedings of the AAAI Conference on Artificial Intelligence, vol. 31 (2017)
15. Persiani, M., Hellström, T.: Intent recognition from speech and plan recognition. In: Demazeau, Y., Holvoet, T., Corchado, J.M., Costantini, S. (eds.) PAAMS 2020. LNCS (LNAI), vol. 12092, pp. 212–223. Springer, Cham (2020). https://doi.org/10.1007/978-3-030-49778-1_17
16. Rabinowitz, N., Perbet, F., Song, F., Zhang, C., Eslami, S.A., Botvinick, M.: Machine theory of mind. In: International Conference on Machine Learning, pp. 4218–4227. PMLR (2018)

17. Raileanu, R., Denton, E., Szlam, A., Fergus, R.: Modeling others using oneself in multi-agent reinforcement learning. In: International Conference on Machine Learning, pp. 4257–4266. PMLR (2018)
18. Ramírez, M., Geffner, H.: Plan recognition as planning. In: Twenty-First International Joint Conference on Artificial Intelligence (2009)
19. Shvo, M., Klassen, T.Q., Sohrabi, S., McIlraith, S.A.: Epistemic plan recognition. In: Proceedings of the 19th International Conference on Autonomous Agents and MultiAgent Systems, pp. 1251–1259 (2020)

SMASH: A Semantic-Enabled Multi-agent Approach for Self-adaptation of Human-Centered IoT

Hamed Rahimi[1,2,3]($\boxtimes$) ⓘ, Iago Felipe Trentin[1,3] ⓘ, Fano Ramparany[1] ⓘ,
and Olivier Boissier[3]

[1] Orange Labs, Meylan, France
{hamed.rahimi,iagofelipe.trentin}@orange.com
[2] Université de Lyon, Université Jean Monnet, Saint-Etienne, France
[3] Mines Saint-Etienne, Univ. Clermont Auvergne, CNRS, UMR 6158 LIMOS,
Institut Henri Fayol, Saint-Etienne, France

Abstract. As the number of IoT applications increases, IoT devices are becoming more and more ubiquitous. Therefore, they need to adapt their functionality in response to the uncertainties of their environment to achieve their goals. In Human-centered IoT, objects and devices have direct interactions with human beings. Self-adaptation of such applications is a crucial subject that needs to be addressed in a way that respects human goals and human values. This paper presents SMASH: a multi-agent approach for self-adaptation of IoT applications in human-centered environments. SMASH agents are provided with a 4-layer architecture based on the BDI agent model that integrates human values with goal-reasoning, planning, and acting. It also takes advantage of a semantic-enabled platform called Home'In to address interoperability issues among non-identical agents and devices with heterogeneous protocols and data formats. This approach is compared with the literature and is validated by developing a scenario as the proof of concept. The timely responses of SMASH agents show the feasibility of the proposed approach in human-centered environments.

Keywords: Multi-agent systems · Self-adaptation · Internet of Things · Semantic web · Human-centered IoT · Smart home · Human values

1 Introduction

The Human-Centered Internet of Things (HCIoT) is a domain of IoT applications that focuses on the accessibility of interactive IoT systems to human beings. Smart Home applications are one of the emerging use cases of the HCIoT that has been directly impacting the lifestyle of people [1]. According to policyAdvice, the IoT market will have over $520 billion revenue in the market by 2027 and Statista estimates Smart Home applications occupy 12.2% of the market in 2021 that are expected to grow up to 21.4% by 2025. As the number of Smart Home applications

© Springer Nature Switzerland AG 2021
F. Dignum et al. (Eds.): PAAMS 2021, LNAI 12946, pp. 201–213, 2021.
https://doi.org/10.1007/978-3-030-85739-4_17

increase, IoT devices are becoming more and more ubiquitous. These objects are responsible for controlling various tasks such as sensing and computing, planning, learning, and acting [2]. Hence, IoT objects in Smart Home applications need to use self-adaptation techniques to manage run-time uncertainties in their dynamic environment. One of these techniques is planning and acting [3], which allows intelligent agents, goal-driven entities capable of perceiving and acting upon their environment [4], to plan for their goals and to adapt their behavior at the run-time for achieving them. The integration of planning and acting advocates an agent's deliberation functions, in which online planning takes place throughout the acting process. In Smart Home applications, where HCIoT consists of several devices, intelligence can be integrated into two levels. The first is in the device layer where we embed intelligence in each device to control its functionality correspond to the behavior of other connected devices. The second level is to implement the intelligence in a CPU that is connected to devices and controls their functionality. In this research, we run deliberation functions on multiple intelligent agents with various coordination models at the system level. Therefore, we can describe these applications as a Multi-Agent System (MAS) [5] that is designed to manage such environments with several intelligent agents controlling domestic artifacts of IoT objects. These agents require access to the information of IoT objects for decision-making and handling data exchanges. Semantic Web Technology [6] is an effective way that simplifies information exchange and enhances the interoperability among various devices.

This paper introduces SMASH: a multi-agent approach for self-adaptation of IoT applications in Smart Home. SMASH agents have a 4-layer agent architecture that autonomously adapts Smart Home devices to uncertainties of their environment by planning and acting of user-centric agents that respect human values and are supported by value-reasoning and goal-reasoning mechanisms. SMASH agents are integrated with a semantic-enabled platform for Smart Home applications called Home'In to create a Multi-agent System capable of autonomous decision-making. The rest of the paper is organized as follows. The state-of-the-art is investigated in Sect. 2 and the proposed approach is presented in Sect. 3. In Sect. 4, we demonstrate the feasibility of the proposed approach by modeling a Smart Home scenario, whose implementation and validation serve as a proof of concept. In Sect. 5, we compare our results with the related works. Finally, in Sect. 6 we present our conclusions.

2   Literature Review

HCIoT applications are closely incorporated with humans and their environment and have a lot of benefits for society, the environment, and the economy. A Smart Home [7] is a living environment that is equipped with artificial intelligence that controls the functionality of a house such as heating, lighting, and other devices. Smart Home is one of the HCIoT applications that play an important role in human lives, and the lifestyle of people has a huge dependency on their existence. However, due to direct interaction with human, these applications come with various issues that need to be addressed. Self-Adaptation is one of the issues that focus on functional control elements that interact with the human environment and enabling dynamic adjustment to run-time uncertainties to provide some QoS requirements. Planning and Acting [3] is one of the strong solutions, in which an agent with proactive behavior, that has planning and deliberation capabilities, is more loosely tied to its environment. By knowing which goals to seek, it can reason upon context and create plans to achieve them. Such reasoning models that integrate planning and acting are explored in [8–11]. In [3], an agent is capable of performing planning and deliberative acting. Deliberative acting is defined as an understanding of the surrounding context and intelligently decision-making in a given situation. Deliberative planning is defined as a way to seek the achievement of goals by executing plans, through the realization of tasks, reaching a contextual state, or the maintenance of a condition. In [12–16], the challenges of merging planning and acting are addressed. Besides, some approaches are presenting goal-reasoning architectures [17,18] that are practical for adaptation of intelligent agents, which may control IoT objects of the smart environment. Although, these architectures do not consider human values that may directly affect decision-making in different conditions. There are some works on value-reasoning models [19,20,27].

Fig. 1. Continuum of values

However, these works have not explored the integration challenges between planning, acting, goal-reasoning, and value-reasoning functions for human-centric smart environments. These solutions are not commonly self-adapted to human behaviors and uncertainties of the environment, and in some cases perform based on tasks that are once programmed by the administrator. In dynamic environments, where IoT objects have direct interactions with human beings and devices need to have access to the online contextual information, the system requires to adapt its execution to user needs and context evolution of the environment including humans. More specifically, a Smart Home has to be context-aware and adapt its user-centric services at run-time in order to increase human comfort. For instance, it easies answering a call while the user is watching a movie. Ideally, a Smart Home should minimize its direct input from users and be autonomous in the pursuit of user-centric goals to satisfy users' needs.

Human values are an aspect of human subjectivity, which can be described as the criteria used by humans to select and justify actions, as well as evaluate people and events [21]. Values are stable over time [22], therefore all value-related configurations of a system need to be performed only once for a long period. They are also intrinsic to each human being, influencing daily activities and long-term decisions. In our approach, which is presented in the next section, we have used the 19 human values defined by Theory of Basic Human Values [23] that have brought a refinement of the initial theory from [24]. This theory has been supported by recent cross-national tests [25], and results show that human values can be organized in a continuum (Fig. 1) based on the compatibility of their pursuit.

Our approach integrates human values with goal-reasoning, planning and acting of user-centric agents in Smart Home applications. In the next section, we propose a reasoning architecture for intelligent agents that improves user-centricity by applying the new dimension of human values in the goal-reasoning, planning and acting layers. We also explain the integration of these agents with the Home'In platform. The proposed system is able to act autonomously, allowing agents to independently perform actions whilst respecting users' values.

3   The Proposed Architecture

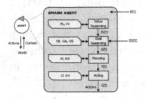

Fig. 2. SMASH agent architecture

SMASH is a user-centric agent architecture that adapts its reasoning and functioning based on value-driven reasoning and deliberation process consisting of 4 context-aware layers: 1) Value-Reasoning Layer, 2) Goal-Reasoning Layer, 3) Planning Layer, and 4) Acting Layer. The first layer is dedicated to reasoning upon human values, ordering them according to the context of the environment and the user's personal preferences (Sect. 3.1). The second is dedicated to goal reasoning and identifying goals to be achieved, based on the context and values from the first layer (Sect. 3.2). The third layer is for run-time planning given the context of the environment, selected goals, and the given values respectively from the second and first layer (Sect. 3.3). And the last layer is for initiation of acting upon given plans and values, selecting actions to be performed (Sect. 3.4). This agent architecture supports a high degree of autonomy while respecting the human values of users.

3.1   Value-Reasoning Layer

This layer is provided with a set of ordered values $IV_D(t)$, which shows the Default Importance of Values and indicates the user's priorities and preferences toward these human values at time t. This set of values alongside with a set of value ordering rules (VO) are able to autonomously reorder the values based on the context of the environment and the preferences of the user. This layer provides the next layers with a set of totally ordered values $IV(t)$. In (1), $B(t)$ is the set of beliefs that represents the context of the system at time t.

$$IV(t) = ValueReasoning\ (B(t), IV_D(t), VO)$$

Value-Ordering Rules. Each rule of VO has the format *"condition $\rightarrow$ body"*, where *condition* is a first-order logical formula stating if the rule is active in the current context. The *body* is a formula with a binary or unary operator that aims to sort the values.

3.2 Goal-Reasoning Layer

This layer manages to activate a set of goals $G(t)$ from the belief base $B(t)$ and the set of ordered values $IV(t)$ that is the output of the previous layer. The goal-reasoning performs on the goals given by the user $GG(t)$ and the set of existing goals called Goal Status $GS(t)$. These given goals along with the context of environment $B(t)$ update and filter $GS(t)$ based on activation rules GA and goal impact rules GI. Note that the impact of activated goals on the user's values is also based on the given values $IV(t)$ and the current context $B(t)$.

$$G(t) = GoalReasoning(B(t), GG(t), IV(t), GS(t), GA, GI)$$

As shown above, $G(t)$ is an ordered subset of goal statuses $GS(t)$ that contains newly created or updated goals at time t. Besides, GS(t), subset of B(t), is a set of beliefs of the form $state(goal, status, source)$ that describes the $status$ of a $goal$ that is from a $source$. $source \in \{user, self\}$ indicating the source of the goal that could be directly given by the user or could be autonomously activated by the reasoning of the agent. The goal-activation rules from GA are able to change the status of goals as shown in Fig. 3.

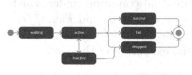

Fig. 3. State diagram of goal states

Goal-Activation Rules. GA rules have the format $(condition \rightarrow body)$, where $condition$ is a first-order logical formula, that checks the state of the environment through $B(t)$. The $body$ is a list of first-order propositions with the format $state(goal, status, source)$ that updates the status of the goal issued of the source in $GS(t)$.

Goal-Impact Rules. The GI rules are responsible to define the impact that a goal with a certain status, under a certain contextual condition, has over a value. These rules check if goals are respecting the values. The format of these rules is expressed as $(condition \rightarrow body)$, where $condition$ is a first-order logical formula that checks the context of the environment, and $body$ is a tuple of $(goal, impact, v)$ that checks the positive, neutral or negative $impact$ of a $goal$ on the value v.

Figure 4 presents a visual representation of goal reasoning layer. The elements *update*, *select* and *sort* are the functions executed during one reasoning cycle. The function *update* adds all goals in $GG(t)$ with the status *waiting* to $GS(t)$, in case their *source* is equal to *user*. The function *select* applies all goal-activation rules from GA whose condition is satisfied in $B(t)$, i.e. the *body* of these rules are used to update $GS(t)$ (setting statuses to *active*, *inactive*, or *dropped*). These rules allow the activation of goals based upon context, and these new goal statuses have *self* as their *source*. The function *sort* filters all the elements in GS, which represent the goals and their statuses; the only goals sorted are those whose *source* is equal to *self*, and the sorting is based upon GI rules that are initiated in current context.

3.3   Planning Layer

The Planning Layer generates a set of plans to achieve goals of $G(t)$ provided by the previous layer. The set of plans $P(t)$ is created based upon the context $B(t)$, the ordered set of values $IV(t)$, the ordered set of goals $G(t)$, the Action Impact rules AI, and a set of tuples Know-What (KW), which shapes the action model depending on the context by providing a set of right actions of the system. The action-impact rules AI describe the impact of actions over the values of IV. A plan $(goal, body)$ in $P(t)$ is a tuple, where $body$ is the list of actions that need to be executed by the acting layer in order to achieve the $goal$.

$$P(t) = planning(B(t), IV(t), G(t), KW, AI)$$

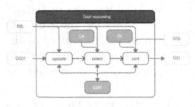

Fig. 4. The goal-reasoning layer

Know-What. The elements of KW are tuples of the form $KW = \{kw_i \ / \ kw_i = (action, condition, effect)\}$. They express the action models, where $kw_i.action$ describes the name of action and its parameters, the $kw_i.condition$ is a first-order logical formula with contextual condition under which the action can be executed, and $kw_i.effect$ includes the tuple $(add, delete)$ that define the action add or $delete$ on agent's beliefs after the execution of the plan.

Action-Impact Rules. The Action-Impact AI represents the impact of an action, under a certain contextual condition, over a value. They are defined as $(condition \rightarrow body)$, where $condition$ is a first-order logical formula based on the current context, and $body$ is the tuple $(action, impact, v)$, presenting the positive, neutral or negative $impact$ of the action $action$ over the value v.

The Fast Downward (FD) planner [26] is a configurable forward state-space search planner responsible to perform the planning in this layer. The planning layer translates the necessary information into Planning Domain Definition Language (PDDL), giving to the planner two inputs: 1) a domain definition PDDL file, where elements from $B(t)$ are added as *predicates*, and elements from KW are translated as *actions*; 2) a problem definition PDDL file, where $B(t)$ are translated into propositions representing the *initial state*, and goal statuses from $G(t)$ are translated into individual *goals*.

Before translating KW elements into *actions*, the set AI is used to filter all actions that have a negative impact over values presented in $IV(t)$ in order to respect the values of the user. The planner is responsible to compute plans to goals in $G(t)$ and pass to acting layer for execution. If planner doesn't succeed, it will then update its goal state in $GS(t)$ with the status $fail$.

3.4   Acting Layer

Acting layer receives a set of plans $P(t)$ and is responsible to execute a set of actions aiming to achieve the goals. The plan execution consists of the constant refinement of selected action until it obtains a list of commands $C(t)$. For this refinement, the acting layer requires a set of tuples Know-How (KH: the execution model of actions according to the contextual condition), and Command Impact rules (CI: the impact of commands over the user's values).

$$C(t) = acting(B(t), IV(t), P(t), KH, CI)$$

Know-How. The tuples $KH = \{kh_j \mid kh_j = (action, condition, body)\}$ are the execution bodies of actions, where $kh_j.action$ is the action name and its parameters, the $kh_j.condition$ is the first-order logical formula with contextual condition under which the action can be executed, and $kh_j.body$ is an ordered set of commands to be executed, and actions to be refined into commands.

Command-Impact Rules. The CI defines the impact of command, under a certain contextual condition, over a value. They are expressed as $(condition \rightarrow body)$, where *condition* is a first-order logical formula bearing on the current context, and *body* is the tuple $(command, impact, v)$, presenting the *command* being considered, and positive, neutral or negative impact over the value v.

4   Proof of Concept

In this section, we aim to design a scenario in Smart Home applications and implement the proposed approach to address self-adaptation of IoT devices. The scenario and the SMASH agents are implemented in a multi-agent oriented programming platform [28] called JaCaMo. The acting layer uses the built-in BDI engine as previously explained, the planning layer uses the PDDL language and the FD planner [26] as described in Sect. 3.3, and the goal- and value-reasoning layers are implemented in Java and are available to agents as internal actions in JaCaMo. An internal action allows JaCaMo to call Java functions defined by the developer. As shown in Fig. 5, There are a PC, a Smart Phone, a Smart TV, and a Smart Sofa in the smart environment of the scenario.

4.1   Scenario

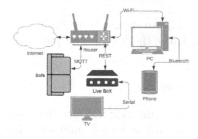

Fig. 5. Technical infrastructure

In this short scenario, we have a scene where Max, the user, asks the Intelligent system of the house through his phone to play a program on TV. Assuming TV is off, the intelligent systems initially turns TV on and once Max arrives in the living room and sits on the smart sofa, which identifies him, TV starts playing the program. After a few minutes, Max receives a phone call from his boss. Considering Max is out of duty, the pleasure of continuing watching TV (that is represented by the value Hedonism in Theory of Human Values) is more important than answering the working call (that is represented by the value Conformity-Rules in Theory of Human Values). Therefore, the system automatically puts his call on the voice mail. A few minutes later, Max receives a call from his mother. Respecting Max's value, in which the value Benevolence-Caring that represents family relations is more important than Hedonism in his value base, the phone starts ringing and the TV goes on mute. The sofa detects the absence of Max due to his leave toward answering the phone. Max, after responding to the phone call, comes back to the living room and sits on the sofa. Right away, the television unmutes itself and continues playing the program.

4.2 Technical Overview

Using the above scenario, we will go through the reasoning process of SMASH agents and show the transition of states and exchange of messages. Max is in his leisure time at home, therefore, value reasoning layer compute the order of the values corresponding to his current context. In his belief base, the value 'Benevolence-Caring' noted vbc is the most important value, and the 'Hedonism' noted vhe is more important that the value 'Conformity-Rules' noted vcr.

$$V_{vbc} > V_{vhe} > V_{vcr}$$

Max sends a request to SMASH through his phone that is connected to Home'In platform for watching "Canal+". This request is translated as a goal in the set GG(t) of the system. In result, a JSON message is sent to the IoT Device Manager of Home'In over MQTT and Goal reasoning layer starts its computation. The messages exchanged are as follows:

$$Goal\ to\ achieve:\ watch(TV, Canal+)$$

IoT device manager shares this message with agents to achieve the goal $watch(TV, Canal+)$. Considering that TV is off, the goal activation rules activate another goal to turn the TV on and save another goal for broadcasting the program once the user sits on the sofa.

$$TV\ is\ OFF \implies goalActivation(turnOn(TV), active, self)$$

The planning layer find the right functions to achieve the goals received from the goal reasoning later. Then, the Acting layer, turns the TV on and put it on the Standby Status to save energy.

$$+deviceStatus(TV, Standby)$$

Sofa is intelligent and can identify the user through his weight. Once the Max sits on Sofa, the goal reasoning layer and planning are activated, and then by acting layer, the TV starts displaying the "Canal+".

$$+beSeated(Max, Sofa) \implies deviceStatus(TV, Playing)$$

While watching TV, Max receives a call from boss. So, it adds a new belief.

$$+callerType(Boss, Work)$$

Considering the user's current values, in which pleasure (vhe) is more important than subordination (vcr), the goal reasoning layer doesn't notify Max and activates a goal to set the call on Voicemail.

$$V_{vhe} > V_{vcr} \implies goalActivation(Voicemail(Phone), active, self)$$

Therefore, the acting layer puts the call directly on Voicemail.

$$+deviceStatus(Phone, Voicemail)$$

Later, when Max receives a call from his mother, the goal reasoning layer activate a goal for muting the TV and notifying the user by putting his phone on the Ringing Status based on his value at the moment, which is family (vbc) is important than pleasure (vhe).

$$+callerType(Mom, Family);$$
$$V_{vhe} < V_{vbc} \implies goalActivation(notifyUser(Phone, User), active, self)$$

The planning and acting layer find a sequence of actions to satisfy the goals.

$$+deviceStatus(TV, Mute)$$
$$+deviceStatus(Phone, Ringing)$$

Once the user gets up from Sofa to go to his room to answer the call, Sofa detects his absence and the goal activation rules activates a goal to record the program that Max was watching.

$$+isStand(User) \implies goalActivation(recording(TV, Program), active, self)$$

After a while when he comes back and sits on the Sofa, the process of reasoning is repeated and in result, TV umutes and user can resume watching the program.

$$+beSeated(Max, Sofa) \implies$$
$$goalActivation(resume(TV, Program), active, self)$$
$$+deviceStatus(TV, Playing);$$

4.3   Discussion and Validation

Our main objective is to push forward the research interest and development of smart environments, specially the smart home, a residential space that takes into account more subjective user aspects such as human values, creating an intelligent autonomous home that better understands its users. The BDI (Belief-Desire-Intention) agent has a basic reasoning function that can be mapped to the deliberative acting function described in the paper. The plan refinement in a BDI architecture is performed by using the agent's procedural plans, which are action models i.e. methods with contextual conditions, to execute plan steps according to the context. It means that a plan can be adapted at run-time thanks to the acting function. Our approach presents the SMASH intelligent agent architecture, which is composed of context-aware reasoning functions. Our result represents a functional proof-of-concept for a multi-agent approach for a Smart Home.

In the Table 1, we have shown the reasoning time of the execution of an agent for two different planning cycle. The execution is repeated four times, in order to show the consistency of the reasoning time of the agent for the same reasoning cycle. For instances, in the second execution, the total reasoning time is equal to 2.008 s, in which 0.844 s is for the planning of the goal A that is the request of Max for watching "Canal+", 0.834 s for the planning of the goal B that is turning on the TV, and 0.330 s for the value- and goal-reasoning of the agent. The performance of the agent, with the additional reasoning steps, showed no significant processing overhead in all studied scenarios. This proof-of-concept validates the feasibility of the proposed approach and shows the agent usability and timely responses in human-centered smart environments.

Table 1. Reasoning Time of an agent for two planning cycles

Time (s)	Execution #1	Execution #2	Execution #3	Execution #4
Planning Time for Goal A	0.828	0.844	0.808	0.950
Planning Time for Goal B	0.837	0.834	0.791	1.124
Value- and Goal-Reasoning Time	0.425	0.330	0.339	0.408
Total Time (s)	**2.090**	**2.008**	**1.938**	**2.482**

5   Related Work

The aforementioned work presents a new approach to improve the reasoning process of an intelligent agent designed for smart environments. Such reasoning process includes planning and acting deliberative functions. The proposed approach presents a new reasoning method to improve the self-adaptation process of a multi-agent system for the management of IoT objects in human-centered environments such as Smart Home. Such reasoning process includes planning and acting deliberative functions. This section elaborates the main similarities and differences among related literature, specially concerning the goal-reasoning, planning and acting, whether or not they present a value-driven approach. An extensive definition and theoretical models for planning and acting are presented in [3]. Also, in [8] authors proposed a decentralized multi-agent planning and acting, and in [29] Torreno et al. surveyed about cooperative multi-agent planning. In [10], Ciortea et al. designed a Multi-agent System for the Web of Things using planning and acting, and in [11] authors surveyed about the integration of planning algorithms and agent. In all these works, the goal- and value-reasoning functions are not present. The planning and acting functions are implemented using different technologies and platforms. In our architecture the acting function is matched with built-in elements present in the BDI agent model [30], where for instance *refinement methods* in acting are *plans* in BDI. And our planning function translates to the known PDDL standard for execution in the FD planner [26]. The used planning language contains *domain actions* that matches to the *know-what* of the proposed agent architecture, and the *problem initial state* is built upon the set of *beliefs* present in our agent. Furthermore, there are works illustrating how flexible the planning and acting functions are, covering integrations with hierarchical operational models [12], with hierarchical task networks (HTN) [14], with first-principles planning (FPP) [15], with BDI agent model [16], and with other deliberation functions like monitoring, observing, and learning [13].

The lack of a goal-reasoning function in the BDI model was already identified in previous research [18], which proposes a goal deliberation strategy to mainly avoid conflict in the pursuit of goals. A goal reasoning model is proposed in [17] that aims at enabling reasoning about the organization and representation of the program flow of planning and execution. The main difference with the SMASH agent architecture is the value-reasoning function and the consideration of human values, meanwhile the common aspects are the explicit representation of goals, the existence of a goal lifecycle, and formalisms to model the transition of a goal through its lifecycle's states. Propositions of value-driven designs for intelligent agents are increasingly studied in the literature. Previous works explored the integration of values in the agent reasoning: [19] aimed at supporting coordination through values; and [20] treated values as goals that are activated when context reveals they are at stake, whereas in our architecture values are first-class citizens and are used in every reasoning function and processes.

6   Conclusion

In this paper, we presented an approach for self-adaptation of IoT objects in human-centered smart environments. This approach manages to autonomously adapt the ubiquitous devices to the uncertainties of the environment by performing a reasoning based on planning and acting that respects the values of the user. The proposed approach takes advantage of Semantic Web technologies using a platform called Home'In, which addresses interoperability issues and makes a common format for the exchange of beliefs among agents and services in Smart Home. The incorporation of values in the reasoning process presented some advantages such as an autonomy lesser dependent on human input. The flexibility of the architecture is maintained, as the engines of the planning and acting layers can be replaced by any engines that might be needed. This approach has been validated by performing a scenario as the proof of concept, which shows the high timely performance of SMASH agents compared with the literature.

References

1. Jiang, L., Liu, D.-Y., Yang, B.: Smart home research. In: Proceedings of 2004 International Conference on Machine Learning and Cybernetics, vol. 2. IEEE (2004)
2. Muccini, H., et al.: Self-adaptive IoT architectures: an emergency handling case study. In: Proceedings of the 12th European Conference on Software Architecture: Companion Proceedings (2018)
3. Ghallab, M., Nau, D., Traverso, P.: Automated Planning: Theory and Practice. Elsevier, New York (2004)
4. Russell, S., Norvig, P.: Artificial intelligence: a modern approach (2002)
5. Wooldridge, M.: An Introduction to Multiagent Systems. John Wiley & Sons, Hoboken (2009)
6. Berners-Lee, T., Hendler, J., Lassila, O.: The semantic web. Sci. Am. **284**(5), 34–43 (2001)
7. Trentin, I., Boissier, O., Ramparany, F.: Insights about user-centric contextual online adaptation of coordinated multi-agent systems in smart homes. In: Rencontres des Jeunes Chercheurs en Intelligence Artificielle 2019 (2019)
8. Li, R., Patra, S., Nau, D.: Decentralized Acting and Planning Using Hierarchical Operational Models (2020)
9. Jordán, J., Torreño, A., de Weerdt, M., Onaindia, E.: A better-response strategy for self-interested planning agents. Appl. Intell. **48**(4), 1020–1040 (2017). https://doi.org/10.1007/s10489-017-1046-5
10. Ciortea, A., Mayer, S., Michahelles, F.: Repurposing manufacturing lines on the fly with multi-agent systems for the web of things. In: Proceedings of the International Conference on Autonomous Agents and MultiAgent Systems (2018)
11. Meneguzzi, F., De Silva, L.: Planning in BDI agents: a survey of the integration of planning algorithms and agent reasoning. Knowl. Eng. Rev. **30**(1), 1–44 (2015)
12. Patra, S., et al.: Integrating acting, planning, and learning in hierarchical operational models. In: Proceedings of the International Conference on Automated Planning and Scheduling, vol. 30 (2020)
13. Ingrand, F., Ghallab, M.: Deliberation for autonomous robots: a survey. Artif. Intell. **247**, 10–44 (2017)
14. de Silva, L.: HTN acting: a formalism and an algorithm. In: Proceedings of the International Conference on Autonomous Agents and MultiAgent Systems (2018)
15. Xu, M., Bauters, K., McAreavey, K., Liu, W.: A formal approach to embedding first-principles planning in BDI agent systems. In: Ciucci, D., Pasi, G., Vantaggi, B. (eds.) SUM 2018. LNCS (LNAI), vol. 11142, pp. 333–347. Springer, Cham (2018). https://doi.org/10.1007/978-3-030-00461-3_23
16. Sardina, S., Padgham, L.: A BDI agent programming language with failure handling, declarative goals, and planning. Auton. Agents Multi-agent Syst. **23**(1), 18–70 (2011)
17. Niemueller, T., Hofmann, T., Lakemeyer, G.: Goal reasoning in the CLIPS executive for integrated planning and execution. In: Proceedings of the International Conference on Automated Planning and Scheduling, vol. 29 (2019)
18. Pokahr, A., Braubach, L., Lamersdorf, W.: Jadex: a BDI reasoning engine. In: Bordini, R.H., Dastani, M., Dix, J., El Fallah Seghrouchni, A. (eds.) Multi-Agent Programming. MSASSO, vol. 15, pp. 149–174. Springer, Boston (2005). https://doi.org/10.1007/0-387-26350-0_6
19. Vanhée, L.C.B.C.: Using Cultures and Values to Support Flexible Coordination. Utrecht Univ, Diss (2015)

20. Battaglino, C., Damiano, R., Lesmo, L.: Emotional range in value-sensitive deliberation. In: AAMAS International conference on Autonomous Agents and Multiagent Systems, vol. 2. IFAAMAS (2013)

21. Rohan, M.J.: A rose by any name? The values construct. Pers. Soc. Psychol. Rev. 4(3), 255–277 (2000)

22. Bardi, A., et al.: The structure of intraindividual value change. J. Pers. Soc. Psychol. 97(5), 913 (2009)

23. Schwartz, S.H.: An overview of the Schwartz theory of basic values. Online Read. Psychol. Culture 2(1), 0919–2307 (2012)

24. Schwartz, S.H.: Universals in the content and structure of values: theoretical advances and empirical tests in 20 countries. In: Advances in experimental social psychology. Academic Press (1992)

25. Cieciuch, J., et al.: The cross-national invariance properties of a new scale to measure 19 basic human values: a test across eight countries. J. Cross-Cultural Psychol. 45(5), 764–776 (2014)

26. Helmert, M.: The fast downward planning system. J. Artif. Intell. Res. 26, 191–246 (2006)

27. Boshuijzen-van Burken, C., et al.: Agent-based modelling of values: the case of value sensitive design for refugee logistics. JASSS 23(4), 345 (2020)

28. Boissier, O., et al.: Multi-Agent Oriented Programming: Programming Multi-agent Systems Using JaCaMo. Intelligent Robotics and Autonomous Agents Series, MIT Press, Cambridge (2020)

29. Torreno, A., et al.: Cooperative multi-agent planning: a survey. ACM Comput. Surv. (CSUR) 50(6), 1–32 (2017)

30. Rao, A.S.: AgentSpeak(L): BDI agents speak out in a logical computable language. In: Van de Velde, W., Perram, J.W. (eds.) MAAMAW 1996. LNCS, vol. 1038, pp. 42–55. Springer, Heidelberg (1996). https://doi.org/10.1007/BFb0031845

Agent-Based Modelling and Simulation of Airport Terminal Operations Under COVID-19-Related Restrictions

Gregory Sanders, S. Sahand Mohammadi Ziabari$^{(\boxtimes)}$ ⓘ, Adin Mekić, and Alexei Sharpanskykh ⓘ

Delft University of Technology, Delft, The Netherlands
{A.Mekic,O.A.Sharpanskykh}@tudelft.nl

Abstract. The worldwide COVID-19 pandemic has had a tremendous impact on the aviation industry, with a reduction in passenger demand never seen before. To minimize the spread of the virus and to gain trust from the public in the airport operations' safety, airports implemented measures, e.g., physical distancing, entry/exit temperature screening and more. However, airports do not know what the impact of these measures will be on the operations' performance and the passengers' safety when passenger demand increases back. The goal of this research is twofold. Firstly, to analyze the impact of current (COVID-19) and future pandemic-related measures on airport terminal operations. Secondly, to identify plans that airport management agents can take to control passengers' flow in a safe, efficient, secure and resilient way. To model and simulate airport operations, an agent-based model was developed. The proposed model covers the main airport's handling processes and simulates local interactions, such as physical distancing between passengers. The obtained results show that COVID-19 measures can significantly affect the passenger throughput of the handling processes and the average time passengers are in contact with each other. For instance, a 20% increase in check-in time (due to additional COVID-19 related paperwork at the check-in desk) can decrease passenger throughput by 16% and increase the time that passengers are in contact by 23%.

Keywords: Multi-agent system · Airport operations · COVID-19 · Physical distancing · Walking behavior

1 Introduction

The outbreak of the COVID-19 pandemic has led to a worldwide crisis and presents us today unprecedented challenges in our life. The aviation industry has been impacted like no other industrial sector. When in March 2020 large clusters of COVID-19 cases were identified in Europe, many countries started to impose travel restrictions. As a result, the travel demand dropped and global air traffic decreased by 80% compared to the preceding year [1]. The aviation industry has never faced a challenge this large. To minimize the spread of the COVID-19 virus and regain the public's trust in the aviation industry's safety, airports needed to be made safe. Since at airports passengers are

© Springer Nature Switzerland AG 2021
F. Dignum et al. (Eds.): PAAMS 2021, LNAI 12946, pp. 214–228, 2021.
https://doi.org/10.1007/978-3-030-85739-4_18

often exposed to many interactions with other people, airport operators implemented measures. Some examples of measures are physical distancing, entry/exit temperature screening, prevention of queuing, use of personal protective equipment. To help airports implement measures, the European Aviation Safety Agency released in June 2020 their "COVID-19 Aviation Health Safety Protocol" [2]. This report lists measures that airport operators can take for safe operations to guarantee the passengers' safety. These measures, for instance social distancing, are widely considered as a new part of our life. These recommended measures from EASA already helped many airports in providing safe operations. However, many airports still do not know the impact of these measures on their operations when passenger demand will increase. For example, Charleroi Airport faced a sudden increase in passenger demand during the Christmas Holiday of 2020. As a result, the airport was too crowded and passengers could not perform physical distancing [3]. Also, airports are very complex because they involve many processes (e.g., check-in, security, boarding) and many stakeholders (airlines, airport operators), resulting in conflicting objectives. On the one hand, airports operators have the financial intent to increase revenue and decrease costs. On the other hand, they also need to make sure that operations are safe for the passengers. While airports are now under financial pressure, it is hard for them to make decisions primarily since they do not understand the impact of these measures. To address this problem agent-based modelling and simulation was used in this research. These emergent properties can be translated into system-wide key performance indicators (KPIs), for example passenger throughput, and can be used to asses, e.g., the system's performance and safety. Altogether, agent-based modelling is a suitable paradigm to model airport terminal operations.

This paper is organized as follows. In Sect. 2 the related work is discussed. The agent-based model is discussed in Sect. 3. The different case studies and the results are given in Sect. 4. Finally, Sect. 5 is Discussion and Conclusion.

2 Related Work

Related works should at least cover two main categories namely, different pedestrian dynamics models to simulate passenger walking behavior, and pandemic modeling and analysis. We will briefly go through each of them.

In general pedestrian dynamics models can be categorized into microscopic models and macroscopic models [4]. In microscopic models, every pedestrian is treated as an individual unit and is given a certain amount of characteristics, for instance direction and speed. The changes in movement of each pedestrian is influenced by other pedestrians and by the environment. Gips et al. proposed the benefit-cost cellular model for modelling pedestrian flows [5]. Blue et al. proposed cellular automata microsimulation for modeling bi-directional pedestrian walkways [6]. These two models are cellular automata-based models which means that the environment of the model is discretized in a grid. The downside of this type of models is that the simulation does not reflect the real behavior of pedestrians because updates in the grid are done heuristically [4, 7]. The queueing network model was introduced in [8]. In this model the environment is discretized into links and nodes. Pedestrians move from one node to another node. The movement is stochastic because it uses Monte Carlo simulations. This model has several drawbacks. Firstly, movement is unidimensional and therefore it is not so realistic because pedestrians walk bi-dimensional. Secondly, the model cannot not deal with high density environments, like airport terminals. Thirdly, because of the discretized environment, the model lacks the ability to analyze local interactions between the different agents. Okazaki introduced a magnetic force model for pedestrian movement simulation with evacuation and queueing [9]. This model is based on the magnetic field theory to simulate pedestrian movement. Helbing et al. came up with the social force model [10]. The social-force model uses psychological forces that drive pedestrians to move towards their goal as well as keep a proper distance from other pedestrians and objects. The values of the parameters of the social forces have a physical meaning and therefore calibrating these parameters for social distancing is easier.

The second category investigates the studies which used agent-based models to analyze the impact of COVID-19 on the performance of airport terminal operations and on the associated passenger health safety. Kierzkowski et al. uses a discrete event simulation model for different security lane configurations to analyze the impact of social distancing on the performance of the security [11]. However, this model lacks the ability to model local interactions between passengers because it is a discrete event simulation model. Furthermore, they only evaluate the performance of the security lanes and not the associated health safety of the passengers. Schultz et al. used a cellular automata model to simulate different aircraft boarding strategies under COVID-19 related restrictions [12]. He assessed for each boarding strategy the impact on total boarding time, the feasibility of the procedure and the associated risk of virus transmission. Schultz et al. used a transmission model which was based on the work of [13]. The study of Schultz et al. lacks to analysis of other processes and activities at the airport such as check-in or security. Ronchi et al. developed a model-agnostic approach to perform a quantitative assessment of pedestrian exposure using the outputs of existing microscopic crowd models, namely the trajectories of pedestrians over time [14]. The model uses a general formulation instead of relying on a specific disease transmission. For instance, the quantification of the pedestrian exposure is based on the distances between pedestrians, the time pedestrians are exposed and reference points (e.g. pedestrian face each other). It is therefore universal and can be tailored to new pandemics when there is no compelling understanding in the transmission of the pandemic.

3   The Agent-Based Model

The model used in this paper is an extension of the baseline "Airport And Terminal Operations Model" (AATOM) with features to simulate passengers adhering to COVID-19 measures and to analyze passengers health safety [15]. In this model, passengers and airport operators are represented as autonomous intelligent entities, called agents. These agents are modelled with a particular behavior approximating humans and placed in a partially observable airport environment. An overview of the agent-based system is provided in Fig. 1.

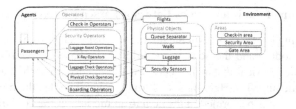

Fig. 1. Overview of the multi-agent system including the different types of agents and their interactions with each other and the environment.

3.1 Specification of the Environment, and the Agents

The model's environment represents an airport terminal under COVID-19 conditions, as seen in Fig. 2. It resembles an existing regional airport from the Netherlands. The environment consists of three main areas: the check-in area, the security checkpoint area and the gate area. The check-in area consists of four sets of check-in desks, each with three desks and one designated queue. There is a check-in operator (red dot), which checks-in passengers, behind each check-in desk. Three check-ins are using a common zig-zag queue. One check-in is using three single straight queues. There are four types of security operators (A, B, C, D) as indicated in the lower part of Fig. 2. Operators A assist passengers in their luggage drop activity. Operators B perform the x-ray scan activity. Operators C perform the luggage check-activity and operators D perform a physical check when a passenger is suspicious. The black dots represent the luggage divest and luggage collect positions. Figure 2 shows three divest and three collect positions per lane, respectively. The number of divest and collect positions can vary depending on the input to the model. The model contains three types of agents: passenger agents adhering to COVID-19 rules, passenger agents not adhering to COVID-19 rules and operator agents. These three types all share the AATOM cognitive architecture described by [15] and shown in Fig. 3. The shaded blocks of Fig. 3 show the extensions and improvements made to the baseline AATOM model. The security checkpoint area consists of four security lanes and one large common queue. The checkpoint lanes have a luggage belt, an X-ray sensor and a walk-through metal detector.

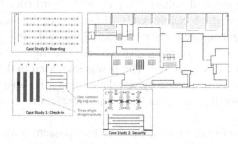

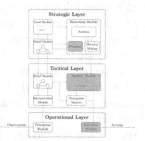

Fig. 2. The environment of the agent-based model. (Color figure online)

Fig. 3. Cognitive architecture of AATOM.

3.2 Specification of the Interactions Between Passenger Agents

Physical distancing has an impact on the interaction between passengers. For this study, the movement module and the activity module of the baseline AATOM model were revised to include physical distancing between the agents when they are walking and when they are queuing. The Helbing social force model handles the movement of passenger agents [10]. It is performed in the actuation module of the cognitive architecture presented in Fig. 3. The model assumes that the passengers' movement is guided by a superposition of attractive and repulsive forces, determining the passengers' walking behavior. The pushing force and a friction force refer to the forces when passengers collide with each other. These forces are not important for the model because passengers are not allowed to touch each other; they need to keep their distance. The social repulsion force $\vec{f}_{\text{social rep}}$, on the other hand, is important for simulating physical distancing. The social repulsion force $\vec{f}_{\text{social rep}}$ is modelled by Eq. 1 and was calibrated in order to simulate physical distancing between the agents. It models the psychological tendency of two pedestrians i and j to stay away from each other. r_{ij} is the sum of the radii of pedestrian i with radius r_i and pedestrian j with radius j. d_{ij} is the absolute distance between the pedestrians i and j (taken from their center of mass). $\vec{n}_{ij}$ is the normalized vector from pedestrian j to i and is calculated by: $\vec{n}_{ij} = \left(n_{ij}^1, n_{ij}^2\right) = (\vec{r}_i - \vec{r}_j)/d_{ij}$. A_i and B_i are the "Helbing" constants [10]. These Helbing constants define the distance between passengers and are therefore crucial in modelling physical distancing.

$$\vec{f}_{\text{social rep.}} = A_i e^{(r_{ij}-d_{ij})/B_i} \vec{n}_{ij} \tag{1}$$

In the baseline AATOM model, no difference was made between the social repulsion force of two agents and the social repulsion force of an agent and an object. The values of A and B for both scenarios were taken 250 [N] and 0.1 [m], respectively. The values of A and B for both scenarios were taken 250 [N] and 0.1 [m], respectively. However, in the model for this research study, the distinction is made between both. In this model, every passenger agent that performs physical distancing is given two sets of Helbing parameters. One set of parameters to simulate the social repulsion force of a passenger agent with the environment. Another set of parameters to simulate the social repulsion force of a passenger agent with other passenger agents. For the first set, the values of A and B were taken to be equal to the original values 250 [N] and 0.1 [m] such that emergence of the interactions is similar to the baseline AATOM model. For the second set, the B value was calibrated to represent physical distancing between agents. In Fig. 4 one can see the impact of parameter B on the social repulsion force. The higher the B value, the earlier the social repulsion force is activated. The B was increased to 0.5 m (while A remains 250 [N]). It was visually inspected by simulation that a B value 0.5 m guarantees a physical distancing between passengers while still representing correct walking behavior.

The agent-based model is able to identify at each time point which passenger agents are not performing physical distancing, this will be referred to as using "agents that are in contact". One analyzer was implemented in the model that represents the number of passengers that are in contact at every time step. This is shown in Fig. 5(a). This analyzer is used to determine the contact locations. A second analyzer, presented in Fig. 5(b),

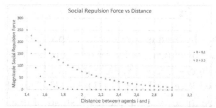

Fig. 4. Plot of social repulsion force $f_{social\ repulsion}$ [N] vs distance between the passengers d_{ij} [m]. The blue graph is the social repulsion force of the baseline AATOM model (when agents are not physically distancing). The orange graph is the social repulsion force for the extended AATOM model where agents are physically distancing. (Color figure online)

integrates the first and represents the total time of all passengers that were in contact. This analyzer is used as a metric for results of the case studies presented in Sect. 4. A third analyzer, in Fig. 5(c), shows the summed contact time but with a distinction between 'face-to-face' contacts and 'everything-back contacts'.

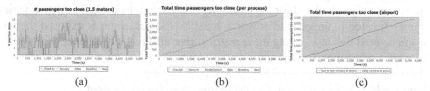

(a)   (b)   (c)

Fig. 5. The passenger contact analyzers. (a) Analyzer showing the amount of agents that are in contact at every time step and at which location. Case study 1: scenario 5. (b) Analyzer showing summed time of all passengers that were in contact. The amount of contacts (figure on the left) are integrated over time. Case study 1: scenario 5. (c) Analyzer showing summed time of all passengers that were in contact. Case study 1: scenario 5.

4   Case Studies

For this research, three different case studies are performed. The check-in process is analyzed in Sect. 4.1. The security process is analyzed in Sect. 4.2 and finally, the boarding process is analyzed in Sect. 4.3. In each case study, different hypotheses are answered by simulating various scenarios in which different COVID-19 measures are modelled. Every scenario is simulated 450 times. These three case studies all share a common goal: they aim to analyze the impact of the COVID-19 measures on the performance of the process and the passengers' health safety. The model set-up and the used metrics are explained in the following three sections.

4.1   Case Study 1: Check-In

In this case study only the check-in is considered, as presented in Fig. 2. This case study aims to analyze the impact of three COVID-19 measures: Firstly, the impact of physical distancing between passengers. Secondly, the impact of longer waiting times at the desk due to additional paperwork related to COVID-19. Thirdly, the impact of a different queue lay out, for instance three straight queues instead of one common zig-zag queue. The following three metrics are developed to analyze the effect of these measures on the system's performance and the associated health safety of the passengers: 1. Check-in throughput T_C, calculated in passengers per hour. Check-in throughput is defined as the number of passengers that were served by a check-in area in a specific time period. Note a check-in area consists out of three check-in desks. 2. Average contact time per passenger C_{pax}, calculated in seconds. Contact time per passenger is defined as the time duration for which a passenger agent is not able to perform at least 1.5 m physical distancing. For the check-in case study, two variants of this metric were designed. Namely, A) the average contact time per passenger in the check-in queue $C_{pax_{CQ}}$. This metric only considers the contact time of a passenger for which the passenger was in the queue during the check-in process. B) The average contact time per passenger at the check-in desk $C_{pax_{CD}}$. This metric is thus only calculated for the passengers that are at the desk. These two variants were implemented to understand at which location the passenger is exposed the most: in the queue or at the desk. Using these metrics, five different hypotheses were found to be the most interesting to analyze:

- **Hypothesis 1:** Physical distancing decreases check-in throughput T_C.
- **Hypothesis 2:** Physical distancing decreases average contact time per passenger in the queue $C_{pax_{CQ}}$.
- **Hypothesis 3:** A 20% increase in check-in time t_{Ci} increases the average contact time per passenger in the queue $C_{pax_{CQ}}$.
- **Hypothesis 4:** Three single straight queues (instead of one common zig-zag queue) result in a higher check-in throughput T_C.
- **Hypothesis 5:** Three single straight queues (instead of one common zig-zag queue) result in a lower average contact time per passenger $C_{pax_{CQ}}$.

These four hypotheses are tested by simulating five different scenarios. Passenger agents are generated in front of check-in queue and they only perform the check-in activity and the queue activity. The inputs to the model for each scenario are given in Table 1. Scenario 1 models a pre-COVID-19 situation. No COVID-19 measures are modelled in this scenario. Thus, passenger agents do not perform physical distancing. No extra paperwork is required. Therefore, the check-in time t_{Ci} follows a normal distribution with a mean of 60 min and a variance of 6 min. This is based on data that is gathered before COVID-19 [16, 17]. Passenger agents are using a common zig-zag queue. In scenario 2, the 1.5-m physical distancing measure is modelled. Scenario 1 and 2 are used to test hypotheses 1 and 2. In scenario 3, a 20% increase in check-in time t_{Ci} is modelled, thus N(72,6), in order to account for additional health questions and more paperwork related to COVID-19. This scenario is used to test hypothesis 3. In scenario 4, the measures of scenario 2 and 3 are modelled together. Lastly, in scenario 5 passenger agents use a straight check-in queue instead of a common zig-zag queue. This scenario is used to test hypotheses 4 and 5.

Results for Check-In

Table 1 presents the results of the check-in case study, Sect. 4.1. For hypothesis 1, Table 1 shows that scenario 1 and 2 result in the same check-in throughput T_C, namely 167 passengers per hour. This means that physical distancing PD does not influence the check-in throughput T_C. This was confirmed by the coefficient of correlation ρPD, T_C = −0.11 with p-$value$ = 0. Since the ρPD, T_C < 0.4 (rule of thumb) we can say there is no significant correlation between these two variables. Thus, we can reject hypothesis 1. For hypothesis 2, Table 1 shows that in scenario 1 a passenger is on average 4 s in contact at the desk C_{paxCD} and 1 min and 25 s in contact with other passengers in the queue C_{paxCQ}. For scenario 2, C_{paxCD} is the same but C_{paxCQ} reduced with 41%. This means that physical distancing does decrease C_{paxCQ}. This is confirmed by the strong negative correlation coefficient: $\rho PD, C_{paxCQ}$ = −0.9 with p-value = 0. Therefore, we can support hypothesis 2. For hypothesis 3, it can be deduced from scenario 3 in Table 1 that an extra 20% more check-in time t_{ci} (due to e.g., extra COVID-19 related paper work) increases the average contact time per passenger in the queue C_{paxCQ} by 23%. The coefficient of correlation ρt_{ci}, C_{paxCQ} = +0.72 with p = 0. This means there is a significant positive correlation between t_{ci} and C_{paxCQ}. Therefore, we can support hypothesis 3. This is reasonable because t_{ci} also reduces the check-in throughput T_C with 16% which results in longer waiting times for passengers in the queue. For hypothesis 4 and 5, three single queues were implemented in scenario 5 instead of one common zig-zag queue. Table 1 reveals that straight queues increase passenger throughput with a small 3%. The coefficient of correlation ρQT, T_C equals 0.24, which is lower than 0.4, meaning there is no significant correlation. We can reject hypothesis 4. The introduction of three single queues also reduced C_{paxCD} by 50% and C_{paxCQ} by 42%. The coefficients of correlation ρQT, C_{paxCD} and ρQT, C_{paxCQ} are −0.86 and −0.74. This confirms that single queues reduce the average contact time per passenger C_{pax}. Hypothesis 5 can be supported. The reason for this reduction is threefold: 1. Due to the three straight queues, the passenger flow from the end of the queue towards the check-in desk is more efficient. Fewer passengers interfere with each other because there are three queue exits instead of one. 2. The absence of corners in a straight queue. Figure 6 shows that in a zig-zag most contacts occur in the corners (dark blue dots). In a straight queue, Passengers do not need to turn while queuing. When passengers are turning, they focus less on other passengers than when they walk in a straight line. 3. The model implementation: a passenger agent is programmed to stop when observing other passenger agents that are in queueing mode and are at 1.5 m distance. At corners, the passenger's observation can be blocked by a wall which causes that other passenger agents are observed too late (when the passengers are already closer than 1.5 m).

4.2   Case Study 2: Security Check Point

Case study 2 only considers the security process. This case study's environment is the security checkpoint area, as shown in Fig. 2. This case study aims to analyze the impact of the COVID-19 measures on the performance of the security checkpoints and the

Fig. 6. Heatmap scenario 2. The dark blue areas represent the hot spots of passenger contacts. (Color figure online)

Table 1. Results of case study 1: check-in. PD means physical distancing, t_{ci} means time to check-in. Note that percentages are given w.r.t. the baseline scenario 1. For every scenario 450 simulations were performed.

Check-in scenario	Input to Model			T_C			$C_{pax_{CD}}$		$C_{pax_{CQ}}$	
	Queue Type	PD	t_{ci} [sec]	μ [pax/h]		σ^2 [pax^2/h^2]	μ [min:sec]	σ^2 [sec^2]	μ [min:sec]	σ^2 [sec^2]
1	One common	No	N(60,6)	167		0.3136	00:04	0.0410	01:25	1.6543
2	One common	Yes	N(60,6)	167	0%	0.3548	00:04	0.0365	00:50	-41%	3.1109
3	One common	No	N(72,6)	140	-16%	0.4750	00:04	0%	0.0334	01:45	23%	1.9986
4	One common	Yes	N(72,6)	140	-16%	0.6131	00:04	0%	0.0337	01:03	-26%	6.2027
5	Three single	Yes	N(72,6)	145	-13%	0.3422	00:02	-50%	0.0194	00:27	-68%	23.773

associated passenger health safety. Similar metrics as for the check-in case study are used, namely: 1. Average security throughput T_S, calculated in passengers per hour. Security throughput is defined as the number of passengers that were served by two security lanes in a specific time period. 2. Average contact time per passenger $Cpax$, calculated in seconds. Two variants of this metric were designed to identify at which location most contacts occur. Namely, A) the average contact time per passenger in the security queue $C_{pax_{SQ}}$. B) The average contact time per passenger at the security lane $C_{pax_{SL}}$. Also, for this case study some hypotheses were found interesting to be analyzed:

- **Hypothesis 6:** An increase in luggage divest time td and luggage collect time tc result in a lower security throughput TS.
- **Hypothesis 7:** An increase in luggage divest time td and luggage collect time tc result a higher average contact time per passenger $C_{pax_{SL}}$ and $C_{pax_{SQ}}$.
- **Hypothesis 8:** Less luggage divest n_d and luggage collect n_c positions result in a lower average contact time per passenger $C_{pax_{SL}}$ and $C_{pax_{SQ}}$.

To test these hypotheses seven different scenarios were designed. In each scenario, only two security lanes are open. Passenger agents are generated in front of the queue of the security checkpoint. They only perform the queue activity and the security checkpoint activity. The inputs to the model for each scenario are given in Table 2. Scenario 1 is the baseline scenario with parameters simulating the pre-COVID19 situation, thus without any COVID-19 measures. Three luggage divest n_d and three luggage collect n_c positions are implemented per lane. Thus, passenger agents are standing there close to each other. Scenario 2 considers an increase of 20% in divest time td and collection time t_c. From interviews with airport stakeholders it was revealed that security operators do not actively support passengers anymore during divesting which results in more time needed for passengers. When passengers place items incorrectly in the trays, operators try to minimize contact with the passengers' belongings. Therefore, they let passengers rather reorganize their items themselves which results in additional time. This scenario is used to test hypothesis 6 and 7. Scenario 4, 5, 6 and 7 consider different number divest n_d and collect positions n_c. Since the divesting and collection area is generally very crowded, pre-COVID-19 configurations with three divest positions and three collect positions per lane do not correspond to physical distance regulations any longer. These scenarios are used to test hypothesis 8.

Results for Security Check Point
Table 2 presents the results for this case study. In the baseline scenario, where the parameters from [19] were used, the throughout for the 2 lanes T_S is 230 passengers per hour. This is equal to 1.92 passengers per minute per lane, which is in line with the findings of [19]. As for the check-in case study, we observe from scenario 3 that physical distancing PD does not influence the security's throughput. Because the physical distancing is already analyzed in the previous case study, no further analysis is needed. For hypotheses 6 and 7, scenario 1 and 2 can be compared. In scenario 2, a 20% increase in divest t_d and collect t_c time was implemented (because operators do not actively support passengers to diminish the interactions). From Fig. 7, it was observed that most contacts happen at the luggage divest and collect area of the security system, therefore different number of luggage divest n_d and collect n_c positions were implemented.

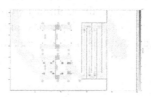

Fig. 7. Heatmap scenario 3. The dark blue areas represent the hot spots of passenger contacts. (Color figure online)

Table 2 shows that an increase in t_d and t_c has a negative influence on the throughput T_S. Throughput reduces by 10%. This reduction is supported by the coefficient of correlation $\rho t_d, T_S = \rho t_c, T_S = -0.51$ with a p-value of 0. Therefore hypothesis 6 can be supported. The average contact time per passenger at the security lane C_{paxSL} and in the queue C_{paxSQ} increased by around 13% and 15%. The coefficients of correlation are 0.42 and 0.39. Since this is lower than 0.4 (rule of thumb), we can't say there is a significant correlation. Therefore, we need to reject hypothesis 7. For hypothesis 8 we can compare scenario 4, 5, 6 and 7 in Table 2. Table 2 shows that a reduction in n_d and n_c lowers the average contact time per passenger at the security lane C_{paxSL}. This correlation is confirmed by the coefficients: $\rho n_d, C_{paxSL} = 0.9$ and $\rho n_c, C_{paxSL} = 0.76$ (both with $p = 0$).

Table 2. Results of case study 2: security. PD means physical distancing, t_d luggage drop time, t_c luggage collect time, n_d number of divest positions per lane and n_c number of collect positions per lane. Note that percentages are given w.r.t. the baseline scenario 1.

Security scenario	PD	t_d [sec]	t_c [sec]	n_d	n_c	μ [pax/h]		σ^2 [pax^2/h^2]	μ [min:sec]		σ^2 [sec^2]	μ [min:sec]		σ^2 [sec^2]
1	No	N(54, 36)	N(71, 54)	3	3	230		15.9250	01:05		3.1485	01:52		4.9035
2	No	N(65, 36)	N(85, 54)	3	3	206	-10%	12.9633	01:13	13%	2.9601	02:09	15%	3.2523
3	Yes	N(65, 36)	N(85, 54)	3	3	206	-10%	15.0640	01:13	12%	4.9906	01:13	-35%	31.879
4	Yes	N(65, 36)	N(85, 54)	2	3	165	-28%	13.8631	00:28	-57%	7.6131	01:36	-15%	68.954
5	Yes	N(65, 36)	N(85, 54)	3	2	155	-33%	16.8833	00:59	-9%	7.9570	01:51	-1%	75.153
6	Yes	N(65, 36)	N(85, 54)	2	2	137	-40%	10.1974	00:09	-86%	3.9940	02:01	8%	78.221
7	Yes	N(65, 36)	N(85, 54)	1	1	69	-70%	17.7884	00:02	-97%	0.2418	04:20	132%	559.09

The table header spans: **Input to Model** over t_d, t_c, n_d, n_c; T_S over μ and σ^2; $C_{pax_{SL}}$ over μ and σ^2; $C_{pax_{SQ}}$ over μ and σ^2.

Hypothesis 8 can be supported. However, Table 2 also shows that a reduction in n_d and n_c lowers the security throughput T_S. To find an optimal between the positive influence of n_d and n_c on the C_{pax} and the negative influence on T_S, some more analysis of the scenarios is needed: Comparing scenario 4 with scenario 5 shows that a "one divest position less" measure improves the $C_{pax_{SL}}$ better than "one collect position less". From this, we can conclude in the luggage divest area more passenger contacts happen than in the collect area. Both measures have almost the same impact on security throughput T_S, around 160 passengers per hour. In scenario 6, one divest position less (scenario 4) and one collect position less (scenario 5) were implemented together. Table 2 shows that throughput reduces to 137 passengers per hour. The contact time at the security lane is reduced to 9 s per passenger, which means that almost no contacts occur at the security lane. Lastly, in scenario 7 only 1 divest position and 1 collect position per lane was implemented. For this scenario, the throughput T_S dropped even further to only 69 passengers per hour. The average contact time per passenger at the security lane dropped to 2 s per passenger while the contact time in the queue increased to 4 min and 20 s.

4.3 Case Study 3: Boarding

For case study 3, only boarding is considered. One gate area is considered and shown in Fig. 2. This case study aims to analyze the impact of the COVID-19 measures on the boarding procedure. For this case study, 50 passengers are considered representing a regional flight with a B737 with a load-factor of 1/3, based on expert knowledge. It is assumed that 50 passengers are all sitting at the start of the simulation. For this case study two metrics are considered, namely:1. The average time to board 50 passengers TB, calculated in minutes. Note: the time starts when the first passenger agent starts the boarding process (when the passenger agent leaves the seat) and it ends when the last (50th) passenger agent is boarded. 2. The average contact time per passenger $Cpax$, calculated in minutes. Using these metrics, four different hypotheses were found interesting to be analyzed:

- **Hypothesis 9:** Physical distancing increases the total time to board 50 passengers T_B.
- **Hypothesis 10:** Boarding in smaller groups increases the total time to board 50 passengers T_B.
- **Hypothesis 11:** Boarding in smaller groups decreases the average time passengers are in contact $Cpax$.

• **Hypothesis 12:** A higher average boarding pass check-time tbc increases the average time passengers are in contact $Cpax$.

These hypotheses are tested by simulating four different scenarios. The inputs to the model for each scenario are given in Table 3. Scenario 1 is the baseline scenario in which passengers do not maintain physical distance, they board in groups of 10 and the t_{bc} follows a normal distribution with mean 10 s and variance 1 s. In scenario 2, passengers board in smaller groups of 5 passengers. This scenario is used to test hypotheses 10 and 11. In scenario 3 physical distancing is modelled to test hypothesis 9. Lastly, for hypothesis 12 scenario 4 simulates the impact of a higher t_{bc} because airlines often ask health questions before checking the boarding pass.

Results for Boarding
In case study, 3 different boarding strategies were analyzed. In total 5 scenarios were simulated. The results are shown in Table 3. For hypothesis 9, scenario 2 and 3 are compared. Scenario 2 in Table 3 shows that when passengers are not performing physical distancing PD, the time to board 50 passengers T_B is 4 min and 49 s. When passengers are performing physical distancing the time to board 50 passengers is 4% higher. This is also confirmed by the coefficient of correlation $\rho PD,T_B$ equal to 0.61 and the p-value equal to 0 which means there is a significant positive correlation. Thus hypothesis 9 can be supported. This makes sense because passengers need more time to organize themselves in the queue, especially at the beginning of the queue.

For hypotheses 10 and 11, scenario 1 and 2 are compared. Scenario 2 shows that when passengers are boarding in smaller groups GS (five passengers instead of ten) the time to board 50 passengers TB increases by 12%. The average contact time per passenger $Cpax$ decreases by 52%. This is also reflected by the coefficients of correlation which are $\rho GS, TB = -0.8$ (p-value of 0) and $\rho GS, Cpax = 0.9$ (p-value of 0). Therefore hypothesis 10 and 11 can be supported. We can conclude that splitting a boarding group in two does not imply that the total boarding time doubles. This finding is important for airports with limited space at gates for queueing. Since some airlines ask additional questions related to COVID-19 during scanning of the boarding pass, passengers need to wait longer at the gate counter. Therefore, an increase of 10 s in boarding pass check time tbc was implemented in scenario 4. To check hypothesis 12, scenario 3 and scenario 4 can be compared. Scenario 4 in Table 3 shows that an in increase in boarding check time tbc increases the average time a passenger is in contact $Cpax$ with 4 s. The coefficient of correlation $\rho t_{bc}, C_{pax} = 0.6$ with a p-value of 0. Therefore, hypothesis 12 can be supported. Moreover, it can also be seen from Table 3 that the total boarding time T_B significantly increases. Thus, the waiting time at the gate counter should be minimized as much as possible because it significantly influences the total boarding time and the average contact time per passenger. We can recommend that administrative questions should be asked in advance, for example, during online check-in.

Table 3. Results of case study 3: boarding. GS means boarding group size, PD means physical distancing and t_{bc} means boarding pass check time.

Boarding	Input to Model			T_B			C_{pax}		
scenario	GS	PD	t_{bc} [sec]	μ [min:sec]		σ^2 [sec^2]	μ [min:sec]		σ^2 [sec^2]
1	10 pax	No	10	10:45		10.9984	01:04		1.1028
2	5 pax	No	10	12:03	12%	21.5824	00:31	-52%	1.2914
3	5 pax	Yes	10	12:28	16%	24.4984	00:08	-88%	5.6517
4	5 pax	Yes	20	20:49	94%	25.3051	00:12	-81%	18.645
5	1 pax	Yes	20	34:25	220%	37.7517	00:00	-100%	0

5 Discussion and Conclusion

The proposed agent-based model simulates the main airport handling processes of passengers at an airport under COVID-19 circumstances. This study can help airport operators in their decision-making and make airports more resilient for future crises. The results from the three case studies are airport specific because the parameters used were specific to a particular regional airport. Data was taken from [16, 17] to calibrate the parameters for the case studies done with the model. As every airport has different distributions of passenger types and different infrastructure and personal, the used parameters can thus not per se be copied to represent other airports. Also, since there is not much work done in the field of agent-based models used for both the analysis of the airport operations performance and for the associated passenger health safety, it is difficult to compare the results with other studies. Although this study has proven to be useful in analyzing the impact of the COVID-19 measures, this study also made some assumptions. The contact time metric used in this research study takes into account distance (a contact happens when passengers are closer than 1.5 m from each other) and time (the time of a contact). However, the model does not distinguish between contacts that happen at 1 m and contacts that happen at 1.4 m. Lastly, the model only considers check-in desks staffed with operators. However, in reality many airports have self-check-in desks as these can spread over the passenger demand and decrease costs. This research study does not consider how self-check-in desks can contribute to safer operations for passengers.

This study aimed to analyze the impact of COVID-19 restrictions on airport operations' performance and the associated health safety of the passengers. The agent-based model was used to explore three different case studies to analyze the impact of these measures on the check-in, the security and the boarding process, respectively. The measures' effects were all tested in different scenarios for each case study by analyzing the maximum throughput and the average contact time per passenger for check-in and security. The results show that physical distancing during queueing does not affect the throughput of the check-in and the security process. Physical distancing does lead to passengers being less in contact with each other, and it also decreases the capacity of queues. The implementation of single queues instead of one common queue had a positive impact on the throughput of the check-in and the passengers' health safety. The flow towards desks is more efficient (with less interfering flows of passengers), and it is easier for physical distancing in single queues because no turning is required. Furthermore, it was shown that in a pre-COVID-19 security lane set-up many passengers are too close at the luggage divest and collect area. The case study results showed that a decrease from three luggage divest and collect positions per lane to two positions of each per lane leads to a significant positive impact on passenger health safety while the throughput is still acceptable. However, to obtain the same throughput with one drop off and one collect position less it is advised to open an extra security lane. Implementing only one divest and one collect position per lane is unnecessary because it does not appropriately improve passenger health safety. Thus, two passengers per divest area and two per collect area is perfectly possible. Then, passengers can move without being closer than 1.5 m from each other. The boarding case study results showed that boarding in smaller groups positively impacts the average contact time per passenger. In contrast, it negatively affects the total boarding time. The results also showed that physical distance has a relatively small impact on the total boarding time because the organization of the passengers lining up during queueing takes a bit more time.

References

1. Covid19 airport status. https://www.icao.int/safety/Pages/COVID-19-Airport-Status.aspx. Accessed 14 Feb 2021
2. EASA: Covid-19 aviation health safety protocol - operational guidelines for the management of air passengers and aviation personnel in relation to the covid-19 pandemic. Technical report, European Union Aviation Safety Agency (2020)
3. De Herdt, C.: Massa mensen afgelopen weekend op luchthaven van Charleroi, viroloog Steven Van Gucht reageert verbaasd: Jammer dat dit gebeurt (2020). https://www.nieuwsblad.be/cnt/dmf20201221_98258870. Accessed 21 Mar 2021
4. Teknomo, K., Takeyama, Y., Inamura, H.: Review on microscopic pedestrian simulation model. arXiv e-prints arXiv:1609.01808 (2016)
5. Gipps, P.G., Marksjö, B.: A micro-simulation model for pedestrian flows. Math. Comput. Simul. **27**(2), 95–105 (1985)
6. Blue, V., Adler, J.: Cellular automata microsimulation for modeling bidirectional pedestrian walkways. Transp. Res. Part B Methodol. **35**, 293–312 (2001)
7. Ma, W.: Agent-based model of passenger flows in airport terminals. Ph.D. thesis, Queensland University of Technology, Brisbane, Australia (2013)
8. Løvås, G.G.: Modeling and simulation of pedestrian traffic flow. Transp. Res. Part B Methodol. **28**(6), 429–443 (1994)
9. Okazaki, S., Matsushita, S.: A study of simulation model for pedestrian movement with evacuation and queuing. In: Engineering for Crowd Safety, p. 432 (1993)
10. Helbing, D., Farkas, I., Vicsek, T.: Simulating dynamical features of escape panic. Nature **407**(6803), 487–490 (2000)
11. Kierzkowski, A., Kisiel, T.: Simulation model of security control lane operation in the state of the COVID-19 epidemic. J. Air Transp. Manag. **88**, 101868 (2020)
12. Schultz, M., Soolaki, M.: Analytical approach to solve the problem of aircraft passenger boarding during the coronavirus pandemic. Transp. Res. Part C: Emerg. Technol. **124**, 102931 (2021)
13. Müller, S.A., Balmer, M., Neumann, A., Nagel, K.: Mobility traces and spreading of COVID-19, pp. 1–22. medRxiv (2020)
14. Ronchi, E., Lovreglio, R.: EXPOSED: an occupant exposure model for confined spaces to retrofit crowd models during a pandemic. Saf. Sci. **130**, 104834 (2020)

15. Janssen, S., Knol, A., Blok, A.-N.: AATOM - An Agent-based Airport Terminal Operations Model (2018). http://stefjanssen.com/AATOMarchticeture.pdf. Accessed 2021
16. Janssen, S., Sharpanskykh, A., Curran, R.: Agent-based modelling and analysis of security and efficiency in airport terminals. Transp. Res. Part C Emerg. Technol. **100**, 142–160 (2019)
17. Janssen, S., van der Sommen, R., Dilweg, A., Sharpanskykh, A.: Data-driven analysis of airport security checkpoint operations. Aerospace **7**(6), 69 (2020)

Semantic Services Catalog for Multiagent Systems Society

Gabriel Santos[1,2(✉)] ⓘ, Alda Canito[1,2] ⓘ, Rui Carvalho[1,2] ⓘ, Tiago Pinto[1,2] ⓘ,
Zita Vale[2] ⓘ, Goreti Marreiros[1,2] ⓘ, and Juan M. Corchado[3] ⓘ

[1] GECAD Research Group, Porto, Portugal
[2] Institute of Engineering, Polytechnic of Porto, Porto, Portugal
{gajls,alrfc,rugco,tcp,zav,mgt}@isep.ipp.pt
[3] BISITE Research Group, University of Salamanca, Salamanca, Spain
corchado@usal.es

Abstract. Agent-based simulation tools have found many applications in the field of Power and Energy Systems, as they can model and analyze the complex synergies of dynamic and continuously evolving systems. While some studies have been done w.r.t. simulation and decision support for electricity markets and smart grids, there is still a generalized limitation referring to the significant lack of interoperability between independently developed systems, hindering the task of addressing all the relevant existing interrelationships. This work presents the Semantic Services Catalog (SSC), developed and implemented for the automatic registry, discovery, composition, and invocation of web and agent-based services. By adding a semantic layer to the description of different types of services, this tool supports the interaction between heterogeneous multiagent systems and web services with distinct capabilities that complement each other. The case study confirms the applicability of the developed work, wherein multiple simulation and decision-support tools work together managing a microgrid of residential and office buildings. Using SSC, besides discovering each other, agents also learn about the ontologies and languages to use to communicate with each other effectively.

Keywords: Multiagent semantic interoperability · Semantic services · Service catalog · Society of multiagent systems

1 Introduction

Power and Energy Systems (PES) worldwide underwent significant changes in the last two decades [1]. The increased and continuous penetration of renewable and distributed energy sources brought uncertainty and variation to the system, weakening its security and reliability, leading to a significant restructuring of the sector, changing its operation and competitiveness. Simultaneously, new players come into play, along with new market and negotiation models, with consumers becoming active players in the sector. Players must now deal with constantly changing rules and data to get the best possible outcomes from the market, which must be processed to predict consumers' behavior and provide

© Springer Nature Switzerland AG 2021
F. Dignum et al. (Eds.): PAAMS 2021, LNAI 12946, pp. 229–240, 2021.
https://doi.org/10.1007/978-3-030-85739-4_19

users with the best possible deals. To this end, data mining (DM) approaches and agent-based simulation tools have been proposed and proven to be particularly well suited [2, 3]. These different approaches are further combined, creating heterogeneous data processing workflows. In Service-Oriented Architectures (SOA), these different responsibilities are supposed to be encapsulated through means of (web) services.

Semantic web technologies have been proposed to describe web services, as they provide richer and machine-readable descriptions, facilitating the process of discovering and composing services performed by software agents [4, 5]. However, the design and development of atomic service's composition are very time-consuming due to the heterogeneity of interaction protocols, lack of proper description of workflows, input and output models, and the need for automated solutions to identify and discover those services [5, 6]. The proper semantization of services potentializes their discovery and invocation according to specified requirements. It is possible to identify and suggest potential solutions for specific scenarios using queries, such as discovering which machine learning (ML) and DM algorithms can be applied to a given dataset, knowing their characteristics and the desired outcomes. There are several semantic models in the literature for semantic service description [7–10]. However, there is no standardized description format for exposing services provided by software agents. Agent gateways are one option to disclose these services on the web. Still, because they are static and configured programmatically beforehand, they restrict some of the agents' capabilities, such as mobility. [11]. The Software Agent ontology proposed in [12] enables a dynamic exposure of agent-based services, describing the properties that an entity must know to interact with the agent or multiagent system (MAS) providing the service. This work also demonstrates how to extend the Software Agent ontology to describe agents developed with different frameworks, focusing on agents developed with the Java Agent DEvelopment (JADE) [13] framework.

Although ontologies ease the correct interpretation of messages, systems still must be aware of each other. They must know what type of services other systems provide, which ontologies they understand, the language (syntax) they use, and where to send the messages when starting the interactions. One possible solution is to configure systems with these details before starting their execution. However, this can become a burden if there is the need to reconfigure every system before each simulation, especially when the user needs to try different approaches and combinations of tools at each iteration. On the other hand, some agent-based tools may require other systems to work, such as external services (e.g., web or agent-based), whose location may be volatile.

To overcome these issues, this work proposes and develops the Semantic Services Catalog (SSC) for MAS societies. SSC is a registration and search platform where tools can register to provide a service or search for a specific type of service to accomplish their goals. It eases the interaction between heterogeneous systems by providing a service where each registered tool details its capabilities, the type of service it provides, where it can be reached, what ontologies and languages are accepted, and what are the expected inputs and outputs. This way, an enhanced and highly dynamic simulation infrastructure is conceived where various components are available at different times, while guaranteeing the interoperability between heterogeneous simulators, systems, and decision support methodologies.

The remaining document is structured as follows: Sect. 2 presents the background context and related work. Section 3 introduces SSC, its architecture, and available functionalities. Section 4 demonstrates the use of the SSC in a case study scenario. Finally, Sect. 5 exposes the conclusions and future work.

2 Background

Semantic technologies have been applied to the description and discovery of web services. The existing approaches share a common goal of adding a semantic layer to describe inputs, outputs, and aims of the services, which, in turn, facilitate the tasks of identifying which services fulfill a set of requirements. Software agents often provide services within a MAS or a single agent-based system, and their interoperability and coordination principles follow the semantic web vision [4]. In [10], the importance of the semantic description of services is discussed, pointing out the similarities between agents and web services w.r.t. their discovery and that matching between distinct service groundings should rely on semantic abstractions. We consider that this vision is materializable in a system that allows for the seamless integration between web and agent-based services. The following subsections will introduce some solutions regarding service discovery and semantic service description.

2.1 Semantic Service Discovery

Existing approaches for discovering semantically annotated web services vary according to the description types in use and the matching of inputs and outputs. In recent years, this research focuses on combining logic-based approaches, which aim to find exact or subsumed matches, or on joining logic and syntactic methods, which employ Natural Language Processing (NLP) algorithms for similarity computation [14–16]. The combination of NLP with logic-based approaches has also found application in [17, 18]. The discovery and ranking of services through the use of ML and DM algorithms has been explored in [19], and the use of search constraints in [20] and [21]. Finally, regarding the topic of web service composition, [22] focuses on a personalization-based approach for finding the ideal invocation sequence of services, with the similarity of terms computed by combining lexical and semantic similarities.

2.2 Semantic Service Description

There are four main models available in the literature regarding the semantic description of web services. The Web Service Modeling Ontology (WSMO) [7] is "a conceptual framework and a formal language for semantically describing all relevant aspects of Web services", facilitating automatic discovery, combination, and invocation. It describes services capabilities, interfaces, internal behavior, goals, the ontologies applied, and mediators to solve interoperability. The Semantic Annotations for Web Services Description Language (SAWSDL) and Extensible Markup Language (XML) Schema [9] is a W3C recommendation defining a set of extension attributes to add semantic annotations to WSDL and XML Schema documents. It is not a language specification to represent semantic models but instead provides ways to reference concepts from existing semantic models within these documents. The Semantic Web Services Ontology (SWSO) [8] is part of the Semantic Web Services Language (SWSL). SWSO follows the high-level structure of OWL-S with three major components to describe services, promote their automated discovery, and supply concrete details, including message formats, communication protocols, and network addresses. The OWL-S ontology [10] describes services, enabling their automatic discovery, invocation, composition, and interoperation. It details the service's requirements, limitations, preconditions, inputs, outputs, and interaction details such as the communication protocol, port number, message format, among others. Although OWL-S has been developed to describe Simple Object Access Protocol (SOAP) services, there are already in the literature extensions to specify Representational State Transfer (REST) services [23, 24].

3 Semantic Services Catalog

SSC is a service registration and search platform developed to provide the means for the automatic interaction between several systems, resulting in an enhanced society of MAS capable of simulating, studying, and analyzing problems of very distinct natures. SSC is the materialization of the architecture proposed in [12], using OWL-S for the semantic description of services and the proposed extensions to describe services supplied by software agents. This system works as a catalog, presenting semantic queries and finding services that answer the specified needs of the requesting party. SSC outstands other systems by providing a common platform to register, discover, and compose both web and agent-based services. The semantic layer gives meaning to syntactic data, allowing to achieve service matching and composition through reasoning processes. Additionally, by providing clear meaning to the requirements of each service, it enhances interoperability, making the co-simulation configuration of systems more straightforward and less error-prone while also potentiating its automation.

SSC enables simple and advanced searches: the former searches services by keywords, while the latter expects a SPARQL[1] query, which allows the user to present the search constraints as they see fit. All registered services are listed publicly. The Resource Description Framework (RDF) languages accepted by the SSC depend on the triple-store used as the knowledge base. Since the triple-store is configurable, it is essential to update the RDF languages accordingly. SSC has a modular and distributed architecture, as depicted in Fig. 1.

The core module of SSC is the *Backend*, providing the necessary endpoints to accomplish the established requirements. Connections to external APIs are configurable to ensure the system's flexibility, namely to the triple store, relational database, LDAP server, and SPARQLer[2] service.

The relational database stores the SPARQL templates for each SSC's activity, the RDF languages accepted by the triple-store, and the LDAP usernames of the authorized administrators. The triple-store stores the semantic description of the registered services

---

[1] https://www.w3.org/TR/sparql11-query/.

[2] http://sparql.org/.

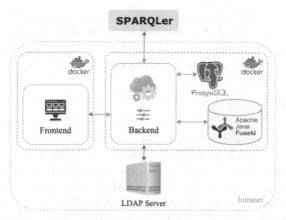

Fig. 1. SSC architecture.

while SPARQLer is exclusively used to validate the SPARQL queries/updates of SSC. The *Frontend* provides a user interface with simple and advanced search options and a documentation page for developers detailing the API to register web or agent-based services in SSC. Authorized users have access to the administration user interface. Figure 2 introduces the application-level architecture.

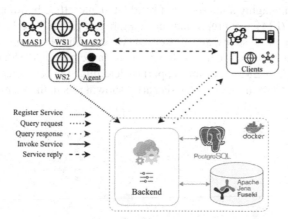

Fig. 2. Application-level architecture.

On the left-top corner of Fig. 2 are the service providers. These can be web services, MAS, or a software agent able to execute a specific task. These service providers must specify their input and output parameters according to an ontology. Description of the processes they execute, such as the technologies or algorithms implied, is encouraged and, whenever possible, should also be described semantically. On the other hand, the client systems (on the top-right corner) can search for registered services and use the information provided by a search query to connect directly to the service provider. The data provided by SSC includes the type of service, its capabilities and where to reach it, what ontologies and RDF languages it accepts, input and output parameters, among others. Finally, there is no order of interactions between the tools displayed in Fig. 2 since these are asynchronous communications that may occur at any time. Additionally, only registered services are available to be invoked by client tools.

4 Case Study

The following case study demonstrates the advantages of using SSC for MAS and web services co-simulation. It will show how SSC facilitates the automatic interaction between the several simulation and decision-support tools. To this end, we perform a joint simulation between three MAS previously developed in the authors' research group. The Multi-Agent Smart Grid Platform (MASGriP) [25] is a multiagent modeling and simulation tool proposing a set of possible coalitions for the management and operation of smart grids (SG) that considers the typically involved players. The Multi-Agent Simulator of Competitive Electricity Markets (MASCEM) [26] is a modeling and simulation tool developed to study the restructured, complex, and competitive whole-sale electricity markets (EM) and models the main market stakeholders. The Adaptive Decision Support for Electricity Markets Negotiations (AiD-EM) [3] provides decision support to EM negotiations, including auction-based markets, bilateral contracts, and portfolio optimization for electronic market participation.

The case study scenario considers a SG operator from MASGriP, named Network Manager (NM), managing a microgrid of residential and office buildings. A MASGriP Facility Manager (FM) agent represents each microgrid player. The 17 FMs totalize 90 loads, 17 photovoltaic systems, and 17 storage systems. The NM aggregates its players' consumption, generation, and demand-flexibility to participate in MASCEM's wholesale EM and requires AiD-EM's decision support to determine the best price for each period bid. Figure 3 illustrates the case study scenario, showing its main agents.

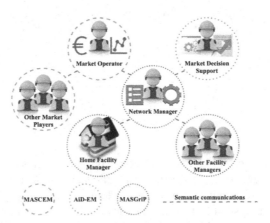

Fig. 3. Case study scenario.

The Market Operator (MO) and the Market Player agents are from MASCEM, the Market Decision Support (MDS) agent is from AiD-EM, and the remaining agents are from MASGriP. The Home Facility Manager (Home FM) agent uses the real-time monitoring and controllable loads of the authors' research group lab. The remaining FMs and market player agents use historical data. All messages exchanged between agents use semantic content. This case study gives special attention to the NM and Home FM. Both agents use Intelligent Decision Support (IDeS) (web) services previously developed, namely the energy resources management (ERM) [27] optimization algorithm and the SCADA House Intelligent Management (SHIM) [28] algorithm.

Without SSC, before each simulation starts, the user must ensure that the required web services are online, that each agent is configured accordingly, and that the agent-based systems start in the correct order to guarantee the proper communications flow. If these requirements are not met, the tools may fail to communicate with each other, and the simulation fails. Another issue comes with users often introducing incorrect configurations that are hard to track when dealing with the co-simulation of multiple MAS. Using SSC, in turn, reduces the user's error-prone configuration of co-simulation MAS since the agents only need to know the URL of SSC and the service to search for to automatically find and communicate with each other and with web services. Besides, if a (web or agent-based) service is not available, the (client) agent can decide if it should search for another service or wait a predetermined amount of time to search for the same service again. This flexibility thus ensures the correct communication flow. Thus, each agent automatically registers in SSC at startup, and the web services use a request URI for their registration. At registration, each tool provides details about the service(s) they provide, the languages or serializations they accept, their location, among others. This way, they can be searched and found without configuration errors. Figure 4 illustrates the registration of services and agents in our case study scenario.

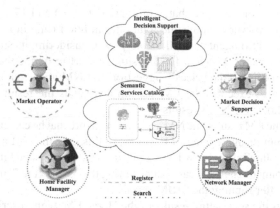

Fig. 4. Agents and services registration and discovery.

The registrations made at SSC, the services' searches performed and respective responses, the SPARQL queries made to obtain the different tools locations, input, and output models, and the de-registrations made at the end of the simulation are publicly available at [29]. For this case study, the ERM and SHIM services, the MO, MDS, and

NM agents register in SSC[3]. Before the simulation starts, the NM agent searches for the ERM service, the MO agent, and the MDS agent, while the FM agents search for the NM agent and SHIM[4] service. Using the endpoint available in the search response, the NM and Home FM agents receive the services' complete semantic descriptions and query them to get the agents and services locations and the input and output models when applicable[5]. The NM agent registers within the MO agent for the day-ahead market and within the MDS agent for decision support in the bids' prices definition. In the same way, all FM agents join the NM agent.

The simulation starts after all agents are ready and the services available. It begins with the MO agent sending the call for proposals to each participating player. Before sending his bids to the MO agent, the NM agent runs the ERM optimization service for the next day, determining the available or required amount of energy for each hourly period. Figure 5 presents ERM results.

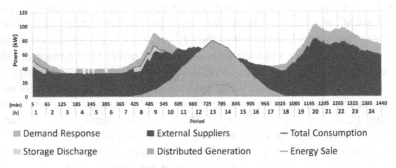

Fig. 5. ERM optimization results.

Observing Fig. 5, one can see that, from period 1 to 10 and 17 to 24, the demand response amount of power is above the total consumption (line in red). It means that in those periods, the NM agent can sell the surplus. Considering its surplus energy, the NM agent requests the MDS agent for decision support to define the prices for each period bid. After receiving the prices' suggestion, the NM agent sends his proposal to the MO agent, which executes the EM session and sends the results to each market player. Figure 6 shows the NM's results.

According to the EM results, the NM agent must ensure that he can gather the required energy amount from its aggregated FM agents. To this end, the NM agent requests his players for energy flexibility. Each FM agent, in turn, runs a scheduling algorithm to determine the amount of energy it can reduce during the day. Figure 7 presents the Home FM agent results after running the SHIM service.

Figure 7 shows the scheduling results of the Home FM agent discriminated by consumption device in one-minute periods. The chart's red line determines the consumption limit set by the optimization algorithm of the NM agent. The amount of power above

---

[3] see folder ***POST register.***

[4] searches and results are available at folder ***POST search.***

[5] see folder ***SPARQL query.***

this line represents the surplus available to reduce. The NM agent remunerates each FM agent according to its effective reduction.

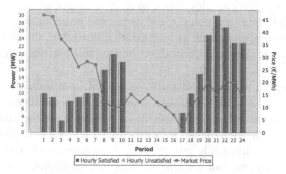

Fig. 6. NM's satisfied supply.

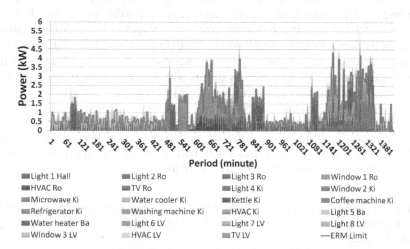

Fig. 7. Home FM's scheduling results.

At the end of the simulation, each agent automatically deregisters from SSC before shutting down[6].

5 Conclusions

This work presents the Semantic Services Catalog, a framework to register, discover, invoke, and compose web and agent-based services using semantic web techniques. From the various semantic models available for services description, OWL-S has been used, with existing extensions, to describe RESTful and agent-based services.

---

[6] see folder *PUT deregister*.

SSC overcomes interoperability and service discovery and invocation issues while reducing the configuration burden before each simulation. It eases heterogeneous systems interactions by providing a service where each registered tool details its capabilities, the type of service it provides, where to reach it, which ontologies and languages it accepts, expected inputs and outputs, and its pre and postconditions. Its modular and distributed architecture, along with its configuration flexibility, allows to deploy the system with a few simple steps and keeps the system agnostic to the semantic model used to describe the services.

The case study shows agents interacting with SSC in a simulation scenario ran at our facilities with real and simulated data, presenting the requests made and responses received, and the results achieved through the interoperation of the different tools. SSC is an enhanced and highly dynamic infrastructure where various components can be available at different times while guaranteeing the interoperability between heterogeneous simulators, systems, and decision support methodologies. The use of semantic web technologies facilitates the discovery, invocation, and composition of services in runtime, without the need to configure the services mappings programmatically.

Future work includes enabling registering a service with any service description semantic model and studying the advantages/disadvantages of using explicit semantics to describe the service's grounding instead of mappings to WADL/WSDL files. On one side, these files may change rapidly over time; on the other, there's the advantage of using semantic queries to get all the necessary details without the need to interpret extra files. Furthermore, combinations of logic and syntactic-based approaches will be explored for service matching and ranking.

Acknowledgments. The authors would like to acknowledge the support of the Fundação para a Ciência e a Tecnologia (FCT) through the SFRH/BD/118487/2016 and SFRH/BD/147386/2019 Ph.D. studentships and the project CEECIND/01811/2017.

Funding. This work was supported by the MAS-Society Project co-funded by Portugal 2020 Fundo Europeu de Desenvolvimento Regional (FEDER) through PO CI and under grant UIDB/00760/2020.

References

1. BEUC: The Future of Energy Consumers - Bright or Burdensome? (2019)
2. Niu, L., Ren, F., Zhang, M.: Feasible negotiation procedures for multiple interdependent negotiations. In: Proceedings of the International Joint Conference on Autonomous Agents and Multiagent Systems, AAMAS, pp. 641–649 (2018). https://doi.org/10.5555/3237383.3237479.
3. Pinto, T., Vale, Z.: AID-EM: adaptive decision support for electricity markets negotiations. In: IJCAI International Joint Conference on Artificial Intelligence, pp. 6563–6565. International Joint Conferences on Artificial Intelligence (2019). https://doi.org/10.24963/ijcai.2019/957
4. Huhns, M.N.: Agents as web services. IEEE Internet Comput. **6**, 93–95 (2002). https://doi.org/10.1109/MIC.2002.1020332
5. Klusch, M., Kapahnke, P., Schulte, S., Lecue, F., Bernstein, A.: Semantic web service search: a brief survey. KI - Künstliche Intelligenz **30**(2), 139–147 (2015). https://doi.org/10.1007/s13218-015-0415-7

6. Lemos, A.L., Daniel, F., Benatallah, B.: Web service composition. ACM Comput. Surv. **48**, 1–41 (2015). https://doi.org/10.1145/2831270
7. Roman, D., et al.: Web service modeling ontology. Appl. Ontol. **1**, 77–106 (2005)
8. Battle, S., Bernstein, A., Boley, H., Grosof, B.: Semantic web services ontology (SWSO). Memb. Submission **68** (2005)
9. Kopecký, J., Vitvar, T., Bournez, C., Farrell, J.: SAWSDL: semantic annotations for WSDL and XML schema. IEEE Internet Comput. **11**, 60–67 (2007). https://doi.org/10.1109/MIC.2007.134
10. Martin, D., et al.: OWL-S: semantic markup for web services. W3C Memb. Submiss. 22 (2004)
11. Canito, A., Santos, G., Corchado, J.M., Marreiros, G., Vale, Z.: Semantic web services for multi-agent systems interoperability. In: Moura Oliveira, P., Novais, P., Reis, L.P. (eds.) EPIA 2019. LNCS (LNAI), vol. 11805, pp. 606–616. Springer, Cham (2019). https://doi.org/10.1007/978-3-030-30244-3_50
12. Gunasekera, K., Zaslavsky, A., Krishnaswamy, S., Loke, S.W.: Service oriented context-aware software agents for greater efficiency. In: Jędrzejowicz, P., Nguyen, N.T., Howlet, R.J., Jain, L.C. (eds.) KES-AMSTA 2010. LNCS (LNAI), vol. 6070, pp. 62–71. Springer, Heidelberg (2010). https://doi.org/10.1007/978-3-642-13480-7_8
13. Zhang, N., Wang, J., Ma, Y., He, K., Li, Z., Liu, X., Frank F.: Web service discovery based on goal-oriented query expansion. J. Syst. Softw. **142**, 73–91 (2018). https://doi.org/10.1016/j.jss.2018.04.046
14. Fang, M., Wang, D., Mi, Z., Obaidat, M.S.: Web service discovery utilizing logical reasoning and semantic similarity. Int. J. Commun. Syst. **31**, e3561 (2018). https://doi.org/10.1002/dac.3561
15. Wagner, F., Ishikawa, F., Honiden, S.: QoS-aware automatic service composition by applying functional clustering. In: Proceedings - 2011 IEEE 9th International Conference on Web Services, ICWS 2011, pp. 89–96. IEEE (2011). https://doi.org/10.1109/ICWS.2011.32
16. Kaufer, F., Klusch, M.: WSMO-MX: a logic programming based hybrid service matchmaker. In: Proccedings of ECOWS 2006: Fourth European Conference on Web Services, pp. 161–170 (2006). https://doi.org/10.1109/ECOWS.2006.39
17. Klusch, M., Fries, B., Sycara, K.: OWLS-MX: a hybrid Semantic Web service matchmaker for OWL-S services. Web Semant. **7**, 121–133 (2009). https://doi.org/10.1016/j.websem.2008.10.001
18. Gmati, F.E., Ayadi, N.Y., Bahri, A., Chakhar, S., Ishizaka, A.: A framework for parameterized semantic matchmaking and ranking of web services. In: WEBIST 2016 - Proceedings of the 12th International Conference on Web Information Systems and Technologies, pp. 54–65. SCITEPRESS - Science and and Technology Publications (2016). https://doi.org/10.5220/0005907300540065
19. Aggarwal, R., Verma, K., Miller, J., Milnor, W.: Constraint driven Web service composition in METEOR-S. In: Proceedings - 2004 IEEE International Conference on Services Computing, SCC 2004, pp. 23–30 (2004). https://doi.org/10.1109/SCC.2004.1357986
20. Ben Hassine, A., Matsubara, S., Ishida, T.: A constraint-based approach to horizontal web service composition. In: Cruz, I., et al. (eds.) ISWC 2006. LNCS, vol. 4273, pp. 130–143. Springer, Heidelberg (2006). https://doi.org/10.1007/11926078_10
21. Abidi, S., Fakhri, M., Essafi, M., Ben Ghezala, H.H.: A personalized on-the-fly approach for secure semantic web services composition. In: Proceedings of IEEE/ACS International Conference on Computer Systems and Applications, AICCSA, pp. 1362–1369. IEEE Computer Society (2018). https://doi.org/10.1109/AICCSA.2017.138
22. Filho, O.F.F., Ferreira, M.A.G.V.: Semantic Web services: a restful approach. In: Proceedings of the IADIS International Conference WWW/Internet 2009, ICWI 2009, Rome, Italy, pp. 169–180 (2009)

23. Kopecký, J., Gomadam, K., Vitvar, T.: hRESTS: an HTML microformat for describing REST-ful web services. In: 2008 IEEE/WIC/ACM International Conference on Web Intelligence and Intelligent Agent Technology, pp. 619–625. IEEE (2008). https://doi.org/10.1109/WIIAT.2008.379
24. Gomes, L., Faria, P., Morais, H., Vale, Z., Ramos, C.: Distributed, agent-based intelligent system for demand response program simulation in smart grids. IEEE Intell. Syst. **29**, 56–65 (2014). https://doi.org/10.1109/MIS.2013.2
25. Santos, G., Pinto, T., Praça, I., Vale, Z.: MASCEM: optimizing the performance of a multi-agent system. Energy. **111**, 513–524 (2016). https://doi.org/10.1016/j.energy.2016.05.127
26. Silva, M., Morais, H., Sousa, T., Vale, Z.: Energy resources management in three distinct time horizons considering a large variation in wind power. In: Proceedings of EWEA Annual Event 2013 (2013)
27. Fernandes, F., Morais, H., Faria, P., Vale, Z., Ramos, C.: SCADA house intelligent manage-ment for energy efficiency analysis in domestic consumers. In: 2013 IEEE PES Conference on Innovative Smart Grid Technologies, ISGT LA 2013. IEEE Computer Society (2013). https://doi.org/10.1109/ISGT-LA.2013.6554494
28. Santos, G., et al.: Semantic Services Catalog: Demonstration of Multiagent Systems Society co-simulation (2021). https://doi.org/10.5281/ZENODO.4717828

Fully Decentralized Planner-Guided Robot Swarms

Michael Schader[✉] and Sean Luke

George Mason University, Fairfax, VA 22030, USA
{mschader,sean}@gmu.edu

Abstract. Robot swarms hold great potential for accomplishing missions in a robust, scalable, and flexible manner. However, determining what low-level agent behavior to implement in order to meet high-level objectives is an unsolved inverse problem. Building on previous work on partially-centralized planner-guided robot swarms, we present an approach that achieves total decentralization of executive and deliberator functions, adds robustness and performance optimization through dynamic task switching, and employs agent-initiated superrational planning to coordinate agent activity while responding to changes in the environment. We demonstrate the effectiveness of the technique with three swarm robotics scenarios.

Keywords: Coordination and control models for multi-agent systems · Knowledge representation and reasoning in robotic systems · Swarm behavior

1 Introduction

Since Beni [3] first developed the idea of robot swarms in 2004, researchers have tried to control large groups of robots in ways that accomplish complex tasks while preserving swarm virtues such as redundancy, parallelism, and decentralization. Despite years of effort since then, Dorigo et al. [11] observed in 2020, "[T]he deployment of large groups of robots, or robot swarms, that coordinate and cooperatively solve a problem or perform a task, remains a challenge". Most existing solutions to this challenge either rely on some degree of centralization, which introduces single points of failure and limits scalability, or address only basic missions such as area coverage and shape formation, which are far short of the complex tasks that swarm engineers aspire to perform.

Dorigo predicted that "Hybrid systems mixing model-free and model-based approaches will likely provide additional power". In previous work [25], we employed that philosophy in creating *planner-guided robot swarms*, a hybrid deliberative/reactive approach to swarm management. A central automated planner produced plans for each group of agents within the swarm. At runtime, an *orchestrator* existing outside the swarm issued the plans to the agents,

© Springer Nature Switzerland AG 2021
F. Dignum et al. (Eds.): PAAMS 2021, LNAI 12946, pp. 241–254, 2021.
https://doi.org/10.1007/978-3-030-85739-4_20

collected success reports, monitored sensor data, determined when actions were complete, and instructed the agents when to advance to the next plan step.

That architecture enabled a human programmer to specify complex missions in a high-level planning language for a swarm to execute. However, the centralized deliberator and executive components were potential single points of runtime failure, reducing the benefits of swarm decentralization. Here we build on that work by modifying the architecture to push the deliberative and executive functions down into the swarm agents themselves. This involves solving problems with action synchronization, task allocation, and replanning without resorting to outside entities or differentiated swarm members. Ultimately our *distributed executive* accomplishes the same missions that the centralized version can, preserving scalability and robustness without any single points of failure.

In this paper we first review the work done by other researchers on swarm control, showing that no one else has integrated classical planning into a swarm or induced a swarm to accomplish complex actions without central direction or an agent hierarchy. Next, we explain our approach with a formal definition of the system, descriptions of the components of the architecture, and background on the design philosophy behind it. Finally, we report the results of three experiments performed on different scenarios: decentralized shape formation, swarm recovery from loss of agents, and agent-initiated replanning in response to changes in the environment. We demonstrate the fully decentralized swarm's robustness and scalability, validating the effectiveness of our method.

2   Previous Work

Published research touching upon our work can be organized into three groups, based on the degree of decentralization and on whether or not there are separate layers specifying the mission goals and the individual agent behaviors:

Partially Centralized. These methods lead to hub and spoke or hierarchical architectures. Becker et al. [2] explored how a single signal broadcast to all agents in a massive swarm could be used to guide them to collectively accomplish a task. Kominis et al. [15] translated uncertain, multi-agent planning problems into classical, single-agent ones that could be centrally solved and then given to the agents. Corah et al. [10], Nissim et al. [20], and Torreño et al. [28] implemented methods to break preliminary plans into parts and have agents refine them through multiple planning rounds. Choudhury et al. [8] and Riyaz et al. [24] created hybrid systems, with a centralized task planner to assign tasks to individual robots combined with an onboard control system enabling each robot to refine and execute its task. All these methods rely on some central component, which represents a single point of failure and a limiting factor on scalability.

Decentralized Single-Layer. These approaches amount to control laws which must be developed prior to runtime. Atay et al. [1], Li et al. [16], and Sheth [26] created emergent task allocation methods in which each robot only used information from its neighbors to select tasks, then sent coordination messages to resolve conflicts, possibly including adversarial interactions. Chaimowicz et al. [7], Ghassemi et al. [12], and Michael et al. [19] used combinations of bidding and recruitment to determine role assignments and when they should be changed. Each of these methods involves designing integrated high- and low-level activities, limiting flexibility when developing solutions matching swarm platforms to specific problems.

Decentralized Multi-Layer. Such systems combine the elimination of single points of failure with the relative ease of separately addressing domain-level and behavior-level concerns. Birattari et al. [4] and Bozhinoski et al. [5] proposed "automatic offline design": enumerating likely missions within a problem domain, using reinforcement learning or evolutionary computing to generate suitable low-level behaviors in simulation, and deploying the best solution available for the problem at hand when needed. Coppola [9] explored this approach extensively. Although promising, this family of solutions requires the development of a large library of pre-generated behaviors to match to missions when needed. Our method falls into the same decentralized multi-layer category, but does not depend on having prebuilt solutions to new mission requirements.

3   Method

In our earlier work, we introduced a novel approach to swarm control: framing the high-level domain and problem using Planning Domain Definition Language (PDDL) [18], generating a plan to achieve the goal state with an automated planner, and having a central executive orchestrate the agents' activities by adjusting their behavioral parameters and synchronizing their plan step advances. In this new work, we move the executive and deliberative functions into the swarm agents themselves, thus eliminating all single points of failure and enabling truly decentralized operations. We add dynamic task switching based on action completion information shared by neighbors, enhancing robustness. Finally, we incorporate agent-initiated replanning to allow the swarm to respond to changes in the environment.

In our revised formulation, a planner-guided swarm scenario definition can be represented by a tuple:

$$S_{def} = \langle A, domain, M_{act}, M_{pred} \rangle \tag{1}$$

where the agent class $A = \langle sensors, behaviors \rangle$ represents the capabilities of a swarm robot platform, the $domain = \langle predicates, actions \rangle$ is the PDDL representation of the planning domain, the action mapping $M_{act} : actions \rightarrow \langle behaviors, parameters, criteria \rangle$ translates each PDDL action to a specific parameterized agent behavior with success criteria, and the predicate mapping $M_{pred} : predicates \rightarrow \langle sensors, parameters, criteria \rangle$ ties predicates needed for replanning to observed states (Fig. 1).

A specific run of a scenario starts with scenario definition S_{def} and adds three items:

$$S_{run} = \langle S_{def}, problem, n, g \rangle \tag{2}$$

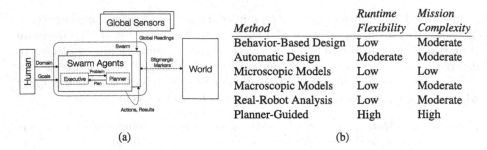

Method	Runtime Flexibility	Mission Complexity
Behavior-Based Design	Low	Moderate
Automatic Design	Moderate	Moderate
Microscopic Models	Low	Low
Macroscopic Models	Low	Moderate
Real-Robot Analysis	Low	Moderate
Planner-Guided	High	High

(a)   (b)

Fig. 1. (a) Fully decentralized planner-guided robot swarm architecture with optional global sensors. (b) Comparison of robot swarm management approaches per Brambilla et al. [6].

which are the PDDL expression of the planning *problem*, the count of agents n, and the number of groups g. If g is set to zero, the group count decision is delegated to each agent's deliberator, which will attempt to generate plans with various numbers of groups, choosing the smallest g that produces a minimum-length sound plan.

3.1   Definitions

Domain and Problem. The PDDL domain defines how the world works from the swarm's top-level perspective: what constants will always be present, what predicates can be true or false, and what actions can be performed in terms of their preconditions and effects. The PDDL problem specifies the objects to consider, the initial conditions of the situation, and the goal state to be achieved. The scenario designer creates these two files to control the swarm.

Agent Class. The agent class defines the capabilities of the agents as they relate to other parts of the scenario in terms of sensors and behaviors. All agents of the swarm belong to this single class. The sensors include all the ways an agent can receive information from the world around it: its own local readings, data it receives from global sensors, and information exchanged with other agents in its neighborhood. The behaviors are the micro-behaviors that each swarm agent performs (e.g. "find item A", "discover site B", "deposit item A at site B"), which lead to emergent phenomena such as coverage and foraging. A given agent class can be used in multiple scenarios, with different domains and problems.

Each instantiated agent has its own planner, which takes PDDL domain and problem files as input and produces PDDL plans as output. The specific planner implementation can be changed at scenario start time, but it must be identical for all agents, be able to process the domain file constructs, and be deterministic (always producing the same output for given inputs). We employ parallel planning to generate plans with multiple simultaneous actions that are assigned to *virtual agents*, groups of real agents within the swarm. Note that this is not multi-agent planning in the sense of generating joint actions or violating classical planning assumptions; rather, we achieve parallelism by taking advantage of partially ordered plans in which the actions at each given plan step are independent.

An agent's executive manages its specific movements, manipulations, and communications. Our own software uses a state machine with states EXPLORING, CARRYING, and DONE, but this is just an implementation detail that is not demanded by the planner-guided swarm framework. The executive also determines when sensor inputs should drive replanning based on an updated set of initial conditions in the problem statement.

Action and Predicate Mappings. The bridge between the high-level view of the world in the planning domain and the low-level configuration of the swarm agents' micro-behaviors is the mapping layer. When an agent class is paired with a domain file, the programmer builds two mappings. The first mapping translates domain actions (e.g. "pick up block A") into parameterized agent behaviors that will lead to the desired effect ("use the foraging behavior with the target item set to bricks of type A"). Bundled with this are the success criteria that must be met to infer that the action has been completed. The second mapping translates grounded domain predicates ("site D is full") into sensor conditions that will reveal its truth or falsehood ("check if the count of bricks deposited in site D equals the size of site D", or "determine if a sensor indicates site D is full").

The action mapping is critical in that it translates the abstract actions of a plan into the configuration of each agent's behaviors. The predicate mapping is not needed if the scenario designer specifies all initial conditions and there is no need for replanning; however, if the agents will need to assess conditions to plan or replan, then the relevant predicates do indeed need to be mapped to sensor readings and shared knowledge.

3.2   Decentralized Plan Monitoring

The agents keep track of their individual successes executing behaviors tied to plan actions, generating a *success token* each time they finish a granular activity (e.g. "remove item A from site B", "discover site C"). By exchanging these success tokens with each other in the course of their local interactions, sometimes along with factoring in data from their own sensors or global ones, the agents can determine when the plan action assigned to their group is complete. In addition, they keep track of other groups' progress toward task completion. When an agent learns that all groups have finished the current plan step, it advances to the next plan step. As the same knowledge spreads, other agents will make the same decision, ending up with all agents on the same next step.

3.3   Dynamic Task Switching

Since each agent knows the action completion status of its own group as well as that of the other groups, it can choose to temporarily switch groups when certain criteria are met. If an agent's current action is complete, and it is not in a state that precludes switching tasks (e.g. already carrying a certain item), it can identify other groups that have not finished their actions. If there is such a group, then the agent will switch to it based on a configured probability (0.1 in our experiments; the exact value has little effect on performance as long as it is positive). This task switching serves both to optimize the swarm's allocation of agents to actions, as well as to provide a fallback capability in case a portion of the swarm is destroyed or disabled.

3.4   Agent-Initiated Replanning

Hofstadter [13] named and refined the notion of *superrational groups* in 1983: when participants in an interaction know that all the others think the same way as they do, and that each recursively knows that the others know this, then they should independently arrive at identical conclusions aimed at maximizing joint benefit. In 2019, Tohmé et al. [27] developed a formal analysis of the concept and determined it to be sound. In our situation of building homogeneous swarms in which all the agents have the same software and goals, the necessary conditions for superrationality do indeed hold, given enough time for the agents in the swarm to converge on the same knowledge of the state of the world. With a deterministic planner, we can be sure that subject to information propagation delay, the agents will produce the same updated plans as each other.

4   Experiments

We conducted three experiments designed to test the novel aspects of our fully decentralized planner-guided robot swarm implementation, seeking to verify that the new mechanisms succeeded reliably while scaling efficiently as agents were added to the swarm. First, we exercised basic operations with all centralized components eliminated. Second, we tested agent-initiated task switching to see if it led to robust recovery from agent failures. Third, we evaluated the effectiveness of decentralized replanning spurred by detected changes in the world state.

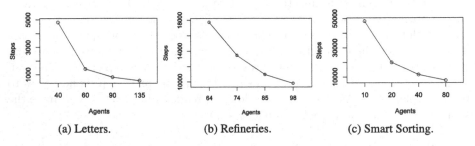

| (a) Letters. | (b) Refineries. | (c) Smart Sorting. |

With 1000 runs of each treatment, the confidence intervals are too small to see.

Fig. 2. Mean steps to completion of scenario for various swarm sizes.

All of our experiments were conducted in the MASON multiagent simulation toolkit [17], in which we modeled non-point robots, each exclusively occupying a nonzero area, so as to reduce the reality gap with actual robots. Agents navigated using virtual pheromone trails, an established swarm mechanism [21] that was just one of several methods with which they could find their way.

4.1 Letters: Runtime-Decentralized Planning, Coordination, and Monitoring

The Letters scenario is a straightforward mission to have robots arrange themselves to spell out a three-letter sequence (Fig. 3). The locations of the pixels of each letter are marked in advance, and the agents know when they have entered such a designated region. The purpose of the experiment is to show the effectiveness and scalability of a completely decentralized planner-guided swarm. Once the robots are launched, they have no special base to which to return or overseer with which to communicate. They have only the domain and problem presented by the operator to the swarm.

This experiment used the PDDL4J sequential planner [22] with the fast-forward heuristic search option. We varied the number of agents from 40 up to 135 to observe the effect on the average number of steps needed to reach the goal state (Fig. 2a). We performed 1000 runs of each treatment with 100% success and verified for statistical significance using the two-tailed t-test at $p = 0.05$ with the Bonferroni correction.

A minimum of 39 agents was necessary to finish this mission, 13 for each of the three letters. The first treatment with 40 agents took an average of 4809 steps to complete. With 60 agents, that dropped dramatically to 1422, since there were more available to find and remain in the designated areas, especially for the later spaces to be filled in. With 90 and 135 agents, the steps needed were further reduced to 828 and 573; the speedup from more agents leveled off due to physical interference with each other as well as diminishing returns from having many potential fillers for each needed position.

(a) The swarm agents explore the area, stopping when they reach a location within the specified destination region.

(b) News that Step 1 is complete has propagated through the swarm, and the agents move onto their next action.

(c) The swarm finishes Step 2 and that word begins to spread.

(d) Ultimately, the agents finish Step 3 and the task is completed.

The green and blue dots represent agents on odd- and even-numbered steps. They turn black when plan execution is complete.

Fig. 3. Stages of the Letters scenario.

4.2   Refineries: Dynamic Task Switching in Response to Group Failure

Refineries is a stress test of agent task-switching (Fig. 4). There are three square piles of bricks, each consisting of three different layers. One group of agents is assigned to disassemble each pile. The agents need to bring the bricks to a refinery area, where they will be processed and removed from the environment. The outer bricks must all be processed first, then the middle ones, and finally the central bricks. Partway through the first step, however, all the agents initially assigned to one of the groups are disabled: rendered permanently immobile. The only way for the swarm to succeed is for the agents to determine via their short-range interactions that one task group is not succeeding, and to choose to switch into that group in order to accomplish the mission.

This experiment used the Blackbox parallel planner [14] with its Graphplan solver ensuring deterministic output. We varied the number of agents from 64 up to 98 to observe the effect on the average number of steps needed to reach the goal state (Fig. 2b). We performed 1000 runs of each treatment with 100% success and verified for statistical significance using the two-tailed t-test at $p = 0.05$ with the Bonferroni correction.

A minimum of 64 agents was needed to complete this assignment: 16 in each of three groups to gather the outermost layers, plus another 16 in the spare group. With the minimum number it took an average of 17,744 steps to finish. Using 80 agents reduced that to 13,444, and with 85 it took 10,957; the additional workers allowed the swarm to perform the discovery and moving jobs more quickly. 98 agents only improved the step count to 9807. The limited space around the pickup and dropoff sites placed an upper bound on the scalability of the swarm, as too many agents on the field blocked each other from moving around as needed.

The ability of the agents to temporarily switch task groups was critical to the swarm's recovery from the externally-imposed disaster, the disabling of all the agents in Group 3. Figure 5 shows the number of agents working in each group through one run of the simulation. Early on, members of the unassigned Group 4 switched to Group 2, which had the job of collecting bricks from the site farthest from the launch point and so needed the help. At step 3000, the Group 3 members were immobilized and their numbers disappeared from the graph. Soon after step 5000, some Group 2 members switched to Group 3 to make up for the lost effort. Around step 7000, the numbers in each group equalized, then from step 11,000 onward the numbers fluctuated based on which groups had completed their assigned actions at the time. The low-level task switching behavior made the swarm robust and able to finish its job even when an entire task group was lost.

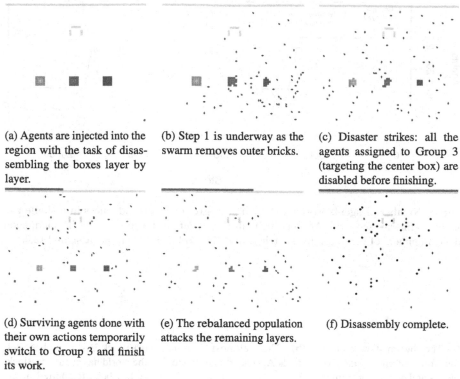

(a) Agents are injected into the region with the task of disassembling the boxes layer by layer.

(b) Step 1 is underway as the swarm removes outer bricks.

(c) Disaster strikes: all the agents assigned to Group 3 (targeting the center box) are disabled before finishing.

(d) Surviving agents done with their own actions temporarily switch to Group 3 and finish its work.

(e) The rebalanced population attacks the remaining layers.

(f) Disassembly complete.

Green and blue dots are working agents. Gray dots are permanently disabled ones. The brown progress bar at the top shows how many bricks have been dropped off at the gray-walled refinery.

Fig. 4. Stages of the Refineries scenario.

4.3   Smart Sorting: Self-initiated Replanning to Handle Changed Situation

The Smart Sorting scenario exercises the agents' coordinated replanning abilities (Fig. 6). The swarm starts with the mission of gathering four different kinds of randomly scattered bricks and assembling them in order into blocks in a walled area. As soon as they finish the first two layers (A and B), though, the A block is teleported outside to a different location. The agents continue with their planned actions, but upon checking sensor readings, they determine that conditions have changed, so they replan and begin taking apart the outer blocks so as to reassemble the correct structure.

This experiment used the Madagascar parallel planner [23], specifically its MpC implementation. We varied the number of agents from 10 up to 80 to observe the effect on the average number of steps needed to reach the goal state (Fig. 2c). We performed 1000 runs of each treatment with 100% success and verified for statistical significance using the two-tailed t-test at $p = 0.05$ with the Bonferroni correction.

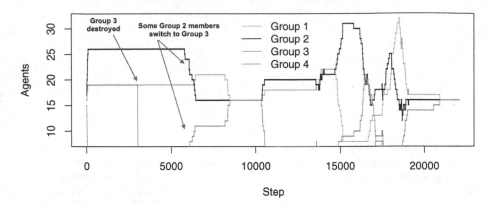

Fig. 5. Number of agents working in each task group as time advances in a single run of the Refineries scenario. At step 3000, all the agents in Group 3 were disabled; soon after, members of other groups switched in order to finish Group 3's assigned tasks.

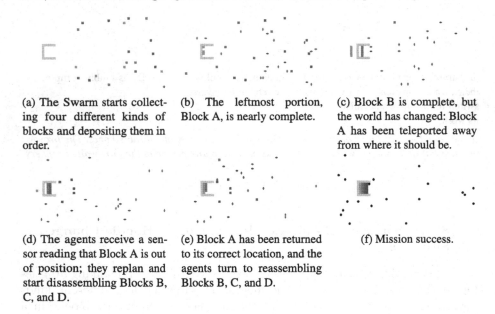

(a) The Swarm starts collecting four different kinds of blocks and depositing them in order.

(b) The leftmost portion, Block A, is nearly complete.

(c) Block B is complete, but the world has changed: Block A has been teleported away from where it should be.

(d) The agents receive a sensor reading that Block A is out of position; they replan and start disassembling Blocks B, C, and D.

(e) Block A has been returned to its correct location, and the agents turn to reassembling Blocks B, C, and D.

(f) Mission success.

The green and blue dots represent agents on odd- and even-numbered steps. The gray/brown shaded squares make up the four different blocks. The gray lines are walls.

Fig. 6. Stages of the Smart Sorting scenario.

The minimum number of agents needed to complete this scenario with two groups was ten, enough for each group to collect all five bricks of a single type. With that smallest possible population, the swarm took 48,230 steps on average to finish. With 20 agents, that was slashed to 20,018; with 40 it dropped to

11,686; and with 80 it was 7766. This excellent scalability was due to more agents being available to explore and move bricks around, along with faster information dissemination caused by increased agent density in the simulation work area.

5 Conclusions and Future Work

Modifying our previously published planner-guided robot swarm architecture to achieve complete decentralization was a success. Each scenario explored in our experiments showed a different area of improvement. Eliminating all central components ensured there were no single points of failure. Introducing dynamic task switching provided robustness against agent failure. Superrational planning enabled the swarm to incorporate flexibility into swarm behavior. We conducted all the experiments using the same agent code, further demonstrating the generality of our method.

In future work, we will attack the problem of retrograde behavior (agents getting out of sync with each other's plan steps), quantify aspects of the speed of communications in a swarm environment, and implement different agent classes with varying navigation and sensing mechanisms. We will also conduct a large-scale demonstration using real robots. This work will show for the first time a widely-applicable approach to building robot swarms that can collectively accomplish complex tasks.

6 Appendix: PDDL Files

Letters domain, problem, and plan

```
(define (domain LETTERS) (:requirements :strips :typing) (:types group site)
  (:constants site-g site-m site-u - site) (:predicates (visited ?s - site) (dummy))
  (:action visit-g :parameters (?g - group)  :precondition () :e ect (visited site-g))
  (:action visit-m :parameters (?g - group)  :precondition (visited site-g) :e ect (visited site-m))
  (:action visit-u :parameters (?g - group)  :precondition (visited site-m) :e ect (visited site-u)))
(define (problem GMU) (:domain LETTERS) (:objects group1 - group) (:init (dummy))
  (:goal (and (visited site-g) (visited site-m) (visited site-u))))

;;;; Plan for one group
1 ( (visit-g group1) )    2 ( (visit-m group1) )    3 ( (visit-u group1) )
```

Refineries domain, problem, and plan

```
(define (domain REFINERIES) (:requirements :strips :typing) (:types group item site)
  (:constants site-1a site-1b site-1c site-2a site-2b site-2c site-3a site-3b site-3c refinery - site
    item-1a item-1b item-1c item-2a item-2b item-2c item-3a item-3b item-3c - item)
  (:predicates (empty ?s - site) (all-at ?i - item ?s - site) (uncarrying ?g - group) (carrying ?g - group ?i - item))
  (:action collect-from-1a :parameters (?g - group) :precondition (and (uncarrying ?g) (all-at item-1a site-1a)
    (empty site-1b) (empty site-1c)) :e ect (and (not (uncarrying ?g)) (carrying ?g item-1a) (empty site-1a)))
  (:action deposit-at :parameters (?g - group ?i - item ?s - site) :precondition (and (carrying ?g ?i))
    :e ect (and (uncarrying ?g) (not (carrying ?g ?i)) (all-at ?i ?s))))  ;; actions repeated for all sites and items
(define (problem DISPOSE) (:domain REFINERIES) (:objects group1 group2 - group group3 - group)
  (:init (uncarrying group1) (uncarrying group2) (uncarrying group3)
    (all-at item-1a site-1a) (all-at item-1b site-1b) (all-at item-1c site-1c)) ;; predicates repeated for all
  (:goal (and (all-at item-1a refinery) (all-at item-1b refinery) (all-at item-1c refinery)))) ;; predicates repeated for all

;;;; Plan for four groups (three groups would be optimal, one is added for redundancy)
```

```
1 ( (collect-from-3c group1 ) (collect-from-1c group2 ) (collect-from-2c group3 ) nil )
2 ( (deposit-at group1 item-3c refinery) (deposit-at group2 item-1c refinery) (deposit-at group3 item-2c refinery) nil )
3 ( (collect-from-3b group1 ) (collect-from-1b group2 ) (collect-from-2b group3 ) nil )
4 ( (deposit-at group1 item-3b refinery) (deposit-at group2 item-1b refinery) (deposit-at group3 item-2b refinery) nil )
5 ( (collect-from-3a group1 ) (collect-from-1a group2 ) (collect-from-2a group3 ) nil )
6 ( (deposit-at group1 item-3a refinery) (deposit-at group2 item-1a refinery) (deposit-at group3 item-2a refinery) nil )
```

Smart Sorting domain, problem, initial plan, and revised plan

```
(define (domain SMART-SORTING) (:requirements :strips :typing :equality :disjunctive-preconditions)
(:types group item site) (:constants site-a site-b site-c site-d - site item-a item-b item-c item-d - item)
(:predicates (empty ?s - site) (all-at ?i - item ?s - site) (some-at ?i - item ?s - site)
  (uncarrying ?g - group) (carrying ?g - group ?i - item))
(:action collect :parameters (?g - group ?i - item) :precondition (and (uncarrying ?g))
  :e ect (and (not (uncarrying ?g)) (carrying ?g ?i)))
(:action clear-out :parameters (?g - group ?s - site) :precondition (and (uncarrying ?g)
  (or (= ?s site-d) (and (= ?s site-c) (empty site-d)) (and (= ?s site-b) (empty site-d) (empty site-c))
  (and (= ?s site-a) (empty site-d) (empty site-c) (empty site-b))))
  :e ect (and (not (all-at item-a ?s)) (not (all-at item-b ?s)) (not (all-at item-c ?s)) (not (all-at item-d ?s))
  (not (some-at item-a ?s)) (not (some-at item-b ?s)) (not (some-at item-c ?s)) (not (some-at item-d ?s))
  (empty ?s) (uncarrying ?g)))
(:action deposit :parameters (?g - group ?i - item ?s - site) :precondition (and (carrying ?g ?i) (empty ?s)
  (or (= ?s site-d) (and (= ?s site-c) (empty site-d)) (and (= ?s site-b) (empty site-d) (empty site-c))
  (and (= ?s site-a) (empty site-d) (empty site-c) (empty site-b))))
  :e ect (and (uncarrying ?g) (not (carrying ?g ?i)) (all-at ?i ?s) (some-at ?i ?s) (not (empty ?s)))))
(define (problem REPLAN) (:domain SMART-SORTING) (:objects group1 group2 - group)
(:init (uncarrying group1) (uncarrying group2) (empty site-a) (empty site-b) (empty site-c) (empty site-d))
(:goal (and (all-at item-a site-a) (all-at item-b site-b) (all-at item-c site-c) (all-at item-d site-d))))


;;;; Initial plan for two groups
1 ( (collect group1 item-a) (collect group2 item-b) )     2 ( (deposit group1 item-a site-a) nil )
3 ( nil (deposit group2 item-b site-b) )     4 ( (collect group1 item-d) (collect group2 item-c) )
5 ( nil (deposit group2 item-c site-c) )     6 ( (deposit group1 item-d site-d) nil )
;;;; Revised plan for two groups (after item-a moved out of correct position)
1 ( (clear-out group1 site-d) nil )     2 ( (collect group1 item-a) (clear-out group2 site-c) )
3 ( nil (clear-out group2 site-b) )     4 ( (deposit group1 item-a site-a) (collect group2 item-b) )
5 ( (collect group1 item-c) (deposit group2 item-b site-b) )     6 ( (deposit group1 item-c site-c) (collect group2 item-d) )
7 ( nil (deposit group2 item-d site-d) )
```

References

1. Atay, N., Bayazit, B.: Emergent task allocation for mobile robots. In: Proceedings of Robotics: Science and Systems. Atlanta, June 2007
2. Becker, A., Demaine, E.D., Fekete, S.P., Habibi, G., McLurkin, J.: Reconfiguring massive particle swarms with limited, global control. In: Flocchini, P., Gao, J., Kranakis, E., Meyer auf der Heide, F. (eds.) ALGOSENSORS 2013. LNCS, vol. 8243, pp. 51–66. Springer, Heidelberg (2014). https://doi.org/10.1007/978-3-642-45346-5_5
3. Beni, G.: From swarm intelligence to swarm robotics. In: Şahin, E., Spears, W.M. (eds.) SR 2004. LNCS, vol. 3342, pp. 1–9. Springer, Heidelberg (2005). https://doi.org/10.1007/978-3-540-30552-1_1
4. Birattari, M., et al.: Automatic off-line design of robot swarms: a manifesto. Front. Robot. AI **6**, 59 (2019)
5. Bozhinoski, D., Birattari, M.: Designing control software for robot swarms: Software engineering for the development of automatic design methods. In: 2018 IEEE/ACM 1st International Workshop on Robotics Software Engineering (RoSE), pp. 33–35 (2018)
6. Brambilla, M., Ferrante, E., Birattari, M., Dorigo, M.: Swarm robotics: a review from the swarm engineering perspective. Swarm Intell. **7**(1), 1–41 (2013)

7. Chaimowicz, L., Campos, M.F.M., Kumar, V.: Dynamic role assignment for cooperative robots. In: Proceedings 2002 IEEE International Conference on Robotics and Automation (Cat. No.02CH37292). vol. 1, pp. 293–298 (2002)
8. Choudhury, S., Gupta, J., Kochenderfer, M., Sadigh, D., Bohg, J.: Dynamic multi-robot task allocation under uncertainty and temporal constraints. In: Proceedings of Robotics: Science and Systems, July 2020
9. Coppola, M.: Automatic design of verifiable robot swarms. Ph.D. thesis, Delft University of Technology (2021)
10. Corah, M., Michael, N.: Efficient online multi-robot exploration via distributed sequential greedy assignment. In: Proceedings of Robotics: Science and Systems, July 2017
11. Dorigo, M., Theraulaz, G., Trianni, V.: Reflections on the future of swarm robotics. Sci. Robot. **5**(49), eabe4385 (2020)
12. Ghassemi, P., Chowdhury, S.: Decentralized task allocation in multi-robot systems via bipartite graph matching augmented with fuzzy clustering. In: International Design Engineering Technical Conferences and Computers and Information in Engineering Conference. vol. 51753, V02AT03A014. American Society of Mechanical Engineers (2018)
13. Hofstadter, D.R.: Dilemmas for superrational thinkers, leading up to a luring lottery. Sci. Am. **248**(6), 739–755 (1983)
14. Kautz, H., Selman, B.: Blackbox: A new approach to the application of theorem proving to problem solving. In: AIPS98 Workshop on Planning as Combinatorial Search. vol. 58260, pp. 58–60 (1998)
15. Kominis, F., Geffner, H.: Beliefs in multiagent planning: From one agent to many. In: Proceedings of the International Conference on Automated Planning and Scheduling. vol. 25 (2015)
16. Li, J., Abbas, W., Shabbir, M., Koutsoukos, X.: Resilient Distributed Diffusion for Multi-Robot Systems Using Centerpoint. In: Proceedings of Robotics: Science and Systems, July 2020
17. Luke, S., Cioffi-Revilla, C., Panait, L., Sullivan, K., Balan, G.: MASON: a multi-agent simulation environment. Simulation **81**(7), 517–527 (2005)
18. McDermott, D., et al..: PDDL: the planning domain definition language (1998)
19. Michael, N., Zavlanos, M., Kumar, V., Pappas, G.: Distributed multi-robot task assignment and formation control. In: 2008 IEEE International Conference on Robotics and Automatio (2008)
20. Nissim, R., Brafman, R.I., Domshlak, C.: A general, fully distributed multi-agent planning algorithm. In: Proceedings of the 9th International Conference on Autonomous Agents and Multiagent Systems: vol. 1, pp. 1323–1330 (2010)
21. Panait, L., Luke, S.: A pheromone-based utility model for collaborative foraging. In: Proceedings of the Third International Joint Conference on Autonomous Agents and Multiagent Systems, 2004 (AAMAS 2004), pp. 36–43. IEEE (2004)
22. Pellier, D., Fiorino, H.: PDDL4J: a planning domain description library for Java. J. Exp. Theor. Artif. Intell. **30**(1), 143–176 (2018)
23. Rintanen, J.: Madagascar: Scalable planning with sat. In: Proceedings of the 8th International Planning Competition (IPC-2014), vol. 21 (2014)
24. Riyaz, S.H., Basir, O.: Intelligent planning and execution of tasks using hybrid agents. In: 2009 International Conference on Artificial Intelligence and Computational Intelligence. vol. 1, pp. 277–282 (2009)

25. Schader, M., Luke, S.: Planner-guided robot swarms. In: Demazeau, Y., Holvoet, T., Corchado, J.M., Costantini, S. (eds.) Advances in Practical Applications of Agents, Multi-Agent Systems, and Trustworthiness. The PAAMS Collection 18th International Conference, PAAMS 2020, October 7–9, 2020, LNCS, vol. 12092, pp. 224–237. Springer (2020)
26. Sheth, R.S.: A decentralized strategy for swarm robots to manage spatially distributed tasks. Ph.D. thesis, Worcester Polytechnic Institute (2017)
27. Tohmé, F.A., Viglizzo, I.D.: Superrational types. Logic J. IGPL **27**(6), 847–864 (2019)
28. Torreño, A., Onaindia, E., Sapena, O.: An approach to multi-agent planning with incomplete information (2015). arXiv preprint arXiv:1501.07256

Winning at Any Cost - Infringing the Cartel Prohibition with Reinforcement Learning

Michael Schlechtinger[1]([✉])(iD), Damaris Kosack[2](iD), Heiko Paulheim[1](iD), and Thomas Fetzer[2](iD)

[1] Chair of Data Science, University of Mannheim, 68159 Mannheim, Germany
schlechtinger@uni-mannheim.de
[2] Chair of Public Law, Regulatory Law and Tax Law, University of Mannheim, 68159 Mannheim, Germany

Abstract. Pricing decisions are increasingly made by AI. Thanks to their ability to train with live market data while making decisions on the fly, deep reinforcement learning algorithms are especially effective in taking such pricing decisions. In e-commerce scenarios, multiple reinforcement learning agents can set prices based on their competitor's prices. Therefore, research states that agents might end up in a state of collusion in the long run. To further analyze this issue, we build a scenario that is based on a modified version of a prisoner's dilemma where three agents play the game of rock paper scissors. Our results indicate that the action selection can be dissected into specific stages, establishing the possibility to develop collusion prevention systems that are able to recognize situations which might lead to a collusion between competitors. We furthermore provide evidence for a situation where agents are capable of performing a tacit cooperation strategy without being explicitly trained to do so.

Keywords: Multi agent reinforcement learning · Pricing agents · Algorithmic collusion

1 Introduction

Dynamic reinforcement learning based pricing strategies supersede static ones in terms of average daily profits [16]. As 27% of the respondents of a 2017 study by KPMG identified price or promotion as the factors that are most likely to influence their decision regarding which product or brand to buy online [15], it is to be expected that successful companies (such as Amazon [5]) base their decisions on these algorithms to learn from and react to their competitor's pricing policies as well as to adjust to external factors, such as a transformation of demand or

The work presented in this paper has been conducted in the *KarekoKI* project, which is funded by the *Baden-Württemberg Stiftung* in the *Responsible Artificial Intelligence* program.

© Springer Nature Switzerland AG 2021
F. Dignum et al. (Eds.): PAAMS 2021, LNAI 12946, pp. 255–266, 2021.
https://doi.org/10.1007/978-3-030-85739-4_21

product innovations [12]. Monitoring these AIs is getting increasingly complex as the market is distributed worldwide, the barriers of entry are minimal, and the amount of created pricing data grows quicker by the day.

Primarily legal scholars have commented on the possibility of self-learning algorithms to quickly learn to achieve a price-setting collaboration especially within oligopolies (e.g., [10–12]). With the power of modern hardware, AIs would be able to monitor the market in which they act, resulting in a rapidly arising tacit collusion. Researchers investigated the issue by creating game theory like scenarios with the intention of pushing the agents towards a Nash equilibrium (e.g., [12,23]). In essence, it seems to be "incredibly easy, if not inevitable" to achieve "such a tacitly collusive, profit-maximizing equilibrium" [20]. While collusion has been presumed to appear in enclosed multi agent reinforcement learning scenarios, scholars have neither studied how to spot the origin of collusion nor if competitors can apply tacit collusion by displacing the others.

In an effort to simplify the dynamic pricing data analysis, we aim to train a competitive multi agent reinforcement learning (MARL) game simulation. In this game, the agents play a three-player version of rock paper scissors (RPS). We aim to analyze the effect of the competitive RPS scenario on the agents' learning performances and potential collaboration strategies. In specific, we aspire to analyze whether RL agents are capable of performing a tacit cooperation or communication strategy without being explicitly trained to do so.

2   Related Work

2.1   Infringing the Cartel Prohibition

In its most recent proposal for an Artificial Intelligence Act, the European Commission emphasises the importance of the safety and lawfulness of AI systems, of legal certainty with regard to AI, the governance and effective enforcement of existing law on fundamental rights and the installation of safety requirements [8]. In line with these goals, AI price policies must oblige to competition law just as prices that are set by humans. Both European and German competition law distinguish three possible conducts of infringing the cartel prohibition, see Article 101 (1) Treaty on the Functioning of the European Union ("TFEU")[1]: (a) *agreements between undertakings*, (b) *decisions by associations of undertakings*, and (c) *concerted practices*. Independent undertakings shall independently decide over their market behavior and must not coordinate it with their competitors ("requirement of independence"). This requirement does strictly preclude any direct or indirect contact by which an undertaking may influence the conduct on the market of its actual or potential competitors or disclose to them its decisions or intentions concerning its own conduct on the market where the object or effect of such contact is to create conditions of competition which do not correspond to the normal conditions of the market [9].

---

[1] Corresponding provision under German law: § 1 Act against Restraint of Competition; corresponding provision under US law Sect. 1 Sherman Antitrust Act of 1890.

The independently chosen intelligent adaption of an undertaking's market behavior to the observed market behavior of its competitors (generally) is permitted. Drawing a clear line between the adaption of an observed market behavior and a conduct through which competition knowingly is replaced by a practical cooperation and therefore constitutes a concerted practice within the meaning of Article 101 (1) TFEU[2] is often difficult and sometimes even impossible. Especially on transparent markets with few market participants, the market outcome of collusion can often hardly be traced back to be (or not to be) the product of a concerted practice (cf. petrol station market). Although collusion as a market outcome can be detrimental to consumers, innovation and economic growth and is therefore undesirable from a welfare economic point of view, the difficulty from a dogmatic perspective is that legal responsibility cannot be attached to a market outcome as such [24].

Our goal is to disclose whether a certain sequence of actions or a specific pattern can be identified as a situation in which the uncertainty about the competitor's next moves is replaced by a practical cooperation. It is conceivable that such accurate determination might not be possible due to the increased market transparency achieved by the self-learning algorithms: their ability to quickly process large amounts of competition-relevant data and to react to price movements in an almost unlimited frequency might lead to such a high degree of transparency on a market that makes it impossible to determine from its outcome whether or not the result of collusion is due to intelligent market observation and parallel behavior or a concerted practice.

2.2 Multi Agent Reinforcement Learning

A tacit collaboration between some reinforcement learning agents can only occur in certain situations. The agents have to interact within a multi agent reinforcement learning (MARL) environment, where competing agents and prices are recognized as a part of such [4]. Due to that, the environment is usually subjective for every agent, resulting in a differing learning performance and a diverse landscape of achieved competencies. It is unclear whether one of these competencies might arise in the skill to communicate with specific other agents to adjust their pricing policies accordingly; resulting in a higher producer's pension and a displacement of a competitor.

Researchers have investigated circumstances which can be juxtaposed with collusion between pricing agents, such as bidding processes [7,21] or economy simulations [25]. However, the authors did not control for or induce communication or collaboration. To combat this shortcoming, scholars within the economics realm created oligopolistic models (particularly Cournot oligopolies) to show collusion between agents. A Cournot oligopoly is characterized by an imperfect competition, where firms individually have some price-setting ability but are constrained by rivals [3]. Izquierdo and Izquierdo [14] show that simple iterative procedures, such as the win-continue, lose-reverse (WCLR) rule are able

---

2 For US law see [6,13].

Table 1. Three player RPS combinatorics.

Agent 1	Agent 2	Agent 3	r_1	r_2	r_3
Rock	Paper	Scissors	0	0	0
Rock	Rock	Rock	0	0	0
Scissors	Scissors	Scissors	0	0	0
Paper	Paper	Paper	0	0	0
Scissors	Rock	Rock	−1	0.5	0.5
Rock	Paper	Paper	−1	0.5	0.5
Paper	Scissors	Scissors	−1	0.5	0.5
Paper	Rock	Rock	2	−1	−1
Rock	Scissors	Scissors	2	−1	−1
Scissors	Paper	Paper	2	−1	−1
...	...	...	...	...	...
Expected reward r			0	0	0

to achieve collusive outcomes. However, the results are not robust in terms of minor, independent perturbations in the firms' cost or profit functions. Similar results were achieved with basic Q-learning [23]. As a case in point, using a price-setting duopoly model with fixed production, in which two firms follow a Q-learning algorithm, Tesauro and Kephart [22] observed convergence to prices higher than the competitive level. Major takeaways from these studies are, that cooperation is more likely to occur in simplified, static environments with a homogeneous good and that communication is vital to achieve collusive outcomes, particularly when more than two firms operate in a market. Such results suggest that the ability to communicate could also be pivotal for algorithmic collusion to occur [20].

3   Methodology

3.1   Problem Definition

Oroojlooy and Hajinezhad [19] recommend to model a MARL problem based on (i) centralized or decentralized control, (ii) fully or partially observable environment and (iii) cooperative or competitive environment. Our case demands for a decentralized control, with a partially to fully observable environment, so that every agent is able to make its own decisions based on the information given by the environment. Lastly, we apply a cooperative inside of a competitive environment, so that agents are able to team up against other agents.

3.2   Approach

With the intention of simplifying a realistic economy simulation, we choose to build a MARL-game based on a three player version of RPS. Every agent

$i = \{1, ..., 3\}$ represents a player with a set of legal game actions $A = \{1, ..., 3\}$ comprising the moves of rock, paper and scissors. The agents interact with a stochastic environment E which solely contains the chosen actions of every agent of the current time step t. Hence, a state at t can be described as $s_t = \{a'_1, ..., a'_i\}$. Following a collective action, every agent receives a reward out of $R = \{-1, 0, 0.5, 2\}$ mapped to the possible game outcomes presented in Table 1, resulting in a direct association between input and output. This formalism gives rise to a finite Markov decision process (MDP) in which every t relates to a distinct state, encouraging an application of standard reinforcement learning methods for MDPs. The goal of the agent is to interact with E by selecting actions in a way that maximises future rewards. As the agents receive a reward at the end of every timestep, we will not apply any discount to future rewards. We define the optimal action-value function $Q^*(s, a)$ as the maximum expected return achievable by following any strategy, after seeing some sequence s and then taking some action a, $Q^*(s, a) = \max_\pi \mathbb{E}[R_t | s_t = s, a_t = a, \pi]$, where π is a policy that maps sequences to actions (or distributions over actions). In an attempt to induce strategic behavior, resulting in a tacit communication within this competitive MARL environment, we utilize a Deep Q-Network (DQN) [18] with an experience replay and a target network [17]. After performing experience replay, the agent selects and executes an action according to an ϵ-greedy policy. The agents select the action a^t that maximizes the expected value of $r + Q^*(s', a')$, updating the Q-values by:

$$Q^*(s, a) = \mathbb{E}_{s' \sim \varepsilon}[r + \max_{a'} Q^*(s', a') | s, a] \tag{1}$$

Our main argument for the selection of this specific scenario is the controlled, unambiguous reward allocation in combination with the restricted moveset of the agents. Thus, every step t develops into a zero-sum game (as shown in Table 1). On the one hand, we create an environment, where no agent can earn a profit, if it does not communicate with another agent. On the other hand, we counteract the poor learning performance of MARL [2] (due to the defined equilibrium/local optimum) as well as increase the comprehensibility of the neural network's predictions. We expect the agents to converge to a collusive state after several episodes, as described by economics and law scholars (e.g., [12,23]).

We also attempt to induce a displacement of one agent due to the actions selected by the other two agents. In our use case, they need to learn a specific policy which would force two colluding agents to not repeat their allied agents' actions. While this would not necessarily result in a better short term step reward for these agents, it would however eliminate the ability to achieve a "big win" (e.g., playing Paper if the opponents play Rock and Rock) for the third, competing agent. Generally speaking, if two agents avoid choosing the same action, the expected reward for the third player is negative. We aim to simulate this circumstance in diverging settings.

In *mode 1*, collusion is induced by explicit communication as suggested by Schwalbe [20]. More specifically, we designate two 'cheating' agents $i_c \subset i$ and a 'fair' agent $i_f \in i$, $i_f \notin i_c$ ahead of a training session. Before its turn, one of

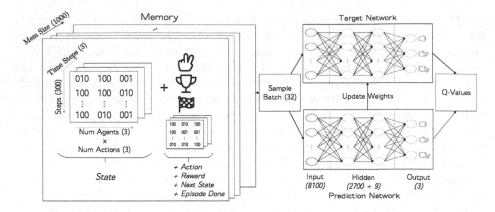

Fig. 1. DQN architecture

the cheating agents transmits his picked action to the other cheating agent. The message will be enclosed to input to the receiver's DQN.[3] In *mode 2*, instead of making the players communicate explicitly, we provoke tacit communication by adjusting the reward of the cheating agents $r_{i_c}^t$ to $r_{i_c}^t = -r_f^t$. In other words, they will try to maximize their *joint* instead of their *individual* reward, which is equivalent to minimizing i_f's reward. We additionally *denoise* the rewards; hence, i_c will receive 1 for a loss or a tie with i_f and -1 for a win of i_f. To further stress this issue, we perform control-runs, where i_f is replaced with an agent that plays random actions (which is the best strategy in a competitive 3-player version of RPS).

3.3   Implementation

The main weakness of RPS in a real world scenario is the unpredictability of an opponent's move. The best player would just play random, however since playing this game is psychologically based on personal human short-term memory behavior, there is a tendency to follow specific patterns, like not repeating moves or trying to play unpredictably [1]. In an artificial MARL-problem, we can model that by not only reacting to an opponent's last move, but learning from a history of its last moves. After testing, we chose to apply a history size of 100 games to accommodate for a stable learning process. Regarding the experience replay, we chose to use the last 3 timesteps as an input for the neural net. The network is made up of four dense layers (input, two hidden layers, output), whose main task is to compress the given information and provide the chosen action. For that matter, we design a DQN with an input layer comprising 8100 neurons (300 steps * 3 one-hot encoded actions * 3 players * 3 time steps), two

---

[3] It is important that in the eyes of the receiving agent, this is just a variable with the values of A which does *not* have the specific semantics of *this is the other agent's next move.*

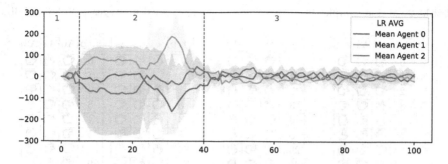

Fig. 2. Episode reward distribution within the different learning rate scenarios.

hidden layers with 2700 and 9 neurons and a dense output with 3 neurons to choose either rock, paper or scissors (cf. Fig. 1). The neurons required for the number of players will increase by 1 for the cheating player to accommodate for the action received by the messaging agent. We use TensorFlow 2 to build and train the DQNs; the code can be found on Github[4].

4   Results

To counter inconsistent MARL outcomes, we chose to train the agents for 10 runs with 100 episodes each (300 steps per episode), comprising three different learning rates (0.001, 0.005, 0.01), resulting in 30 runs with 900.000 games of RPS per scenario. We picked learning rates that are fairly small to counteract quickly developing local optima, causing repetitions of the same action, due to the straightforward connection between action and reward. For every scenario with i_c involved, we also performed another 15 runs (5 per learning rate) where i_f is replaced with an agent that randomly picks actions in order to further stress the issue by simulating a perfect RPS policy.

4.1   Collusion Between All Agents

In our series of simulations, we were able to achieve collusive results within every of the chosen learning rate scenarios (cf. Fig. 2). When averaged, the different action sequences can be visually divided into three learning stages. In *stage 1*, the agents basically acted random, due to the epsilon-greedy algorithm. After approximately 5 episodes (*stage 2*), one of the agents achieved a better outcome due to a lucky action selection. The agents stuck to their learned strategy while randomly delving into different policies. Upon further examination, we discovered that the strategies usually involve a single action which will be repeated in the next turns, even if this might not be the best action. This sub-optimal behavior stems from the first few episodes being mostly played randomly due

---

[4] https://gitfront.io/r/user-7017325/1eb2ef3332343def1c7f67d5fce5953f1e003681/AiC ollusionDQN/.

Table 2. Action samples from two different runs, divided in stages 1, 2, 3a and 3b

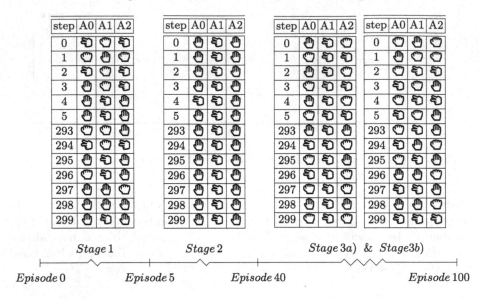

			Stage 1				Stage 2			Stage 3a)	&	Stage 3b)

Episode 0   Episode 5   Episode 40   Episode 100

to the epsilon-greedy strategy. Thus, the agents were only able to learn from a short history, which taught them to repeat the most successful action, rather than a certain sequence of actions. *Stage 3* establishes a collusive sequence of actions from episode 40 onwards with two different scenarios (**3a** and **3b**).

As presented in Table 2, the agents try to avoid a negative reward over a long-term, resulting in an average episode profit of zero. However, stages 3a and 3b differ significantly in their way of achieving this. In 3a, one of the players repeated one action (e.g., scissors) and occasionally deviated from that due to the epsilon-greedy strategy, while the others predominantly alternate between two moves that change over time. In stage 3b, the agents played seemingly random. However if examined more closely, specific alternation patterns occurred. A specific pattern can be identified, when observing the actions of agent 1 in Fig. 2. The player oscillated between choosing rock and scissors in the first moves and transitions to scissors and paper towards the end of the episode. The remainder of the agents follow more elaborate patterns, however specific repetitions can be discovered by scanning the history.

4.2   Collusion Between Two Agents

Mode 1: Explicit Communication. We successfully trained a displacing collusion policy with the help of explicit communication between the cheating agents i_c. The results represented in Fig. 3 indicate that the agents were able to learn the suggested policy of not repeating their collaborator's action after a few episodes. After about 5 episodes, i_c achieve a higher reward on average. Thus, for the next 30 Episodes i_f is only rarely able to achieve a "big win". However, just

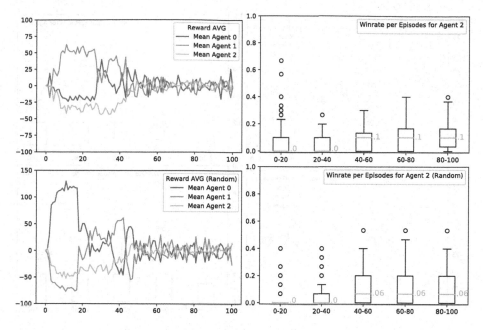

Fig. 3. Episode reward distribution within *mode 1* including control runs where i_f is choosing random actions (lower half).

like when colluding with all agents, after approximately 45 episodes, they tend to converge to an average game reward of 0. While it would be feasible to prolong this behavior by including variable learning rates or reducing the target update frequency during later episodes, we chose to encourage a long-term formation of a zero-centered equilibrium. Our reasoning behind this is the comparison to a real-world oligopoly, where two market participants could only uphold a displacement by reducing the price up to a certain point, before damaging themselves.

In order to further stress the issue, we chose to replace i_f with an agent that chooses actions randomly. While i_c were able to successfully learn a displacement strategy in every training session, the results within the first 40 episodes were less significant than when i_f acted on behalf of the DQN. Nevertheless, we were able to observe slightly better results in the later stages, due to the added randomness.

Mode 2: Implicit Communication. The agents i_c successfully learned the suggested implicit collusion policy. After about 5 episodes, i_c achieve a higher game reward on average. This circumstance is especially prominent in the section between 20 episodes and 40 episodes (cf. the upper right half of Fig. 4). On average, i_f is rarely able to exceed a reward of 0. Again, after about 40 episodes, the agents converge to an average game reward of 0.

We were able to observe a less prevailing, but still effective policy when implementing a randomly acting agent i_f. As demonstrated in Fig. 7, the median

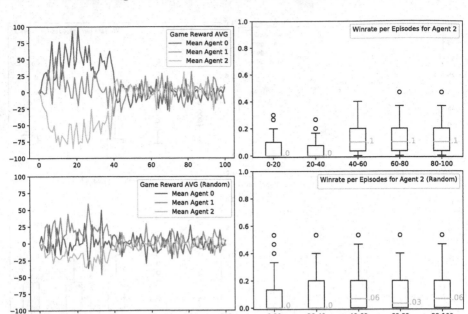

Fig. 4. Episode reward distribution within *mode 2* including control runs where i_f is choosing random actions (lower half).

of i_f's winrate was still 0 in between episodes 0 to 40, yet the interquartile range is greater than before, indicating a less stable learning due to the added randomness of i_f's action selection. We also experience a few runs, where the agents were able to learn the displacement policy and not unlearn it in later episodes. In those specific runs, agent 1 repeated the same actions from episode 22 onward while agent 0 played the action that would lose against that one in a regular game. Hence, the joined rewards i_c turn out greater than those of i_f.

5   Discussion

Our research successfully confirmed the hypothesis from law and economics scholars (e.g., [23] or [14]) about a possible collusion between reinforcement learning based pricing agents in MARL scenarios without being especially trained to do so. We furthermore extended these findings by providing specific learning stages that could be translated into real world scenarios to possibly set a foundation for a system that is capable to detect collusion in early stages. Moreover, we were able to show that with the appropriate reward function, deep reinforcement learning can be used to learn an effective displacement strategy in a MARL environment.

Based on the results of the experiments, we derive several implications. Due to the noticeable segmentation of action selection in different learning stages, one could argue that the transition episodes in between a fair and a collusive state can be seen as a signaling process, where agents agree on specific patterns to increase the joint reward. This proposition is supported by the fact, that a repeating action selection pattern of another agent could be predicted and punished by the DQN due to its experience replay [17]. In a real world scenario, a malicious AI could be trained to repeat patterns, that are less recognizable for humans. We would like to emphasize that within inelastic selling conditions (as they appear in collusive markets), a cooperation between two agents will be facilitated as the existing communication strategy will furthermore ease the displacement of a competitor. From a legal perspective, the question whether the cartel prohibition can be applied to such factual achieved, however non-volitional, state of collusion, is subject to this project's further legal research.

6   Limitations and Outlook

As every study, the results are beset with limitations, opening the door for future research. As aforementioned, our experiment is a simplified, gamified version of an economy simulation game. As such, it lacks the data complexity of a real world pricing AI as well as the scaling opportunities. To further develop our research, we intend to apply the gained knowledge to a MARL environment resembling the one of real pricing AIs, where we can further highlight specific moments in which the agent's behavior tips over from independence to collusion. Especially the division into distinct stages should be investigated in a context of realistic pricing agents environments. While we focused on highlighting the possible dangers of pricing AIs in a MARL environment, we opened the opportunity for research explicitly investigating measures to avoid it. As such, law and IT scholars alike could benefit from this research as a foundation for guidelines, law amendments, or specific laws concerning the training and behavior of pricing AIs.

References

1. Ali, F.F., Nakao, Z., Chen, Y.W.: Playing the rock-paper-scissors game with a genetic algorithm. In: Congress on Evolutionary Computation, Piscataway, NJ, pp. 741–745 (2000). https://doi.org/10.1109/CEC.2000.870372
2. Allen, M., Zilberstein, S.: Complexity of decentralized control: special cases. In: International Conference on Neural Information Processing Systems, NIPS 2009, Curran Associates Inc., Red Hook, NY, USA, pp. 19–27 (2009)
3. Augustin, A.: Cournot: Recherches sur les principes mathématiques de la théorie des richesses. L. Hachette, Paris (1836)
4. Charpentier, A., Elie, R., Remlinger, C.: Reinforcement learning in economics and finance. https://arxiv.org/pdf/2003.10014
5. Chen, L., Mislove, A., Wilson, C.: An empirical analysis of algorithmic pricing on amazon marketplace. In: Bourdeau, J. (ed.) Proceedings of the 25th International Conference on World Wide Web, Montreal, Canada, Geneva, 11–15 May 2016, pp. 1339–1349 (2016). https://doi.org/10.1145/2872427.2883089

6. DOJ and FTC: Algorithms and collusion - note by the united states. In: OECD Contributions Received for the Discussion on Algorithms and Collusion, 127th Competition Committee Meeting, 21–23 June 2017. https://one.oecd.org/document/DAF/COMP/WD(2017)41/en/pdf

7. Dütting, P., Feng, Z., Narasimhan, H., Parkes, D.C., Ravindranath, S.S.: Optimal auctions through deep learning. https://arxiv.org/pdf/1706.03459

8. European Commission: Proposal for a regulation of the European parliament and of the council - laying down harmonized rules on artificial intelligence (artificial intelligence act) and amending certain union legislative acts

9. European Court of Justice: Case c-8/08 - t-mobile netherlands v raad van bestuur van de nederlandse mededingingsautoriteit, ecli:eu:c:2009:343 (2009)

10. Ezrachi, A.: Virtual Competition: The Promise and Perils of the Algorithm-Driven Economy. Harvard University Press, Cambridge (2016). http://gbv.eblib.com/patron/FullRecord.aspx?p=4742341

11. Ezrachi, A., Stucke, M.E.: Artificial intelligence & collusion: when computers inhibit competition. SSRN Electron. J. (2015). https://doi.org/10.2139/ssrn.2591874

12. Ezrachi, A., Stucke, M.E.: Two artificial neural networks meet in an online hub and change the future (of competition, market dynamics and society). SSRN Electron. J. (2017). https://doi.org/10.2139/ssrn.2949434

13. Gulati, A.: How much is no longer a simple question - pricing algorithms and antitrust laws. SSRN Electron. J. (2018). http://dx.doi.org/10.2139/ssrn.3682486

14. Izquierdo, S.S., Izquierdo, L.R.: The "win-continue, lose-reverse" rule in cournot oligopolies: robustness of collusive outcomes. Adv. Complex Syst. 18(05n06), 1550013 (2015). https://doi.org/10.1142/S0219525915500137

15. KPMG: The truth about online consumers: 2017 global online consumer report

16. Kropp, L.A., Korbel, J.J., Theilig, M., Zarnekow, R.: Dynamic pricing of product clusters: a multi-agent reinforcement learning approach. In: ECIS (2019)

17. Lin, L.J.: Reinforcement Learning for Robots Using Neural Networks. Technical report, DTIC Document. Carnegie Mellon University, USA (1992)

18. Mnih, V., et al.: Playing Atari with deep reinforcement learning. https://arxiv.org/pdf/1312.5602

19. Oroojlooy, A.J., Hajinezhad, D.: A review of cooperative multi-agent deep reinforcement learning. http://arxiv.org/pdf/1908.03963v3

20. Schwalbe, U.: Algorithms, machine learning, and collusion. J. Competition Law Econ. 14(4), 568–607 (2018). https://doi.org/10.1093/joclec/nhz004

21. Schwind, M.: Dynamic Pricing and Automated Resource Allocation For Complex Information Services: Reinforcement Learning and Combinatorial Auctions. Springer, Heidelberg (2007). https://doi.org/10.1007/978-3-540-68003-1

22. Tesauro, G., Kephart, J.O.: Pricing in agent economies using multi-agent q-learning. Auton. Agent. Multi-Agent Syst. 5(3), 289–304 (2002). https://doi.org/10.1023/A:1015504423309

23. Waltman, L., Kaymak, U.: Q-learning agents in a Cournot oligopoly model. J. Econ. Dyn. Control 32(10), 3275–3293 (2008). https://doi.org/10.1016/j.jedc.2008.01.003

24. Weche, J., Weck, T.: Neue möglichkeiten impliziter kollusion und die grenzen des kartellrechts. Europäische Zeitschrift für Wirtschaftsrecht 21, 923–929 (2020)

25. Zheng, S., et al.: The AI economist: improving equality and productivity with AI-driven tax policies. https://arxiv.org/pdf/2004.13332

Swarm of Satellites: Implementation and Experimental Study of Multi-Agent Solution for Adaptive Scheduling of Large-Scale Space Observation Systems

Petr Skobelev[1]([⊠]) [iD], Elena Simonova[2] [iD], Vladimir Galuzin[3] [iD],
Anastasiya Galitskaya[4] [iD], and Vitaly Travin[4] [iD]

[1] Samara Federal Research Scientific Center RAS, Institute for the Control
of Complex Systems RAS, Sadovaya Street, 61, 443020 Samara, Russia
[2] Samara National Research University, Moskovskoye Shosse, 34, Samara 443086, Russia
[3] Samara State Technical University, Molodogvardeyskaya Street, 244, Samara 443100, Russia
[4] SEC «Smart Solutions», Moskovskoye Shosse, Office 1201, 17, Samara 443013, Russia
`{galitskaya,travin}@smartsolutions-123.ru`

Abstract. The paper dwells on solution to the problem of planning large-scale space observation systems, which can include from several dozens to hundreds of small spacecrafts. These systems are created in response to massive increase in the load on currently operating systems. New space systems, in comparison with traditional single spacecrafts, impose much more tough requirements on methods of planning, and only a few of the existing solutions can at least partially correspond to them. Thus, there is a need for new planning approaches that take into account domain semantics more deeply. The paper presents expanded application of multi-agent technology. Its essence lies in negotiations between agents of imaging through mutual compromises and concessions. The desired efficiency is achieved by searching for the near-to-global optimum for each application and using this information in a targeted search for a solution for the entire system. Experiments have demonstrated that approach helps promptly draw up a schedule for dozens of spacecrafts and thousands of observation objects.

Keywords: Small spacecraft · Space system · Ground stations · Observation objects · Multi-agent technologies · Adaptive planning

1 Introduction

Satellite systems based on small spacecrafts for Earth remote sensing (ERS) belong to a new generation of space observation systems (SpOS) designed to obtain images of the earth's surface in various spectral ranges. The obtained data is more and more in demand in various areas of human activity, such as military, forestry and agriculture, cartography, climate research, disaster recovery operations, etc. [1]. Thus, there is a need to build up the ERS orbital group and put into operation a large-scale constellation of small spacecrafts

© Springer Nature Switzerland AG 2021
F. Dignum et al. (Eds.): PAAMS 2021, LNAI 12946, pp. 267–278, 2021.
https://doi.org/10.1007/978-3-030-85739-4_22

along with traditional large-mass ones. Depending on the task of SpOS, they can vary from several dozens [2] to hundreds [3, 4] of satellites. Consequently, the number of ground stations for receiving and transmitting information (GS) also increases. They are part of the ground complex for servicing the orbital group.

To ensure targeted functioning of the space observation system, it is required to solve the problem of planning execution of incoming imaging applications, which is an NP-complete task [5]. At the same time, large-scale orbital constellations impose much more rigid requirements on methods and means of planning in comparison with traditional single ERS satellites. Among the main requirements are the following [6]:

- scalability: planning thousands of applications on a significant horizon without losses in processing speed with a growing number of applications and resources;
- adaptability: changing plans according to incoming events in a mode close to real time without stopping and completely recalculating the schedule;
- flexibility: taking into account individual characteristics of applications and resources to build the most optimal solution for multi-criteria optimization;
- efficiency: the time for placing new applications should be measured in minutes;
- reliability and survivability: in case of failure of some of the SpOS resources.

Most of existing developments such as SaVoir [7], STM [8], STK Scheduler [9], etc. are centralized, monolithic, hierarchical and sequential solutions. They only partially satisfy requirements, which makes them poorly applicable for large-scale SpOS. Thus, there is a need either for serious revision of existing software and algorithmic solutions, taking into account the emerging requirements, or for development of new approaches to planning orbital groups, taking into account domain semantics more deeply.

One of such approaches to resource management in complex systems is the use of virtual market methodology based on multi-agent technology (MAT) [10, 11], allowing flexible adaptation of schedules by events in real time. MAT also takes into account individual characteristics of orders and resources. The model of demand-resource network (DR-network) helps create high-performance, distributed, fault-tolerant solutions for resource management of SpOS in comparison with traditional methods.

The purpose of this work is to present the implementation and experimental study of a two-stage hybrid method for planning large-scale SpOS: 1st stage - building an initial plan using a greedy optimization algorithm (conflict-free planning); 2nd stage - multi-agent adaptation and optimization (proactive planning).

This approach develops the initial solution [12, 13] by improving architecture of multi-agent system (MAS) and introducing additional heuristics, significantly reducing complexity of combinatorial search for a solution for virtual market and DR-networks.

The second section of this paper proposes a SpOS model and formulation of the planning problem. Section 3 provides an overview of the current state of solutions. The fourth section describes the developed adaptive scheduling method. Section 5 examines a prototype SpOS planning system and presents experiment results. Section 6 provides a conclusion on development and application of the described solution.

2   The Problem of Planning Space Observation Systems

2.1   Model

The SpOS model consists of a set of small spacecrafts $Sat = \{sat_i\}$, $i = \overline{1, L}$ and a set of ground stations $GS = \{gs_j\}$, $r = \overline{1, G}$. Each sat_i spacecraft has its own orbit O_i (the orbits of satellites can be located both in one plane, and in different planes; in the first case they have a similar trajectory), limiting roll angle $maxRollAngle_i$ and pitch angle $maxPitchAngle_i$, as well as parameters of imaging equipment (f - focal length, $matx$ - matrix dimensions, minimum angle of sun elevation $minSunAngle_i$, $memVol_i$ memory capacity). And each gs_j is characterized by geographic location $coord_j$ and parameters of antenna (opening angle and data reception rate). The composition of spacecrafts and GS may change over time. Each satellite may have restrictions for data transfer to a certain GS. Besides, time intervals of inaccessibility can be indicated.

The targeted functioning of SpOS consists in execution of a set of applications $R = \{r_p\}$, $p = \overline{1, P}$. The r_p application can have its priority pr_p and restrictions (execution period $t_p = [t_p^{start}; t_p^{end}]$, admissible image linear resolution $minR_p$ and $maxR_p$ and admissible sun angle $minSunAngle_p$ and $maxSunAngle_p$). Besides, R can also change.

In the described model, two operations are performed:

- imaging of the observation object (OO), characterized by execution interval $t_p^{imag} = [t_p^{imagStart}; t_p^{imagEnd}]$, roll and pitch angles $rollAngle_p$ and $pitchAngle_p$.
- transfer of the images $drop_p$, characterized by execution interval $t_p^{drop} = [t_p^{dropStart}; t_p^{dropEnd}]$ and data transmission speed $baudRate_p$.

2.2   Problem Statement

It is necessary to provide adaptive scheduling of incoming applications, redistributing them between spacecrafts in order to increase the SpOS productivity, obtain images of the highest quality, minimize the lead time for individual orders and ensure fulfillment of other criteria. The system's objective function (OF) has the following form:

$$OF = \frac{1}{S} \sum_{k=1}^{N} OF_k \rightarrow max, \tag{1}$$

$$OF_k = \sum_{m=1}^{M} c_m F_m^k \rightarrow max, \tag{2}$$

where

OF is the system's objective function,
OF_k – is the OF of the k-th application,
S is the total number of applications,
N is he number of placed applications,
M is the number of optimization criteria,

c_m is the weighting factor of the m-th optimization criterion, such that $0 \le c_m \le 1$, $\sum_{m=1}^{M} c_m = 1$,
F_m^k is evaluation of the m-th optimization criterion for the k-th application.

Minimization of the imaging time F_1^k (3) and maximization of image quality F_2^k (4) are chosen as optimization criteria.

$$F_1^k = \frac{t_k^{end} - t_k^{imagEnd}}{t_k^{end} - t_k^{start}}, \tag{3}$$

$$F_2^k = \frac{minR_k - r\left(f, \text{matx}, \text{rollAngle}_k, \text{pitchAngle}_p\right)}{minR_k - maxR_k}, \tag{4}$$

where r is the function for linear resolution of the image for the k-th application [14].

3 State of the Art Review

Various classical and metaheuristic optimization algorithms are proposed for solving the problem of planning space imagery. Application of machine learning (ML) methods is also studied. One of the most famous metaheuristic algorithms is the ant colony one [15, 16]. Other equally popular algorithms are the local search method [17, 18] and the genetic algorithm [19, 20]. Heuristic and metaheuristic algorithms show higher performance in comparison with traditional optimization methods, however, heuristics requires strict specifications for problem conditions. Meanwhile, operation time and quality of obtained solutions can strongly depend on the initial data. Attempts of using ML methods are described in [21–23]. ML has great potential because it allows for training on data but does not require users to hard-code parts of the algorithm. However, ML algorithms currently have limited interpretability (e.g., there is no way to explicitly specify constraints) and require quite a large amount of data for training.

Recently, approaches to planning ERS data using agents have begun to develop [24–26]. The planning process proposed in [24] consists in interaction between agents of the survey strip and agents of the spacecraft. It is based on heuristics of programming in constraints together with virtual market approach. Results of its comparison with the currently used greedy algorithm show advantages of the proposed approach. However, performance of this solution is still insufficient for the task proposed in this paper. [25] describes the mechanisms of market auctions for distribution of orders for OO imaging between spacecrafts. They are operated by their own mission centers, coordinating their schedules using auction protocols, bidding on vacant orders based on the influence on the onboard plan and forecasted profits. [26] discusses the idea of fully autonomous planning on board a spacecraft. Its main advantages lie in using the current actual data on the state of the spacecraft and its resources to respond to emerging events in real time. However, in order to create a full-fledged MAS using a spacecraft in orbit, it is necessary to overcome limitations of the computing capabilities of onboard equipment. It is also important to build a stable communication system with several spacecrafts.

Complexity and dynamics of the market of ERS services leads to the fact that traditional, centralized, hierarchical and sequential methods based on heuristic algorithms do not effectively solve the problem of adaptive resource management for large-scale SpOS with acceptable quality and within the required time. A promising area is the use of methods and algorithms based on artificial intelligence and an agent-based virtual market, taking into account the domain semantics, conflict analysis, non-deterministic behavior, self-organization and adaptation in real time. However, currently these methods are at the stage of initial development, therefore, integral solutions, suitable for practical digital implementation, have not yet been designed and implemented [26, 27].

4 Adaptive Planning Method

Figure 1 shows a diagram of the adaptive planning method, which consists of preparing initial data (visibility intervals and placement options) and hybrid scheduling, combining a greedy optimization algorithm (conflict-free scheduling) with multi-agent adaptation and optimization (proactive scheduling).

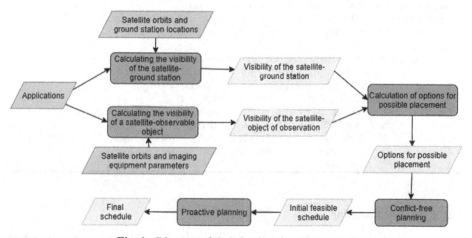

Fig. 1. Diagram of the adaptive planning method

Before planning is initiated, calculation of the satellite-GS and satellite-OO visibility intervals is performed on the specified planning horizon $[t_{min}^{start}, t_{max}^{end}]$. Next, possible placement options po_k for each application are calculated. The possible placement option is a combination of both visibility intervals within which imaging and dropping operations can be performed. The exact operation time is determined during planning.

Calculation of possible placement options is implemented based on the method of successive concessions between optimization criteria. A sequence of possible placement options is formed, sorted in descending order of objective functions of applications (2). The first place is for the placement option at the global optimum point.

4.1 Conflict-Free Planning

At this stage, an initial feasible schedule is constructed using a greedy optimization algorithm. The quality of the schedule does not really matter. The purpose is to form an initial state for the next stage of proactive planning. Applications occupy the first vacant placement option, without trying to displace those that are already allocated.

Algorithm 1 presents the pseudocode for conflict-free planning method. The list of applications is organized and grouped according to the value of the pr_p priority (lines 1–2). Then, for each group of applications, an attempt of planning is made (line 4–11). Options for placing each application are sequentially sorted out (line 7–11). For the next option, a search is performed for specific intervals of imaging and transmitting operations within the specified visibility intervals (line 8), for which there are no conflicts with other previously placed applications. If such intervals are found, the imaging job is formed (line 10–11). Otherwise, the algorithm proceeds to the next placement option.

Algorithm 1: Conflict-free planning algorithm

```
Input: applications, ImgJobOpts is set of possible placement
options for the problem
Output: ImgJobs is set of planned jobs
1:   groupedApplications = group(applications, 'priority')
2:   sort(groupedApplications, 'priority', 'desc')
3:   ImgJobs = []
4:   for applicationGroup in groupedApplications
5:     parallel for application_j in applicationGroup
6:       ImgJobOpts_j = ImgJobOpts[application_j]
7:       for imgJobOpt_k in ImgJobOpts_j
8:         imgAndDropInters = findImgAndDropInters(imgJobOpt_k)
9:         if imgAndDropInters not empty
10:          imgJob= createImgJob(ijo_k, task_j, imgAndDropInters)
11:          ImgJobs.push(imgJob)
12: return ImgJobs
```

4.2 Proactive Planning

At this stage, the resulting schedule is optimized using a multi-agent approach, which consists in competition and cooperation of agents with certain resources or demands [12]. Agents interact via negotiations on the virtual market through mutual compromises and concessions and arrive at a locally optimal solution.

Two types of agents are introduced: an application agent with the goal of occupying the most advantageous placement, and a scene agent, designed to control the activity of application agents and interact with external systems. The application agent is responsible for making changes to the schedule: it can move another agent from a more advantageous position or change its own position upon the request of another agent. To assess the current position of an agent, its satisfaction function $SF_k(po_k)$ (5) is used, which is the difference between the value of the task's OF (2) at the global optimum point $OF_k(p\dot{o}_k)$ and the OF value for the current accommodation option $OF_k(po_k)$:

$$SF_k(po_k) = 1 - (OF_k(p\dot{o}_k) - OF_k(po_k)). \tag{5}$$

During proactive planning, the scene agent grants the proactive right to application agents, starting with those with the least advantageous position ($SF_k(po_k) = min$). Figure 2 shows the negotiation protocol of agents during proactive planning.

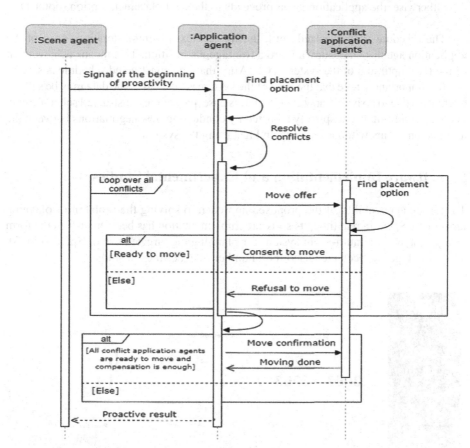

Fig. 2. Negotiation protocol at the stage of proactive planning

An agent that is launched for proactivity acts according to the following algorithm:

1. Sequentially search through placement options that are better than the current one.
2. For the next placement option, determine the list of conflicting applications and send a message to their agents with a proposal to find another placement, using compensation equal to the increment of the agent's OF $\Delta F = F_j\left(\tilde{po}_j\right) - F_j(po_j)$. Upon receipt of this message, the agent of the conflicting application R_c recursively searches for another placement option using a similar algorithm (embedded proactivity) and sends its solution in a response message. It indicates the agent's willingness to change its position in the schedule and the ΔF_c losses in case of agreement.

3. If all agents of conflicting applications agree to move, the total losses $\sum \Delta F_c$ are evaluated, and if the agent of a proactive application can compensate for them due to the increase of its OF, i.e. $\Delta F > \sum \Delta F_c$, the resulting permutation is applied.
4. Otherwise, the application agent proceeds to the next placement option (point 1).

The schedule is synthesized until, during the next planning iteration, none of the application agents can occupy a more advantageous position. This means achievement of the local optimum of the system's OF. After that, the constructed schedule is saved.

It is important to note that the state of the system is not static. The data may be subject to changes due to arrival of new events. In this case, part of the constructed schedule may become irrelevant and adaptively adjusted by conducting new negotiations between the application agents without stopping and restarting the system.

5   Software Implementation and Experimental Studies

To test the applicability of the proposed approach to solving the problem of planning large-scale SpOS in real time, its software implementation has been created in the form of a prototype of a multi-agent system for planning the targeted use of SpOS (Fig. 3). This prototype has been then used for a number of experimental studies.

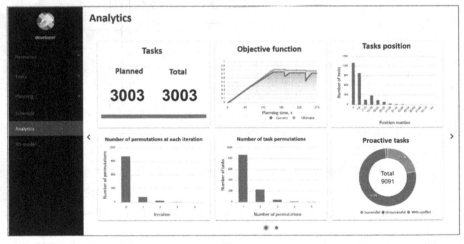

Fig. 3. System user interface

The prototype has a client–server network architecture. The server side of the system is written in Java using the Spring framework. The user interface is a one-page web application through which the initial data is loaded and modified (spacecrafts, GS, applications, calendars, resource availability restrictions, etc.). The interface also helps manage the planning progress, monitor resources, view reports and planning results.

5.1 Investigation of the Method's Performance and Ability to Adapt the Schedule

This study evaluated performance of the presented method and its ability to adapt the schedule damaged by failure of one of the spacecrafts. During the experiments, the scheduling of applications for OO imaging has been carried out first, the number of applications varied from 100 to 20,000 for a different number of small spacecrafts (15, 25, or 35). The system's OF value (1) (Fig. 4a) and the planning time (Fig. 4b) were measured. Then, one of the spacecrafts was excluded from the system and the time spent on restoring the solution was also measured (Fig. 5). The experiments were carried out on a PC with a 4-core CPU Intel Core i7-3770 and 8 GB RAM. The number of GS in all experiments was the same - 20. The planning horizon was 21 days.

Experimental results have shown that the developed method meets performance requirements when working with large volumes of applications. In this case, the quality of the obtained solution weakly depends on the number of small spacecrafts and applications in the system. The time spent on restoring a schedule damaged by failure of one of the spacecrafts is a much smaller fraction of the total planning time and increases proportionally with the growing number of applications and spacecrafts. Comparison of the obtained results with those presented in [12, 17, 24] shows that the developed algorithm demonstrates higher performance and scalability, allowing for a similar time interval to process a much larger number of incoming applications (by 5–10 times).

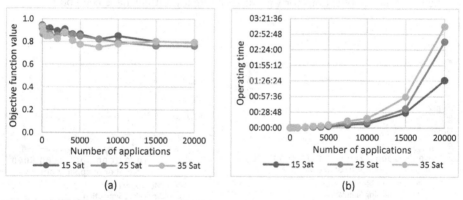

Fig. 4. Graphs of dependence of the OF value (a) and the planning time (b) on the number of applications and spacecrafts in the system

5.2 Comparison with Centralized Scheduling Algorithms

In this study, the effectiveness of the developed method has been analyzed in comparison with centralized scheduling algorithms based on traditional optimization methods, such as the simulated annealing algorithm and the Tabu Search algorithm, implemented in the Optaplaner open-source Java scheduling framework. They have been compared based on the quality of the resulting schedule and the time required for its compilation.

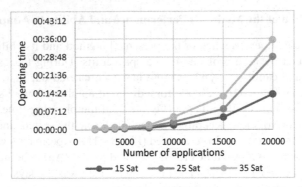

Fig. 5. Graphs of dependence of the schedule recovery time on the number of applications and spacecrafts in the system

In the course of the study, a series of experiments have been carried out, in which the number of applications for OO imaging varied from 100 to 5000. At the same time, the time spent on drawing up the schedule and the system OF value have been measured (1). The PC configuration and the number of ground stations are similar to the previous experiment, the number of spacecrafts is 25. Based on the results of the experiments, graphs of dependence of the system OF value (Fig. 6a) and the planning time (Fig. 6b) on the number of applications for various planning algorithms have been built.

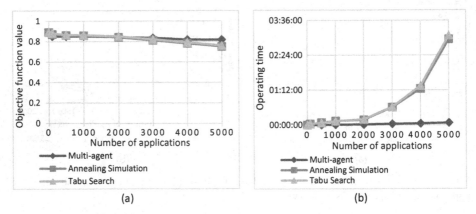

Fig. 6. Graphs of dependence of the OF value (a) and planning time (b) on the number of applications for various planning algorithms

The obtained experimental results show that the proposed method is comparable with centralized scheduling methods in terms of the scheduling quality. While with an increase in the number of planned applications, it demonstrates a more linear growth in the processing time without any loss of quality.

6 Conclusion

The authors of the paper proposed a method for adaptive planning of large-scale space observation systems based on multi-agent technologies. Results of experimental studies on the developed prototype demonstrate compliance of the presented approach with requirements for methods and tools of planning large-scale SpOS in terms of scalability, adaptability, flexibility, efficiency, reliability and survivability. As the next step, it is proposed to introduce the concepts of more advanced virtual market and ontology of space observation systems into the multi-agent system to provide the possibility of more flexible and adaptive planning settings. All these actions will ultimately create an actual platform for planning space observation systems.

Acknowledgements. The paper has been prepared based on materials of scientific research within the subsidized state theme of the Samara Federal Research Scientific Center RAS, Institute for Control of Complex Systems RAS for research and development on the topic: № AAAA-A19-119030190053-2 "Research and development of methods and means of analytical design, computer-based knowledge representation, computational algorithms and multi-agent technology in problems of optimizing management processes in complex systems".

References

1. Shimoda, H.: Remote sensing data applications. In: Handbook of Satellite Applications, pp. 1–70 (2016)
2. Henely, S., Baldwin-Pulcini, B., Smith, K.: Turning off the lights: aAutomating SkySat mission operations. In: Small Satellite Conference (2019)
3. Irisov, V., Nguyen, V., Duly, T., et al.: Recent Ionosphere collection results from Spire's 3U CubeSat GNSS-RO constellation, American Geophysical Union Fall Meeting (2018)
4. Kopacz, J., Herschitz, R., Roney, J.: Small satellites an overview and assessment. Acta Astronautica **170**, 93–105 (2020)
5. Wang, M., Dai, G., Vasile, M.: Heuristic Scheduling Algorithm Oriented Dynamic Tasks for Imaging Satellites. Hindawi Publishing Corporation (2014)
6. Galuzin, V., Matyushin, M., Kutomanov, A., Skobelev, P.: A review of modern methods for planning and scheduling of the operations in advanced space systems. Mekhatronika, Avtomatizatsiya, Upravlenie **21**(11), 639–650 (2020)
7. SaVoir. https://www.taitussoftware.com/products/applications/savoir. Accessed 30 Mar 2021
8. STM. https://www.stm.com.tr/en/our-solutions/satellite-and-aerospace. Accessed 30 Mar 2021
9. AGI: STK Scheduler. https://www.agi.com/products/stk-specialized-modules/stk-scheduler. Accessed 30 Mar 2021
10. Rzevski, G., Skobelev, P.: Managing Complexity. WIT Press, Boston (2014)
11. Gorodetsky, V., Skobelev, P.: System engineering view on multi-agent technology for industrial applications: barriers and prospects. Cybernet. Phys. **9**(1), 13–30 (2020)
12. Belokonov, I., Skobelev, P., Simonova, E., et al.: Multiagent planning of the network traffic between nanosatellites and ground stations. Proc. Eng. Sci. Technol. Exp. Autom. Space Veh. Small Satellites **104**, 118–130 (2015)
13. Skobelev, P., Simonova, E., Zhilyaev, A., Travin, V.: Multi-agent planning of spacecraft group for earth remote sensing. In: Borangiu, T., Trentesaux, D., Thomas, A., McFarlane, D. (eds.) Service Orientation in Holonic and Multi-Agent Manufacturing. Studies in Computational Intelligence, vol. 640, pp. 309–317 (2016)

14. Vallado, D.A.: Fundamentals of Astrodynamics and Applications, 4th edn., vol. 12. Springer, New York (2013)
15. Iacopino, C., Palmer, P., Policella, N., et al.: How ants can manage your satellites. Acta Futura 9, 59–70 (2014)
16. He, L., Liu, X., Xing, L., Liu, K.: Hierarchical scheduling for real-time agile satellite task scheduling in a dynamic environment. Adv. Space Res. 63(2), 897–912 (2019)
17. He, L., Liu, X., Laporte, G., et al.: An improved adaptive large neighborhood search algorithm for multiple agile satellites scheduling. Comput. Oper. Res. 100, 12–25 (2018)
18. Peng, G., Dewil, R., Verbeeck, C., et al.: Agile earth observation satellite scheduling: an orienteering problem with time-dependent profits and travel times. Comput. Oper. Res. 111, 84–98 (2019)
19. Niu, X., Tang, H., Wu, L.: Satellite scheduling of large areal tasks for rapid response to natural disaster using a multi-objective genetic algorithm. Int. J. Disaster Risk Reduc. 28, 813–825 (2018)
20. Hosseinabadi, S., Ranjbar, M., Ramyar, S., et al.: Scheduling a constellation of agile Earth observation satellites with preemption. J. Qual. Eng. Prod. Optim. 2(1), 47–64 (2017)
21. Peng, S., Chen, H., Du, C., et al.: Onboard observation task planning for an autonomous Earth observation satellite using long shortterm memory. IEEE Access 6, 65118–65129 (2018)
22. Song, Y., Zhou, Z., Zhang, Z., et al.: A framework involving MEC: imaging satellites mission planning. Neural Comput. Appl. 32 (2019)
23. Du, Y., Wang, T., Xin, B., et al.: A data-driven parallel scheduling approach for multiple agile Earth observation satellites. IEEE Trans. Evol. Comput 24, 679–693 (2020)
24. Bonnet, J., Gleizes, M., Kaddoum, E., et al.: Multi-satellite mission planning using a self-adaptive multi-agent system. In: Proceedings of the SASO 2015, pp. 11–20 (2015)
25. Phillips, S., Parra, F.: A case study on auction-based task allocation algorithms in multi-satellite systems. In: AIAA 2021-0185. AIAA Scitech 2021 Forum (2021)
26. Picard, G., Caron, C., Farges, J., et al.: Autonomous agents and multiagent systems challenges in earth observation satellite constellations. Proc. AAMAS 2021, 39–44 (2021)
27. Wang, X., Wu, G., Xing, L.: Agile earth observation satellite scheduling over 20 years: formulations, methods, and future directions. IEEE Syst. J., 1–12 (2020)

Towards an Online Agent Based Collision Avoidance by Mobile Edge Computing

Igor Tchappi[1,2,3]([email]), André Bottaro[1], Frédéric Gardes[1], and Stéphane Galland[2]

[1] Orange Labs, 6 Avenue Albert Durand, 31700 Blagnac, France
[2] CIAD, Univ. Bourgogne Franche-Comté, UTBM, 90010 Belfort, France
[3] Faculty of Sciences, The University of Ngaoundere, Ngaoundere, Cameroon

Abstract. Even before the ongoing recent deployment of 5G technology, Mobile Edge Computing was already considered as a key driver towards the development of vehicular use cases having stringent latency and bandwidth requirements. This paper relies on 5G and proposes an agent-based collision avoidance system focusing on the Mobile Edge Computing. The general architecture of the proposal is described as well as the interactions between the involved entities of the system. The integration of trust used in social relationship brings out the flexibility of the proposal. Moreover, while some approaches neglect data preprocessing, in this paper we present the results of the online preprocessing of the data received by vehicles as a first step towards collision avoidance.

Keywords: Mobile Edge Computing · Multiagent system · Collision avoidance system · 5G

1 Introduction

Nowadays, road safety is a major public health issue. According to the World Health Organization, every year, the lives of approximately 1.4 million people are shortened as a result of road accidents [14]. More efficient and more safer transportation solutions are therefore essential for the functioning and prosperity of modern society. To this end, the automotive industry is moving towards a vision where vehicles are becoming increasingly automated, connected, and cooperative with each other for safer and more efficient driving. Actually, the trend towards connected vehicles is more and more possible nowadays thanks to the integrated sensors of vehicles and to the recent deployment of 5G (fifth generation technology standard for broadband cellular networks). 5G is widely announced as a key tool for cooperative connected vehicles, being considered instrumental as an enabler of vehicular services, as it guarantees low latency and reliability under high mobility and densely connected scenarios. One of the main pillars of 5G is Mobile Edge Computing (MEC). MEC brings processing, storage and networking capabilities closer to the edge of the cellular networks. MEC is a suitable solution for collision avoidance system [5].

© Springer Nature Switzerland AG 2021
F. Dignum et al. (Eds.): PAAMS 2021, LNAI 12946, pp. 279–290, 2021.
https://doi.org/10.1007/978-3-030-85739-4_23

Collision avoidance in vehicular networks has emerged as one of the most prominent and effective applications to tackle safety in transportation systems [5,7]. Collision avoidance is about alerting a driver through a message, a light, a sound, etc. and/or taking immediate actions like an emergency brake before a plausible collision. To this end, vehicles are equipped by an on-board unit (OBU) that periodically sends Cooperative Awareness Messages (CAM) containing information, such as the vehicle's speed, acceleration, direction, position, etc. This data is usually analyzed in order to check whether a collision is plausible or not [5]. Here, MEC - precisely an edge server - hosts the collision detection algorithms due to its substantial processing, storage and network resources.

Despite the interest of this research area, connected vehicles' cooperation is still at its early stage, particularly using 5G. In this paper, we propose a first step towards an architecture based on the powerful resources of MEC to online predict the future positions of vehicles, and therefore anticipate and avoid collision events between nearby vehicles. To this end, this paper focuses on the multiagent system field [13]. Multiagent systems have shown a great potential for solving problems in distributed environment by their ability to decompose a complex system into multiple autonomous entities (called agents) that interact with each other to achieve a desired global goal [13]. Moreover, multiagent systems have proven their efficacy of modeling mobile agents in transportation systems [11], as well as the objects used and shared by the agents. To enable a clear separation between the agents and the objects of the system, the paper uses the Agent & Artifact (A&A) framework [9]. In A&A, agents are intelligent entities, which are capable of flexible actions while artifacts are any type of resource or tool that agents can dynamically create, share, use, or manipulate.

The rest of this paper is organized as follows. Section 2 presents the related work. Section 3 presents the framework of our proposal and the description of involved entities. Section 4 is devoted to the experimental validation of the proposal. Finally Sect. 5 concludes this paper and presents future works.

2   Related Work

Safety in transportation systems is widely studied in literature [3]. Recently, MEC-based collision avoidance systems have started to get attention in Research. For instance, Vázquez-Gallego et al. [12] propose the general guidelines of a MEC-based cooperative collision avoidance system, which is designed to detect and track road hazards. In this approach, thanks to their sensors, vehicles send their status and detected hazards to a service allocated in the MEC infrastructure. This infrastructure processes provided information, and selectively informs every vehicle that comes close to a road hazard or to other vehicles. In these papers, due to the fact that their research is still ongoing, the authors do not present experiments of their proposals. Moreover, although detection of road hazards is an interesting point inside a collision avoidance system, predicting the future behavior of entities is also a very interesting point to tackle.

To tackle the problem of predicting the behaviors of vehicles or vulnerable road users for avoiding collision, Malinverno et al. [5] propose a MEC-based collision avoidance system allowing an alert to be sent in the case of a potential risk to either vehicles or vulnerable road users. To this end, the authors use a linear analytical approach for their collision avoidance system. However, linear models cannot describe the non stochastic nature of traffic [1]. Some recent results have brought out the added value of non parametric models such as deep learning models for traffic forecasting. However, most of the deep learning models applied for traffic forecasting nowadays focus on predicting macroscopic variables of traffic such as flow, average speed, density [4]. Therefore, deep learning models (supervised learning) applied for traffic forecasting of microscopic variables of traffic such as speed, position, acceleration etc. of vehicles in a real road traffic scenario for collision avoidance system are still an open issue.

Nguyen et al. [8] focus on vulnerable road users such as pedestrians. They explore possibilities for the exchange of safety mechanisms between pedestrians and cars. They use users smartphones to run collision detection algorithms. However, although the authors use MEC, many key computations are still on the smartphone side, having limited energy capacity, while MEC is wired. Moreover, since it is not the focus of the authors, they do not take into account, neither the autonomous characteristic of human drivers or autonomous cars, nor the trust in the interaction between vehicles and the infrastructure. To the current state of our knowledge, even with the best resources, an alert could be wrong, i.e., false positive (an alert is issued without actual risk) or false negative (an alert is not issued while there is a risk) [5]. We advocate using trust in order to improve the quality of alerts issued by MEC.

3   System Architecture

As stated before, the architecture relies on a multiagent system with an artifact based perspective (A&A). A&A framework is one of the standard metamodels that enable a clear separation between agents - here MEC and vehicles - and passive objects - here Base Stations (BS), as illustrated on Fig. 1 [9].

The agents of the system are autonomous and sociable, i.e., they are capable to communicate between them. The artifacts are used and shared by agents to make the communication possible. MEC agents communicate with vehicle agents using BS artifacts, that means a direct communication between a MEC agent and a vehicle agent is not possible since they are not co-located.

A vehicle agent can communicate with another vehicle agent directly, i.e., without passing by any BS artifact (e.g., using WiFi). Meanwhile, a MEC agent can communicate with another MEC agent directly (wired) without passing by BS artifacts. Detailed implementations of the coordination and cooperation between agents of the same type are out of the scope of this paper, as it focuses on interactions between agents of different types, i.e., interactions between vehicle agents and MEC agents. In the following, these entities are described.

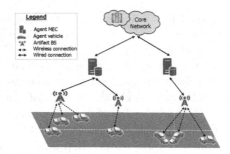

Fig. 1. The proposed multiagent MEC architecture

3.1   Base Station Artifact

A base station (BS) is a device in the land mobile service. It is a core equipment of the 5G network, providing wireless coverage and realizing wireless signal transmission between the wired communication network and the wireless terminals. In our proposal, BSs are passive and reactive entities in charge of the services and functions, those are enabling agents to work together in the multiagent system. Following this idea, the interactions between agents and artifacts are based on the notion of use, i.e., agents use artifacts to exploit their functionality [9].

Vehicle agents use BS artifacts to send their CAMs to the MEC agents. CAMs are sent by vehicle agents. Meanwhile, MEC agents use the artifact to communicate with vehicle agents to send the alerts.

3.2   Vehicle Agent

The vehicles are entities that could be involved in a collision: they are critical entities. Vehicles are equipped with an OBU. We propose here an agentification of the pair vehicle—driver. In other words a vehicle agent represents the pair vehicle—driver or an autonomous vehicle. The motivation of the agentification of a vehicle comes from the autonomy of the driving activity [6]. The agentification of a vehicle is still an active research field [10].

The vehicle agent behavior is depicted on Fig. 2 and described as follows. On the one hand, vehicle agents periodically broadcast their CAMs. Every CAM is composed by the uuid of the vehicle, a timestamp, a position (longitude, latitude, heading, yaw rate), speed, lateral, longitudinal and vertical accelerations, vehicle type, length, width, etc. On the other hand, vehicle agents could receive a warning, named DENM (Decentralized Environmental Notification Message), from MEC agents. A DENM typically contains data describing the warning, and the area the situation is valid for. What is done by vehicle agents upon receiving a DENM from a MEC agent depends on the situation. The receiving agent determines whether the warning is relevant or not, based on the included path history. If a warning is not relevant according to a given vehicle agent, the latter emits a DENM negation. Otherwise, if the warning sounds relevant, it may display a warning to the driver or perform an emergency braking.

In the proposal, we advocate performing most computations by the MEC agent in order to reduce the computations from the vehicle agents (keeping vehicle behaviors basic) due to their limited resources and energy.

3.3 MEC Agent

The paper proposes a general framework of the MEC agent able to fit with different types of collision algorithms. To this end, a MEC agent is structured by three layers: an online preprocessing layer, a collision detection layer, and a trust layer. This structure and the data flow between the layers are depicted in Fig. 2. A MEC agent receives CAMs from vehicle agents, process them, and predict the future positions of the vehicles. If a collision is plausible, then the agent creates a new DENM or updates a previous DENM, sends this latest DENM to vehicle agents. Using DENMs, MEC agents send alerts about on-road events such as potential collisions. MEC agent layers are detailed below.

Online Preprocessing Layer: The online preprocessing layer focuses on the creation and management of the dataset composed of CAMs over time. This includes checking whether any new CAM received from the vehicle agent is up-to-date and whether it is redundant. This checking is run every time a new CAM is received to prevent dataset from being corrupted. Moreover, CAMs with outliers such as *speed* < 0 are discarded.

Usually, the dataset is built with data recorded from sensors and stored in dedicated files or databases. Traditional dataset are therefore built around disk-based processing and batch data pipelines, making them insufficient for streaming online data as required in collision avoidance systems. Actually, disk-based technologies are not fast enough to process online streams. To solve this problem, recent applications in the field of business intelligence rely on in-memory processing. The decreasing price of computer memory chips makes in-memory computing increasingly viable to support online data streaming. This paper focuses on in-memory computing with an online preprocessing. The preprocessing steps are: feature selection, encoding, feature scaling and imputation.

- **Feature selection:** Each CAM broadcast by a vehicle agent is usually composed of about 50 variables. Some of these variables are useless for collision detection, e.g., vehicle length, width. They are dropped.
- **Encoding:** The goal is to encode the categorical data of the CAM such as the uuid of the vehicle. Our paper focuses on one-hot encoding techniques because it is easy to be designed and modified.
- **Normalization:** The values measured on various scales are adjusted to a notionally common scale. To normalize the dataset online, min-max normalization technique is used. The main drawback of the latter is the sensitivity to outliers. Presently however, by discarding the CAMs with wrong values such as *speed* < 0 and > 200 km/h, the number of outliers is reduced. Equation 1 defines min-max normalization, bringing values into $[0, 1]$ range.

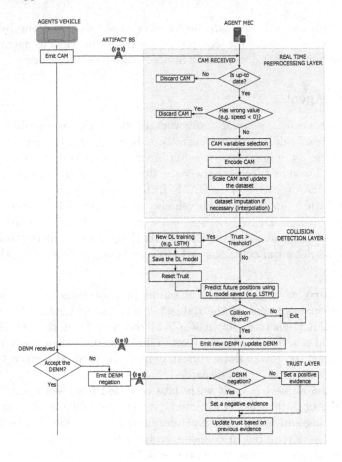

Fig. 2. Interaction between MEC agent and vehicle agent

$$X_{norm} = \frac{X - X_{min}}{X_{max} - X_{min}} \tag{1}$$

Since new CAMs arrive over time, the min-max normalization presented in Eq. 1 is not enough due to the in-memory processing. To take into account the online constraints, min-max normalization has to be reversed sometimes to get the original dataset, then min-max normalization is applied again to get a new maximum and minimum. Equation 2 presents the round trip min-max normalization suitable to fit with in-memory preprocessing. In Eq. 2, X_{max}^{old}, X_{min}^{old} are the old parameters used for the previous min-max normalization while X_{max}^{new}, X_{min}^{new} are the new parameters used for the current min-max normalization.

$$X_{norm}^{new} = \frac{X_{norm}^{old}(X_{max}^{old} - X_{min}^{old}) + X_{min}^{old} - X_{min}^{new}}{X_{max}^{new} - X_{min}^{new}} \tag{2}$$

Algorithm 1 is proposed for online min-max normalization (for each CAM). In this algorithm, when the dataset is empty (line 2 –line 7), the new CAM is added to the dataset and Eq. 1 is applied. After the initialization phase, Eq. 1 is applied (line 9 – line 12) when the data of the new CAM are lower than the current dataset maximum and higher than the current dataset minimum. In other situations, Eq. 2 is applied—here called MinMaxRound—to the dataset and Eq. 1 to the new CAM.

Algorithm 1. Min-Max Online Normalization

1: **function** NORMALIZATION($dataset, new\_CAM$)
2:     **if** $dataset = \emptyset$ **then**
3:         $min\_dataset \leftarrow min(new\_CAM)$
4:         $max\_dataset \leftarrow max(new\_CAM)$
5:         $scaled\_CAM = MinMax(new\_CAM)$ ▷ cf. Eq. 1
6:         $dataset \leftarrow dataset \cup scaled\_CAM$
7:         **return** $dataset, min\_dataset, max\_dataset$
8:     **else**
9:         **if** $min\_dataset \leq min(new\_CAM)$ & $max\_dataset \geq max(new\_CAM)$ **then**
10:            $scaled\_CAM = MinMax(new\_CAM)$ ▷ cf. Eq. 1
11:            $dataset \leftarrow dataset \cup scaled\_CAM$
12:            **return** $dataset, min\_dataset, max\_dataset$
13:        **else**
14:            **for all** $CAM \in dataset$ **do**
15:                $CAM \leftarrow MinMaxRound(CAM)$ ▷ cf. Eq. 2
16:            **end for**
17:            $min\_dataset \leftarrow min(min\_dataset, new\_CAM)$
18:            $max\_dataset \leftarrow max(max\_dataset, new\_CAM)$
19:            $scaled\_CAM = MinMax(new\_CAM)$
20:            $dataset \leftarrow dataset \cup scaled\_CAM$ ▷ cf. Eq. 1
21:            **return** $dataset, min\_dataset, max\_dataset$
22:        **end if**
23:    **end if**
24: **end function**

Collision Detection Layer: According to the flow chart presented in Fig. 2, below the online preprocessing layer, the dataset can be used for traffic forecasting. Traffic forecasting is the first goal of the collision detection layer. Traffic forecasting can be made by machine learning algorithms or deep learning algorithms such as LSTM (Long short-term memory) [2]. The proposal is intended to be general, therefore compatible with several types of deep learning algorithms.

Deep learning models are non parametric models that are sensitive to the data used to build them. Actually, the weights of deep learning models are directly linked to the dataset. Changes within the dataset could sometimes lead to reduce the performance of a deep learning model. Since the dataset is here dynamically built by vehicle CAMs, there are frequent changes in the dataset. Therefore, a fixed deep learning model for traffic forecasting could provide inconsistent results due to the frequent dataset update. Moreover, due to the high computational cost of the training phase of any deep learning model, and the high rate of CAMs arrival, training the deep learning model for each CAM does not seem appropriate. To deal with this issue, we advocate for the use of trust. Based on the value of trust, two possibilities are presented as depicted in Fig. 2. For readability sake, Fig. 2 does not account trends, cyclicity and seasonality management, sliding window creation, data conversion etc.

- *trust < threshold*: a new training is made to get the new weights of the deep learning model. Then, this model is saved and the trust value is reset.
- *trust ≥ threshold*: the last saved model is applied for traffic forecasting.

The second goal of the collision detection layer is to establish, based on the predictions made before, whether any two vehicles are susceptible to collide, emit a new alert or update an existing alert, i.e., with a standard DENM message.

Trust Layer: This layer manages the value of trust over time. The feedbacks received from vehicle agents are used to update the trust value. This property allows the definition of a centralized approach, described below, to manage the trust value over time. The approach is inspired by [15] works.

Let T_t the rating trust at time t. We require that $-1 < T_t < 1$ and $T_0 = 0$. Let α denotes a positive evidence ($\alpha \geq 0$) and β a negative evidence ($\beta < 0$). A negative evidence is applied when a vehicle agent denies an alert and a positive evidence in the other case. Equation 3 presents the update of trust in the case of positive evidence, and Eq. 4 in the case of negative evidence.

$$T_{t+1} = \begin{cases} T_t + \alpha(1 - T_t), & \text{if } T_t \geq 0. \\ (T_t + \alpha)/(1 - min\{|T_t|, |\alpha|\}), & \text{otherwise.} \end{cases} \quad (3)$$

$$T_{t+1} = \begin{cases} (T_t + \beta)/(1 - min\{|T_t|, |\beta|\}), & \text{if } T_t \geq 0. \\ T_t + \beta(1 + T_t), & \text{otherwise.} \end{cases} \quad (4)$$

4   Experimentation

This work is a first step towards a full system relying on the powerful resources of MEC and 5G capacity. Experiments are carried out on the preprocessing layer. The experiments on the two other layers will be presented in future works.

4.1   Time Lag of 5G for Vehicle—MEC Interaction

Present experiments have been carried out in Montlhéry, France within the trials of 5GCroCo European project. The goal of this project is to experiment

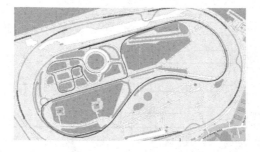

Fig. 3. Montlhéry study area with a small set of the trajectory of three vehicles

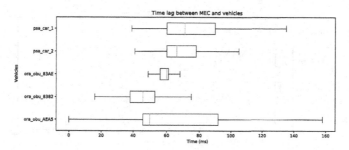

Fig. 4. Time lag between vehicles and MEC interaction without outliers

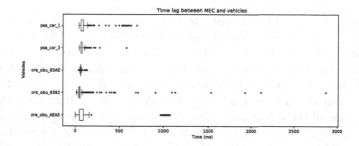

Fig. 5. Time lag between vehicles and MEC interaction with outliers

5G on real vehicles on the field. The project defines a path towards the provision of connected, cooperative and automated mobility services and reduces the uncertainties of a real 5G deployment.

Figure 3 depicts the trajectory of three vehicles: a vehicle in black for about 6.1s, a vehicle in green for about 1, 89s and a vehicle in blue for about 1.1s. Vehicles move on the track in one direction . 5G is used with 3600 Mhz frequency.

Several experiments have been made. On September 15th, 2020, 5 vehicles of the companies PSA, Renault and Orange are deployed. These vehicles were represented by their uuid psa_car_1, psa_car_2, ora_obu_83AE, ora_obu_8382 and ora_obu_AEA5. During the trials, these vehicles broadcast their CAMs at a fixed frequency depending on the vehicle type. The goal was to measure the latency

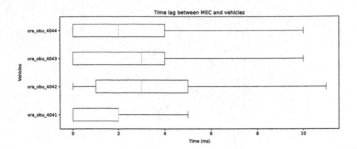

Fig. 6. Time lag between vehicles and MEC interaction without outliers (simulation)

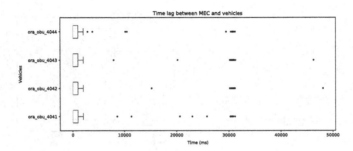

Fig. 7. Time lag between vehicles and MEC interaction with outliers (simulation)

from the vehicle to the MEC in order to bring out the added value of 5G in a real experiment. Figures 4 and 5 present the results of this latency. Work to reduce it is still ongoing. Note that Fig. 4 and Fig. 5 outline the same latency with the difference that, in Fig. 5, outliers (CAMs outside date) are drawn, while in Fig. 4; they are not. This choice is done because outliers prevent the visualization of quartiles. In fact, we can see that there are some CAMs with more than 2500 ms of time lag while most of the CAMs has a time lag below 100 ms (this is because for all the vehicles, the third quartile is below 100 ms). Because 2500 ms are too high for a collision avoidance system [5], such CAMs are discarded automatically in our online preprocessing as presented in Fig. 1 of the general architecture.

Another trial has been done November 13th, 2020. In the trial, there were 4 vehicles represented by their uuid those are ora_obu_4041, ora_obu_4042, ora_obu_4043, ora_obu_4044. In the trial, in order to preprocess the data online, the data of ora_obu_4041, ora_ob5u_4042, ora_obu_4043, ora_obu_4044 were gotten from the field, and replay in loop to simulate the online dataset preprocessing during about 4 h. Figure 6 and 7 present the time lag of the CAMs for the simulation. Even though the time lag are reduced compared to the real network lag of September experiment presented above, there are still some outliers appearing.

4.2 The Added Value of In-Memory Preprocessing

In the trial of November, for 4 vehicles and about 4 h of experiment, more than 170 000 CAMs were received. This raised out the need of dealing with an

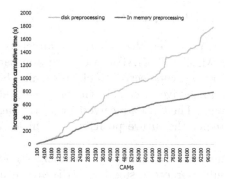

Fig. 8. A comparison between hard drive disk and in-memory preprocessing

increasing dataset. Moreover, because collision avoidance system is a critical system, CAMs are not processed by batch in our proposal as outlined in literature [5]. CAMs are preprocessed one by one [5]. Therefore, in this section we present the comparison between two approaches:

- **Hard drive disk preprocessing:** Each CAM received by vehicles (using JSON format) is stored in the dataset file within the disk. Then the entire dataset is loaded in memory from the dataset file for the preprocessing and collision avoidance checking. After collision avoidance checking, the memory is freed and the previous is repeated for the next CAM. The normalization is done by the classical min-max normalization presented in Eq. 1.
- **In-memory preprocessing:** For each CAM received by vehicles, there is an update of the dataset loaded in memory. As CAMs arrive, outliers are discarded, categorical variable of CAMs are encoded, and CAMs are normalized in memory without writing to the hard drive disk. The normalization is done by the online MinMax normalization presented by Eq. 2. The dataset is always ready to be used by a deep learning algorithm such as LSTM (since the dataset is always preprocessed and cleaned). In this approach, the whole dataset is stored on the disk only one time viz. at the end of the simulation.

Figure 8 presents the execution time of hard drive disk and in-memory preprocessings. The latter has noticeably a better computation time than hard drive disk preprocessing, which leads in-memory preprocessing to be a better solution for critical time constraints application such as collision avoidance systems. However, it should be noted that the experiments were done only with four vehicles. If the number of vehicles increase considerably for a long-term horizon, the number of received CAMs will also considerably increase and therefore bring out the issue of the scalability of the proposal. To deal with this issue, a trade-off could be a solution, i.e., save the too old CAMs, which are becoming useless for prediction, in disk and keep in memory only the useful CAMs. To this end, a static approach defining a time interval of writing data to the disk could be a possible solution. Moreover, a dynamic approach enabling the system to be adapted according to the traffic scenario could be also a plausible approach.

5   Conclusion and Future Works

In this paper, we have presented the general architecture of a collision avoidance system based on MEC and 5G. The proposed approach relies on a multiagent system with an artifact perspective to clearly make the distinction between autonomous entities and passive objects. In the proposal, vehicle agents exchange CAMs with MEC agents. The CAMs received by a MEC agent are preprocessed online in order to predict the future position of vehicles and therefore enable collision avoidance.

Future work will involve three main areas, namely, (i) defining the time interval required for the online preprocessing layer, (ii) presenting the outputs of the collision layer, and (iii) presenting the outputs of the trust layer as well as the impact of trust in MEC agent.

References

1. Fu, R., Zhang, Z., Li, L.: Using LSTM and GRU neural network methods for traffic flow prediction. In: 31st Youth Academic Annual Conference of Chinese Association of Automation (2016)
2. Hochreiter, S., Schmidhuber, J.: Long short-term memory. Neural Comput. **9**(8), 1735–1780 (1997)
3. Hughes, B.P., Newstead, S., Anund, A., Shu, C.C., Falkmer, T.: A review of models relevant to road safety. Accid. Anal. Prev. **74**, 250–270 (2015)
4. Lana, I., Del Ser, J., Velez, M., Vlahogianni, E.I.: Recent advances and new challenges. IEEE Intell. Transp. Syst. Road Traffic Forecast. (2018)
5. Malinverno, M., Avino, G., Casetti, C., Chiasserini, C.F., Malandrino, F., Scarpina, S.: Edge-based collision avoidance for vehicles and vulnerable users: an architecture based on MEC. IEEE Veh. Technol. Mag. **15**, 27–35 (2019)
6. Michon, J.A.: A critical view of driver behavior models: what do we know, what should we do? In: Evans, L., Schwing, R.C. (eds.) Human Behavior and Traffic Safety, pp. 485–524. Springer, Boston (1985). https://doi.org/10.1007/978-1-4613-2173-6_19
7. Mukhtar, A., Xia, L., Tang, T.B.: Vehicle detection techniques for collision avoidance systems: a review. IEEE Trans. Intell. Trans. Syst. **16**, 2318–2338 (2015)
8. Nguyen, Q., Morold, M., David, K., Dressler, F.: Car-to-pedestrian communication with MEC-support for adaptive safety of vulnerable road users. Comput. Commun. **150**, 83–93 (2020)
9. Omicini, A., Ricci, A., Viroli, M.: Artifacts in the A&A meta-model for multi-agent systems. Auton. Agent. Multi-Agent Syst. **17**, 432–456 (2008)
10. Pico-Valencia, P., Holgado-Terriza, J.A.: Agentification of the internet of things: a systematic literature review. Int. J. Distrib. Sens. (2018)
11. Tchappi, I., et al.: A critical review of the use of holonic paradigm in traffic and transportation systems. Eng. Appl. Artif. Intell. (2020)
12. Vázquez-Gallego, F., et al.: A mobile edge computing-based collision avoidance system for future vehicular networks. In: INFOCOM Workshops (2019)
13. Wooldridge, M.: An Introduction to Multiagent Systems. Wiley, Hoboken (2009)
14. World Health Organization: Mortality 2016 and 2060 - baseline scenario (2016)
15. Yu, B., Singh, M.P.: A social mechanism of reputation management in electronic communities. In: International Workshop on Cooperative Information Agents (2000)

Formal Specification of Fault-Tolerant Multi-agent Systems

Elena Troubitsyna$^{(\boxtimes)}$

KTH – Royal Institute of Technology, Stockholm, Sweden
elenatro@kth.se

Abstract. Multi-agent systems (MAS) are increasingly used in critical applications. To ensure dependability of MAS, we need to formally specify and verify their fault tolerance, i.e., to ensure that collaborative agent activities are performed correctly despite agent failure. In this paper, we present a formalisation of fault tolerant MAS and use it to define specification and refinement patterns for modelling MAS in Event-B.

Keywords: Formal modelling · MAS · Fault tolerance · Event-B

1 Introduction

Mobile multi-agent systems (MAS) are complex decentralised distributed systems composed of agents asynchronously communicating with each other. Agents are computer programs acting autonomously on behalf of a person or organisation, while coordinating their activities by communication [8,14]. MAS are increasingly used in various critical applications such as factories, hospitals, rescue operations in disaster areas etc. [1,6,7,9]. However, widespread use of MAS is currently hindered by the lack of methods for ensuring their dependability, and in particular, fault tolerance.

In this paper we focus on studying fault tolerance of agent cooperative activities. However, ensuring correctness of complex cooperative activities is a challenging issue due to faults caused by agent disconnections, dynamic role allocation and autonomy of the agent behaviour [4,5,10,11]. To address these challenges, we need the system-level modelling approaches that would support formal verification of correctness and facilitate discovery of restrictions that should be imposed on the system to guarantee its safety.

In this paper we propose a formalisation of properties of fault tolerant MAS and then demonstrate how to specify and verify them in Event-B [3]. The main development technique of Event-B is refinement. It is a top-down approach to formal development of systems that are correct by construction. The system development starts from an abstract specification which defines the main behaviour and properties of the system. The abstract specification is gradually transformed (refined) into a more concrete specification directly translatable into a system implementation. Correctness of each refinement step is verified by proofs.

© Springer Nature Switzerland AG 2021
F. Dignum et al. (Eds.): PAAMS 2021, LNAI 12946, pp. 291–302, 2021.
https://doi.org/10.1007/978-3-030-85739-4_24

These proofs establish system safety (via preservation of safety invariant properties expressed at different levels of abstraction) and liveness (via the provable absence of undesirable system deadlocks). Transitivity of the refinement relation allows us to guarantee that the system implementation adheres to the abstract and intermediate models. The Rodin platform [15] provides the developers with automated tool support for constructing and verifying system models in Event-B.

Our reliance of abstraction and stepwise refinement allows us to rigorously define and verify correctness of agent cooperative activities in presence of agent failure. We consider a hierarchical agent system, i.e., distinguish between the supervisor and subordinate agents. This introduces intricate details into handling the failures of different kinds and performing cooperative error recovery. Event-B allowed us to consider fault tolerance as a system-level property that can be verified by proofs. Hence,we argue that Event-B offers a useful formalisation framework for specification and verification of complex fault tolerant MAS.

2   Fault Tolerant MAS

2.1   Fault Tolerance

The main aim of fault tolerance is to ensure that the system continues to provide its services even in presence of faults [13]. Typically, fault occurrence leads to a certain service degradation. However, it is important to ensure that the system behaves in a predictable deterministic way even in presence of faults.

The main techniques to achieve fault tolerance are error processing and fault treatment [13]. Fault treatment is usually performed while the system is not operational, i.e., during the scheduled maintenance. In this paper, we focus on error processing part of fault tolerance.

Error processing comprises the fault tolerance measures applied while the system is operational. The purpose of error processing is to eliminate an error from the computational state and preclude failure occurrence. Error processing is usually implemented in three steps: error detection, error diagnosis, and error recovery. Error detection determines the presence of error. Error diagnosis evaluates the amount of damage caused by the detected error. Error recovery aims at replacing an erroneous system state with the error-free state.

There are three types of error recovery methods: backward recovery, forward recovery and compensation. Backward recovery tries to return the system to some previous error-free state. Typically, backward recovery is implemented by checkpointing, i.e., periodically, during the normal system operation, the state of the system is stored in the memory. In case of a failure, the system retrieves the information about the error-free state from the memory and resumes its functioning from this states. When implementing forward recovery, upon detection of an error, the system makes a transition to a new error-free state from which it continues to operate. Exception handling is a typical example of forward error recovery. Compensation, typical for complex transactions, is used when the erroneous state contains enough redundancy to enable its transformation to error-free state.

To implement fault tolerance, it is important to understand the types of faults that might occur in the system. A fault can be characterized by their nature, duration or extent [13]. When considering the nature of a fault, we distinguish between random, e.g., hardware failures and systematic faults, e.g., design errors.

Faults can also be classified in terms of their duration into permanent and transient faults. Once permanent fault has occurred, it remain in the system during its entire operational life, if no corrective actions are performed. Transient faults can appear and then disappear after a short time. Moreover, faults can be categorised according to their effect on the system as localized and global ones. Localized faults affect only a single agent. Global faults permeate throughout the system and typically affect some set of agents.

2.2 Fault Tolerant MAS

To achieve fault tolerance while developing MAS, we formally define MAS and the properties that its design should ensure.

Definition 1. A multi-agent system $\mathcal{MAS}$ is a tuple $(\mathcal{A}, \mu, \mathcal{E}, \mathcal{R})$, where $\mathcal{A}$ is a collection of different classes of agents, μ is the system middleware, $\mathcal{E}$ is a collection of system events and $\mathcal{R}$ is a set of dynamic relationships between agents in a MAS.

Each agent belongs to a particular class or type of agents A_i, $i \in 1..n$ such that $A_i \in \mathcal{A}$. An agent $a_{ij} \in A_i$ is characterised by its local state that consists of variables determining its behaviour and static attributes. Since agent might fail and be replaced by other agents, the set of agents in each class is dynamic. An agent might experience a transient failure and hence spontaneously disappear from the class and reappear again. Moreover, an agent might fail permanently, i.e., permanently disappear from its class. In a system with redundancy, a failed agent can be replaced by another agent, i.e., a new agent can appear in a class instead of the failed one. An agent might also leave a class in a normal predefined way when its function in the system is completed.

The system middleware μ can be considered as an agent of a special kind that is always present in the system and belongs to its own class. Middleware is fault free, i.e., it always provides its services. The responsibility of the middleware is to maintain the communication between the agents and provide some basic fault tolerance. For instance, middleware is responsible for detecting agent failures. Initially, a failure is considered to be transient. However, if an agent does not recover within a certain deadline then the middleware considers this agent to be failed permanently. When a new agent appears in the system, e.g., to replace the failed agent, middleware provides it with the connectivity with the rest of the agents.

Often some agents in MAS experience a transient loss of connectivity. In this case, middleware maintains their status and state to resume normal operation when the connection is re-established, i.e., provides a backward recovery service.

The system events $\mathcal{E}$ include all internal and external system reactions. An execution of an event may change the state of the middleware or agents.

Usually, a failure of an agent affects it capability to perform its functions, i.e., it might prevent a progress in some collaborative activities with the other agents. Each collaborative activity between different agents (or an agent and the middleware) is composed of a set of events. Hence, an agent failure might disable some events. Therefore, while modelling the behaviour of a MAS, we should also define the functions of the middleware as a set of events and reactions specifying the behaviour in case of transient and permanent faults, as well as explicitly specify the events representing error detection and recovery. Moreover, we should represent the impact of failures on collaborative activities via constraining the set of enabled events. Now we are ready to introduce the first property that a fault tolerant MAS should preserve.

The collaborative actions of fault tolerant MAS should preserve the following enabledness property:

Property 1. *Let $\mathcal{A}_{act}$ and $\mathcal{A}_{ina}$ be sets of active and inactive agents correspondingly, where $\mathcal{A} = \mathcal{A}_{act} \cup \mathcal{A}_{ina}$ and $\mathcal{A}_{act} \cap \mathcal{A}_{ina} = \varnothing$. Let $\mathcal{E}\mathcal{A}\mathcal{A}$ and $\mathcal{E}\mathcal{A}\mu$ be all the collaborative activities (sets of events) between agents and agents and between agents and middleware respectively. Moreover, for each $A \in \mathcal{A}$, let $\mathcal{E}A$ be a set of events in which the agent A is involved. Then*

$$\forall A \cdot \ A \in \mathcal{A}_{act} \Rightarrow \mathcal{E}A \in \mathcal{E}\mathcal{A}\mathcal{A}$$

and

$$\forall A \cdot \ A \in \mathcal{A}_{ina} \Rightarrow \mathcal{E}A \in \mathcal{E}\mathcal{A}\mu$$

This property defines the restrictions on agent behaviour in presence of failures. Essentially, it postulates that if an agent failed, i.e., has become inactive then it cannot participate in any collaborative activities until it recovers, i.e., becomes active. This property can be ensured by checking the status attributes of each agent that should be involved into a collaborative activity.

A collection of system events $\mathcal{R}$ consists of dynamic relationships or connections between active agents of the same or different classes. An agent relationship is modelled as a mathematical relation

$$R(a_1, a_2, ..., a_m) \subseteq C_1^* \times C_2^* ... \times C_m^*,$$

where $C_j^* = C_j \cup \{?\}$. A relationship can be *pending*, i.e., incomplete. This is indicated by question marks in the corresponding places of R, e.g., $R(a_1, a_2, ?, a_4, ?)$. Pending relationships are typically occur during the error recovery. If an agent fails then the middleware detects it, saves the status of an agent and actives the timer bounding the time of error recovery. If an agent recovers before the timeout then the relationships become complete, i.e., all the corresponding events become enabled. However, if an agent fails to recover, its failure is considered to be permanent. Then the middleware tries to replace the failed agent by a healthy one. If it succeeds in doing this then the relationships become complete.

Property 2. *Let $\mathcal{A}_{act}$ be a set of active agents. Let $\mathcal{E}\mathcal{A}\mathcal{A}$ be all the collaborative activities in which these active agents are involved. Moreover, for each agent $A \in$*

$\mathcal{A}_{act}$, let $\mathcal{R}_A$ be all the relationships it is involved. Finally, for each collaborative activity $CA \in \mathcal{EAA}$, let $\mathcal{A}_{CA}$ be a set of the involved agents in this activity. Then, for each $CA \in \mathcal{EAA}$ and $A_1, A_2 \in \mathcal{A}_{CA}$,

$$\mathcal{R}_{A_1} \cap \mathcal{R}_{A_2} \neq \varnothing$$

This property restricts the interactions between the agents – only the agents that are linked by relationships (some of which may be pending) can be involved into cooperative activities.

The system middleware μ keeps a track of pending relationships and tries to resolve them by enquiring suitable agents to confirm their willingness to enter into a particular relationships. Additional data structure $Pref_R$ associated with a relationship $R \in \mathcal{R}$ can be used to express a specific preference of one agents over other ones. The middleware then enforces this preference by enquiring the preferred agents first. Formally, $Pref_R$ is an ordering relation over the involved agent classes. Thus, for $R \subseteq C_1^* \times ... \times C_m^*$,

$$Pref_R \in C_1 \times ... \times C_m \leftrightarrow C_1 \times ... \times C_m.$$

A responsibility of the middleware is detect situations when some of the established or to be established relationships become pending and guarantee "fairness", i.e., no pending request will be ignored forever, as well as try to enforce the given preferences, if possible.

While developing a critical MAS, we should ensure that certain cooperative activities once initiated are successfully completed. These are the activities that implement safety requirements. The ensure safety we have to verify the following property:

Property 3. *Let* $\mathcal{EAA}_{crit}$, *where* $\mathcal{EAA}_{crit} \subseteq \mathcal{EAA}$, *be a subset containing critical collaborative activities. Moreover, let* $\mathcal{R}_{pen}$ *and* $\mathcal{R}_{res}$, *where* $\mathcal{R}_{pen} \subseteq \mathcal{R}$ *and* $\mathcal{R}_{res} \subseteq \mathcal{R}$, *be subsets of pending and resolved relationships defined for these activities. Finally, let* $\mathcal{R}_{CA}$, *where* $CA \in \mathcal{EAA}$ *and* $\mathcal{R}_{CA} \subseteq \mathcal{R}$, *be all the relationships the activity* CA *can affect. Then, for each activity* $CA \in \mathcal{EAA}_{crit}$ *and relationship* $R \in \mathcal{R}_{CA}$,

$$\square((R \in \mathcal{R}_{pen}) \leadsto (R \in \mathcal{R}_{res}))$$

where $\square$ *designates "always" and* $\leadsto$ *denotes "leads to".*

This property postulates that eventually all pending relationships should be resolved for each critical cooperative activity. It guarantees that error recovery terminates (either successfully or not).

"The system state p always leads to the state q" or, using the temporal logic notation, "$\square(p \leadsto q)$".

3 Formal Specification in Event B

We start by briefly describing our formal development framework. The Event-B formalism is a variation of the B Method [2], a state-based formal approach that promotes the correct-by-construction development paradigm and formal verification by theorem proving. Event-B has been specifically designed to model and reason about parallel, distributed and reactive systems.

Modelling in Event-B. In Event-B, a system specification (model) is defined using the notion of an *abstract state machine* [3]. An abstract state machine encapsulates the model state represented as a collection of model variables, and defines operations on this state, i.e., it describes the dynamic part (behaviour) of the modelled system. A machine may also have the accompanying component, called *context*, which contains the static part of the system. In particular, a context can include user-defined carrier sets, constants and their properties, which are given as a list of model axioms.

The machine is uniquely identified by its name M. The state variables, v, are declared in the **Variables** clause and initialised in the $Init$ event. The variables are strongly typed by the constraining predicates I given in the **Invariants** clause. The invariant clause might also contain other predicates defining properties that should be preserved during system execution.

The dynamic behaviour of the system is defined by the set of atomic events specified in the **Events** clause. Generally, an event can be defined as follows:

$$\textbf{evt} \mathrel{\widehat{=}} \textbf{any } vl \textbf{ where } g \textbf{ then } S \textbf{ end}$$

where vl is a list of new local variables (parameters), the guard g is a state predicate, and the action S is a statement (assignment). In case when vl is empty, the event syntax becomes **when** g **then** S **end**. If g is always true, the syntax can be further simplified to **begin** S **end**.

The occurrence of events represents the observable behaviour of the system. The guard defines the conditions under which the action can be executed, i.e., when the event is *enabled*. If several events are enabled at the same time, any of them can be chosen for execution non-deterministically. If none of the events is enabled then the system deadlocks.

In general, the action of an event is a parallel composition of assignments. The assignments can be either deterministic or non-deterministic. A deterministic assignment, $x := E(x, y)$, has the standard syntax and meaning. A non-deterministic assignment is denoted either as $x :\in Set$, where Set is a set of values, or $x :| P(x, y, x')$, where P is a predicate relating initial values of x, y to some final value of x'. As a result of such a non-deterministic assignment, x can get any value belonging to Set or according to P.

Event-B Semantics. The semantics of an Event-B model is formulated as a collection of *proof obligations* – logical sequents. Below we describe only the most important proof obligations that should be verified (proved) for the initial and refined models. The full list of proof obligations can be found in [3].

The semantics of Event-B actions is defined using so called before-after (BA) predicates [3]. A before-after predicate describes a relationship between the system states before and after execution of an event, as shown in Fig. 1. Here x and y are disjoint lists (partitions) of state variables, and x', y' represent their values in the after-state.

Action (S)	$BA(S)$
$x := E(x,y)$	$x' = E(x,y) \ \wedge \ y' = y$
$x :\in Set$	$\exists z \cdot (z \in Set \wedge x' = z) \ \wedge \ y' = y$
$x :\mid P(x,y,x')$	$\exists z \cdot (P(x,z,y) \wedge x' = z) \ \wedge \ y' = y$

Fig. 1. Before-after predicates

The initial Event-B model should satisfy the event feasibility and invariant preservation properties. For each event of the model, evt_i, its feasibility means that, whenever the event is enabled, its before-after predicate (BA) is well-defined, i.e., exists some reachable after-state:

$$A(d,c), \ I(d,c,v), \ g_i(d,c,v) \ \vdash \ \exists v' \cdot BA_i(d,c,v,v') \qquad \text{(FIS)}$$

where A is model axioms, I is the model invariant, g_i is the event guard, d are model sets, c are model constants, and v, v' are the variable values before and after the event execution.

Each event evt_i of the initial Event-B model should also preserve the given model invariant:

$$A(d,c), \ I(d,c,v), \ g_i(d,c,v), \ BA_i(d,c,v,v') \ \vdash \ I(d,c,v') \qquad \text{(INV)}$$

Since the initialisation event has no initial state and guard, its proof obligation is simpler:

$$A(d,c), \ BA_{Init}(d,c,v') \ \vdash \ I(d,c,v') \qquad \text{(INIT)}$$

Event-B employs a top-down refinement-based approach to system development. Development starts from an abstract system specification that models the most essential functional requirements. While capturing more detailed requirements, each refinement step typically introduces new events and variables into the abstract specification. These new events correspond to stuttering steps that are not visible at the abstract level. Moreover, Event-B formal development supports data refinement, allowing us to replace some abstract variables with their concrete counterparts. In that case, the invariant of the refined machine formally defines the relationship between the abstract and concrete variables.

To verify correctness of a refinement step, we need to prove a number of proof obligations for a refined model. The Event-B refinement process allows us to gradually introduce implementation details, while preserving functional correctness. The verification efforts, in particular, automatic generation and proving of the required proof obligations, are significantly facilitated by the Rodin platform [15]. Proof-based verification as well as reliance on abstraction and decomposition adopted in Event-B offers the designers a scalable support for the development of such complex distributed systems as multi-agent systems.

In the next section, we outline main principles of formal reasoning about MAS and their properties.

4   Specification of Fault Tolerant MAS in Event-B

In the Event-B specification of fault tolerant MAS, we are interested in verifying the properties related to convergence and correctness of fault tolerance:

- all pending relationships are eventually resolved;
- the given relationship preferences are enforced.

Properties of the first kind, i.e., eventuality properties, are especially important for multi-agent systems. Such properties are often of the form "The system state p always leads to the state q" or, using the temporal logic notation, "$\square(p \rightsquigarrow q)$".

Often we are interested in formulating the properties similar to the examples below:

- $\square$(new subordinate agent $\rightsquigarrow$ assigned supervisor agent);
- $\square$(an agent leaves the system $\rightsquigarrow$ all its relationships are removed);
- $\square$(a supervisor agent leaves the system $\rightsquigarrow$ all its subordinates are re-assigned);
- $\square$(a supervisor agent fails $\rightsquigarrow$ all its subordinate agents are re-assigned).

The responsibility of the middleware is detect situations when some of the established/ or to be established relationships become pending due to failres and guarantee "fairness", i.e., no pending request for collaboration will be ignored forever.

Next we present modelling patterns that allow us to express properties described above in the Event-B framework. The abstract machine MAS (omitted for brevity) defines two general types of agents defined by sets $ATYPE1$ and $ATYPE2$, which are subsets of the generic type $AGENT$. The status of agents (i.e., whether they active or not, i.e., failed) is stored in a function variables $status1$ and $status2$, which for agents of different types returns a value of the enumerated set $STATUS = \{active, inactive\}$. We encapsulate the other variables of the machine by the abstract variable $state$. The machine models recovery of the agents in the location, i.e. the operating system, and non-deterministic changes of their statuses due to failure or recovery. In Fig. 2 we define a machine $MAS1$. Essentially, the specification $MAS1$ introduces a new event $CooperativeActivity$ in the machine MAS. The we can define the following proposition:

Proposition 1. The machine $MAS1$ refines MAS and preserves Property 1, where
$\mathcal{A}_{act} = \{a \mid a \in a\_t1 \wedge status1(a) = active) \vee (a \in a\_t2 \wedge status2(a) = active\}$
and $\mathcal{A}_{ina} = \{a \mid (a1 \in a\_t1 \wedge status1(a1) = inactive) \vee (a \in a\_t2 \wedge status2(a) = inactive)\}$ and $\mathcal{EAA} = \{CooperativeActivity\}$
and $\mathcal{EA}\mu = \{Status1, Status2\}$

Proof: The proof of the proposition follows from two facts:

1. The rules REF_INV, REF_GRD and REF_SIM defined in Sect. 2 are satisfied
2. The event $CooperativeActivity$ is enabled only for active, i.e., healthy agents, i.e., the agents whose status evaluates to $TRUE$

In a MAS, the agents often fail only for a short period of time. After the recovery, the agent should be able to continue its operations. Therefore, after detecting an agent failure, the middleware should not immediately disengage the disconnected agent but rather set a deadline before which the agent should recover. If the failed agent recovers before the deadline then it can continue its normal activities. However, if the agent fails to do so, the location should permanently disengage the agent.

In the refined specification we define the variable $failed$ representing the subset of active agents that are detected as transiently failed $failed \subseteq coop\_agents$.

Moreover, to model a timeout mechanism, we define the variable $timer$ of the enumerated type $\{inactive, active, timeout\}$. Initially, for every active agent, the $timer$ value is set to $inactive$. As soon as active agent fails, its id is added to the set $failed$ and its timer value becomes $active$. This behaviour is specified in the new event $FailedAgent$.

An agent experiencing a transient failure can succeed or fail to recover, as modelled by the events $RecoverySuccessful$ and $RecovertFailed$ respectively. If the agent recovers before the value of timer becomes $timeout$, the timer value is changed to $inactive$ and the agent continues its activities virtually uninterrupted. Otherwise, the agent is removed from the set of active agents. The following invariant ensures that any disconnected agent is considered to be inactive:

$$\forall a \cdot (a \in coop\_agents \land timer(a) \neq inactive \Leftrightarrow a \in disconnected)$$

The introduction of an agent failure allows us to make a distinction between two reasons behind leaving the system by a supervisory agent – because its duties are completed or due to the disconnection timeout. To model these two cases, we split the event $AgentLeaving$ into two events $NormalAgentLeaving$ and $DetectFailedFreeAgent$ respectively.

While modelling failure of a supervisory agent, we should again have to deal with the property stating that if a supervisory agent fails then all its subordinate agents are re-assigned. In a similar way as above, the event $ReassignSupervisor$ is decomposed into two events $NormalReassignSupervisor$ and $DetectFailedAgent$. The second refinement step resulted in a specification ensuring that no subordinate agent is left unattached to the supervisor neither because of its normal termination or failure.

The second refinement step resulted in a specification ensuring that no subordinate agent is left unattached to the supervisor neither because of its normal termination or failure.

5   Related Work

Formal modelling of MAS has been undertaken by [6, 8, 10–12]. Our approach builds on these work. It is different from numerous process-algebraic approaches used for modelling MAS. Firstly, we have relied on proof-based verification that does not impose restrictions on the size of the model, number of agents etc. Secondly, we have adopted a system's approach, i.e., we modelled the entire system and extracted specifications of its individual components by decomposition. Such an approach allows us to express and formally verify correctness of the overall

```
Machine MAS1
Variables a_t1, a_t2, status1, status2, state
Invariants
    inv₁ : a_t1 ⊆ ATYPE1
    inv₂ : a_t2 ⊆ ATYPE1
    inv₃ : status1 ∈ a_t1 → STATUS
    inv₄ : status2 ∈ a_t2 → STATUS
    inv₅ : state : STATE
Events
    Initialisation ≙
        begin
            a_t1 := ∅
            a_t2 := ∅
            status1 := ∅
            status2 := ∅
            state :: STATE
        end

    Populate1 ≙
        any a1
        when
            a1 ∈ ATYPE1
            a1 ∉ a_t1
        then
            a_t1 := a_t1 ∪ {a1}
            status1(a1) := active
        end

    Status1 ≙
        any a1
        when
            a1 ∈ a_t1
        then
            status1(a1) :∈ STATUS
            state :∈ STATE
        end

    CooperativeActivity ≙
        any a1, a2
        when
            a1 ∈ a_t1
            a2 ∈ a_t2
            status(a1) = active
            status(a2) = active
        then
            state :∈ STATE
        end
    END
```

Fig. 2. Specification of a MAS with cooperative activity

$FailedAgent \cong$
  any a
  when
    $a \in coop\_agents \wedge a \notin failed$
  then
    $failed := failed \cup \{a\}$
    $timer(a) := active$
  end

$RecoveryFailed \cong$
  any a
  when
    $a \in failed \wedge timer(a) = active$
  then
    $timer(a) := timeout$
  end

Fig. 3. Failed agent and recovery failed events

$DetectFailedAgent \cong$
  Refines $ReassignSupervisor$
  any a, a_new
  when
    $a \in ran(assigned\_supervisor) \wedge a \notin last\_cooperated[cooperated] \wedge$
    $a\_new \in coop\_agents \wedge a\_new \neq a \wedge$
    $a \in disconnected \wedge timer(a) = timeout \wedge$
    $a\_new \notin disconnected \vee (a\_new \in disconnected \wedge timer(a\_new) = active)$
  then
    $coop\_agents := coop\_agents \setminus \{a\}$
    $assigned\_supervisor := assigned\_supervisor \Lsh$
        $(dom(assigned\_supervisor \vartriangleright \{a\}) \times \{a\_new\})$
    $disconnected := disconnected\{a\}$
    $timer := \{a\} \Lsh timer$
  end
$DetectFailedFreeAgent \cong$
  Refines $AgentLeaving$
  any a
  when
    $a \in coop\_agents \wedge a \notin ran(assigned\_supervisor) \wedge$
    $a \notin last\_cooperated[cooperated] \wedge a \in disconnected \wedge timer(a) = timeout$
  then
    $coop\_agents := coop\_agents \setminus \{a\}$
    $disconnected := disconnected\{a\}$
    $timer := \{a\} \Lsh timer$
  end

system, i.e., we indeed achieve verification of fault tolerance as a system level property. Finally, the adopted top-down development paradigm has allowed us to efficiently cope not only with complexity of requirements but also with complexity of verification. We have build a large formal model of a complex system by a number of rather small increments. As a result, verification efforts have been manageable because we merely needed to prove refinement between each two adjacent levels of abstraction.

6   Conclusion

In this paper, we have presented an approach to formal specification of fault tolerant MAS. We formalised the main properties of fault tolerant MAS that perform cooperative activities and supported by the middleware to achieve fault tolerance. We defined the specification and refinment patterns for the formal development of fault tolerant MAS in Event-N.

In our development we have explicitly modelled the fault tolerance mechanism that ensures correct system functioning in the presence of agent failures. We have verified by proofs the correctness and termination of error recovery. Formal verification process has not only allowed us to systematically capture the complex error detection and recovery but also facilitated derivation of the constraints that should be imposed on the behaviour of the agents of different types to guarantee a correct implementation of fault tolerant. As a future work, we are planning to apply the proposed approach to modelling interaction of autonomous agents that are subject of malicious rather than random faults.

References

1. Majd, A., Ashraf, A., Troubitsyna, E.: Online path generation and navigation for swarms of UAVs. In: Scientific Computing, pp. 1–12 (2020)
2. Abrial, J.-R.: The B-Book: Assigning Programs to Meanings. Cambridge University Press, Cambridge (2005)
3. Abrial, J.-R.: Modeling in Event-B. Cambridge University Press, Cambridge (2010)
4. Majd, A., Troubitsyna, E.: Data-driven approach to ensuring fault tolerance and efficiency of swarm systems. In: Proceedings of Big Data, vol. 2017, pp. 4792–4794 (2017)
5. Majd, A., Troubitsyna, E.: Towards a realtime, collision-free motion coordination and navigation system for a UAV fleet. In: Proceedings of ECBS, vol. 2017, pp. 111–119 (2017)
6. Troubitsyna, E., Pereverzeva, I., Laibinis, L.: Formal development of critical multi-agent systems: a refinement approach. In: Proceedings of European Dependable Computing Conference, pp. 156–161 (2015)
7. Vistbakka, I., Troubitsyna, E.: Modelling autonomous resilient multi-robotic systems. In: Calinescu, R., Di Giandomenico, F. (eds.) SERENE 2019. LNCS, vol. 11732, pp. 29–45. Springer, Cham (2019). https://doi.org/10.1007/978-3-030-30856-8_3
8. Vistbakka, I., Troubitsyna, E.: Modelling resilient collaborative multi-agent systems. J. Comput. **103**(4), 1–23 (2020)
9. Vistbakka, I., Troubitsyna, E.: Pattern-based goal-oriented development of fault-tolerant MAS in Event-B. In: Proceedings of International Conference on Practical Applications of Agents and Multi-Agent Systems, pp. 327–339 (2020)
10. Vistbakka, I., Majd, A., Troubitsyna, E.: Deriving mode logic for autonomous resilient systems. In: Sun, J., Sun, M. (eds.) ICFEM 2018. LNCS, vol. 11232, pp. 320–336. Springer, Cham (2018). https://doi.org/10.1007/978-3-030-02450-5_19
11. Majd, A., Vistbakka, I., Troubitsyna, E.: Formal reasoning about resilient goal-oriented multi-agent systems. Sci. Comput. Program. **148**, 66–87 (2019)
12. Majd, A., Vistbakka, I., Troubitsyna, E.: Multi-layered safety architecture of autonomous systems: formalising coordination perspective. In: Proceedings of 9th International Symposium on High Assurance Systems Engineering (HASE), pp. 58–65 (2019)
13. Laprie, J.C.: From dependability to resilience. In: 38th IEEE/IFIP International Conference on Dependable Systems and Networks, pp. G8–G9 (2008)
14. OMG Mobile Agents Facility (MASIF). www.omg.org
15. Rigorous Open Development Environment for Complex Systems (RODIN). IST FP6 STREP project. http://rodin.cs.ncl.ac.uk/

Integrating Valence and Arousal Within an Agent-Based Model of Emotion Contagion

Erik van Haeringen[(✉)] ⓘ, Charlotte Gerritsen ⓘ, and Koen Hindriks ⓘ

Vrije Universiteit Amsterdam, De Boelelaan 1111, 1081 HV Amsterdam, The Netherlands
e.s.van.haeringen@vu.nl

Abstract. Existing agent-based models of emotion contagion that account for the emotional diversity in groups have mostly focussed on the spread of categorical emotions (happy, sad, angry). In practice this raises problems with regard to how the spread of different emotions should interact. Can one be both very happy and very angry at the same time, or shift quickly between these states? And which emotion should determine the behaviour of an agent?

The present paper explores an alternative where dimensional emotions spread in a crowd and the emotional state of an agent equals its location in the valence-arousal space, corresponding to a single emotion. We propose an agent-based model that is an extension of the ASCRIBE model. Furthermore, building on recent work that found an attention bias in participants toward emotionally salient stimuli, we examine the effects of attention bias in the context of emotion contagion at the crowd level.

We have simulated a crowd in a soccer arena wherein several types of visitors react differently to the same events in the game (goals), with and without attention bias. Our results give a first indication that a dimensional approach to emotion contagion has the potential to solve these challenges without the need to model mood as an extra layer, though further study is required with regard to model validation and the translation from emotional state to behaviour in order to accurately simulate the complexity of real-world crowds that are emotionally diverse.

Keywords: Emotion contagion · Dimension theory · Attention bias · Agent-based model · Crowd simulation

1 Introduction

When a comedian tells a joke to a single listener this may evoke a different emotional response than when it is told in front of a packed theatre. The alignment of emotion at the group level is often called collective emotion. While in this example it can be assumed the members of the audience responded to the comedian, their emotion may also be affected directly by the emotions of other members of the audience, a phenomenon known as emotion contagion.

A growing number of studies over the past decade have used agent-based models to study the spread of emotion in large groups as the result of emotion contagion. They have focussed mainly on incidents where the safety of people in the crowd was in danger

© Springer Nature Switzerland AG 2021
F. Dignum et al. (Eds.): PAAMS 2021, LNAI 12946, pp. 303–315, 2021.
https://doi.org/10.1007/978-3-030-85739-4_25

and emotion contagion caused or contributed to the collective behavioural response. Accordingly, the spread of a single negative emotion, usually either fear or anger, is studied most frequently in the crowd. However, studies have indicated that positive emotions also spread via contagion in groups [1, 2]. This raises the question whether emotional interaction between group members in many scenarios may be too complex to capture using a single emotion.

Indeed, several agent-based models have been proposed where multiple emotions spread via emotion contagion [3]. Most of these models investigate the contagion of categorical emotions, often based on the OCC model that distinguishes 22 emotions based on appraisal [4]. However, the spread of multiple categorical emotions allows for complex states where an agent experiences multiple and even seemingly contradictory emotions simultaneously. This poses a challenge in translating such a state to a behavioural response of the agent and the contagion process among agents. Does the strongest emotion determine the behaviour and is this therefore the only emotion that is contagious, or do all emotions affect behaviour and the contagion process? And can a person experience high levels of two (opposite) emotions simultaneously?

A solution proposed by several studies is to use the Pleasure-Arousal-Dominance model to simulate the mood of an agent along three continuous axes [5, 6]. In this setup, mood acts like an intermediary between the emotions and behaviour of an agent. Emotion is mapped to affect the mood of the agent slightly and in turn affects the behaviour of the agent, thereby preventing erratic behaviour from fast changes in emotion.

In the present paper we propose a more parsimonious alternative by modelling emotions directly along two continuous axes, valence and arousal, based on the circumplex model of emotion [7]. The emotional state of an agent equates to a single location in this two-dimensional space. Areas in this space are labelled as a type of emotion to facilitate human interpretation, thus resulting in a single emotion label for the state of an agent at any time. For this purpose, the ASCRIBE model [8], an often used model of emotion contagion that is agent-based, was extended for valence and arousal to spread simultaneously and independently among agents. The ASCRIBE model was chosen because contrary to epidemiological-based models, it considers contagion on a continuous scale [3]. Also, it has been validated using footage of real crowds and was found to compare favourably in relation to several other models of emotion contagion.

Our aim is to investigate the dynamics of the proposed model and test whether it remedies the problems encountered with categorical emotions. For this purpose, we simulate a crowd in a soccer arena wherein several types of visitors react differently to the same events in the game (goals) and multiple emotions spread among the stationary agents. We expect that the transitions in the emotion state of an agent due to contagion occur gradually, where an agent under the influence of others with an opposite emotional state first becomes less emotional or transitions to an emotional state that is nearby its original state.

Furthermore, in a recent publication Goldenberg et al. (2020) let participants estimate the emotion of the crowd and found that this estimation was biased towards others with stronger facial expressions, thus resulting in a skewed assessment in the presence of strong emotions [9]. We hypothesize that if observing emotions triggers an emotional response and this observation is an overestimation, this results in amplification at the group level of the strongest emotions in the crowd. Therefore, in the present paper we also investigate the effect of an attention bias towards agents with a strong expression of emotion.

2 Methods

2.1 Emotion Contagion in the ASCRIBE Model

With the ASCRIBE model the authors considered the spread of a single categorical emotion among agents [8]. Emotion is expressed as a continuous number between 0 and 1, where 0 represents the lowest level or absence and 1 the highest level of emotion. The contagion process is divided in two aspects, 1) the emotion channel through which emotion flows and 2) the potential emotional influence the sender has on the receiver.

The first aspect, the width of the emotion channel, is determined by the personality of the agents that are involved and the social or physical distance between them. The second aspect, the influence the emotional expression of the sender has on the receiver in ASCRIBE, is determined by a blend of two processes: absorption and amplification. Absorption represents the tendency for the receiving agent to adjust its emotion to its surroundings. When considering only absorption in a group, over time the emotions of its members approach each other and eventually reach an equilibrium, the value of which always lays within the range of emotion that was present at the start. Amplification, despite its name, represents the ability for emotional escalation or de-escalation of the emotion of the receiver when its emotion matches that of its surrounding. Whether the amplification process escalates or deescalates emotion or behaves similar to absorption is determined by a characteristic of the receiving agent. Note that amplification can therefore result in collective emotion beyond the emotional range that was present at the start, providing the ability to simulate emotional spirals like a spontaneous outbreak of panic in a crowd due to emotion contagion.

2.2 The Proposed Model

In the present paper we extend the ASCRIBE model and propose a model for emotion contagion in two dimensions of emotion, namely valence and arousal. Different from ASCRIBE, both dimensions range from strongly negative at -1 to strongly positive at 1, where 0 represents a neutral state. Contagion of valence and arousal occurs simultaneously and independently among agents.

The change in valence and arousal of an agent (ΔE_r) due to contagion is the result of the total connection strength between the receiver and its neighbours, times the emotional influence for that dimension of emotion.

$$\Delta E_{r_{valence}} = \langle connection \rangle * \langle influence_{valence} \rangle$$
$$\Delta E_{r_{arousal}} = \langle connection \rangle * \langle influence_{arousal} \rangle \tag{1}$$

Connection Strength. How much of the emotional influence can flow from the senders to the receiver is determined by the strength of the connection between each sender and the receiver. We assume that there is only one channel between a receiver and a sender.

Therefore, the connection strength influences contagion of valence and arousal equally. The total connection strength (Γ_r) between a receiver and its neighbours is given by the sum of the individual connection strengths between the receiving agent and each of the senders (γ_{sr}) in the group Nr.

$$connection = \Gamma_r = \sum_{s \in N_r} \gamma_{sr} \tag{2}$$

The strength of the connection between two agents (γ_{sr}), a sender and a receiver, is determined by three components. The first is the personality characteristic openness (δ_r) of the receiver that represents the tendency to take up affective information. The second is the channel strength between both agents (α_{sr}), which in the present paper is defined as the inverse distance between the agents in space. Last is the weighted attention (θ_s^*) of the receiver for the sender. We assume that an agent has a limited amount of attention and distributes this among its neighbours [10]. The weighted attention (θ_s^*) represents the share of attention a sender claims in the context of competition.

$$\gamma_{sr} = \theta_s^* \alpha_{sr} \delta_r \tag{3}$$

To calculate the weighted attention θ_s^* for a sender, we take the potential attention (θ_s) the sender could receive plus a basic level of attention every sender receives ($1/N$) and weigh this to that of all senders in group N_r. The relative importance of the potential attention (θ_s) is determined by the constant κ_1, that is set to 1 in the present paper.

$$\theta_s^* = \frac{\frac{1}{N} + \kappa_1 \theta_s}{1 + \kappa_1 \sum_{c \in N_r} \theta_c} \tag{4}$$

Without a bias in attention towards emotional stimuli, the potential attention (θ_s) a sender claims is equal to the personality characteristic expressiveness (ε_s) of the sender, that represents its tendency to show or voice its affective state.

$$\theta_s = \varepsilon_s \tag{5}$$

Emotional Influence. The emotional pressure from a group of neighbours on a receiver is determined by the nett emotion the receiver observes and the tendency of the receiver to dampen, absorb or amplify this perceived nett emotion. Note that the term emotion here can be replaced by either valence or arousal that are calculated independently. To get the nett emotion (E_s^*) of the group of senders (N_r) as observed by the receiver, the emotion of each sender is weighed by the channel strength of the sender (γ_{sr}) against the overall channel strength (Γ_r) of the group.

$$E_s^* = \sum_{s \in N_r} \frac{\gamma_{sr} E_s}{\Gamma_r} \tag{6}$$

In ASCRIBE the tendency of the receiver to amplify or absorb was based on two separate processes, the balance of which was set via two parameters. However, because the amplification process in ASCRIBE can mimic the result of the absorption process with the setting of a single parameter (see appendix 1 for an example), in the proposed model we simplified the emotional influence to one process based on the amplification process in ASCRIBE. In the proposed model, one characteristic of the receiver determines the tendency of a receiver to dampen ($\beta_r < 0.5$), absorb ($\beta_r = 0.5$) or amplify ($\beta_r > 0.5$) the emotions of its neighbours. To accommodate for the extended range of emotion in the proposed model (from -1 to 1), the total emotional influence of the senders on the receiver is calculated differently depending on three conditions. First, when both the emotion of the receiver (E_r) and the weighted average of the senders (E_s^*) is on the positive side of the scale, the influence is calculated in the same manner as the amplification process was in ASCRIBE. Second, if both the receiver and the average of its neighbours are on the negative end of the scale, influence is calculated like in ASCRIBE and then inverted. Lastly, when the receiver and its neighbours have an opposite polarity, the emotion is the difference between the weighted emotion of the senders modulated by β_r and the emotion of the receiver modulated by $1 - \beta_r$.

$$IF\,(E_s^* \geq 0)\&(E_r \geq 0)$$
$$influence = \beta_r(1 - 1(-|E_s^*|)(1 - |E_r|)) + (1 - \beta_r)E_s^*E_r - E_r$$
$$ELSE\ IF\,(E_s^* \leq 0)\&(E_r \leq 0)$$
$$influence = -(\beta_r(1 - (1 - |E_s^*|)(1 - |E_r|)) + (1 - \beta_r)E_s^*E_r) - E_r$$
$$ELSE$$
$$influence = \beta_r * E_s^* - (1 - \beta_r) * E_r \tag{7}$$

Figure 1 shows the emotional influence for different levels of emotion of the receiver and its neighbours for three levels of characteristic β_r of the receiver. The lower-left and upper-right quadrants show that the reaction of a receiver to neighbours with the same emotion polarity depends on the setting of β_r. A positive β_r amplifies the emotion of the receiver (towards 1 or -1 depending on the polarity), a neutral β_r pulls the emotion of the receiver towards that of the senders (absorption), and a negative β_r dampens the emotion of the receiver (towards 0). The upper-left and lower-right quadrants show the scenarios where the polarity of emotion differs between the receiver and senders. In this case the emotion of the receiver is pulled towards that of the senders, the rate of which is determined by β_r. Note that the amount of influence that can flow towards the receiver is determined by the connection strength as shown in Eq. 1.

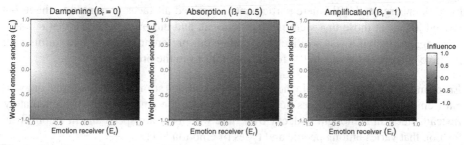

Fig. 1. Emotional influence as a function of the emotion of the receiving agent and the weighted emotion of the senders, shown for three levels of characteristic β_r.

Bias Towards Salient Emotional Stimuli. Judging the emotional state of a crowd requires fast evaluation of many stimuli, while people are generally assumed to have a limited capacity to do so. In recent work, Goldenberg et al. performed an experiment in which participants had to judge the average emotion of a set of faces with varying emotional expressions on a monitor [9]. The authors found that people overestimated the average emotion in a crowd, especially when this emotion was negative, and did so increasingly with a larger crowd and longer exposure time.

Then to explore what mechanism underlies this overestimation, Goldenberg and colleagues tracked the eye movement of the participants and found that emotional expression of a face did not affect whether a face was examined by the participant. Yet, when considering the dwell time, the duration with which a participant examined each face was found to be correlated with the strength of the emotional expression on the face. Moreover, the estimation error increased rather than decreased with the number of presented faces and longer exposure time to the faces. According to the authors, this hints at a preference in attention for faces that express strong emotions, rather than a selection bias for expressive faces due to constraints in how many faces could be processed in the given time.

Following these findings, we investigate the effect of attention bias on the spread of emotions in the crowd. We implemented a bias towards emotional salient stimuli in the proposed model via the potential attention (θ_s) a sender receives, replacing Eq. 5. The potential attention θ_s an agent receives is determined by both the expressiveness of the sender (ε_s) and its emotional state (E_d). To determine a single value for the potential attention of a sender over multiple dimensions of emotion (here dim = {valence, arousal}), we calculate the distance towards the neutral state of zero. To model a preference of the receiver for negative or positive stimuli two components are added, the balance between which is set by parameter μ_r, where $\mu_r < 0.5$ represents a preference towards negative emotions and $\mu_r > 0.5$ towards positive emotions.

$$\theta_s = \sum_{d \in dim} \left(|E_d| * \varepsilon_s + \mu_r * \left(2 - \frac{E_d + 1}{2} \right) + (1 - \mu_r) * \left(\frac{E_d + 1}{2} \right) \right)^2 \quad (8)$$

The result of attention bias is that a larger share of the attention goes to agents with a stronger expression of emotion, yet all agents receive a basic level of attention and no agents are ignored by the receiver (Fig. 2). This description corresponds to the findings by Goldenberg et al. [9] where participants examined all faces presented to them, but looked longer at those that were more emotional, and did more so when that emotion was negative than if it was positive. To simulate this preference for negative stimuli over positive stimuli, we set μ_r to 0.4 for all simulations in the present paper.

Emotional Self-regulation. In the absence of emotional stimuli (either internal or external), emotion in a person does not persist, nor does the emotion vanish immediately. Instead, emotion is thought to decay over time with a certain speed and in a non-linear fashion that varies among people and types of emotion [11].

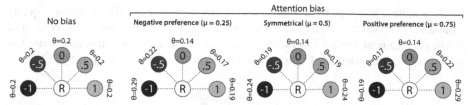

Fig. 2. Effect of attention bias in the distribution of attention of receiver R towards a group of senders (surrounding circles) for three preferences of stimuli type (μ_r). For simplicity only one dimension of emotion is shown. The emotions of the senders are indicated in the circles and the attention (θ_s) that the sender receives is indicated outside of the circle. In this example all senders have the same expressiveness ε_s set to 0.5.

In the proposed model, an agent can become less emotional, i.e. closer to the zero point on the axes of valence and arousal, when it meets others with an opposite emotion or via dampening ($\beta_r < 0.5$). Yet based on these processes, when an agent would not meet other agents, it would maintain its level of emotion indefinitely. Hence, we have added a function of emotion decay to the proposed model. According to Hudlicka [11] an exponential or logarithmic decline is more realistic than a linear decline for emotional decay. Therefore, we chose a logit function, as this is similar to an exponential relation that is mirrored in the negative direction to account for the decay of negative valence and arousal.

Preceding the contagion process, the emotion of the receiver is reduced depending on the decay rate λ_r of the receiver and its current level of emotion (E_r). A higher λ_r results in a faster decay of emotion, while at a decay rate of zero there is no decay of emotions (See appendix 2 for an example). The constant κ_2 sets the curve of the line, where a value approaching one results in a more curved line while a value approaching infinity results in a line that is approx. linear. In the present paper κ_2 was set to 1.1.

$$\Delta E_r = -\lambda_r * \log \frac{\frac{1}{2}\left(1 + \frac{E_r}{\kappa_2}\right)}{1 - \frac{1}{2}\left(1 + \frac{E_r}{\kappa_2}\right)} \tag{9}$$

Mapping to Categorical Emotions. To improve human interpretability of the results, locations in the valence and arousal space are commonly mapped to categorical emotions. However, currently there exists no clear consensus about how indicative the dimensions of valence and arousal are for specific categorical emotions, nor a generally agreed upon model of how continuously measured emotion should be translated to emotion labels that are used in everyday life.

As a starting point, we have chosen eight emotions and a neutral state that are equally separated in the valence-arousal space and we estimate to be relevant in the context of crowd management. Figure 3 shows the area that is associated with these emotions. The locations of the emotion labels are a simplification of the space described by [12].

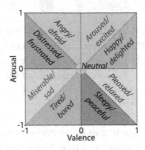

Fig. 3. Mapping of the valence-arousal space to emotion labels.

3 Results

To study the spread of continuous emotion in an emotion-rich environment, we simulated a soccer match that is visited by 2900 agents in an arena. The agents respond emotionally to the events on the field, specifically to a goal for the home team after 50 steps and a goal for the away team after 500 steps. How an agent responds to these events depends on what type of visitor the agent is. Agents with the same type are placed together in sections of the arena inspired by the arrangement in some Dutch soccer arenas (Fig. 4). There are three types of agents that support the home team. The valence of these agents increases when the home team scores and decreases when the away team scores, where the family-type agents respond mildly, regular supporters at an intermediate level and fanatic supporters respond strongly (Table 1). For the away team we assume mostly the highly motivated fans travelled to support their team and thus behave similarly to the fanatic supporter except the valence reaction is reversed to the home and away goal. Arousal increases for all agents after each goal, where family-type agents stay relatively calm, regular supporters get somewhat excited and the fanatic and away supporters become most excited. Lastly the family-type agents have a tendency to absorb emotion, thereby adjusting to their environment, while regular and to a higher degree fanatic and away supporters have the tendency to amplify emotional stimuli when they match their own emotion.

Since the simulations did not contain any stochastic elements, one run was performed per condition. Each simulation was run for 1000 timesteps, recording the levels of valence and arousal of every agent. To focus on the contagion mechanism, behaviour was not considered. See Appendix 3 for a complete list of parameter settings.

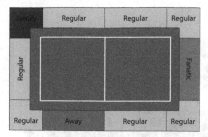

Fig. 4. Distribution of agent types over sections of the soccer arena.

Table 1. Parameter settings for agent types

Agent type	N	β_r	Response home goal		Response away goal	
			E_{val}	E_{aro}	E_{val}	E_{aro}
Regular	2000	0.6	0.3	0.3	−0.3	0.3
Fanatic	330	0.7	0.5	0.5	−0.5	0.5
Family	240	0.5	0.3	0.1	−0.1	0.1
Away	330	0.7	−0.5	0.5	0.5	0.5

3.1 Contagion in a Multi-emotion Environment

To first investigate the contagion of continuous emotions, Fig. 5 shows the results of a run without an attention bias. At the start of the run, all agents have a neutral emotional state and no contagion takes place until an event (goal) evokes an emotional response in all agents at step 50. After this step only contagion and decay affect the emotions of the agents until the second event at step 500.

Several differences can be observed among the types of agents in Fig. 5B, not only in the one-step response to the event, but also in the contagion and decay process that follows. The family-type agents react mildly happy/delighted to the events and afterwards their emotional response quickly fades. This happens because these agents have the tendency to absorb instead of strengthen similar emotions and the emotional influence of the surrounding supporters is less than the decay due to self-regulation. Their emotion however does impact the regular supporters that are close, who become less aroused and change from aroused/excited to happy/delighted.

In contrast, the fanatic- and away-type of agents respond strongly to the events and, while there is some decay after the initial emotional stimulus, these supporters amplify each other enough to compensate for emotion decay, finding an equilibrium. Notable is the difference between the fanatic and away supporters in the response to the (to them) negative event. While their initial emotion response is the same, the valence of the away supporters is reduced stronger (towards 0) due to contagion than in the fanatic supporters. This is because both groups are bordered by the regular supporters that express a similar though less extreme sentiment to the fanatic supporters while contrasting the away supporters. This also effects the regular supporters, as can be seen in Fig. 5A, where at step 150 and 600 in the areas where the away and regular supporters border the emotion of some regular agents was extinguished and those closest to the away group adopted the emotion of the away group, though to a lesser degree. Oppositely, at the border between the fanatic and regular supporters the emotion of the regular supporters is stronger compared to other regular supporters.

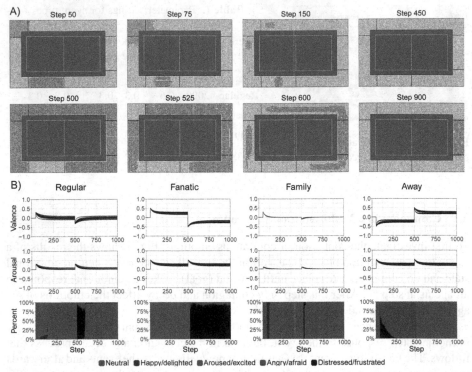

Fig. 5. Simulation of visitors to a soccer game without attention bias. A) Illustration of the spread of emotions among agents over time. Note that the colours correspond to Fig. 3 and do not express the strength of the emotion. B) Development of emotion over time per agent-type, shown as a line per agent for valence and arousal and as the percentage of agents with an emotion label.

3.2 Attention Bias Towards Emotional Salient Stimuli

Next, to study the effect of an attention bias in the context of emotion contagion in a crowd, Fig. 6 shows the results of the same experiment as before but with attention bias. Comparing Fig. 5 to Fig. 6, it can be observed that there is amplification of the agents that express strong emotions (fanatic & away supporters), with less decay of emotion and less influence of the bordering agent type (regular supporters). The regular supporters are influenced more strongly by the fanatic and away supporters with attention bias enabled (see for example the larger group of regular supporters that adopts the sentiment of the away supporters). The family-type supporters do not express strong emotions, yet still impact the emotions of nearby regular supporters. This most likely is because each sender always receives a basic share of attention and, as both family and regular supporters do not express strong emotions, the impact of attention bias is relatively small.

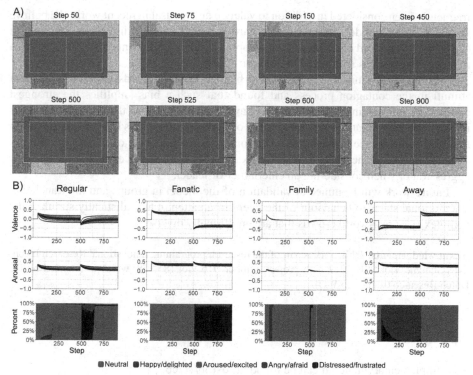

Fig. 6. Simulation of visitors to a soccer game with attention bias.

4 Discussion

With the present paper we took a dimensional approach to the spread of emotions in large groups, where valence and arousal spread independently yet together represented the emotional state of an agent. The location in valence-arousal space was mapped to a categorical emotion label to make the results more interpretable for humans.

Our results demonstrate that a dimensional approach to emotion contagion has the potential to solve problems arising from the contagion of multiple categorical emotions without the need to model mood as an extra layer. Because the dimensional emotions spread independently but together form a single emotional state, this results in more stable transitions of emotion over time. Although we do not model mood explicitly, it can be argued that mood is an emergent property that arises from the tendency to keep the same emotional state in the proposed model (e.g., frustrated) or shift to a nearby state following emotional input (angry), instead of an emotion that is distant in the valence-arousal space (peaceful). Important to note is that while mapping the multi-dimensional space to categorical emotion labels makes the results easier to interpret for humans, currently there exists no consensus on what dimensions of emotion should be considered and what the exact locations are of emotion labels in the space these dimensions form. Future work may therefore also consider exploring additional or alternative dimensions of emotion in the context of contagion. The dimension of dominance for example has frequently been considered in addition to valence and arousal in recent work. We believe that the proposed model offers a suitable starting point for this as dimensions of emotion can easily be replaced or added and the mapping used in the present paper can be refined to more precise areas in the chosen emotion space.

Further, we examined the effect of a bias of agents towards emotionally salient stimuli in the contagion process and found that such a bias amplifies the strongest emotion in surrounding agents, yet does have a large impact on the contagion process in an environment that is emotionally poor or homogeneous. This kind of amplification may be of importance in scenarios where one or some members of the crowd strongly deviate from the general sentiment, for example in the case of a sudden calamity or aggression or when considering an entertainer or leader.

Future work will be aimed at validation of the model in groups and the translation of emotional states to behaviour of the agent in an attempt to realistically simulate the complexity of real-world crowds that are emotionally diverse.

Acknowledgements. This work is part of the research programme Innovational Research Incentives Scheme Vidi SSH 2017 with project number 016.Vidi.185.178, which is financed by the Dutch Research Council (NWO).

Appendix

The supplementary material can be found at: osf.io/vt7c6.

References

1. Bono, J.E., Ilies, R.: Charisma, positive emotions and mood contagion. Leadersh. Quart. **17**, 317–334 (2006)
2. Kramer, A.D.I., Guillory, J.E., Hancock, J.T.: Experimental evidence of massive-scale emotional contagion through social networks. Proc. Natl. Acad. Sci. U.S.A. **111**, 8788–8790 (2014)
3. van Haeringen, E.S., Gerritsen, C., Hindriks, K.V.: Emotion contagion in agent-based simulations of the crowd. Vrije Universiteit Amsterdam, Technical report (2021)
4. Ortony, A., Clore, G.L., Collins, A.: The Cognitive Structure of Emotions. Cambridge University Press, New York (1988)
5. Durupinar, F., Gudukbay, U., Aman, A., et al.: Psychological parameters for crowd simulation: from audiences to mobs. IEEE Trans. Visual Comput. Graph. **22**, 2145–2159 (2016)
6. Bordas, J., Tschirhart, F.: Contaminating crowds' emotional states. In: Proceedings of the 2014 Summer Simulation Multiconference, vol. 46, pp. 300–308. The Society for Modeling and Simulation International, San Diego (2014)
7. Russell, J.A.: A circumplex model of affect. J. Pers. Soc. Psychol. **39**, 1161–1178 (1980)
8. Bosse, T., Hoogendoorn, M., Klein, M.C.A., et al.: Modelling collective decision making in groups and crowds: integrating social contagion and interacting emotions, beliefs and intentions. Auton. Agent. Multi-Agent Syst. **27**, 52–84 (2013)
9. Goldenberg, A., Weisz, E., Sweeny, T., et al.: The crowd emotion amplification effect. Psychol. Sci. **31**, 437–450 (2021)
10. Whitney, D., Yamanashi, L.A.: Ensemble perception. Annu. Rev. Psychol. **69**, 105–129 (2018)

11. Hudlicka, E.: Computational analytical framework for affective modeling: towards guidelines for designing computational models of emotions. In: Handbook of Research on Synthesizing Human Emotion in Intelligent Systems and Robotics, pp. 1–62. IGI Global, Hershey (2014)
12. Russell, J.A., Barrett, L.F.: Core affect, prototypical emotional episodes, and other things called emotion: dissecting the elephant. J. Pers. Soc. Psychol. **76**, 805–819 (1999)

Towards a Versatile Intelligent Conversational Agent as Personal Assistant for Migrants

Leo Wanner[1,2(✉)], Matthias Klusch[3], Athanasios Mavropoulos[4],
Emmanuel Jamin[5], Víctor Marín Puchades[5], Gerard Casamayor[2],
Jan Černocký[6], Steffi Davey[7], Mónica Domínguez[2], Ekaterina Egorova[6],
Jens Grivolla[2], Gloria Elena Jaramillo Rojas[3], Anastasios Karakostas[4],
Dimos Ntioudis[4], Pavel Pecina[8], Oleksandr Sobko[5], Stefanos Vrochidis[4],
and Lena Wertmann[9]

[1] Catalan Institute for Research and Advanced Studies, Barcelona, Spain
[2] Pompeu Fabra University, Barcelona, Spain
`leo.wanner@upf.edu`
[3] Deutsches Forschungszentrum für Künstliche Intelligenz (DFKI),
Saarbrücken, Germany
[4] Centre for Research and Technology Hellas, Thessaloniki, Greece
[5] Everis Inc., Madrid, Spain
[6] Brno University of Technology, Brno, Czech Republic
[7] Centric, Sheffield Hallam University, Sheffield, UK
[8] Charles University Prague, Prague, Czech Republic
[9] Nurogames GmbH, Cologne, Germany

Abstract. We present a knowledge-driven multilingual conversational agent (referred to as "MyWelcome Agent") that acts as personal assistant for migrants in the contexts of their reception and integration. In order to also account for tasks that go beyond communication and require advanced service coordination skills, the architecture of the proposed platform separates the dialogue management service from the agent behavior including the service selection and planning. The involvement of genuine agent planning strategies in the design of personal assistants, which tend to be limited to dialogue management tasks, makes the proposed agent significantly more versatile and intelligent. To ensure high quality verbal interaction, we draw upon state-of-the-art multilingual spoken language understanding and generation technologies.

Keywords: Conversational agent · Agent service coordination · Dialogue management · Ontologies · Multilingual

Supported by the European Commission in the framework of its Horizon 2020 R&D Program under the contract number 870930.

F. Dignum et al. (Eds.): PAAMS 2021, LNAI 12946, pp. 316–327, 2021.
https://doi.org/10.1007/978-3-030-85739-4_26

1   Introduction

With Siri, Cortana, Alexa, Google Assistant, etc. the concept of a virtual conversational assistant reached the general public, and with it also rose the demands for more intelligence, versatility, and a broader coverage of background information. However, data-driven models underlying assistants like those mentioned above are naturally limited in terms of the scope of their memory, interpretative intelligence and cognition. Thus, although one can ask Siri about the weather prediction, one will not obtain a satisfactory answer when the inquiry concerns the location "where my mother lives" or even just whether "it will get warmer". Notwithstanding, for some contexts, such skills are highly desirable, in particular, when the assistant is supposed to be personalized, i.e., be aware of the profile, needs and capabilities of a specific user. Such contexts, include, e.g., assistance in healthcare or education, interaction with elderly, or support of migrants during their reception and integration in the host country.

Knowledge-driven conversational agents are in this sense an alternative to data-driven assistants. The design of a state-of-the-art knowledge driven conversational agent usually foresees a dialogue manager (DM) as the central knowledge-processing module, which accesses and reasons over an underlying ontology to plan the dialogue moves, possibly taking into account the context and the profile of the addressee; cf., e.g., [6,12,21,22]. Recently, neural reinforcement learning-based DMs proved to achieve an impressively good performance in well-defined, limited contextual setups such as restaurant reservation [24], travel booking [23], movie ticket purchase [11], etc. Still, while they cope well with the management of the dialogue history and the belief states, planning of dialogue moves, control of the coherence of the generated discourse, etc., they are not designed to carry out tasks such as, e.g., retrieval of useful information based on the profile of the user, identification of the closest office for residence application submission, or assessment of health data and determination of the adequate reaction. And they are even less designed to interact with each other. To cover these tasks, techniques for multi-agent coordination such as coalition formation and clustering, semantic service selection and composition planning can be used.

In what follows, we present work in progress on Embodied Conversational Agents (ECA) in the context of the WELCOME Project, henceforth referred to as "MyWelcome agent", whose design foresees the separation of the agent behavior and dialogue management tasks in two different modules. The agents are intended to act as personalized virtual companions of migrants or refugees (henceforth *Third Country Nationals*, TCNs) in specific contexts related to reception and integration in the host country.

The reception, administration and integration of TCNs imply a variety of tasks that can be roughly grouped as follows:

(1) registration and guidance through the administrative procedures and documentation needed for registration as well as provision of information on basic healthcare, legal, and social services;

(2) language courses and civic and social education;

(3) cultural and societal integration;

(4) coaching in daily life contexts, including, e.g., filling out a form or submission of an application; job interview training, legal consultation, etc.

Personalized embodied conversational agents that are capable of covering these tasks must show the following characteristics: (i) dispose of targeted background knowledge in a number of areas (including, among others, host country-specific migrant reception and integration procedures, prominent local cultural, civic, and social facts, everyday life contexts, etc.) as well as of the personal profile of a user (TCN, in our case); (ii) command situational awareness in interaction with the user; (iii) understand and interpret the verbal statements of the user; (iv) plan the actions to be undertaken by the agent in order to act respectively react appropriately to the statement of the user under given situational circumstances and the dialogue to be conducted by the agent; and (v) communicate with the user in the language of their preference.

Consider a fragment of a sample conversation as targeted by the MyWelcome agent:

U: *Hello, I would like to register for the First Reception Service.*
A: *Hello! What is your name?*
U: *Karim*
A: *Very good Karim! I need some basic information from you. Since when are you in the country and what is your current address?*
U: *I am still staying with friends.*
A: *In this case, I need your friends' address.*
U: *It is Lepant, 142 in Terrassa.*
A: *And since when do you live there?*
   . . .

In the next section, we outline the design of the MyWelcome agent. Section 3 presents the corresponding knowledge and data models and the agent services, and Sect. 4 the language technologies. Section 5, finally, summarizes the current state of our work and sketches its ongoing extension.

2   Design of the MyWelcome Agent

Each user is assigned their own personalized MyWelcome agent realized in terms of a mobile cloud application. Figure 1 shows the global MyWelcome agent platform architecture, which is grounded in the concept of services.[1] The backbone of the platform is the *Dispatcher* service, which channels the communication between the different platform services. Due to the challenging system reaction time restrictions on the one side and a required 1:n control flow efficiency on the

---

[1] We use the notion of *service* in order to highlight the functionality perspective on the individual software modules or components of the platform.

other side, a Dispatcher is preferred to a central Bus service or direct interaction between the services. From the perspective of their function, the individual platform services can be grouped into *message understanding* services, which include language identification (LIS), automatic speech recognition (ASR), language analysis (LAS); *message interpretation and reaction* services, which consist of one or multiple personal MyWelcome agents for agent-driven semantic service coordination (ADSC) and a dialogue management service (DMS); and *message generation* services, which are composed of the natural language generation (NLGS) and text-to-speech (TTS) services. For multi-agent coordination tasks, the MyWelcome agents communicate directly with each other via their endpoints, without leveraging the Dispatcher service.

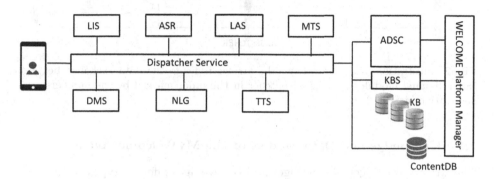

Fig. 1. Architecture of the MyWelcome agent platform.

Figure 2 displays the data flow between the individual MyWelcome services for the first two turns of our dialogue in Sect. 1. The user speaks to the avatar that embodies the MyWelcome agent in the mobile MyWelcome Application. The spoken turn is passed to the Dispatcher, which dispatches its analysis by the LID, ASR and LAS services. The outcome of the analysis, which consists of a predicate argument structure and the corresponding speech act (i.e., *communicative intent* of the speaker), is mapped onto an OWL representation and introduced into the local knowledge repository of the ADSC, where it is used for context-aware semantic service selection and planning. The output of the ADSC is passed via the Dispatcher to the DMS, which decides on the next dialogue move. The syntactic structure and the exact wording of the move is synthesized by the NLG service, spoken by the TTS service and played on the MyWelcome application.

3 Knowledge and Data Models and Agent Services

The quality of a knowledge-driven personalized conversational agent decisively depends on the coverage of its ontologies and the extent to which the personal features of the users are captured. In this section, we first present the knowledge and data models drawn upon by the agent and then the realization of the agent interaction services.

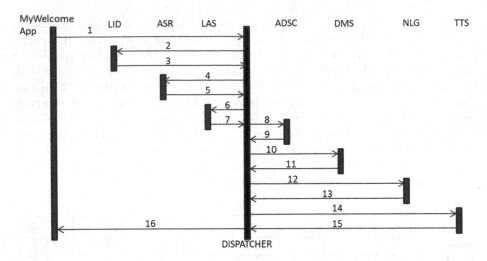

Fig. 2. Illustration of the data flow (the arrows indicate the data exchange between the individual modules and the Dispatcher in the order marked by the numbers); see description in Sect. 2.

3.1   Knowledge and Data Models of the MyWelcome Agent

The MyWelcome agent knowledge models leverage different types of information: (i) background information on migrant reception and integration policies and procedures, language learning curricula, social services, etc.; (ii) user-specific data, initially provided during user registration and subsequently distilled from the natural language interaction of the TCN with the MyWelcome agent; (iii) temporal properties of user resources, dialogue strategies and dialogue history, cultural integration activities, language learning advances, etc., and (iv) information obtained via reasoning and decision making on the available information.

To ensure GDPR-compliance with respect to the maintenance of personal TCN data, we distinguish between local and global agent knowledge repositories, which are realized as separate partitions of a semantic graph DB. Each MyWelcome agent is assigned its own **Local agent repository** realized as a tri-partite RDF triple store: the *Local Agent Knowledge Repository* (LAKR), which manages the personal data of its "TCN master", the *Local Agent Repository* (LAR), which keeps the internal states of the agent, and the Local Service Repository (LSR), which maintains the services of the agent. Each triple store can be accessed only by its owner agent.[2] The population and management of local repositories are handled by the Knowledge Management Service (KMS), which is a service responsible for initially converting external knowledge into RDF triple store-compliant representations, and then mapping them to the respective ontologies. The **Global Knowledge Repositories** contain RDF triple stores

---

[2] The LAKRs can be also accessed via secure interface by the TCN whose data it contains and the responsible authority.

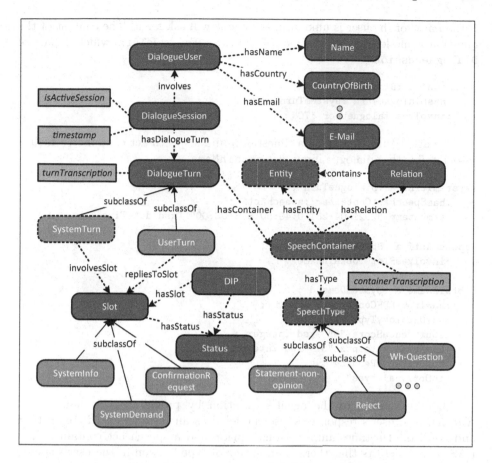

Fig. 3. Abstract representation of the WELCOME ontology.

that concern all agents, again separated into three partitions: the *WELCOME Domain Knowledge Repository* (WDRK), which contains the content of the scenarios covered by the agents, the *Semantic Service Descriptions* (WSR), and the *WELCOME Agent Repository* (WAR) with the ids of all created agents. A KMS-like service called *Knowledge Base Service* (KBS) facilitates the conversion into RDF and introduction of new information into WDKR or LAKR via the Platform Manager and initiates the LSR of a newly created agent. In addition to the knowledge repositories, a **content database** is included into the knowledge/data model of the MyWelcome Application. The content DB contains, e.g., sentence templates used for the agent move generation, relevant textual material pointed to in the generated moves, etc.

A fragment of the ontology, which forms the backbone of LAKR is shown in Fig. 3. It depicts the vocabulary that supports the dialogue with the user to inquire information on the profile of the user. The fact that a user exists in the ontology is modeled in terms of an instance of the class DialogueUser.

If the name of the user is unknown, the agent will ask for it. The content of the question is modeled as an instance of the class `DialogueTurn`, which is part of `DialogueSession`:

```
:session1 a :DialogueSession ;
    :hasDialogueTurn :systemTurn1 ;
    :involvesDialogueUser :TCN .
```

The agent turn consists of a timestamp and a speech act container, which is associated with a dialogue input slot `obtainName`:

```
:systemTurn1 a :DialogueTurn ;
    :hasSpeechActContainer :speechAct1 ;
    :timestamp "2021-04-28T10:46:50.623+03:00"^^xsd:dateTime .

:speechAct1 a :SpeechActContainer ;
    :involvesSlot :obtainName .

:obtainName a :SystemDemand ;
    :hasInputRDFContents :Unknown ;
    :hasOntologyType :Name ;
    :confidenceScore "0"^^xsd:integer ;
    :hasNumberAttempts "0"^^xsd:integer ;
    :hasStatus :Pending ;
    :isOptional "yes" .
```

The user replies to the agent's question by providing their name (e.g., *Karim*). The user's response is also modeled as an instance of `DialogueTurn` and consists of a timestamp, a transcription and a speech act container. The LAS service detects that there is an entity of type `Person` in the user's speech act. Cf. the corresponding codification in ontological terms:

```
:session1 a :DialogueSession ;
:hasDialogueTurn :systemTurn1 ;
:hasDialogueTurn :userTurn1 ;
:involvesDialogueUser :TCN .

:userTurn1 a :DialogueTurn ;
    :hasTurnTranscription "Karim"^^xsd:string ;
    :hasSpeechActContainer :speechAct2 ;
    :timestamp "2021-04-28T10:47:00.300+03:00"^^xsd:dateTime ;
    :prevTurn :systemTurn1 .

:speechAct2 a :SpeechActContainer ;
    :hasContainerTranscription "Karim"^^xsd:string ;
    :hasDetectedEntity :entity1 .
    :repliesToSlot :obtainName .

:entity1 a :DetectedEntity ;
    :hasEntityType "Person"^^xsd:String .
```

Finally, the KMS infers that this particular entity of the user's speech act is an expected response for the particular question, creates a new instance of type Name that is associated with the user's profile and updates the status of the dialogue input slot to *Completed*.

```
:TCN a :DialogueUser ;
    :hasName :Karim .
:Karim a :Name .
```

3.2   Agent Interaction Services and Dialogue Management

The TCN shall be intelligently assisted in the execution of the different procedures (referred to as *social services*) associated to the reception and integration, such as first reception, language learning, asylum application, etc. The actions of the agent in the context of social services are determined by two different modules. The first of them (ADSC) plans all "interaction" moves of the agent and coordinates its behavior; the second (DMS) plans the verbalization of the communication-oriented moves. In what follows, both are briefly introduced.

The behavior of an agent is determined by its *Behavior Trees* (BTs), which are conditioned by the facts stored in its LAKR. The facts are accessed via SPARQL queries attached to the nodes of the tree. The agent core, which is implemented in an *Access Java Agent Nucleus* (AJAN) server[3], encodes targeted sub-BTs that determine how to react to speech acts (cf. Sect. 4) that request specific social services. To react to a request, the agent core invokes its internal *Semantic Service Computing* (SSC), which identifies the corresponding service in its *Local Service Repository* (LSR). The LSR encodes the representation of the services in OWL-S 1.1. In this context, two different and complementary strategies are implemented inside the SSC for semantic service coordination: service selection and service composition.

To select a service, the agent core launches a service request that contains all relevant information (speech act and facts) from the user's move (passed by LAS to the KMS of the agent). The request is taken up by the *iSeM matchmaker* [9], which retrieves top-k semantically relevant services from the LSR.

If no relevant service is found in the LSR, the agent core invokes the SSC to call its semantic service composition planner to satisfy the given request of a service. This planner works as an offline state-based action planner [4,5]. Its action plan corresponds to the desired service plan; the initial state is a set of facts in OWL extracted by the KMS from the LAKR (its fact base), which describes the current state of the world; the goal state is a set of facts in OWL that shall persist after performing the plan. If a service composition matches the goal, the planner solves the given semantic service composition problem. If no service composition matches the goal, the agent asks DMS to inform the user that the service request cannot be satisfied and to propose to check the information available in the Frequently Asked Questions also provided in the MyWelcome

---

[3] https://asr.dfki.de/ajan/.

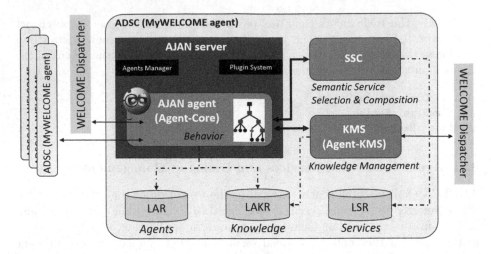

Fig. 4. Architecture of the MyWelcome agent (ADSC).

Application. On the other hand, the agent-core performs the atomic or composed service by collecting or providing information from/to the user. To create the dialogue strategies, the agent-core and DMS interact with each other based on a specific data structure called *Dialogue Input Package* (DIP). A DIP is created by the agent-core describing what the particular information that needs to be asked or communicated (slots in the DIP) is, and some meta-information such as the number of times that a piece of information has been sent to the user, and the type of the information (System Info or System Demand). DMS, together with the message generation service, decides what information (slot) to communicate to the user and how to do it. The current version of the DMS is based on the KRISTINA dialogue manager [21]. Its next version will incorporate a versatile neural network-based repair strategy of the dialogue faulted by ASR errors or misleading user information.

4   Language Technology Services

The MyWelcome agent is projected to be multilingual, speaking Syrian (Levantine) and Moroccan (Darija) Arabic, Catalan, English, German, Greek, and Spanish. In its current state, it is tested in English

Spoken Language Understanding. The spoken language understanding technologies cover language identification (LI), automatic speech recognition (ASR), language analysis (LAS), and machine translation (MT). **The LI service** is based on [16], which utilizes a robust generative concept of i-vectors, i.e., utterance embeddings, based on generative models. Acoustic features, which serve as input for i-vector training, are multiligually trained on stacked bottleneck features [2]. After the extraction of i-vectors, a Gaussian Linear Classifier is applied. **The ASR module** is based on the kaldi toolkit [17] and [8]. **The LAS**

module consists of the surface language analysis and deep language analysis modules. The distinction between surface and deep analysis is made in order to ensure word sense disambiguation and entity identification and linking at the deep side of the analysis. For surface language analysis, [19] is used. For word sense disambiguation and entity linking, we use BabelFy [14]; for entity (concept) identification, we adapt [18]. The relations that hold between the concepts are identified applying rule-based grammars to the results of these analysis submodules; the grammars are implemented in the graph transduction framework [1]. LAS outputs a predicate argument structure, which is mapped by the KMS onto an RDF-triple structure in the local knowledge repository of the agent, and the speech act (e.g., 'suggest', 'commit', 'complain', etc.) that characterizes the analyzed statement of the user. The speech act classification is done with https://github.com/bhavitvyamalik/DialogTag. For illustration, Fig. 5 shows some sample structures as provided by LAS. **The MT service** [7] ensures that the agent is able to converse with users who speak a language not covered by the language analysis/production modules.

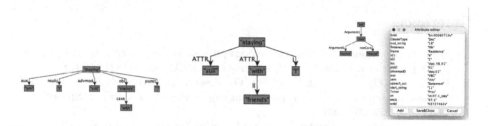

Fig. 5. Sample language analysis structures for "I am still staying with friends".

Spoken language synthesis. The spoken language synthesis technologies comprise multilingual natural language generation (NLG) and text-to-speech synthesis (TTS). The NLG module is an extension of the multilayer FoG generation module [13], which uses the same types of structures as depicted in Fig. 5. We adapt FoG for dialogue generation and use of sentence templates for scenarios in which the reactions of the agent differ only in terms of provided data. For TTS, we use a flexible multilingual service that comprises different off-the-shelf Tacotron-based TTS applications [20]. Coqui.ai[4] pre-trained models are used for English, German, and Spanish. For Arabic, Catalan, and Greek, smaller off-the-shelf models [3,10,15] are currently being worked on.

5   Conclusions and Ongoing Work

We presented the first prototypical implementation of a personalized knowledge-based ECA. In contrast to the overwhelming majority of the state-of-the-art

---

[4] https://coqui.ai/.

ECAs, its interaction core consists of an agent planning service, which plans the overall interaction with the user (including actions not related to communication) and a dialogue management service, which plans the dialogue moves of the agent. This separation ensures that the agent is capable of also performing actions that are not directly related to communication – a prerequisite of a genuine personal assistant, which is expected to be not only communicative, but also intelligent. The first assessment of the functionality of the prototype by TCNs, NGOs and governmental institutions indicates that the information provided by the MyWelcome agent is useful, supports the TCNs in their concerns and alleviates the workload of NGO workers and officers. Formal evaluation trials are planned to obtain a more detailed picture on the performance of the agent. The future efforts will target the consolidation of the modules of MyWelcome agent and the extension of the topics in which the agent can support the TCNs.

Acknowledgements. Many thanks to our colleagues from the NGOs PRAKSIS and CARITAS, Generalitat de Catalunya, Mind Refuge, KEMEA, and ISocial Foundation for their guidance and constant constructive feedback!

References

1. Bohnet, B., Wanner, L.: Open source graph transducer interpreter and grammar development environment. In: Proceedings of LREC, pp. 211–218 (2010)
2. Fér, R., Matějka, P., Grézl, F., Plchot, O., Veselý, K., Černocký, J.: Multilingually trained bottleneck features in spoken language recognition. Comput. Speech Lang. **2017**(46), 252–267 (2017)
3. Halabi, N.: Modern standard Arabic phonetics for speech synthesis. Ph.D. Diss. (2016)
4. Helmert, M.: The fast downward planning system. J. Artif. Int. Res. **26**(1), 191–246 (2006)
5. Helmert, M., Röger, G., Karpas, E.: Fast downward stone soup: a baseline for building planner portfolios. In: ICAPS 2011 Workshop on Planning and Learning, pp. 28–35 (2011)
6. Janowski, K., Ritschel, H., Lugrin, B., André, E.: Sozial interagierende Roboter in der Pflege, pp. 63–87. Springer Fachmedien Wiesbaden, Wiesbaden (2018). https://doi.org/10.1007/978-3-658-22698-5_4
7. Junczys-Dowmunt, M., et al.: Marian: Fast Neural Machine Translation in C++. In: Proceedings of ACL 2018, System Demonstrations, pp. 116–121 (2018)
8. Karafiat, M., Karthick, B., Szoke, I., Vydana, H., Benes, K., Černocký, J.: BUT OpenSAT 2020 speech recognition system. In: Proceedings of the InterSpeech 2021 (2021)
9. Klusch, M., Kapahnke, P.: The ISEM matchmaker: a flexible approach for adaptive hybrid semantic service selection. J. Web Seman. **15**, 1–14 (2012)
10. Külebi, B., Öktem, A., Peiró-Lilja, A., Pascual, S., Farrús, M.: CATOTRON – a neural text-to-speech system in Catalan. In: Proceedings of the Interspeech, pp. 490–491 (2020)
11. Li, X., Chen, Y.N., Li, L., Gao, J., Celikyilmaz, A.: End-to-end task-completion neural dialogue systems. In: Proceedings of the IJCNLP, pp. 733–743 (2017)

12. Mencía, B.L., Pardo, D.D., Trapote, A.H., Gómez, L.A.H.: Embodied Conversational Agents in interactive applications for children with special educational needs. In: Griol Barres, D., Callejas Carrión, Z., Delgado, R.L.C. (eds.) Technologies for Inclusive Education: Beyond Traditional Integration Approaches, pp. 59–88. IGI Global, Hershey (2013)

13. Mille, S., Dasioupoulou, S., Wanner, L.: A portable grammar-based NLG system for verbalization of structured data. In: Proceedings of the 34th ACM/SIGAPP Symposium on Applied Computing, pp. 1054–1056 (2019)

14. Moro, A., Raganato, A., Navigli, R.: Entity linking meets word sense disambiguation: a unified approach. Trans. Assoc. Comput. Linguist. (TACL) **2**, 231–244 (2014)

15. Park, K., Mulc, T.: CSS10: a collection of single speaker speech datasets for 10 languages (2019)

16. Plchot, O., et al.: Analysis of BUT-PT Submission for NIST LRE 2017. In: Proceedings of Odyssey 2018 the Speaker and Language Recognition WS, pp. 47–53 (2018). https://www.fit.vut.cz/research/publication/11762

17. Povey, D., et al.: The Kaldi speech recognition toolkit. In: IEEE 2011 Workshop on Automatic Speech Recognition and Understanding, December 2011

18. Shvets, A., Wanner, L.: Concept extraction using pointer–generator networks and distant supervision for data augmentation. In: Keet, C.M., Dumontier, M. (eds.) EKAW 2020. LNCS (LNAI), vol. 12387, pp. 120–135. Springer, Cham (2020). https://doi.org/10.1007/978-3-030-61244-3_8

19. Straka, M.: UDPipe 2.0 prototype at CoNLL 2018 UD shared task. In: Proceedings of the CoNLL 2018, pp. 197–207 (2018)

20. Wang, Y., et al.: Tacotron: Towards end-to-end speech synthesis (2017)

21. Wanner, L., et al.: KRISTINA: a knowledge-based virtual conversation agent. In: Demazeau, Y., Davidsson, P., Bajo, J., Vale, Z. (eds.) PAAMS 2017. LNCS (LNAI), vol. 10349, pp. 284–295. Springer, Cham (2017). https://doi.org/10.1007/978-3-319-59930-4_23

22. Wargnier, P., Carletti, G., Laurent-Corniquet, Y., Benveniste, S., Jouvelot, P., Rigaud, A.S.: Field evaluation with cognitively-impaired older adults of attention management in the Embodied Conversational Agent Louise. In: Proceedings of the IEEE International Conference on Serious Games and Applications for Health, pp. 1–8 (2016)

23. Wei, W., Le, Q., Dai, A., Li, L.J.: AirDialogue: an environment for goal-oriented dialogue research. In: Proceedings of the EMNLP, pp. 3844–3854 (2018)

24. Weisz, G., Budzianowski, P., Su, P.H., Gašić, M.: Sample efficient deep reinforcement learning for dialogue systems with large action spaces. IEEE/ACM Trans. Audio Speech Lang. Process. **26**(11), 2083–2097 (2018)

Comparing Thread Migration, Mobile Agents, and ABM Simulators in Distributed Data Analysis

Maxwell Wenger, Jonathan Acoltzi, and Munehiro Fukuda[✉]

Computing and Software Systems, University of Washington,
Bothell, WA 98011, USA
{mdwenger,jacoltzi,mfukuda}@uw.edu

Abstract. Many scientific datasets are generated in a given data structure (e.g., a graph) and are reused for various analyses. From this viewpoint, instead of streaming these datasets into conventional big-data tools such as MapReduce or Spark, we should maintain their data structures over distributed memory and repeat deploying mobile computing units to the datasets. Since thread migration, mobile agents, and parallel ABM (agent-based modeling) simulators enable migration of execution entities, this paper looks at four Java-based representative systems: JCilk, IBM Aglets, Repast Simphony, and the MASS library. Our analysis of their programmability and parallel performance demonstrates that MASS can competitively perform distributed data analysis in an emergent collective group behavior among reactive agents.

Keywords: Thread migration · Mobile agents · Agent-based modeling · Distributed memory

1 Introduction

In contrast to typical big-data computing in text datasets, scientific computing generates structured datasets and repetitively applies different analyses to the same data. For instance, biological network analysis may apply different topological and clustering algorithms to the same protein-to-protein reaction network (PPN) [1], which results in identifying important proteins and their motifs. Climate data analysis scans NetCDF historical and simulation datasets back and forth along their time line [17], for the purpose of forecasting the time of emergence in global warming. Environmental analysis stores multimedia datasets in multi-dimensional semantic spaces and wants to retrieve only data items in a user-defined context [9]. The key to these scientific data analyses is to maintain the structure of a given dataset in memory for different analytic purposes.

From this viewpoint, our previous work [4] pointed out challenges of conventional data-streaming approaches such as MapReduce and Spark, all in need of preprocessing structured datasets into a text format. As alternatives, thread

© Springer Nature Switzerland AG 2021
F. Dignum et al. (Eds.): PAAMS 2021, LNAI 12946, pp. 328–340, 2021.
https://doi.org/10.1007/978-3-030-85739-4_27

migration [8,13] and mobile agents [11] can be considered for hunting target data items from a distributed dataset. Yet, they are not the best option: the coarse granularity of execution entities (e.g., processes and threads) and unawareness of the underlying data structure. Based on these observations, we proposed in [4] that parallel ABM (agent-based modeling) simulators including Repast[1] and MASS[2] have the best capability of deploying many agents over a distributed, structured dataset as well as analyzing its attributes and shapes in a collective group behavior among agents.

However, we understand the importance of demonstrating empirical evidences rather than theoretical discussions, strong enough to support ABM's superiority to the other entity-migration systems in analysis of structured, scientific datasets. For this reason, we conducted an experimental verification through the following four steps: (1) selected JCilk [3] from thread migration, IBM Aglets[3] from mobile agents, and Repast Simphony and the MASS library from an ABM system; (2) considered the closet-pair-of-points and the triangle counting problems, each representing a 2D geometric analysis and a graph problem respectively; (3) parallelized them with JCilk, Aglets, Repast Simphony, and MASS; and (4) compared their programmability and execution performance.

The contribution of this paper is to show that the MASS library, a parallel ABM library equipped with parallel I/O, advanced agent management, and distributed data structures, serves as a promising alternative to conduct in-memory analysis of distributed, structured datasets.

The rest of this paper consists of the following sections: Sect. 2 considers several systems that support migration of execution entities over distributed memory; Sect. 3 discusses how to apply these migration systems to parallelized analysis of structured datasets; Sect. 4 compares their programmability and execution performance in two data-science benchmarks; and Sect. 5 summarizes our achievements with a brief discussion of our plan to keep enhancing agent intelligence.

2   Migration of Execution Entities over Memory

We observe two extreme approaches to distributed data analysis: one is data streaming that partitions a dataset into multiple data streams, each fed to parallel computing units, (e.g., map/reduce functions in MapReduce), whereas the other is migration of computing unites where threads or agents are repetitively dispatched to a dataset structured and maintained in distributed memory. Since our previous research in [4] compared the MASS library with data-streaming tools, this section focuses on migration of execution entities from programming and functional viewpoints. We look at the following three migration systems: (1) thread migration, (2) mobile agents, and (3) ABM simulators

---

[1] https://repast.github.io/.
[2] http://depts.washington.edu/dslab/MASS/.
[3] http://aglets.sourceforge.net/.

2.1 Thread Migration

Thread migration intends to reduce remote memory accesses. Many libraries including Nomadic Thread systems [8] move their threads by system when their memory access latencies become unacceptably higher, when too many threads complete for local memory, or when a thread needs to access a remote critical section. Their threads have no navigational autonomy unlike MASS. On the other hand, PM2 [12] allows its threads to autonomously move to remote pages. Threads in Olden [13] can create and traverse a distributed tree. However, their threads are too coarse to move frequently. They do not consider graph construction, either. As operating systems are in control of their execution and migration, data-science applications have little chances of fine-tuning their execution performance, which we observe later in Sect. 4.

Only an exception is EMU [2] that creates a large-scale graph over distributed memory and orchestrates thread migration over the graph. EMU takes the closest approach to agent-navigable distributed graph analysis that we are aiming for. On the other hand, it differs from the MASS library in: (1) EMU's graph emulation does not support incremental graph modifications; (2) thread migration in Cilk Plus[4] only spawns child threads remotely but does not move active threads; and more importantly (3) EMU needs its custom hardware. Thread migration does not focus on interactive computation nor parallel I/O by itself, which should be supported by additional software.

2.2 Mobile Agents

Mobile agents have been once highlighted as an SSH/RPC replacement to automate network management, information retrieval, and Internet surfing. For instance, IBM Aglets expected its use for automating eCommerce of airline tickets [10]. They are intelligent agents, capable of navigational autonomy, equipped with network security features, and thus instantiated as coarse-grained execution entities such as processes or threads. To implement collaboration among agents, D'Agents [7] facilitates one-on-one agent meeting and IBM Aglets supports message multicast among agents. However, their migration is based on IP addresses and thus does not distinguish distributed data structures, their computation typically takes the master-worker model and collective communication (e.g., divide and conquer) by allocating a different range of data to each agent.

Most Java-based agents such as IBM Aglets and JADE[5] are based on so-called *weak migration* that restarts agents from the top of a given function every time they have migrated to a new site. This is because of the difficulty in capturing an agent's stack and program counter from JVM. As mobile agents are expected to keep running from top to down of their migration itinerary, users would prefer *strong migration* that resumes agent execution at every new site right after their last migration function. D'Agents supports this feature by hacking the original Tcl/Tk interpretor, which risks being outdating their language

---

[4] http://www.cilkplus.org/.
[5] http://jade.tilab.com/.

platforms. Furthermore, strong migration contradicts event-oriented function calls such as invocations upon agent departure, arrival, and message delivery, which we have demonstrated are useful for agent-based data analysis in [14].

2.3   ABM Simulators

ABM views its computation as an emergent collective group behavior among reactive agents. Two representative simulators are FLAME[6] and RepastHPC, both parallelized with MPI and available in C. If we apply biologically inspired optimizations such as ant colony optimization and grasshopper optimization algorithm to these systems by simulating their agent collaboration on a data space, this can be considered as agent-based data analysis. However, they are not designed for big-data computing but micro-simulation. FLAME implements ABM as a collection of communicating agents, each carrying an entire spatial information, which does not allow distributed data analysis. Although RepastHPC populates and moves agents on a user-defined graph and contiguous space, its file inputs are distributed through the main. Even when too many agents traverse a dataset, they cannot be temporarily frozen to prevent memory exhaustion.

In summary, we believe that reactive and light-weight agents are potential to carry out repetitive analysis of scientific dataset, structured over distributed memory. Yet, existing ABM simulators do not assume their uses in data sciences. This is our motivation to apply the MASS library to structured data analysis.

2.4   MASS Java

The MASS library was originally intended to parallelize ABM micro-simulation at each level of Java, C++, and CUDA. Focusing on architectural independence, we have tuned up the MASS Java version (simply say MASS in the following discussion) to parallel data analysis. MASS constructs a distributed, multi-dimensional array (named *Places*), populates mobile objects (named *Agents*), and parallelizes their array-indexed migration and execution on places, using a cluster of multithreaded computing nodes. The main program schedules places/agents' parallel function call with *callAll( )*, inter-places data exchange with *exchangeAll( )*, and agents' commitment on cloning, termination, and migration with *manageAll( )*.

For parallel data analysis, MASS reads input data into places simultaneously [16], constructs distributed graphs, trees, and 2D contiguous space over a cluster system [5], controls agent population to prevent memory exhaustion [4], and facilitates event-driven function calls using Java annotations such as *@onDeparture*, *@onArrival*, and *@onMessage* [14]. To simplify the main program, MASS prepares additional agent functions: *doAll( )*, *doUntil( )*, and *doWhile( )*, each repeatedly executing a pair of agent callAll and manageAll, in burst until a given condition gets satisfied, or while the condition stays true.

---

[6] http://www.flame.ac.uk.

3   Parallelization of Benchmark Programs

We empirically demonstrate that the MASS library is a competitive tool among thread migration, mobile agents, and ABM simulation systems when being applied to structured data analysis. Our choices of competitors are: (1) JCilk from thread migration, (2) IBM Aglets from mobile agents, and (3) Repast Simphony from ABM simulators, all running in Java. Although JCilk and Repast Simphony are only available for a single computing node with multi-cores, they are Java versions corresponding to Cilk Plus used in EMU and RepastHPC in C++, and we can project their execution performance for cluster computing, based on their thread/object management overheads within a single computer. Please note that our former comparison between MASS and RepastHPC looked into their behavioral, social, and economical micro-simulations in C++ [15], which is different from this paper's focus on agent-based big data. For our comparative work, we use the following two benchmark programs:

1. **Closet Pair of Points:** finds the closet pair of points among many data points mapped over a 2D space. It is a typical computational geometric problem that can be extended to Voronoi diagram construction [6]. Our agent-based algorithm populates an agent at each data point, propagates them over a 2D space, and observes their collisions, among which the first occurrence finds the closet pair of points.
2. **Triangle Counting:** identifies the number of triangles in a given graph. It is a typical graph problem that can be extended to any sub-graph problems such as biological network motif identification [1]. We walk agents from each vertex along three cascading edges and count how many of them have come back to their source vertex, which equals the number of triangles.

3.1   2D Contiguous Space Problem: Closet Pair of Points

We use either our agent-based algorithm (with agent propagation and collision), a conventional divide-and-conquer parallelization, or a master-worker model where each worker executes a partial divide-and-conquer. The parallelization on each platform looks at the following three viewpoints: (1) data distribution, (2) entity (i.e., threads or agents) population, and (3) problem parallelization.

JCilk. Our preliminary experiment showed that spawning a thread at each of 32K data points could not finish our agent-based algorithm in a reasonable time. Therefore, as shown in Fig. 1(a), we used divide and conquer:

1. **Data distribution:** generates and sorts 2D data points on shared memory;
2. **Entity population:** spawns JCilk threads recursively, each in charge of the left and right of a repetitively halved space until a partition gets at most two points whose distance becomes the shortest in it; and
3. **Problem parallelization:** selects the shortest distance from a pair of left and right partitions as well as examine if there is even a shorter pair of points over their boundary, which will be repeated back to the original space.

More specifically, the divide phase spawns two child JCilk threads with JCilk's *spawn* construct, whereas the conquer phase automatically terminates them upon a return from the recursive function call.

IBM Aglets. We encountered two obstacles to coding either an agent-based or a divide-and-conquer algorithm entirely with Aglets. First, IBM Aglets was meant to be managed from their GUI built into the program. Second, their inter-agent messaging gave partial support to object serializations. To address these problems, we set up an SSH tunnel to forward X11, (i.e., Aglets GUI) from a remote cluster system to a local machine. We also implemented a socket-based broker that collects messages sent from remote Aglets. With these solutions, we chose the master-worker model where the main program dispatched Aglets as workers, which would not unfairly penalized Aglets' execution.

1. **Data distribution:** generates 2D data points in an NFS file;
2. **Entity population:** spawns a given number of Aglets, each hopping to a different computing node to read the entire data file into memory, to sort the data points, and to focus on a different range of the dataset;
3. **Problem parallelization:** engages each worker Aglet in a partial divide-and-conquer algorithm to find the shortest distance so far in its own range of points (see Fig. 1(a) while the main program collects partial results from all the Aglets to find the minimum value.

The actual implementation uses Aglets' *createAglet( )* and *dispatch(remoteIp)* to start an Aglet remotely; and *onArrival( )* to have the Aglet invoke its divide-and-conquer function as well as establish a Java client socket back to the main program's broker instance.

Repast Simphony. We applied our agent-based approach to Repast. Figure 1(b) describes how the approach finds the closet pair of points, based on agent propagation and collision.

1. **Data distribution:** distributes data points over a 2D grid simulation space and embeds this space into a Repast context;
2. **Entity population:** populates *Point* agents, each moving to a different data point in the grid and spawning a *Turtle* agent; and
3. **Problem parallelization:** has each *Turtle* keep propagating itself to its von Neumann and Moore neighborhoods in turn, which approximates a radical propagation with a growing octagon. The first collision of two octagons finds the shortest pair of points

Unlike the circle, the octagon has different distances from its center to the edges where the longest and shortest distance ratio is 1.0824. Therefore, the simulation must run further for assuring that the shortest distance catches up this difference.

MASS. AS MASS is an ABM platform, it takes our agent-based approach.

1. **Data distribution:** distributes data points over *SpacePlaces*, a 2D contiguous space derived from *Places*;
2. **Entity population:** uses the *SpaceAgent* class that is derived from *Agents* and is specialized for populating agents over *SpacePlaces*; and
3. **Problem parallelization:** repetitively invokes *SpaceAgent.propagate Agent( )* to simulate the agents' 2D propagation.

Since agent propagation and collision detection are automated in *SpacePlaces*, the logic is much simpler than Repast.

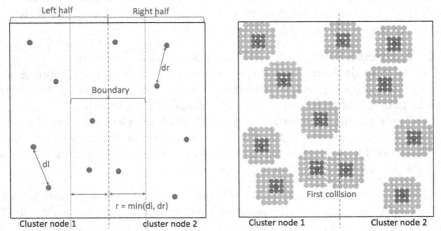

(a) Divide and conquer in JCilk and Aglets (b) Agent propagation in Repast and MASS

Fig. 1. Closet pair of points with migration of execution entities

3.2   Graph Problem: Triangle Counting

Unlike our previous parallelization for the closet pair of points, we applied our agent-based approach, (i.e., walking agents three times) to all the four platforms: JCilk, IBM Aglets, Repast Simphony, and MASS. This is because our test graph of 3,000 vertices, each connected to up to 1000 neighbors is large enough but does not exponentially increase the population of threads or agents. Below is the summary of each platform's (1) graph construction, (2) entity population, and (3) problem parallelization.

JCilk. We represented each JCilk thread as a mobile entity that hops over a graph (see Fig. 2(b)).

1. **Data distribution:** creates in shared memory a 1D array of vertices, each with an adjacency list of its neighbors;

2. **Entity population:** populates a JCilk thread at each vertex, (i.e., associated with each array element); and
3. **Problem parallelization:** makes each thread pick up only neighboring vertices whose index is smaller than the current vertex (i.e., array) index, so that it dispatches an offspring to each of these neighbors. This hop must be repeated twice. Thereafter, for the third hop, each thread seeks for its source vertex in the adjacency list of the current vertex where it resides.

If threads come to a dead-end or cannot find their source index for their third hop, they get terminated. Therefore, threads that have survived through their three hops eventually traveled along a triangle.

IBM Aglets. Since IBM Aglets' GUI is not practicable of managing 3,000 Aglets (each starting from a different graph vertex), we combined the master-worker model and our agent-based approach, as shown in Fig. 2(a)

1. **Data distribution:** generates graph adjacency lists in an NFS file;
2. **Entity population:** spawns a given number of Aglets, each migrating to a different computing node to read the file and to take charge of a different range of adjacency lists; and
3. **Problem parallelization:** starts with an Aglet that examines one by one vertex from its task and checks if there are three cascading edges coming back to the source vertex.

Unlike the other platforms, an Aglet does not clone nor terminate itself. Upon a failure to find a triangle in the current route, the Aglet backtracks to a previous vertex and explores a different route. This is the same as depth-first search.

Repast Simphony. We walked Repast agents named *Turtles* over a graph as shown in Fig. 2(b).

1. **Data distribution:** creates two Repast projections: (1) a grid projection that maps 3,000 vertices over its $1,000 \times 1,000$ space and (2) a network projection that defines a graph edge from one vertex to another in the graph;
2. **Entity population:** instantiates a *Turtle* agent at each vertex when the vertex was mapped to the 2D grid projection; and
3. **Problem parallelization:** schedules repetitive invocations of *migrateTurtles( )* at each vertex by annotating the method with Repast's *@ScheduleMethod* type. It scans *Turtles* residing on each vertex and moves them to their next destination.

The *TurtleMonitor* class was prepared to monitor active *Turtles*, to delete idle *Turtles*, and to increment the number of triangles when a *Turtle* completes a successful walk.

MASS. Its original triangle-counting program [4] was revised for better programmability and faster execution by using the *GraphPlaces* class to construct a graph as well as agent annotations to invoke agents' onArrival and onDeparture functions asynchronously.

1. **Data distribution:** constructs a graph with GraphPlaces as a 1D array of places, each representing a vertex with its adjacency list of neighbors;
2. **Entity population:** starts an agent from each vertex; and
3. **Problem parallelization:** walks each agent twice from one vertex to another with a lower ID and lets it seek for an edge going back to its source vertex upon the third walk.

Agents' onArrival and onDeparture functions are automatically invoked before and after their migration to a new vertex, each choosing the next destination and initiating an actual migration.

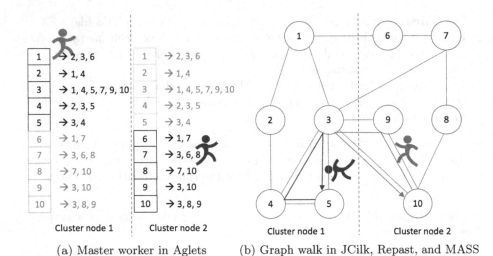

(a) Master worker in Aglets   (b) Graph walk in JCilk, Repast, and MASS

Fig. 2. Triangle counting with migration of execution entities

4   System Comparisons

Our comparisons look into the four systems' programmability and execution performance when parallelizing and running the two benchmark programs. The actual code and raw results are available through the MASS library website.

4.1   Programmability

We first discuss how the four systems can naturally apply the concept of ABM to distributed analysis of a 2D space and a graph. Thereafter we compare their code quantitatively.

Qualitative Analysis. Table 1 summarizes if each system was able to use any of ABM behaviors as well as to maintain a data structure in memory for repetitive analyses. Although IBM Aglets are agents, the platform cannot be used more than simply dispatching agents to remote computing nodes for one-time parallel computing. JCilk can maintain a data structure in memory but suffers from managing too many coarse-grain threads, which results in using the conventional divide-and-conquer algorithm in the closest pair of points. On the other hand, Repast Simphony and MASS can naturally apply their ABM computation to the two benchmark programs. Their drawback is however a burden of adjusting a hexagonal agent propagation to a circle with additional computation.

Quantitative Analysis. Table 2 counts the lines of code (LoC) for the two benchmark programs when they are parallelized with each platform. The notations of total, main, entity, and space respectively refer to LoC of the entire program, main/utility functions, thread/agent functions, and 2D/graph construction functions. BP refers to the boilerplate code that is necessary for parallelization but irrelevant to actual algorithms. Since JCilk is based on shared-memory programming, it shows the easiest transition from sequential algorithms. IBM Aglets uses its agents as remote computing servers and thus their logic is simple. However the BP percentage is in the 38%–57% range due to our additional coding that facilitates inter-agent communication to collect the results. MASS demonstrates shorter code than Repast and even shorter than Aglets in triangle counting, in support with its graph construction features.

Table 1. Distributed data analysis with JCilk, Aglets, Repast, and MASS

System	Closest pair of points		Triangle counting	
	Algorithms	Data maintenance	Algorithms	Data maintenance
JCilk	Divide-and-conquer (D& C)	Yes	Agent triangle walk	Yes
Aglets	Master-worker (MW) and D& C	No	MW and adjacency-list scan	No
Repast & MASS	Hexagonal agent propagation (must be adjusted to a circle)	Yes	Agent triangle walk	Yes

Table 2. Code comparison among JCilk, Aglets, Repast, and MASS

Closet pair of points						Triangle counting				
Platforms		Total	Main	Entity	Space	Platforms		Total	Main	Entity	Space
JCilk	LoC	199	62	101	36	JCilk	LoC	134	30	36	68
	BP (%)	4 (1%)	2	2	0		BP (%)	4 (3%)	2	2	0
Aglets	LoC	297	176	94	27	Aglets	LoC	246	190	44	12
	BP (%)	113 (38%)	108	5	0		BP(%)	140 (57%)	135	5	0
Repast	LoC	383	165	146	72	Repast	LoC	300	71	84	145
	BP (%)	16 (4%)	2	12	2		BP (%)	5 (2%)	3	2	0
MASS	LoC	336	146	118	102	MASS	LoC	209	43	92	74
	BP (%)	10 (3%)	8	2	0		BP (%)	8 (4%)	4	2	2

4.2 Execution Performance

Our performance evaluation used a cluster of eight Linux machines, each with
8-core 2.33 GHz CPU (Intel Xeon E5410) with 16 GB memory. Figures 3(a) and
(b) compare the execution performance of the four platforms respectively when
running the closet pair of points and triangle counting programs. We have chosen the best execution performance for each platform as IBM Aglets fluctuated
its agent-transfer speed. NFS took 0.05 and 0.45 s to retrieve 32,768 points and
3,000 vertices respectively, which did not affect Aglets' ranking in our evaluation. In the closest paper of points, IBM Aglets performed fastest, which was
however its maximum speed by running three agents within a single computing
node. Similarly, parallel execution of Repast and JCilk was limited to a single
computing node with six and eight CPU cores respectively. In triangle counting, IBM Aglets could not handle 3,000 vertices by exhausting 16GB memory at
each cluster node. Therefore, we estimated its performance, using a polynomial
regression of executions with 600, 1,000, 1,500, and 2,000 vertices, each respectively spending 0.225, 0.766, 2.147, and 4.293 s with 16 agents running over four
computing nodes. Repast and JCilk also suffered from their overheads incurred
by too many agents or threads in a single machine. On the other hand, MASS

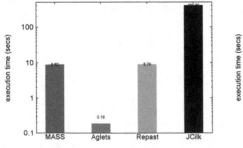
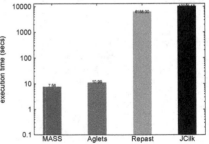

(a) Closet pair of points with 32,768 points (b) Triangle counting with 3,000 vertices

Fig. 3. Performance comparison among JCilk, Aglets, Repast, and MASS

took advantage of distributed memory to handle 32,768 data points over four computing nodes and a graph of 3,000 vertices over eight computing nodes.

5 Conclusions

In contrast to the conventional data-streaming tools, we apply ABM to distributed analysis of structured datasets whose attributes or shapes are computed from agent group behaviors. Since the key to our approach is migration of execution entities, this paper picked up the four platforms from thread migration, mobile agents, and ABM simulators, all moving their threads or agents over computing nodes. Our measurements of their programmability and parallel executions show that MASS minimizes the semantic gap between ABM-based analysis and its parallelization, reasonably (but not optimally) reduces the code size, and performs competitively in a larger dataset. We plan on embedding more intelligence in graph-walking agents, e.g., with a capability of walking toward network hubs rather than in a pure breadth-first fashion, which we expect will benefit analysis of scale-free network, (e.g., biological network motif search).

References

1. Andersen, A., Kim, W., Fukuda, M.: Mass-based nemoprofile construction for an efficient network motif search. In: IEEE International Conference on Big Data and Cloud Computing in Bioinformatics - BDCloud 2016, Atlanta, GA, pp. 601–606, October 2016
2. Belviranli, M.E., Lee, S., Vetter, J.S.: Designing algorithms for the EMU migrating-threads-based architecture. In: Proceedings of the 22nd IEEE High Performance extreme Computing Conference (HPEC), pp. 1–7, Waltham, MA, Septmeber 2018. https://doi.org/10.1109/HPEC.2018.8547571
3. Danaher, J.S., Lee, I.T.A., Leiserson, C.E.: The JCilk language for multithreaded computing. In: Workshop on Synchronization and Concurrency in Object-Oriented Languages (SCOOL), San Diego, CA, October 2005
4. Fukuda, M., Gordon, C., Mert, U., Sell, M.: Agent-based computational framework for distributed analysis. IEEE Comput. **53**(4), 16–25 (2020)
5. Gilroy, J., Paronyan, S., Acoltz, J., Fukuda, M.: Agent-navigable dynamic graph construction and visualization over distributed memory. In: 7th International Workshop on Big Graphs, pp. 2957–2966. IEEE, December 2020
6. Gokulramkumar, S.: Agent based parallelization of computationl geometry algorithms. Master's thesis, University of Washington Bothell, June 2020
7. Gray, R.S., et al.: D'Agents: applications and performance of a mobile-agent system. J. Softw. Pract. Exp. **32**(6), 543–573 (2002)
8. Jenks, S., et al.: Nomadic threads: a migrating multi-threaded approach to remote memory accesses in multiprocessors. In: Proceedings of the 5th International Conference on Parallel Architectures and Compilation Techniques, pp. 2–11 (1996)
9. Kiyoki, Y., et al.: Multi-dimensional semantic computing with spatial-temporal and semantic axes for multi-spectrum images in environment analysis. In: Proceedings of 27th International Conference on Information Modeling and Knowledge Bases, Maribor, Slovenia, pp. 14–30, June 2015

10. Lange, D.B., Oshima, M.: Programming and Deploying Java Mobile Agents with Aglets. Addison Wesley Professional (1998)
11. Milojicic, D., Douglis, F., Wheeler, R. (eds.): Mobility: Processes, Computers, and Agents, 1st edn. Addison-Wesley Professional (1999)
12. Namyst, R., Méhault, J.: PM2: parallel multithreaded machine. A computing environment for distributed architectures. In: ParCo, Gent, Belgium, pp. 279–285, September 1995
13. Rogers, A., et al.: Supporting dynamic data structures on distributed-memory machines. ACM TOPLAS **17**(2), 233–263 (1995)
14. Sell, M., Fukuda, M.: Agent programmability enhancement for rambling over a scientific dataset. In: PAAMS 2020, L'Aquila, Italy, pp. 251–263, October 2020
15. Shih, C., Yang, C., Fukuda, M.: Benchmarking the agent descriptivity of parallel multi-agent simulators. In: International Workshops of PAAMS 2018, Highlights of Practical Application of Agents, Multi-Agent Systems, and Complexity, Toledo, Spain, pp. 480–492, June 2018
16. Shih, Y., et al.: Translation of string-and-pin-based shortest path search into data-scalable agent-based computational models. In: Proceedings of Winter Simulation Conference, Gothenburg, Sweden, pp. 881–892, December 2018
17. Woodring, J., et al.: A multi-agent parallel approach to analyzing large climate data sets. In: 37th IEEE International Conference on Distributed Computing Systems, Atlanta, GA, pp. 1639–1648, June 2017

Demonstrating Exception Handling in JaCaMo

Matteo Baldoni[1], Cristina Baroglio[1], Olivier Boissier[2], Roberto Micalizio[1], and Stefano Tedeschi[1(✉)]

[1] Dipartimento di Informatica, Università degli Studi di Torino, Turin, Italy
{baldoni,baroglio,micalizio}@di.unito.it, stefano.tedeschi@unito.it
[2] Laboratoire Hubert Curien UMR CNRS 5516, Institut Henri Fayol,
MINES Saint-Etienne, Saint-Etienne, France
Olivier.Boissier@emse.fr

Abstract. Current models for multi-agent organizations offer effective abstractions to build distributed systems, but lack a systematic way to address exceptions. This demonstration presents an exception handling mechanism in the context of the JaCaMo framework, based on the notions of responsibility and feedback. The mechanism is seamlessly integrated within organizational concepts, such as goals and norms.

Keywords: Exception handling · Multi-agent organizations · JaCaMo

1 Introduction

System robustness is a main concern in software engineering practice. It is "the degree to which a system or component can function correctly in the presence of invalid inputs or stressful environmental conditions" [1]. It refers to the ability of a computer system to cope with *perturbations* occurring during execution, keeping an acceptable behavior [7]. *Exception handling* has been successfully proposed as a powerful technology to achieve robustness. When a perturbation is detected (e.g., missing parameters, or unknown data format) an *exception* breaks the normal flow of execution, and deviates it to a pre-registered *handler*, that is executed to manage the perturbation. Notably, the seminal work by Goodenough [8] points out how exceptions are a viable mechanism for structuring and modularizing software, separating concerns into components that interact. Exceptions permit to extend an operation's domain or its range. They tailor an operation's results to the purpose in using it, making them usable in a wider variety of contexts. The invoker of an operation controls the response to an exception to be activated; this increases the generality of an operation because the appropriate "fixup" will vary from one use to the next. Multi-Agent Systems (MAS), and organizations (MAOs) in particular, bring software modularization, and separation of concerns to an extreme. Key features of many organizational models (see e.g., [4–6]), are a functional decomposition of an organizational goal and a normative system. Norms shape the scope of the responsibilities that agents

© Springer Nature Switzerland AG 2021
F. Dignum et al. (Eds.): PAAMS 2021, LNAI 12946, pp. 341–345, 2021.
https://doi.org/10.1007/978-3-030-85739-4_28

take within the organization, capturing what they should do to contribute to the organizational goal. Surprisingly, exception handling has almost never been applied in MAS as postulated in [8]. A critical point is that the availability of *feedback* concerning the perturbation is crucial for treating exceptions, and hence for robustness [2,3], but not easy to obtain in distributed systems. This demonstration shows how exception handling can be grafted inside the normative system of a MAO by explicitly distributing the responsiblities of rising and handling exceptions among agents, so making a perturbation feedback flow properly within the organization. We introduced exception handling in JaCaMo [4], integrating it at a conceptual level, within the abstractions of its meta-model, and at a software level, by enriching its infrastructure.

2   Main Purpose

The discussion above highlights two main aspects of exception handling: (i) it involves two parties: one is *responsible* for raising an exception, another is *responsible* for handling it, and (ii) it captures the need for some *feedback* from the former to the latter that allows coping with the exception. Since MAOs are built upon responsibilities, we claim that exception handling – in essence, a matter of responsibility distribution – can be integrated seamlessly. We interpret an exception as an event which denotes the impossibility, for some agent, to fulfill its responsibilities – e.g., a failure in goal achievement – causing the suspension of the distributed execution. We propose to leverage responsibility not only to model the duties of the agents in relation to the organizational goal, but also to enable them report about exceptions, occurring within the organization operation, and to identify the ones entitled for handling them. When agents join an organization, they will be asked to take on the responsibilities not only for organizational goals, but also: (i) for providing feedback about the context where exceptions are detected while pursuing goals, and (ii) if appointed, for handling such exceptions once the needed information is available. In our perspective, responsibilities also define the scope of exceptions, expressed with respect to the state of the organization, that agents ought to raise or treat. As a result, the normative system enables the coordination of the activities that concern not only the normal behavior of the system, but also its exceptional one, uniformly.

3   Demonstration

JaCaMo [4] is a platform that integrates agents, environments and organizations. Its organization model comprises a *structural* dimension, a *functional* dimension, including a set of schemes that capture how the organizational goals are decomposed into subgoals, grouped into missions, and a *normative* dimension binding the other two. Agents are held to commit to missions, taking responsibility for mission goals. We enriched the scheme specification with a few new

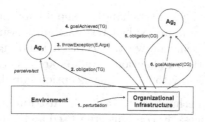

Fig. 1. Interaction between agents and organization for exception handling.

concepts[1]. Shortly, **Recovery Strategy** enables the treatment of an exception by binding a **Notification Policy** with one, or many, **Handling Policy**. **Notification Policy** specifies (i) when an exception must be raised by means of a **Throwing Goal**, enabled when a given perturbation occurs, and (ii) the kind of feedback to produce via **Exception Spec**. **Handling Policy**, instead, specifies how an exception must be handled, once the needed information–the exception feedback–is available, by enabling an appropriate **Catching Goal**. Notably, throwing and catching goals specialize the JaCaMo **Goal** concept, and are incorporated into mission like standard ones. In this way, our extension is seamlessly integrated into the organization management infrastructure, enabling a uniform approach in agent programming. Agents, entering an organization, take some responsibilities by committing to missions. Then, the infrastructure issues *obligations* to achieve goals, which may concern the normal functioning or the raising/handling of exceptions. Agent developers are required to implement the set of plans to make agents able to fulfill their responsibilities, achieving the goals expressed by the obligations directed to them. Figure 1 shows the typical interaction schema, between the involved agents and the organizational infrastructure, for handling the occurrence of an exception. As soon as a perturbation is detected, a suitable recovery strategy is searched and its notification policy activated: an obligation to achieve the corresponding throwing goal TG is issued. The agent responsible for TG will fulfill the obligation by throwing an exception (i.e., providing feedback) compliant with the specification. This enables one (or more) handling policy(ies), and the obligation(s) for the related catching goal(s) CG is issued. The agent in charge of CG leverages the exception feedback, made available through the infrastructure, to actually handling the exception. During the demonstration, we will present a set of use cases that take inspiration from real-world scenarios – coming from the fields of, e.g., business processes, and smart factories.

4   Conclusions

We evaluated the proposal with respect to a set of features that, in our view, should be exhibited by an exception handling mechanism to be suitable for MAS.

---

[1] The extension is available at http://di.unito.it/moiseexceptions.

Autonomy Preservation. Exception handling should not interfere with the agents' autonomy. In our proposal, an explicit responsibility assumption creates expectation on the agents' behavior w.r.t. exception handling. Nonetheless, agents remain free to violate their obligations. Agents are also autonomous in deliberating the most suitable way to carry out exception handling.

Decentralization. The mechanism leverages the distributed nature of MAS in the exception handling process. Exceptions are raised and handled in synergy by the society of agents in the organization. At the same time, the exception handling mechanism is integrated within the organizational infrastructure, which is reified in the environment in a distributed way.

Responsibility Distribution. Following Goodenough, exception handling is a mechanism to widen the scope of operations. Our proposal aims at creating a bridge between the agents responsible for raising exceptions and the ones responsible for their handling. The responsibility for exception handling is then moved outside the failing agent, increasing the generality of the applied recovery.

Importance of Feedback. A feedback coming from an informed source allows to increase the situational awareness about a perturbation, with straightforward benefits in its handling. This is especially true in a multi-agent setting, where each agent may have a different and partial view of the environment and of the overall ongoing execution. Our proposal systematize the way in which this relevant information is produced, encoded, delivered, and exploited for recovery.

Platform Integration. Together with the conceptual and theoretical soundness, we believe that the presence of a concrete programming support is fundamental for any application of exception handling. We then decided to implement the proposed model in the context of JaCaMo. The resulting solution proved to be effective in dealing with a wide range of situations, in multiple applications.

Acknowledgements. Stefano Tedeschi's research project has been carried out thanks to the grant "Bando Talenti della Società Civile" promoted by Fondazione CRT with Fondazione Giovanni Goria.

References

1. ISO/IEC/IEEE International Standard - Systems and software engineering - Vocabulary. ISO/IEC/IEEE 24765:2010(E) (2010)
2. Alderson, D.L., Doyle, J.C.: Contrasting views of complexity and their implications for network-centric infrastructures. IEEE Trans. Syst. Man Cyber. **40**(4), 839–852 (2010)
3. Baldoni, M., Baroglio, C., Micalizio, R., Tedeschi, S.: Robustness based on accountability in multiagent organizations. In: AAMAS 2021: 20th International Conference on Autonomous Agents and Multiagent Systems, pp. 142–150. ACM (2021)
4. Boissier, O., Bordini, R.H., Hübner, J.F., Ricci, A., Santi, A.: Multi-agent oriented programming with JaCaMo. Sci. Comput. Program. **78**(6), 747–761 (2013)
5. Bresciani, P., Perini, A., Giorgini, P., Giunchiglia, F., Mylopoulos, J.: Tropos: an agent-oriented software development methodology. JAAMAS **8**(3), 203–236 (2004)

6. Dardenne, A., van Lamsweerde, A., Fickas, S.: Goal-directed requirements acquisition. Sci. Comput. Program. **20**(1), 3–50 (1993)
7. Fernandez, J.C., Mounier, L., Pachon, C.: A model-based approach for robustness testing. In: Proceedings of TestCom 2005, pp. 333–348 (2005)
8. Goodenough, J.B.: Exception handling: issues and a proposed notation. Commun. ACM **18**(12), 683–696 (1975)

Dial4JaCa – A Demonstration

Débora Engelmann[1,3]($\boxtimes$)(iD), Juliana Damasio[1](iD), Tabajara Krausburg[1,4](iD),
Olimar Borges[1](iD), Lucca Dornelles Cezar[1](iD), Alison R. Panisson[2](iD),
and Rafael H. Bordini[1](iD)

[1] School of Technology, Pontifical Catholic University of Rio Grande do Sul,
Porto Alegre, Brazil
{debora.engelmann,juliana.damasio,tabajara.rodrigues,olimar.borges,
lucca.cezar}@edu.pucrs.br, rafael.bordini@pucrs.br
[2] Department of Computer Engineering, Federal University of Santa Catarina,
Florianópolis, Brazil
alison.panisson@ufsc.br
[3] DIBRIS, University of Genoa, Genoa, Italy
[4] Department of Informatics, Technische Universität Clausthal (TUC),
Clausthal-Zellerfeld, Germany

Abstract. Multi-Agent Systems (MAS) have become a powerful approach to the development of complex AI systems. However, the community faces the challenge of developing communication interfaces between software agents and humans, for instance, using natural language. In this paper, we demonstrate an approach to the integration of MAS and chatbot technologies named Dial4JaCa. Dial4JaCa enables the implementation of MAS integrated with chatbots, which can be applied to a variety of domains. In this particular work, we demonstrate how it is possible to integrate a JaCaMo application (agent system) with Dialogflow (a chatbot platform) using Dial4JaCa.

Keywords: Multi-agent systems · Natural language · Chatbots

1 Introduction

A conversational agent (chatbot) is a computer program that interacts with users through natural language. With the advances of Natural Language Processing (NLP), conversational agents have started to play an important role in a variety of contexts. As a result, many platforms are available to provide mechanisms for NLP and dialog management. On the other hand, Multi-Agent Systems (MAS) are built upon core concepts such as distributed systems and reactivity, as well as individual rationality. Thus, agent technology is a promising way to provide strong reasoning capabilities to chatbot platforms.

In this paper, we demonstrate the use of Dial4JaCa, a communication interface between MAS and chatbot platforms. In particular, we demonstrate the implementation of a communication interface between a JaCaMo [3] application for supporting hospital bed allocation and Dialogflow[1]. Our communication

---

[1] https://dialogflow.com/.

F. Dignum et al. (Eds.): PAAMS 2021, LNAI 12946, pp. 346–350, 2021.
https://doi.org/10.1007/978-3-030-85739-4_29

interface makes it possible to implement multi-agent systems in which agents and humans are able to have dialogues in natural language.

```
1  +request(ResponseId, IntentName, Params, Contexts)
2     : (IntentName == "Reply With Context")
3  <- contextBuilder(ResponseId, "test context", "1", Context);
4     replyWithContext("Hello, I am your Jason agent, and I am
5                                responding with context ", Context).
```

Listing 1: An example of a plan to reply to a request with a context.

2   Main Purpose

Dial4JaCa provides an integration[2] of the JaCaMo framework [3] and Dialogflow, and it allows developers to implement intelligent agents that are able to communicate with humans through natural-language interaction. We aim at making our approach as modular as possible so that it can be imported into any MAS project developed in JaCaMo. Figure 1 depicts the Dial4JaCa architecture.

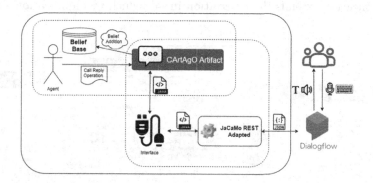

Fig. 1. The Dial4JaCa architecture.

Our approach is built upon a resource-oriented abstraction provided by the JaCaMo REST project[3] [2]. We integrate it with *fulfillment* services available in Dialogflow. Our interface allows all agents that are observing a particular CArtAgO artefact to receive requests from Dialogflow. Then, it is up to the agents to decide whether they are going to react to such requests or not. We show in Listing 1 an example of a Jason plan to react to a request. In a request, Dial4JaCa makes an agent perceive contexts and parameters captured by Dialogflow. *Parameters* is a list containing the pattern parameter(key, value). *Contexts* is a list in which each element contains a context name, a lifespan, and a list of parameters.

---

[2] https://git.io/Dial4JaCa.
[3] https://git.io/jacamoRest.

To reply to a request, the agents have at their disposal an operation in the Dial4JaCa artefact which may take in addition to the intended response a *context* or an *event*. The response is just plain text to be shown to the user. A reply with a context is important to provide to Dialogflow additional information besides the response to the user. To do so, an agent first creates a new context (line 3) in the same pattern as described above. Then it sends the information back through Dial4JaCa (lines 4–5). A reply with an event is useful in cases an agent is running out of time to reply to a request (e.g., if the chatbot platform has a predefined waiting timeout). In that case, Dial4JaCa automatically replies with an event for Dialogflow to reestablish the intention. Doing so, it gets more time for the agent to finish its reasoning. This mechanism can be used at most three times in a row.

Note that we can also use, given some small changes in Dial4JaCa, other natural language processing platforms such as Rasa, Watson, or Luis.

3   Demonstration

We use Dial4JaCa as a decision support system for hospital bed allocation[4]. This application extends the integration in [4], which was application specific.

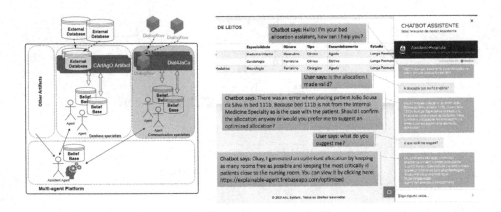

Fig. 2. Bed allocation system.

We show in Fig. 2 an overview of the application architecture (left) and part of the application interface[5] (right). In it, the `assistant agent` is responsible for communicating with other agents to assist a user in a search for bed availability. The `database specialist` agents take care of any database query needed. These agents use a CArtAgO artefact to connect to hospital databases (in this application in particular).

---

[4] https://git.io/bedAlloSystem.
[5] https://git.io/bedAllocSimul.

Communication specialist agents use Dial4JaCa to provide a communication layer between an end user and the assistant agent. For instance, it is possible to instantiate an agent for each user of the system. This allows customised responses according to a user profile. This way an application can avoid giving too many explanatory answers to a user who has a specialist background, as well as avoid giving superficial answers to users with little background. The ability to instantiate multiple communication expert agents, one for each user of the system, also allows the Assistant Agent to engage in multiparty conversations, helping a team or a group of users to make joint decisions.

Moreover, there are two other agents populating the MAS application: the optimiser agent and the validator agent. The optimiser agent is responsible for communicating with a GLPK solver to generate optimal bed allocations. The validator agent uses a PDDL (Planning Domain Definition Language) validator[6] and a CArtAgO artefact[7] to validate bed allocation plans made by the user.

The current version of this MAS application has not been evaluated by professionals responsible for allocating beds in hospitals yet. However, we intend to do it in the near future. Dial4JaCa fulfilled its role in our preliminary tests, supporting communication and other functionalities as expected, and providing a complete integration between the MAS application and Dialogflow. In the next version of this multi-agent system application, we intend to use argumentation theory and ontology techniques, allowing agents to explain their suggestions for bed allocation. Explainability becomes an essential part of decision support systems, and Dial4JaCa can support this type of sophisticated interactions.

4 Conclusions

We made considerable progress towards natural language communication interfaces between humans and multi-agent systems. The scenario presented in this paper demonstrate the use of Dial4JaCa in practice, also showing promising preliminary results. We believe that several applications for various domains can be developed using Dial4JaCa, for example, ambient intelligence and law. Also, our approach provides support to the development of applications in the context of hybrid intelligence [1], in which human-agent collaboration is fundamental. In our future work, we intend to explore the integration with other chatbot development platforms. We also intend to apply Dial4JaCa in other domains.

References

1. Akata, Z., et al.: A research agenda for hybrid intelligence: augmenting human intellect with collaborative, adaptive, responsible, and explainable artificial intelligence. Computer **53**(8), 18–28 (2020)

---

[6] https://git.io/PDDLPlanValid.
[7] https://git.io/PDDLPlanValidArtif.

2. Amaral, C.J., Hübner, J.F., Kampik, T.: Towards Jacamo-rest: a resource-oriented abstraction for managing multi-agent systems. arXiv preprint arXiv:2006.05619 (2020)
3. Boissier, O., Bordini, R.H., Hübner, J.F., Ricci, A., Santi, A.: Multi-agent oriented programming with Jacamo. Sci. Comput. Programm. **78**(6), 747–761 (2013)
4. Engelmann, D.C.: An interactive agent to support hospital bed allocation based on plan validation. dissertation, PUCRS (2019)

Experiments on User-Centered Control of Lights in Open-Plan Office Spaces Using IoT Devices and Distributed Constraint Optimization

Farousi Nuha[1](✉), Atrache Meryem[2](✉), Stahl Christoph[2](✉), and Najjar Amro[1](✉)

[1] University of Luxembourg, Esch-sur-Alzette, Luxembourg
amro.najjar@uni.lu
[2] Luxembourg Institute of Science and Technology (LIST),
Esch-sur-Alzette, Luxembourg
christoph.stahl@list.com

Abstract. Our solution learns the relationship between lamps and desks to minimize conflicts between neighbours. We adopt an IoT infrastructure with light sensors and a Distributed Constraint Optimisation (DCOP) algorithm as scalable solution to this problem.

Keywords: Smart lighting · Open-plan office space · DCOP algorithm · IoT

1 Introduction

Based on the user's activity and age, different light settings may be desired. Our approach uses a fine-grained array of ceiling lights based on LED light bulbs that can be individually dimmed by RF (Zigbee) connectivity.

2 Our Approach to Solve the Problem

Our prototype follows a user-centered and self-calibrating approach. The light calibration procedure uses wireless light sensors (lux meter) on each desk surfce to measure the effect of each lamp. As user interface, office workers use a smartphone app to select a desk by scanning a QR code and choose a desired activity with associated light level. Each time a new request is made by a user, the system computes the optimal configuration (dimming level) of each ceiling lamp to provide the required light level per desk and user, while minimizing overall brightness to avoid potential glare and save energy. Furthermore, a certain contrast between bright and dark areas is perceived as more natural and comfortable for the eye than a uniform light distribution.

Supported by University of Luxembourg and Luxembourg Institute of Science and Technology (LIST).

F. Dignum et al. (Eds.): PAAMS 2021, LNAI 12946, pp. 351–354, 2021.
https://doi.org/10.1007/978-3-030-85739-4_30

The Demonstrator Environment. The demonstrator is currently implemented in one of LIST's labs, equipped with light spots (GU10 socket light bulbs, 5W, warm white, dimmable in 255 steps via a zigbee gateway), among other lamps, and two desk locations for the users, as shown in Fig. 1

Fig. 1. The lab environment with several spotlights and desks with integrated light sensors.

The spots are mounted on a high cross beam structure that is generally used to equip the lab with sensors and actuators for experiments. In our test setting, Lamps L_1 and L_2 are positioned to illuminate the desk referred by $Desk1$, and lamps L_3 and L_4 are directed to the desk referred by $Desk2$. Lamps L_5 and L_6 are located in between and have an effect on both desks.

We are using a MQTT message broker for the communication between IoT devices in our lab, including the lamps and light sensors (luxmeter). Different applications can publish or subscribe to data using topics.

3 Demonstration Scenario

Let's assume that user A is participating in a video chat using the PC at Desk 2 in the open space of our scenario, with lights slightly dimmed to 350 lux of luminosity, according to her preference for this activity. Now user B arrives at Desk 1 to read the manual for a sensor. His preferred light level for reading tasks is 600 lux. He scans the QR code and chooses his personalized reading activity using the app. The DCOP, based on the constrains, comes up with a solution that provides the proper dimming levels, based on the calibration information.

4   Implementation

The application for our experiment is implemented with Python using Kivy, which is a free and open-source Python framework for developing mobile apps and other multi-touch application software with a natural user interface. We use the pydcop library to find the optimal solution for our problem, and the paho.mqtt library is used for the communication with the MQTT broker. Controlling the lights involves the following steps:

1. Self-calibration procedure: Every night, when the office is empty, the automatic calibration sequentially turns on single lamps an measures their impact on the lux sensors of all desks.
2. Sign in: The user registers with a simple procedure and sign in to be able to use the application and manage personal preferences.
3. Choose a desk: After signing in, the user must choose a desk by scanning the QR code that sticks on the table.
4. Choosing an activity: The application provides a list of activities with associated brightness (lux) levels, which can be personalized as well.

DCOP Algorithm

Applying DCOP on Our Scenario

- A set of agents $A = \{A_1, A_2, A_3\}$ represents the micro-controllers used to solve DCOP (in our case Arduino-compatible boards with built-in WiFi, running PyDcop on Micropython.
- The variables $X = \{L_1, L_2, L_3, L_4, L_5, L_6\}$ represent the spotlights' dimming level;
- The domain: we have only one domain, which is the spotlight dimming level with values [0 to 255];
- For the mapping μ between agents and lamps (it depends on the Desk the user is choosing, and the measured effect per spotlight and desk): A_1 controls L_1 or L_4; A_2 controls L_2 or L_3; A_3 controls L_5 and L_6.

The constrains are written in a way that direct DCOP to find the optimal solution by using the maximum values from the dedicated lights and the least it can get from the mutual ones. We do this by setting a maximum value and giving a high-cost to the mutual lights, in this way the DCOP will avoid using them as much as it can since the objective of the algorithm is to minimize the cost. In our example, Fig. 2 shows the constraints for $Desk_1$ with $Reading$ activity, where we control L_1, L_2, L_5, L_6 to reach the luminosity level of 600 lux.

The DCOP Solution: Once the user chooses his Desk and activity, DCOP will run and decides what values to send to the lights, the decision is made by the DCOP based on the constrains we deployed. In our example, the user has chosen $Desk1$ and $Reading$, so the luminosity level in this case is 600 lux and the variables L_1, L_2, L_6 and L_5 are the ones who should be affected.

```
constraints:
# nc are the constraint that bind the light bulb to the physical model

nc1:
    type: intention
    function: 0 if round(0.001*l1 + 0.001*l2 + 0.7*l5 + 0.7*l6 ) == 600 else 10
nc2:
    type: intention
    function: 0 if round(0.7*l5) <= 50 else 10
nc3:
    type: intention
    function: 0 if round(0.7*l6) <= 50 else 10
nc4:
    type: intention
    function: 0 if round(0.001*l2) <= 150 else 10
```

Fig. 2. The DCOP defines lighting constraints for *Desk*1 with *Reading* activity (600 lux).

After running the algorithm for this scenario on 3 agents, we get the solution $[L_1 : 250, L_2 : 250, L_5 : 50, L_6 : 50]$: L1 and L2 got a dimming value of 250 since they are directed to *Desk*1 and have the bigger effect, while L5 and L6 got a dimming value of 50, which is the maximum value you can get from these 2 lights without disturbing the neighbour at *Desk*2.

5   Summary and Outlook

In this demonstration paper, we described an experiment with 6 light bulbs, 3 agents and 2 desks, in order to see the effect of each user on his neighbour, and based on that we gave the lights their weights and wrote the constraints. The next steps will make the scenario more complex by adding more lights and desks, and involve other ceiling lights, and window blinds actuators to control the amount of outside light. Also, it would be promising to apply image recognition, which could decide the user activity by analysing objects around the user.

References

1. Rust, P., Picard, G., Ramparany, F.: Using message-passing DCOP algorithms to solve energy-efficient smart environment configuration problems (2016)
2. Aji, S.M., McEliece, R.J.: The generalized distributive law (2000)
3. Fioretto, F., Pontelli, E., Yeoh, W.: Distributed constraint optimization problems and applications: a survey (2018)
4. Zhang, W., Wang, G., Xing, Z., Wittenburg, L.: A comparative study of distributed constraint algorithms (2003)
5. Rust, P., Ramparany, F.: Distributed constraint optimization for the Internet-of-Things (2016)

A DBDN with the MAS Ellipsis

Marianne Mauch[(✉)]

Department of Computer Science, Friedrich Schiller University Jena, Jena, Germany
marianne.mauch@uni-jena.de
https://swt.informatik.uni-jena.de/Mitarbeiter/Mauch+Marianne.html

Abstract. This demonstration paper aims to present the multi-agent system (MAS) Ellipsis, which has been enhanced within the joint research project SMART DISTRIBUTION LOGISTICS (SDL) to build a distributed agent-based Big Data network (DBDN) between the cooperating media logistics companies [5]. The goal was to enable an e-mobility focused TCO (total cost of ownership) analysis on a broad data basis while keeping the original data itself securely within the control of each company. With the help of mobile agents and a BDI concept, agents are able to react independently to unforeseen events. They are able to decide in an autonomous fashion, to travel and to transfer algorithms from one system to another. Thus, the system enables asynchronous communication between the logistics entrepreneur and the agent acting on its behalf in the TCO study. Proactive and distributed systems with autonomous units (acting deputies) on heterogeneous data meet the unbroken demand of companies and stakeholders for the sovereignty of their data and their underlying business models. These business models express themselves in dynamic structures and different types of negotiation.

Keywords: Mobile agent · Multi-agent system · Migration · Logistic

1 Introduction

Mobile agents offer innovative approaches for complex and distributed data structures. The Chair of Software Engineering (https://swt.informatik.uni-jena.de) at the Institute of Computer Science at Friedrich Schiller University Jena (FSU Jena) has been researching mobile agents for many years and has developed various multi-agent systems such as Tracy, Tracy2 and Ellipsis [2,7]. Using the project SMART DISTRIBUTION LOGISTICS (SDL) project (http://sdl-projekt.de) as an example, MAS Ellipsis, was further developed in such a way that it can be integrated into historically grown solutions for loosely cooperating logistics companies and telematics solutions. Media logistics is on the verge of a complete restructuring of its logistics systems and a change from part-time to full-time delivery, which is seen as necessary in the industry. The media and publishing industry has to cope

Supported by the W. Rossak, the SDL project team and the Bachelor theses of M. Rauppach, P. Langisch and H. Legner.

F. Dignum et al. (Eds.): PAAMS 2021, LNAI 12946, pp. 355–358, 2021.
https://doi.org/10.1007/978-3-030-85739-4_31

with changing customer demands. More and more people are using digital media. The number of people using printed media is continuously decreasing. To compensate for this trend, media logistics companies are expanding their business fields to include services such as postal delivery. Against this background, media logistics companies deliver newspapers, letters, parcels and take over goods deliveries for local retailers. In addition, there is a significant shortage of staff for delivery. It is becoming increasingly difficult to find low-paid staff willing to work in the early hours of the morning from 3 am. Since introducing the minimum wage in Germany, delivery staff are no longer paid by piece but per time unit. Time expenditures must now be estimated based on delivery quantities, the number of households to be delivered to, kilometers traveled, or other parameters. The exchange of information is mostly done with digital spreadsheet programs and paper. The challenge in media logistics is to reposition itself in terms of ICT, business processes and logistics concepts. Due to already high levels of particulate matter and nitrogen oxide in German inner cities and the resulting threat of driving bans, media logistics is facing a further challenge and ,thus, moving towards e-mobility.

2   Main Purpose

There are various off-the-shelf systems for different tasks in media logistics, and each of the companies involved employs its own flavor. In mail collection of one project partner, customer data is maintained in CodX, scheduling information such as time windows and the collection status of orders in an Excel spreadsheet. In delivery, orders for newspapers and weeklies come from Vi & Va. Letter deliveries are administered in CodX. There is digital access to the software program, which calculates the optimal route for the delivery staff once a month. The letters intended for delivery are pre-sorted electronically and assigned to the delivery districts. Here, too, there is a software program that stores all addresses, but again without a usable interface to the outside world. It is easy to see that this use case is appropriate for a MAS. In the ideal conception of a distributed Big Data network, there are three nodes, the logistics partners and only one type of edge - the migration interface. In this network, each contractual partner retains sovereignty over its data and negotiations can be carried out at each node of this network. Each actor can decide when, to whom and how pre-processed data is transferred. Furthermore, it is possible to enter into negotiations with other logistics partners about possible orders - in the sense of car and cargo sharing. The IT-systems of the logistics partners each have a MAS infrastructure that enables data processing and serves as basis of negotiations. Negotiations on one's own system are thus also possible if necessary, while negotiations on external systems could be avoided. In addition, data does not have to be exchanged in large quantities, and analyses can be carried out on site. Data are pre-processed on the own system, and only what is required for the current negotiation is transmitted. In this way, redundancies are also avoided from the point of view of data security and data minimization. Thus, as the owner of the data, the logistics partner also retains sovereignty over his data and does not have to make sensitive company data available for analysis on external systems. Another advantage is a homogeneous environment with low maintenance requirements, which can also be expanded ad-hoc during running operations. For the overall development of such a distributed Big Data network, fitting interfaces to all the existing IT-systems had to be generated. Based on the experiences in the project, this approach will now be generalized in further research and the essential components will be identified in the form of a reference architecture proposal. A. Schäfer presents such an approach for a modified Multi-Agent System (MAS) as a network-independent adaptive framework for a distributed logistic network [6]. The main components are mobile and autonomous agents, which will behave as acting deputies, a completely decoupled graphical interface for a bidirectional human-agent interaction, and a user administration, which mapped the human-agent relationship and a management of a distributed network. The goal is to develop a general approach to exchange and negotiate services within a generalized DBDN from this very domain-specific approach. There are a lot of Multi-Agent-Systems also in the logistics domain [1,3,8]. Not all these systems have all these components. The decisive factor here is the characteristics of the mobile and autonomous agents, which will behave as acting deputies in a media logistics use case. The MAS Ellipsis is to be understood as a research approach.

3 Demonstration

This demonstration is intended to show the mobile and autonomously acting agents in several instances of MAS Ellipsis. In one example, agents travel according to a set of goals and plans and collect information from several instances of MAS Ellipsis. Mobile agents as an artificial intelligence concept offer exciting approaches to processing algorithms and data in distributed systems. In contrast to conventional software architectures, algorithms are transmitted in a network with the help of migration, and the processing of a resource (e.g., data) takes place where it is available. With the migration component Kalong [2] can several integrated migration strategies be used. They differ depending on when and where how much code is transferred. The pre-processing of the data is done with an agent society in which agents connect to data sources. Agents can read in Excel tables, request SQL servers and connect other data sources. These agents, which function as data adapters, are then triggered by other agents with a functional focus. This makes it easy to integrate heterogeneous data sources and present them homogeneously to the outside world. The information on how the data should be transformed comes in turn from an ontology agent. For this purpose, requests are made to the ontology agent, which provides a suitable answer to the request from its knowledge base. Direct human-agent interaction is also supported. This is achieved with the help of a bidirectional and graphical user-interface for the MAS Ellipsis. The interface itself has been implemented to be technically decoupled from the specifics of our MAS. For the negotiation with the help of agents between different logistics partners, the data obtained had to be integrated into one interface. HTML, CSS, JavaScript, and a double REST API can establish asynchronous communication with one or more Ellipsis instances. Since an agent's task scope is not defined precisely, each agent requires a different representation on the frontend. A user interface according to the modular principle of many small microservices was built to serve this purpose. The layout was arranged in a grid, a tiled layout. Users can largely determine the interfaces themselves and only have to evaluate and manage the incoming data.

4   Conclusions

In this project, partners who trusted each other cooperated in a well-defined scenario and exchanged crucial information based on the MAS Ellipsis. This type of trust will not always be available. To support also more critical cases, improved security is crucial and will be further expanded with adequate mechanisms, e.g., by an SSL - based communication during agent migration.

References

1. Anand, N., van Duin, R., Tavasszy, L.: Framework for modelling multi-stakeholder city logistics domain using the agent based modelling approach. Transp. Res. Procedia **16**, 4–15 (2016). https://doi.org/10.1016/j.trpro.2016.11.002
2. Braun, P., Rossak, W.: Mobile Agents. Morgan Kaufmann, San Francisco (2005). https://doi.org/10.1016/B978-155860817-7/50002-7
3. Davidsson, P., Henesey, L., Ramstedt, L., Törnquist, J., Wernstedt, F.: An analysis of agent-based approaches to transport logistics. Transp. Res. Part C Emerg. Technol. **13**(4), 255–271 (2005). Ronneby. https://doi.org/10.1016/j.trc.2005.07.002
4. Lorenzen, L.-E., Woelk, P.-O., Denkena, B., Scholz, T., Timm, I.J., Herzog, O.: Integrated Process Planning and Production Control. Springer, Heidelberg, pp. 91–113 (2006) https://doi.org/10.1007/3-540-32062-8_6
5. Mauch, M., et al.: Distributed agent-based big data network for secure e-mobility TCO analysis: A use case for multi-agent systems in logistics environment. In: 2019 International Conference on Computational Science and Computational Intelligence (CSCI), Las Vegas, pp. 1151–1155. IEEE (2019). https://doi.org/10.1109/CSCI49370.2019.00217
6. Schäfer, A., Schau, V., Mauch, M., Amme, W.: Two layer approach: a modified multi agent system (mas) as a network-independent adaptive framework for a distributed logistic network. In: 13th International KES Conference: Agents and multi-agent systems: Technologies and Applications in Malta, Malta (2019). http://nimbusvault.net/publications/koala/assr/605.html
7. Schau, V.: Ellipsis-Konzeption und Implementierung einer vereinheitlichten und leistungsfähigen Architektur für Multi-Agenten Systeme (MAS) auf Basis frei verfügbarer IT-Infrastrukturkomponeneten unter besonderer Berücksichtigung internationaler Standards. Ph.D. thesis, FSU Jena (2012)
8. Timm, I.J., Woelk, P.-O., Knirsch, P., Tönshoff, H.-K., Herzog, O.: Flexible Mass Customisation: Managing Its Information Logistics Using Adaptive Cooperative Multi-agent Systems. Palgrave Macmillan London, pp. 203–211 (2016) https://doi.org/10.1057/9781137541253_18

Demo Paper: A Tool for Analyzing COVID-19-Related Measurements Using Agent-Based Support Simulator for Airport Terminal Operations

S. Sahand Mohammadi Ziabari$^{(\boxtimes)}$ ⓘ, Gregory Sanders, Adin Mekic,
and Alexei Sharpanskykh ⓘ

Delft University of Technology, Delft, The Netherlands
A.Mekic@tudelft.nl

Abstract. This paper presents a demonstration of our PAAMS 2021 paper using data-driven analysis of airport terminal operations and An Agent-based Airport Terminal Operations Model Simulator (AATOM). The goal of this paper is to demonstrate and analyze the impact of the current COVID-19 and future pandemic-related measures on airport terminal operations and to identify plans that airport management agents can take into account to control the flow of passengers in a safe, efficient, secure and resilient way. To analyze the impact of the identified COVID-19 measures on the airport operations, the existing agent-based AATOM model was need to be modified in order to implement these measures. In this paper, we illustrate a demo of a developed simulator tool by investigating the effects of different degrees of physical distancing rules among agents on the performances of the airport. In the demo session the attendees will have the possibility to (i) work with the simulator tool on different relevant parameters regarding different sections and agents in the airport; (ii) view and analyze different performance indicator analyzers of the simulator.

Keywords: Airport operations · Physical distancing · Analyzer · AATOM

1 Introduction

Due to the COVID-19, many countries closed their borders to mitigate the spread of the virus and to reduce COVID-19 deaths. As a result, global passenger demand of April 2020 (in revenue passenger kilometer or RPK) plunged with 94.3% compared to last year [5]. A vaccine is considered as the only solution to completely eradicate the spread of COVID-19. Moreover, the COVID-19 situation is dynamic as restrictions are modified regularly, to study these restrictions we need a model that is able to capture this highly complex system and is able to adapt to varying conditions. Agent-based modelling is a suitable paradigm to model and study complex socio-economic systems, such as airport operations [2]. Agent based models are also very suited to study the resilience of the

© Springer Nature Switzerland AG 2021
F. Dignum et al. (Eds.): PAAMS 2021, LNAI 12946, pp. 359–362, 2021.
https://doi.org/10.1007/978-3-030-85739-4_32

system [2], for example what is the effect of a sudden disruption in the flight schedule on the airport operations.

To address this problem agent-based modelling and simulation is used. In agent-based modelling, humans can be modelled as intelligent entities, called agents. These agents can be given certain traits and behavior that organize their interaction with the environment. This bottom-up approach allows for modelling complex sociotechnical systems, such as an airport terminal. It also allows for simulating local interactions in the system, for instance, physical distancing between passengers and analyzing the emergent properties of the global system. These emergent properties can be translated into system-wide key performance indicators.

The airport is a highly complex socio-technical system that consists of many different processes that are linked with each other. The passenger flow can be generally split up in departing passengers, arriving passengers and connecting passengers. An airport terminal generally consists out of three areas: the transit hall, the departure hall and the arrival hall. The transit hall is the area where departing passengers enter the airport and arrived passengers leave the airport. In this area the departing passengers can check in at the check-in desks or make use of other facilities such as shopping or restaurants. The transit hall and the departure hall are connected by the security check area. In the departure hall the gates are located where the departing passengers can wait for their flight. The arrival hall is solely used by the arriving passengers and connecting passengers. Based on the work of Schultz et al. [4] it was found that the passenger characteristics have an impact on their walking speed. It was concluded that passenger speed is significantly influenced by age, gender, group size and travel purpose such as business or leisure.

This paper presents a demonstration of our PAAMS 2021 paper on modeling the effects of COVID-19 measures in airports terminal using an agent-based airport terminal operations simulator (AATOM) [1]. Figure 1 shows the environment of this simulator. It consists of different sections such as check-in, security check point and gates. In this demo paper we propose a model that can be used to asses airport's efficiency and passenger safety.

2 Main Purpose

The passengers and airport staff are modelled as autonomous intelligent entities, called agents. These agents can be modelled with a particular behavior approximating passengers/staff and located in an environment, in our case the airport. The behaviors and interactions of the agents may be formalized by equations, but also more generally by decision rules such as if-then kind of rules. Global system-wide emergent properties can be generated and studies without having to make assumptions in advance regarding the system as a whole. The simulation fills the gap between the individual behavior of the passengers and the collective effects on the airport operations performance. Furthermore, the behavioral rules of agents can be varied (heterogeneity) or random influences can be incorporated (stochasticity). Agents characteristics can also be varied. For passenger one can define: gender, age, business vs leisure and the walking speed. Furthermore, agent-based simulation can be well used interdependencies between agent types and emergent properties in the model [2], for instance which passenger type has a higher risk of COVID-19 infection. It can be considered as a sort of magnifying glass to understand the reality better. The results of the interdependencies between passenger speed and passenger characteristics were given by Schultz et al. [4] in the form of statistical distributions. These distributions are implemented in AATOM such that different passenger types are created. Then also a risk-analysis will be done in the model output analysis to observe for different types of passengers.

There are different agents and interactions possible in AATOM. Firstly, check-in operators are able to interact with the environment, especially the flights. For example, they can update the state of a certain flight when everyone has checked-in [3]. Secondly, operators can interact with each other. For example, operator responsible for X-Ray scanning and the operator responsible for luggage checking can communicate with each other. Thirdly, operators and passenger agents can interact with each other. For instance, a check-in agent can order a passenger to wait for a specific time at the check-in desk. Lastly, an orchestration agent can be implemented overall for coordination of terminal operations, such as optimizing physical distance between agents. To coordinate, the orchestration needs to interact with operators, passengers and the environment [3]. Helbing et al. came up with the social force model for analyzing physical distancing [2]. The social-force model uses psychological forces that drive pedestrians to move towards their goal as well as keep a proper distance from other pedestrians and objects.

3   Demonstration

AATOM contains calibrated templates of basic airport terminal configurations that can be easily adjusted and used for analysis of airport operations. The model simulates the main handling processes for departing passengers in the airport terminal, this includes check-in, security checkpoint and border control. Figure 2 illustrates performance indicators of the airport. That consist of passenger agents in queue, average time in queue, activity distribution, time to gate, number of passenger agents, number of missed flights, and finally average physical distancing. Furthermore, there is a need for additional passenger safety indicators. Since currently the transmission of the respiratory syndrome COVID-19 is not fully understood yet, many experts assume that the spread is found by physical contact, droplets and airborne routes [6]. In the proposed model, the proposed safety indicator is the physical distancing. Therefore, there is a need for a flexible model that does not rely on specific assumptions of the disease and initial condition's such as the amount of infected people enter the terminal. We implemented the proposed model using AATOM simulator. During the demonstration, the simulator for one run will be used. Attendees will be able to see the live run of the simulator with some predefined configuration (and can change) for different sections in the airport such as check-in, security checkpoint, and gates. These configurations are for instance the walking speed, number of lanes at the security checkpoint, number of check-in desks, and passenger arrival distribution.

The outputs of the AATOM model can be investigated in this demonstration. These output indicators are purely performance based, such as: amount of passengers in a queue, average time in a queue, time to gate, average physical distancing and others.

Fig. 1. AATOM environment.   **Fig. 2.** AATOM analyzers.

4 Conclusion

The purpose of the developed simulator tool was to model and provide a proper under-standing of the impact of the COVID-19 measures on airport operations' performance and the associated safety of passengers. The model is an extension of the existing AATOM model and includes a redefined passenger dynamics model based on the social force model of Helbing to simulate physical distancing. The agent-based model also consists of a new model environment (check-in, security and boarding infrastructure) to represent realistically an airport under COVID-19 conditions. The metrics to assess the health safety of the passengers are based on existing studies regarding COVID-19 trans-mission. Because of the COVID-19 pandemic, passenger safety has become an essential topic on airport operators' agenda. With the possibility of new pandemics arising, this study is not only relevant for today but also for the future. This study can help airport operators in their decision-making and make airports more resilient for future crises.

1. References

1. Janssen, S., Sharpanskykh, A., Curran, R., Langendoen, K.: AATOM: an agent-based airport terminal operations model simulator. In: SummerSim, pp. 20–1, July 2019
2. Helbing, D., Balietti, S.: How to do agent-based simulations in the future: from modeling social mechanisms to emergent phenomena and interactive systems design. Technical report 11-06-024 (2015)
3. Janssen, S., Blok, A.N., Knol, A.: Aatom-an agent-based airport terminal operations model (2018)
4. Schultz, M., Oreschko, B., Schulz, C., Fricke, H.: Tracking Passengers at Airports for User Driven Terminal Design
5. ACI launches accreditation program to assess airport health measures. Airport Council International ACI (2020). https://aci.aero/news/2020/07/24/. Accessed 03 Mar 2021
6. Yu, I.T., et al.: Evidence of airborne transmission of the severe acute respiratory syndrome virus. N. Engl. J. Med. **350**(17), 1731–1739 (2004)

Using AGADE Traffic to Analyse Purpose-Driven Travel Behaviour

Johannes Nguyen[1,2]([⊠]), Simon T. Powers[2], Neil Urquhart[2],
Thomas Farrenkopf[1], and Michael Guckert[1]

[1] KITE, Technische Hochschule Mittelhessen, 61169 Friedberg, Germany
{Johannes.Nguyen,Thomas.Farrenkopf,michael.guckert}@mnd.thm.de
[2] School of Computing, Edinburgh Napier University, Edinburgh EH10 5DT, UK
{S.Powers,n.urquhart}@napier.ac.uk

Abstract. AGADE Traffic is an agent-based traffic simulator that can
be used to analyse purpose-driven travel behaviour of individuals that
leads to the emergence of systemic patterns in mobility. The simulator
uses semantic technology to model knowledge of individuals and thus is
able to capture individual preferences and personal objectives as determining factors of travel decisions. This creates a deeper understanding
of the individuals and allows for new analysis options. Using an example,
we give an overview of analysis instruments implemented in our simulator that are particularly suitable to examine results of individual-based
simulations.

Keywords: Traffic simulation · Behaviour analysis · Agent systems

1 Introduction

Current state of road traffic is a system in overload mode that requires a fundamental change in the concepts of everyday mobility. Frequent traffic jams
and the perpetual lack of parking space are obvious consequences of this situation. Private companies and public institutions are already working intensely
on solutions that exploit contemporary technological innovation [4]. Measures in
complex public systems are threatened by rebound effects [1], e.g. car sharing
services at first sight encourage people to abandon their private vehicles thus
freeing up space in urban areas. However, if they apply to the wrong audiences
effects may even end up worsening the traffic situation. It has been observed
that car sharing services were accepted as an alternative to *public transport*,
which in consequence has increased the number of people travelling in individual vehicles [5]. In order to prevent counterproductive effects from happening,
traffic planners need more elaborate tools for working out new ideas on mobility.
Computer-based simulations can be applied to predict and investigate effects
of planned measures in complex traffic systems. More specifically, agent-based
simulation models that focus on simulating individuals and their purpose-driven
travel behaviour are particularly suitable for analysing causal changes that have
led to the emergence of new systemic patterns.

© Springer Nature Switzerland AG 2021
F. Dignum et al. (Eds.): PAAMS 2021, LNAI 12946, pp. 363–366, 2021.
https://doi.org/10.1007/978-3-030-85739-4_33

2   Main Purpose

AGADE Traffic is an agent-based traffic simulator that places modelling of individuals at the center of attention. The simulator focuses on individuals pursuing personal objectives which determines purpose of their trips. Travel purpose plays a crucial role in the perception of personal preferences and thus has an effect on individual travel behaviour. For example, *time/punctuality* has a different value when commuting to work as compared to a social visit. Hence, travel behaviour is specific to the context of travel which is why in AGADE Traffic agents are modelled to have knowledge not only about traffic but also about the simulated domain (see [7]). The application of semantic methods creates flexibility in modelling of agent knowledge which allows simulation and analysis of a wide range of scenarios that cover more than just transport related research questions. In [2], we have demonstrated effectiveness and efficiency of this approach. By adding more details to the modelling of individuals, simulation results can produce more insight about the individuals and their decision-making processes. AGADE Traffic implements a series of analysis instruments that can be used to examine this type of individual-based simulation models.

3   Demonstration

During our research activities we have dealt with environmental impact caused by urban mobility. Private shopping is a travel purpose that accounts for a significant share of urban mobility (see [6] Table 3.2) which is why we have chosen a scenario that simulates mobility of individuals during their grocery shopping. Our scenario is situated in the area around the German city of Wetzlar. Given that Wetzlar has circa 50.000 inhabitants and assuming that one person shops for one household and 20% of the household shop during the simulated time interval, simulation has been performed for a set of 2130 agents. During the simulation, agents are assigned a list of food items to be procured. Agents are then required to make decisions about *selection of supermarkets* as well as *mode of travel*. Modelled supermarkets not only differ in product supply, but also their stock may vary in price tendency, product quality and sustainability. Consequently, in some cases agents will not purchase all items on the grocery list at a selected grocery store, which requires them to visit subsequent target locations. Details of simulation data as well as source code of the simulation are available at GitHub.[1] Based on research activities around this scenario, we have implemented a series of analysis instruments that can also be used for other simulation scenarios.

Simulation results include *routing information* that describe where the agents have travelled. This is visualised with a heat map that colour-codes traffic load on road sections (see [3] Fig. 1). Details on global system behaviour such as temporal distribution of traveller volume, visited target locations as well as selected modes of travel are visualised using appropriate charts. When comparing results

---

[1] See https://github.com/kite-cloud/agade-traffic.

of two simulations with identical agent populations, AGADE Traffic allows side-by-side visualisation of simulation results. Using provided filter options it is possible to examine specific groups of agents that are particularly relevant for the analysis. This helps to identify systemic changes and to pinpoint areas that require more in-depth analysis (see Fig. 1). For example, identifying a significant shift in modal choices when looking at the relevant pie charts leads to questions on the extent of how this shift affects environmental impact of road traffic on the global system. Explanation for this lies in the comparison of calculated performance indicators. Environmental impact is measured by the indicators *global travel distance* which is the sum of the overall distances travelled by the set of all agents, and *combustion distance* that only considers modes of travel that produce exhaust gases.

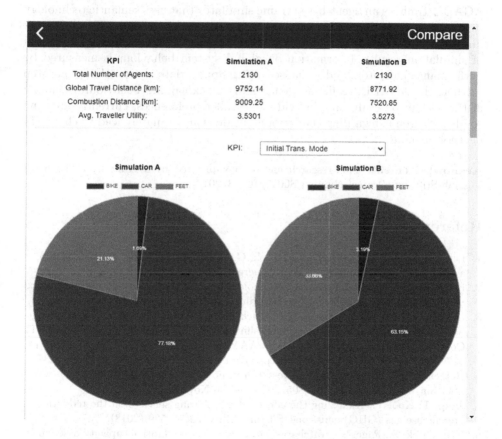

Fig. 1. Side-by-side visualisation of simulation results.

Meanwhile, another question arises as to what causal chains have led to this type of behavioural changes. This is where the strength of AGADE Traffic becomes apparent. The detailed modelling of individuals makes it possible to explain behavioural changes by evaluating their individual preferences. Currently, we are able to output and compare preference values, hence it is possible to identify trends regarding change of attitude that ultimately lead to change in decision-making. As our simulator makes use of semantic technology to compute preferences, we are also able to produce a detailed protocol of firing and non firing rules that can later be used to explain how preferences of an individual were determined. We are working on visualisation options that improve knowledge extraction from this protocol in order to enhance analysis capabilities of AGADE Traffic simulator.

4 Conclusion

AGADE Traffic is an agent-based traffic simulator that uses semantic technology to model individuals and their purpose-driven travel behaviour. The simulator implements a series of analysis instruments allowing for side-by-side comparison of simulation results. Information on global system behaviour is measured by performance indicators and visualised using appropriate charts. Going one step further, the AGADE Traffic approach aims at explaining behavioural changes of the system by evaluating individual traveller preferences, currently allowing to identify trends regarding change of attitude that ultimately lead to change in decision-making.

Acknowledgement. This research has been supported by a grant from the Karl-Vossloh-Stiftung (Project Number S0047/10053/2019).

References

1. Dimitropoulos, A., Oueslati, W., Sintek, C.: The rebound effect in road transport: a meta-analysis of empirical studies. Energy Econ. **75**, 163–179 (2018)
2. Farrenkopf, T.: Applying semantic technologies to multi-agent models in the context of business simulations. Ph.D. thesis, Edinburgh Napier University (2017)
3. Geyer, J., Nguyen, J., Farrenkopf, T., Guckert, M.: AGADE traffic 2.0 - a knowledge-based approach for multi-agent traffic simulations. In: Demazeau, Y., Holvoet, T., Corchado, J.M., Costantini, S. (eds.) PAAMS 2020. LNCS (LNAI), vol. 12092, pp. 417–420. Springer, Cham (2020). https://doi.org/10.1007/978-3-030-49778-1_38
4. Hotten, R.: BMW and daimler invest 1bn in new car venture (2019). https://www.bbc.com/news/business-47332805. Accessed 30 Nov 2019
5. Jung, J., Koo, Y.: Analyzing the effects of car sharing services on the reduction of greenhouse gas (GHG) emissions. Sustainability **10**(2), 539 (2018)
6. Krumdieck, S., Page, S., Watcharasukarn, M.: Travel adaptive capacity assessment for particular geographic, demographic and activity cohorts. NZ Transport Agency Research report (2012)
7. Nguyen, J., Powers, S.T., Urquhart, N., Farrenkopf, T., Guckert, M.: Using semantic technology to model persona for adaptable agents. In: ECMS (2021, page in press)

re:Mobidyc - Reconstructing MOdeling Based on Individual for the DYnamics of Community

Tomohiro Oda[1]([✉]), Gaël Dur[2], Stéphane Ducasse[3], and Sami Souissi[4]

[1] Software Research Associates, Inc., Tokyo, Japan
tomohiro@sra.co.jp
[2] Creative Science Unit (Geoscience), Faculty of Science, Shizuoka University,
Shizuoka, Japan
dur.gael@shizuoka.ac.jp
[3] Inria - Univ. Lille, CNRS, Centrale Lille, UMR 9189 - CRIStAL, Lille, France
stephane.ducasse@inria.fr
[4] Université de Lille, CNRS, Université du Littoral Côte d'Opale, UMR 8187 LOG,
Laboratoire d'Océanologie et de Géosciences, Station Marine de Wimereux,
59000 Lille, France
sami.souissi@univ-lille.fr

Abstract. The MOBIDYC platform has been used in the study of population dynamics in biology for about two decades. MOBIDYC employs modeling features specific to population dynamics. However, MOBIDYC has not been updated for more than ten years. This paper presents a reconstruction of the design and the implementation of MOBIDYC. The re:Mobidyc platform has a new modeling language, a new runtime architecture and a new modeling environment, inheriting the design principles of the original MOBIDYC.

Keywords: Population dynamics · Individual-based modeling · Modeling language · Memory models · Mobydic · Pharo

1 Introduction

Every multi-agent simulation tool has a specific programming syntax and semantics for the agents, and each is unique in terms of generality, usability, modifiability, scalability, and performance [1]. Among these tools, MOBIDYC, which stands for "MOdeling Based on Individual for the DYnamics of Community", aims to promote Agent-Based Models as an accompanying tool for scientific research in the field of ecology, biology, and environment [6]. Although the software has proven its usefulness for conducting scientific studies on several occasions [4,5], the development of MOBIDYC has been stalled for more than ten years.

The authors started to develop re:Mobidyc as MOBIDYC's modernized successor. The strength of MOBIDYC was in its modeling language design dedicated to the specific scientific fields, and the easy-for-non-programmer modeling

© Springer Nature Switzerland AG 2021
F. Dignum et al. (Eds.): PAAMS 2021, LNAI 12946, pp. 367–371, 2021.
https://doi.org/10.1007/978-3-030-85739-4_34

environment. The goal of re:Mobidyc is to push those properties further with modernized design and implementation.

2 Main Purpose

The development of re:Mobidyc is not a mere porting or refactoring of MOBIDYC, but the modeling language, modeling UI, and runtime mechanism have been re-designed from scratch based on the following design principles inherited from MOBIDYC.

1. The modeler can visually construct a model with graphical interfaces.
2. The modeling language does not impose imperative or procedural programming skills, and provides a higher abstraction to the modeling.
3. The modeling language supports three different types of agents: located agents, cells, and the global agent.

We use Pharo, a cutting-edge object-oriented programming environment, as a basis for development. Pharo has the flexibility to host the modeling language and has been used in programming language research for realizing new language features [2,3].

3 Demonstration

The modeling language and runtime mechanisms of re:Mobidyc will be explained.

3.1 Modeling Language

An example definition of an animat named `Goat` is shown below.

```
Goat is Animat with
    blood_sugar [kcal]
```

The animat `Goat` has an attribute named `blood_sugar` measured in `kcal`. The re:Mobidyc platform automatically converts the values of `blood_sugar` into its SI unit Joule, evaluates expressions in SI, and displays the values in `kcal` for the user. The system checks the expressions used in a model are sound with the units. The unit checking helps the users to find errors in their definitions and to avoid erroneous conversions of units. All animats has two implicit attributes: x [m] and y [m].

The task definition in re:Mobidyc is declarative and the states are updated synchronously. Below is a definition of the *move* task that changes its location according to its `heading` and `speed` attributes.

```
to move is
    my d/dt x' = cos(theta) * r
    my d/dt y' = sin(theta) * r
where
    theta = my heading
    r = my speed.
```

The **move** task above is general and needs adaptation to a particular animat. Please note that the attributes **heading** and **speed** referred to in the above definition are not declared in the definition of **Goat**. In re:Mobidyc, the user defines replacement rules to adapt general tasks to a particular animat.

Goat move **where**
    my heading —> **direction neighbor**'s grass
    my speed —> 1[km/day].

The above definition adapts the general **move** task to the **Goat** animat by replacing the reference to **heading** attribute with a primitive operation to compute the direction of the cell with the richest **grass** around it. The **speed** attribute is also replaced with 1 [km/day]. As the result, the adapted task is equivalent to the definition below.

to move **is**
    my d/dt x' = cos(theta) * r
    my d/dt y' = sin(theta) * r
where
    theta = **direction neighbor**'s grass
    r = 1[km/day].

The adapted task is then unit checked. The unit checker infers the SI unit of local variable **theta** be radian, and the SI unit of **r** be [m/s]. The unit checker then checks the two difference equation in the second and the third lines. The right-hand sides of the difference equation are in [m/s] because cos(theta) and sin(theta) has no dimension and **r**'s SI unit is inferred to be [m/s]. So, re:Mobydic will confirm that the units of the left-hand side and the right-hand side agree. Figure 1 shows the screenshot of a simulation with the Goat animat.

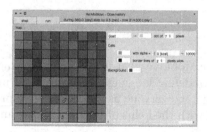

Fig. 1. Overview of re:Mobidyc's memory model

3.2 Memory Model

Re:Mobidyc has a unique memory model that equips with automated history recording of its memory image and differential write access to each memory slot. Figure 2 illustrates the memory model of re:Mobidyc. The memory provides value slots addressed by slot numbers. Individual agents are allocated in the address space. The interpreter can read the value of the slot at the specified address,

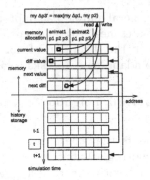

Fig. 2. Overview of re:Mobidyc's memory model

and also the difference value from the previous value of the slot. The memory accepts write access to a slot and will update the memory slot synchronously at the end of the time step. The memory also accepts differential write access that will accumulate the deltas until the end of the simulation time step, and the accumulated deltas will be added to the value of the memory slot.

The memory is attached with history storage that records a snapshot of the memory at every time step. The interpreter can have the memory loaded with the snapshot of the specified point of time. The re:Mobidyc's memory model encapsulates the history management of the simulation. This design simplifies the implementation of the interpreter by isolating the history and synchronous memory updates. The current implementation supports on-memory history and persistent storage on the filesystem. We are also planning to provide a storage backend to relational database systems.

4   Conclusions

The development of re:Mobidyc is still at the early stage of its lifecycle. We have re-designed the modeling language and created a unique memory model. Re:Mobidyc is accessible to everyone as an open source project and we will continue the development with the helps of both biologists and computer scientists.

References

1. Abar, S., Theodoropoulos, G.K., Lemarinier, P., O'Hare, G.M.: Agent based modelling and simulation tools: a review of the state-of-art software. Comput. Sci. Rev. **24**, 13–33 (2017)
2. Bergel, A., Cassou, D., Ducasse, S., Laval, J.: Deep into Pharo. Square Bracket Associates (2013). http://books.pharo.org
3. Black, A.P., Ducasse, S., Nierstrasz, O., Pollet, D., Cassou, D., Denker, M.: Pharo by Example. Square Bracket Associates, Kehrsatz (2009). http://books.pharo.org

4. Dur, G., Jiménez-Melero, R., Beyrend-Dur, D., Hwang, J.S., Souissi, S.: Individual-based model of the phenology of egg-bearing copepods: application to Eurytemora affinis from the Seine estuary, France. Ecol. Model. **269**, 21–36 (2013)
5. Dur, G., Won, E.J., Han, J., Lee, J.S., Souissi, S.: An individual-based model for evaluating post-exposure effects of UV-B radiation on zooplankton reproduction. Ecol. Model. **441**, 109379 (2021)
6. Ginot, V., Le Page, C., Souissi, S.: A multi-agents architecture to enhance end-user individual-based modelling. Ecol. Model. **157**(1), 23–41 (2002)

Mobile Device Approach for the Measurement of Jump Flight Time

Ivan Miguel Pires[1,2,3](✉) (iD), Nuno M. Garcia[1] (iD),
and Maria Cristina Canavarro Teixeira[4,5] (iD)

[1] Instituto de Telecomunicações, Universidade da Beira Interior, Covilhã, Portugal
impires@it.ubi.pt, ngarcia@di.ubi.pt
[2] Computer Science Department, Polytechnic Institute of Viseu, Viseu, Portugal
[3] UICISA:E Research Centre, School of Health, Polytechnic Institute of Viseu, Viseu, Portugal
[4] UTC de Recursos Naturais e Desenvolvimento Sustentável, Polytechnic Institute of Castelo Branco, Castelo Branco, Portugal
ccanavarro@ipcb.pt
[5] Environment and Society, CERNAS - Research Centre for Natural Resources, Polytechnic Institute of Castelo Branco, Castelo Branco, Portugal

Abstract. Teenagers are mainly sedentary with the use of technological devices. However, technological devices may be part of recreational activities to challenge people to achieve better results. This paper described the acquisition of accelerometer data from mobile devices and BioPlux devices, measuring the correct jump flight time with the help of a pressure sensor in a jump platform. Also, this paper tested different methods for adjusting the calculation of the jump flight time, including the least-squares method, the subtraction of average error, and the multilayer perceptron. Currently, a mobile application is available with the Least Squares methods, but it will use the best method soon. Also, the method presented can be also incorporated in a game to stimulate the physical activity practice.

Keywords: Mobile application · Jump flight time · Accelerometer · Vertical jump · Machine learning · Statistical analysis

1 Introduction

According to the World Health Organization (WHO), 80% of the worldwide teenagers do not perform at least one hour of physical activity per day, where it is more accent in girls [6]. Also, the physical activity level is continually decreasing, due to the high daily use of technology [1].

These devices included different sensors that may enable the acquisition of physical functional parameters [4]. Thus, the teenagers will increase the movements and physical activity with the equipment that is the cause of the sedentarism. One of the activities that can be promoted is vertical jumping, which consists of pushing oneself off a surface and into the air using the muscles in the legs and feats [2]. It is a simple exercise that the teenagers may practice anywhere, creating and promoting a challenging activity with the interaction between teenagers [5].

© Springer Nature Switzerland AG 2021
F. Dignum et al. (Eds.): PAAMS 2021, LNAI 12946, pp. 372–375, 2021.
https://doi.org/10.1007/978-3-030-85739-4_35

2   Main Purpose

The primary purpose of the presented method implemented in a mobile application is to measure the jump flight time as a recreational activity accurately. Next, it allows the implementation of gamification techniques to reduce sedentarism in teenagers. Several methods were implemented to validate and adjust the measurement of the jump flight time to avoid the need for a pressure sensor. This activity may be disseminated using a unique mobile device correctly positioned in the front pocket of the user's pants. Due to the easy use, it is expected to promote challenges to the teenagers with jumps, where some rewards can be given. This project is related to the execution of vertical jumps.

A vertical jump is composed of three phases. These are:

- **Take-off:** Time interval when the person is preparing the jump;
- **Flying:** Time interval when the teenager is on the air;
- **Landing:** Time interval when the person is returning to the initial position.

The different phases were identified by the accelerometry signal of the mobile device with the comparison of the accelerometer and pressure sensors with the BioPlux device.

3   Demonstration

Based on the accelerometer data acquired from the mobile device and the pressure and accelerometer data from the BioPlux device, a sample of a vertical jump is presented in Fig. 1 with the clear identification of the different vertical jump phases. For the data acquired from the mobile device accelerometer, the real gravity was subtracted.

After identifying the phases of a vertical jump with the different devices used, the experimental setup was prepared, and a battery of tests was performed with 25 individuals aged between 15 and 25 years old with different lifestyles. Thus, the data is heterogeneous to validate the method for identifying the jump flight time. The final dataset is available at [3]. The proposed method is composed of the following rules:

1. After the data collection, the data is validated by the following conditions:

   a. The acceleration of the initial time must be lower than the acceleration of final time plus one;
   b. The acceleration of the final time must be lower than 2 m/s^2.

2. When a local maximum is found, the instant and acceleration are saved;
3. The process is repeated for the remaining values are three or more peaks;
4. Verify if the mean of all peaks is comprehended between zero and one;
5. Calculate the average of the peaks, and discard the peaks below the average;
6. Verify if the number of peaks is higher or equals to three;
7. The algorithm searches the two minima between the first three peaks;
8. The difference between instants of the two minima is the jump flight time.

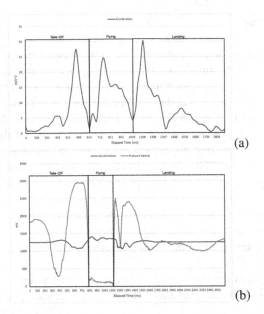

Fig. 1. Accelerometer and Pressure sensors' data from mobile (a) and BioPlux devices (b).

Thus, the algorithm is tested with a battery of tests and adjusted with three different methods: the least-squares method, the subtraction of average error, and the multilayer perceptron. The various participants executed 550 jumps, removing 10% of the experiments due to involuntary movements. The error values between the sensors connected to the BioPlux device and the sensors available in the smartphone are presented in Table 1, verifying that the subtraction of the average error is the worst method. However, comparing the Artificial Neural Networks (ANN) with the least squares' method, the ANN are slightly better than others. Still, the increasing number of inputs for the ANN does not clearly benefit the results.

Table 1. Results of the validation of calculation of jump flight time with mobile accelerometer.

Method	Parameters	Average of the error	Standard deviation of the error	Maximum of the error
Least-squares method	By duration	5.53%	4.53%	27.98%
Subtraction of average error	By duration	6.63%	4.86%	28.20%
Multilayer Perceptron	By duration	4.98%	4.10%	27.39%
	By duration, height, age, and weight	4.91%	4.11%	28.34%

4   Conclusion

The objective of the method for the measurement of the jump flight time with the mobile devices is to prove that it can be accurate, and the measures will be performed with a commodity. The mobile application named JumpTimeCalc is available for iOS devices at [7]. Currently, the Least-squares method is implemented, but the best method was the Multilayer Perception considering the time, height, age, and weight that will be applied to the mobile application soon.

As future work, we intend to implement the jump flight time measurement in a mobile application with gamification to stimulate the physical activity practice.

Acknowledgments. This work is funded by FCT/MEC through national funds and, when applicable, co-funded by the FEDER-PT2020 partnership agreement under the project **UIDB/50008/2020**. This work is also funded by National Funds through the FCT - Foundation for Science and Technology, I.P., within the scope of the project **UIDB/00742/2020**. This article is based upon work from COST Action IC1303-AAPELE—Architectures, Algorithms, and Protocols for Enhanced Living Environments and COST Action CA16226–SHELD-ON—Indoor living space improvement: Smart Habitat for the Elderly, supported by COST (European Cooperation in Science and Technology). COST is a funding agency for research and innovation networks. Our Actions help connect research initiatives across Europe and enable scientists to grow their ideas by sharing them with their peers. It boosts their research, career, and innovation. More information in www. cost.eu.

References

1. Lewis, B.A., Napolitano, M.A., Buman, M.P., Williams, D.M., Nigg, C.R.: Future directions in physical activity intervention research: expanding our focus to sedentary behaviors, technology, and dissemination. J. Behav. Med. **40**(1), 112–126 (2016). https://doi.org/10.1007/s10865-016-9797-8
2. Petrigna, L., et al.: A review of countermovement and squat jump testing methods in the context of public health examination in adolescence: reliability and feasibility of current testing procedures. Front. Physiol. **10**, 1384 (2019). https://doi.org/10.3389/fphys.2019.01384
3. Pires, I.M., Garcia, N.M.: accelerometer data collected during jumping activity. Mendeley V1. https://doi.org/10.17632/cvfy8gtfn9.1
4. Sanders, J.P., et al.: Devices for self-monitoring sedentary time or physical activity: a scoping review. J. Med. Internet Res. **18**, e90 (2016). https://doi.org/10.2196/jmir.5373
5. Zuckerman, O., Gal-Oz, A.: Deconstructing gamification: evaluating the effectiveness of continuous measurement, virtual rewards, and social comparison for promoting physical activity. Pers. Ubiquit. Comput. **18**(7), 1705–1719 (2014). https://doi.org/10.1007/s00779-014-0783-2
6. New WHO-led study says majority of adolescents worldwide are not sufficiently physically active. https://www.who.int/news/item/22-11-2019-new-who-led-study-says-majority-of-adolescents-worldwide-are-not-sufficiently-physically-active-putting-their-current-and-future-health-at-risk. Accessed 31 May 2021
7. JumpTimeCalc. In: App Store. https://apps.apple.com/pt/app/jumptimecalc/id654811255. Accessed 31 May 2021

Nego-Bot: A Human-Robot Negotiation System

J. A. Rincon[1(✉)], A. Costa[2(✉)], V. Julian[1(✉)], C. Carrascosa[1(✉)],
and P. Novais[3(✉)]

[1] Institut Valencià d'Investigació en Intelligència Artificial (VRAIN),
Universitat Politècnica de València, Valencia, Spain
{jrincon,carrasco}@dsic.upv.es, vjulian@upv.es
[2] MVRLab, University of Alicante, Alicante, Spain
angelogoncalo.costa@ua.es
[3] ALGORITMI Centre, Universidade do Minho, Braga, Portugal
pjon@di.uminho.pt

Abstract. In this paper we present a platform composed of a low-cost
robot and a multi-agent system that uses deep learning algorithms, whose
objective is to establish a negotiation process and persuasively sell items,
maximising their price, thus gain. To do this, we have focused on developing an interactive process that is able to interact with humans using
a camera, microphone and speaker, to establish all negotiation process
without physical contact. This is relevant due to the current COVID-19
situation and arisen issues of human contact. Validation processes with
university students have revealed high interest and success in products'
negotiation.

Keywords: EDGE AI · Assistant robot · Emotion detection ·
Automated negotiation

1 Introduction

In the process of human-machine interaction, there is a feeling of displeasure
on the part of the human. This feeling is due, in some cases, to the feeling of
wanting to trust the decisions that the machine makes. The discomfort felt is
not because they think that the robot can deceive them. It is because they are
not sure if the robot has the necessary knowledge to validate the decision [1]. An
inherent distrust towards these systems arises, leaving them aside and omitting
their recommendations. Studies have shown that providing an embodiment of
a person, whether video-based or robot-based, can improve human acceptance
values [2].

For this project we have designed and built a low-cost robot expert in trading
and sales tasks. The goal is to provide a complete human-like shopping experience by visually identifying the object that the user (in this case acting as
a buyer) wants to buy, to interact orally with the user while negotiating the

© Springer Nature Switzerland AG 2021
F. Dignum et al. (Eds.): PAAMS 2021, LNAI 12946, pp. 376–379, 2021.
https://doi.org/10.1007/978-3-030-85739-4_36

price. To infer the negotiation process we use a multi-agent system that levels current prices, availability and demand and calculates the lowest possible price, the utility function being profit maximisation. Thus, the negotiation follows a bazaar-like style, where user and robot try to maximise their utility functions in each interaction. While, in the current phase, the visual appearance of the robot is bare, the features are enriched and designed to maintain a fluid conversation without the user having to touch any kind of screen or control to interact with it.

2   Robot Trading Assistant

This section describes the operation of the robot trading assistant, detailing the different software and hardware tools used for the creation of the system. The proposed system is shown in the Fig. 1.

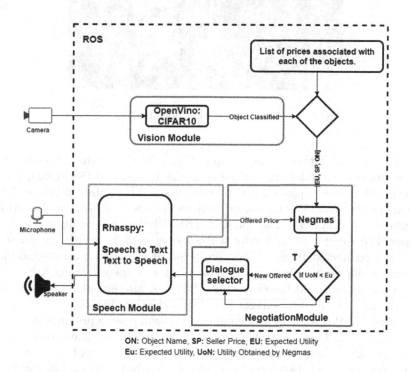

ON: Object Name, **SP**: Seller Price, **EU**: Expected Utility
Eu: Expected Utility, **UoN**: Utility Obtained by Negmas

Fig. 1. Proposed system architecture.

The proposed robot (see Fig. 2) uses ROS (Robot Operating System) as the control and interaction tool. ROS provides a set of libraries and software tools to help the creation of robotic applications, aiding in the easy integration of motor control systems, AI algorithms, among other tools. ROS was designed to be a loosely coupled system in which a process is called a node and each node must

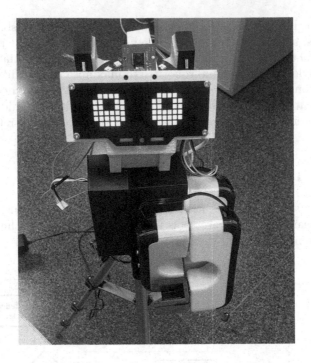

Fig. 2. A general view of the robot trading assistant

be responsible for a task. In our proposal, each of the modules (speech, vision and negotiation module) runs on independent nodes, and the system makes a subscription to the topics offered by each node. This subscription is the way to manage the flow of information between nodes, achieving a decentralized execution of the system. The robot described below was built using low-cost devices. The robot was built with a Raspberry pi 3, to which several sensors have been connected to allow the perception of the environment. Specifically, the sensors allow the robot to recognize the user's speech, using a hat with 6 MEMS microphones. At the same time, the robot also includes a camera, which helps the robot to capture images in order to classify objects.

The use of a Raspberry pi as a computing system poses a problem, since it cannot be upgraded. This is a problem when trying to use applications that involve the integration of deep learning models. Fortunately, in recent years companies like Google and Intel, have developed specific hardware that allow the integration of these models in devices with low power performance. In our case, we used the Intel device as an external system to optimize object classification using the Raspberry Pi 3B+. In this way, the robot was able to classify objects from the CIFAR-10 database in a relatively short time. As the main purpose of the robot is to interact with a person, it was necessary to incorporate LED arrays. These arrays allow the robot's eyes to be displayed, which helps to improve the interaction with the human. The robot can represent up to five expressions (see Fig. 3).

Fig. 3. An overview of the different robot expressions.

3   Conclusions and Future Work

This paper explores the use of physical presence, via a robot, in a system with human interaction. This physical presence that facilitates the interaction is carried out by a low-cost robot described along the paper. The prototype has been used in a negotiation process for trading objects with humans. In the current stage, the robot is engaged to sell the user the object he chooses and shows to the robot. During the negotiation process, both negotiate the price to reach an agreement.

Experiments with real users have shown that using the robot and an speech-based dialogue system to interact with it, makes the user more comfortable and more interested in participate in the negotiation process than if this negotiation is made by a system with a more typical interface.

Acknowledgements. This work was partly supported by the Spanish Government (RTI2018-095390-B-C31) and Universitat Politecnica de Valencia Research Grant PAID-10-19.

References

1. Aseeri, S., Interrante, V.: The influence of avatar representation on interpersonal communication in virtual social environments. IEEE Trans. Visual Comput. Graphics **27**(5), 2608–2617 (2021)
2. Pan, Y., Steed, A.: A comparison of avatar-, video-, and robot-mediated interaction on users' trust in expertise. Front. Robot. AI **3**, 12 (2016)

Fully Decentralized Planner-Guided Robot Swarm Demonstration

Michael Schader$^{(\boxtimes)}$ and Sean Luke

George Mason University, Fairfax, VA 22030, USA
{mschader,sean}@gmu.edu

Abstract. Robot swarms hold great potential for accomplishing missions in a robust, scalable, and flexible manner. However, determining what low-level agent behavior to implement in order to meet high-level objectives is an unsolved inverse problem. Building on previous work on partially-centralized planner-guided robot swarms, we present an approach that achieves total decentralization of executive and deliberator functions, adds robustness and performance optimization through dynamic task switching, and employs agent-initiated superrational planning to coordinate agent activity while responding to changes in the environment. We demonstrate the effectiveness of the technique with three swarm robotics scenarios.

Keywords: Coordination and control models for multi-agent systems · Knowledge representation and reasoning in robotic systems · Swarm behavior

1 Introduction

Robot swarms hold great potential for accomplishing missions in a robust, scalable, and flexible manner. However, determining what low-level agent behavior to implement in order to meet high-level objectives is an unsolved inverse problem. Our approach builds on previous work on partially-centralized planner-guided robot swarms. It achieves total decentralization of executive and deliberator functions, adds robustness and performance optimization through dynamic task switching, and employs agent-initiated superrational planning to coordinate agent activity while responding to changes in the environment. We demonstrate the effectiveness of the technique with three swarm robotics scenarios.

Since Beni [1] first developed the idea of robot swarms in 2004, researchers have tried to control large groups of robots in ways that accomplish complex tasks while preserving swarm virtues such as redundancy, parallelism, and decentralization. Despite years of effort since then, Dorigo et al. [2] observed in 2020, "[T]he deployment of large groups of robots, or robot swarms, that coordinate and cooperatively solve a problem or perform a task, remains a challenge". Most existing solutions to this challenge either rely on some degree of centralization, which introduces single points of failure and limits scalability, or address only

© Springer Nature Switzerland AG 2021
F. Dignum et al. (Eds.): PAAMS 2021, LNAI 12946, pp. 380–384, 2021.
https://doi.org/10.1007/978-3-030-85739-4_37

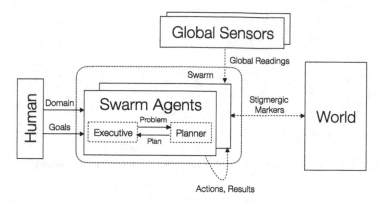

Fig. 1. Fully decentralized planner-guided robot swarm architecture with optional global sensors.

basic missions such as area coverage and shape formation, which are far short of the complex tasks that swarm engineers aspire to perform.

Dorigo predicted that "Hybrid systems mixing model-free and model-based approaches will likely provide additional power". In previous work [7], we employed that philosophy in creating *planner-guided robot swarms*, a hybrid deliberative/reactive approach to swarm management. A central automated planner produced plans for each group of agents within the swarm. At run-time, an *orchestrator* existing outside the swarm issued the plans to the agents, collected success reports, monitored sensor data, determined when actions were complete, and instructed the agents when to advance to the next plan step (Fig. 1).

That architecture enabled a human programmer to specify complex missions in a high-level planning language for a swarm to execute. However, the centralized deliberator and executive components were potential single points of runtime failure, reducing the benefits of swarm decentralization. Here we build on that work by modifying the architecture to push the deliberative and executive functions down into the swarm agents themselves. This involves solving problems with action synchronization, task allocation, and replanning without resorting to outside entities or differentiated swarm members. Ultimately our *distributed executive* accomplishes the same missions that the centralized version can, preserving scalability and robustness without any single points of failure.

2   Main Purpose

In our earlier work, we introduced a novel approach to swarm control: framing the high-level domain and problem using Planning Domain Definition Language (PDDL) [5], generating a plan to achieve the goal state with an automated planner, and having a central executive orchestrate the agents' activities by adjusting their behavioral parameters and synchronizing their plan step advances. In this

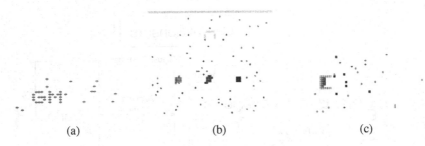

(a)   (b)   (c)

Fig. 2. (a) Letters scenario. (b) Refineries scenario. (c) Smart sorting scenario.

new work, we move the executive and deliberative functions into the swarm agents themselves, thus eliminating all single points of failure and enabling truly decentralized operations. We add dynamic task switching based on action completion information shared by neighbors, enhancing robustness. Finally, we incorporate agent-initiated replanning to allow the swarm to respond to changes in the environment.

In our revised formulation, a planner-guided swarm scenario definition can be represented by a tuple:

$$S_{def} = \langle A, domain, M_{act}, M_{pred} \rangle \tag{1}$$

where the agent class $A = \langle sensors, behaviors \rangle$ represents the capabilities of a swarm robot platform, the $domain = \langle predicates, actions \rangle$ is the PDDL representation of the planning domain, the action mapping $M_{act} : actions \rightarrow \langle behaviors, parameters, criteria \rangle$ translates each PDDL action to a specific parameterized agent behavior with success criteria, and the predicate mapping $M_{pred} : predicates \rightarrow \langle sensors, parameters, criteria \rangle$ ties predicates needed for replanning to observed states.

A specific run of a scenario starts with scenario definition S_{def} and adds three items:

$$S_{run} = \langle S_{def}, problem, n, g \rangle \tag{2}$$

which are the PDDL expression of the planning *problem*, the count of agents n, and the number of groups g. If g is set to zero, the group count decision is delegated to each agent's deliberator, which will attempt to generate plans with various numbers of groups, choosing the smallest g that produces a minimum-length sound plan.

3   Demonstration

We will demonstrate three simulated scenarios that expose the novel aspects of our fully decentralized planner-guided robot swarm implementation. First, we will exercise basic operations with all centralized components eliminated. Second, we will show agent-initiated task switching and how it leads to robust recovery from agent failures. Third, we will exhibit the effectiveness of decentralized replanning spurred by detected changes in the world state [3]. All of our demonstrations will be conducted using the MASON multiagent simulation toolkit [4], in which we model non-point robots, each exclusively occupying a nonzero area and navigating using virtual pheromone trails [6].

The Letters scenario is a straightforward mission to have robots arrange themselves to spell out a three-letter sequence (Fig. 2a). The locations of the pixels of each letter are marked in advance, and the agents know when they have entered such a designated region. The purpose of the demonstration is to show the effectiveness and scalability of a completely decentralized planner-guided swarm. Once the agents are launched, they have no special base to which to return to or overseer with which to communicate. They have only the domain and problem presented by the operator to the swarm.

Refineries is a stress test of agent task-switching (Fig. 2b). There are three square piles of bricks, each consisting of three different layers. One group of agents is assigned to disassemble each pile. The agents need to bring the bricks to a refinery area, where they will be processed and removed from the environment. The outer bricks must all be processed first, then the middle ones, and finally the central bricks. Partway through the first step, however, all the agents initially assigned to one of the groups are disabled: rendered permanently immobile. The only way for the swarm to succeed is for the agents to determine via their short-range interactions that one task group is not succeeding, and to choose to switch into that group in order to accomplish the mission.

The Smart Sorting scenario exercises the agents' coordinated replanning abilities (Fig. 2c). The swarm starts with the mission of gathering four different kinds of randomly scattered bricks and assembling them in order into blocks in a walled area. As soon as they finish the first two layers (A and B), though, the A block is teleported outside to a different location. The agents continue with their planned actions, but upon checking sensor readings, they determine that conditions have changed, so they replan and begin taking apart the outer blocks so as to reassemble the correct structure.

4   Conclusion

Modifying our previously published planner-guided robot swarm architecture to achieve complete decentralization was a success. Each scenario explored in our experiments showed a different area of improvement. Eliminating all central components ensured there were no single points of failure. Introducing dynamic task switching provided robustness against agent failure. Superrational planning enabled the swarm to incorporate flexibility into swarm behavior. We conducted all the experiments using the same agent code, further demonstrating the generality of our method.

In future work, we will attack the problem of retrograde behavior (agents getting out of sync with each other's plan steps), quantify aspects of the speed of communications in a swarm environment, and implement different agent classes with varying navigation and sensing mechanisms. This work will show for the first time a widely-applicable approach to building robot swarms that can collectively accomplish complex tasks.

References

1. Beni, G.: From swarm intelligence to swarm robotics. In: Şahin, E., Spears, W.M. (eds.) SR 2004. LNCS, vol. 3342, pp. 1–9. Springer, Heidelberg (2005). https://doi.org/10.1007/978-3-540-30552-1_1
2. Dorigo, M., Theraulaz, G., Trianni, V.: Reflections on the future of swarm robotics. Sci. Robot. **5**(49), 1–3 (2020)
3. Hofstadter, D.R.: Dilemmas for superrational thinkers, leading up to a luring lottery. Sci. Am. **248**(6), 739–755 (1983)
4. Luke, S., Cioffi-Revilla, C., Panait, L., Sullivan, K., Balan, G.: MASON: a multi-agent simulation environment. SIMULATION **81**(7), 517–527 (2005)
5. McDermott, D., et al.: PDDL: the planning domain definition language (1998)
6. Panait, L., Luke, S.: A pheromone-based utility model for collaborative foraging. In: 2004 Proceedings of the Third International Joint Conference on Autonomous Agents and Multiagent Systems, AAMAS 2004, pp. 36–43. IEEE (2004)
7. Schader, M., Luke, S.: Planner-guided robot swarms. In: Demazeau, Y., Holvoet, T., Corchado, J.M., Costantini, S. (eds.) PAAMS 2020. LNCS (LNAI), vol. 12092, pp. 224–237. Springer, Cham (2020). https://doi.org/10.1007/978-3-030-49778-1_18

An Agent-Based Game Engine Layer
for Interactive Fiction

Markus Schatten[✉][iD], Bogdan Okreša Đurić[iD], and Tomislav Peharda[iD]

Artificial Intelligence Laboratory, Faculty of Organization and Informatics,
University of Zagreb, Pavlinska 2, 42000 Varaždin, Croatia
{markus.schatten,dokresa,tomislav.peharda}@foi.unizg.hr
http://ai.foi.hr

Abstract. Interactive fiction (IF) is a type of computer game in which players use text commands inside a literary narrative in order to influence the environment, the story and/or characters. We have developed an agent based game engine layer that allows us to introduce intelligent agents into such games including but not limited to chatbots, autonomous agents, expert systems as well as implement ontology based content generation. We provide demo implementations of games which include the implemented methods and show the benefits of using them.

Keywords: Interactive fiction · Artificial intelligence · Computer games · Multiagent systems

1 Introduction

IF, text adventures, gamebooks and even in some cases visual novels comprise computer games in which players interact with the game using text commands. These narrative worlds usually consist of a number of rooms (whereby the term "room" is very broadly defined and can include any kind of imaginable space or even states of mind) connected by doors (again very broadly defined), and in which objects or things can be placed that can be examined and interacted with. Such things can, for example include non-playing characters (NPCs) that the player can communicate with, containers that might have other objects within, edibles that can be consumed, wearables that can be used as clothes or equipment, etc. As opposed to most computer games focused on graphics, interactive fiction (IF) is focused on the story and narrative which makes it an interesting and different medium similarly as printed novels differ from movies.

2 Main Purpose

An important aspect of game engine design is the integration of artificial intelligence (AI) [2]. Integrating AI into IF seemingly presents an interesting challenge

This work has been supported in full by Croatian Science Foundation under the project number IP-2019-04-5824.

© Springer Nature Switzerland AG 2021
F. Dignum et al. (Eds.): PAAMS 2021, LNAI 12946, pp. 385–389, 2021.
https://doi.org/10.1007/978-3-030-85739-4_38

due to specifics of the medium. Most games in industry often use very limited capabilities of (especially modern) AI which is why we decided to introduce a game engine layer that allows for the implementation of fairly advanced concepts.

We have developed our game engine layer above Inform 7,[1] a declarative programming language for the development of IF based on natural language syntax. The following listing shows a way to describe a world in Inform 7:

```
"The Dungeon" by "Markus Schatten, Bogdan Okreša Đurić & Tomislav Peharda".
When play begins:
    say "You find yourself in a dungeon surrounded by darkness. " ;
The pit is a room. The description is "This is where you woke up."
A torch is here. The description is "You can see a dim light flickering a few
    ↪ steps away from you." ...
```

An example interpreter session is shown in the following listing:

```
You find yourself in a dungeon surrounded by darkness.
The Dungeon
An Interactive Fiction by Markus Schatten,Bogdan Okreša Đurić & Tomislav
    ↪ Peharda
The pit
This is the place where you woke up.
You can see a torch and a Chest (closed) here.
--> open chest
You open the Chest, revealing an old smelly cheese.
--> take torch and cheese
torch: Taken.
old smelly cheese: Taken. ...
```

Whilst such an interface allows a player to use numerous commands based on natural language processing (NLP), the implementation of game actors like NPCs or mobs and the interaction with them is fairly limited to predefined mechanics.

3   Demonstration

We have developed an agent-based Python interface[2] to the glulxe IF interpreter shell that can execute a number of IF formats in terminal sessions. The developed interface allows us to place filters in front of the IF shell and thus interact with the player on one side and control the game on the other (see Fig. 1).

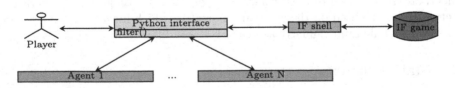

Fig. 1. Python interface to an IF shell

---

[1] Available here: http://inform7.com/.
[2] Available here: https://github.com/AILab-FOI/python-glulxe.git.

For the implementation we have used the Smart Python Agent Development Environment (SPADE) [1]. In the following, we will show proof-of-concept games building upon this interface.

3.1   Chatbot Agents

Whilst NLP has since its beginning been a part of IF, the textual interface to the player has always been constrained to a certain number of commands. Also, it does not recognize any possible synonyms of objects or artifacts defined in the game (if they are not explicitly encoded into the game) nor does it recognize common phrases. To implement a chatbot agent we have used Chatterbot[3] as can be seen in the following code excerpt.

```
def train( bot ):
    bot.set_trainer( ListTrainer )
    bot.train( [ 'where_am_i', 'look' ] )
    bot.train( [ 'what_is_this_place', 'look' ] )
    bot.train( [ 'give_me_that_torch', 'take_torch' ] )
    bot.train( [ 'i_want_that_torch', 'take_torch' ] )
    bot.train( [ 'what_is_in_that_chest', 'open_chest' ] )
    bot.train( [ 'let_me_open_that_chest', 'open_chest' ] )
    bot.train( [ 'yay_cheese', 'take_cheese' ] )
    bot.train( [ 'take_the_cheddar', 'take_cheese' ] ) ...
```

In this way we were able to train the chatbot to understand a number of common phrases that may be used by the player and turn them into the previously mentioned predefined commands, as shown in the following game session:

```
--> where am i
This is the place you woke up.
You can see a torch and a Chest (closed) here.
--> gimme the torch
Taken.
--> what's in that chest
You open the Chest, revealing an old smelly cheese.
--> take the cheddar
Taken.
```

Besides using chatbots as a means of achieving user friendliness of the interface, we could have used it to add additional personality traits to in-game NPCs. For example, we could train one chatbot for each NPC including various special types of conversations that can be understood and performed by each of them to boost player experience.

3.2   Autonomous (Background) Agents

Autonomous background agents can provide us with additional dynamics in IF environments. In the following example we show how IF games can be manipulated by an external agent that randomly generates actions thus directly impacting the game-play regardless of the player's actions. In our example, there is an

---

[3] Available at: https://chatterbot.readthedocs.io/.

agent that generates actions at random times. We have built in two actions that can teleport or disarm a player. The following listing shows the implementation of these two actions in Inform 7:

```
Disarming is an action applying to nothing. Understand "disarm" as disarming.
Instead of disarming:
    if the player carries anything:
        say "The elf disarmed you";
        now everything carried by the player is in the location;
    otherwise:
        say "The elf tried to disarm you, but you carry nothing"
Teleporting is an action applying to nothing. Understand "teleport" as
    ↪ teleporting.
Instead of teleporting:
    say "Elf teleported you to a different room...";
    move the player to a random room
```

When the autonomous agent decides to interrupt the game by invoking a command, the agent that communicates with the game receives the command and processes it by sending an appropriate command to the interpreter. This provides interesting dynamics to IF games which are usually static, i.e. can only be changed by user actions or special types of events.

3.3 Expert Systems

ES can be of great value to IF game design especially for the implementation of certain "expert" NPCs that can help the player to decide about certain situations. As an example we have developed a very simple decision tree based expert system (ES) that can recognize four types of cheese. By using our interface we can allow the player to interact with the ES agent in-game when they for example ask some NPC (in our example the orc lady) about cheese as shown in the following listing:

```
--> ask orc lady about cheese
Orc Lady: Is the cheese soft?
--> no.
Orc Lady: Does is taste very umami?
--> yes.
Orc Lady: Ahh... parmesan, king of all cheeses!
```

3.4 Generating Content

Although a narrative of an IF instance could be considered similar to a book, and therefore unalterable, the digital context of IF encourages the idea of having parts of such a narrative, or indeed narrative as a whole, generated automatically, as opposed to having been written by a human.

The approach herein is based on a developed ontology that consists of concepts that can be used to describe the world that should be generated. The concepts existing in the generated world represent a subset of all the concepts that are modelled as available in the observed world. The following listing shows an example random generated world using the developed ontology:

```
Meduseld is a room. The description of Meduseld is "You are now in the Golden
   ↪ Hall of Meduseld, the seat of power in Rohan." Understand "The Golden
   ↪ Hall" as Meduseld.
A metal throne is a thing in Meduseld. The description of the metal throne is
   ↪ "This is the throne of the ruling House of Rohan."
A large chest is a container in Meduseld. The description of the large chest
   ↪ is "A large chest that can house many items." It is opaque and
   ↪ openable.
```

4 Conclusion

In this paper we have implemented an agent based game engine layer and shown
a number of possible use cases. With Python being one of the most popular
programming languages for AI with thousands of libraries an modules available
this opens a wide set of possibilities for testing various approaches. Our future
research will be focused on the implementation of multiplayer features for IF.

References

1. Palanca, J., Terrasa, A., Julian, V., Carrascosa, C.: Spade 3: Supporting the new
   generation of multi-agent systems. IEEE Access **8**, 182537–182549 (2020)
2. Yannakakis, G.N., Togelius, J.: Artificial Intelligence and Games, vol. 2. Springer,
   Cham (2018). https://doi.org/10.1007/978-3-319-63519-4

Sim-Env: Decoupling OpenAI Gym Environments from Simulation Models

Andreas Schuderer[1,2(✉)], Stefano Bromuri[1], and Marko van Eekelen[1,3]

[1] Open University of the Netherlands, Valkenburgerweg 177,
Heerlen, The Netherlands
{andreas.schuderer,stefano.bromuri,marko.vaneekelen}@ou.nl
[2] APG Algemene Pensioen Groep N.V., Oude Lindestraat 70,
Heerlen, The Netherlands
[3] Radboud University, Houtlaan 4, Nijmegen, The Netherlands

Abstract. Reinforcement learning (RL) is being used to create self-adaptive agents, where RL researchers commonly create and employ simulations of the problem domains to train and evaluate various RL algorithms and their variants. This activity is in need of methodological and tool-based support, particularly concerning the reuse of model- and simulation-related code across various RL experiments. We propose a workflow and tool for the decoupled development and maintenance of multi-purpose agent-based models and derived single-purpose RL environments, enabling the researcher to swap out environments with ones representing different perspectives or different reward models, all while keeping the underlying domain model intact and separate.

Keywords: Software engineering in AI · Reinforcement learning · Simulation · Models

1 Introduction

Reinforcement learning (RL) is a field of artificial intelligence concerned with the problem of modelling situated agents which can learn by receiving rewards from an environment [3], without explicitly programming the behaviour of the agents. In spite of thriving development from the algorithmic perspective, the software engineering methodology is still lagging behind. While advances such as the *OpenAI Gym* initiative [1] have created a de-facto standard RL API which caused large numbers of reusable RL environments to become widely available, developers still need more support when creating these environments.

Creating a new OpenAI-Gym-compatible RL environment (or any type of RL environment) still requires custom software development. This can lead to code duplication and hard-to-maintain bridging code, particularly in cases of a non-trivial matrix of research problems and if parameter sweeps in the problem domain are desired. While sweeps are well-supported on the side of parametrising RL algorithms, this is less so for the environments that are used to evaluate those RL algorithms.

© Springer Nature Switzerland AG 2021
F. Dignum et al. (Eds.): PAAMS 2021, LNAI 12946, pp. 390–393, 2021.
https://doi.org/10.1007/978-3-030-85739-4_39

2   Main Purpose

This work approaches aforementioned issues from a software engineering perspective. Its main contributions are a workflow which reduces the coupling between the domain model and the RL environment(s) (Fig. 1), and a Python library called *Sim-Env* as a tool to facilitate this workflow.

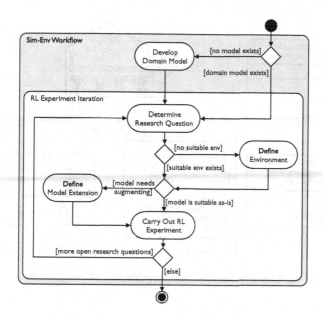

Fig. 1. Cyclic workflow for creating a simulation-based OpenAI-Gym-compatible environment which is in turn based on a reusable domain model.

This workflow results in a generic domain model that is independent from any associated RL environments. Thus, any effort to validate the model is only needed once, and the model can be reused in a variety of applications.

The Sim-Env Python library offers mechanisms to facilitate the workflow, specifically its steps *Define Environment* and *Define Model Extension*. It has been developed with the following goals in mind:

- **Convenience for simple cases, extensibility for complex cases.**
- **Separation between domain model and RL problem environment.**
- **Flexible agency.** There should be no precluded perspective of which modelled entities will act as agents, and which decisions will be handled by a RL algorithm.
- **Extensibility.** It should be possible to update the RL problem without having to change the model's code or require the model to follow a particular software engineering paradigm.

3   Demonstration

As a motivating example, we will assume the need to evaluate the suitability of different RL algorithms for a simplified greenhouse watering system (Fig. 2) by means of simulation. The domain model for the greenhouse setting is implemented in Python, as shown below.

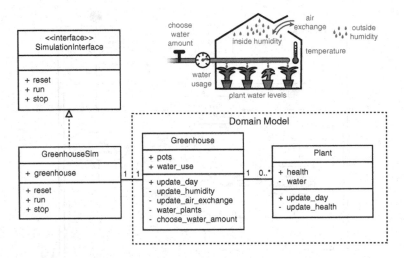

Fig. 2. Main components and UML representation of the greenhouse example.

For running the simulation, we implement Sim-Env's `SimulationInterface`, which makes it controllable by Sim-Env and eventually OpenAI Gym.

We define the RL environment using Sim-Env's `make_step` and applying it to our decision function `choose_water_amount`. Any definitions created this way are registered as environments in the OpenAI Gym framework and available through `gym.make`.

```
Greenhouse.choose_water_amount = make_step(
    observation_space=spaces.Box(
      low=np.array([0.0, 0.0, 0.0, 0.0]),
      high=np.array([1.0, 1.0, 1.0, 1.0])
    ),
    observation_space_mapping=obs_from_greenhouse,
    action_space=spaces.Box(low=0.0, high=1.0, shape=(1,)),
    action_space_mapping=lambda w: min(max(0, w*1000), 1000),
    reward_mapping=reward_from_greenhouse
)(Greenhouse.choose_water_amount)
```

The resulting generated greenhouse environment can be used like any other OpenAI Gym environment:

```
from random import random
import gym

def rand_policy(obs):
    return random()

env = gym.make("env_def:Greenhouse-v0")
obs0 = env.reset()
obs1, rew1, done, info = env.step(rand_policy(obs0))
obs2, rew2, done, info = env.step(rand_policy(obs1))

# day 0 alive: 200, dead: 0
# day 1 alive: 200, dead: 0
# day 2 alive: 182, dead: 18
```

Sim-Env provides a simple plugin system, where any function in the simulation code can be made extendable using expose_to_plugins and at a later point be extended with additional functionality without having to adapt the simulation's code base or assuming specific software engineering paradigms like inheritance. It is important to note that Sim-Env does not assume the researcher extending the model or defining the environments to have full access to the domain model code base. Authoring the domain model is different from using it. This is by design to foster the sharing of existing domain models between researchers for simulation-based RL research. A detailed explanation and implementation of the greenhouse example can be found in [2].

4   Conclusions

This paper illustrates the Sim-Env workflow and library. Our approach decouples domain model maintenance from RL environment maintenance and thereby aids the acceleration of simulation-based RL research. We expect Sim-Env to contribute as a RL research tool which not only makes it easier, but also encourages users to develop environments that use the de-facto standard OpenAI Gym interface and that are more broadly reusable (as are their components).

Acknowledgement. This work is supported by APG Algemene Pensioen Groep N.V. The Sim-Env package is available at https://github.com/schuderer/bprl.

References

1. Brockman, G., et al.: OpenAI gym. arXiv e-prints (2016). https://doi.org/10.1021/am3026129
2. Schuderer, A., Bromuri, S., van Eekelen, M.: Sim-Env: decoupling OpenAI gym environments from simulation models. Preprint at arXiv e-prints, February 2021. http://arxiv.org/abs/2102.09824
3. Van Seijen, H., Mahmood, A.R., Pilarski, P.M., Machado, M.C., Sutton, R.S.: True online temporal-difference learning. J. Mach. Learn. Res. **17**(145), 1–40 (2016)

SIMALL Demonstration: Emotional BDI Simulation of a Mall

Daniel S. Valencia P.[1], Jairo E. Serrano[2]([⊠]) [iD], and Enrique González[1] [iD]

[1] Pontificia Universidad Javeriana, Bogotá, Colombia
{daniel.valencia,egonzal}@javeriana.edu.co
[2] Universidad Tecnológica de Bolívar, Cartagena, Colombia
jserrano@utb.edu.co

Abstract. The following is a description of the design, development, and implementation process of the SIMALL shopping mall simulator. Created in order to carry out a study of the behavior of shoppers inside a shopping mall in order to create a better distribution of warehouses in the mall. A short description showing how the simulator was implemented based on a Multi-agent System with an emotional BDI architecture is also included.

Keywords: Shopping centers · Agentes-based · Emotional BDI · Purchasing intention

1 Introduction

Shopping malls attract different demographic groups to engage in all kinds of activities or make various types of purchases. A report on UK productivity stated that "the key to productivity remains what happens inside the firm and this is something of a 'black box'" [1]. In this context, it is extremely important to define the elements that make up the shopping center to model it more accurately.

In order to design the simulator, the AOPOA methodology [4] was used as the analysis and modeling multi-agent system tool. JAVA and JAVAFX were used for its development, together with a library for the implementation of multi-agent systems developed at the Pontificia Universidad Javeriana, called BESA [2]. The resulting simulator is an application that can be run in text or visual mode, depending on the environment in which it is executed.

2 Main Purpose

The behavior of a person regarding the use of their money in some opportunities may go beyond meeting their needs, to understand this decision-making process and predict a purchase intention that maximizes the possible profits of a trade, can not be seen only from a traditional perspective in a simulation. This process goes beyond that and involves reasons, emotions, and experiences [6].

© Springer Nature Switzerland AG 2021
F. Dignum et al. (Eds.): PAAMS 2021, LNAI 12946, pp. 394–397, 2021.
https://doi.org/10.1007/978-3-030-85739-4_40

This denotes that the solution should be treated as a non-deterministic problem, which should include the resolution of conflicting emotional and/or experiential conflicting impulses that coexist within the simulation actors [5].

For this application purpose of this simulator is to study the behavior of a focal group of customers, which would allow the identification of opportunities to improve the sales of stores operating within a shopping mall. In particular, the main technical challenge of SIMALL was to take into account in a explicit way, in the simulation model, the emotional and the ambiguity involved in the decision process of a buyer when dealing with conflicting and concurrent buying alternatives.

Studying customer behavior to analyze the factors that influence sales is a complex and emerging scenario. Therefore, the simulator was implemented as a multi-agent system where customers are BDI agents, in order to model the decision making, the spatial location of stores, the emotional and unpredictable human behavior, the implicit fuzziness of the customer's decision process. The model has a micro level approach that allows analyzing the result of the interactions and behavior at the macro-level [3]. In this case, each agent represents a store, a customer, and even the mall aisles.

3   Demonstration

In order to run the simulator it is necessary to modify the simall.xml file, which contains the configuration parameters for the services offered, the fuzzy decisions, the customer's demographic distribution, the stores with their location, and the product's categories. The experiment presented below is configured as shown in Table 1.

This experiment was designed to verify the correct operation of the simulator by analyzing if the results obtained using the simulator, presented in Table 1, correspond to the expected behavior. The dependent variable was defined as the total sales, this will allow evaluating the performance in the different test scenarios. The independent controlled experimental variables were defined to create several mall operating scenarios. Finally, the intervening variables, which generate a direct or indirect effect on the simulation results, have no change configuration during the experiments.

When running the simulator, 10 runs were performed for each experimental setting; by default, each one of them simulates 8 h of real-time in approximately 40 s on a Linux server with 12 cores and 16 gigabytes of memory. Once the simulation process is finished, a TXT report file is generated including detailed data of the behavior of the customers and also more general data as the shown in the Table 2. As can be noted by analyzing the obtained results, if the physical location of the stores is clustered, as expected, the level of sales on average is higher compared to a random distribution of the same. This variable directly impacts the design of the shopping center with a holistic perspective. The results obtained, while modifying the other independent experimental variables are also coherent with the expected behavior.

Table 1. Simall Experiment

Dependent	Values
Sales realized	?
Independent	**Values**
Number of needs	[Low] – less that 3, [High] – more that 20
Purchasing capacity	[Low] less that 100, [High] – more that 2000
Distribution of premises	[Clustered] o [Random]
Intervening	**Values**
Demography	Age and gender distribution
Brokers	5
Halls per broker	4
Simulation total time	8
Categories	237
Retailers	13
Products	103
Entrance	1
WC	2
Information centers	2

Table 2. Experiment results

Money	Needs	Distribution	Average sales	Variance	Square error
High	High	Clustered	957	8.90	2.98
High	High	Random	882	4.40	2.09
High	Low	Clustered	584	10.48	3.23
High	Low	Random	443	5.11	2.26
Low	High	Clustered	74	2.71	1.64
Low	High	Random	65	1.82	1.34
Low	Low	Clustered	37	6.54	2.55
Low	Low	Random	32	8.17	2.85

The simulator also generates different visualizations of the detailed data related to the shop distribution and customers' behavior, as the ones shown in Fig. 1. On the left, it is presented the internal layout of the shopping center and the location of the warehouses. In the center, it is shown the location of the "anchor" stores, the ones that have the most traction for potential customers. On the right, a heat map linking the anchor stores and customer journeys within the mall can be observed, showing a complete picture of behavior and possible overlooked points in the journeys that need attention to improve productivity. In the experiment presented, the areas not close to the anchor stores are less visited by customers, as it was expected.

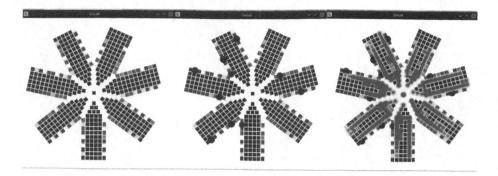

Fig. 1. SIMALL interactions SMA

4 Conclusions

The project was successfully concluded, it was possible to build and verify the correct operation of a multi-agent system that simulates the behavior of a focal group of customers inside a shopping mall. This allowed identifying possible opportunities for improvement in business sales by changing the location of commercial premises and adjusting the interaction between customers and stores.

Acknowledgements. The author Jairo Enrique Serrano Castañeda thanks MIN-CIENCIAS, the PONTIFICIA UNIVERSIDAD JAVERIANA and the UNIVERSIDAD TECNOLOGICA DE BOLIVAR for the support received to pursue a doctoral degree within "Becas de la Excelencia Doctoral del Bicentenario (corte 1)".

References

1. Delbridge, R., Edwards, P., Forth, J., Miskell, P., Payne, J.: The Organisation of Productivity: Re-thinking Skills and Work Organisation. Tech. Rep., December 2006
2. González, E., Avila, J., Bustacara, C.: BESA Behav.-Orient. Social-Based Agent Framework. undefined, Event-Driven (2003)
3. Pourdehnad, J., Maani, K., Sedehi, H.: System dynamics and intelligent agent-based simulation: where is the synergy? In: The 20th International Conference of the System Dynamics Society, pp. 1–16 (2002)
4. Rodríguez, J., Torres, M., González, E.: LA METODOLOGÍA AOPOA. Avances en Sistemas e Informática **4**(2) (2007)
5. Roux, G.: Quenches in quantum many-body systems: one-dimensional Bose-Hubbard model reexamined. In:4th Workshop on Emotion and Computing, pp. 1–8, October 2008. https://doi.org/10.1103/PhysRevA.79.021608
6. Singh, H., Sahay, V.: Determinants of shopping experience. Int. J. Retail Distrib. Manag. **40**(3), 235–248 (2012). https://doi.org/10.1108/09590551211207184, https://www.emerald.com/insight/content/doi.org/10.1108/09590551211207184/full/html

Author Index

Printed in the United States
by Baker & Taylor Publisher Services

Printed in the United States
by Baker & Taylor Publisher Services